Can Democracy and Capitalism Be Reconciled?

Can Democracy and Capitalism Be Reconciled?

Edited by

SIDNEY M. MILKIS
SCOTT C. MILLER

OXFORD
UNIVERSITY PRESS

Oxford University Press is a department of the University of Oxford.
It furthers the University's objective of excellence in research, scholarship,
and education by publishing worldwide. Oxford is a registered trade mark of
Oxford University Press in the UK and in certain other countries.

Published in the United States of America by Oxford University Press
198 Madison Avenue, New York, NY 10016, United States of America.

Library of Congress Cataloging-in-Publication Data

Names: Milkis, Sidney M. editor | Miller, Scott C. editor
Title: Can democracy and capitalism be reconciled? / edited by Sidney M. Milkis and Scott C. Miller.
Description: New York, NY : Oxford University Press, 2025. |
Includes bibliographical references and index.
Identifiers: LCCN 2025007055 (print) | LCCN 2025007056 (ebook) |
ISBN 9780197774700 paperback | ISBN 9780197774694 hardback |
ISBN 9780197774731 | ISBN 9780197774724 epub
Subjects: LCSH: Democracy—Economic aspects | Capitalism—Political aspects |
Comparative government | Comparative economics
Classification: LCC JC423 .C2495 2025 (print) | LCC JC423 (ebook) |
DDC 320.473—dc23/eng/20250415
LC record available at https://lccn.loc.gov/2025007055
LC ebook record available at https://lccn.loc.gov/2025007056

DOI: 10.1093/9780197774731.001.0001

Paperback printed by Integrated Books International, United States of America

Hardback printed by Lightning Source, Inc., United States of America

The manufacturer's authorized representative in the EU for product safety is
Oxford University Press España S.A., Parque Empresarial San Fernando de Henares,
Avenida de Castilla, 2 – 28830 Madrid (www.oup.es/en) or product.safety@oup.com).
OUP España S.A. also acts as importer into Spain of products made by the manufacturer).

CONTENTS

SECTION III. GOVERNANCE AND CONSOLIDATION OF PRIVATE POWER

SECTION IV. INEQUALITY AND OPPORTUNITY

SECTION V. POLARIZATION

PREFACE

SIDNEY M. MILKIS AND SCOTT C. MILLER

The ambition for this volume springs from a recognition that both democracy and capitalism are under siege today. Both critics and friends of democratic capitalism perceive that this is a pivotal moment, a "crossroad" at which values, parties, and policies will realign for years to come. We charged the contributors to this volume to develop ideas and evidence that will address today's challenges at the confluence of the economy, government, and society. We believe that the chapters in this volume confirm that this is the right moment to analyze what is and isn't going well in democratic capitalism, and what might be done to treat the pathologies that threaten the fraught relationship between self-government and free markets.

We are fortunate to have exceptional scholars join us in this endeavor, which began with a conference at the University of Virginia on March 7–9, 2023. At that gathering, participants explored the philosophical relationship between a free enterprise system and self-government, probed the deep historical roots of the bonds between the two, and considered policy proposals that promise a reimagining of the relationship. With the benefit of the rich conversation and insightful commentary that ensued in Charlottesville, our authors prepared essays that interrogate the relationship between these two principal elements of liberal society with a rare blend of synoptic reasoning and empirical evidence.

The question "can democracy and capitalism be reconciled?" is multifaceted and complex—both concepts are relatively new in human history, and have undergone considerable change since their inception. As such, scholars and the public alike struggle to understand the precise meaning of these ideas and how they interact. We believe that democracy is far more than a system of electing leaders—it is a civic ecology anchored to liberal principles of personal freedoms, the rule of law, and civic and electoral justice. Likewise, capitalism is not simply commerce beyond the reach of the state. It is an ecosystem of economic production based on free markets, competition, and private enterprise. The evolution of these ideas—and their practical implementation amid changing cultural, economic, and political norms—makes an evaluation of their relationship an even more vexing question.

Taking account of major political and economic developments in the United States, our introduction to this volume argues that Americans have never agreed over the proper balance between equality and free markets. Since the Colonial period there have been foundational conflicts that have made forging a consensus on how to achieve democratic capitalism a chimera. Nevertheless, despite the uneasy connection between capitalism and democracy, and the sharp conflicts they have agitated throughout history, reformers have routinely reimagined the American political economy in ways that have allowed for the coexistence of self-government and a dynamic economy that tolerates degrees of inequality. Put simply, a struggle between democracy and capitalism is not new in American history, nor is a battle of ideas about how that relationship should evolve.

Our collaborators in this volume, examining the United States and other comparable political systems, have concluded that there can be a co-existence between democracy and capitalism. Several essays demonstrate that there is a distinct correlation between the most capitalist and most democratic countries in the world. At the same time, almost every essay agrees that this relationship is fragile—the synthesis between capitalism and democracy can rapidly corrode and endanger each institution in the process. Numerous authors conclude that capitalism has a greater propensity to impinge on democracy than vice versa, and that only a well-calibrated set of institutions can prevent capture of democratic systems by capitalist impulses. In the end, this volume shows that both democracy and capitalism are human inventions, created to serve the broader purpose of human dignity and well-being. Yet these human creations need human upkeep to ensure that the relationship maintains proper balance. The countries that best sustain their institutions maintain the working relationship between democracy and capitalism that, when working well, contains remarkable potential. Nevertheless, the devil is in the details. Democratic capitalism certainly *can* exist and thrive; whether they *will* or not in the future is a different question entirely.

To tackle this vexing query, we have organized this volume with the hope of remedying some of the problems that have plagued previous studies of democracy and capitalism: the vagueness of the terms themselves, the siloed nature of studies, and the failure to build a research agenda focused on democracy and capitalism as interlocutors.

The chapters that follow address all three. First, they provide common intellectual ground on the very nature of democracy, capitalism, and where they interact. While seemingly basic, deficient definitions prevent scholarly investigation and rigorous debate across fields. Most agree that capitalism entails some degree of private ownership of the means of production, with the object being increased productivity and the attainment of profits. However, definitions beyond that remain a black box. Should capitalist systems emphasize minimal government intervention or the freest markets possible? What does "free market" even mean? Is entrepreneurialism and new firm development essential, or is the maximizing of capital efficiency all it takes? Are monopolies legitimate features of capitalist systems, or must competition define how capitalist structures operate? These are just a few of the questions that scholars repeatedly fail to answer and for which there is no consensus. The result has been a literature on "capitalism" that is discordant because scholars rarely refer to the same thing despite using the same vocabulary.

Second, the lack of adequate definitions often results in siloed and segmented studies. Seeking to address the prevailing segmentation, this volume features 24 essays from scholars across 9 academic fields. Democracy is not simply an issue of politics, but also social relations, legal structures, and a complex system of cultural norms that vary across time and political systems. Likewise, capitalism is far from a section of economics. It incorporates philosophical frameworks about how the world works, fundamental assumptions of "the good," and prescriptions, which also vary across time and space, about how to allocate resources. We believe that these two concepts are deeply interrelated and interreliant, but studies of democracy and capitalism remain cloistered in individual disciplines. This volume's multidisciplinary and comparative approach eliminates this balkanization by including scholars who specialize in multidisciplinary work and by including essays from scholars across at least nine disciplines.

Third, the cross-disciplinary approach of this volume addresses the intersection of democracy and capitalism on its own terms, free from modes of investigation imposed by arbitrary scholarly boundaries. Not to say that disciplinary boundaries are meaningless; indeed, we favor multidisciplinary to interdisciplinary approaches. The relationship between democracy and capitalism is multidimensional, encompassing economics, law, politics, business, public policy, and numerous other modes of study. For this reason, we believe that a full understanding of the relationship between democracy and capitalism requires an examination as multifaceted and nuanced as the subject itself. This volume aims to provide a *lingua franca* that will make further scholarship and debate possible while contributing its own conclusions and analysis.

The volume is organized into six sections, each of which serve as a benchmark challenge to which democratic capitalism will need to respond in the coming age. The careful reader will see that many of the issues and pathologies covered by these sections resemble ones that came before. Nevertheless, they retain a distinct character in today's world. They are:

1. The Nature of Democratic Capitalism
2. Environmental Degradation
3. Governance and Consolidation of Private Power
4. Inequality and Opportunity
5. Polarization
6. Frictions at the Intersection of Democracy and Capitalism

Sections 1 and 6 address broad themes about the meaning of, and relationship between democracy and capitalism; Sections 2 through 5 analyze the pathologies that threaten the tenuous ties between self-government and markets. Each section features an introductory essay that lays the intellectual groundwork for the chapters that follow, while synthesizing core arguments and proposed solutions. The component chapters address different elements of the section's theme. So organized, this volume provides a rounded understanding of why these issues and pathologies arose, how they have influenced society, and how free people can reform their political economy to bring it more in line with their values. Underlying the examination of these questions is the belief that it is possible to understand the dissonance in societies, know that humans have wrestled with these questions before, and combine the tools of theory and history to chart a course for democratic capitalism into a new age.

In Section 1, Isabel Sawhill's (Brookings Institution) synthetic essay charts the tense relationship between democracy and capitalism in the contemporary era, suggesting that capitalism is in much better shape than democracy; the chapters she reviews offer support for, and challenges to this proposition. In Chapter 1, Alex Tabarrok and Vincent Geloso (George Mason University) demonstrate significant complementarities between capitalism and democracy, with their empirical tests suggesting that, in the end, most democracies are capitalist, and most capitalist countries are democracies. In Chapter 2, Didi Kuo of Stanford University argues that one of the biggest challenges facing democratic capitalist states is the inability, or unwillingness, of governments to organize countervailing power, most often through political parties. Like Sawhill, Kuo concludes that democratic backsliding is largely a problem of capitalism, and trends toward autocracy cannot be resolved if governments do not also address the problems of economic insecurity and inequality. This resolution, she argues, is hindered by the absence of political parties in the United States and comparable political systems that countervail the dominion of powerful business interests. Chapter 3 features Carles Boix's (Princeton University) suggestion that instead of thinking about one capitalism, we should talk about different capitalisms. Each capitalism is defined by the nature of its production technologies and organization, and, above all, by the kind of labor skills that were (and are) complementary to capital. Those varying capital-labor complementarities have a different impact on employment patterns, wages, the distribution of income, and capitalism's likelihood of establishing democratic institutions.

Section 2 explores the "wicked problem" of climate change and the role of capitalist systems in addressing it. Michael James Lenox's (University of Virginia's Darden School of Business) introduction to this pathology argues that democratic capitalist nations are best positioned to deliver the changes necessary to avert, or at very least, moderate a crisis. This view is partially supported in Chapter 4, in which Barry G. Rabe (University of Michigan) explores emerging technological options such as direct air capture, modular nuclear reactors, and underground carbon storage, where democracies and capitalist systems will remain in the lead on research and future deployment. However, Rabe fears these advantages will fail to meaningfully address climate change unless polarization within nations and intense rivalries between nation states can be sufficiently moderated to solve a severe collective action problem. Chapter 5 features Shi-Ling Hsu's (Florida State University College of Law) more optimistic take on the profound challenges posed by climate change. He argues that that the large social and environmental costs suffered under capitalist systems have been failures of government, not failures of capitalism. Fortunately, Hsu argues, capitalism has demonstrated a capacity for dramatic transformation and re-orientation in the past and that a system of environmentally friendly taxes could not only preclude the externalization of environmental costs but stimulate much needed innovation.

Section 3 examines government's role as rule maker in capitalist economies, and the ramifications of both action and inaction in policing industry. Focusing on concepts of antitrust and legislative capture, this section looks at the historical role government has played in promoting, and preventing, the function of free markets. Kenneth G. Elzinga's (University of Virginia) essay frames the adjacent but contrasting nature of economic and political markets, arguing that, in the United States at least, the former have worked far better than the latter. While not disagreeing, the authors whose chapters appear in this section argue that free markets presuppose political conflict and purposeful government action. In Chapter 6 Laura Phillips-Sawyer (University of Georgia School of Law) revives and reassesses the democratic content of American antitrust law since 1945, emphasizing how the law changed in response to democratic protest movements as well as perceived threats to democratic accountability. In Chapter 7, Naomi Lamoreaux (Yale University) and John Joseph Wallis (University of Maryland) provide empirical evidence for the strong link between democracy and capitalism, but only among advanced democracies with strong and long-lasting democratic institutions. Simply put, Lamoreaux and Wallis find that the most democratic countries are almost all relatively wealthy, while lesser democracies show little to no correlation between democracy and capitalism.

Section 4 examines the tensions between social and economic liberalism, as well as complexities of making traditional liberal values sustainable in the twenty-first century. Christine Mahoney (University of Virginia) frames the challenge of balancing the inequality that often comes with capitalism with the equal opportunity that most associate with contemporary democracies. She warns that there is a "vicious cycle at play, where wealth inequality drives political inequality, as wealthy and corporate interests finance the campaigns of business-friendly candidates and pour untold amounts of money into lobbying for policies that protect the status quo of inequity and further exacerbates it." To resolve this conundrum, she prescribes not only political reform that ameliorates economic and racial inequality, but also corporate social responsibility, which has been abetted by investment strategies that reward businesses that are responsible employers and stewards of the environment. The chapters in this section elaborate on the potential of our democratic institutions and our capitalistic economy to deliver the equity needed for a thriving democracy. In Chapter 8, Joel Mokyr (Northwestern University) examines the historical consequences of greater tolerance and diversity. Mokyr concludes that greater diversity in many historical environments was not necessarily economically beneficial, and that well-meaning calls for "more diversity at any cost" may have to be qualified, depending on institutional quality and societal values. Deondra Rose (Duke University) offers a different perspective on inclusiveness in Chapter 9, recounting the injustices that follow from the power that capitalist institutions have in shaping government efforts to expand or limit access to education in the United States. In Chapter 10, Danielle Allen (Harvard University) argues that economic questions are critical to laying a foundation for political equality and human freedom, but not as ends in themselves. Allen suggests that whereas political equality and human freedom are intrinsically valuable, economic justice is an instrumental objective, and suggests that societies should seek economic justice to secure political equality and human freedom.

Section 5 looks at how schisms in American society—political, geographic, and cultural—are skewing traditional left-right divides in American politics, and in so doing casting doubt on the core tenants of the American capitalist system. Robert C. Lieberman (Johns Hopkins University) suggests in his synthetic essay that "the neoliberal push toward the marketization of, well, pretty much everything" has fueled a hyperpolarization in the United States and around the world. In the United States, these recurring struggles have typically played out against the backdrop of the country's foundational and continuing history of racial inequality, and if Americans are to coexist and flourish in the future, they will have to confront that history. The chapters that follow offer distinctive takes on the trauma of polarization. In Chapter 11, Jacob S. Hacker (Yale University) and Paul Pierson (University of California-Berkeley) explore how the two

US political parties are shaped, in different ways, by their internal class divides, which in turn reflect the rise of an increasingly geographically unequal political economy. In Chapter 12, Suzanne Mettler and Trevor E. Brown (Cornell University) probe the impact of trade liberalization, financial deregulation, and other policies in the late twentieth century and early twenty-first century on political change in rural areas. While these liberalizations did not single-handedly undermine democracy, Mettler and Brown argue, they have triggered developments that have transformed the rural-urban divide into the most dangerous fault line in contemporary American politics. Taking a bit more hopeful view of these disruptive tendencies in Chapter 13, William A. Galston (Brookings Institution) explores how shifts in conservative sentiment regarding market regulation have impacted party coalitions and the operation of American democracy. Some prominent "New Right" intellectuals and public actors have become highly critical of globalization and unfettered markets for ravaging conservative values such as family and community. Given that the market has generated grievances that have contributed to the rise of anti-democratic tendencies in recent decades, Galston suggests, the New Right's critique of contemporary capitalism might create opportunities for progressives and conservatives to form uneasy coalitions that pursue policies that impose constraints on markets—and, possibly, help rebuild support for democratic institutions and norms.

Section 6 explores what happens when the popular will conflicts with "sound" policy, and how policy makers have (or have not) smoothed frictions at the interface of democracy and capitalism. Jennifer Bair (University of Virginia) identifies throughlines for successful alignments of democracy and capitalism across time, stressing flexibility and the ability to shape solutions to their specific time and place. Exploring the deep historical roots of democratic capitalism's viability in Chapter 14, Kara Dimitruk (Hamilton College) and Dan Bogart (University of California-Irvine) demonstrate the effect of Parliamentary changes on liberalizations in British imperial policy before and after the Glorious Revolution of 1688. Dimitruk and Bogart show how the consistent push and pull—or "friction"—between the earliest democratic and capitalist institutions shaped the frameworks in which British liberalism operated for decades, if not centuries. Chapter 15 features a theoretical reconceptualization of economic and political freedom across time. Hannah Knox Tucker (Copenhagen Business School) and R. Daniel Wadhwani (University of Southern California) argue that a series of "entrepreneurial imaginaries" have resolved the inherent tension between positive and negative freedom in capitalist democracies. While the contents of these imaginaries change, Tucker and Wadhwani argue, their function does not. The imaginaries reemerge across democratic-capitalist societies to aid actors in navigating the tension between economic invention and political constraint. Chapter 16 features Robert F. Bruner's (University of Virginia's Darden School of Business) exploration of the effect of financial crises on America's civic ecology. Using the Panic of 1907 as a lens, Bruner focuses on the imposing challenges of crisis management, and how moments of crisis have spurred solutions to four major impediments to efficient political and economic action.

In the concluding chapter, James A. Morone (Brown University) draws on the lessons of the volume's authors to offer 10 conclusions about the profound challenges that now strain the relationship between democracy and capitalism and to ponder the potential paths ahead. Together, they add up to a sobering view of the United States's beleaguered political economy and an urgent call for change. As in the past, there are serious doubts about whether the United States—obsessed with privacy, property, and how government power threatens them—can address the pathologies that currently plague the nation. Like many authors, Morone views polarization in the United States as the heart of the fraught relationship between self-government and free markets. All the challenges that test this relationship—social, political, and economic inequality; climate change; and monopolization—require an active and competent government. However, Morone warns, the current tribalism that disrupts democracy in America makes meeting these challenges extraordinarily difficult.

Yet Morone joins the other authors of this volume in the hope that capitalism and democracy can be reconciled. We share his observation that "they are deeply intertwined." Self-government depends on constraining the inevitable excesses of an unfettered capitalist economy; a free and prosperous economy depends on cultural and institutional constraints on what James Madison called "the mischiefs of factionalism." If the past is prologue, we should not expect the current cause of our present discontents to be cured; what we can reasonably hope for, as Morone elegantly prescribes, "is the courage to imagine a more virtuous way forward."

ACKNOWLEDGMENTS

We are grateful to Brian Kettenring and the Hewlett Foundation for their generous support of the conference that made this ambitious volume possible. The warm friendship and intellectual engagement of our amazing colleagues in the Project on Democracy and Capitalism—Robert F. Bruner, Melody Barnes, Michael James Lenox, and Margaret Riley—have been a constant source of inspiration as we tackled the imposing challenges of organizing an unusually wide-ranging conference and forging a coherent volume from such a diverse array of intellectual and disciplinary approaches. Special thanks go to William Antholis, the CEO and president of the Miller Center at the University of Virginia, who has provided the Project on Democracy and Capitalism with a congenial and vibrant home over the past four years. It had been a great pleasure to work with Dave McBride, senior editor at Oxford University Press. Dave expressed enthusiasm for this project from the beginning, solicited very helpful reviews as this volume gradually took shape, and patiently helped us navigate the complex obstacles we faced in moving the manuscript into production. Emily Benitez, Oxford's Senior Project Editor, expertly guided us through the final nettlesome steps of publication. Finally, we are very fortunate to have had the indispensable help of our program's Project Manager, Christine Linsinbigler, in all phases of the painstaking process that has led us to our final destination. We will always be grateful for Chrissy's friendship, intelligence, and patience as we struggled to the finish line. She is truly the guardian angel of the Democracy and Capitalism program.

LIST OF CONTRIBUTORS

Danielle Allen is the James Bryant Conant University Professor, Harvard University, Cambridge, MA, US. https://scholar.harvard.edu/danielleallen/home

Jennifer Bair is Professor of Sociology, University of Virginia, Charlottesville, VA, US. https://orcid.org/0000-0002-5083-1385

Dan Bogart is Professor, UC Irvine, CA, US. https://orcid.org/0000-0002-0011-3190

Carles Boix is Robert Garrett Professor of Politics and Public Affairs, Princeton University, Princeton, NJ, US. https://orcid.org/0000-0002-2154-2701

Trevor E. Brown is Ph.D. Candidate, Cornell University, Ithaca, NY, US. https://orcid.org/0000-0003-4418-1619

Robert F. Bruner is University Professor Emeritus, Distinguished Professor Emeritus, and Dean Emeritus, University of Virginia, Charlottesville, VA, US.

Kara Dimitruk is Assistant Professor, Economics Department, Hamilton College, Clinton, NY, US.

Kenneth G. Elzinga is Robert C. Taylor Professor of Economics, University of Virginia, Charlottesville, VA, US. https://orcid.org/0000-0001-9988-0148

William A. Galston is Senior Fellow, The Brookings Institution, Washington, DC, US.

Vincent Geloso is Assistant Professor, George Mason University, Fairfax, VA, US.

Jacob S. Hacker is Stanley Resor Professor of Political Science, Department of Political Science, Yale University, New Haven, CT, US. https://orcid.org/ 0000-0002-3686-2513

Shi-Ling Hsu is D'Alemberte Professor, Florida State University College of Law, Tallahassee, FL, US. https://orcid.org/0000-0003-4057-7480

Didi Kuo is Center Fellow, Freeman-Spogli Institute for International Studies, Stanford University, CA, US.

Naomi Lamoreaux is Senior Research Scholar, University of Michigan, Ann Arbor, MI, US and Stanley B. Resor Professor Emeritus of Economics and Professor Emeritus of History, Yale University, New Haven, CT, US.

Michael James Lenox is University Professor, Darden School of Business, University of Virginia, Charlottesville, VA, US. https://orcid.org/0000-0002-4600-2517

Robert C. Lieberman is Krieger-Eisenhower Professor of Political Science, Johns Hopkins University, Baltimore, MD, US. https://orcid.org/0000-0002-9677-8946

Christine Mahoney is Professor of Public Policy and Politics, Batten School of Leadership and Public Policy, University of Virginia, Charlottesville, Virginia, US. https://batten.virginia.edu/people/christine-mahoney

Suzanne Mettler is John L. Senior Professor of American Institutions, Cornell University, Ithaca, NY, US. https://orcid.org/0000-0002-5165-3349

Sidney M Milkis is White Burkett Miller Professor of Politics, University of Virginia, Charlottesville, VA, US.

Scott C. Miller is Assistant Professor, Darden School of Business and Director, Project on Democracy & Capitalism, Miller Center of Public Affairs, University of Virginia Charlottesville, VA, US.

Joel Mokyr is Robert H. Strotz Professor of Arts and Sciences and Professor of Economics and History, Northwestern University, Evanston, IL, US.

James A. Morone is Professor Emeritus of Political Science, Brown University, Providence, Rhode Island, US. https://polisci.brown.edu/people/james-morone

Laura Phillips-Sawyer is Jane W. Wilson Associate Professor of Business Law, University of Georgia, School of Law, Athens, GA, US.

Paul Pierson is Professor of Political Science, University of California-Berkeley, CA, US.

Barry G. Rabe is Professor of Public Policy, Gerald Ford School of Public Policy, University of Michigan, Ann Arbor, MI, US.

Deondra Rose is Kevin D. Gorter Associate Professor of Public Policy and Associate Professor of Political Science and History, Sanford School of Public Policy, Duke University, Durham, NC, US.

Isabel Sawhill is Senior Fellow, Brookings Institution, Washington, DC, US.

Alex Tabarrok is Bartley J. Madden Chair in Economics at the Mercatus Center, George Mason University, Fairfax, VA, US. https://orcid.org/0000-0003-2200-2851

Hannah Knox Tucker is Assistant Professor of History, Copenhagen Business School, Copenhagen, Denmark. https://www.cbs.dk/en/research/departments-and-centres/department-of-business-humanities-and-law/staff/htubhl:

R. Daniel Wadhwani is Professor of Entrepreneurship and History, University of Southern California, Sacramento, CA, US. https://orcid.org/0000-0003-4221-4077

John Joseph Wallis is Research Associate, National Bureau of Economic Research, Cambridge, MA, US, Professor of Economics, University of Maryland, College Park, MD, US and Research Fellow, CEPR, Paris, France.

Introduction

Sidney M. Milkis and Scott C. Miller

Figure 0.1 National Association of Manufacturers sign in Dubuque, Iowa. Source: Photograph taken by John Vachon, 1940, Library of Congress. Accessed January 30, 2025, https://loc.gov/pictures/resource/fsa.8a05458/

At the apex of the Great Depression's second wave in 1937, the National Association of Manufacturers unleashed a national campaign of billboards and advertisements. Trade associations regularly promote their goods, services, and firms, but this 1937–1940 campaign stood out. Instead of promoting products for sale,

Sidney M. Milkis and Scott C. Miller, *Introduction*. In: *Can Democracy and Capitalism Be Reconciled?*. Edited by: Sidney M. Milkis and Scott C. Miller, Oxford University Press. © Oxford University Press (2025).
DOI: 10.1093/9780197774731.003.0001

the Association invested millions of dollars trumpeting Americans democratic and capitalist values. The billboards presented "representative democracy" and "private enterprise" as "the American Way." The existence of the campaign revealed much more; the United States was experiencing an ideological battle about the future of democratic capitalism itself. Despite the rhetoric on all sides, this was not unprecedented or new. Nor is it today.

The compatibility of democracy and capitalism remains a flashpoint of modern American civic dialogue. Polling in 2022 by Pew Research found that 40 percent of Americans have unfavorable views of capitalism. If you ask people under 40 years old, those numbers almost double. Likewise, a recent poll by Quinnipiac University found that 69 percent of Americans believe the nation's democracy is on the brink of collapse. In our experience, young people largely believe that democracy and capitalism are structurally incompatible. Even many students at elite business schools believe this to be the case.

Although current conditions entail new challenges, we believe that a proper understanding of our present discontents requires engagement with the American tradition of debating the meaning and compatibility of democracy and capitalism. We reject frameworks that assume Americans have always agreed on the right mix of democracy and capitalism. Such assertions are often cynical and ahistorical. Americans have long questioned the value of consumer economies, private property, and universal political liberty. Americans have long disputed the effect of wage labor on personal freedom, and land ownership on social and economic mobility. Americans have long argued about how to create a democratic culture or even if one should exist in the first place. Modern policy disputes including the role of finance, the extent of universal rights, monopoly power and government oversight, and the provision of public goods have, in fact, polarized American opinion for generations. The myth that we are in a particularly volatile debate about socialism and capitalism, or democracy and authoritarianism, fails to stand amid historical investigation. For centuries, Americans have contested the balance between equality and wealth, government and the private sector, consumption and investment, and labor and management. In many ways, the fight over democracy and capitalism is as American as democracy and capitalism themselves.

Colonial Battles

When the fight for American independence erupted in 1775, debates over the balance between what we would now call democracy and capitalism already had a long history. "Capitalism" as an economic ideology would not arise until the mid-nineteenth century. Economic liberalism even remained a relatively novel concept. English mercantilism, in which the state coordinated systems of economic output, dominated economic thought. "According to the mercantilist view," writes historian Alan Taylor, "the government had every right, indeed the duty, to shape the economy to serve its needs for more revenue, ships, and men for use in war . . ."[1] Commerce and trade existed to boost the wealth and prestige of the state, not the individual. Private markets, free trade, and consumption-based economies remained anathema. Of course, British citizens—and those on the home island in particular—benefited from this regime. Nevertheless, the economic paradigm that dominated colonial America remained focused on consolidating, not expanding, as much of the globe's limited wealth in metropolitan England as possible.

The economic paradigm in the North American colonies remained even less "capitalist" than in the broader empire. Rather than growth, diversification, and productivity, most seventeenth-century colonial Americans embraced an extraction economy in which North Americans exported raw materials such as tobacco, wheat, and wood products for processing and reexport in the metropole. American mercantilists considered economic growth to be corrupting and believed that foreign trade remained the only legitimate source of wealth. According to this view, banking institutions, local currency, and internal markets diverted resources away from the Empire and were thus frowned upon or outlawed. The British North American economic system carried a distinct ethic. "Bank credit and internal trade did not increase wealth," mercantilist North Americans thought, "but rather encouraged [them] to spend beyond their means and to pledge their lands and goods recklessly so they could consume rather than invest or improve."[2] Civic leaders argued that the procurement of credit, debt, and consumption would corrupt character and harm the social fabric. If the colonists went down what could be retrospectively called a "capitalist" path of financialization, market integration, and free trade, Americans would fall victim to the vice of "luxury" and "dissipated manners."[3] In other words, many seventeenth-century American colonists viewed principles of modern capitalism as toxic, corrupting, and deleterious to the public good.

Still, many new English colonies began pursuing what could be called an early or "pre-capitalism" by the mid-seventeenth century. The Puritans of Massachusetts Bay eliminated guilds, commercial monopolies, and wage and price controls, while establishing money markets and private property rights via land reforms. As a result, the Puritans encouraged acquisition, profit-making, and productivity enhancements that dramatically increased their output. While Massachusetts Bay did lack some elements of advanced financial capitalism, "the Puritans were moving 'crab-like' into the new capitalist world," writes historian Stephen Innes, by "creat[ing] an economy increasingly based on the principles of economic freedom."[4] This freedom produced profound advances in general well-being, in everything from rising incomes, falling infant mortality, and the rapid expansion of economic security across the colony.

Despite their "capitalist" successes, the Puritans were keenly aware that money-making and efficiency needed a countervailing force. Like other colonists, the Puritans believed that the accumulation of wealth could tear at the social fabric, leading to corrosive disparities among members of the commonwealth. The Puritans foresaw that "capitalist" enterprise could be a remarkable means to commonwealth building but could and should not be an end in and of itself. As such, Puritan culture encouraged a "civic ecology" anchored in religious traditions that mandated care for "the least of these," even at the expense of personal economic advancement. "Ministers sermons, as well as the daily devotional labors of mothers and fathers within the New England household," Innes writes, "provided a cultural counterweight to unbridled capitalist behavior, the moral ballast of the developmental state. They helped ensure that the ethics of the marketplace were never unchallenged, never became those later identified with—and castigated as—social Darwinism."[5] In short, the Puritans harnessed the immense potential of individual enterprise, but they knew that capitalism could quickly run away with itself. The Puritans believed that only a communal capitalism in which money-making was encouraged but subject to community and religious obligation, could prevent the corrosive effects that would eventually lead to its downfall.

Yet by the early eighteenth century, a reconceptualization of political economy began to emerge. Colonial leaders like John Colman and Oliver Noyes began advocating for specialization and diversification, domestic market development, and paper money issuances that could finance such ventures. Rather than serving as extractive "ghost acres" for the British imperial machine, Americans would begin investing in ironworks, naileries, timber mills, and facilities for producing woolen goods.[6] British mercantilism, its advocates argued, would meet its match in a liberal entrepreneurialism fueled by the new technology of finance.

The emergence of this new, liberal faction sparked an ideological war in colonial America. Advocates for "investment capital, internal development, diversification, [and] manufactures" like Noyes and Colman argued that this new liberal regime would enlarge the sphere of home rule by eliminating the coercive power brought by dependence on the British empire. Their opponents such as Paul and Thomas Dudley argued that the new course would elevate individuals above the group and make Americans slaves of mammon. Americans would become hostages to the vicissitudes of financial speculation and crisis, and the social unrest that would inevitably follow. While supposedly free, new liberal adventurers would succumb to uncertainty and instability, and thus be more willing to surrender their liberties to populist demagogues preaching equality and revolution. Even advocates of greater commercial freedom split among themselves. Merchants in different colonies contested the wisdom of financialization, banks, and paper money.[7] Throughout the eighteenth century, both groups lashed out at each other, claiming that their opponents' policies would make the colonies less free and less prosperous.

It is alluring to frame the Revolution as the forces of democratic capitalism against royalist mercantilism. Yet we must remember that few revolutionaries were doctrinaire liberals. Even during the Revolution itself, Americans (literally) fought about how liberal and capitalist they should become. While wanting the right to enhance their financial and commercial systems, they often did so by illiberal acts such as establishing their own trade barriers and enacting state-driven industrial policy. Far from opening America as a democratic and capitalist paradise, the Revolution spawned a long-running battle over whether Americans could become capitalist and free at the same time.

Revolutionary Wars

The post-Revolutionary contest between Alexander Hamilton and Thomas Jefferson embodies early America's lack of consensus about their relationship with free markets and free government. Free from the British yoke, Hamilton, Jefferson, and their supporters engaged in an ideological war over the future of American political economy.

In many ways, Hamilton embodied the industrialized financial capitalism that would not take hold in America for a century. Hamilton believed that American independence depended on a rapid transition to industrial capitalism backed by liquid financial markets. The United States needed to diversify its economic base to protect against embargos, trade shocks, and the changes in labor productivity flowing from Europe's Industrial Revolution. Hamilton financed this conversion by mobilizing the vast national debt into a stock of liquid capital. By refinancing America's wartime obligations, Hamilton transformed the national debt into liquid securities that expanded the money supply and served as stable collateral for loans. For the first time ever, money and credit ceased being a constraint and activated the large-scale investment needed to make industrial development possible. On the production side, Hamilton emphasized the use of machinery to save labor, increase productivity, and capitalize on America's natural wealth. Hamilton also argued that domestic manufactures would provide an outlet for excess agricultural supply, benefiting farmers who invested in their land and updated their production methods. Hamilton channeled Adam Smith in suggesting that industry would unleash the energies of the entrepreneur. As Hamilton saw in the United Kingdom, manufacturing benefited existing sectors and created entirely new ones.

Despite Hamilton's emphasis on capitalist production methods, he did not adhere to laissez-faire principles of political economy. Hamilton disagreed with Adam Smith's credo that human industry, "if left to itself, will naturally find its way to the most useful and profitable employment."[8] Hamilton's experience showed him that economic actors adhered to habits formed by custom, opting to stick to traditional and less productive methods of enterprise. Thus, Hamilton believed that reluctant laborers and investors needed "the incitement and patronage of government" to help them overcome initial obstacles to engage in a new manufacturing economy.[9] Smith's principles may have been accurate with all things being equal, Hamilton said. But Hamilton argued that all things were *not* equal. On the theoretical level, the United States had deeply ingrained economic, cultural, and political traditions anchored to agricultural production. On a more practical front, potential manufacturers faced an industrial leviathan in the United Kingdom that could slash prices to undercut American startups, only to reestablish its monopolistic control after driving domestic alternatives out of business. While Hamilton remained an unbridled proponent of private enterprise and the market economy, he believed that the new government had to level the playing field for American entrepreneurs. In short, Hamilton advocated an industrialized system in which the state and private actors work together for the betterment of American citizens.

Jefferson despised Hamilton's "unholy marriage" of state-backed urban manufacturing and financial wizardry. He saw what would later be called "industrial capitalism" as a dual threat to his idea of an agrarian "empire of liberty" in which independent producers cultivated their land and engaged each other as peers. Jefferson embraced large-scale trade, arguing that America should "throw open the doors of commerce . . . giving perfect freedom to all persons for the vent of whatever they may chuse [sic] to bring into our ports, and asking the same in theirs."[10] Jefferson envisioned Americans producing more and more on their independent farms and, in the words of historian Peter Onuf, "trading agricultural surpluses ('what we can spare') for manufactured goods ('what we shall want')."[11] Jefferson warned that anchoring the American economy to the large-scale production of manufactured goods in decrepit factories manned by landless laborers was a recipe for a new form of aristocracy.

While he advocated for "the promotion of . . . household manufacture," Jefferson strongly opposed the prospect of huge factories that produced a vast number of goods in large, coastal cities.[12] First, Jefferson rejected the pools of liquid debt and investment that would make those facilities possible. Theories about Jefferson's aversion to debt abound, but much of it comes down to how to finance converted debts into commodities that could be transferred across time. The conversion of personal obligations into assets that would encumber those who did not initiate them conflicted with Jefferson's notions of personal ownership and generational sovereignty—his ideal that the constitution "belongs to the living." Jefferson charged "that for one generation to encumber its successors with debt, squandering 'the usufruct of the lands for several generations to come', is a form of enslavement, forcing unborn men and women to work for the dead."[13] Financial capitalism, and Hamilton's system anchored to it, rests upon the premise of transferrable, commoditized debt as a capital base for investment. Jefferson rejected this principle, and the capitalist enterprise anchored to it, as slavery.

The issue of labor, and the right of employers to profit from the labor of others, marks perhaps the greatest difference between Hamilton and Jefferson. Hamilton viewed the emergence of wage-labor markets as vital fixes to structural problems in the American economy. First, Hamilton saw the provision of wages as a way to channel liquidity into the perpetually cash-starved economy. Second, Hamilton saw the rise of cash wages as a means of increasing mobility and capital accumulation. Cash provided the common worker ways to invest in relatively small-denomination liquid assets. Thus, the emergence of cash wages supported not only systemic liquidity, but well-functioning capital markets in which investors received a return on their savings while gaining collateral for loans should they choose to start a business. Finally, Hamilton saw wage labor as a way to increase incomes. Hamilton contended that working for wages in manufacturing or artisanal trades would provide off-season work for agricultural laborers who faced several months a year without gainful employment.

In the end, Hamilton saw wage labor and the increasingly liquid labor market as key to addressing the fundamental underproductivity of the American economy. Where Jefferson saw vast acres of undeveloped land as the facilitator of personal liberty, Hamilton saw an unproductive natural asset that locked Americans into an ossified class structure based on landed wealth. He saw agriculture in general as unproductive because weather and seasonal patterns precluded farmers from working to their fullest potential. Hamilton believed that wage work and liquid labor markets would solve this productivity problem, helping the United States, and the workers that comprised it, to become wealthier and more secure.

Hamilton's drive for growth did not arise from an obsession with individual wealth. Hamilton repeatedly turned down schemes that made small fortunes and once told his friend John Laurens, ". . . in perfect confidence I whisper a word in your ear. I hate money-making men . . ."[14] Conversely, Hamilton's efforts to make the United States more "capitalist" emanated from his desire to make the country freer and more mobile. Hamilton was a visionary, but he was also a student of history. He understood that the existing order based on land and other forms of illiquid wealth precluded upstarts like himself from gaining social position and asserting their political will. In other words, Hamilton sought to create a system in which citizens "measured worth and achievement in terms of money and worked to obtain money" as the *best* way to create an equitable, free, and mobile society. "To transform the established order," historian Forrest McDonald writes,

> to make society fluid and open to merit, to make industry both rewarding and necessary, all that needed to be done was to monetize the whole—to rig the rules of the game so that money would become the universal measure of the value of things. For money is oblivious to class, status, color, and inherited social position; money is the ultimate, neutral, and personal arbiter. Infused into an **oligarchical**, agrarian social order, money would be the leaven, the fermenting yeast, that would stimulate growth, change, prosperity, and national strength.[15]

Hamilton thus saw the spirit of capitalism as liberation from the constrained social and political order of the day. Class would never be eliminated, but the accumulation of wealth through capitalist enterprise would make the class structure more open and fluid. As they accrued wealth and power, traditionally disenfranchised Americans would gain electoral access and political opportunities, making a more liberal and diverse society.

Jefferson's opposition to Hamilton's plans for the political economy was not just theoretical; he saw financial capitalism as antithetical to the American experiment. Jefferson believed that the cultivation of individual plots by freeholders fortified and perpetuated "competency," their capacity "to be fed abundantly, clothed above mere decency, to labor moderately and raise their families."[16] Holding conservative, pre-capitalist conceptions of wealth and the power that came with it, Jefferson cared little about productivity. He viewed the moneyed wealth cultivated by merchants, bankers, and "capitalists" as vapid, volatile, and devoid of real value. Channeling one's labor toward agricultural self-sufficiency was not a means to an end; it was the essence of freedom itself. Abandoning the land to work for wages, even if that meant increasing one's standard of living, struck at the heart of Jefferson's vision of a free America.

Jefferson believed that an economic system built upon a landless working class would entrench a system of reliance and dependence. "Compelling individuals to relinquish the right to direct their labor," Claudio J. Katz writes, summarizing Jefferson, "is equivalent to compelling them to relinquish the right to direct their government: both are inconsistent with independence."[17] Once a worker subjected their labor to an employer, they would be more likely to subject their will to that employer as well. Subjugation would not flow simply from physical intimidation, but also from employers' ability to threaten their workers' livelihoods. "Does not the moral coercion of want," Jefferson asked Dr. Thomas Cooper, "subject their will as despotically to that of their employer, as the physical constraint does to the soldier, the seaman, or the slave?"[18] To Hamilton, possessing the free choice as to whether or not to work for wages was sufficient. In contrast, writes Katz, Jefferson "contend[ed] that laborers are meaningfully free only if they employ their own property and work for themselves . . . To be constrained by necessity, to subject oneself to another's will [was] equivalent to wage-slavery."[19] By making them reliant on the market as opposed to the land, Jefferson thought, laborers would be as unfree as the enslaved people he himself owned.

Jefferson derived his reasoning from the principle of collusive monopoly. Men of capital would draw workers away from their farms with elevated wages. Once laborers lost their agricultural sufficiency, managers would drive down wages to the point where laborers could not provide for themselves. While Jefferson suggested that working for a wage could be acceptable in isolated and temporary circumstances, he believed that it should be avoided and coupled with immediate recourse to agricultural labor on one's own property. Removing workers from the land, paying them a wage, and extracting increasing levels of productivity through "factory discipline" would produce a society like England or France in which "paupers cannot provide for themselves, even by labor," and the laboring poor, "whether employed in agriculture or the arts," are reduced "to the maximum of labor which . . . the human body can endure, and to the minimum of food . . . which will preserve it in life."[20] Workers' desperation would eventually force them into even more arduous conditions and open them to manipulation by those able to exploit their poverty.

Hamilton and Jefferson also clashed over the role of private property and inequality in American society. Jefferson believed that all men had the equal right to work the earth in usufruct, with ownership arising from the investment of labor in improving the land. Government then had the duty to secure the fruits of that labor to those who produced it. In this way, the right to property was tangible. "It is agreed by those who have seriously considered the subject," Jefferson wrote, "that no individual has, of natural right, a separate property in an acre of land, for instance . . . [W]hatever, whether fixed or movable, belongs to all men equally and in common, is the property for the moment of him who occupies it, but when he relinquishes the occupation, the property goes with it."[21] In fact, Jefferson argued that the accumulation of property that produced an unnecessary scarcity of resources and "violate[d] others' rights to the means of subsistence," was illegitimate. As he told James Madison, "extending 'the laws of property' to protect the aristocracy's extravagant waste of resources . . . is to 'violate natural right.'"[22]

Unrealistic as it may seem—especially given his enslavement of 400 human beings at Monticello—Jefferson worked hard to melt away class distinctions. Jefferson favored policy, such as the Louisiana Purchase that doubled the land mass of the United States, that would buttress "the small land holders

[that] are the most precious part of a state."[23] He advocated the distribution of Western lands to farmers, believing that unequal accumulation of property could be diluted or even eliminated by rapid distribution of freeholds. This policy would fuel the extension of suffrage, and thus make the American political economy more democratic. It would also prevent workers from resorting to wage labor, which Jefferson believed would inevitably enslave them. Finally, it would provide steady increases in well-being, as more people cultivated more crops for consumption and trade. Jefferson also "proposed a steeply graduated tax" that would provide public goods while ensuring that "the poor man in this country . . . pays not a farthing of tax to the general government . . . [while] the farmer will see government supported, his children educated, and the face of his country made a paradise by the contributions of the rich alone."[24] In the end, Jefferson sought a society in which class and inequality melted away into an egalitarian ethos focused on liberty and competency, rather than productivity and competition. By continuing to expand their holdings into the seemingly "empty" western frontier, Jefferson believed that America could grow increasingly wealthy without the draconian measures of industrial capitalism.

Hamilton viewed Jefferson's vision as one of "paradoxical imagination."[25] Hamilton told the Constitutional Convention in 1787 that "In every community where industry is encouraged, there will be a division of it into the few and the many." He believed that the goal of society should not be to eliminate classes; such attempts would be fanciful. Rather, the United States should aim to make those classes as fluid as possible. Hamilton believed that, as much as Jefferson sought to distribute land to small holders, the industrious would still work harder, be more productive, cultivate more crops, and accumulate more wealth. Stratification would occur in the West just like it did in the East. Indeed, class stratification would be more intractable if land remained the baseline asset and determinate of political viability. Land would always remain less liquid than money or other financial assets, and thus wealth and political power would accumulate with those who did not necessarily deserve it. Where Jefferson saw a commercial but not necessarily capitalist system dissolving America's inequalities into the vast expanse of the West, Hamilton saw the beginning of a gold rush that would eventually solidify the wealth and power of a landed aristocracy.

Contrary to Jefferson's view of property rights as rooted in labor, Hamilton viewed property rights as founded in contract. In the early 1790s, Hamilton rejected the policy of "discrimination" that favored Revolutionary soldiers, suppliers, and pensioners who had sold depreciated continental IOUs to speculators for pennies on the dollar. Jefferson's political ally in his opposition to Hamiltonian nationalism, James Madison, wanted the government to divide the benefits among current owners and the original holders of continental debt. While Hamilton sympathized with his former comrades who had sold their notes cheap, the original debt holders parted with their securities willingly and of their own volition. Consequently, the right of ownership had legally and justly passed to the speculators. In addition to the practical fact that foreign capital would not invest in a system that risked the arbitrary redistribution of property, Hamilton saw Jefferson's law of property as against the principle of just governance itself. If ownership did not rest on contract, government or oligarchs could cancel ownership at will. Such a system would be ripe for corruption by elites that sought to preserve their waning power.

The Madisonian (and Jeffersonian) position rested on an old theory of contract law in which everything held an objective value and a just price, with courts adjudicating rights based on that value. Whereas theorists like E. P. Thompson argue that the social body shapes the "moral economy," Hamilton insisted that oligarchic land—and slaveholders held the power to determine—or manipulate—"just" prices through their networks of wealth and privilege. As such, Hamilton believed that the market should determine value and price. While Hamilton was not naïve about the flaws in market functions, he believed it worked better than a system that allowed oligarchs to pull strings in the name of objectivity and justice. "Only by incorporating such changes into law," historian Forrest McDonald wrote, "could a modern, dynamic market economy replace the static, fixed economy that had been rooted in feudalism."[26] Anchoring property rights to the free agreement of willing parties circumvented the oligarchy's ability to bend the rules in their favor. Having property rights determined by a non-arbitrary standard, Hamilton believed, would open the doors to a flood of investment and entrepreneurial activity.

The fundamental conflict between Hamilton and Jefferson revolved around their view of growth. Both men believed that the United States would become an empire of "liberty and freedom." However, their view of how the United States would grow into that empire of liberty could not have been more different. Jefferson saw the process as one of extensive growth, the continual adding of resources to increase output. In many cases this simply referred to Western lands—Americans would cultivate more acres, produce more crops, and in so doing secure their freedom and liberty from the malign powers of industrial empires. Hamilton saw this view as chimerical. He argued that intensive growth, the constant increasing of productivity through capital investment, was America's path to supremacy. Hamilton believed that as America's economy became more dynamic and open, its political system would follow. In both visions America becomes more wealthy and more free. However, Jefferson viewed Hamilton's capitalist vision as a futuristic dystopia, while Hamilton saw Jefferson's as the continuation of Europe's feudal past.

Antebellum Fracture

Hamilton and Jefferson's struggle reveals that resolving the fraught relationship between markets and self-government was bounded by a consensus that America must chart a different path than feudal Europe. Yet slavery was the serpent in the Garden of Eden that the Framers' grand experiment in self-rule imagined. Consequently, as the founding generation faded into history, their successors became more divided on the integration of democracy and capitalism, not less. The rising ideological conflict over slavery and its role in the American capitalist system severely tested the idea that democratic capitalism could buttress the political economy. As Jefferson feared, American industrialism catalyzed conflicts between capital and labor, and raised doubts that they could co-exist as the United States emerged as an industrial power. Voices like Alexis de Tocqueville viewed American democracy and capitalism as symbiotic, while ("small-d") democrats like Daniel Webster held distinct reservations about the co-existence of free markets and free peoples. Both, however, viewed slavery as a stain on the American Constitution that could halt the march toward a just commercial republic. At the same time, a not insignificant number of Americans adopted the views of radicals like the slavery apologist George Fitzhugh who argued that both democracy and capitalism could, and in fact should, not endure in America. The mid-nineteenth century thus witnessed a violent conflict over not simply the balance between democracy and capitalism, but whether they could co-exist at all.

Tocqueville traveled to "the great young Republic" from his native France in the tumultuous wake of the July Revolution of 1830. For Tocqueville, the co-existence of democracy and industrial capitalism was not academic. He sought to understand how, or *if*, a liberal Republic could survive the historical forces set against it. To the surprise of many in Europe, Tocqueville's mid-1830s analysis of the young American republic argued that the Hamiltonian synthesis of democratic capitalism had become a reality in the North. Tocqueville posed a strong link between America's rising commercial prowess and its democratic culture. While still more agrarian than Hamilton may have preferred, Tocqueville described a striving, entrepreneurial economy with a dynamic and fluid class structure. While Tocqueville believed "that . . . a [democratic] society can be composed of distinct social classes, there must be a non-zero probability of social mobility from one class to another."[27] In fact, Tocqueville made this fluidity a, if not *the*, critical element of what made the United States the vanguard of a new individual-based democracy arising from the Enlightenment. In contrast with Tocqueville's native France, still hobbled by its feudal past, the equality of opportunity made possible by American capitalism both reinforced, and was reinforced by, the young republic's democratic values.

The specter of aristocracy loomed large over Tocqueville's analysis of American democratic capitalism. Tocqueville described aristocratic society as static and ossified in both political and economic terms. But Americans were "excited, uncertain, breathless, [and] ready to change will and place."[28] For Tocqueville, the fluidity provided by democratic society destroyed aristocratic barriers, thus providing opportunity for the churn of business-oriented initiative. Relieved of the stasis, rent seeking, and capture of aristocratic politics, Americans were freed to pursue their taste for material "comfort."[29] Tocqueville believed that the lack of social constraints incentivized the American work ethic at which he marveled. Tocqueville theorized that Americans worked so hard because they believed that "at any moment a servant may become a master, and he aspires to rise to that condition."[30]

In addition to the catalytic effects of democratic culture, social mobility, and incentives for profit making, Tocqueville argued that the practicalities of widespread political participation produced a self-reinforcing cycle of liberty, equality, and commercialism. Democratic politics helped balance the obsessive pursuit of self-interest, while also building skills and networks useful for commercial growth. Tocqueville also suggested that commerce provided avenues for ambition, giving talented individuals multiple theaters to win acclaim. He believed that entrepreneurial growth in democratic societies would ameliorate the negative tendency of commercial power to consolidate. Effectively a capitalist version of Madison's argument in Federalist 10, Tocqueville suggested that a nation of entrepreneurs would diffuse economic interest and prevent the vast consolidation of power backed by corporate money.

Despite his optimism, Tocqueville held several concerns about the future of democratic capitalism in America. He feared that slavery—"the most dreadful of all evils that threatened the United States"—would produce a "revolution" that could leave America in a state of "senile imbecility."[31] Even if the United States managed to avoid a fatal civil war, Tocqueville worried that the dynamics of democratic capitalism, if unchecked, might denigrate economic freedoms. The continued division of labor in American industry would produce extreme inequalities and concentrate wealth. Inequality would diminish the social mobility that activated American "restiveness," entrepreneurial vigor, and democratic spirit. Tocqueville believed that the stratification and solidification of class structure would prove the death knell to successful capitalist enterprise. While he did not believe that the productivity that arose from division of labor would inevitably produce class ossification and conflict, he argued that "a manufacturing aristocracy" posed a significant threat to American democratic culture.[32] Nevertheless, Tocqueville remained cautiously optimistic, believing that American religious and cultural mores would preserve the tenuous balance between free markets and free people.

As Tocqueville relayed his optimistic vision of American democratic capitalism to his readers in France, George Fitzhugh relayed a starkly different vision to his domestic audience. A staunch proslavery advocate from Prince William County, Virginia, Fitzhugh ranked among the most widely read essayists in the antebellum South. His two pre-Civil War books, *Sociology of the South* and *Cannibals All!*, circulated widely and ran in influential southern periodicals, like the *Richmond Examiner* and *DeBow's Review*. While Fitzhugh espoused common paternalist views in favor of perpetuating slavery in the United States, he also lambasted the capitalist regimes of Europe and the Northern States. Fitzhugh spewed venom at Adam Smith, free trade, and what he caustically called "free society," and systems of industrial and financial capital. Arguing in favor of socialism and even communism in America, Fitzhugh presented a synthesis of what could only be called neo-fascism. In contrast to Tocqueville who sought democracy and capitalism as fundamentally compatible, Fitzhugh viewed both as fundamental failures that should be done away with.

At his core, Fitzhugh argued that the liberal project had failed. Economic freedom allowed the strong to prey on the weak, with liberal political systems being too passive or corrupt to protect those subjugated by men of capital. As such, the white laboring class of the North became even more worse off than the African slaves of the south. In slave society, Fitzhugh argued, masters had the obligation and interest in providing a basic livelihood to those they enslaved. In contrast, "free enterprise" relieved the employers and investors of the North of such social obligations, allowing them to discard their workers at will. Northern capitalist society simply made its citizens slaves in another form, subjects of unquenchable class oppression. "The world is divided between two philosophies," Fitzhugh wrote, "the one, the philosophy of free trade and universal liberty—the philosophy adapted to promote the interests of the strong, the wealthy and wise. The other, that is Socialism; intended to protect the weak, the poor and the ignorant. The Former is almost universal in free society; the Latter prevails in the slaveholding States of the south."[33] Southern society would triumph because Northern capitalism was "an ahistorical, inherent contradiction." Slavery, Fitzhugh provocatively claimed, "is a form, and very best form, of socialism."[34]

In reality, Fitzhugh argued, democratic capitalism was illusory, especially in a diverse nation like America. Liberal institutions would descend into chaos as self-interest divided families, while capitalist systems "place[d] those classes in positions of antagonism and war."[35] He insisted that "free competition" in economics walked hand-in-hand with that individual liberty that he derided as degraded and dangerous. Liberal rule of law was an anachronism that should be done away with. "The mass of mankind cannot be governed by law," Fitzhugh wrote. "More of despotic discretion and less of law is what the world wants."[36]

Only in slavery could society embrace "true democracy," the patriarchal socialism that he argued would protect the people from capitalist oppression.

As much as Fitzhugh derided democracy, he held special invective for American capitalism. Fitzhugh argued that capitalist wage labor made people slaves by another name. In such a society, Fitzhugh reasoned, "all the laborers must live by the wages they receive from the capitalists. The capitalist cheapens their wages; they compete with and underbid each other, for employed they must be on any terms. This war of the rich with the poor and the poor with one another, is the morality which [capitalism] inculcates."[37] Contrary to the "nonsensical" rhetoric of individual liberty and free markets that he pins on the American Founders and Adam Smith, Fitzhugh suggests that capitalist society turns all but the elite into slaves. The difference arises in the safety net that exists in "socialist" slave society. "Slaves never die of hunger; seldom suffer want," Fitzhugh spuriously claims, unlike the industrial workers of the North.[38] In fact, "God makes masters and gives them affections, feelings and interests that secure kindness to the sick, aged and dying slave."[39] In this way, Fitzhugh suggests, "the people of the North and of Europe are proslavery men in the abstract; those of the South are theoretical abolitionists."[40] Northern capitalism and its associated "free society" would only continue to subjugate and wear down the American populace. To Fitzhugh, the North's unholy marriage of democracy and capitalism not only justified Confederate separation from the United States, but it also destined the northern Republic for collapse.

Of course, more moderate voices filled the space between Tocqueville and Fitzhugh. The legendary orator and Massachusetts congressman Daniel Webster embodied a classically American advocacy for economic development in service of shared prosperity, while retaining healthy skepticism of many core tenants of capitalist enterprise. As a Whig, the party that celebrated a version of Hamiltonian capitalism, Webster believed in a substantial role for the state in economic development. Only a strong Union committed to economic prosperity could cultivate a prosperous economy and sectional harmony that might put the country on a path to end slavery. Much of this prosperity would come in the form of infrastructure investment and public services, which Webster believed were essential and unlikely to come from the private sector. Webster argued that the state should cultivate republicanism in an age of Jacksonian populist democracy. Pushing back against an onslaught of liberal individualism, Webster saw a cozy relationship between government and private capital as a nationalist opposition to what he saw as democracy running amok. In contrast to the class conflict espoused by the Jacksonian Democrats and emancipation championed by a rising abolitionist movement, Webster articulated a vision in which capital and labor unified in service of a national political economy.

Webster saw protectionism as the easiest way to connect workers and industrialists. He argued that high tariff rates would protect American capital and American labor, leading both to unify in strengthening American institutions. While not capitalist in a liberal sense, Webster's protectionism became a tool for broadening American civil society. Webster's America looked very different from that of Tocqueville—where Tocqueville lauded the individualistic entrepreneurialism of the everyday American, Webster preached the value of a politico-economic machine in which labor, capital, and the state work together to build a distinct and uniquely American commercialism. To Webster, this meant not just greater individual prosperity but the expansion of suffrage and civic participation. Webster remained skeptical of the populist impulses of the demos and sought to temper their increasing involvement in politics with stronger state institutions. Nevertheless, he had great faith in the ability of democratic culture to foster the expansion of a free and just society.

To build this democratic culture however, Webster understood that the lower classes needed to own a stake in society. Continued economic prosperity was vital, and Webster saw American industry as the best way to secure material security in a rapidly changing nation. As such, Webster advocated for the country's rededication to a national bank, which the Jacksonians had eliminated, to provide credit to "men of small capital." Improved systems of finance would also enable large capitalists to provide better goods at a lower price for working people. Webster saw the American capitalist machine as a means to an end, a mechanism that would provide the baseline prosperity that made democratic society possible. Under the potent slogan "everyman a capitalist," "Webster and the Whigs of the 1830s and 1840s thus propounded their own embryonic version of the 'people's capitalism' so popular in the 1920s and post-World War II America."[41]

Gilded Cages

The American Civil War instigated the collision of industrialism versus agrarianism, finance versus commerce, and free versus slave society. The Union's struggle, Abraham Lincoln told a joint session of Congress in July 1861, was "to maintain that form and substance whose leading object was to elevate the conditions of men—to lift artificial weights from all shoulders—to clear the paths of laudable pursuit for all—to afford all an unfettered start, and a fair chance, in race of life."[42] The stubborn tumor of white supremacy would prevail in the form of Jim Crow—a disease that would obstruct efforts to reconcile self-government and free labor—until the 1960s. Nevertheless, the Civil

War resulted in the Hamiltonian north subduing the Jeffersonian south, with widespread implications for America's future as a democratic capitalist state. In addition to the very tangible effects of death, destruction of property, and freedom for millions of previously enslaved human beings, the Civil War closed the door on one era of ideas and opened the door for another. Questions of whether the Union would endure had been answered. The United States was now a consolidated national republic, if still a large, dispersed, and unruly one. Its greatness had always been prophesied, but now it became a tangible possibility. To become a true world power, Americans needed to decide what a truly "American" political economy should be. No longer an upstart republic, the balance between American democracy and capitalism would affect its place in the brotherhood of nations.

The Civil War ensconced major changes in thought about American political economy. Classic English whiggism that viewed "bigness" in government, business, or religion as inherently dangerous largely evaporated. The war made bigness necessary, even if many Americans had misgivings about it. The "Yankee Leviathan" that marshalled military, industrial, and financial power during the war laid the groundwork for the world of Standard Oil, J. P. Morgan, and American Steel, as well as the state-centered progressivism that sought to corral them half a century later.[43] The war and the lengths taken to win it led many to feel that the American political economy had fundamentally changed. The tumultuous postbellum years only intensified the feeling. Financial crises in 1866, 1873, 1884, 1890, and 1893, connected by the "Long Depression" of consistent unemployment and bankruptcy, coincided with America's emergence as an industrial power. Gilded Age-scale fortunes and pervasive poverty were truly unprecedented in American history, and the victory of Hamiltonian capitalism led Americans to grapple with the loss of Jeffersonian agrarianism.

Into this new world came the desperate voices of Henry George and William Graham Sumner. While they came to wildly different conclusions, each grappled with the compatibility of democracy and capitalism in the postbellum world. Sumner, the Yale lecturer and Episcopal priest who avoided Civil War service when his father purchased him a replacement, became the American prophet of laissez-faire capitalism. Sumner considered capitalism the chief cultural achievement of Western civilization. It not only produced unprecedented material well-being but proved the best means yet discovered to promote and sustain civil liberty. Capitalism fostered social order without the threat of force and provided the best way for people of varying abilities to complement each other. Sumner marveled at the simple logic of market systems, price mechanisms, and social cooperation resulting from the mutual drive for profit. He remained concerned about the rising threat of socialism that, he argued, would enslave Americans in dependency and pave the way for demagogic elites. Against these adversaries stood Sumner's independent capitalist, the "forgotten man" of American society, who remained caught between the "pauper" on one side and the "plutocrat" on the other.

While mid-twentieth century progressives like Richard Hofstadter painted Sumner a "Social Darwinist" defender of the rich, careful analysis shows that Sumner feared subversion of liberty by the rich just as much as the poor.[44] "Although Sumner was very concerned about creeping socialism," writes William F. Byrne, "he argues at least as stridently against 'plutocracy'. This refers not just to government by the wealthy but, more specifically, to the dominance of the state by moneyed interests. The plutocrats would amass the political clout to manipulate public policies and dip into the public coffers for their own enrichment."[45] Sumner argued that plutocracy posed the greatest threat to the capitalist ethos because it could be veiled in the language of free markets. In the United States, this came in the form of massive railroad subsidies, national banking systems, protective duties, and vast public debts.[46] To Sumner, this system of state-sponsored graft was "crony capitalism" at its finest, a veiled shadow of the laissez-faire free market system that made humans most free. "Instead of devoting their efforts to becoming more competitive in a free marketplace," Byrne writes, "plutocrats devote their efforts to influencing government . . . [and] tilting the playing field in their favor."[47] In this process, material well-being fades as the ambitious devote energy to fighting over rents, while independent capitalists get crushed by the combined force of government power and plutocratic monopoly.

To Sumner's dismay, he believed that democracies, and American democracy in particular, were most vulnerable to plutocrats and the violations to civil liberty they engendered. Sumner argued that America's democratic instincts and weakness for the narrative of the self-made man opened the door for elected plutocracy. Sumner rejected "the popular notion . . . that we have a free country because we select our political officers."[48] Elections were mechanisms for civil liberty, but by no means guarantees of it. Americans imbued their government with tremendous authority because they felt safe in the refining power of the electoral process. This, Sumner argued, was ultimate folly. Secure in the assumption that elected governments would safeguard the rights of the majority, Americans would surrender increasing amounts of sovereignty to the plutocratic class who ran for and won public office. From this process would arise a plutocratic elite that enslaved people with bread and circuses while crushing the capitalist wellspring that gave rise to American economic well-being and political liberty. As he saw populist and socialist movements gain prominence under the leadership of Edward Bellamy and Henry George, Sumner became increasingly pessimistic about the ability to maintain a free market economic system and a liberal democracy in the same nation.

Whereas Sumner concluded that democracy would likely consume and corrupt capitalism, Henry George sought to eliminate the systemic flaw that separated them. A self-taught political economist, George became a cultural phenomenon with the publication of *Progress and Poverty* in 1879. In his best-selling book, George proposed a "Single Tax" on the unimproved value of all land in the United States. George saw the monopolization of land as the fundamental driver of poverty and unearned wealth, as monopolists extracted rents and prevented the deployment of entrepreneurial and intellectual capital by the lower classes. George's plan would eliminate all other taxes while providing the government sufficient revenue to deliver public goods. George conceived of this as a sort of "start-up utopia," an environment in which laborers and entrepreneurs of little capital could pull themselves out of poverty.

In part, George's theory was a post-bellum version of Jeffersonianism—he believed all citizens held an equal right to access and work the land in usufruct. Poverty and disenfranchisement arose when voracious landholders denied others that right in defiance of the laws of nature, resulting in vast inequalities of wealth and power. Monopolies on land would lead to an unproductive economy of rent-seeking aristocrats who deprived workers, farmers, and entrepreneurs of the basic right to improve their lives. By taxing the unimproved value of all land, George sought to socialize the non-productive benefits of real property. At the same time, the absence of any other taxation would incentivize holders to invest in and make the land more productive. This quasi-elimination of property rights on land, George argued, would consolidate populations, incentivize people to work with one another, and improve societal bonds. In effect, Christopher England writes, George argued "that private ownership of land was at the root of inequality and posed an existential threat to democracy."[49]

Although his Single Tax drew howls of socialism, George repeatedly said that he aimed to elevate capitalism to its truest form. "George believed in competition, in the free market, in the unrestricted operation of the laws of supply and demand," Robert V. Andelson argues. "He distrusted government and despised bureaucracy. He was no egalitarian leveler; the only equality he sought was equality of opportunity." In essence, Andelson suggests, "what he intended was to make free enterprise truly free, by ridding it of the monopolistic hobbles which prevent its effective operation."[50] George also remained a lifetime proponent of free trade, arguing that protectionism only buttressed the interests of price-gouging monopolists. It is thus not surprising that Karl Marx regularly criticized George, calling his work an attempt "to *save capitalist domination* and indeed to *establish it afresh on an ever wider basis* than its present one."[51]

In fact, George did seek to create a tax system that would least impact, and actually encourage, the productive application of capital. He argued that while most taxes discouraged work and production, a tax on unimproved land would not reduce the quantity available or people's demand to employ it. Rather, the Single Tax would prevent people from hoarding land in an unimproved state, encourage them to invest in it, and prevent the monopolistic stranglehold large landowners had on entrepreneurial and productive behavior. To achieve this, George argued, "[i]t is not necessary to confiscate land; it is only necessary to confiscate rent."[52] In response to his laissez-faire critics, George wrote, "We have no fear of capital, regarding it as the natural hand-maiden of labor; we look on interest in itself as natural and just; we would set no limit to accumulation, nor impose on the rich any burden that is not equally placed on the poor; we see no evil in competition, but deem unrestricted competition to be as necessary to the health of the industrial and social organism as the free circulation of the blood is to the bodily organism." To George, the Single Tax empowered meritocracy—it allowed people to accumulate wealth based on what they produced, not how much of a natural monopoly they controlled.

George's refinement of the capitalist system also had profound effects on his view of American democracy. George believed that democracy could only flourish in an egalitarian, integrated, and cohesive society.[53] While he echoed Jefferson's instincts about land access, George viewed the Jeffersonian vision of a dispersed agrarian republic as a structural impediment to democracy. Viable democracies required a functional "public" in which people engaged with and learned from each other. "American democracy had been born in small-town meetings, out of similar face-to-face exchanges," England writes. "The problem with modern democracy was that the vast size of the nation made this sort of organic community less viable." George argued that his Single Tax incentivized the efficient use of space and would lead to denser communities more conducive to democratic action. Like Tocqueville, George saw democracy as a culture that thrived in communities. Communities would not form amid the scramble of poverty or the stratified landowner relations that George likened to lords and surfs. In this way, George echoed Hamilton's concerns about great landlords sitting atop a static land-based social pyramid.

By preventing the monopoly of land and, effectively giving each citizen equal access to it, George sought to make each citizen a stakeholder in society. Whereas Jefferson sought to build democratic involvement by parceling cheap land to freeholders, George aimed to create stakeholders by giving all equal access to it through the elimination of rents. In this way, dense cities would become the bastions of interactive democracy. While society would retain gradations of wealth and power, no individual would gain an advantage through the hoarding of a natural monopoly.

In the end, George believed that democracy and capitalism could thrive together if government prevented the consolidation of land ownership from stratifying the public into haves and have nots. He viewed the quest to elevate all Americans to their rightful place as equal heirs to the American promise as his Christian duty. "How I long for the Golden Age—for the promised Millennium," George wrote, "... when the poorest and meanest will have a chance to use all his God-given faculties, and not be forced to drudge away the best part of his time in order to support wants but little above those of the animal."[54] George's collectivist vision of democratic capitalism reprised the commonwealths of puritan New England. The Puritans and George welcomed profit and gain but believed that communal values including stakeholderism and participatory government would prevent capitalism from running away with itself. If they could accomplish this, the combination of free people and free markets would have a fighting chance.

As Americans approached the advent of the twentieth century, they knew that the balance between democracy and capitalism would define their future. While they did so in very different ways, both Sumner and George sought to prevent the everyday capitalist from being suppressed by undemocratic monopolists. George's disregard for private property rights on land repulsed Sumner, but both saw the value of unleashing the market mechanisms that plutocrats suppressed and co-opted. That American capitalism developed the range from Sumner's laissez-faire and George's collectivist capitalism reveals its indelible hold on American society, even in the face of challenges from patriotic socialists like Edward Bellamy and Eugene Debs. Nevertheless, both men remained far more skeptical of democracy's ability to endure. Sumner saw democracy and capitalism as potential adversaries whereas George viewed them as vulnerable to the same landed monopolists. At the dawn of the American century, thinkers perceived a greater threat to the institutions that kept us free than those that made us rich.

Building an American State

During the first three decades of the new century, an ascendant America searched for a new equilibrium between its economic success and the increasingly democratic impulses of its citizens. This search began in earnest with the Progressive Era, which witnessed the first comprehensive efforts to come to terms with fundamental conflicts raised by the industrial revolution. Above all, reform leaders that arose in the early part of the twentieth century had to grapple with the troubling question of how to curb the excesses of large corporations—the giant "trusts" that, according to Progressives, constituted uncontrolled and irresponsible bastions of power. The foremost figure of the era, Theodore Roosevelt, acknowledged that American capitalism had produced remarkable advances in economic prosperity. However, dynamic growth created new leviathans that aroused fears that growing corporate influence would diminish economic opportunity. Moreover, many people believed that great business interests had captured and corrupted national and state governments for their own profit.

Unlike George, who distrusted centralized power, Progressive reformers argued that only national administrative authority could constrain the dangerous impulses of America's largest capitalists, those Theodore Roosevelt called the "malefactors of great wealth." As Roosevelt stated in a 1907 address invoking America's puritan roots, "In the man of great wealth who has earned his wealth honestly and uses it wisely we recognize a good citizen of the best type, worthy of all praise and respect." However, he continued, "there is no individual and no corporation so powerful that stands above the possibility of punishment under the law. Our aim is to try to do something effective; our purpose is to stamp out the evil . . . [and] when we thus take action against the wealth which works iniquity, we are acting in the interest of every man of property who acts decently and fairly by his fellows."[55] In the first decades of the twentieth century, government would assert its new role as a referee, regulating powerful industries with the purpose of serving the public interest.

Reformers' efforts to forge a strong national state took on a new urgency with the Great Depression, which portended the collapse of both democracy and capitalism. As Franklin D. Roosevelt prepared to take the oath of office on March 4, 1933, the ranks of the unemployed numbered 15 million, about one-third of the workforce. In 32 states, every bank had been closed by state government edict. On the morning of FDR's inauguration, the New York Stock Exchange shut its doors. Merle Thorpe, the editor of the *Nation's Business*, wrote ominously, "Fear Bordering on panic, loss of faith in everything, our fellow man, our institutions, private and government. Worst of all, no faith in ourselves, or the future."[56]

Other alarmed commentators looked toward the apparent social stability and economic revival of Nazi Germany under Adolf Hitler, fascist Italy under Benito Mussolini, and (among those on the political left) the Communist Soviet Union under Joseph Stalin. Given the raging Depression, observers increasingly argued that liberal democracy may have had its day. Nicholas Murray Butler, the president of Columbia University, told students that dictatorships were producing "men of far greater intelligence, far stronger character and far more courage than the system of elections."[57] One month before Roosevelt's inauguration, the respected columnist Walter Lippmann told the president, "You may have to assume dictatorial powers."[58] According to the political scientist Ira Katznelson, "Parliamentary democracies were widely thought to be weak and incapable compared to the assertive regimes," led by the new dictators. "This problem seemed especially acute in the United States, whose government reflected the most radical separation of powers between the executive and legislative branches of government in the world."[59]

However, Roosevelt recognized the rich possibilities for reform that would renew, rather than denigrate, the idea of liberalism in the United States. Indeed, like many reformers who sought solutions to the challenges posed by the Industrial Revolution, he looked back to the struggle between Jefferson and Hamilton for inspiration. During the "Roaring 20s," when Progressive reforms were threatened by a renascence of pro-business policies, Roosevelt argued that it was necessary to "apply [the] fundamental differences between Jeffersonian and Hamiltonian ideals . . . to present-day policies of our two great parties."[60] Roosevelt's fascination with the struggle between these two Founders was not unusual. Most progressive reformers during the first three decades of the twentieth century believed that the sweeping changes wrought by American capitalism called for a new founding that resolved the contending Jeffersonian and Hamiltonian theories of government. Just as Jefferson believed that Hamilton's program would restrict the voice of the people and advantage commercial interests, so progressive reformers believed that the Republican Party's program of high tariffs and business-friendly policies vitiated popular rule and economic opportunity. "I wonder if a century and a quarter later the same contending forces are not again mobilizing," Roosevelt speculated. "Hamiltonians we have today. Is a Jefferson on the horizon?"[61]

Yet it was not possible simply to resurrect Jeffersonian ideals. Progressive thinkers like Herbert Croly, who championed a New Nationalism that inspired Theodore Roosevelt's reform vision, considered the Jeffersonian tradition the cardinal vice of American politics. Although he loathed Hamilton's distrust of democracy, Croly and Theodore Roosevelt had believed that the resurrection of Hamiltonian nationalism and its faith in strong government formed an essential prerequisite to the reconciliation of democracy and capitalism in the twentieth century. Taking a lesson from his cousin, FDR concluded that Jeffersonian ideals would have to be applied to the economic and political problems spawned by the concentration of private power in such a way that these principles were respectful of Hamilton's "genius" for sound administrative practice.[62]

Roosevelt believed that the dire circumstances of the Great Depression prepared the country for a "bold experiment" that would redefine the social contract and reconcile big government and free enterprise. This new understanding of liberty involved, as one presidential scholar wrote, "a careful process of grafting [the welfare state] on the stalk of traditional American values."[63] Roosevelt first spoke of the need to modernize the old faith of American democratic capitalism in his famous Commonwealth Club Address, delivered during the 1932 campaign. Understood to be a manifesto for the New Deal, Roosevelt argued for "new terms of the old social contract." The new terms would acknowledge that

American capitalism had changed, making possible a concentration of economic power that even Hamilton could not have imagined. To preserve the union of individual liberty and economic prosperity, the new contract would establish a countervailing power—a stronger national state—lest the United States steer "a steady course toward economic oligarchy." Protection of national welfare had to shift from the private citizen to the government. As FDR put it, in an alluring turn of phrase, "The day of enlightened administration has come."[64]

FDR acknowledged that the creation of a national state would be a "long, slow task." He was sensitive to the uneasy fit between an energetic central government and the Constitution's separation and division of power. Even in the teeth of economic disaster, Roosevelt feared the resonance of Herbert Hoover's warning that the New Deal threatened "regimented men and extended bureaucracy" that would denigrate the dignity of the democratic individual. Therefore, Roosevelt and his political allies crafted the New Deal to embody a new concept of state power that would interlock with earlier conceptions of American government. While Croly and Theodore Roosevelt excoriated Americans' obsession with individual rights, Adolf Berle, a member of FDR's celebrated "Brains Trust" and author of a well-known volume on the power of corporations, urged Roosevelt to reimagine individualism to fit the social and economic stresses of the twentieth century.[65]

Given the task of assisting Roosevelt in preparing the Commonwealth Club speech, Berle's draft decried Hoover's idea of "rugged individualism" as the "cornerstone of our national happiness and the great purpose of the future." Roosevelt's principal objective, Berle argued, was to explain the "real understanding of the role of American individualism" in the country's national life. "The word individualism," Berle insisted, has "no content when divorced from society."[66] The protection of liberty in the twentieth century, Roosevelt pronounced, was "to assist the development of an economic declaration of rights, an economic constitutional order."[67] The traditional emphasis in American politics on limited government should give way to a new understanding of the social contract, in which the government guaranteed individual men and women protection from the uncertainties of the marketplace. Security, as the 1936 platform pronounced, was to be the new self-evident truth of political life in the United States. As Roosevelt would put it during the 1936 campaign, "necessitous men are not free men."

The new social contract FDR proposed not only required a safety net against the vicissitudes of the market, but it also demanded that business recognize the authority of the national government. This authority would not oppose private enterprise, Roosevelt argued, but strengthen it by curbing its most abusive practices and ameliorating the most extreme economic hardship. As the National Association of Manufacturers' campaign made clear, a significant segment of the business community opposed granting the federal government additional power to regulate commercial activity. As Roosevelt complained in a letter to law professor Felix Frankfurter (who he would appoint to the Supreme Court), "It is the same old story of those who have property to fail to realize that I am the best friend the profit system ever had, even though I add my denunciation of unconscionable profits."[68]

As James Morone notes in his conclusion to this volume, Roosevelt conceived of economic constitutional order as a *second bill of rights* during World War II—to clarify, he said, what America was fighting for. The new rights that Roosevelt pledged the federal government to protect included "the right to a useful and remunerative job" and "the right to adequate protection from the fears of old age, sickness, accident and unemployment."[69] These new rights were not to supplant, but to "supplement," those in the original Constitution. However, signature programs like Social Security came to be thought of as "entitlements" beyond the vagaries of partisanship and public opinion. Moreover, the idea of programmatic rights became the foundation of political dialogue, redefining the role of the national government and setting in motion the rise of a far-flung administrative state that defied, in fact if not in theory, America's exceptional hostility to centralized power. The New Deal thus unleashed a new struggle over the very meaning of liberalism that reverberates through our own political time.

Can Democracy and Capitalism Co-Exist in the Twenty-first Century?

The previous sections show that Americans' long debate about democracy and capitalism is much more heterodox than current political opinion allows. Democracy and capitalism are a series of institutions that interact with public challenges that are unique to their time. The American colonists reacted to feudalism and the revolutionaries to early modern mercantilism. Antebellum Americans contested democracy and capitalism amid the nation's emergence as an industrial behemoth, whereas Gilded Age thinkers debated their society in an era in which the American continent had been conquered, slavery expunged, and previously unimaginable fortunes became a possibility. In later years, the New Deal would emerge in an ascendant but humbled America whose liberal orthodoxy was challenged by two world wars and the Great Depression. Put simply, the challenges facing American democratic capitalism always shaped and formed it. The same is true today. Indeed, the globalization of the political economy requires scholars to consider and reconsider the inherent tensions between self-government and markets roiled by international developments.

It thus seems that we again find ourselves in an era of profound change. Old challenges like political polarization, rising market concentration, racial and ethnic battles over identity, and vast gaps between rich and poor are exacerbated by new circumstances. At the same time, new crises like climate change pose profound threats to the sustainability of economic and political systems. The changing forces shaping democracy and capitalism require nimble investigations that adequately frame the legacy of previous struggles with the challenges of modern circumstances. The chapters that follow offer a careful analysis of both the enduring and emerging challenges that make reconciling democracy and capitalism in our own time extraordinarily difficult.

In pondering the prospects of renewing democratic capitalism in the United States, we should return to where this chapter began. Americans have always fought over how to balance self-government and free markets; indeed, searching for an enduring consensus may be a fool's errand. This volume, we believe, is a persuasive representation of the inherently contentious relationship between democracy and capitalism. Yet the uneasy connection between capitalism and democracy—and the sharp conflicts they have agitated throughout history—have encouraged periodic and vital reimaginings of America's political economy. We hope the chapters in this volume not only contribute to a better awareness of the causes of our present discontents, but also encourage "dreams of change," as Morone puts it, that "gather velocity and, over time, create waves." Reconciling equality and individual self-interest is a never-ending challenge that poses opportunities as well as peril. It is a generational conceit to think that our perils are unprecedented, and mischievous to believe they cannot be addressed by transfusing with new meaning the rich possibilities of a liberal democracy.

Notes

1. Alan Taylor, *American Colonies* (New York: Penguin Books, 2001), 258.
2. Margaret Ellen Newell, *From Dependency to Independence: Economic Revolution in Colonial New England* (Ithaca: Cornell University Press, 1998), 147.
3. *An oration on the advantages of American independence: spoken before a publick assembly of the inhabitants of Charlestown in South-Carolina, on the second anniversary of that glorious area. By David Ramsay, M.B.; [Five lines in Latin from Virgil]*, Ramsay, David, 1749–1815, Charlestown [i.e., Charleston, S.C.]: Printed by John Wells, Jun., MDCCLXXVIII. [1778]. Accessed at http://name.umdl.umich.edu/N12684.0001.001.
4. Stephen Innes, *Creating the Commonwealth: The Economic Culture of Puritan New England* (New York: W. W. Norton, 1995), 27–28.
5. Innes, *Creating the Commonwealth*, 31.
6. The term "ghost acres" is used by Kenneth Pomeranz in *The Great Divergence: China, Europe, and the Making of the Modern World Economy* (Princeton: Princeton University Press, 2000).
7. Newell, *From Dependency to Independence*, 232–233.
8. Adam Smith, *An Inquiry into the Nature and Causes of the Wealth of Nations, Volume 1* (The Clarendon Press, 1869).

9. Stanley Elkins and Eric McKitrick, *The Age of Federalism: The Early American Republic, 1788–1800* (New York: Oxford University Press, 1994), 260.
10. Thomas Jefferson, Notes XXII, https://web.archive.org/web/20231012010229/http://xroads.virginia.edu/~Hyper/hypertex.html.
11. Peter S. Onuf, *Jefferson's Empire: The Language of American Nationhood* (Charlottesville, VA: University of Virginia Press, 2000), 71.
12. Thomas Jefferson to Benjamin Hawkins, February 18, 1803, in *The Papers of Thomas Jefferson Digital Edition*, ed. James P. McClure and J. Jefferson Looney (Charlottesville: University of Virginia Press, Rotunda, 2011).
13. Claudio J. Katz, "Thomas Jefferson's Liberal Anticapitalism," *American Journal of Political Science* 47, no. 1 (January 2003): 8.
14. Alexander Hamilton to Henry Lee, December 1, 1789, in *The Papers of Alexander Hamilton Digital Edition*, ed. Harold C. Syrett (Charlottesville: University of Virginia Press, Rotunda, 2011); "From Alexander Hamilton to Lieutenant Colonel John Laurens, 22 May 1779," *Founders Online*, National Archives, https://founders.archives.gov/documents/Hamilton/01-02-02-0151. [Original source: *The Papers of Alexander Hamilton*, vol. 2, *1779–1781*, ed. Harold C. Syrett (New York: Columbia University Press, 1961), 52–54.]
15. Forrest McDonald, *Alexander Hamilton, A Biography* (New York: W. W. Norton, 1979), 4.
16. Thomas Jefferson to Dr. Thomas Cooper, September 10, 1814, in *The Papers of Thomas Jefferson Digital Edition*, ed. James P. McClure and J. Jefferson Looney (Charlottesville: University of Virginia Press, Rotunda, 2011).
17. Claudio J. Katz, "Thomas Jefferson's Liberal Anticapitalism," *American Journal of Political Science* 47, no. 1 (2003): 12.
18. Thomas Jefferson to Dr. Thomas Cooper, September 10, 1814, in *The Papers of Thomas Jefferson Digital Edition*, ed. James P. McClure and J. Jefferson Looney (Charlottesville: University of Virginia Press, Rotunda, 2011).
19. Katz, "Thomas Jefferson's Liberal Anticapitalism," 13.
20. Katz, "Thomas Jefferson's Liberal Anticapitalism," 13.
21. Thomas Jefferson to Isaac McPherson, August 13, 1813, in *The Papers of Thomas Jefferson Digital Edition*, ed. James P. McClure and J. Jefferson Looney (Charlottesville: University of Virginia Press, Rotunda, 2011).
22. Thomas Jefferson to James Madison, October 28, 1785, in *The Papers of Thomas Jefferson Digital Edition*, ed. James P. McClure and J. Jefferson Looney (Charlottesville: University of Virginia Press, Rotunda, 2011).
23. Jefferson to Madison, October 28, 1785.
24. Thomas Jefferson to DuPont de Nemours, April 15, 1815, in *The Papers of Thomas Jefferson Digital Edition*, ed. James P. McClure and J. Jefferson Looney (Charlottesville: University of Virginia Press, Rotunda, 2011).
25. Alexander Hamilton to Charles Coatsworth Pinckney, October 2, 1792, in *The Papers of Alexander Hamilton Digital Edition*, ed. Harold C. Syrett (Charlottesville: University of Virginia Press, Rotunda, 2011).
26. McDonald, *Alexander Hamilton*, 311–312.
27. Debra Satz, "Tocqueville, Commerce, and Democracy," in David Copp, Jean Hampton, and John E. Roemer, ed. *The Idea of Democracy* (New York: Cambridge University Press, 1993), 65.
28. Alexis de Tocqueville, *Democracy in America*, ed. Olivier Zunz (New York: Library of America, 2012), 616.
29. Richard Swedberg, "Tocqueville and the Spirit of American Capitalism," in *On Capitalism*, ed. Victor Nee and Richard Swedberg (Stanford: Stanford University Press, 2007), 46–47.
30. Tocqueville, *Democracy in America*, book III, ch. 5.
31. Tocqueville, *Democracy in America*, 326, 368.
32. Tocqueville, *Democracy in America*, 532.
33. George Fitzhugh, *Sociology of the South, or the Failure of Free Society* (Richmond, VA: A. Morris, Publisher, 1854), 80.
34. Fitzhugh, *Sociology of the South*, 27.
35. Fitzhugh, *Sociology of the South*, 43.

36. George Fitzhugh, *Cannibals All! or, Slaves Without Masters* (Richmond, VA: A. Morris, Publisher, 1857), 361.
37. Fitzhugh, *Sociology of the South*, 22.
38. Fitzhugh, *Sociology of the South*, 48. Here Fitzhugh displays a striking lack of understanding for his southern slave society. Earlier in *Sociology of the South*, Fitzhugh writes, "The wages of the poor diminish as their wants and families increase, for the care and labor of attending to the family leaves them fewer hours for profitable work. With negro slaves, their wages invariably increase with their wants. The master increases the provision for the family as the family increases in number and helplessness. It is a beautiful example of communism, where each one receives not according to his labor, but according to his wants."
39. Fitzhugh, *Sociology of the South*, 68.
40. Fitzhugh, *Sociology of the South*, 80.
41. Melvyn Dubofsky, "Daniel Webster and the Whig Theory of Economic Growth: 1828–1848," *The New England Quarterly* 42, no. 4 (December 1969): 569–570.
42. R. N. Current, *The Political Thought of Abraham Lincoln* (Indianapolis, IN: Bobbs-Merrill, 1967), 187–188.
43. See Richard Bensel, *Yankee Leviathan: The Origins of Central State Authority in America, 1859–1877* (New York: Cambridge University Press, 1990); and Nancy Cohen, *The Reconstruction of American Liberalism, 1865–1914* (Chapel Hill: The University of North Carolina Press, 2003).
44. Richard Hofstadter, "William Graham Sumner, Social Darwinist," *The New England Quarterly* 14, no. 3 (1941): 457–77.
45. William F. Byrne, "William Graham Sumner and the Problem of Liberal Democracy," *The Review of Politics* 72, no. 4 (Fall 2010): 576.
46. H. A. Scott Trask, "William Graham Sumner: Against Democracy, Plutocracy, and Imperialism," *Journal of Libertarian Studies* 18, no. 4 (Fall 2004): 11.
47. Byrne, "William Graham Sumner," 577.
48. William Graham Sumner, *What Social Classes Owe To Each Other* (New York: Harper & Brothers, Franklin Square, 1883), 28.
49. Christopher England, "John Dewey and Henry George: The Socialization of Land as a Prerequisite for a Democratic Public," *American Journal of Economics and Sociology* 77, no. 1 (January 2018): 170.
50. Robert V. Andelson, "Henry George and the Reconstruction of Capitalism: An Address," *The American Journal of Economics and Sociology* 52, no. 4 (October 1993): 495.
51. Karl Marx to Friedrich A. Sorge, June 20, 1881, in *Karl Marx and Frederick Engels: Letters to Americans 1848–1895, A Selection* (New York: International Publishers, 1953), 127–128.
52. Henry George, *Progress and Poverty: An Inquiry into the Cause of Industrial Depressions and of the Increase of Want with Increase of Wealth* (New York: Sterling Publishing Company, 1879), 364.
53. England, "John Dewey and Henry George," 170.
54. Henry George to Caroline Jennie, Barker, September 15, 1861, in Morris D. Forkosch, "Henry George: The Economist as Moralist," *The American Journal of Economics and Sociology* 38, no. 4 (1979): 359.
55. *Address of President Roosevelt on the occasion of the laying of the cornerstone of the Pilgrim Monument, Provincetown, Massachusetts, August 20, 1907*. Theodore Roosevelt Collection.
56. Quoted in R. M. Collins, *The Business Response to Keynes* (New York: Columbia University Press, 1981), 28.
57. Quoted in Ira Katznelson, *Fear Itself: The New Deal and the Origins of Our Time* (New York: Liveright Publishing Corporation, 2013), pp. 115, 118, 12.
58. Katznelson, *Fear Itself*.
59. Katznelson, *Fear Itself*.
60. Franklin D. Roosevelt, "Is There a Jefferson on the Horizon?," in Basil Rauch, ed., *The Roosevelt Reader: Selected Speeches, Messages, Press Conferences and Letters of Franklin D. Roosevelt* (New York: Rinehart, 1957), 44.
61. Roosevelt, "Is There a Jefferson on the Horizon," 47.
62. Roosevelt, "Is There a Jefferson on the Horizon," 45.

63. E. E. Cornwell, Jr., *Presidential Leadership of Public Opinion* (Bloomington, IN: Indiana University Press, 1955), 131.
64. Franklin D. Roosevelt, in Samuel I. Rosenman, ed., *The Public Papers and Addresses of Franklin D. Roosevelt*, 13 vols. (New York: Random House, 1), 751–752.
65. Herbert Croly, *Progressive Democracy* (New York: MacMillan, 1915), 15.
66. Adolph Berle, "Memorandum to Governor Franklin D. Roosevelt," August 15, 1932, *The Adolph Berle Papers*, Box 15; "American Individualism: Romantic and Realistic," *Berle Papers*, Box 17, Folder: Speech Draft: Individualism," Franklin D Roosevelt Library, Hyde Park, New York. Berle's counsel to redefine liberalism owed a great deal to a six-part series the philosopher John Dewey contributed to the *New Republic* in 1929 and 1930, entitled "Individualism, Old and New," which anticipated many of the ideas of the Commonwealth Club address. Reprinted in *John Dewey: The Later Writings, Vol. 5, 1925–1953* (Carbondale and Edwardsville: Southern Illinois University Press, 1984), 41–123.
67. Roosevelt, *Public Papers and Addresses*, 1, 753.
68. Franklin D. Roosevelt to Felix Frankfurter, February 9, 1937, *The Felix Frankfurter Papers*, microfilm reel 60, Manuscript Department, Library of Congress, Washington, D.C.
69. Roosevelt, *Public Papers and Addresses*, 13, 40–41.

SECTION I

THE NATURE OF DEMOCRATIC CAPITALISM

Capitalism and Democracy

Will They Survive?

Isabel Sawhill

This essay addresses the relationship between democracy and capitalism. Can a healthy capitalism live side by side with an autocracy or dictatorship? Can a nation be a democracy but also one in which the government owns the means of production and runs the economy? Because most readers of this book likely live in a nation that fits neither description, but instead has a democratic government and a market-based economy, these questions may seem odd. But by describing the tensions between capitalism and democracy, I hope to highlight the strengths and weaknesses of each, as well as their dependence on one another. Like many marriages, the combination of capitalism and democracy may be fraught with conflict and the survival of this particular marriage may not be assured but, as I hope to show, it should be preserved.

Let me start with a few definitions.

By democracy, I mean a system in which a broad swath of the public is entitled to choose their own representatives and to hold them accountable through regular elections. Political power is decentralized, limited, and its legitimacy based on the will of the people. Its antithesis would be an autocracy or dictatorship in which power is held by one person or a small elite and in which elections, if held, are not free and fair.

By capitalism, I mean a market system in which individual property rights are secured by law and in which individuals are free to contract with one another for the sale of both goods and labor services. Its antithesis would be a pure form of communism or socialism in which the means of production are government owned and the allocation of resources and incomes is determined by the state.[1]

Of course, there are many variations on these definitions. Freedom House uses 25 indicators of democracy, encompassing political rights such as fairness of the political process or the rule of law, as well as civil liberties such as freedom of speech and the press, freedom from arbitrary arrest and detention, freedom of assembly and protest. As noted below, according to Freedom House, democracy in the United States is declining. That assessment was made before Donald Trump was elected President for the second time; and what his second term holds was unclear as this book went to press.

As for capitalism, we can distinguish between Nordic-style capitalism and US-style capitalism in which the former involves a greater emphasis on social solidarity, stronger safety nets, more worker rights, higher taxes, and more involvement of government in the economy and the latter more emphasis on individual liberty, limited government, smaller safety nets, less regulation, and lower taxes.

Still, what I will call democratic capitalism is what we most often see in high income countries and to which many people around the globe aspire. But are they always compatible?

In more recent times, the concern has been that an over-active government will kill the goose that lays the golden eggs, that taxes and regulation will impede growth and stifle innovation. This view was ascendant in the United States during the gilded age around the turn of the twentieth century and again in the United States and the United Kingdom during the Reagan/Thatcher era. My own discipline of economics has contributed to this view. Scholars such as Friedrich Hayek and Milton Friedman have argued that unless democratic governments are very limited, capitalism cannot flourish. It will be stifled and even if it survives, it will be greatly weakened by the constraints imposed by a regulatory and redistributional state. These constraints, it is argued, discourage incentives to save and invest, to work, and to take the kind of risks that lead to innovation and prosperity.

Because democracy unlike autocracy is based on the will of the people, it may undermine capitalism for another reason. If the population is uneducated and unable to select leaders capable of governing wisely, the result may be a set of policies that end up hobbling capitalism. If the electorate believes, for example, that vaccines are dangerous, causing many people to become unnecessarily ill, the economy and the education system will feel the effects and mortality will rise. In short, democracy requires an informed electorate. Some issues, such as the regulation of artificial intelligence (AI) or nuclear power or the conduct of monetary policy require a level of expertise that most citizens do not possess and should be at least partially isolated from democratic decision-making, although the Supreme Court has recently been tilting toward curbing the so-called administrative state or what some populists like to call "the swamp." Education prepares people to choose their leaders wisely. Without it, experiments in self-government are likely to fail. Even in the contemporary United States where the public is more educated than ever, many voters are surprisingly ignorant, leading to calls for more civic education, less misinformation, and a more engaged electorate. As Thomas Jefferson said, "Whenever the people are well informed, they can be trusted with their own government."

While it's possible for democracy to undermine capitalism, another and widely-held view holds that it is the other way around; it is capitalism that subverts democracy. The accumulation of wealth under capitalism can lead to oligarchy or to business interests having extra clout in political decision-making, and those beholden to monied interests may have little or no interest in distributing that wealth more broadly. Wealth inequality in the United States has reached virtually unprecedented levels, and efforts to raise taxes on the wealthy have been blocked by conservative politicians and their allies.

Another reason that capitalism might not be compatible with democracy is if the electorate is mostly poor and thus resentful of capitalist wealth and power. Without a thriving middle class and some hope of upward mobility, enfranchising the masses might simply lead them to conclude that the system is unfair, and motivate them to take away the private property and wealth on which capitalism depends, using violence if necessary.

More generally, there are many reasons why democracy is needed to supplement private markets. Only government can deal effectively with such issues as the environment, national security, and access to education, health care, jobs, and a minimum level of economic security. Thus, if government is captured by the wealthy few, and if it fails to protect the interests of the wider public, it may lose its legitimacy. One interpretation of the continuing popularity of President Trump in the United

States is that an important segment of the electorate (about a third) are fed up with the status quo and no longer even believe in the legitimacy of elections. When that happens, when democracy fails to respond to the resentments or misfortunes of ordinary people, when they lose faith in the electoral process itself, when they are so angry or misguided that they want to wipe the slate clean, they will be more likely to select extreme leaders, those who recognize their frustrations and promise to overturn the status quo.

What I hope to convince you of in this essay is that there needs to be a healthy balance between private and public interests, between capitalism and democracy, that in too many countries that balance has been lost, that democracy is in far greater peril than capitalism, and that the United States is the current poster child for democratic backsliding. I focus mainly on the United States not only because it is currently a country in which the threats to democracy seem especially high but also because it is the country I know best. I will argue that if democracy falters, capitalism may fail as well. Without a stable government in which people feel represented and in which their elected leaders are able to find the kind of compromises that respect the divergent views inevitable in a pluralistic society, we will not be able to address the major challenges facing the nation. The private sector could then become a victim of this failure of governance. Whether it is severe weather events, internal violence, a new war in Europe or the Middle East, the fallout from AI, the opioid epidemic, or the slow erosion of American advantages in education, technology, and science, the private sector cannot escape the consequences.

In what follows, I will expand on these conclusions by making five major points. First, capitalism and democracy complement each other. Second, they need to evolve with the times. History matters. Third, I will show that in recent decades, government has become less responsive to the electorate in the United States, and there appears to have been some capture of the political process by business interests. Fourth, democracy is in deeper trouble than capitalism, beset by not just a lack of broadly shared prosperity and unresponsive political institutions but cultural anxieties and a lack of confidence in institutions as well. Fifth, I will argue that we need fundamental reform of the political system in the United States; but because those currently in office benefit from the status quo, it may take pressures from voters and from business and civic society to make this happen.

Capitalism and Democracy Complement Each Other

As two of this volume's authors, Geloso and Tabarrok, argue, capitalism and democracy each address a weakness in the other and together they are stronger than either could be alone. These authors' empirical analysis is persuasive in showing that the two are like "two peas in a pod." I agree. As I have written elsewhere, capitalism is a good way to organize markets; it is not a good way to organize society. Democratic government can deal with challenges that markets cannot address, but it is not good at allocating resources, coordinating the many different aspects of a well-functioning economy, or encouraging risk taking and innovation.

That said, capitalism is dependent on a well-functioning democracy to provide guardrails against growing inequality, environmental damage, gun violence, and other social ills that if allowed to persist for too long eventually create widespread public dissatisfaction. That dissatisfaction sets the stage for illiberalism, for populism, and for autocracy. Debates about the guardrails themselves—where, why, and how much they are needed—are what a liberal democracy should resolve. When it ceases to do its job and instead becomes some mixture of mass entertainment, cultural grievances run amok, the protection of inherited privileges, or a platform for would-be autocrats or oligarchs, that dysfunction will eventually destroy the fragile balance between capitalism and democracy.

We need a private sector that is free to innovate and compete in a way that produces widespread prosperity, and a government whose job it is to constrain or direct that competition in socially beneficial ways. In the words of Charles Lindblom, we need to marry the nimble fingers of the market with the strong, if often clumsy, thumb of government.[2] Historically, there is a reason why most democracies have had market-based economies and why most market-based economies have been democracies.[3] They depend on each other for success. State-run economies have some advantages but usually succumb to inefficiency, a failure to innovate, and to reallocate resources in response to shifting preferences and technologies.

The combination of capitalism and democracy has produced a level of prosperity unfathomable as recently as 150 years ago. Daron Acemoglu and his colleagues at MIT have found that countries experiencing a switch from dictatorship to democracy experience a 20 percent increase in GDP over a 25-year period.[4] These gains seem to be the result of greater investment and less corruption. In his book, *Slouching Toward Utopia,* Brad Delong estimates that average living standards have risen eight-fold since 1870 in industrialized democracies.[5] As someone who grew up in the first half of the twentieth century, I can remember when blocks of ice were delivered to keep food cold, when chicken was a luxury, when TV, computers, and cell phones didn't exist, and when passenger air travel was not yet common. But rising affluence creates new demands, including demands on government to provide more economic security and more public goods. The share of government spending in GDP has risen sharply over the past century in virtually all high-income countries, regardless of which political party was in power, suggesting that public expectations and aspirations rise with income.[6] In the United States, that share rose from 7 percent in 1870 to 36 percent in 2019.[7] Did this growth in the size of the public sector and the revenues needed to sustain it undermine growth and prosperity? There is almost no empirical evidence that it did.[8]

The best way to see what capitalism and democracy each contribute to creating a healthy society is to imagine or observe what happens when one is missing.

Capitalism without democracy would produce too much inequality, no checks on monopoly, on environmental damage or other market failures, no way to manage macroeconomic and financial instability, or to deal with the personal insecurity of the elderly, the disabled, the unemployed, the poor, and those whose lives are shattered by natural disasters. It would mean little or no investment in education, basic research, infrastructure, and little or no protection against external threats. In their impressively wide-ranging and historically-grounded book, *Why Nations Fail,* Daron Acemoglu and James A. Robinson argue that "countries such as Great Britain and the United States became rich because their citizens overthrew the elites who controlled power and created a society where political rights were much more broadly distributed, where the government was accountable and responsive to citizens, and where the great mass of people could take advantage of economic opportunities."[9] But as I noted earlier, there are many varieties of democracy and the path from autocracy to democracy is often long and difficult.

Democracy without capitalism, on the other hand, implies government ownership of the means of production, leading to inefficiency, waste, corruption, and failure to innovate or adjust to change. State-led capitalism—as found, for example, in China—has some record of success and may invite new versions of industrial policy in the West to secure supply chains and protect technologies vital to national security; but China's state-led capitalism has weaknesses that now appear to be slowing growth in that country.[10]

At a more basic level, critics of capitalism have argued that rising inequality of income and wealth is an inherent problem with capitalism, that a theory that says that wages are determined by each worker's contribution and not by institutional norms, discrimination, or power imbalances between capital and labor is naïve.[11] These critics suggest that there is much less of a trade-off between equity and efficiency than proponents of capitalism believe, and that economic growth that does not also produce human dignity or flourishing may not be worth having. To speak of capitalism or democracy in isolation from the goals we want to achieve is to substitute means for ends, structure for values.[12] As Washington Post columnist and author, Steve Pearlstein puts it, drawing on the earlier wisdom of Adam Smith, the pursuit of self-interest must be "tempered by moral sentiments such as compassion, generosity, and a sense of fair play."[13]

Democracy has its own set of weaknesses. The Founders recognized that the passions of the electorate might be its downfall, so they created a representative rather than a popular democracy with many checks and balances. Another problem with democracy is that it is hard to maintain. Benjamin Franklin's worry was that without an informed and active citizenry, it would not last—calling it "a republic if you can keep it," while Winston Churchill said "it is the worst form of government except for all the others." Less well known is Franklin's suggestion that "democracy is two wolves and a lamb voting on what to have for lunch." Then, he added: "Liberty is a well-armed lamb contesting the vote." Yet, we all know that most lambs don't have much power. Forbearance by the wolves is essential. That forbearance involves upholding unwritten democratic norms, such as peaceful transitions of power, treating one's opponents with some degree of respect, and abiding by the rule of law.

Critics on both sides of this debate should note that historically most democracies have had market-based economies and most market-based economies have been democracies. That's a key message in the Geloso and Tabarrok chapter in this volume and also in Martin Wolf's book,

The Crisis of Democratic Capitalism. However, the necessary balance between the two is not self-enforcing, and needs to adjust to new developments. Each generation must re-assess and renegotiate the social contract.

Both Capitalism and Democracy Need to Evolve with the Times

Historically, democratic governments in the West have taken on new responsibilities in response to the kind of technological changes and rising prosperity described by Charles Boix in this volume. As he notes, during the nineteenth century, the industrial revolution depended heavily on unskilled labor to operate the new machinery then being applied to the manufacturing process. Wages fell during this period and health declined (men actually got shorter). As even the enlightened intellectuals of the day, such as John Stuart Mill, argued, suffrage (and thus democracy) had to be limited to those who were not only sufficiently well educated to vote but also would not rebel against the declining living standards among the less-skilled workers of that era. Arguably then, capitalism and a fulsome democracy were not entirely compatible during this period. However, by the mid-twentieth century—the so-called "Detroit era" in the United States—we saw the emergence of modes of production that relied on more skilled or semi-skilled workers, many of whom had benefited from the expansion of education in the first half of the twentieth century, with the result that productivity and wages rose. This version of capitalism along with strong unions and more activist governments that enacted measures to deal with economic insecurity and inequality helped to create a middle-class society. Thus, both capitalism and democracy each played a distinct and complementary role in creating widespread prosperity from the end of World War II until the early 1980s. The term "a mixed economy" became popular among economists who argued that saving capitalism paradoxically required that government step in to smooth the rough edges of a market economy. But as technology has continued to evolve, the demand for highly skilled labor has accelerated and is now outpacing its supply, in part because of the inability of the education system to do the necessary upskilling. It is too soon, Boix says, to predict how this new era will affect democracy. On the one hand, automation and AI could lead to a much greater concentration of capital along with widespread joblessness. On the other hand, if the new technologies are used to augment rather than replace existing skills and to fuel a new round of innovation, the gains could surpass those of the original industrial revolution.

One clear lesson from history, I think, is that education and training are critical and that without the public investments that enable people to adjust to whatever the technology of a particular era requires, the complementarity of democracy and capitalism will fray. The private sector will not be able to find the workers it needs while confidence in government will fall in the wake of lower employment rates, stagnant wages, a declining middle class, and communities racked by so-called "deaths of despair." This imbalance between the skills that the private sector needs and the ones that the education and training system are supplying is, in my view, growing worse in the United States. As evidence I would point to declining test scores, and the poor performance of US students on international tests, complaints from employers about what new hires know and can do, and a rising wage premium for the best-educated among us along with a decades-long stagnation of wages for less educated men.[14] American middle class families' incomes have only risen because of the entry of women into the labor market but we are now running out of second earners.[15]

In addition to changes in technology that require a more skilled work force, and the public investments to create those skills, there have also been changes in globalization, in demography (e.g. aging and declining fertility), in immigration, in the climate, and in demands for new protections against economic insecurity. These, too, are creating fresh challenges to democratic governance. New technologies will not only change modes of production and the distribution of income, they will also require new regulations to protect privacy, to align AI or genetic engineering with human values, to curb the manipulation of political opinion via social media, to address pandemics, and to manage the proliferation of cyber warfare, just to mention a few.[16]

The problem is not just democracy, it is governance writ large. Without a supranational government, globalization in particular poses huge challenges. For example, should corporations be allowed to avoid taxes by moving production to low-tax jurisdictions? Can national governments be counted on to treat pandemics in ways that prevent their spread? Will it be possible to prevent the further proliferation of nuclear weapons? Will climate change lead to new waves of immigration and the kind of conflict this is likely to engender? Will increasingly frequent and seriously damaging natural catastrophes overwhelm already over-indebted governments with the need to spend trillions on mitigation and response? Will AI destroy so many jobs so quickly that new forms of support such as a universal basic income will be needed as a replacement? These kinds of questions need far more discussion if capitalism and democracy are to evolve with the times.

From the end of World War II until the late 1970s, capitalism and democracy worked hand-in-hand to create a middle-class society. The economy not only grew more rapidly than it has in recent years but that prosperity was widely shared. Income inequality declined, most children achieved a higher standard of living than their own parents, and many barriers to opportunities for minorities and women were dismantled as the result of the Civil Rights movement of the 1960s. A new generation of economists argued for Keynesian tax cuts to spur the economy when it performed below its potential. During this postwar era, business and government often worked in tandem to improve people's lives. The national highway system was built, the GI bill ensured that many more people were able to access a college education, Medicare and Medicaid provided health benefits to millions, and factories in the United States provided well-paid jobs that enabled the communities in which they were located to flourish. To be sure, much of the progress of this era was aided by the fact that Europe had been devasted by the war and the United States had an expanding export market with little competition from other countries.

During this postwar period, both government and unions provided some of the countervailing power to capitalists, emphasized by Dedi Kuo in this volume. As she emphasizes, political parties at that time were more aligned with people's economic or class interests. Republicans represented business interests and Democrats the working class. This contrasts sharply with our own era. Republicans now draw the bulk of their support from the white working class while the Democratic Party is losing the support of this group. So right and left no longer split neatly along economic lines and thus cannot provide the same kind of countervailing power that Kuo argues is needed in a capitalist system. As I argued in my own book, *The Forgotten Americans*, President Donald Trump spoke to this group of less educated Americans. However, his policies while in office further damaged their economic prospects, raising questions about the basis for their support.[17] That support may have more to do with their general anger at their government and their cultural anxieties than it does with their economic interests.

But returning to the 1960s, there were growing problems. The Vietnam War tore the country apart and two oil price shocks produced stagflation. President Johnson's attempt to finance both the War in Vietnam and his Great Society agenda at home led to double digit inflation. That in turn led the Federal Reserve to tighten the economy and produced a very deep recession in the early 1980s. The savings and loan crisis in which banks took on too much risk and had to be bailed out demonstrated that capitalism could produce financial instability in the absence of sensible regulations on the private sector.

At about the same time, there was a sea change in ideas about the nature of markets and the good society. Its most forceful advocates were Milton Friedman and like-minded economists and lawyers at the University of Chicago. They argued that markets would produce not only prosperity but individual freedom as well. The responsibility of corporations and businesses was to stay focused on making money for their shareholders or owners.

This view—a strong faith in markets, sometimes referred to as neoliberalism—soon came to dominate public discussion and became the mantra of President Reagan, Margaret Thatcher, and many others. Translated into policy terms, it came to be known as supply-side economics. The goal was to cut taxes and regulation and to limit domestic spending. Taxes on top incomes which had been over 90 percent in the immediate postwar period and as high as 70 percent when Reagan took office were sharply reduced.[18] Additional tax cuts were enacted under President George W. Bush and later in 2017, under President Trump. Such tax cuts were supposed to produce so much new economic growth that they would end up paying for themselves. Instead, history and analysis show they ballooned deficits and added to growing inequality. If this was good governance, there were few lambs singing its praises.

The 2017 tax cut bill is a case in point. It added about $2 trillion to the debt, exacerbated inequality, produced a short Keynesian-style bump to the economy but did little or nothing for longer-term growth.[19]

More recently, spending bills have also added trillions to the debt but were temporary and justified on the grounds that they were needed to fight the economic effects of a pandemic. Whether they were responsible for later inflationary pressures remains somewhat disputed, but it seems likely that they were at least partially to blame. In the meantime, the Republican love-affair with tax cuts for corporations and the wealthy seem to be as strong as ever despite the party's dependence on working class voters to remain in power. At the same time, some Republican intellectuals and elected officials are now sounding like Democrats in their opposition to trade, their support for manufacturing workers, and their dismissal of economic growth as a top priority. [20]

The election of Biden in 2020 ended—at least temporarily—the neoliberal faith in markets.[21] In fact, polls showed that by this time the public wanted more government involvement in their lives. But for something like forty years, the dominant paradigm had been a firm belief that markets were good and government, if not evil, was at least suspect. Even President Clinton, a Democrat, famously said "the era of Big Government is over." He reformed welfare, got tough on crime, and argued for freer trade with Canada and Mexico under NAFTA. Glass-Steagall, a law prohibiting banks from making potentially speculative investments was rescinded as part of Gramm-Leach-Bliley that also allowed more consolidation in financial markets. When the financial crisis of 2008 tanked the economy, the big banks were given a pass while people lost their homes and main street suffered. We can debate whether these actions were justified or not; my only point is that the limitations of government were recognized even among Democrats, while Republicans have now pivoted to a much more intrusive form of government, especially where social issues such as immigration, abortion or the rights of some minorities are concerned.

What is striking about a comparison between the first three decades after the war and the last three or four is the extent to which the zeitgeist shifted from a belief in a mixed economy with an important role for government to one focused much more on faith in unfettered markets.[22] The belief during this latter period in market fundamentalism has, in turn, raised the questions this volume seeks to address. Can capitalism survive in the absence of a well-functioning democracy? The belief that markets know best, that government should stay out of the way, that the best way to ensure efficiency and prosperity is to cut taxes, reduce regulation, and keep the government as small as possible has had major implications not just for the kinds of laws enacted during this period *but more importantly for the laws that weren't enacted* and the challenges that went unaddressed. This last point bears emphasizing. By capturing and effectively promulgating a free market ideology, its proponents not only deprived the government of revenue that might have been used for public investments in basic research, infrastructure, or skill-building, they also ignored growing problems such as rising inequality, climate change, and people and places that got left behind as the result of the march of technology and globalization. These opportunity costs are large and have left a backlog of problems that had they been addressed earlier would not now be so hard and expensive to address. And if Boix is right, as I think he may be, that the lack of widely shared prosperity took its toll on democracy itself, then the costs have been incalculable.

True, we are now in a new era in which supply-side economics has faded, Democrats managed a narrow and disputed political win in 2020, and a more active and pragmatic government has scored some wins. However, Democrats themselves remain divided about how far the government should go to supplement the market, while Republicans are no longer defending free trade or the free movement of people across borders (immigration) and are calling for more government in some areas—even going so far as to get cross-wise with, or penalize, businesses viewed as too "woke." But it is not just the political discourse that has changed; there are new and potentially existential threats that only government has the power and the motivation to address. These include climate change, AI, genetic engineering, cyber terrorism, and the spread of nuclear weapons.[23] So it's a good time to be taking stock. But first, we need to look at the effects of this history on public attitudes and on democracy itself.

Political Institutions Are Unresponsive to Popular Concerns

It is the task of a democracy to adopt policies that a majority of the electorate wants, as long as these policies do not infringe on fundamental individual rights. But right now, according to leading political scientists, the problem is that government in the United States is not responsive to citizen concerns. Research by Page and Gilens shows that there is no correlation between the public's stated policy preferences and what has been enacted by their political representatives in recent decades.[24] There is, on the other hand, a strong correlation between the preferences of organized interests, especially business interests, and what has been enacted. That suggests that democracy is not working as intended, that it has been at least partially captured by special interests and that public disillusionment with government and talk of a rigged system is not completely ill-founded. Trust in government has plummeted since the 1960s when about three-quarters of Americans trusted the federal government to do the right thing almost always or most of the time. By 2023, this figure had fallen to 16 percent.[25]

In their interesting book, *The Captured Economy*, Brink Lindsey, a libertarian, and Steven Teles, a progressive, argue that this is one reason democracy is in peril.[26] Their work is only the latest in a long literature about democratic sclerosis by Mancur Olson, Jonathan Rauch, and various public choice theorists.[27] When government is captured by special interests and unable to respond flexibly to new challenges, confidence will wane and democracy itself be put at risk.

At least half of younger people in the United States say they are no longer in favor of capitalism as an economic system and say instead that they prefer socialism. Among all adults in the United States, more than one third does not support capitalism.[28] The two most important reasons for this lack of support are the belief that capitalism benefits only a few while producing an unequal distribution of wealth and that it is exploitive or corrupt in nature.[29] The lambs are not happy with the wolves.

In my book, *The Forgotten Americans*, written in an attempt to explain the election in 2016 and the continued popularity of President Trump, I focused on the 30 percent of the population that was white, lacked a college degree, and had incomes above the poverty level but below the average income for the country as a whole. In 1962, this group received 18 percent of all the income in the economy. By 2014 their share had fallen to 11 percent, while the share held by those in the top income decile rose from 31 percent to 47 percent over the same period. There has been a massive shift in income between the working class and the professional or managerial class. Is it any surprise, then, that "the forgotten Americans" feel left behind and angry at their government?

Along with my book, I also conducted focus groups with working-class citizens. These were eye-opening interviews.[30] The main themes were: the importance this group of working-class Americans attach to pay and benefits and feeling respected on the job; their distrust and cynicism about government, especially the federal government; and their concern that the education and training system was not producing the skills needed in today's labor market. In my book I recommended a variety of policies that might speak to these concerns. Especially relevant to this essay, I recommended a bigger role for the private sector in training workers (in collaboration with community colleges or others), and in aligning worker and management interests via profit sharing or ownership shares for workers.[31] I called for tax credits for businesses that provided on-the-job training to their workers, arguing that employers are in a better position than government to know what skills are most needed but who need a carrot to overcome an understandable reluctance to train people who might then leave to work for a competitor. What we would get under such a strategy is a more worker-friendly form of capitalism and one that would not require as much social welfare or redistribution via taxes and transfers after the fact. It's a strategy that relies on government to provide the kind of countervailing power Kuo supports, and it is very "light-touch" since government's only role is to incentivize the private sector to do what both our politics and our future productivity require. We could under such policies revive the kind of broad-based prosperity of the immediate postwar period and do so while simultaneously respecting the strengths of the private sector. To me, it is a form of capitalism that fits the times—building skills and worker engagement while preserving the private sector's ability to take the lead in creating long-term value and a strong economy.

Democracy Is in Deeper Trouble than Capitalism, Beset by Cultural and not Just Economic Anxieties

What we are seeing at present in high-income countries like the United States is, in part, a backlash against the disappearance of well-paid blue-collar jobs and the stable communities they created along with growing resentments against cultural elites and their "wokeness." Along with declining confidence in government and other mainstream institutions such as the media, there has been a general decline in trust of other people, and a new fixation with group identity.[32]

Democracies that had been advancing across the globe until recently are now backsliding, with the United States being a prominent example.

Freedom House's democratic score for the United States slipped by 11 points on a 100-point scale between 2010 and 2020, with an accelerated slide during Tump's first term.[33] The areas of backsliding were many but included voting rights, lack of trust in elections, concerns about the independence of the judiciary and the legislature, concerns about the influence of special interests, and the treatment of minorities and women along with the weakening of worker protections.

Some blame this backsliding on economic developments. The Financial Times' Martin Wolf, for example, sees the financial crisis and long post-crisis recovery as a key trigger for the rise of Donald Trump in the United States, and of Brexit in the U.K. Others, such as political scientists John Sides, Michael Tesler, and Lynn Vavreck, believe that cultural anxieties caused by immigration, a decline in religion, in traditional families and gender roles, and a more racially diverse population are more to blame.[34] Larry Bartels places the blame more on populist leaders themselves rather than on any major change in attitudes among the public.[35] These leaders have exploited a submerged tribalism that has always existed but was kept in check until recently and is now being manipulated by political elites with nefarious goals. Of course, all of these may have played a role and they likely interact in ways that exacerbate their individual effects.[36]

The solutions to these problems of declining social trust and a deepening cultural divide are not evident. Some have called for greater regulation of social media. It has exacerbated mistrust, spewed forth misinformation, and drowned out facts and reason. One could start by limiting accounts to those over age 18, requiring that account holders be identified, and disallowing the use of cell phones in school.

Others, including myself, have advocated for universal national service—a call for all young people to serve their country in a civic or military activity for a year, getting to know and respect one another in the process.[37] Those who served might become eligible for a year or two of publicly financed postsecondary training linked to their service. Richard Reeves and I call this "scholarships for service" and it could replace some portion of existing student loans or grants.[38]

Still another response might be to return more responsibilities to state and local governments, where public trust and involvement are greater than at the federal level, and where it would be possible to design diverse solutions better aligned with the preferences of local communities.

Reform of Political Institutions in the United States Is Needed

The American political system is badly in need of reform. The list of issues that need to be addressed is well known. It includes gerrymandering or redistricting, the electoral college, campaign finance, and a primary system favoring the extremes.[39] Some political scientists believe that a system in which legislative or congressional districts were larger but had multiple members, primaries were used to select the top two or the top four candidates on a nonpartisan basis to compete in a general election, and in which ranked choice voting was used to select the best person at the end, would be an improvement over the current system. It would incentivize candidates to make broader appeals, reduce extremism, and give moderates or other distinct groups more influence and greater reason to stay engaged.

Needed reforms are stymied because those currently in power have too much of a stake in the status quo. We have a very narrowly but deeply divided electorate. That kind of narrow divide provides each party with the hope that they can regain power in the next election, leading to a focus on winning rather than governing.

Meanwhile, ordinary citizens are poorly informed about their own government. On a test of civic knowledge, the proportion passing the test was 90 percent among immigrants but only 36 percent for native-born Americans, and knowledge of civics has declined as shown by the fact that senior citizens know far more than those under the age of 45.[40]

My pessimism about the ability of elected leaders or ordinary citizens to reform the system leads me to suggest that leaders in other sectors—especially the private sector—have a role to play. What businesses should recognize is that if democracy fails, so too may capitalism. Populists or autocrats, whether of the left or the right, have no compunction about using the private sector as a tool to achieve their own ends—whether it is to amass excessive wealth and power (on the right), or to excessively redistribute incomes downward (on the left). In addition, the Chinese model of state capitalism may spread to other parts of the globe unless liberal democracies—the United States in particular—improve on their performance.

In this context, the business community has a role to play. Evidence of their changing views is apparent in the movement to incorporate environmental, social, and governance (or ESG) issues into business decision-making and in the Business Roundtable's embrace of stakeholder in place of shareholder capitalism. Some scholars are now calling on the business sector to play a more active role in saving democracy itself (while also worrying that some types of political interference in company affairs may cross a line into improper, even authoritarian, territory).[41]

Unlike ordinary citizens, the business sector has money, power, and influence. I'm not suggesting that they get caught up in the issue du jour—that is, supporting environmentally-friendly packaging, scholarships for the disadvantaged, or trans rights. Instead, they should recognize that while such efforts are laudable, they will not preserve democratic capitalism. I was an adviser to the Committee for Economic Development in the 1970s and can recall the kind of leadership that they and other business organizations provided on major public policy questions. Those who actively participated in these discussions were not just business leaders: they were statesmen (virtually all men at that time). What will help now is not just more leadership from this sector, but a refusal to support candidates who fail to recognize the legitimate winner of an election. Put differently, too much focus on what is good for General Motors and too little on what is good for the country will not help to restore a healthy democracy, and without a healthy democracy, capitalism cannot flourish.

Conclusions

We have an economic system that works well to produce the goods and services people want but distributes the rewards very unequally and with little or no regard for the social costs it generates on the environment, on workers and communities left behind, or the insecurities associated with low wages, or inadequate benefits. The inability of the political system to address such problems is, in turn, undermining the legitimacy of the economic system itself. As the polls I cited earlier show, support for capitalism is eroding, especially among the young.

Rising prosperity has historically led to greater demands on the public sector. Added to this general affluence and the demands it creates are the challenges posed by other developments such as climate change, AI, genetic engineering, the mass manipulation of attitudes via social media, and cyber warfare. Democracies will be hard pressed to respond to such challenges unless reforms are made. There will be, and should be, continuing debate about the role of government, but if democracies don't address these evolving demands in some way, the public frustration that ensues may undermine or even end democracy and eventually capitalism itself.

Notes

1. These are process-oriented definitions. We can contrast them with the philosophical traditions of classical liberalism or libertarianism in which the emphasis is on individual liberty and the right to control one's own life and thus to strict limits on government itself, and a belief that free markets organize themselves and that capitalism allows for this. Classical liberals believe in democracy but with strong limits on its powers. Contrast this to a view in which individuals are believed to be in need of strong guidance or supervision whether by the church, a king, a lord, or a dictator with absolute or near-absolute power. This may be combined with state planning of the economy or ownership of the means of production as under communism or socialism. However, mixed systems can be found. An example would be state-led capitalism as in China or a benign form of autocracy devoted to the well-being of the broader public as in Singapore. Philosophically, democracy vs autocracy grows out of different conceptions of human nature. If as Rousseau believed, individuals are naturally good, then they should be as free as possible to live the good life. If they are born in sin, or naturally prone to evil, as Hobbes believed, then they must be controlled for their own good.
2. Charles Lindblom, *Politics and Markets: The World's Political-economic Systems* (New York: Basic Books, 1977).
3. Martin Wolf, *The Crisis of Democratic Capitalism* (London: Penguin Press, 2023); Daron Acemoglu and James Robinson, *Why Nations Fail: The Origins of Power, Prosperity, and Poverty* (New York: Currency, 2012).
4. Daron Acemoglu, Suresh Naidu, Pascual Restrepo, and James Robinson, "Democracy Does Cause Growth," *Journal of Political Economy* 127, no. 1 (February 2019): 47–100. https://doi.org/10.1086/700936.
5. J. Bradford DeLong, *Slouching Towards Utopia: An Economic History of the Twentieth Century* (New York: Basic Books, 2022).
6. Wolf, *Crisis of Democratic Capitalism*, p. 53.
7. Wolf, *Crisis of Democratic Capitalism*, p. 53.
8. Wolf, *Crisis of Democratic Capitalism*, p. 303.
9. Daron Acemoglu and James A. Robinson, *Why Nations Fail: The Origins of Power, Prosperity, and Poverty* (New York: Crown Publishing, 2012), 3–4.
10. Michael Strain, "Why Industrial Policy Fails," *Project Syndicate*, August 15, 2023, https://www.project-syndicate.org/commentary/industrial-policy-why-it-fails-biden-subsidies-trump-tariffs-by-michael-r-strain-2023-08?barrier=accesspay; Jesús Fernández-Villaverde and Lee Ohanian, "The Neoclassical Growth of China," *VoxEU CEPR*, September 29, 2023, https://cepr.org/voxeu/columns/neoclassical-growth-china; Alicia García-Herrero, "Can Chinese Growth Defy Gravity?," *Bruegel*, June 20, 2023, https://www.bruegel.org/policy-brief/can-chinese-growth-defy-gravity; Peter Goodman, "The Rise and Fall of the World's Most Successful Joint Venture," *New York Times*, November 14, 2023, https://www.nytimes.com/2023/11/14/business/us-china-economy-trade.html.
11. For a more detailed discussion of these issues, see Isabel Sawhill, "Capitalism and The Future of Democracy," in *Community Wealth Building and the Reconstruction of American Democracy: Can We Make American Democracy Work?*, ed. Melody C. Barnes, Corey D.B. Walker, Thad M. Williamson (Cheltenham: Edward Elgar Publishing, 2020), where I discuss intellectual challenges to the neoclassical model of an economy taught in most universities. See

also Thomans Piketty, *Capital in the Twenty-First Century* (Cambridge: The Belknap Press of Harvard University Press, 2014), where Piketty argues that inequality is an inherent feature of capitalism.

12. See especially Robert Skidelsky and Edward Skidelsky, *How Much is Enough?: Money and the Good Life* (London: Penguin Random House, 2013); Steven Pearlstein, *Can American Capitalism Survive?: Why Greed Is Not Good, Opportunity Is Note Equal, and Fairness Won't Make Us Poor* (New York: St. Martin's Press, 2018); Piketty, *Capital in the Twenty-First Century*; Sawhill, "Capitalism and The Future of Democracy."
13. Pearlstein, *Can American Capitalism Survive?*, p. 205.
14. Isabel Sawhill, *The Forgotten Americans: An Economic Agenda for a Divided Nation* (New Haven: Yale University Press, 2018); Eric Hanushek, G. William Hoagland, Douglas Holtz-Eakin, et al., "Toward a Potential Grand Bargain for the Nation," *Bipartisan Policy Center*, July 2024, 11–13, https://bipartisanpolicy.org/download/?file=/wp-content/uploads/2024/08/BPC_Grand_Market_Committee_Paper-3.pdf
15. Isabel Sawhill and Katherine Guyot, "The Middle Class Time Squeeze," *Brookings Institution*, August 18, 2020, https://www.brookings.edu/wp-content/uploads/2020/08/The-Middle-Class-Time-Squeeze_08.18.2020.pdf.
16. For a more extended discussion of the misalignment between technology and governance, see Isabel Sawhill, "Saving Democracy," *Democracy Journal*, no. 67 (Winter 2023), https://democracyjournal.org/magazine/67/saving-democracy/.
17. Sawhill, *Forgotten Americans.*
18. James Fallows, "When the Top U.S. Tax Rate was 70 Percent—or Higher," *The Atlantic*, January 25, 2019, https://www.theatlantic.com/ideas/archive/2019/01/tax-rates-davos/622220/
19. Robert Barro and Jason Furman, "Macroeconomic Effects of the 2017 Tax Reform," *Brookings Papers on Economic Activity*, March 8, 2018, https://www.brookings.edu/wp-content/uploads/2018/03/BarroFurman_Text.pdf.
20. Oren Kass, *The Once and Future Worker: A Vision for the Renewal of Work in America* (New York: Encounter Books, 2018).
21. By 2019, a small majority of the public was in favor of a more active government. Pew Research Center, "Views of government and the nation," December 17, 2019, https://www.pewresearch.org/politics/2019/12/17/views-of-government-and-the-nation/.
22. Jacob S. Hacker and Paul Pierson, *American Amnesia: How the War on Government Led Us to Forget What Made America Prosper* (New York: Simon & Schuster, 2016).
23. For more detail on these threats, see Sawhill, "Saving Democracy."
24. Martin Gilens and Benjamin I. Page, "Testing Theories of American Politics: Elites, Interest Groups, and Average Citizens," *Perspectives on Politics* 12, no. 3 (2014): 564–581, https://doi.org/10.1017/S1537592714001595; Larry M. Bartels, *Unequal Democracy: The Political Economy of the New Gilded Age* (Princeton: Princeton University Press, 2016). Bartels argues that "the folk theory of democracy" is wrong. Elected officials don't respond to public opinion as much as they shape it in ways that achieve their own ends and to the extent that they respond to citizens' preferences, that response favors the affluent.
25. Pew Research Center, "Public Trust in Government: 1958–2023," September 19, 2023, https://www.pewresearch.org/politics/2024/06/24/public-trust-in-government-1958-2024/.
26. Brink Lindsey and Steven M. Teles, *The Captured Economy: How the Powerful Enrich Themselves, Slow Down Growth, and Increase Inequality* (Oxford: Oxford University Press, 2017).
27. Mancur Olson, *The Rise and Decline of Nations: Economic Growth, Stagflation, and Social Rigidities* (New Haven: Yale University Press, 1982); Jonathan Rauch, *Demosclerosis: The Silent Killer of American Government* (New York: Random House, 1995).
28. Pew Research Center, "Modest Declines in Positive Views of 'Socialism' and 'Capitalism' in U.S.," September 19, 2022, https://www.pewresearch.org/politics/2022/09/19/modest-declines-in-positive-views-of-socialism-and-capitalism-in-u-s/.
29. Pew Research Center, "Many Across the Globe Are Dissatisfied With How Democracy is Working," April 29–May 13, 2019, https://www.pewresearch.org/global/2019/04/29/many-across-the-globe-are-dissatisfied-with-how-democracy-is-working/.

30. Isabel Sawhill, "What the forgotten Americans really want—and how to give it to them," Brookings Institution, October 2018, https://www.brookings.edu/articles/what-the-forgotten-americans-really-want-and-how-to-give-it-to-them/; Yasha Mounk, *The Identity Trap: A Story of Ideas and Power in Our Time* (New York: Penguin Random House, 2023); Ezra Klein; *Why We're Polarized*, (New York: Avid Reader Press, 2020; Isabel Sawhill, "Social Capital: Why we need it and how we can create more of it," Brookings Institution, July 16, 2020, https://www.brookings.edu/articles/social-capital-why-we-need-it-and-how-we-can-create-more-of-it/.
31. Sawhill, "A Bigger Role for the Private Sector," in *Forgotten Americans*, 139–159
32. Isabel Sawhill, "How Biden can Rebuild a Divided and Distrustful Nation," *Foreign Affairs*, January 4, 2021, https://www.foreignaffairs.com/articles/how-biden-can-rebuild-divided-and-distrustful-nation.
33. Sarah Repucci, "Reversing the Decline of Democracy in the United States," *Freedom House*, 2022, https://freedomhouse.org/report/freedom-world/2022/global-expansion-authoritarian-rule/reversing-decline-democracy-united-states.
34. John Sides, Michael Tesler, and Lynn Vavreck, *Identity Crisis: The 2016 Presidential Campaign and the Battle for the Meaning of America* (Princeton: Princeton University Press, 2018).
35. Larry Bartels, "The Wave of Right-wing Populist Sentiment Is a Myth," *Washington Post*, June 21, 2017, https://www.washingtonpost.com/news/monkey-cage/wp/2017/06/21/the-wave-of-right-wing-populist-sentiment-is-a-myth/.
36. Wolf, *Crisis of Democratic Capitalism*; John Sides, Michael Tesler, and Lynn Vavreck, *Identity Crisis: The Presidential Campaign and the Battle for the Meaning of America* (Princeton: Princeton University Press, 2018).
37. Isabel Sawhill and John Bridgeland, "Here's a Cost-effective National Service Proposal That Could Bridge our Deep Divisions," *Washington Post*, February 21, 2020, https://www.washingtonpost.com/opinions/2020/02/21/heres-cost-effective-national-service-proposal-that-could-bridge-our-deep-divisions/.
38. Richard Reeves and Isabel Sawhill, *A New Contract with the Middle Class* (Washington, D.C.: Brookings Institution, 2020).
39. See, for example, Larry Diamond: "Saving Democracy: Realistically," *Democracy Journal*, no. 65 (Summer 2022). For a useful ongoing synthesis of the status of these reforms and their likely effectiveness, see "Solutions Landscape: A New Holistic Resource on American Political Reforms," *FixUS*, August 31, 2023, https://docs.google.com/document/d/1lfhQLd2y6yjJcfa_NdyX0TgaTJoH5rX6/edit.
40. Institute for Citizens and Scholars, "National Survey Finds Just 1 in 3 Americans Would Pass Citizenship Test," October 3, 2018, https://citizensandscholars.org/resource/national-survey-finds-just-1-in-3-americans-would-pass-citizenship-test/.
41. On the relationship between corporate America and the political system, see Rebecca Henderson, "The Business Case for Saving Democracy," *Harvard Business Review*, March 10, 2020, https://hbr.org/2020/03/the-business-case-for-saving-democracy; and William Galston and Elaine Kamarck, "Is Democracy Failing and Putting Our Economic System at Risk?," *Brookings Institution*, January 4, 2022, https://www.brookings.edu/articles/is-democracy-failing-and-putting-our-economic-system-at-risk/.

1

Two Peas in a Pod

Democracy and Capitalism

VINCENT GELOSO AND ALEX TABARROK

Introduction

It seems that hardly anyone thinks that democracy and capitalism are compatible.[1] If we go by the average pundit, the average politician, or even the average voter, capitalism and democracy are in tension. Tension that may eventually lead to societal collapse. However, beyond this agreement about incompatibility, little else can be agreed upon. The arguments regarding the causes, consequences, and normative evaluations of such tensions can be broken into two broadly defined categories.

The first category is "democracy undermines capitalism". Proponents of this view argue that voters will vote for socialist policies or give in to jingoist, nativist, or interventionist policies that create conflicts, breed bad policies, or slow down economic growth that eventually occasions a turn toward authoritarianism. In the first case, the end of capitalism at the hands of democracy is considered by some to be a boon. In the second, neither capitalism nor democracy survive and the death of both is seen as undesirable yet inevitable.

The second category is "capitalism undermines democracy". For proponents of this view, the mechanism is more straightforward: Capitalists' wealth gives them proximity to political power, enabling them to tilt societal rules in their favor, in some cases so much as to end democracy or make it an illusion. Democracy dies directly because of capitalism. For proponents of this category, the death of democracy is bad and capitalism needs to be restrained to prevent its homicidal tendencies. The range of policies they propose is wide: from limits on campaign finance and a mild interventionist government that redistributes according to some basic notions of fairness to full-blown socialism.

Vincent Geloso and Alex Tabarrok, *Two Peas in a Pod*. In: *Can Democracy and Capitalism Be Reconciled?*. Edited by: Sidney M. Milkis and Scott C. Miller, Oxford University Press. © Oxford University Press (2025). DOI: 10.1093/9780197774731.003.0002

However, the evidence for both categories is—surprisingly given how frequently they are reiterated in the public sphere by academics, pundits, and politicians—weak. In fact, there is stronger evidence for a third category of arguments, which is that capitalism and democracy are mutually reinforcing.

In this chapter, we first summarize the arguments for incompatibility, citing the proponents of each theory and giving the historical background. Then, we examine the empirical evidence for incompatibility and find that there is far more evidence supporting the argument of mutual reinforcement. Finally, we explain some of the mechanisms of mutual reinforcement, but also why mutual reinforcement may fail and where future research should direct its attention.

We define capitalism as an economic system in which individuals and organizations are broadly free to use their capital, labor, and resources however they see fit.[2] More generally, a capitalist system is one in which a large fraction of total resources is owned privately and allocated according to voluntary exchange, and individuals have the freedom to enter markets and compete, with both conditions legally protected. Later we will operationalize this definition using the Fraser Index of Economic Freedom.[3] As for democracy, we define it as a political system in which leaders are elected in free and fair elections. Later we will operationalize this concept using the Varieties of Democracy index which further distinguishes electoral, liberal, majoritarian, consensual, participatory, deliberative, and egalitarian versions of democracy. We discuss both indexes at greater length further below.

Democracy Undermines Capitalism

The fear that democracy will trample capitalism has been a constant concern of classical liberal political economy from Locke through to Hume, Smith, the Mills, and Madison.[4] For some classical liberals, those discussed in this section, the forces that lead to the end of capitalism are immensely powerful. For other classical liberals—discussed in the "capitalism and democracy are mutually reinforcing" section—it is possible to create a reasonable set of *de jure* and *de facto* constraints that limit the possibility of the catastrophe scenario described by others. However, they all agree that tensions exist.

For Locke (1690) governments were justified to the extent that they protected the inalienable rights of the governed, most importantly life, liberty, and property.[5] The immediate implication was that the rights of kings were limited. Monarchs *might* act consistently with the rights of the governed (those that did not could be legitimately overthrown), and in this sense monarchy was not inconsistent with capitalism and liberty but it was more likely that rights would be protected by some form of democracy. Democracy, however, was no guarantee of liberty, and thus also had to be limited. Locke thus supported representative government with the franchise limited to property owners. In Burke's words "neither the few nor the many have the right to govern by their will" and thus any type of government had to be limited.[6]

Adam Smith said little about the form of government per se, but was clear that for government to serve its purpose of increasing the wealth of nations it had to protect the rich from the poor:

> The affluence of the rich excites the indignation of the poor, who are often both driven by want, and prompted by envy, to invade his possessions. It is only under the shelter of the civil magistrate that the owner of that valuable property, which is acquired by the labour of many years, or perhaps of many successive generations, can sleep a single night in security. He is at all times surrounded by unknown enemies, whom, though he never provoked, he can never appease, and from whose injustice he can be protected only by the powerful arm of the civil magistrate continually held up to chastise it. The acquisition of valuable and extensive property, therefore, necessarily requires the establishment of civil government.[7]

James Madison argued similarly that "[pure] democracies have ever been . . . found incompatible with personal security or the rights of property."[8] Protecting liberty and property meant checking government and limiting the franchise. This concern was shared by scholars inside the classical liberal tradition outside of the English-speaking world, such as the French economist Jean-Baptiste Say who expressed concerns that liberal democracies needed capitalism to thrive, but that capitalism could be throttled by democratic tendencies.[9]

Throughout the classical period two mutually supporting but slightly different versions of the "democracy tramples capitalism" view circulated, which we might label the cupidity and stupidity views. The cupidity view was that the poor would trample the rights of the rich out of avarice, that is, a demand for redistribution.[10] The stupidity view was that the poor would trample the rights of the rich out of envy, short-sightedness, and ill-founded beliefs. Adam Smith neatly summarized both when he wrote that the poor may invade the possessions of the rich "driven by want and prompted by envy."[11] Both views, which are not mutually exclusive, may also be seen in John Stuart Mill's *Considerations on Representative Government.*[12] Mill writes:

> . . . the dangers incident to a representative democracy are of two kinds: danger of a low-grade intelligence in the representative body, and

> in the popular opinion which controls it; and dangers of class legislation on the part of the numerical majority, these being all composed of the same class.

To limit the latter, class legislation, Mill argued for division of powers, and also to limit the franchise. It was obvious to Mill, for example, that:

> . . . the assembly which votes the taxes, either general or local, should be elected exclusively by those who pay something towards the taxes imposed. Those who pay no taxes, disposing by their votes of other people's money, have every motive to be lavish and none to economize. As far as money matters are concerned, any power of voting possessed by them is a violation of the fundamental principle of free government, a severance of the power of control from the interest in its beneficial exercise. It amounts to allowing them to put their hands into other people's pockets.

Taxes should be broadly conceived so as not to limit the franchise unjustly, but anyone on welfare should be excluded from the vote.

> I regard it as required by first principles, that the receipt of parish relief should be a peremptory disqualification for the franchise. He who cannot by his labor suffice for his own support has no claim to the privilege of helping himself to the money of others.

Cupidity, however, wasn't the only problem. Democracies also had to deal with stupidity or more generally, lack of education, short-term thinking, and possible misanthropy. Thus, Mill recognizes that it's natural for workers to think that interferences with the free market, such as minimum wage laws, immigration restrictions, tariffs, taxes on capital and restrictions on innovation are good for workers even when they are contrary to their long-term interests. But "It is not what their interest is, but what they suppose it to be, that is the important consideration with respect to their conduct." The majority may be confused about their true interests, or they may simply regard their interests as different from those the economist-philosopher thinks they should have.

> It would be vain to attempt to persuade a man who beats his wife and ill-treats his children that he would be happier if he lived in love and kindness with them. He would be happier if he were the kind of person who could so live; but he is not, and it is probably too late for him to become that kind of person.

Mill is not confident of any solution, but in addition to proportional representation and divided government he also considers giving educated people more than one vote.[13] Some classical liberals also defended property-related qualifications for voting.[14]

The apotheosis of the cupidity view is perhaps found in Meltzer and Richard's 1981 paper, *A Rational Theory of the Size of Government,* and that of the stupidity view in Caplan's 2008 book, *The Myth of the Rational Voter.*

Using Anthony Down's median voter theorem, Meltzer and Richard formalize when voters will want to tax to redistribute income.[15] In essence, the greater mean income is to median income the higher the median voter's ideal tax rate. Thus, the Meltzer and Richard model implies that greater inequality will lead to greater redistribution, and that extending the franchise to lower income voters will result in greater redistribution. Note, however, that Meltzer and Richard build into their model a natural limit to redistribution—as the tax rate increases, workers choose to work fewer hours. Thus, even purely avaricious voters won't raise taxes too high for fear of killing the goose laying the golden eggs.

The stupidity view finds its modern statement in Caplan.[16] Like Mill, Caplan contrasts the views of the economists with those of the public on what is in the public's interest.[17] The economists tend to take a more long-term, promarket view of what is in the public's interest. Unlike Mill, however, Caplan locates the irrationality of voting not primarily in poor education but in the vote mechanism itself.[18] Since the chances of a single vote changing the outcome of an election are miniscule there is no incentive to be informed (hence rational ignorance) or to vote rationally (hence rational irrationality). A consumer choosing a phone chooses carefully because their choice determines what phone they get. A consumer choosing a politician doesn't choose carefully because their choice is nugatory, other people's choices determine what they get. It's no surprise, therefore, that political choices are swayed by appeals to emotion, tribalism, and short-term thinking. While these factors influence all choices, emotionalism is disciplined in the market by the utility of rational thinking. In politics, emotionalism rules because rational thinking is impotent. Thus, a consumer will buy a product from China because it has a lower price and at the same time vote for tariffs on Chinese products because they don't like Asians.[19]

The upshot of the Smith/Mill/Meltzer-Richard/Caplan view is that democracy undermines private property and free exchange through a combination of avarice that leads to taxes and redistribution and irrational, tribalistic, envious policies that destroy the foundations for economic growth, thereby harming the rightly understood interests even of the majority.

The Marxist view of capitalism and democracy is very similar to that of the classical economists and Meltzer-Richard, only differing in regarding the end goal of socialism positively. In the Communist Manifesto, Marx and Engels consider democracy to be "the first step in the revolution."[20] Under democracy:

> The proletariat will use its political supremacy to wrest, by degree, all capital from the bourgeoisie, to centralise all instruments of production in the hands of the State, i.e., of the proletariat organised as the ruling class.

Capitalism Undermines Democracy

The second category of argument—namely that capitalism undermines democracy—is a more heteroclite assembly of viewpoints. Proponents of the view that democracy undermines capitalism are largely classical liberals. But among those holding the opposite view, one finds conservatives such as Russell Kirk, socialists like Gunnar Myrdal, social democrats like Thomas Piketty, and centrist liberals such as Amartya Sen. Assigning them a common denominator is virtually impossible, and so it is preferable to break their argument in three groups according to the types of solutions they propose. At one end of the spectrum, we find those like Amartya Sen who propose mild redistributive schemes in order to counter what they see as the effect of capitalism on socio-economic inequalities. At the other end, we find outright socialists who believe that the commanding heights of the economy should be nationalized. In-between, we find conservatives who argue that capitalism erodes shared values that sustain democracy, which makes necessary occasional interventions to curtail capitalism.

The first of the three groups—represented by say Amartya Sen and Martha Nussbaum—is the closest to the classical liberals in terms of core principles, but they depart from or wish to extend that tradition beyond negative liberty.[21] Economic freedom is a negative liberty—the absence of legal barriers. They argue that negative liberty is not the full definition of freedom. Freedom must include the *ability* to make choices. Being free to open a business is of little use for an illiterate and crippled man as he is unable to exercise agency. This opens the door to what Sen calls "legal entitlements" that allow the rearrangement of the allocation of economic resources in order to allow a basic level of "capabilities" that allow people to exercise their freedoms.[22]

Inequality in capabilities creates economic inequality. From there it is easy to argue for an incompatibility between capitalism and democracy; viz. capitalism increases inequality beyond acceptable levels, which creates social tensions that threaten democracy.

The most common contemporary exposition of this argument can be seen in the so-called Great Gatsby curve, which depicts a negative relationship between inequality and intergenerational income mobility—more inequality leads to less mobility.[23] Societies with high inequality lead to fixed classes such that children born to parents in the lowest income classes will be unable to exit their relative positions even as society as a whole increases in absolute income. If capitalism breeds too much inequality and if lower intergenerational mobility is associated with weaker democratic commitments (something for which there is evidence), the loop is completed as there is a causal chain tying capitalism to collapsing democracies.[24]

Another illustration of this worldview is Robert Reich who suggests quite straightforwardly that "capitalism is killing democracy."[25] Reich's primary argument is that capitalism creates economic inequality, and economic inequality creates political inequality, and political inequality destroys democracy. "Corporations" and "billionaire capitalists," Reich argues, "have invested ever greater sums in lobbying, public relations, and even bribes and kickbacks, seeking laws that give them a competitive advantage over their rivals. The result is an arms race for political influence that is drowning out the voices of average citizens" or even worse "drowning democracy in giant campaign donations to authoritarian candidates."

Reich's primary argument is that it is capitalism's winners that destroy democracy—it's the corporations and the billionaires and the "1%," who use their money and influence to increase and cement their wealth and place in society. In contrast, Robert Kuttner, building on Polanyi, argues that it's capitalism's losers that destroy democracy—the workers who are cruelly abandoned by global capitalism rise up to vote for populist and fascist governments.[26] Capitalism thus destroys democracy through democratic backlash.

One can also see elements of this view in the work of Jayadev and Bowles, and Bowles on guard labor and inequality.[27] They posit a simple relationship between inequality and the share of the workforce employed in guard duties which include anyone who must be employed in a supervisory capacity (e.g., security guards, police officers, judges, forensic accountants, parole officers). Where inequality is greater, there is greater social distance between rich and poor. This distance translates into lesser trust and more opportunistic/violent behavior. More resources must be employed to neutralize potential threats, hence the greater share of the workforce employed in guard duties. More resources spent on non-productive deterrence and guarding means slower economic growth. Slower economic growth, in turn, fragilizes democratic institutions as they are seen as unable to deliver results desired by lower—but demographically larger—income groups. Ergo, redistribution from rich to poor reduces social distance that increases trust, reduces guard labor and increases growth.

From these examples, the remedies are evident—use income redistribution to alleviate economic inequality and preserve democracy. The second group—socialists who advocate far more extreme measures—also argue that capitalist-generated inequality harms democracy, but they ramp up the degree. Indeed, their argument is that capitalism *fails* to raise the standard of living at the bottom, whereas scholars like Sen allow for varying increases along the income ladder (i.e., gains for all, but bigger gains for those nearer to the top of the income ladder).[28] In the view of Sen, capitalism need not harm the poor to create undesirable outcomes. In contrast, socialists argue that "democratic" capitalism gives capitalists power to shape the rules of societies in ways that are exploitative of the poor. As the sins are greater, the remedies must be harsher. Rather than only advocating mild forms of redistribution, such as transfers to fund human capital acquisition, socialists advocate the complete takeover of the means of production by the state. This remedy, by taking away the power of the rich to make the rules, returns balance to democratic life.

The last and final group is that of conservatives. Here, the argument is that capitalism's success is at the root of its own collapse, which brings democracy along with it.[29] As it raises living standards, individuals feel like they can more easily renounce traditional institutions, and the result is that they seek to liberate themselves "from all forms of associations and relationships, from family to church, from schools to village and community, that exerted control over behavior through informal and habituated expectations and norms." The gradual erosion of informal institutions, it is argued, eventually leads to a hyper-individualized society which in turn seeps into political behavior in ways that make Bryan Caplan's "stupidity" view operate. Mainstream conservatives like George Will appear to share this view, and sometimes do so by invoking Karl Marx's idea that capitalism erodes social structures.[30] Eventually, democracy is brought crashing down because it has eroded its own foundation.

Capitalism and Democracy Are Mutually Reinforcing

The third category is that capitalism and democracy are generally mutually reinforcing. This view has been mostly held by economists like Milton Friedman, Ludwig von Mises, and Friedrich Hayek and by sociologists like Peter Berger.[31] It is simply summarized in Mises when he stated that "liberalism must necessarily demand democracy as its political corollary," or by Berger when he states that the answer to the question of whether political democracy requires a market economy is "a resounding yes."[32]

Their argument is, however, largely an empirical one. Milton Friedman stated that economic freedom was generally followed by political freedom. Berger stated flat out that he could find no lasting case of a "political democracy that has *not* been a market economy" (emphasis in original), and that nondemocratic market economies were eventually pressured into democratizing themselves.[33] Empirical regularities suggest capitalism and democracy are compatible, but the arguments were anecdotal, and few mechanisms were discussed.

What theory the compatibilists invoked was based on the idea of Lipset that by promoting development, capitalism legitimizes democracy.[34] In return, democratic oversight and constraints upon power legitimize capitalism. The relation is symbiotic. However, beyond that theoretical invocation, the compatibilists tend to eschew elaborations of mechanisms—something that we will return to later, after reviewing that empirical evidence.

Empirical Evidence

Capitalism and Democracy are Highly Correlated

We operationalize capitalism with the Fraser Institute's Economic Freedom of the World (EFW) index. The EFW Index is designed:

> . . . as a measure of the degree to which scarce resources are allocated by personal choices coordinated by markets rather than centralized planning directed by the political process. It might also be thought of as an effort to identify how closely the institutions and policies of a country correspond with the classical liberal ideal of a limited government, where the government protects property rights and arranges for the provision of a limited set of "public goods" such as national defense and access to money of sound value, but little beyond these core functions.[35]

The index thus corresponds well with our definition of capitalism.[36] Similar results can be found using alternative indexes such as The Heritage Foundation's Economic Freedom Index.

We operationalize democracy using the Varieties of Democracy index. For convenience we focus on the liberal democracy index but as we describe below, any of the indexes of democracy would have worked equally well, as would have alternative democracy indexes such as Polity V.

In Table 1.1, we present descriptive statistics for EFW and V-DEM. Figure 1.1 shows that there is a strong and positive correlation between democracy and capitalism. In addition to the correlation (ρ=.64) it's notable that there are no strong democracies with very low levels of economic freedom (say below 5) and,

Table 1.1 **Descriptive statistics**

Variable	*Obs*	*Mean*	*Std. Dev.*	*Min*	*Max*
V-DEM Liberal democracy index	179	.405	.26	.009	.883
Fraser Institute Economic Freedom Index	165	6.894	.997	2.87	8.87

Note: 2019.

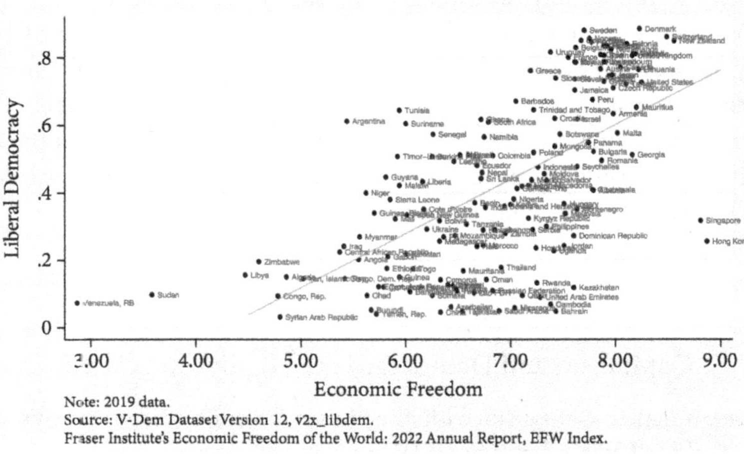

Figure 1.1 Economic freedom and liberal democracy are highly correlated.

with the exceptions of Singapore and Hong Kong, there are no countries with very high levels of economic freedom (say 8 or higher) that are not also strong democracies.

In Figure 1.1, the V-Dem's score for liberal democracy attempts to index democracies according to the following idea:

> The liberal principle of democracy emphasizes the importance of protecting individual and minority rights against the tyranny of the state and the tyranny of the majority. The liberal model takes a "negative" view of political power insofar as it judges the quality of democracy by the limits placed on government. This is achieved by constitutionally protected civil liberties, strong rule of law, an independent judiciary, and effective checks and balances that, together, limit the exercise of executive power. To make this a measure of liberal democracy, the index also takes the level of electoral democracy into account.

In addition to liberal democracy, V-Dem also offers indexes for participatory democracy, deliberative democracy, and egalitarian democracy. Each of these indexes emphasizes different ideas of democracy. Participatory democracy, for example, tries to index the following idea:

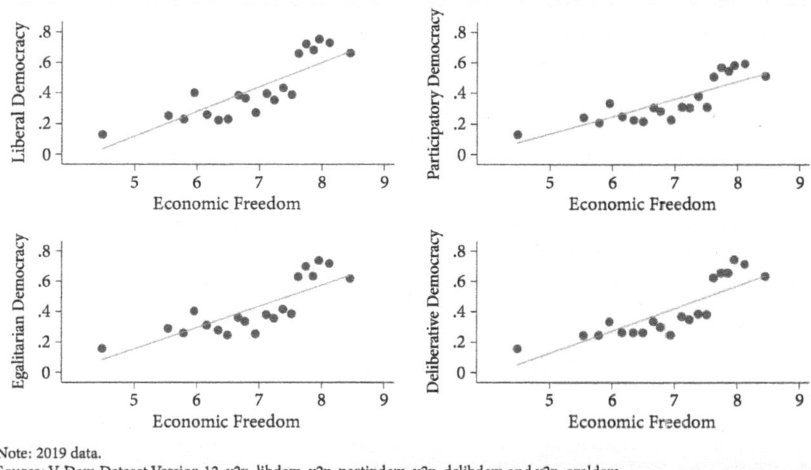

Note: 2019 data.
Source: V-Dem Dataset Version 12, v2x_libdem, v2x_partipdem, v2x_delibdem and v2x_egaldem.
Fraser Institute's Economic Freedom of the World: 2022 Annual Report, EFW Index.

Figure 1.2 Economic freedom and all types of democracy are highly correlated.

> The participatory principle of democracy emphasizes active participation by citizens in all political processes, electoral and non-electoral. It is motivated by uneasiness about a bedrock practice of electoral democracy: delegating authority to representatives. Thus, direct rule by citizens is preferred, wherever practicable. This model of democracy thus takes suffrage for granted, emphasizing engagement in civil society organizations, direct democracy, and subnational elected bodies. To make it a measure of participatory democracy, the index also takes the level of electoral democracy into account.

As a result of these different definitions, one could argue that Figure 1.1 might be the result of some form of cherry-picking on our part. To circumvent that potential criticism, we produce Figure 1.2 that shows the correlation between each measure of democracy and capitalism, as measured by economic freedom. For clarity Figure 1.2 use binned scatterplots. Binned scatterplots divide the x-axis variable into equal-sized bins, compute the mean of the x-axis and y-axis variables within each bin, then create a scatterplot of these data points. A binned scatterplot is a non-parametric method of plotting the conditional expectation function.[37] The top-left binned scatterplot is the same data as in Figure 1.1. Moving clockwise we then have the participatory, deliberative, and egalitarian conceptions of democracy against economic freedom in each case. Each of the binned scatterplots looks identical, but in fact they are different measures. Each measure of democracy correlates highly with every other measure and perforce with economic freedom. Indeed, even egalitarian democracy, which emphasizes economic equality, correlates highly with economic freedom (ρ=.62). Since all measures of democracy correlate highly with economic freedom in what follows we focus on liberal democracy for convenience.

In fact, if there are to be concerns with the data, it's not on the side of the democracy data. Rather, it's on the side of the economic freedom data. If one returns to Figure 1.1 and looks at countries that have economic freedom between 7 and 8, one will find a cluster of countries that seem to have high economic freedom but low political liberty such as Bahrain and the United Arab Emirates. As Rosemarie Fike pointed out in her work, the EFW has long failed to incorporate consideration of how the law in certain countries may create differentiation of property rights (one of the components of the Economic Freedom Index) according to gender.[38] For example, the property rights of women in countries like Bahrain and the United Arab Emirates are far less extensive and secure than those of men. If half the population enjoys lower *de jure* economic freedom than the other half, Fike argues, the EFW should be recalculated. When she does, these countries move down significantly in the ranking of economically free countries. This means that many countries in that strange cluster move toward the mean value of economic freedom at that level of political liberty. Essentially, the fit improves when we are able to improve the economic freedom data.

Democracy and capitalism are highly correlated—this doesn't prove causation in either direction, but it is enough to refute both of the incompatibility views discussed in the introduction. The theory that democracy undermines capitalism and the theory that capitalism undermines democracy both predict a negative correlation between democracy and capitalism. That prediction finds itself at odds with strong correlative evidence that the incompatibility theorists fail to address seriously (beyond sometimes offering entertaining hyperbolized anecdotes).

Growth in Democracy is Correlated with Growth in Capitalism and Vice-Versa

Capitalism and democracy are correlated today and were correlated in the past, but the causal connections are not obvious. In addition to bi-directionality there are likely also exogenous variables (third variables) that promote both capitalism and democracy. We do not intend to resolve these issues here. We can begin to get some intuition, however, by examining whether growth in democracy is correlated with growth in capitalism. That is, if a society grows more democratic does it grow more capitalist?

In Figure 1.3 we look at how changes in a country's democracy index correlate with changes over the same period in its economic freedom index. In most

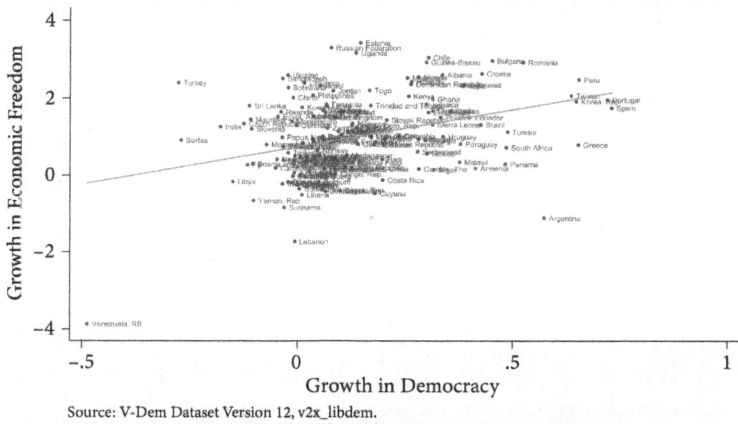

Figure 1.3 Growth in democracy and growth in economic freedom.

Table 1.2 **Changes in Democracy are Positively Correlated with Changes in Economic Freedom**

Variables	*(1)* *Change in Economic Freedom*
Change in democracy	1.937***
	(0.394)
Constant	0.744***
	(0.0930)
Observations	160
R-squared	0.133

Standard errors in parentheses
*** p<0.01, ** p<0.05, * p<0.1

cases, we have 40–50 years of data although some newer countries have fewer data points. In each case we take the longest difference available in the data. Figure 1.3 shows that countries where democracy increased also tended to see increases in economic freedom. Most countries over this time period clustered around the mean levels with small increases in democracy (+.13 on a 0–1 scale) and small increases in economic freedom (+.98 on a 0–10 scale). The countries with the biggest increases in democracy—namely, Peru, Taiwan, Portugal, Spain, and Greece—all increased in economic freedom. Only Argentina grew significantly in democracy but fell in economic freedom.

The correlation between growth in democracy and growth in capitalism is positive (.36) and highly statistically significant, albeit not as large as the correlation in levels. Table 1.2 shows the regression of growth in democracy on growth

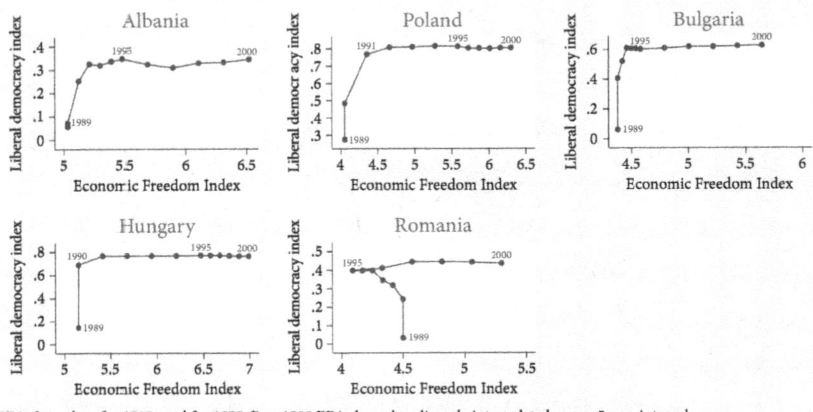

EF index values for 1990 used for 1989. Post 1990 EF index values linearly interpolated across 5 year intervals
Source: V-Dem Dataset Version 12, v2x_libdem, v2x_partipdem, v2x_delibdem and v2x_egaldem.
Fraser Instiute's Economic Freedom of the World: 2022 Annual Report, EFW Index.

Figure 1.4 The Berlin Wall Shock and the evolution of democracy and capitalism: Eastern Europe.

in economic freedom. A .1 increase in democracy tends to increase economic freedom by .1*1.94=.194 points in economic freedom, a result that is statistically significant at the greater than 1% level. A one standard deviation increase in democracy (~.2 units) thus increases economic freedom by approximately .37 of a standard deviation (.2*1.94=.388 units). Overall, this evidence is consistent with the mutual reinforcement thesis: liberal democracy has a symbiotic relationship with economic freedom.

The Berlin Wall Shock and the Evolution of Democracy and Economic Freedom

We can get another perspective on growth in democracy and growth in economic freedom by looking at shocks. In November of 1989 the Berlin Wall fell, a key event in the opening of the Iron Curtain and the reintegration of Eastern European countries with Western Europe and away from the communist system and the Soviet Union. Shortly thereafter, the Soviet Union broke apart into constituent parts. We look at what happened to democracy and economic freedom following the collapse of the Berlin Wall. For the countries for which data is available we start with the year closest to 1989 and then plot the evolution of democracy and economic freedom through to 2000.[39]

Figure 1.4 shows the evolution of democracy and economic freedom for the Eastern Europeans: Albania, Poland, Bulgaria, Hungary, and Romania. In each case, democracy and economic freedom were both substantially larger in

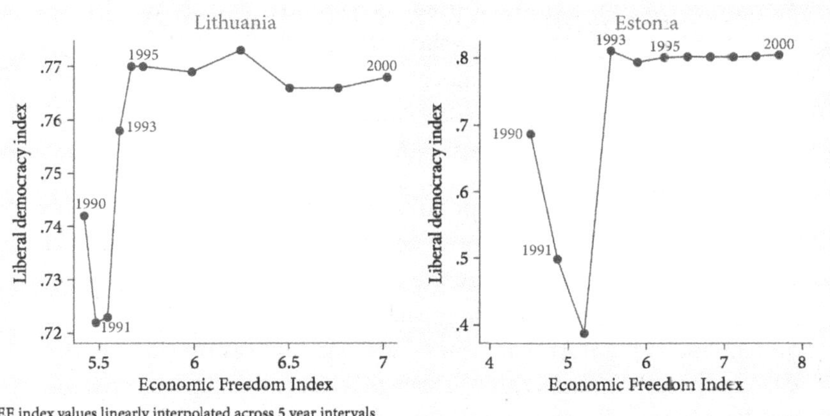

EF index values linearly interpolated across 5 year intervals
Source: V-Dem Dataset Version 12, v2x_libdem.
Fraser Institute's Economic Freedom of the World: 2022 Annual Report, EFW Index.

Figure 1.5 The Berlin Wall Shock and the Evolution of democracy and capitalism Former Soviets.

2000 than at the beginning of the peaceful revolution in 1989. Again, we must reiterate that causality is difficult to identify. However, it is clear that the opening of the Iron Curtain was first a shock to democracy, and then an increase in economic freedom that was sustained over many years after the democracy shock. In other words, the large increases in economic freedom that took place in Eastern Europe happened under democratic regimes. Figure 1.5 shows the same evolution of democracy and economic freedom for the former Soviets: Lithuania and Estonia. These countries were born as high but initially volatile democracies. As democracy stabilized, however, economic freedom increased. Once again, we see substantial increases in economic freedom following democratization.

These results hurt the "democracy undermines capitalism" argument. Consider one subfield of economics today known as persistence studies. This subfield essentially attempts to evaluate the "shadow of history," why long-ago historical factors weigh heavily today.[40] One of the arguments advanced within the field is that "bad institutions" (e.g., serfdom, slavery, segregation, legalized monopsonies, and monopolies) have a long half-life through their effect on culture. For example, Alesina and Fuchs-Schündeln (2007) argue that people who grew up under communism in East Germany preserved and transmitted most of their (differential) preferences even after decades in the free and reunified Germany.[41] If one accepts this result, it means that incorporating these potential voters into a politically free polity should erode economic freedom. Yet, Eastern European countries that have experienced communism appear *more* reluctant than other countries to erode economic freedom. The "democracy undermines capitalism" argument predicts movements in favor of retreating economic freedom in the long run—the opposite of what we see here.

The simultaneous growth of democracy and economic freedom after the fall of the Berlin Wall refutes a common idea that big increases in capitalism require an authoritarian government. Katherine Jones (2022) writes for example that:

> Authoritarianism's growth in popularity in recent years could be due to its perceived superior ability to ensure economic growth. Authoritarian governments can execute the most favorable economic policies without winning elections, compromising with opposition parties, or contending with unfortunate voter decisions (such as Brexit.) In many ways, these authoritarian regimes have experienced unprecedented success.[42]

In contrast, we find that democracy and capitalism tend to grow together. We haven't examined all of the big increases in economic freedom, however. We turn to that in the next section.

Four More Big Increases in Economic Freedom

The increases in economic freedom in the Eastern European economies and the post-Soviets are some of the largest increases in economic freedom in our data. There are, however, other increases, which we depict in Table 1.3. We will be particularly interested in the question whether these increases in economic freedom happened because of authoritarianism or could have happened only under authoritarianism.

Peru

In 1970 Peru had modest economic freedom and was governed by a military junta. Economic freedom declined under the authoritarian regime, and continued to decline modestly under the civilian government beginning in

Table 1.3 **Largest increases in economic freedom 1970–2020**

Peru	4.96
Nicaragua	4.96
Uganda	4.7
Chile	4.39

Source: Fraser Institute's Economic Freedom of the World: 2022 Annual Report EFW Index.

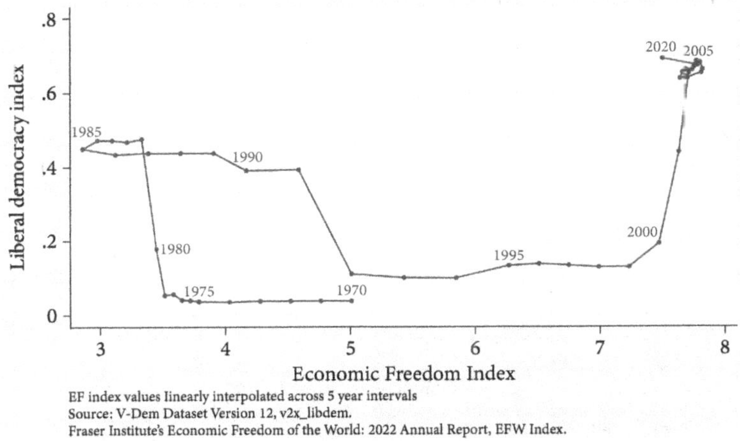

Figure 1.6 The evolution of democracy and economic freedom in Peru 1970–2020.

1980. In the mid-1980s economic freedom began to increase with pressure from the military and notably under President Alberto Fujimori, who became a de-facto dictator. After Fujimori's regime ended in late 2000, liberal democracy increased, and economic freedom remained stable at high levels.

Thus, the Peruvian regime indicates decreases, then substantial increases in economic freedom under authoritarian governments with stabilization under a democratic government.

It's important to note that Peru has more economic freedom under democracy than under any authoritarian government since 1970. Moreover, if we define a modestly democratic country as one standard deviation above the mean (.46 on a 0–1 scale) then no modestly democratic country in our dataset has had an economic freedom index as low as Peru had under military rule.[43] One reason that economic freedom could grow tremendously in Peru under an authoritarian regime is because at its lowest point economic freedom in Peru was well below that of any democratic country. We return to this point further below.

Nicaragua

In 1970 Nicaragua had high to modest economic freedom under the authoritarian Somoza regime but as the Somoza's squeezed the economy there were large decreases in economic freedom, which continued after the Sandinista revolution in 1979. Democracy increased in the 1980s with only a modest increase in economic freedom, but beginning in the 1990s and until 2005 economic freedom increased substantially under more democratic regimes. Sharp decreases in

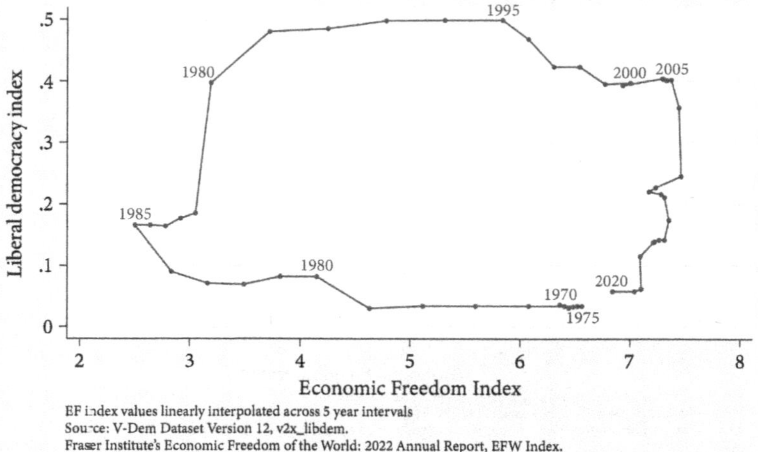

Figure 1.7 The evolution of democracy and economic freedom in Nicaragua 1970–2020.

democracy occurred with the return of President Daniel Ortega in 2006 leading to a return by 2020 to the situation of 1970, modest economic freedom under an authoritarian government. Economic freedom and democracy in Nicaragua had come full circle. Thus, we see in Nicaragua substantial decreases in economic freedom under authoritarian governments and increases in economic freedom under more democratic government, but democracy did not take root.

Uganda

Uganda didn't have a democratic government at any time between 1970 and 2020. Economic freedom was low and falling under the Idi Amin regime but increased substantially in the 1990s under the Yoweri Museveni regime. As such, Uganda's evolution looks akin to that of Hong Kong and Singapore (albeit at lower levels of economic freedom) where economic freedom increases with little gains in political liberty. While these examples of delays in the operation of the symbiotic relationship described by the "mutual reinforcement" thesis suggest a weak point in that thesis, they do not support the idea that capitalism undermines democracy for there was none of the latter to start with.

Chile

The case of Chile is especially interesting because several free market economists, including Milton Friedman, James Buchanan, and Friedrich Hayek, gave talks in Chile after the coup by General Augusto Pinochet. Dark and

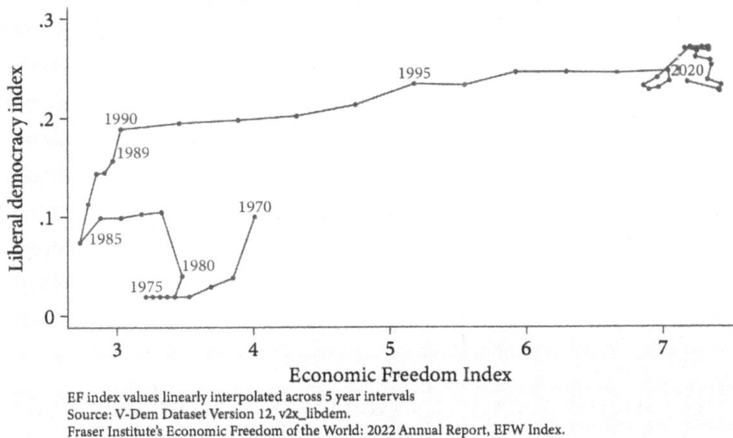

Figure 1.8 The evaluation of democracy and economic freedom in Uganda 1970–2020.

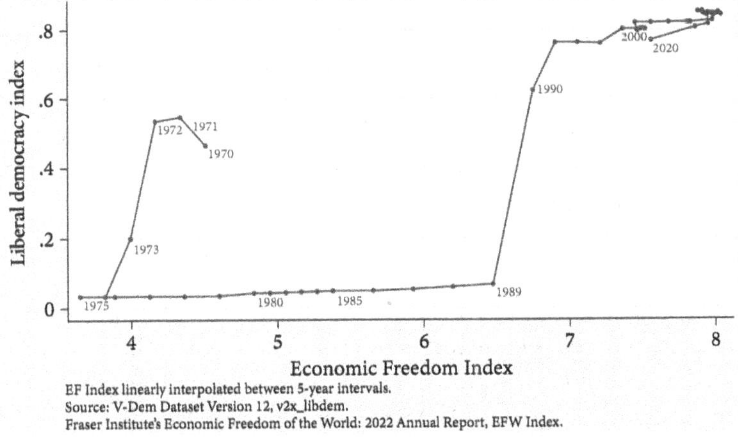

Figure 1.9 The Evolution of democracy and economic freedom in Chile 1970–2020.

lurid theories assert that these thinkers not only supported the Pinochet regime but collaborated in designing it.[44] These are plainly exaggerations both as to the influence of the intellectuals and the extent of their support. Some classical liberals—in line with the view that democracy could strangle capitalism—expressed lukewarm support for Pinochet's regime. However, other classical liberals—such as James Buchanan—criticized these expressions and argued that adherence to liberal democratic ideals could not be compromised.[45]

What is true is that the coup initially *reduced* economic freedom, but beginning around 1975 there was a sustained increase in economic freedom, which was not matched by an increase in democracy. Less remarked upon, however, is that after democracy was restored in Chile, economic freedom continued to increase. The Chile example illustrates that it is possible to increase economic freedom without increasing democracy, but it in no way suggests that democracy is incompatible with economic freedom. Indeed, quite the opposite since under democracy, economic freedom in Chile reached levels considerably higher than at any time under the Pinochet regime. Moreover, a good case can also be made that economic freedom opened up breaches that eventually forced Pinochet to step down or face major political unrest.[46]

Discussion of Big Changes in Democracy and Economic Freedom

Overall, our examination of the largest changes in democracy and economic freedom illustrates three points. First, large increases in economic freedom are possible under democratic governments as illustrated by the Eastern European economies and the ex-Soviets. Second, and consistent with the cross-sectional results we showed earlier, once put into place high economic freedom and democracy are stable. Third, big increases in economic freedom have occurred in democracies, and also under authoritarian regimes, albeit for the latter starting at and typically reaching lower levels than under democracy.

The big increases in economic freedom that have sometimes occurred under authoritarian regimes have led some to think that authoritarianism is necessary for big increases in economic freedom. But this is wrong on two accounts. First, as already noted, big increases in economic freedom have occurred under democracies or with the growth in democracy. Second, economic freedom has changed dramatically under authoritarian regimes in *both* directions. Indeed, one reason that economic freedom has sometimes increased rapidly in authoritarian regimes is because of previous rapid decreases in economic freedom under an equally authoritarian regime. More generally, one reason that economic freedom in authoritarian regimes can increase rapidly is that it typically starts at levels far below those ever found in democracies. Economic freedom in Peru increased tremendously between 1985 and 2020, for example, but it wasn't until 1992 that Peru had as much economic freedom as it had had in 1970. Thus, much of Peru's increase in economic freedom was retracting earlier decreases under other authoritarian governments. Uganda and Chile also illustrate this story, albeit not quite so dramatically. In short, anyone seeking economic freedom from behind a veil of ignorance would be well advised to select a democratic government.

Mechanisms

We think that the correlations we observe between democracy and capitalism are indicative of causal links running both from democracy to capitalism and from capitalism to democracy. We have provided some evidence for causality, but we don't attempt to prove these causal links. In this section, however, we outline some of reasons or mechanisms that could generate causal links.

Democracies Don't Want to Kill the Goose

Our view is that capitalism, broadly conceived, generates economic growth. We don't argue for that here, but to the extent that the connection is causal it provides a link between democracy and capitalism.[47] People living in democracies want economic growth, and thus they have an incentive to support capitalist policies.

The simple argument hides a plethora of subtleties. A collective incentive to support capitalist policies, for example, does not necessarily translate into an individual incentive to support (vote for) capitalist policies because an individual's vote is nugatory.[48] An incentive to support capitalist policies is only one incentive among many and some incentives favor supporting anti-capitalist policies. Voters in a democracy might support anti-immigrant policies, for example, even when immigrants bring economic benefits. Voters might vote against capitalism out of envy, hatred, or as an expression of class warfare.[49] Voters may not know their own interests.[50] Thus, the desire for growth may provide only a weak incentive to vote for capitalist policies. Nevertheless, weak or not, the incentive to support capitalist policies under democracy is likely to be larger than under other systems of governance.

Notice first that growth is the *only* way a large group of people can become wealthy. Redistribution can make a minority rich at the expense of the majority but cannot make the majority rich at the expense of a minority.[51] Thus, the only way a large group of voters in a democracy can become wealthy is by voting for capitalism. In contrast, under any system in which a small percentage rule, redistribution can create great wealth for the few. Mobutu Sese Seko amassed a huge personal fortune as the dictatorial president of one of the poorest countries in the world.

In theory, a small elite could enact capitalist policies and siphon enough of the gains to make themselves and their country rich but in practice there are few examples, probably because there are no enforcement mechanisms for mutually beneficial contracts at the state level, and it's easier to rule poor and uneducated people than rich and educated people.[52] Thus, when elites rule, they typically prefer redistribution to growth.

A closely related point is that in a democracy, the route to becoming rich is not politics. Rich people—George Washington, Silvio Berlusconi, Donald Trump—can certainly become politicians and they may use the state to benefit their economic interests, but few politicians become super-rich, especially in comparison to their power. The US government spends over $5 trillion a year, and only a tiny fraction of this is captured by US political elites. Donald Trump may well have directed government business to his hotels, but the amounts involved were small relative to the trillions of spending by the US government. Moreover, democracies have convincingly shown that these norms and rules are stable, and even small violations are frowned upon and often prosecuted.

A capitalist democracy benefits from a "division of labor"; democracy makes it clear that the route to riches is not politics and capitalism makes it clear that the route to riches is markets. Thus, capitalist democracies send the pecuniary self-interested toward markets where their actions are likely to be guided by the invisible hand toward the social good and not toward the sector where pecuniary self-interest results in rent seeking, monopoly, and stasis. A socialist state, in contrast, has nowhere to channel pecuniary self-interest except toward the state.

Democracies Are a Constraint on Government

Our view of democracy is not that democracy is an ideal way of making decisions—Arrow's Impossibility Theorem and modern political economy preclude that view—but that democracies tend to avoid rare but very bad events. Amartya Sen, for example, argued that "no famine has ever taken place in the history of the world in a functioning democracy."[53] Taken literally, Sen's statement is almost certainly false. Nevertheless, famines are less likely to take place in functioning democracies, that is famines are less likely in democracies with competitive elections and a free press.[54] Famine are very bad events, so this is a clear mark in favor of democracies.

Put the other way, it's undeniable that some famines—such as the Soviet starvation of Ukraine—have been intentionally created by governments as tools of policy.[55] As Ó Gráda points out, hunger-related deaths have waned dramatically from their pre-1800 historical average.[56] Since the 1870s, deaths from hunger have fallen from 142 per 100,000 to 0.5 per 100,000—a 99 percent reduction.[57] Yet, there is a paradox as the ten worst famines in *all* of human history occurred in the same period. Why the paradox? Listing those famines makes us realize that they are all outcomes of dictatorial or colonial regimes or the byproduct of wars involving dictatorial regimes.[58] In essence, only dictatorships do famines. Liberal democracies, on the other hand, prevent exogenous shocks from turning into famines. One part is due to the development of markets that prevented localized supply shocks from becoming detrimental to health.[59] Another part is that liberal democracies are unlikely to starve their own citizens. After all, starving voters tend not to vote for the incumbent. More generally, Bardhan argues:

> Democracy helps development through the accountability mechanisms it installs for limiting the abuse of executive power and provides a system of periodic punishments for undesirable government interventions in the economy and rewards for desirable interventions . . . Accountability mechanisms are particularly important in averting disasters.[60]

In other words, democracy should be conceived of as a tool to constrain government similar to checks and balances, federalism, and a constitution. Democracy limits government to a set of actions in a core of common support or, to be more precise, it excludes actions that are both opposed by a large number of citizens and not supported by a large number of citizens. Excluding actions that are opposed by a large number of citizens and not supported by a large number of citizens would seem to be a weak constraint, and yet there are important examples of policies, such as famines, which are excluded by democracy. Moreover, famines are not the only such policy.

Democracies tend not to kill their own citizens. Again, this would appear to be a weak constraint, and yet the history of government indicates that it is a powerful and desirable constraint. In the twentieth century, hundreds of millions of people were killed by their own governments.[61] The Nazi regime, for example, murdered millions of its own Jewish citizens and hundreds of thousands of Roma and disabled citizens. The Soviet regime murdered tens of millions of its own citizens. Murders in Communist China were at least as high as in the Soviet Union, and perhaps much higher depending on whether one counts famine deaths as intentional.[62] Cambodian, Turkish, and North Korean mass murders were also in the millions. The exact number of mass murders is less important than the comparison across regimes. Democracies are much less likely to murder their own citizens.[63,64]

Democracies are less likely to murder their own citizens, and also less likely to murder citizens of other democracies. That is, democracies are less likely to engage in war with other democracies. Weart's claim illustrated in the title of his book *Never at War: Why Democracies Will Not Fight One Another*, like Sen's claims about democracy and famine, is literally false.[65] Nevertheless, the finding that democracies are less likely to go to war against one another is strongly and consistently supported empirically.[66]

A closely related point is that democracies are less likely to engage in civil wars.[67] Indeed, Ludwig von Mises regarded the peaceful transition of power as the essence of democracy.

> Democracy is that form of political constitution which makes possible the adaption of the government to the wishes of the governed without violent struggle.[68]

Mises's minimalist defense of democracy is very similar to that of Popper, who asked

> How is the state to be constituted so that bad rulers can be got rid of without bloodshed, without violence?[69]

Popper answered, with a democracy. For Popper the virtue of democracy is not the "rule of the people" but simply that under a democracy there is a system of peaceful error-correction. Popper thus drew a connection between democracy and the scientific process.[70] We would add capitalism to that connection. The profit and loss system of capitalism is an error-correction process analogous to voting and the scientific critique. More generally, capitalism, democracy, and science are all examples of open-access orders.[71] Open-access orders are characterized by dispersed power, low barriers to access and transparent rules that apply to all.

Summarizing this section, we may say that compared to other political regimes democracies are less likely to let their citizens die in a mass famine, murder their own citizens, engage in a civil war or foreign war (at least against other democracies). These positive attributes of democracies align well with capitalism in at least two ways. First, stability and peace are good for growth and thus democracy is good for growth. Second, democracy and capitalism correlate so highly that some of these positive attributes of democracy may actually be positive attributes of capitalism—the data isn't dispositive. We discuss each of these points in turn.

Capitalism Prospers with Peace and Stability

Capitalist growth requires investment; investment requires peace and stability. Investors don't want to invest in times and places where their investments can be destroyed or expropriated. As Mises argued:

> There can be no lasting economic improvement if the peaceful course of action of affairs is continually interrupted . . .[72]

Good institutions such as property rights, independent judiciaries, and governments constrained by the rule of law are all about encouraging long-term investments in human and physical capital.[73] It's these types of investments which generate wealth and further investment. Even the weapons manufacturers want domestic peace because with war comes expropriation, price controls, and regulation, not to mention the possibility of destruction and complete loss.[74]

Indeed, the rich and developed capitalist economies are rich and developed not primarily because they have undergone spurts of 10 percent growth but because they have grown slowly but steadily for many decades and even centuries.[75] Growth under democracy is more stable than under other political systems, and so over time tends to result in higher GDP per capita.[76]

Why is growth more stable under democracy? We have already seen that famines, civil wars, and foreign wars disrupt growth; and similar very bad events are less likely under democracies, and naturally the lack of such disruptions is good for growth.

But famines and wars are only one example of policy instability; revolutions and rapid changes in institutions and policies can also harm investment, and democracies tend to have more stable policies than non-democracies.[77] Policies under democracy tend to reflect the policy preferences of the median voter whose preferences are likely to vary less than those of a single leader or the median voter of an oligarchy. More generally, policies under a democracy may be the result of consensus and bargaining more than in other systems. Democracies to the extent that they involve multiple veto players may also simply be slow to make changes. Slow change can be determinantal at times, but the historical evidence recounted earlier indicates that stability is overall beneficial for long-run growth.

While not as deadly as war and famine, capitalist economies probably do perform worse than socialist economies, especially communist economies, on the economic volatility of business cycles and unemployment. Mass unemployment is a threat to the capitalist-democratic order which is one reason why John Maynard Keynes and demand management are often said to have "saved capitalism."[78]

The relative stability of policy under democracy also bears on the issue of authoritarian governments with economic freedom. As we noted earlier, some dictators such as Pinochet in Chile and Museveni in Uganda have increased economic freedom, but the promises of dictators are rarely credible. In contrast, the institutions of liberal democracies make it harder for politicians to reverse course. Thus, the same increase in economic freedom enacted under a democracy may be more powerful in generating long-run economic growth than under a dictatorship. As such, expectations about future institutional conditions are probably more stable under a liberal democracy than under a liberal dictator, making growth faster. This is one explanation for why Escalante found that a counterfactual Chile without Pinochet would have enjoyed the same income growth rate as it did under his dictatorship.[79] Another paper, using the same method as Escalante, finds that it was democratization that sped up economic growth.[80] These results are consistent with the claims of Sebastian Edwards that the second-wave of Chilean liberalizations that took place as democracy was increasing were more successful.[81]

Capitalism and Democracy Promote Human Development and Social Mobility

Human development and social and economic mobility are additional important mechanisms, which create mutual reinforcement between democracy and capitalism.

Amartya Sen and Martha Nussbaum have argued that economic freedom may erode democracy if it fails to increase capabilities (i.e., agency, human development, positive liberty) for all. After the UN created the Human Development Index, which was inspired by their work, however, it became clear that economic freedom was highly correlated with human development, as shown in Figure 1.10

In fact, economic freedom is highly correlated with multiple measures of human development including greater life expectancy, higher educational achievement, better health outcomes, shorter working hours, cleaner air and water, safer neighborhoods, stronger social networks, and higher levels of life satisfaction.[82]

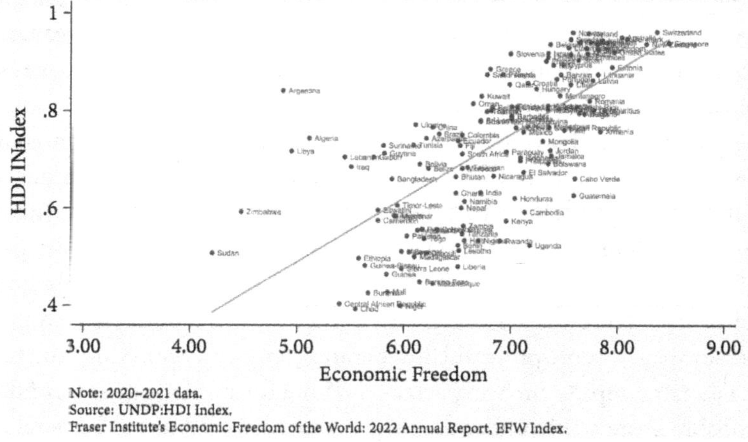

Note: 2020–2021 data.
Source: UNDP:HDI Index.
Fraser Institute's Economic Freedom of the World: 2022 Annual Report, EFW Index.

Figure 1.10 Freedom Economic freedom and human development are highly correlated.

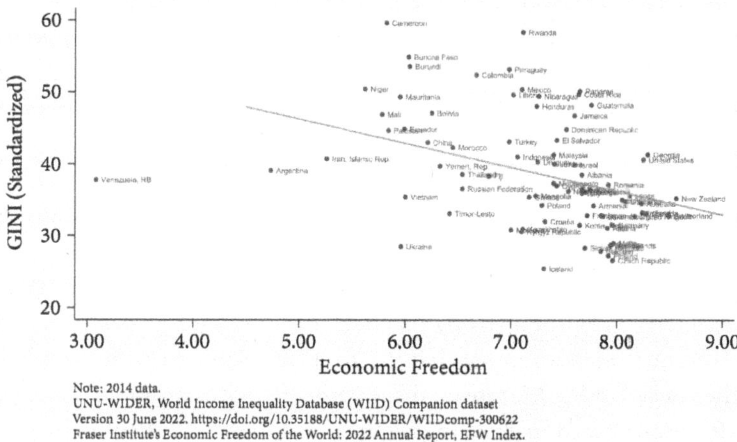

Figure Figure 1.11 Income inequality and economic freedom are negatively correlated.

Both democracy and capitalism create incentives for human development. A small group of rulers can become rich by exploiting a large group of poor people. But, as we noted earlier, the only way that a large group of people can become rich is via economic growth, and a key factor in increasing economic growth is human capital. For example, widespread education serves the democratic goals of informed and intelligent voters and the capitalist goals of a productive workforce. The fact that widespread education may also increase income equality is a bonus.

The connection between inequality and economic freedom may seem like an obvious counter-argument. Indeed, if economic freedom leads to income inequality and income inequality leads to a reduction in support for democracy then it would seem we have a clear case that economic freedom reduces support for democracy.[83] A problem with this argument is the first premise. It is not clear that economic freedom leads to income inequality. It is true that inequality has increased in some of the advanced liberal democracies, albeit probably not as much as some of the more extreme claims.[84] It's also true that there will be inequality under capitalism. The error, however, stems from forgetting to compare with inequality in countries with very little economic freedom. In fact, as Figure 1.11 shows, the raw correlation between economic freedom and income inequality (here measured with the standardized Gini index) is negative!

More sophisticated statistical analyses of the relationship between economic freedom and inequality are mixed.[85] We do not pretend to resolve this debate here, but merely point out that the relationship between economic freedom and inequality is complicated, especially when we add democracy as a third variable. However, as Welch as well as Kufenko and Geloso point out, the social ills of inequality are greater in unfree societies.[86] In unfree societies, greater inequality is harder to overcome, and those born lower down the income ladder cannot escape their relative condition. In free societies, the opportunity of upward mobility is legally present and more plausible. As such, whatever the harm associated with a given level of the Gini coefficient, it will be greater in unfree societies than in free ones.

This particular point has been illustrated by a recent wave of research tying economic freedom to social mobility on net.[87] Rulers in economically unfree countries tend to share the rents of power not with the poor but with richer individuals who can help them to maintain power (see the work of Lant Pritchett, e.g. Pritchett (2020), for a strong illustration).[88] As such, movements toward more economic freedom imply that the fruits are likely to go to people lower down the social ladder. Moreover, if economic freedom promotes intergenerational (or intragenerational) mobility, then that may be a channel by which it legitimizes the political regime in the process. This mechanism has been noted in passing by Milton Friedman and Peter Berger, but these recent works provide the first substantiation of its empirical validity and importance.[89]

Democracy Prospers with Growth

The relationship between capitalism, democracy, and growth is likely bidirectional. Democracy results in stability, which increases growth, and growth increases democratic stability.[90] If an economy isn't growing the only way that some people can become richer is if others become poorer. A zero-sum economy creates fractious politics, potentially even civil wars. In contrast, in a growing economy politics can focus on positive sum games resulting in greater democratic cohesion and stability.[91]

Growth almost always comes with "creative destruction," and creative destruction in the economy means that interest groups take longer to develop and cement into place.[92] Furthermore, creative destruction in the economy is reflected in shifts in political power, new interest groups, new allies, and new enemies. Fewer and changing interest groups means a more fluid politics, which is likely to be beneficial for democracy and economic growth.[93] Similarly, unstable interest groups may create more stable politics by reminding everyone that tomorrow new allies may be needed so today's compromise and fair play pays off tomorrow when roles are reversed.[94]

Moreover, and this is highly underappreciated, capitalism makes exogenous shocks less damaging than they otherwise would be, which minimizes pressures on democratic polities during crises. Christian Bjørnskov made a list of 212 crises from 1993 to 2010.[95] This included natural disasters, recessions, terrorist attacks, and numerous other shocks that one would expect to lead to falling living standards. He hypothesizes that more economically free societies will suffer less from these shocks than less economically free societies. And this is exactly what he finds. The depth of economic downturns was smaller in freer economies and the recovery was faster.[96] By minimizing the damage induced by economic shocks, economic freedom protects democracy through minimizing pressures on politicians to adopt more corrosive measures.[97]

The democracy to growth and growth to democracy mechanisms mean that democracy and capitalism are a stable equilibrium in the long run. Deviations from that equilibrium require large exogenous shocks.

Doux Commerce and Doux Politics

Another reason for the democracy/capitalism symbiosis is that capitalism reduces warfare—one of the main killers of liberal democracies. World War I, for example, weakened democracies that were unable to resist later shocks, such as the Great Depression, leading to democratic regression and the rise of authoritarian states in the first half of the twentieth century. More generally, in *The Spirit of the Laws*, Montesquieu famously argued that

> . . . Peace is the natural effect of trade. Two nations who traffic with each other become reciprocally dependent; for if one has an interest in buying, the other has an interest in selling; and thus their union is founded on their mutual necessities.[98]

The American revolutionary Thomas Paine [1792] also argued that commerce "cordialized" mankind and reduced the probability of war:

> [Commerce] is a pacific system, operating to cordialize mankind, by rendering nations, as well as individuals, useful to each other . . . If commerce were permitted to act to the universal extent it is capable, it would extirpate the system of war, and produce a revolution in the uncivilized state of governments. The invention of commerce has arisen since those governments began, and is the greatest approach towards universal civilization, that has yet been made by any means not immediately flowing from moral principles.[99]

Similar arguments were made by Kant, Cobden, Angell, and others.[100] The effect of free trade on war was perhaps most pithily summarized by the aphorism "when goods don't cross borders, armies will."[101] Indeed, it's unclear whether the democratic peace is better described as a capitalist peace. McDonald and Gartzke provide statistical evidence in favor of capitalist peace and argue that when run head-to-head against the democratic peace hypothesis, the capitalist peace hypothesis is more powerful; Choi argues for the reverse. In our view, democracy and capitalism are so tightly intertwined in the data that it's difficult to disentangle which is responsible for findings such as fewer wars and fewer mass murders under capitalist democracies. The answer is both; capitalism and democracy are mutually reinforcing.

More generally, Montesquieu argued that capitalism moderated not just interactions between states but those between individuals:

> Commerce is a cure for the most destructive prejudices; for it is almost a general rule, that wherever we find agreeable manners, there commerce flourishes; and that wherever there is commerce, there we meet with agreeable manners.[102]

The *doux commerce* thesis was elaborated on by Voltaire:

> Go into the London Stock Exchange – a more respectable place than many a court – and you will see representatives from all nations gathered together for the utility of men. Here Jew, Mohammedan and Christian deal with each other as though they were all of the same faith, and only apply the word infidel to people who go bankrupt. Here the Presbyterian trusts the Anabaptist and the Anglican accepts a promise from the Quaker. On leaving these peaceful and free assemblies some go to the Synagogue and others for a drink, this one goes to be baptized in a great bath in the name of Father, Son and Holy Ghost, that one has his son's foreskin cut and has some Hebrew words he doesn't understand mumbled over the child, others go to their church and await the inspiration of God with their hats on, and everybody is happy.

Voltaire's hypothesis finds support in the modern literature which finds that exposure to markets makes people act in ways which are more pro-social, more altruistic and more universal.[103]

More pro-social, altruistic, and universal action are also key attributes of successful behavior under democracy. In a democracy, different parties with different interests must trade and bargain to come to consensus or agreement—consensus and agreement requires compromise and mutual respect, just as with trade. Indeed, since most people are much more involved in trade than in politics it is almost certainly the case that *doux commerce* precedes and generates *douce politique*. Thus, once again, we see that capitalism and democracy are mutually compatible and self-reinforcing.

Socialism Destabilizes Democracy

We have argued that democracy and capitalism are consistent with one another and in some ways are mutually reinforcing. But that leaves open the possibility that democracy is also consistent with socialism. We now argue that democracy is inconsistent with socialism, which we define as extensive state ownership of the means of production.

The primary reason why democracy is inconsistent with socialism is that socialism destabilizes democracy. Robert A. Dahl explained:

> It is not the inefficiencies of a centrally planned economy . . . that are most injurious to democratic prospects. It is the economy's social and political consequences. A centrally planned economy puts the resources of the entire economy at the disposal of government leaders. To foresee the likely consequences of that fantastic political windfall, we might recall the aphorism that "power corrupts and absolute power corrupts absolutely." A centrally planned economy issues an outright invitation to government leaders, written in bold letters: **You are free to use all these economic resources to consolidate and maintain your power!**[104]

In a socialist democracy, the temptation to use power to maintain power would be immense. Indeed, it would be virtually inevitable because in a socialist state there is no distinction between politics and economics.[105]

For Popper, as we noted earlier, democracy is about error-correction and the peaceful rotation of power.[106] But for this to work the losers must be willing to cede power to the winners. And why should they do so? If the losers can expect to regain power in the future, then the rotation of power can be a self-sustaining equilibrium.[107] But if one party expects the other to take decisions in the future that will diminish their power then they have reason not to give up power today. Thus, abuse of power can also be a self-sustaining equilibrium when the rotation of power is threatened. Even in a capitalist democracy one can see this issue arise in debates over extensions of the franchise, but in a socialist democracy every decision would involve considerations of future power and the rotation of power would continually be threatened. Thus, socialist democracies are bound to be unstable.

Ideology, Contingency, and Mutual Reinforcement

We have outlined a number of reasons why capitalism and democracy are mutually reinforcing but it should be clear that these are tendencies, not laws of social organization. Consider, for example, some of the arguments we noted earlier that democracy undermines capitalism. Voters in a democracy could be so outraged by inequality that they vote for high income and wealth taxes. Indeed, in some times and places they have. Yet, overall, income and wealth inequality are not notably lower in democracies compared to non-democracies.[108] The most extreme redistributions of wealth, such as land redistributions, tend to occur in non-democracies.[109]

One explanation for these results is that the wealthy have captured democracies. A simpler and better supported explanation is that a majority of voters won't demand extreme redistribution if they think the existing distribution is fair.[110] In the democracy undermines capitalism group, the pro-capitalism thinkers feared redistribution while the pro-socialism thinkers hoped for redistribution. But both groups assumed a mechanical connection between inequality and redistribution, which is neither evident in the data nor required by theory. In particular, ideology is a major mediating variable between inequality and redistribution.

In fact, one strand of argument defended by James Buchanan over multiple works starting with the *Calculus of Consent* argues that inequality under a constitutional order in which the rules of the game are seen as fair doesn't generate tension but is seen as *ipso facto* also fair. Rules set in advance determine the fields over which democratic choice holds sway and those fields that are protected from democratic choice. These understandings and protections create certainty and confidence in the regime. Liberal democratic ideologies and justifications emerge that shield both capitalism and democracy from the extreme ideologies of both the left and the right.

Conclusions

Capitalist democracy isn't quite the same as unmarried bachelor, but it is true that democracy and capitalism are highly correlated both today and in the past. Moreover, countries that increase in capitalism also tend to increase in democracy and vice versa. Contrary to both the democracy undermines capitalism and capitalism undermines democracy arguments we find that capitalist democracies tend to be stable. Capitalism and democracy are so highly correlated that it's often difficult to ascribe consequences to one or the other. The democratic peace and the capitalist peace are both supported in the data, for example.

The connections between capitalism and democracy are probably not accidental. Both are examples of open-access orders.[111] Open-access orders are characterized by dispersed power, low barriers to access, and transparent rules that apply to all. Aside from conceptual similarities, capitalism and democracy have a number of mutually reinforcing mechanisms: capitalism promotes economic growth, which is the only way that a large group, the demos, can become wealthy;

democracies are more likely to avoid extreme, wealth-destroying events such as wars, civil wars, famines, and democides; capitalism promotes gentle manners and cooperation that are also valuable mindsets in democracies; dispersed political power allows for more creative destruction in the economy. None of these mechanisms are guarantees, voters must choose capitalism. Nevertheless, our prediction is that capitalist democracies will remain a strong and vital element in the political firmament.

Notes

1. On the right, we have statements such as "I no longer believe that freedom and democracy are compatible," by the capitalist Peter Thiel (2009). On the left, we have essays by Robert Reich (2009) arguing "How Capitalism Is Killing Democracy." Many other examples could be given. A longer discussion placing recent debates in historical context follows.
2. See also Lamoreaux and Wallis this volume.
3. Some have defined capitalism broadly enough to incorporate anything where private enterprise is involved from Nazi Germany and Fascist Italy to liberal-democratic Canada. We find these broad definitions unhelpful. Our use of economic freedom allows us to be more precise.
4. Jerry Muller, "The Democratic Threat to Capitalism," *Daedalus* 136, no. 2 (2007): 77–86.
5. John Locke, *Second Treatise of Government* (1690; repr. Simon & Brown (2012)
6. Edmund Burke, *An Appeal from the New to the Old Whigs, in Consequence of Some Late Discussions in Parliament, Relative to the Reflections on the French Revolution* (London: J. Dodsley, 1791).
7. Adam Smith, *An Inquiry Into the Nature and Causes of the Wealth of Nations* (Cannan ed., 1776).
8. James Madison, "Federalist Papers No. 10" (1787), https://billofrightsinstitute.org/primary-sources/federalist-no-10/.
9. Félix Laget, "La Pensée Politique de Jean-Baptiste Say: Droit et Politique Au Service de l'ordre Libéral" (PhD diss., Lyon 3, 2002).
10. James Madison, "Federalist Papers No. 10" (1787).
11. Smith, *Wealth of Nations*, vol. 2.
12. John Stuart Mill, *Considerations on Representative Government* (London: Parker, Son, and Bourn, 1861).
13. In fact, graduates of Oxford and Cambridge had two votes in the UK until 1948, and Ireland still maintains a special university constituency https://en.wikipedia.org/wiki/University_constituency
14. It is worth noting that most classical liberals appear to have shunned these proposals (David M. Levy, Sandra J Peart, and Michael Albert, "Economic Liberals as Quasi-Public Intellectuals: The Democratic Dimension," in *Documents on Government and the Economy* Vol. 30, Part 2 pp. 1-116 (Emerald Group Publishing Limited, 2012). For estimates of the effects of voting franchise extension see Alejandro Corvalán, Pablo Querubín, and Sergion Vicente, "The Political Class and Redistributive Policies," *Journal of the European Economic Association* 18, no. 1 (2020): 1–48;, and John R. Lott, Jr. and Lawrence W. Kenny, "Did Women's Suffrage Change the Size and Scope of Government?," *Journal of Political Economy* 107, no. 6 (1999): 1163–98, https://doi.org/10.1086/250093.
15. Allan H. Meltzer and Scott F. Richard, "A Rational Theory of the Size of Government," *Journal of Political Economy* 89, no. 5 (October 1981): 914–27.
16. Bryan Caplan, *The Myth of the Rational Voter: Why Democracies Choose Bad Policies* (Princeton, NJ: Princeton University Press, 2008).
17. Caplan, *The Myth of the Rational Voter.*
18. Caplan, *The Myth of the Rational Voter.*

19. See also Jones (2020) and the political philosopher Jason Brennan (Garett Jones, *10% Less Democracy* (Stanford University Press, 2020; Jason Brennan, *Against Democracy*, 1st ed. (Princeton: Princeton University Press, 2016). Jones (2020) argues that the public would be better off with "10% less democracy" and more rule by experts. Brennan (2016) points out that political choice has the characteristics of an externality, that is, it imposes costs (or benefits) on others (see also Buchanan J. M., & Tullock, G. (1965) *The Calculus of Consent: Logical Foundations of Constitutional Democracy*. Ann Arbor, MI: University of Michigan Press.). Imposing costs on others is a significant responsibility that should not be exercised lightly. We require competence in driving, why not competence in voting? Thus, Brennan (2016) advocates that the public would be better off under epistocracy, rule by citizens with political knowledge.
20. Karl Marx and Friedrich Engels, *The Communist Manifesto*, new ed. (New York: International Publishers Co., 1848/1948).
21. Martha C. Nussbaum, *Creating Capabilities: The Human Development Approach* (Cambridge, MA: Harvard University Press, 2011).
22. Amartya Sen, "Democracy as a Universal Value," *Journal of Democracy* 10, no. 10 (1999): 10.
23. Miles Corak, "Income Inequality, Equality of Opportunity, and Intergenerational Mobility," *Journal of Economic Perspectives* 27, no. 3 (2013): 79–102.
24. Christian Houle and Michael K. Miller, "Social Mobility and Democratic Attitudes: Evidence from Latin America and Sub-Saharan Africa," *Comparative Political Studies* 52, no. 11 (2019): 1610–47.
25. Robert B. Reich, "How Capitalism Is Killing Democracy," *Foreign Policy*, October 12, 2009; Robert B. Reich, *The System: Who Rigged It, How We Fix It*, 2nd prt. ed. (New York: Knopf, 2020).
26. Robert Kuttner, *Can Democracy Survive Global Capitalism?*, 1st ed. (New York: W. W. Norton, 2018), 45; Karl Polanyi, *The Great Transformation: The Political and Economic Origins of Our Time* (Boston: Beacon Press, 1944), 102.
27. Arjun Jayadev and Samuel Bowles, "Guard Labor," *Journal of Development Economics* 79, no. 2 (2006): 328–48; Samuel Bowles, *The New Economics of Inequality and Redistribution* (Cambridge: Cambridge University Press, 2012).
28. Donald F. Busky, *Democratic Socialism: A Global Survey* (Westport, CT: Greenwood Publishing Group, 2000); Marc Fleurbaey, *Capitalisme ou démocratie? L'alternative du XXIe siècle* (Paris: Grasset & Fasquelle, 2006); Alain Deneault, *La Médiocratie* (Montréal: Lux éditeur, 2015); and Marcia Watersone and Noam Chomsky, *Les Conséquences Du Capitalisme: Du Mécontentement à La Résistence* (Montréal: Lux, 2021).
29. Peter Kolozi, *Conservatives against Capitalism: From the Industrial Revolution to Globalization* (New York: Columbia University Press, 2017); Patrick J. Deneen, *Why Liberalism Failed* (New Haven, CT: Yale University Press, 2019).
30. https://areomagazine.com/2020/01/22/understanding-conservative-anti-capitalism/
31. Peter L. Berger, *The Capitalist Revolution: Fifty Propositions About Prosperity, Equality and Liberty* (New York: Basic Books, 1986); Peter L. Berger, "The Uncertain Triumph of Democratic Capitalism," *Journal of Democracy* 3, no. 3 (1992): 7–16.
32. Ludwig von Mises, *Liberalism: The Classical Tradition*, 3rd ed., ed. Bettina Bien Greaves (Indianapolis: Liberty Fund, 1927); Berger, "The Uncertain Triumph of Democratic Capitalism."
33. Berger, "The Uncertain Triumph of Democratic Capitalism," 9.
34. Seymour Martin Lipset, "Some Social Requisites of Democracy: Economic Development and Political Legitimacy," *American Political Science Review* 53, no. 1 (1959): 69–105.
35. Fraser Institute, *Economic Freedom of the World: 2022 Annual Report* (Vancouver: Fraser Institute, 2022).
36. James Gwartney and Robert Lawson, "The Concept and Measurement of Economic Freedom," *European Journal of Political Economy* 19, no. 3 (2003), 406.
37. Michael Stepner, "BINSCATTER: Stata Module to Generate Binned Scatterplots," *Statistical Software Components* (Boston: Boston College Department of Economics, 2013).
38. Rosemarie Fike, "Gender Disparity in Legal Rights and Its Effect on Economic Freedom," in *Economic Freedom of the World: 2016 Annual Report* pp. 189-212 (Vancouver: Fraser Institute, 2016).

39. Democracy scores are measured annually but especially, in early years Economic Freedom Index, scores are measured every five years. Democracy scores changed very rapidly in 1989. In order to show the big changes in Democracy we use the 1990 Economic Freedom index score for the 1989 value. We also linearly interpolate post-1990 Economic Freedom scores. Economic Freedom typically changes more slowly than these changes in democracy, so this allows a more complete visualization of the data and appears reasonable.
40. Hans-Joachim Voth, "Persistence–Myth and Mystery," in *The Handbook of Historical Economics*, ed. Alberto Bisin and Giovanni Federico (San Diego: Academic Press, 2021), 243–67.
41. Alberto Alesina and Nicola Fuchs-Schündeln, "Good-Bye Lenin (or Not?): The Effect of Communism on People's Preferences," *American Economic Review* 97, no. 4 (2007): 1507–28.
42. Katherine Jones, "The Free-Market Democracy Scam," *The Generation*, January 31, 2022. URL: https://the-generation.net/the-free-market-democracy-scam/
43. The lowest economic freedom index for modestly democratic countries in our data set is 3.49 for Argentina in 1985.
44. Andrew Farrant and Vlad Tarko, "James M. Buchanan's 1981 Visit to Chile: Knightian Democrat or Defender of the 'Devil's Fix'?," *The Review of Austrian Economics* 32, no. 1 (2019): 1–20.
45. Farrant and Tarko, "James M. Buchanan's 1981 Visit to Chile"; Bruce Caldwell and Leonidas Montes, "Friedrich Hayek and His Visits to Chile," *The Review of Austrian Economics* 28, no. 3 (2015): 261–309.
46. Michael Munger and Viktor Vanberg, "Contractarianism, Constitutionalism, and the Status Quo," *Public Choice* 1 (2021): 1–17; Chile's economic history also confirms the direction from falling economic freedom to falling political liberty if we go beyond the period covered by the EFW Index. The erosion in economic freedom started in the 1930s and 1940s with rising protectionism and state-led industrialization in the 1930s and 1940s (and culminated in the nationalization of copper production by the conservative president Eduardo Frei in 1964) (Marcelo Bucheli and Enrique Salvaj, "Reputation and Political Legitimacy: ITT in Chile, 1927–1972," *Business History Review* 87, no. 4 (2013): 729–56; Marc Badía-Miró and Carlos Yáñez, "Localisation of Industry in Chile, 1895–1967: Mining Cycles and State Policy," Australian Economic History Review 55, no. 3 (2015): 256–76; Jael Goldsmoth Weil, "Facing the State: Everyday Interactions throughout Regime Change: Chile's State Milk 1954–2010," Social Science History 42, no. 3 (2018): 469–94; Juan Pablo Couyoumdjian, Christian Larroulet, and Diego Díaz, "Another Case of the Middle-Income Trap: Chile, 1900–1939," *Revista de Historia Economica-Journal of Iberian and Latin American Economic History* 40, no. 1 (2022): 5–33). But as growth slowed down, there were also losses in political freedom starting in the 1960s (well before Salvador Allende and Augusto Pinochet).
47. Mark Koyama and Jared Rubin, *How the World Became Rich: The Historical Origins of Economic Growth*, 1st ed. (Cambridge, UK Polity, 2022); Mark Dincecco, *State Capacity and Economic Development: Present and Past* (Cambridge: Cambridge University Press, 2017); Randall G. Holcombe, *Political Capitalism: How Political Influence Is Made and Maintained* (Cambridge: Cambridge University Press, 2018); and Naomi R. Lamoreaux and John Joseph Wallis, eds., *Organizations, Civil Society, and the Roots of Development* (Chicago: University of Chicago Press, 2017). The evidence on economic growth and capitalism is biased against capitalism because authoritarian regimes falsify data about living standards more than democracies. An effort to create a generalizable estimate of how much dictatorships fudge the figures has been made by Martinez (2022), who pointed out that while GDP data can be fudged, satellite data about artificial nighttime light intensity (NTL) cannot be trafficked. As there is a well-documented relationship between both GDP per capita and NTL, Martinez was able to backtrack the *true* rate of growth. The result is that dictatorships overstate, on average, their growth rates by factors ranging somewhere between 1.15 and 1.3, which would be the equivalent of bringing a growth rate of 6.6 percent to 5.1 percent. This may not seem like much, but it essentially removes the vast majority of authoritarian regimes that made it into the top tier of countries ranked by pace of economic growth between 1992 and today. These results by Martinez implies that, if we were able to correct estimates of GDP per capita for the lies

of dictators, we would find a *stronger* relationship between democracy and economic growth. Alvarez, S. P., Geloso, V., and Scheck, M. (2024). Revisiting the relationship between economic freedom and development to account for statistical deception by autocratic regimes. *European Journal of Political Economy*, 85, 102577 attempt such a correction using Martinez's data and find that coefficients for the effects of economic freedom on growth are close to being twice as large as those estimated with uncorrected data (Luis R. Martinez, "How Much Should We Trust the Dictator's GDP Growth Estimates?," *Journal of Political Economy* 130 no. 10 (2022): 2731–69).

48. Caplan, *The Myth of the Rational Voter.*
49. Joseph A. Schumpeter, *Capitalism, Socialism, and Democracy* (New York: Harper, 2008).
50. John Stuart Mill, *Considerations on Representative Government* (London: Parker, Son, and Bourn, 1861).
51. For example, if the wealth of every US billionaire were 100 percent expropriated it would not be enough to fund the US government for a single year and, of course, would almost certainly reduce future US growth.
52. Daron Acemoglu, "Why Not a Political Coase Theorem? Social Conflict, Commitment, and Politics," *Journal of Comparative Economics* 31, no. 4 (2003): 620–52; Stanley L. Engerman and Kenneth L. Sokoloff, "Factor Endowments, Inequality, and Paths of Development Among New World Economies," Working Paper 9259 (Cambridge, MA: National Bureau of Economic Research, 2002).
53. Sen, "Democracy as a Universal Value."
54. Francesco Burchi, "Democracy, Institutions and Famines in Developing and Emerging Countries," *Canadian Journal of Development Studies / Revue Canadienne d'études Du Développement* 32, no. 1 (2011): 17–31; Timothy Besley and Robin Burgess, "The Political Economy of Government Responsiveness: Theory and Evidence from India," *The Quarterly Journal of Economics* 117, no. 4 (2002): 1415–51.
55. Anne Applebaum, *Red Famine: Stalin's War on Ukraine*, repr. ed. (New York: Knopf Doubleday Publishing Group, 2018).
56. Cormac Ó Gráda, *Eating People Is Wrong, and Other Essays on Famine, Its Past, and Its Future* (Princeton, NJ: Princeton University Press, 2015).
57. Joe Hasell and Max Roser (2017) - "Famines" Published online at OurWorldinData.org. Retrieved from: 'https://ourworldindata.org/famines' [Online Resource]
58. Natalya Naumenko, "The Political Economy of Famine: The Ukrainian Famine of 1933," *The Journal of Economic History* 81, no. 1 (2021): 156–97.
59. Ó Gráda, *Eating People Is Wrong.*
60. Pranab Bardhan, "Democracy and Development: A Complex Relationship," in *Democracy's Values*, ed. Ian Shapiro and Casiano Hacker-Cordon (Cambridge: Cambridge University Press, n.d.), 102.
61. R. J. Rummel, *Power Kills: Democracy as a Method of Nonviolence* (Routledge, 2002).
62. Rummel, *Power Kills*; Jean-Louis Panné et al., *The Black Book of Communism: Crimes, Terror, Repression*, ed. Mark Kramer, trans. Jonathan Murphy (Cambridge, MA; London: Harvard University Press, 1999).
63. Rummel, *Power Kills*; William Easterly, Michael Kremer, Lant Pritchett, and Lawrence H. Summers, "Good Policy or Good Luck?" *Journal of Monetary Economics* 32, no. 3 (1993): 459–83.
64. Democracies can engage in mass murder, the genocide of native Americans being one example, albeit one that is broadly supportive of the contention since native Americans were not voters.
65. Spencer Weart, *Never at War: Why Democracies Will Not Fight One Another* (New Haven: Yale University Press, 1998).
66. Dan Reiter, "Is Democracy a Cause of Peace?" *Oxford Research Encyclopedia of Politics*, January 25, 2017, https://doi.org/10.1093/acrefore/9780190228637.013.287; James Lee Ray, "Does Democracy Cause Peace?," *Annual Review of Political Science* 1, no. 1 (1998): 27–46.
67. Matthew Krain and Marissa Edson Myers, "Democracy and Civil War: A Note on the Democratic Peace Proposition," *International Interactions* 23, no. 1 (1997): 109–18; Håvard Hegre, "Toward a Democratic Civil Peace? Democracy, Political Change, and Civil War, 1816–1992," *American Political Science Review* 95, no. 1 (2001): 33–48; Uwe Sunde and

Matteo Cervellati, "Democratizing for Peace? The Effect of Democratization on Civil Conflicts," *Oxford Economic Papers* 66, no. 3 (2014): 774–97.

68. Mises, *Liberalism*.
69. Mises, *Liberalism*; Karl R. Popper, "From the Archives: The Open Society and Its Enemies Revisited," *The Economist*, April 23, 1998.
70. Mises, *Liberalism*; Karl R. Popper, *The Open Society and Its Enemies: New One-Volume Edition*, new ed. (Princeton: Princeton University Press, 2013).
71. Douglass C. North, John Joseph Wallis, and Barry R. Weingast, *Violence and Social Orders: A Conceptual Framework for Interpreting Recorded Human History* (Cambridge: Cambridge University Press, 2009).
72. Mises, *Liberalism*.
73. North et al.
74. The weapons manufacturers benefit from the possibility of war, not actual war. Moreover, the manufactures of weapons are only a small part of the capitalist system. The retail sector, for example, is considerably bigger and the retail sector does not do well in war.
75. Easterly et al., "Good Policy or Good Luck?"; Stephen Broadberry and John Joseph Wallis, "Growing, Shrinking, and Long Run Economic Performance: Historical Perspectives on Economic Development," Working Paper (National Bureau of Economic Research, 2017).
76. Heitor Almeida and Daniel Ferreira, "Democracy and the Variability of Economic Performance," *Economics & Politics* 14, no. 3 (2002): 225–57; Daron Acemoglu, Simon Johnson, James Robinson, and Yunyong Thaicharoen, "Institutional Causes, Macroeconomic Symptoms: Volatility, Crises and Growth," *Journal of Monetary Economics* 50, no. 1 (2003): 49–123; Pushan Dutt and Ahmed Mushfiq Mobarak, "Democracy and Policy Stability," *International Review of Economics & Finance* 42 (March 2016): 499–517; and Marco Colagrossi, Domenico Rossignoli, and Mario A. Maggioni, "Does Democracy Cause Growth? A Meta-Analysis (of 2000 Regressions)," *European Journal of Political Economy* 61 (January 2020): 101824.
77. Dutt and Mobarak, "Democracy and Policy Stability."
78. On unemployment under communist regimes and how it was often hidden or obfuscated see Baxandall, Phineas. 2000. "The Communist Taboo against Unemployment: Ideology, Soft-Budget Constraints, or the Politics of De-Stalinization?" *East European Politics and Societies* 14 (3): 597–635. https://doi.org/10.1177/0888325400014003004.
    On Keynes as capitalist savior see Backhouse, Roger E., and Bradley W. Bateman. 2011. *Capitalist Revolutionary: John Maynard Keynes*. Cambridge, Mass: Harvard University Press.
79. Escalante, Eduardo E. 2022. "The Influence of Pinochet on the Chilean Miracle." *Latin American Research Review* 57 (4): 1–17.
80. Escalante, "The Influence of Pinochet"; Daniel Uhr, Julia Uhr, and Regis A. Ely, "A Synthetic Control Approach on Chile's Transition to Democracy," *Economics Bulletin* 37, no. 3 (2017): 2219–33.
81. Sebastian Edwards, *The Chile Project: The Story of the Chicago Boys and the Downfall of Neoliberalism* (Princeton, NJ: Princeton University Press, 2023).
82. Boris Nikolaev, "Economic Freedom and Quality of Life: Evidence from the OECD's Your Better Life Index," *Journal of Private Enterprise* 29, no. 3 (2014): 61–96.
83. Jonathan Krieckhaus, Byunghwan Son, Nisha Mukherjee Bellinger, and Jason M. Wells, "Economic Inequality and Democratic Support," *The Journal of Politics* 76, no. 1 (2014): 139–51.
84. Geloso, V. J., Magness, P., Moore, J., and Schlosser, P. (2022). How pronounced is the U-curve? Revisiting income inequality in the United States, 1917–60. *The Economic Journal*, 132(647), 2366–2391; Geloso, V., and Toda, A. A. (Forthcoming). Pareto's Limits: Improving Inequality Estimates in America, 1917 to 1965. Cliometrica (Vol and No not assigned yet); Geloso, V., and Magness, P. (2020). The great overestimation: Tax data and inequality measurements in the United States, 1913–1943. *Economic Inquiry*, 58(2), 834–855; Auten, G., and Splinter, D. (2024). Income inequality in the United States: Using tax data to measure long-term trends. *Journal of Political Economy*, 132(7), 2179–2227; Thomas Piketty and Emmanuel Saez, "Income Inequality in the United States, 1913–1998," *Quarterly Journal of Economics* 118, no. 1 (2003): 1–39.
85. E.g. compare Carter (2007) with Apergis and Cooray (2015) (John R. Carter, "An Empirical Note on Economic Freedom and Income Inequality," *Public Choice* 130, no.

1 (2007): 163–77, https://doi.org/10.1007/s11127-006-9078-0; Nicholas Apergis and Arusha Cooray, "Economic Freedom and Income Inequality: Evidence from a Panel of Global Economies—A Linear and a Non-Linear Long-Run Analysis," *The Manchester School* 85, no. 1 (2017): 88–105, https://doi.org/10.1111/manc.12137).

86. Finis Welch, "In Defense of Inequality," *American Economic Review* 89, no. 2 (1999): 1–17. https://doi.org/10.1257/aer.89.2.1; Vadim Kufenko and Vincent Geloso, "Who Are the Champions? Inequality, Economic Freedom and the Olympics," *Journal of Institutional Economics* 17, no. 3 (2021): 411–27.

87. Chris J. Boudreaux, "Jumping off of the Great Gatsby Curve: How Institutions Facilitate Entrepreneurship and Intergenerational Mobility," *Journal of Institutional Economics* 10, no. 2 (2014): 231–55; James Dean and Vincent Geloso, "Economic Freedom Improves Income Mobility: Evidence from Canadian Provinces, 1982–2018," *Journal of Institutional Economics* 18, no. 5 (2022): 807–26; Justin T. Callais and Vincent Geloso, "Intergenerational Income Mobility and Economic Freedom," *Southern Economic Journal* 89(3): 732–753(2022); Callais, J. T., Geloso, V., and Plemmons, A. (Forthcoming). Economic Freedom and Intergenerational Educational Mobility. *Journal of Private Entreprise*; Justin T. Callais, Vincent Geloso, and Alicia M. Plemmons, *Intergenerational Mobility, Social Capital, and Economic Freedom* (Washington, D.C.: Archbridge Institute Working Paper Series, 2023); Justin T. Callais and Jamie Bologna Pavlik, "Does Economic Freedom Lighten the Blow? Evidence from the Great Recession in the United States," *Economics of Governance* (2023): 24: 357–398; Dean, J., and Geloso, V. (2024). Poverty spells and economic freedom: Canadian evidence. *Journal of Economic Behavior & Organization*, 224, 282–296; and Geloso, V., and Sharma, P. (2025). Regulation and Income Mobility. *The Economists' Voice*, 22(1), 1–7.

88. Lant Pritchett, "The Tyranny of Concepts: CUDIE (Cumulated, Depreciated, Investment Effort) Is Not Capital," *Journal of Economic Growth* 5, no. 4 (2000): 361–84.

89. It also echoes works suggesting that economic freedom increases the Human Development Index (HDI) (which is another measure of human capabilities) (Nikolaev, "Economic Freedom and Quality of Life"; Cephas Naanwaab, "Does Economic Freedom Promote Human Development? New Evidence from a Cross-National Study," *The Journal of Developing Areas* 52, no. 3 (2018): 183–98; Johan Graafland, "Contingencies in the Relationship between Economic Freedom and Human Development: The Role of Generalized Trust," *Journal of Institutional Economics* 16, no. 3 (2020): 271–86).

90. Yi Feng, "Democracy, Political Stability and Economic Growth," *British Journal of Political Science* 27, no. 3 (1997): 391–418, https://www.jstor.org/stable/194123.; Uk Heo and Alexander C. Tan, "Democracy and Economic Growth: A Causal Analysis," *Comparative Politics* 33, no. 4 (2001): 463–73; and Benjamin M. Friedman, *The Moral Consequences of Economic Growth*, repr. ed. (New York: Vintage, 2006).

91. Friedman, *The Moral Consequences of Economic Growth*.

92. Mancur Olson, *The Rise and Decline of Nations* (New Haven: Yale University Press, 1982).

93. Olson, *The Rise and Decline of Nations*.

94. See Tabarrok (1994) for a related model of term limits Alexander Tabarrok, "A Survey, Critique, and New Defense of Term Limits," *Cato Journal* 14, no. 2 (1994): 333–50.

95. Christian Bjørnskov, "Economic Freedom and Economic Crises," *European Journal of Political Economy* 45 (2016): 11–23.

96. See also for more support and extension to pandemics Callais and Bologna Pavlik, "Does Economic Freedom Lighten the Blow?"; Vincent Geloso and Jamie Bologna Pavlik, "Economic Freedom and the Economic Consequences of the 1918 Pandemic," *Contemporary Economic Policy* 39, no. 2 (2021): 255–63; and Rosolino A. Candela and Vincent Geloso, "Economic Freedom, Pandemics, and Robust Political Economy," *Southern Economic Journal* 87, no. 4 (2021): 1250–66.

97. Vincent Geloso, "Conceptualizing the Cost of COVID Policy: The Role of Institutional Trade-Offs," *The Economists' Voice* 18, no. 1 (2021): 129–36; Geloso, Hyde, and Murtazashvili, "Pandemics, Economic Freedom, and Institutional Trade-Offs"; and Vincent Geloso and Ilia Murtazashvili, "Can Governments Deal with Pandemics?," *Cosmos + Taxis* 9, no. 5–6 (2022): 54–63. It should also be noted that there is evidence of the inverse statement—namely that dictatorships with low economic freedom do not withstand shocks

well. Authoritarian regimes respond poorly to external shocks, and dictators will deploy greater violence to remain in power following these shocks (e.g., P. Verwimp, "The Political Economy of Coffee, Dictatorship, and Genocide," *European Journal of Political Economy* 19, no. 2 (2003): 161–81.). Moreover, dictatorial regimes tend to repurpose potentially growth-enhancing technologies for repressive purposes (J. G. Hariri and A. M. Wingender, Jumping the Gun: How Dictators Got Ahead of their Subjects," *The Economic Journal* 133, no. 650 (2023): 728–60).

98. Charles de Montesquieu, *The Spirit of the Laws*, trans. Thomas Nugent (1750; repr., Digireads.com Publishing, 2020).
99. Thomas Paine, *Rights of Man: Part the Second. Combining Principle and Practice. By Thomas Paine, Secretary for Foreign Affairs to Congress in the American War, and Author of the Work Intitled Common Sense* (1792; repr., Gale ECCO, Print Editions, 2018).
100. Immanuel Kant, *Perpetual Peace* (1795 (2007); repr.,: FQ Classics); Richard Cobden, *The Political Writings of Richard Cobden, Vol. 1* (1835; repr., London: T. Fisher Unwin); and Norman Angell, *The Great Illusion*, 1st ed. (1910 (2015); repr., CreateSpace Independent Publishing Platform).
101. Often attributed to Bastiat but more likely coming from Otto Tod Mallery, *Economic Union and Durable Peace* (Harper & Brothers, 1943).
102. Montesquieu, *The Spirit of the Laws.*
103. Joseph Henrich et al., "In Search of Homo Economicus: Behavioral Experiments in 15 Small-Scale Societies," *American Economic Review* 91, no. 2 (2001): 73–78; Omar Al-Ubaydli et al., "The Causal Effect of Market Priming on Trust: An Experimental Investigation Using Randomized Control," *PLOS ONE* 8, no. 3 (2013); Delia Baldassarri, "Market Integration Accounts for Local Variation in Generalized Altruism in a Nationwide Lost-Letter Experiment," *Proceedings of the National Academy of Sciences* 117, no. 6 (2020): 2858–63; and Gustav Agneman and Esther Chevrot-Bianco, "Market Participation and Moral Decision-Making: Experimental Evidence from Greenland," *The Economic Journal*, September 2022, ueac06.
104. Robert A. Dahl (1998).
105. A good summary of this point has been by recent work in the history of economic thought: Benzecry, G. F., Jensen, N., and Smith, D. J. (2025). The Road to Serfdom and the Definitions of Socialism, Planning, and the Welfare State, 1930–1950. *History of Political Economy*, 11773500; Benzecry, G. F., Reinarts, N. A., and Smith, D. J. (2024). You have nothing to lose but your chains?. *Public Choice*, 1–28; Benzecry, G., Jensen, N., and Smith, D. J. (Forthcoming). The socialists' hypotheses and the road to serfdom. *Journal of the History of Economic Thought.*
106. Popper, *The Open Society and Its Enemies.*
107. Adam Przeworski, "Minimalist Conceptions of Democracy: A Defense," in *Democracy's Value*, ed. Ian Shapiro and Casiano Hacker-Cordon (Cambridge: Cambridge University Press, 1999), 23–55; Alexander Tabarrok, "A Survey, Critique, and New Defense of Term Limits," *Cato Journal* 14, no. 2 (1994): 333–50.
108. Kenneth Scheve and David Stasavage, *Taxing the Rich: A History of Fiscal Fairness in the United States and Europe* (Princeton, NJ: Princeton University Press, 2016); Kenneth Scheve and David Stasavage, "Wealth Inequality and Democracy," *Annual Review of Political Science* 20, no. 1 (2017): 451–68; Daron Acemoglu, Suresh Naidu, Pascual Restrepo, and James A. Robinson, "Democracy, Redistribution, and Inequality," ch. 21, in *Handbook of Income Distribution*, ed. Anthony B. Atkinson and François Bourguignon, vol. 2 (Elsevier, 2015), pp. 1885–1966; and Zlatko Nikoloski, "Democracy and Income Inequality: Revisiting the Long- and Short-Term Relationship," *Review of Economics and Institutions* 6, no. 2 (2015): 1-24. http://dx.doi.org/10.5202/rei.v6i2.138
109. Kenneth Scheve and David Stasavage, "Wealth Inequality and Democracy," *Annual Review of Political Science* 20, no. 1 (2017): 451–68.
110. Scheve and Stasavage, "Wealth Inequality and Democracy."
111. North et al., *Violence and Social Orders.*

2

Political Parties and Democratic Capitalism

DIDI KUO

The roots of contemporary democratic discontent have both political and economic causes. In the United States, partisan polarization and democratic instability have worsened against a backdrop of rising economic insecurity. Around the world, democracy indicators have deteriorated since 2005, and citizens have taken to the streets to protest political corruption, election outcomes, worsening economic conditions, and declining living standards.[1] Concerns about democracy and economic well-being are inseparable, with citizens increasingly cynical that governments are responsive to their material concerns.

Since the end of the Cold War, the world has become both more democratic and more economically integrated. Many nations initiated so-called transitions to democracy—adopting democratic elections and formal representative institutions—alongside economic reforms that liberalized their economies and opened their borders to global trade. But the exuberance around markets and democracy in the 1990s has settled into a general unease. We have little reason to expect that democracy and capitalism cannot coexist, but we also know that the contemporary relationship is not a straightforward one of mutual benefit—as it perhaps was during the postwar period in the West. After 1945, Sheri Berman argues that people "began to perceive states as the guardian of society," with the result being "the reconciliation of things long viewed as incompatible: a well-functioning capitalist system, democracy, and social stability."[2] That reconciliation seems far more precarious today. While neoliberal, globalized capitalism has produced innovation and economic growth, it has also sown greater distrust in both democracy (as a political system) and capitalism (as an economic one).

Didi Kuo, *Political Parties and Democratic Capitalism*. In: *Can Democracy and Capitalism Be Reconciled?*.
Edited by: Sidney M. Milkis and Scott C. Miller, Oxford University Press. © Oxford University Press (2025).
DOI: 10.1093/9780197774731.003.0003

The tensions in democratic capitalism today reveal that something is broken in the way democratic institutions aggregate, mediate, and represent interests. Democracy stabilizes capitalism not by amplifying the already significant economic and political power of capital, but by organizing countervailing power. This chapter therefore focuses on representation—in particular, on political parties—to understand the relationship of democracy and capitalism. In particular, it examines the way party organization changed in a neoliberal era. While parties have remained central to electoral politics, their intermediary capacity—defined as their ability to effectively channel and translate distinct interests—has eroded. This affects the political economy of representation, by making democratic institutions more responsive to the interests of capital than to other economic groups.

Parties may not seem to be directly connected to the relationship of democracy and capitalism. Most scholarship on parties examines how parties seek and maintain power by examining their electoral and legislative priorities. Given contemporary levels of partisan polarization, much of the scholarship on parties also tries to understand the relationship of parties to one another, and to explain how parties became more polarized over time.

However, parties are also embedded intermediary organizations tasked with connecting the amorphous preferences of the electorate to concrete material and economic demands for governance. This is the role parties have played throughout history, yet their capacity to serve as representative intermediaries has not been constant. An analysis of why the relationship of democracy and capitalism has deteriorated must focus on representative organizations, and examine how the work of representation has both shaped, and been shaped by, broader economic changes.

This chapter first discusses theories of democracy and capitalism, arguing that parties are central to understanding how governing institutions manage the economy. It then discusses an erosion of party *intermediary capacity*, particularly regarding political economy concerns. This chapter focuses on changes to party organization from 1970 to 2000, when parties became less distinguished by their market orientation, and began a realignment over class and education. It concludes by discussing partisan polarization today, and the way parties that are polarized and organizationally weak contribute to greater instability in democratic capitalism. When parties are unable to articulate distinct interests, to craft policies that meet the material needs of citizens, or to regulate the downstream effects of capitalist change, democracies lose the capacity to manage capitalism in the long run.

Tensions in Democracy and Capitalism

Scholars have long debated the relationship of democracy and capitalism, with one school of thought delineating the mutual benefit between the two, and with the other detailing tensions that require political and social negotiation. These perspectives, while not exclusive, help us to understand particular stages in the development of democracy and capitalism.

Early periods of democratization, dating to the expansion of suffrage in the eighteenth and nineteenth centuries in North America and Western Europe, occurred alongside a transition from agrarian to industrial forms of economic production. Barrington Moore's famous maxim "no bourgeoisie, no democracy" stemmed from an analysis of middle-class growth preceding the overthrow of the *ancien regime*. Modernization theorists argue that economic development transforms the class structure of society, and the corresponding growth of the middle classes increases demands for representation and public goods.[3] Historically, democracy has produced higher rates of economic growth and lower rates of inequality than authoritarianism.[4] Democracies also have higher levels of social development and better health outcomes because of greater investments in public goods and infrastructure.

Industrialization also expanded the political mobilization of the working classes, who often demanded political and economic rights alongside one another. Labor parties, with strong ties to trades unions, served as important conduits of recruitment and socialization of working-class representatives.[5]

But there has also been skepticism about the relationship of democracy and capitalism. All democratic republics tend to be run by the elite, broadly construed. Marxists argued that democracy could never really transform capitalism: because capitalism creates inevitable divisions of power and material resources between laborers and producers, the state inevitably serves as a mere shell for capitalist interests. Contemporary versions of these critiques usually argue not that democracy will always protect capitalism, but instead that business enjoys special power in democratic regimes. Capitalists are responsible for "the economic security of everyone," given their ability to set prices and wages, and they in turn have structural power in politics.[6] Business can also use tools such as lobbying or state capture to exert power according to quid-pro-quos, and at worse can leverage a public power unmatched by other formal institutions.[7]

The compromise of these perspectives was the democratic capitalism associated with the postwar period, roughly 1940–1970, when many governments across Europe and North America expanded welfare states and social policy while growing their economies. Inequities of capitalism continued to exist, but governments worked to distribute power away from capitalists. Goran Therborn described a state apparatus with a "bourgeois class composition" and state power operating "to maintain and promote capitalist relations of production and the class character of the state apparatus" that was nonetheless democratic.[8]

Democratic Capitalism in a Neoliberal Era

Because many theories of democracy and capitalism were developed to understand transitions to democracy, they do not fully explain the relationship of democracy and capitalism beyond the 1970s. Many advanced capitalist economies are no longer dominated by manufacturing sectors. Further, democratic publics may become dissatisfied with their representative institutions and leaders, even in the absence of active threats to democracy. An account of democracy and capitalism in the neoliberal era therefore needs to take into account the ways that capitalism has evolved, and in turn, how democracies have responded to these changes.

There is reason to believe that democracy and capitalism can continue to coexist effectively. Torben Iverson and David Soskice argue that democracies have fostered growth and investments in contemporary capitalism as a response to the demands of the middle classes, similarly to earlier eras of democratic transition.[9] Financial integration may affect the preferences of economic elites in authoritarian countries, for example, and create incentives for them to embrace democracy in order to become more economically competitive.[10]

But the neoliberal variant of capitalism also seems unsustainable.[11] The profits generated in the knowledge economy sectors of finance and technology have not been evenly distributed. Wealth inequality is exacerbated by high capital mobility and transnational financial networks that shield private money.[12] Meanwhile, communities in advanced industrial societies that cannot reap the benefits of globalization have diminishing economic mobility and higher levels of precarity.[13] These communities, lacking aid or social support, have experienced declining life expectancies.[14] Further, economic inequality disproportionately impacts communities of color that have long been excluded from the benefits of full citizenship. It is not the case that democracy cannot respond to these developments, but instead that representative institutions are not translating material demands into policy outcomes.

Representation and Parties

Democratization is a story of leaders that must do more than win elections: they must serve as representatives, and must also govern effectively. Parties are intermediary organizations that serve as the linkage between amorphous interests and government policies. They are more than just groups of elites competing for power. Instead, parties are the sites where questions of political economy representation are managed. They are able to facilitate the relationship of democracy and capitalism by mobilizing and articulating an interest distinct from that of capital, and by bringing the state's resources to bear on societal and economic problems.

Democracy mediates capitalism through the institution of parties. Parties have typically been the way democracy is associated with improved economic outcomes; they make the government responsive to material demands. Franchise expansion historically leads to greater public goods provision, particularly in areas such as infrastructure, health, and sanitation.[15] For example, the passage of the 19th Amendment enfranchising women led to higher rates of educational attainment in children,[16] and greater infant and maternal health outcomes.[17]

Democratic competition (as opposed to one-party rule) has also been linked to greater investments in human welfare (health and education), both at the state level and globally.[18] The removal of barriers to vote in the United States has been empirically associated with greater public spending and material investments in areas with black voters, after passage of the Voting Rights Act.[19]

Leaders have incentives to mobilize new voters through redistributive measures, but in order to develop ongoing relationships and loyalty, they need to work through the institution of party. In her study of women's enfranchisement, Dawn Teele shows that alliances between women's suffrage groups and parties were critical to securing the vote in the first place, precisely because of bargains that women would vote for specific parties and that parties, in turn, would legislate in their favor.[20] Further, expansions of social policy, such as President Franklin Delano Roosevelt's New Deal, establish longlasting coalitions based on partisan commitments and electoral support. Parties come to occupy meaningful space along a left-right spectrum precisely because of the distinct policy commitments they make. When parties no longer retain connections to communities they serve, or when their policy priorities do not reflect the interests of their base, they may no longer be able to convince voters that are serving as effective intermediaries.

Defining Intermediary Capacity

What is it that parties are doing, or are failing to do, and how might trends in party capacities affect the broader crisis of liberal democracy? Parties, after all, are responsible for most of the work of democracy: they recruit and field candidates, manage election campaigns, aggregate and mediate competing interests, devise and pass policies, and mobilize the citizenry into politics.

An intermediary capacity perspective asks us to examine in greater detail how it is that parties articulate and embody material interests, those that are rooted in, and shaped by, capitalist economics. Many parties originated around divisions around class or territory: social and economic divisions between labor and capital or core (urban) and peripheral (rural) interests were "frozen" into party systems.[21] While parties of course differentiated themselves on more than economic policy, there was a consistency to the way parties occupied the left-right spectrum. Parties became responsible for defining the axes of political competition, for translating the interests of voters into the mandates of government.

As the economic dimension of politics has changed, however—reflecting a deeper structural shift in capitalism—so, too, have party alignments. In particular, a party's orientation toward markets and states, and its class bases, have significant effects on the party system's representation of society overall. Assessing party intermediary capacity requires taking into account not only the programmatic elements of a party's economic agenda, but also the forms of party organization that link these programs to constituencies in need. While mass parties that were built as nations industrialized and expanded democracy had robust intermediary capacity, the parties of the neoliberal era have not prioritized their intermediary functions.

Stephanie Mudge, in her work on neoliberalism, argues that "the key problematic, or concern, of the historical social science of parties, party politics, and party-political institutional order should be representation—as opposed to policies, votes and elections, demographics, or ideas—and within that concern, parties' *capacity to mediate*."[22] For party competition to be meaningful, parties must offer competing visions of state-society relationships, particularly over the roles and responsibility of government.

Building Intermediary Capacity

The relationship of democracy and capitalism was built over centuries, with political parties playing a critical role at each stage of its development. For most of the twentieth century, ideological debates manifested themselves in the party system, with parties competing by offering distinct policies and visions to voters. Mass party organizations created multiple sources of accountability between citizens and politicians; at the same time, parties competed over fundamental issues of state and society, including the creation of new social programs and regulatory institutions. As a result, parties are considered essential to long-term democratic stability and economic growth.[23]

In the era of suffrage expansion in the early democracies, parties often developed their intermediary capacities alongside their electoral ones. Over a century or so, parties evolved from narrow legislative factions to mass parties rooted in the electorate. The "mass" in mass party referred not to the collective masses, that is, a party that wins decisive majorities, but instead denoted a party with extensive networks within specific segments of society. These parties placed a premium on representational integrity—how well they channeled the interests of their base—rather than on how savvily they conducted campaigns.[24] In this era, parties of the left became associated with support for social policy, redistribution, and progressive social values, while parties of the right were associated with less state intervention and redistribution, and traditional social values.

The social bases of politics began a slow but significant change after the economic crises of the 1970s and the conservative revolution of the 1980s. The manufacturing sectors of the industrial democracies started to decline, as the global economy became more integrated and trade expanded. In 1988, Angelo Panebianco described the rise of an "electoral-professional party."[25] These parties were oriented toward issues, rather than ideology, and toward leaders, rather than members. These parties were likely to become more dependent on interest groups and single-advocacy groups to do the work of representing citizens, and to depend on technicians, rather than party bureaucrats, to formulate policy.

Panebianco's description of the electoral-professional party led him to predict the "*dissolution of parties* as organizations . . . [they will] be only convenient tags for independent political entrepreneurs."[26] Mass media and television made campaigns more candidate centered, and as a result, parties would increasingly specialize in public relations and advertising specialists. Communications technology also made parties more dependent on pollsters, who could now gauge public opinion in more efficient, supposedly accurate ways.

By the final decades of the twentieth century, party membership was on the decline. For citizens, belonging to a party was no longer a formal affiliation; people could affiliate with advocacy or interest groups. Writing about Europe, Richard Katz and Peter Mair noted that parties that are financed by the state operate as "cartels," characterized by "collusion and cooperation between ostensible competitors."[27] As Panebianco predicted, these parties are "exclusively capital-" (rather than labor-) "intensive, professional and centralized."[28] In the context of American parties, Daniel Shea worried that the candidate-centered parties of the 1980s would become disconnected from the "mass base," since "the gap between what activists desire and what the voters care about is growing."[29] These kinds of parties would run up the cost of elections, which would likely become more competitive but also more elite.

Intermediary capacity was therefore associated with the period of mass party organization, while scholars of parties documented a shift away from labor-intensive, locally-based parties around the 1980s in many advanced industrial democracies. While postwar economic growth required strong, class-based parties, given economic reliance on manufacturing and industry, liberalization and knowledge-based growth since the 1980s have instead been associated with technocratic, elite parties. These parties have little connection to their traditional mass bases. Parties of the left embraced neoliberal economic policies at the turn of the twenty-first century, no longer the consistent party representing the working class.[30] As the economic policies of the mainstream parties became less differentiated, debates over culture and identity became more salient.[31]

While parties once reached citizens through membership and local party offices, they took advantage of changes to communications technology to rely on a politics industry—pollsters, strategists—to target potential voters. As parties became more professional and campaign oriented, they also became less responsive, shedding the representation and mobilization functions they once performed; they delegate many traditional mobilization functions to outside groups.[32] Interest groups, lobbying firms, and public relations provide messages and information to voters—and they often denigrate parties, rather than tout the benefits of partisanship. While people may continue to vote for parties, trust in parties has nonetheless plummeted, and party membership has reached historic lows.

Given the decline of civic associations and unions that reinforced citizens' relationships to parties, political parties went through a period of growing more similar in their economic priorities, particularly related to growth and globalization. Parties used to reflect differences in the class structure of society, which helped them develop consistent policies reflecting differing ideas of how government should manage the economy. As class differences have become muddled, parties have increasingly tailored their policies toward the center, in ways that obscure rather than clarify their differences. These changes to party organization have had far-reaching consequences, reshaping the architecture and bases of representation itself. And in an unfortunate turn, these changes to parties have also rendered the relationship of democracy and capitalism less tenable.

Parties in the neoliberal era are disengaged from civil society, functioning more as partnerships of professionals. Their power in politics all but assured, these parties made elections little more than legitimating tactics—a "service provided by the state" for citizens.[33] Bernard Manin described this as audience democracy, as opposed to party democracy, whereby voters provide consent to parties rather than active engagement.[34] Russell Muirhead and Nancy Rosenblum warn about ". . . a failure of the elemental linkage function once attributed to parties . . . if parties cannot link the groups vying for power in the legislature with groups in the larger society, then legislatures, which are the heart of representative government, lose their connection to popular interests, wants, and passions, and representative government loses something of its legitimacy."[35]

Trends in advanced industrial nations do not necessarily bode poorly for democracy. However, there are lessons from neoliberal development around the world that helps us understand why party organization affects representation. Since the 1980s, many party systems in developing regions feature parties that do not differ ideologically, or in which parties of the left and right hold similar economic positions. The Washington Consensus led many parties around the world to adopt neoliberal economic policies, including free trade, deregulation, privatization, and welfare austerity. As economic integration accelerated in the late twentieth century, many parties—in particular parties of the left—moved to the right, at least on economic issues. This blurring of programmatic differences between the parties makes it difficult for voters to attribute positions to parties, and in turn to hold them accountable. In other words, when parties have a similar market orientation, they are likely to foster greater distrust in democracy in the long run.[36]

The state has also contracted in many parts of the world, owing either to economic crisis, neoliberal policy, or some combination thereof. As a result, parties are less likely to use social policy to provide resources to citizens. Austerity measures and privatization have further constrained the programs that parties can credibly offer, limiting the state's role and further driving party deinstitutionalization.[37] Similar trends might be at play in the Western democracies, as the project of neoliberalism was embraced by parties across the political spectrum.

Parties in a Neoliberal Era

The years of 1970–2000 reshaped the political economy of representation, as the nationalized, professionalized parties responded to neoliberal economic adjustments. Party systems often experience realignment in the face of demographic and economic change. The neoliberal era has produced a change in the composition of the society, from single-breadwinner households with secure jobs in manufacturing or industry to a postindustrial economy. As Herbert Kitschelt argued, the growing service sector and decline of manufacturing posed a challenge for traditional left parties.[38] Education has become a growing cleavage, both in determining who gets economic opportunities as well as who supports which parties. Those with higher levels of education (i.e., college degrees) are more likely to support parties of the left, while those with a high school education or less are more likely to support parties of the right.[39] This pattern is evident across the industrial economies and advanced democracies.

However, this misalignment has yet to translate into a coherent new mapping of left and right. Realignment is a long process, and requires parties to adapt to changing demographics or attitudes by understanding these interests and funneling them into new policies. Contemporary disagreements about the management of political economy, and the relationship of state to society, have yet to be resolved in the party system, which then creates opportunities for political outsiders.[40]

Social movements, activism around identity and values, and grievance mobilization cannot serve to rectify structural economic concerns unless absorbed into meaningful party contestation. Attention to the ways parties reprioritized their representative functions with their economic concerns reveals how intermediary capacity changed in the final decades of the twentieth century.

Austerity and the Orthodoxy of the Market

After the economic crises of the 1970s, conservative parties ushered in a period of economic retrenchment. They scaled back welfare programs, reduced tax rates, and deregulated the economy. However, this did not simply reflect a conservative ideology. Instead, as the world was becoming more economically integrated, parties on both the left and right became more wary of state action, and more inclined to prioritize economic growth as the foremost responsibility of government. Although many party systems have become more ideologically cohesive (within parties) and polarized (between parties), there is evidence that parties of the left and right have actually moved *closer* in the past half a century. They show a similar market orientation with respect to a neoliberal policy agenda of deregulation, globalization, and growth.[41] Parties of the left, in particular, embraced a "third way" centrism in the 1990s. Leaders such as Bill Clinton, Tony Blair, and Gerhard Schroeder pursued neoliberalism with social democratic characteristics. This entailed, among other things, welfare-to-work policies, "flexible" labor market arrangements, urban renewal via enterprise zones, greater central bank authority, and more offshoring of corporate jobs and profits. Center-right parties continued to pursue an agenda of deregulation, lower corporate taxes, and reduced barriers to trade. All of these reflected a shift toward markets, rather than governments, to manage the economy.[42]

For the most part, the mainstream parties of the advanced industrialized democracies have furthered the project of market liberalization. When social democratic parties won elections throughout the advanced industrial democracies in the 1990s, they embraced the policy agenda around globalization and growth. Stephanie Mudge has shown a "market-centric political logic . . . a cross-partisan *neoliberal politics*" taking hold across parties of the right and left in this period.[43] Rather than using the state to make determinations about redistribution or employment, markets were, in effect, left to make allocative choices under the guise of neutrality.

Because globalization entailed a certain approach to economic management, one that prioritized the free flow of goods and capital and less state intervention in the market, globalization also shaped party dynamics. Political leaders adopted the language of governing "responsibly," that is, in a way that prioritized the health of the economy, over the language of governing responsively. As countries liberalized their economies and signed free trade agreements, western governments promised that capitalism would generate growth regardless of its short-term distributive costs—that a rising tide would lift all boats. The Western economies were also well positioned to benefit from globalization: their corporations could now take advantage of cheaper labor markets or supply chains outside the United States, and tap in to new consumer markets.

The project of the third way was inseparable from the project of globalization, as countries removed barriers to trade, and corporations expanded their operations across borders. John Kenneth Galbraith once described American business as subject to the countervailing power of government and labor: in the postwar era, the relationship of business and democracy was mediated by national governments and domestic regulatory environments. Globalization shifts the loci of power away from states, since national leaders regardless of partisan ideology feel pressure to make their economies attractive to foreign trade and capital.[44]

As parties have become more similar in their market orientation, they have undermined their ability to respond to voters through policy. Evidence from European countries that join the European Union show high degrees of mainstream party convergence, particularly on economic policy.[45] When domestic parties are less differentiated on economic policy, the right and the left become harder to distinguish—with significant political consequences. First, parties may amplify their differences on cultural and social issues.[46] New parties—particularly those with an "anti-system" message—can also mobilize disaffected constituencies, and they are more likely to win when the mainstream parties are similar.[47]

Market liberalization in other parts of the world, such as Latin America, also offer lessons for the advanced democracies in the West. As countries undertook structural adjustment programs to stabilize their economies through the 1980s, leaders who had campaigned on leftist platforms often had to implement policies they explicitly opposed. Susan Stokes describes "bait-and-switch" policies that implemented economic liberalization policies "not approved ex ante by popular mandate."[48] Voters had no way to channel their opposition to these policies through the party system, however, because the parties were in agreement on austerity. As a result, it was harder for democracy to manage capitalism. Citizens took to the streets to protest reforms and rejected mainstream parties, occasionally turning to extremists instead.

The examples of the European Union and Latin American democracies show that when parties change their positions—and in particular when the mainstream parties move closer together on economic policy—they can make it harder for voters to hold them to account. The third way parties coopted some of the issues of the right, such as trade and deregulation.[49] They replaced the language of explicit class conflict, stressing work, "human capital development," and "social investment" rather than class divides or even poverty.[50]

Peter Hall has noted that organizational changes to parties shared electoral affinities with a global economic agenda of liberalization.[51] The economic policies associated with neoliberalism and globalization, which allow a logic of markets to prevail, has also entailed a slow abdication of government from many aspects of public life. Given that prevailing governance relies on the market to resolve distributive decisions, parties are deprived of critical programmatic levers to respond to public concerns, and are displaced as sites of contestation.

Parties replaced the input of members and civic groups with consultants and strategists who could sell these policies to the public. Through new techniques of representation, like polling and message targeting, parties obviated the need to consult with voters. Parties with intermediary capacity must be capable of, or invested in, developing a role for government to mitigate the problems of capitalism. But parties today have little infrastructure or capacity to nurture their representational capacities in order to win elections, and as a result, have weakened the role of the party system in managing democratic concerns.

Class and Education Divides in the Party System

Education has become a significant political cleavage across the advanced capitalist democracies. In the United States, college-educated voters are increasingly more likely to support Democrats than Republicans. While 60 percent of white voters without college degrees voted for Bill Clinton in 1992, in 2020, only 27 percent supported Joe Biden.[52] The traditional base of left parties was the working class, typically understood as people working in manufacturing, or in manual or clerical jobs. The working and middle classes are more difficult to delineate in the new American workforce. Further, sectors such as finance and technology have driven wealth inequality; these sectors are lucrative, and their profits are shared among relatively few highly-skilled workers.

The electoral success of the third way parties showed just how effective a policy of triangulation (between values of the left and economic policies of the right) could be. The traditional constituencies of the social democratic left—blue-collar, unionized workers—have been a declining part of the workforce.[53] More workers pursued college, and women began to constitute a greater share of the workforce.

Class politics seems like a relic of the recent past, but political demands continue to be based in large part on employment and income. The parties of the right and left, however, are undergoing realignment around new sectors and opportunities—such that education is increasingly a predictor of vote share, rather than class per se.[54] The postindustrial economy is characterized by a growing service sector (70–80 percent of the American workforce), which obscures traditional class divisions by encompassing so many types of employment—personal services, retail, hospitality (restaurants and hotels), as well as health care and law. Herbert Kitschelt hypothesized that corporate workers would adopt "left-libertarian" attitudes, making it difficult for parties of the left to cater to educated professionals *and* blue-collar workers—especially in industries requiring protection from trade.[55]

The legacy of third way politics was a social democratic turn toward centrism that appealed to salaried workers in skilled employment who could expect their incomes to rise. Workers in semi-skilled or low-skilled jobs, however, received few protections from the effects of globalization, which included deindustrialization and offshoring. As a result, the political left has lost the faithful votes of the working class.[56] Parties across the political spectrum still try to win these votes, but not necessarily through policies emphasizing redistribution or protectionism.

Parties can also create coalitions around values, rather than bread-and-butter materialism. Younger or 'post-material' voters may care more about, say, social justice, identity, or environmental concerns.[57] Partisan competition may therefore take place over traditional values associated with law-and-order, religion, and family, and cosmopolitan issues associated with rights' protections and inclusion. Educated workers tend to vote Democratic because of their socially liberal and cosmopolitan values. But these affluent voters also support globalization, and therefore may be less likely to support corporate taxation or redistribution.[58] The Republican party has long been closely aligned with business interests, which tend to be unified in their opposition to redistribution and regulation. However, Republicans also increasingly draw support from white voters without college degrees—a trend that drives popular narratives around Republicans mobilizing those "left behind" from globalization. While Republicans use grievance and anger to mobilize a working-class base, they have not yet translated the *class* component into economic policies that are redistributive or pro-labor.[59]

As the educated upper-middle-classes saw their incomes and opportunities grow relative to those with less education, labor parties—which were once crucial for recruiting and electing working-class representatives—became more elite themselves. Legislative representatives are likely to be more educated and command a higher income than their constituents.[60] In 1945, 56 percent of representatives in the House and 75% of Senators had college degrees; today, 94% of House members and all Senators have graduated from college, and 66 percent and 75 percent, respectively, have graduate degrees.[61]

These changes to class and party have reshaped the political advantages available to capitalists. Not only are the wealthy far more wealthy today than they were in the postwar period, but they also seem to secure access to greater representation. For example, affluent voters are more likely to get their preferences implemented into policy, particularly on redistribution and taxation issues.[62] Issues of policy responsiveness are not limited to the United States. Policies tend to reflect the preferences of high-income voters in across many of the advanced industrial democracies, even those with robust social transfers.[63] Macroeconomic policymaking—particularly delegation to central banks—was in part a concession to financial and business elites, a promise that workers' or domestic concerns would be secondary to the need to control inflation. This also allowed politicians to deflect blame when faced with difficult questions of the tradeoff between unemployment and inflation.[64]

Conclusion: Who Solves Problems?

In October 2019, a decade after a global financial crisis and merely months before a global pandemic, Marc Benioff, the CEO of Salesforce, wrote in *The New York Times*: "As a capitalist, I believe it's time to say out loud what we all know to be true: capitalism, as we know it, is dead."[65] Like many other concerned capitalists today, a group that includes Warren Buffett of Berkshire Hathaway, Larry Fink of BlackRock, and Jamie Dimon of JP Morgan, Benioff argues that what we need is a new kind of capitalism—one that works for all stakeholders.[66]

Capitalists see the private sector as capable of reforming itself, with calls for corporate social responsibility and greater commitments to environmental, social, and governance goals. They increasingly devote resources to philanthropic foundations that can shape a civic and policy agenda.[67] While businesses have long protected their economic interests through political means (i.e., campaign finance, lobbying), they increasingly use their resources to support political issues as well. In response to political events, businesses have been vocal in their support of racial justice, women's rights, and immigration; they have supported ballot access and democratic election results. Republican politicians have called on businesses to stay out of politics, denouncing "woke corporations." Meanwhile, consumers and employees expect businesses to respond to social conflicts. Private money often helps nonprofit organizations, social justice groups, and advocates and reformers, but the private sector cannot do the work of government.

Historically, parties have managed democracy and capitalism by articulating a distinct role for the state vis-a-vis its citizens, and by using that role to represent an interest distinct from that of capital. Although there are promising signs that political and economic leaders are worried about the relationship of democracy and capitalism, the erosion of democracy's representative capabilities means there is little mobilized opposition to capital. Further, there are mechanisms for those with resources to dominate political ideas and policies despite the fact that they may represent only a small segment of society. And government itself, through public-private partnerships and reliance on private sector contractors, can directly contribute to business power.[68]

Increasing numbers of voters feel that parties are corrupt and cannot be trusted, or that they care only about short-term goals rather than the public good. Americans trust parties even less than police or the media; the fastest-rising partisan group is independents, many of whom disdain the party system across the board.[69] These trends parallel those in other longstanding democracies, where parties are losing members and people are participating in politics less. Citizens of Asia, Africa, and Europe also feel less trusting of parties today than in previous decades.[70]

Distrust of parties is not just a symptom of a broader erosion of faith in democracy. Instead, the way parties adapted their representative and mobilizing functions in a neoliberal era weakened their ability to respond to the economic concerns of citizens. Focusing on party intermediary capacity may be at odds with contemporary scholarship that views parties exclusively as vote-getting organizations. As Joseph Schumpeter famously argued, parties are engaged in a competitive struggle for the people's vote. Much of the scholarship on parties therefore focus on campaigns, elections, and legislative politics. The foremost theory of parties in the study of American politics tells us that parties are not intermediary organizations at all—they are merely "groups of policy demanders."[71] This theory explains why corporate interests often prevail within parties, but does not capture the shift in parties from dense organizations with linkages to civic groups and unions to porous, elite organizations.

Today's "hollow parties" are a far cry from the organizational party of the mid-twentieth century.[72] Attention devoted to the electoral-legislative dimension of parties neglects an equally important dimension: that of parties as membership and linkage organizations, rooted in society. Parties are critical to democratic stability not because they win elections, but because of their representational integrity—their ability to channel voters' interests and translate them into the substance of party competition and policy. There is a structural imbalance of power at the heart of the capitalist democracies today that may seem impervious to stronger parties. However, addressing problems associated with capitalism will require working through democratic intermediaries. Parties cannot be wished out of existence: they can be renewed and repurposed, but not replaced. Pro-democracy coalitions and factions, as well as mobilization of those without wealth and power, can only be sustained through the representative, intermediary infrastructure of parties.

Notes

1. Sarah Repucci and Amy Slipowitz, *Freedom in the World 2021: Democracy Under Siege* (Freedom House, 2021); Economist Intelligence Unit, *Democracy Index 2020: In Sickness and in Health?* (2020); Larry Diamond, *Ill Winds: Saving Democracy from Russian Rage, Chinese Ambition, and American Complacency* (New York, NY: Penguin Random House, 2019); Robin Wright, "The Story of 2019: Protests in Every Corner of the Globe," *The New Yorker*, 2019, see also the Carnegie Foundation's Global Protest Tracker.
2. Sheri Berman, *The Primacy of Politics: Social Democracy and the Making of Europe's Twentieth Century* (New York, NY: Cambridge University Press, 2006).
3. Seymour M. Lipset, "Some Social Requisites of Democracy: Economic Development and Political Legitimacy," *American Political Science Review* 53, no. 1 (March 1959): 69–105; Dankwart A. Rustow, "Transitions to Democracy: Toward a Dynamic Model," *Comparative Politics* 2, no. 3 (April 1970): 337–363.
4. Daron Acemoglu et al., "Democracy Does Cause Growth," *Journal of Political Economy* 127, no. 1 (2019): 47–100; Daron Acemoglu and James A. Robinson, "Why Did the West Extend the Franchise? Democracy, Inequality, and Growth in Historical Perspective," *The Quarterly Journal of Economics* 115, no. 4 (November 2000): 1167–1199.
5. Dietrich Rueschemeyer, Evelyn Stephens, and John Stephens, *Capitalist Development and Democracy* (Chicago, IL: University of Chicago Press, 1992); Ruth Collier, *Paths Toward Democracy: The Working Class and Elites in Western Europe and South America* (Cambridge, UK: Cambridge University Press, 1999).
6. Charles E. Lindblom, *Politics and Markets* (New York: Basic Books, 1977).
7. Adam Przeworski and Michael Wallerstein, "Structural Dependence of the State on Capital" *American Political Science Review* 82, no. 1 (1988): 11–29.
8. Goran Therborn, "The Rule of Capital and the Rise of Democracy," *New Left Review* 103 (May 1977): 3–41.
9. Torben Iversen and David Soskice, *Democracy and Prosperity: Reinventing Capitalism through a Turbulent Century* (Princeton University Press, 2019); Mads Andreas Elkjær and Torben Iversen, "The Political Representation of Economic Interests: Subversion of Democracy or Middle-Class Supremacy?," *World Politics* 72, no. 2 (2020): 254–290.
10. John R. Freeman and Dennis P. Quinn, "The Economic Origins of Democracy Reconsidered," *The American Political Science Review* 106, no. 1 (2012): 58–80; Michael Albertus and Victor Gay, "Unlikely Democrats: Economic Elite Uncertainty under Dictatorship and Support for Democratization," *American Journal of Political Science* 61, no. 3 (2017): 624–641.
11. Paul Collier, *The Future of Capitalism: Facing the New Anxieties* (New York, NY: Harper Collins, 2018); Fred Block, *Capitalism: The Future of an Illusion* (University of California Press, 2018); Robert Kuttner, *Can Democracy Survive Global Capitalism?* (New York: W. W. Norton, 2018); Wolfgang Streeck, *Buying Time: The Delayed Crisis of Democratic Capitalism* (London: Verso, 2014); Thomas Piketty, *Capital in the Twenty-First Century* (Cambridge, MA: Harvard University Press, 2014).

12. Henry Farrell and Abraham Newman, "BREXIT, Voice and Loyalty: Rethinking Electoral Politics in an Age of Interdependence," *Review of International Political Economy* 24, no. 2 (2017): 232–247.
13. Kathleen Thelen, "The American Precariat: U.S. Capitalism in Comparative Perspective," *Perspectives on Politics* 17, no. 1 (March 2019): 5–27.
14. Anne Case and Angus Deaton, *Deaths of Despair and the Future of Capitalism* (Princeton, NJ: Princeton University Press, 2020).
15. Alessandro Lizzeri and Nicola Persico, "Why did the Elites Extend the Suffrage? Democracy and the Scope of Government, with an Application to Britain's 'Age of Reform'," *The Quarterly Journal of Economics* 119, no. 2 (May 2004): 707–65.
16. Esra Kose, Elira Kuka, and Na'ama Shenhav, "Women's Suffrage and Children's Education," *American Economic Journal: Economic Policy* 13, no. 3 (August 2021): 374–405.
17. Grant Miller, "Women's Suffrage, Political Responsiveness, and Child Survival in American History," *The Quarterly Journal of Economics* 123, no. 3 (August 2008): 1287-1327.
18. Gerald Gamm and Thad Kousser, "Life, Literacy, and the Pursuit of Prosperity: Party Competition and Policy Outcomes in 50 States," *American Political Science Review* 115, no. 4 (2021): 1442–63; Acemoglu et al., "Democracy Does Cause Growth."
19. Elizabeth U. Cascio and Ebonya Washington, "Valuing the Vote: The Redistribution of Voting Rights and State Funds following the Voting Rights Act of 1965," *The Quarterly Journal of Economics* 129, no. 1 (October 2013): 379–433; Gavin Wright, *Sharing the Prize: The Economics of the Civil Rights Revolution in the American South* (Cambridge, MA: Harvard University Press, 2018).
20. Dawn Langan Teele, *Forging the Franchise: The Political Origins of the Women's Vote* (Princeton, NJ: Princeton University Press, 2018).
21. Seymour M. Lipset and Stein Rokkan, *Party Systems and Voter Alignments: Cross-National Perspectives* (New York: Free Press, 1967).
22. Stephanie L. Mudge, *Leftism Reinvented: Western Parties from Socialism to Neoliberalism* (Cambridge, MA: Harvard University Press, 2018).
23. Steven Levitsky and Daniel Ziblatt, *How Democracies Die* (New York: Crown Publishers, 2018); Scott Mainwaring and Timothy Scully (eds), "Party Systems in Latin America" in *Building Democratic Institutions: Party Systems in Latin America* (Cambridge: Cambridge University Press, 1995), 1–34; Nancy Bermeo and Deborah J. Yashar, *Parties, Movements, and Democracy in the Developing World* (New York, NY: Cambridge University Press, 2017); Fernando Bizzarro et al., "Party Strength and Economic Growth," *World Politics* 70, no. 2 (2018): 275–320.
24. Maurice Duverger, *Political Parties: Their Organization and Activity in the Modern State* (London: Methuen, 1951); Moisei Ostrogorski, *Democracy and the Organization of Political Parties* (Garden City, NY: Anchor Books, 1903); Robert Michels, *Political Parties: A Sociological Study of the Oligarchical Tendencies of Modern Democracy*. (New York: Free Press, 1911; 1968); Otto Kirchheimer, "The Transformation of the Western European Party Systems" in *Political Parties and Political Development*, edited by Joseph LaPalombara and Myron Weiner (Princeton, NJ: Princeton University Press, 1966), 177–200.
25. Angelo Panebianco, *Political Parties: Organization and Power* (New York, NY: Cambridge University Press, 1988).
26. Panebianco, *Political Parties*, 274.
27. Richard Katz and Peter Mair, "Changing Models of Party Organization and Party Democracy: The Emergence of the Cartel Party," *Party Politics* 1, no. 1 (1995): 5–28.
28. Panebianco, *Political Parties*, 20.
29. Daniel M. Shea, "The Passing of Realignment and the Advent of the 'BaseLess' Party System," *American Politics Quarterly* 27, no. 1 (January 1999): 33–57.
30. Mudge, *Leftism Reinvented*, 2018.
31. Sheri Berman, "The Specter Haunting Europe: The Lost Left," *Journal of Democracy* 27, no. 4 (2016): 69–76; Peter A. Hall, "The Electoral Politics of Growth Regimes," *Perspectives on Politics* 18, no. 1 (March 2019): 185–99.
32. Bruce E. Cain and Cody Gray, "Parties by Design: Pluralist Party Reform in a Polarized Era," *New York University Law Review* 93 (October 2018): 621–46; Joseph Fishkin and Heather K. Gerken, "The Party's Over: McCutcheon, Shadow Parties, and the Future of the Party

System" *The Supreme Court Review* 2014, no. 1 (2015): 175–214; Richard H. Pildes, "Romanticizing Democracy, Political Fragmentation, and the Decline of American Government," *Yale Law Journal* vol. 122 (2014): 806–52; Samuel Issacharoff, "Outsourcing Politics: The Hostile Takeover of our Hollowed-Out Political Parties," *Houston Law Review Frankel Lecture Series* 54, no. 4 (April 2017): 845–880.

33. Mark Blyth and Richard Katz, "From Catch-all Politics to Cartelisation: The Political Economy of the Cartel Party," *West European Politics* 28, no. 1 (2005): 33–60; Richard Katz and Peter Mair, "The Cartel Party Thesis: A Restatement," *Perspectives on Politics* 7, no. 4 (2009): 753–66.
34. Bernard Manin, *The Principles of Representative Government* (Cambridge University Press, 1997).
35. Russell Muirhead and Nancy L. Rosenblum, "The Political Theory of Parties and Partisanship: Catching Up," *Annual Review of Political Science* 23 (2020):95–110.
36. Noam Lupu, *Party Brands in Crisis: Partisanship, Brand Dilution, and the Breakdown of Political Parties in Latin America* (New York, NY: Cambridge University Press, 2011); Jana Morgan, *Bankrupt Representation and Party System Collapse* (University Park, PA: Pennsylvania State University Press, 2011); Jason Seawright, *Party System Collapse: The Roots of Crisis in Peru and Benezuela* (Stanford, CA: Stanford University Press, 2012).
37. Allen Hicken and Rachel Beatty Riedl, "From the Outside Looking In: Latin American Parties in Comparative Perspective," in *Party Systems in Latin America*, ed. Scott Mainwaring (Cambridge University Press, 2018), 426–440.
38. Herbert Kitschelt, *The Transformation of European Social Democracy* (New York: Cambridge University Press, 1994).
39. Thomas Piketty, *Capital and Ideology* (Harvard University Press, 2020); Amory Gethin, Clara Martinez-Toledano, and Thomas Piketty, "Brahmin Left Versus Merchant Right: Changing Political Cleavages in 21 Western Democracies, 1948–2020," *The Quarterly Journal of Economics* 137, no. 1 (October 2021): 1–48.
40. Jan-Werner Muller, *What Is Populism?* (University of Pennsylvania Press, 2016); Luciano Bardi, Stefano Bartolini, and Alexander H. Trechsel, "Responsive and Responsible? The Role of Parties in Twenty-First Century Politics," *West European Politics* 37, no. 2 (2014): 235–52; Dennis Spies, "Explaining Working-class Support for Extreme Right Parties: A Party Competition Approach," *Acta Politica* 48, no. 3 (2013): 296–325; Kai Arzheimer and Elisabeth Carter, "Political Opportunity Structures and Right-wing Extremist Party Success," *European Journal of Political Research* 45 (2006): 419–443.
41. Mudge, *Leftism Reinvented*; Lily Geismer, *Left Behind: The Democrats' Failed Attempt to Solve Inequality* (Public Affairs, 2022); Elizabeth Popp Berman, *Thinking Like an Economist: How Efficiency Replaced Equality in U.S. Public Policy* (Princeton University Press, 2022); Berman, "The Specter Haunting Europe."
42. Wolfgang Streeck and Kathleen Thelen, eds., *Beyond Continuity: Institutional Change in Advanced Political Economies* (Oxford University Press, 2005); Lucio Baccaro and Chris Howell, *Trajectories of Neoliberal Transformation: European Industrial Relations Since the 1970s* (Cambridge University Press, 2017).
43. Mudge
44. Timothy Hellwig, *Globalization and Mass Politics: Retaining the Room to Maneuver*, Cambridge Studies in Comparative Politics (Cambridge University Press, 2014); Mark Blyth, *Great Transformations: Economic Ideas and Institutional Change in the Twentieth Century* (Cambridge University Press, 2012).
45. Nils D. Steiner and Christian W. Martin, "Economic Integration, Party Polarisation and Electoral Turnout," *West European Politics* 35, no. 2 (2012): 238–265; Helen V. Milner and Benjamin Judkins, "Partisanship, Trade Policy, and Globalization: Is There a Left–Right Divide on Trade Policy?," *International Studies Quarterly* 48, no. 1 (January 2004): 95–119; Hugh Ward, Lawrence Ezrow, and Han Dorussen, "Globalization, Party Positions, and the Median Voter," *World Politics* 63, no. 3 (2011): 509–547.
46. Dalston Ward et al., "How Economic Integration Affects Party Issue Emphases," *Comparative Political Studies* 48, no. 10 (2015): 1227–1259.
47. Jonathan Hopkin, *Anti-System Politics: The Crisis of Market Liberalism in Rich Democracies* (Oxford University Press, 2020); Jae-Jae Spoon and Heike Kluver, "Party Convergence and

Vote Switching: Explaining Mainstream Party Decline across Europe," *European Journal of Political Research* 58 (2019): 1021–1042.

48. Susan Stokes, *Mandates and Democracy: Neoliberalism by Surprise in Latin America* (Cambridge University Press, 2001); Lupu, *Party Brands in Crisis.*
49. Spoon and Kluver, "Party Convergence and Vote Switching"; Niklas Potrafke, "Political Cycles and Economic Performance in OECD Countries: Empirical Evidence from 1951–2006," *Public Choice* 150, no. 1 (2019): 155–179.
50. Julia Lynch, *Regimes of Inequality: The Political Economy of Health and Wealth* (Cambridge University Press, 2020); Geismer, *Left Behind.*
51. Hall, "The Electoral Politics of Growth Regimes."
52. Nate Cohn, "How Educational Differences Are Widening America's Political Rift," *The New York Times*, September 8, 2021. https://www.nytimes.com/2021/09/08/us/politics/how-college-graduates-vote.html
53. In 1975, 25 percent of the labor force in the United States worked in manufacturing; by the 1990s, it was only 15 percent.
54. Tarik Abou-Chadi and Simon Hix, "Brahmin Left versus Merchant Right? Education, class, multiparty competition, and redistribution in Western Europe," *The British Journal of Sociology* 72, no. 1 (2021): 79–92.
55. Kitschelt, *Transformation of European Social Democracy.*
56. Jane Gingrich and Silja Hausermann, "The Decline of the Working-class Vote, the Reconfiguration of the Welfare Support Coalition and Consequences for the Welfare State," *Journal of European Social Policy* 25, no. 1 (2015): 50–75.
57. Russell J. Dalton and Martin Wattenberg, *Parties Without Partisans: Political Change in Advanced Industrial Democracies* (New York: Oxford University Press, 2000); Ronald Inglehart, *Modernization and Postmodernization: Cultural, Economic and Political Change in 43 Nations* (Princeton, NJ: Princeton University Press, 1997).
58. See, for example, David E. Broockman, Gregory Ferenstein, and Neil Malhotra, "Predispositions and the Political Behavior of American Economic Elites: Evidence from Technology Entrepreneurs," *American Journal of Political Science* 63, no. 1 (2019): 212–233.
59. Jacob Hacker and Paul Pierson, *Let them Eat Tweets: How the Right Rules in an Age of Extreme Inequality* (Liveright, 2020).
60. Adam Bonica and Maya Sen, *The Judicial Tug of War How Lawyers, Politicians, and Ideological Incentives Shape the American Judiciary* (Cambridge University Press, 2020); Geoffrey Evans and James Tilley, *The New Politics of Class: The Political Exclusion of the British Working Class* (Oxford University Press, 2017); Jonathan Klick, "The Wealth of Congress," *Harvard Journal of Law & Public Policy* 40, no. 3 (2017): 603–637.
61. Pew https://www.pewresearch.org/fact-tank/2021/03/10/the-changing-face-of-congress/. See also Nicholas Carnes, *White-Collar Government: The Hidden Role of Class in Economic Policy Making* (University of Chicago Press, 2013); Tabatha Abu El-Haj, "Networking the Party: First Amendment Rights and the Pursuit of Responsive Party Government," *Columbia Law Review* 118, no. 1 (2018): 1–76.
62. Jacob Hacker and Paul Pierson, *Winner-Take-All Politics: How Washington Made the Rich Richer—And Turned its Back on the Middle Class* (New York, NY: Simon & Schuster, 2011); Benjamin Page and Martin Gilens, *Democracy in America?: What Has Gone Wrong and What We Can Do About It* (Chicago, IL: University of Chicago Press, 2017).
63. Lea Elsässer and Armin Schäfer, "Political Inequality in Rich Democracies," *Annual Review of Political Science* 26, no. 1 (2023): 469–487.
64. Sheri Berman and Kathleen R. McNamara, "Bank on Democracy: Why Central Banks Need Public Oversight," *Foreign Affairs* 78, no. 2 (1999): 2–8; Lawrence Jacobs and Desmond King, *Fed Power: How Finance Wins* (New York, NY: Oxford University Press, 2017).
65. Marc Benioff, "We Need a New Capitalism," *The New York Times*, October 2019. https://www.nytimes.com/2019/10/14/opinion/benioff-salesforce-capitalism.html
66. Aaron K. Chatterji and Michael W. Toffel, "The New CEO Activists," *Harvard Business Review*. https://hbr.org/2018/01/the-new-ceo-activists
67. Kristin A. Goss, "Policy Plutocrats: How America's Wealthy Seek to Influence Governance," *PS: Political Science and Politics* vol. 49, no. 3 (July 2016): 442–448; Rob Reich, *Just Giving:*

Why Philanthropy Is Failing Democracy and How It Can Do Better (Princeton University Press, 2018).

68. Marius R. Busemeyer and Kathleen Thelen, "Institutional Sources of Business Power," *World Politics* 72, no. 3 (July 2020): 448–480.
69. Samara Klar and Yanna Krupnikov, *Independent Politics: How American Disdain for Parties Leads to Political Inaction* (Cambridge University Press, 2016).
70. International Institute for Democracy and Electoral Assistance, *The Global State of Democracy 2019: Addressing the Ills, Reviving the Promise* (2019). https://www.idea.int/sites/default/files/publications/the-global-state-of-democracy-2019.pdf
71. Kathleen Bawn et al., "A Theory of Political Parties: Groups, Policy Demands and Nominations in American Politics," *Perspectives on Politics* 10, no. 3 (2012): 571–597.
72. Daniel Schlozman and Sam Rosenfeld, *The Hollow Parties: The Many Pasts and Disordered Present of American Party Politics* (Princeton University Press, 2024); Julia R. Azari, "Weak Parties and Strong Partisanship Are a Bad Combination," *Mischiefs of Faction on Vox.com*, Nov. 3, 2016. https://www.vox.com/mischiefs-of-faction/2016/11/3/13512362/weak-parties-strong-partisanship-bad-combination

3

The Varying Fortunes of Democratic Capitalism*

CARLES BOIX

Ulysses, Homer tells us at the very beginning of the Odyssey, was a "complicated man." Democratic capitalism, similarly multifaceted and subject to historically varying fortunes, is too.

At the peak of the first industrial revolution, both the right and the left judged democracy and capitalism to be intrinsically at odds with each other. In the United Kingdom, the Whig historian and politician Thomas Macaulay declared universal suffrage to be "incompatible, not only with this and that form of government, [but] with everything for the sake of which government exists . . . with property and . . . with civilization."[1] In France, Jules Baroche, a leading liberal in the 1848 revolution, opposed it as "necessarily leading, sooner or later, to the triumph of those appalling ideas that are called socialism."[2] Only two years later, and writing from the left, Marx concurred, seeing universal suffrage as a mechanism that "forces the political rule of the bourgeoisie into democratic conditions, which at every moment help the hostile classes [the people] to jeopardize the very foundations of bourgeois society."[3] A hundred years later, however, a growing number of social scientists proclaimed democratic capitalism to be the final stage of economic development or, in even grander terms, the end of History. As Daniel Bell concluded in his influential collection of essays *The End of Ideology*, "in the Western world, there is today a rough consensus among intellectuals on political issues: the acceptance of the Welfare State; the desirability of decentralized power; a system of mixed economy and of political pluralism."[4] Yet, today, in a new intellectual turn, a mounting number of voices point to

* Paper prepared for the Democracy and Capitalism Scholars Conference, University of Virginia, March 7–9, 2023. I thank the comments of participants and, particularly, of Sidney M. Milkis.

Carles Boix, *The Varying Fortunes of Democratic Capitalism*. In: *Can Democracy and Capitalism Be Reconciled?*. Edited by: Sidney M. Milkis and Scott C. Miller, Oxford University Press. © Oxford University Press (2025).
DOI: 10.1093/9780197774731.003.0004

the parallel rise of economic inequality, political polarization, and populism as proof of the inherent instability (and even imminent demise) of democratic capitalism.

In this chapter, I propose a way to reconcile these different, seemingly contradictory, theoretical standpoints, by taking two steps. First, I start by accepting the nineteenth-century vision of capitalism and democracy as two separate 'systems' with different internal logics, potentially in tension with each other. I then point to the fact that the actual level of friction (or incompatibility) between them varies with both the internal structure of capitalism, which has changed over time, and the level of economic prosperity generated by the market system.

While democracy (at least ideally) allocates power according to a principle of strict equality (one person, one vote), capitalism rewards the owners of the factors of production according to the latter's employment and market prices. A democratic decision-making system enables, in principle, a majority to alter the market allocation of returns to factors—redistributing them in such a way as to mirror the political equality of democracy (or, in fact, even to benefit that majority) and, therefore, jeopardizing the welfare and position of the factor owners. The introduction of "equal and universal suffrage" was, for John Stuart Mill, a "violent remedy" because it implied "disfranchising the higher and middle classes . . . who comprise the majority of the most intellectual in the kingdom."[5]

The tension between capitalism and democracy and, hence, the actual level of intervention implemented by a democratic majority have varied, however, with the type of capitalism in place.[6] The technologies and organization of production and, above all, the kind of labor skills that have been complementary to capital have shaped the pattern of employment, wages, the distribution of income, and capital's incentives to invest in public goods. And, as a result, they have had a crucial effect on the likelihood of establishing and maintaining democratic institutions.

The nineteenth-century capitalism that emerged with the first industrial revolution was characterized by a high demand for unskilled labor, low wages, and, at least in the new industrial towns, declining living standards. In a context of raising inequality and considerable social conflict, full democracy remained out of the question. By contrast, twentieth-century capitalism, founded on the use of electricity and the invention of the combustion engine and the assembly line, relied on semi-skilled and skilled individuals as the main type of labor complementary to capital. Fast economic growth, the formation of a broad affluent working class, and the relative equalization of incomes made universal suffrage possible and, with it, the advent of peaceful coexistence of democracy and capitalism. Finally, the information revolution (IT) of the last decades has fueled the demand for high-skilled jobs and widened the wage and income distribution of advanced economies, in the process rattling the political consensus that prevailed during the so-called golden era of democratic capitalism.

I organize the rest of this chapter as follows. Section 1, "Capitalism and Democracy: A Historical Overview," offers a brief history of both the contested but mostly growing hegemony of capitalism and the expansion of democracy in the last two centuries. Section 2, "The Foundations of Democratic Capitalism," discusses the conditions that may explain the emergence of democratic capitalism, validating them with comprehensive data since 1900. Section 3, "Is This Time Different?," turns to consider the political and social challenges of today's IT revolution. Section 4, "Concluding Remarks: Mapping Policy Interventions," concludes by discussing some policy interventions to shore up today's democratic capitalism.

Capitalism and Democracy: A Historical Overview

The story of capitalism over the last two centuries is one of its contested yet, in the long run, successful diffusion across the globe.

Starting in the nineteenth century, industrialization and the triumph of economic liberalism blew up most of the existing regulatory and corporatist structures in place in modern Europe—from feudal rights and guild corporations to domestic trade barriers and distinct jurisdictional structures within nation-states.[7] A fall in the costs of transportation and communication, and the practice of imperialism extended the new laissez-faire economic regime to the rest of the world.[8]

The unfettered capitalism invented in Manchester would then experience a reversal starting in the late 1910s. The Russian Revolution and World War II ushered the imposition of planned economies in the Soviet Union, Eastern Europe, China, and several South East Asian countries. Following the collapse of European empires, numerous former colonies experimented with some variant of heavy state intervention in the form of credit rationing, import substitution policies, and/or state-led industrial policies. In the early 1970s, public-owned enterprises accounted for 27 percent of gross fixed capital formation in developing countries (excluding planned economies)—reaching up to 34 percent in India and Pakistan and 48 percent in Tanzania. Developed countries moved away too from laissez-faire policies in the middle of the century—setting up a comprehensive system of labor market regulations, fostering nationwide wage bargaining between trade unions and business associations, and developing a state-owned business sector. However, their level of public intervention was much more tepid than in low-income countries.

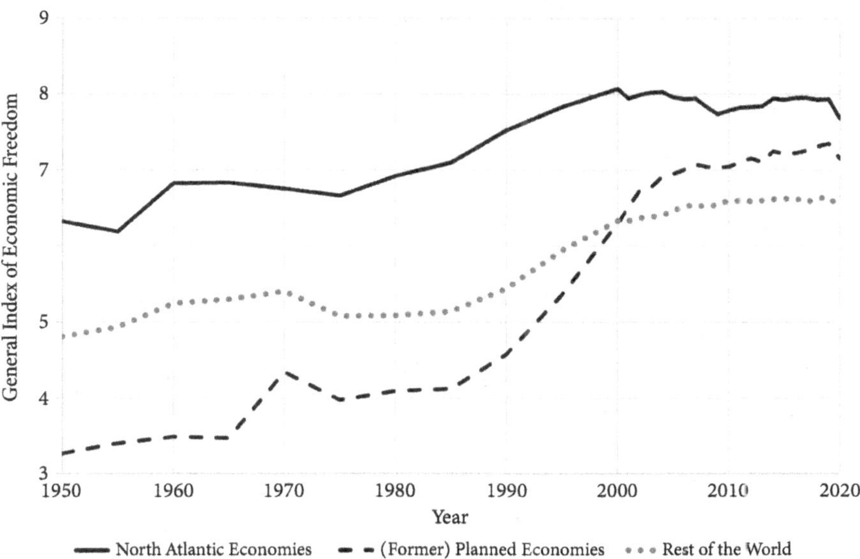

Figure 3.1 Economic freedom, 1950–2020

In the 1970s, state-owned business represented 11 percent of all gross capital formation.[9]

Liberal capitalism then made a comeback in the last third of the twentieth century. The Fraser Institute has developed a comprehensive index of economic freedom at the country level from 1950 to 2020. The overall index ranges from 0 to 10 with a higher number indicating lower levels of public intervention in the economy.[10] Figure 3.1 plots its evolution from 1950 to 2020 for three groups of countries: "North Atlantic" economies (North America and Western Europe), countries that had experienced a socialist planning system at some point in time (before the collapse of the Soviet Union), and the rest of the world. North Atlantic countries led the way in a process of economic liberalization. Starting in the late 1970s, their score rose to around 8 in the twenty-first century. After Gorbachev's perestroika and Deng Xiaoping's liberalization program, former planned economies converged rather quickly from an average of 4 in 1980 to 7 in the early 2000s. The rest of the world also moved, albeit at a slower pace, toward a less regulated economy—from an index of 5.1 in 1980 to about 6.5 in the 2010s.

Historically, capitalism and democracy have had a checkered relationship. During the long nineteenth century of classic liberalism and unconstrained globalization, democracy was uncommon. Before the revolutionary wave of 1848, only a few states in the United States and several cantons in Switzerland had male universal suffrage, and relatively competitive procedures of government selection. In 1848, France and Switzerland extended the suffrage to all men, and by 1914, about one fifth of all independent states had competitive elections and male universal suffrage. In only four, however, women could vote on the same basis as men. In the aftermath of World War I, 28 countries, or 42 percent of all sovereign states, had male universal suffrage and competitive elections. A string of democratic breakdowns and war more than halved that number to 13 countries by 1940.

In the postwar period, between 30 and 40 percent of all sovereign countries had democratic institutions. In contrast to the era of classical liberalism, when suffrage was tightly restricted in almost all countries holding elections, democracy became correlated with the prevalence of a market economy. Whereas among dictatorships the Fraser index of economic freedom was 4.88, for democracies it was 6.09—a difference of 1.21 points. In a linear regression model controlling for per capita income, having a full democracy in 1975 was associated with an increase of 0.90 points in the level of economic freedom.

The process of economic liberalization that started in the 1980s came hand in hand with a prolonged democratization wave. After a long authoritarian interlude, several Southern European countries transitioned to democracy in the later 1970s, followed by Latin America in the following decade. Democratic transitions peaked with the fall of the Soviet Union in the early 1990s. In the early 2000s, the share of democracies plateaued at around 60 percent of all sovereign countries.

At the end of the second decade of the twenty-first century, the association between democracy and the index of economic freedom, which I take here as a proxy of market capitalism, continued to be robust. Having democracy was still associated with an additional point in the Fraser Institute—and the association remained statistically significant even controlling for per capita income. Yet, as I explore in more detail at the end of Section 2, the golden age of democratic capitalism hailed by Daniel Bell has given way to a state of political anxiety among well-established democracies, now buffeted by growing political polarization, the rise of populism, declining levels of voters' trust in both politicians and political institutions, and a much debated process of democratic backsliding.

The Foundations of Democratic Capitalism

If the past is any guide, capitalism and democracy are neither inherently compatible nor intrinsically in conflict with each other. Instead, their evolving relationship appears to have been governed by two key factors, economic inequality and economic development, shaping the extent to which political and economic agents accept combining them or not. First, the organization of production, which, by influencing the societal distribution of wealth, has made it more or less easy to reconcile capitalism with the principle of political equality that animates the idea of democracy. Second, the level of wealth generated by capitalism.

In the rest of this section, I first discuss each factor separately. Then I integrate both of them (inequality and growth) to explain the success of democratic capitalism. Still, as I clarify at the end of this exercise, we should not read the effects of capitalism on the possibility of having democracy in a deterministic way. Making democratic capitalism work depends too on the political and institutional strategies that policymakers develop in response to the technological transformations spurred by the process of creative destruction that defines the market economy. This is particularly true when the level of economic development is such that policymakers have considerable room to reconcile the potentially conflicting logics of democracy and capitalism (for example, using compensatory spending).

Different Capitalisms, Different Distributions of Wealth

Since the rise of industrial capitalism, several waves of technological change have transformed the system of production and, in particular, the kind of labor that was most useful (i.e., complementary) to capital. Broadly speaking, while nineteenth-century firms employed unskilled labor, twentieth-century companies relied on semi-skilled labor (organized around the assembly line). In turn, today's information technologies favor high-skilled labor, while making semi-skilled labor routine tasks redundant.

The evolving technological and institutional configuration of capitalism, resulting in changing rewards for different types of labor and for capital over time, shaped, in turn, the incentives of social and economic agents to cooperate with each other and, in the political realm, accept the possibility of contesting and losing elections (while maintaining the essential attributes of a market economy).

The first industrial revolution, set in motion in Manchester, put an end to a system of production that relied on skilled individuals working in small artisanal shops. British industrialists reorganized the manufacturing process as a sequence of routinized tasks to be performed in large factories. That division of labor into small tasks or routine actions was then gradually mechanized, employing a growing number of machines. By 1850, mechanized factories dominated the production of cotton, a fraction of wool and worsteds, and iron forging in large blast furnaces. Two decades later, manual movements had been eliminated in the refinement of petroleum, and the technologies employed there quickly spilled over to the distilling industry. Around the same time, metalworking industries started to introduce machines to cut and shape metal. Automatizing the manufacture of complex items such as bicycles, clocks, or sewing machines took even longer. Nevertheless, the factory system defined the entire industrial system in Northwestern Atlantic economies by the end of the nineteenth century.[11]

That mechanization process transformed the overall structure of employment. Unskilled individuals, each in charge of a very specific task in the chain of production, became the key type of labor in the new industrial system. The Scottish chemist Andrew Ure proclaimed, in his *Philosophy of Manufactures*, published in 1835, that "the constant aim and tendency of every improvement in machinery [is] to supersede human labour altogether, or to diminish its cost, by substituting the industry of women and children for that of men; or that of ordinary labourers for trained artisans," predicting that "skilled labour (. . .) will, eventually, be replaced by mere overlookers of machines."[12] Within the American manufacturing industry, for example, the proportion of skilled workers fell from 39 percent in 1850 to 23 percent in 1910.

The first industrial revolution came with a decline in the living conditions of workers.[13] The combination of low real wage growth, hard working conditions, overcrowded housing, and bad sanitation conditions resulted in a deterioration of adult mortality rates among British urban and industrial populations after 1800. Life expectancy did not go back to eighteenth-century levels until the 1870s.[14] British men were shorter on average in 1850 than in 1760.[15] By contrast, profits rose, and capital accumulated steadily. The share of national income received by labor fell from around 60 percent in 1800 to 45 percent by 1845. The share of national income in the hands of capital rose from 20 percent in 1770 to 50 percent one hundred years later. In terms of the overall distribution of individual incomes, inequality peaked in the United Kingdom in the first half of the nineteenth century. The income share in the hands of the top quintile of the British population rose from 57 percent in the eighteenth century to 63 percent in 1801, declining to 58 percent in 1867.

In such a socially and politically conflictual environment, universal franchise and competitive elections remained out of the question—opposed by both pre-industrial elites and the new industrial capitalists. Political oligarchies only accepted the extension of the right to vote to well-to-do urban strata holding moderate distributive demands.

By the end of the nineteenth century, a second industrial revolution, resulting from the use of electricity and electric motors and the introduction of the assembly line and of mass-production techniques, generated large productivity gains. After its invention by Henry Ford and the Detroit car industry, the assembly line quickly spread to manufacturing sectors as variegated as household appliances, steel production, fruit canning, or cow-milking. At around the same time, batch-production or continuous-processing machines, which followed the same principle of mechanization and labor substitution, were applied to cigarette–making, soap-making, photographic material, newspaper printing, and glass making, to name a few sectors. Output per hour worked doubled from 1870 to 1913, and again from 1913 to 1950 in the United States. From 1900 onwards, the economy expanded on average at an annual rate of about 2.5 percent in the United States, and almost 3 percent in Western Europe—a pace two times faster than in the previous century. Per capita income doubled in the forty years that preceded World War II. It then doubled again during the Cold War.

The new technologies in place changed the labor market in two fundamental ways. First, the demand for unskilled workers declined sharply. Although exact data on the number of unskilled and skilled workers by industry in the United States before World War II is sparse, in key industries such as iron and steel, the proportion of "common laborers" fell by half from 1910 to 1931.[16] As shown by Claudia Goldin and Lawrence Katz, twentieth-century factories needed individuals capable of reading the operating instructions of machines as well as installing, repairing, and improving them.[17] Second, the second industrial revolution was associated with the formation of large corporations—arguably due to the fall in communication and transportation costs, the emergence of bigger markets, and the possibility of exploiting large economies of scale. Big corporations required a growing number of white-collar jobs needed to manage their production and distribution tasks. The proportion of white-collar employees in the manufacturing sector rose from 14.8 percent in 1920 to 23.5 percent in 1950 and then to 30.5 percent by 1970.[18]

As semi-skilled and medium-skilled workers became central to the process of production—that is, as they became the main type of labor complementary to machines and capital—wages grew across the board, particularly among middle social strata. The American car industry led the way in this regard: its average annual wage rose from $594 in 1904 to $802 in 1914 and exceeded $1,600 by 1924.[19] Similar changes took place across the whole US economy. The average earnings of commerce and industry workers tracked productivity growth throughout the whole period, rising by 69 percent between 1913 and 1937, and more than tripling from 1937 to 1975. The number of working households living under conditions of absolute poverty declined precipitously over the first half of the twentieth century. Buying food and clothing, which had absorbed two thirds of the budget of the average American family just after the Civil War, dropped to about a third of its expenditure in 1940. By the 1960s, life expectancy had almost doubled with respect to that of the middle of the nineteenth century. Average height, a valuable proxy of access to food and good health habits, increased by about four inches in Europe over the span of a century.[20]

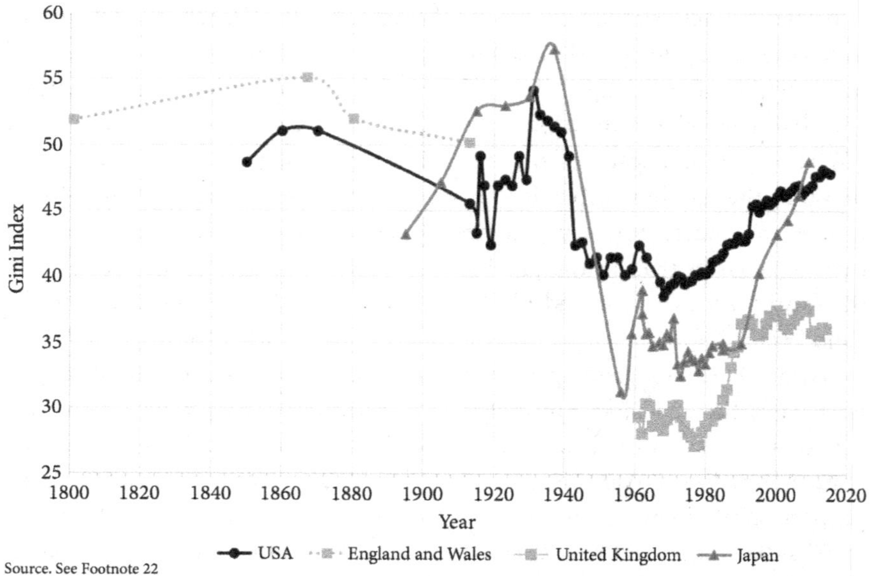

Figure 3.2 Income inequality, 1800–2015 Source: See Footnote 22

The new economic model of production led too to the equalization of both wages and the overall distribution of income in twentieth-century industrial economies.[21] Figure 3.2 shows the evolution of the Gini index over the nineteenth and twentieth centuries for Japan, the United Kingdom, and the United States.[22] During the first stage of the Industrial Revolution, the Gini coefficient was high—at around 50—and rising. In both the United Kingdom, which spearheaded the first industrial revolution, and the United States, which followed England closely, it increased until the last third of the nineteenth century. In Japan, a late industrializer, it rose until World War II. Roughly coinciding with the expansion of the second industrial revolution, inequality declined everywhere throughout the middle decades of the twentieth century. Using other measures to approximate the distribution of income tell a similar story. In England and Wales, the fraction of total income in the hands of the top 10 percent of the population fell from slightly below 50 percent in 1914 to less than 30 percent in the late 1960s. In most advanced countries, it dropped, from different baselines, to around 30 percent by the 1970s.

Higher salaries and a more equal income distribution pacified the politics of the nineteenth century and early twentieth century. As Daniel Bell wrote in 1955, "in the advanced industrial countries, principally the United States, the United Kingdom, and Northwestern Europe, where national income has been rising, where mass expectations of an equitable share in that increase are relatively fulfilled, and where social mobility affects ever greater numbers . . . extremist politics have the least hold."[23]

Starting in the early 1980s, the economy took a new turn. Whereas labor productivity and median earnings had trended together until 1975, they diverged afterwards. US labor productivity continued to grow at a similar rate as in the postwar period, doubling between 1975 and 2016. By contrast, median earnings remained flat throughout the whole period. In Japan and Europe, median salaries performed slightly better, but they still rose much less than the overall economy. While wages for those in the bottom quintile of the earnings distribution dropped in real terms in the United States and the United Kingdom and barely increased in the other advanced economies, earnings grew by almost 50 percent for those holding bachelor degrees, and doubled for individuals with postgraduate education in the United States. Less dramatic but similar wage dynamics took place in the majority of advanced industrial economies. By 2010, the earnings of an individual in the ninetieth percentile of the wage distribution were three to five times greater than the earnings of an individual at the tenth percentile of the same distribution.

As with previous historical shifts in the distribution of income, the changes of the last decades responded to the introduction of new technologies, in this case information technologies (ranging from the personal computer to the internet) that reshaped the labor market. The acceleration of automation—driven by fast microprocessors—made a substantial fraction of qualified blue-collar workers redundant. The number of US factory workers shrunk from a postwar peak of nearly 19.5 million in 1979 to about 12 million in 2014. In Europe, manufacturing jobs fell from over one-fifth of all employment in 1970 to less than one-tenth in the middle of the 2010s. Automation extended to white-collar occupations—replacing an increasing number of the routine tasks that defined those jobs. Whereas routine occupations (i.e., jobs composed of tasks that imply following a well-defined number of procedures), employed almost 45 percent of the working-age population in the United States until the mid-1980s, they employed 31 percent in 2014.[24] By contrast, the complementarity of IT with high-skilled workers raised the proportion of managerial and professional jobs from 28 percent of all civilian employment in 1980 to 39 percent in 2010.[25]

Jointly with a sharp drop in transportation costs, the information and communication revolution globalized trade at a truly worldwide scale after the late 1970s. Globalization then intensified the direct employment effects triggered by the invention of the personal computer. An increasing number of American, European, and Japanese companies—from makers of toys and other consumer goods in the 1970s to electronics companies in the 2000s—unbundled their production operations across the world, moving low-wage jobs to developing countries, in the process eroding the job status and wages of blue-collar industrial workers and the administrative middle class in advanced industrial economies. Recent estimates attribute about one-third of all employment losses in the last few decades to trade and the relocation of production abroad.[26]

Those changes came hand-in-hand with the gradual erosion of the postwar political consensus, initially at the citizen level, in the form of growing voter alienation and lower turnout, and later on at the political elite level too. Despite the social and economic transformations of the last decades, mainstream political forces, from conservatives and Christian democrats to social democratic parties, hardly changed their public discourse and general commitment to globalization and market-led change.[27] Perhaps unsurprisingly, trust in political elites fell to a historical low. Almost 80 percent of Americans thought that politicians cared about their opinions in the late 1950s. Only 20 percent do now. In France, Germany, and the United Kingdom, the proportion is even lower, at around 10–15 percent. In Europe, electoral abstention nearly doubled, encompassing one third of the electorate in the late 2000s. Throughout the postwar era and until 1970, 70 percent of all electors in Western Europe voted for mainstream parties. By 2010, only 45 percent did. Then, following the great recession of 2008, populist parties became an important part of the political landscape. Close to one quarter of European voters are currently casting their ballots for far right and far left parties. In the United States, both the Republican and the Democratic parties house a powerful, often dominant populist faction. Political polarization has risen to levels unseen since at least the 1930s—spurred by Silicon Valley capitalism and reinforced, particularly in the United States, by growing disagreements on cultural and social policy matters.[28]

Still, despite a growing literature on democratic backsliding,[29] there is little evidence of democratic reversals in developed countries.[30] To explain why, we need to consider the stabilization role played by the prosperity generated by capitalism.

Economic Prosperity and Democratic Resilience

The diffusion of industrial capitalism has created extraordinary wealth. In 1820, about 95 percent of the world population earned less than the equivalent of two dollars (in 1990 USD) per day. More than four-fifths had to survive with just one dollar per day. In Western Europe, more than half of the population had a per capita income similar (in real terms) to today's poorest countries in Africa. By contrast, today's average income per person (in real terms) is about ten to fifteen times larger than one century and a half ago in North America, Europe, and Japan, and over 90 percent of the population have an income equal to or higher than the income of an individual in the ninety-fifth percentile of the income distribution back in the nineteenth century. In addition, most of them receive a wide range of publicly provided services, from free schooling to a public health system and pensions, which tend to benefit the poorest strata of society.

Such levels of economic prosperity have raised everyone's incentives to subject themselves to democratic elections, that is, to the possibility of losing power, while accepting the basic rules of a capitalist economy, for at least two reasons.

First, the generation of economic growth through market mechanisms (in absolute terms but also in relative terms, that is, in comparison to non-market economies) has persuaded voters (especially those with lower incomes and therefore with a higher incentive to demand higher wages or to support high tax and spending levels to modify market-based outcomes) to moderate their redistributive demands—precisely in exchange for economic growth. In turn, their moderation or self-restraint, when conveyed in a credible manner, has made it easier for capital owners and high-income individuals to drop their opposition to democracy. We can interpret the European postwar consensus (and even the political deals that undergird the democratization of Latin America in the 1980s and Eastern Europe in the 1990s) as an exercise on political restraint that facilitated the consolidation of democratic capitalism. Although the industrial structure of most European countries in the late 1940s was not that different from the one in the 1920s, a pact (formalized through corporatist institutions in most small countries) between capital and labor pacified Western Europe, in the process contributing partly to unleashing a period of growth that, through some kind of virtuous cycle, reinforced social support for democratic capitalism.[31]

Second, economic growth attenuates the negative effects of democracy among high-income individuals, and therefore their resistance to elections, for the following reason. If the marginal utility of additional income declines,[32] the disutility of losing elections and bearing high taxes falls among high-income individuals (who should be, in principle, the most affected by the decisions of the majority to redistribute) as their per capita income increases. At some point, blocking democracy will generate more disutility than the welfare losses resulting from majority voting.[33]

Checking the Historical Evidence

If our previous discussion is right, an unequal society should hamper the introduction of democracy. Nonetheless, the potential undemocratic effects of economic inequality will be mediated by economic growth. At low and intermediate levels of development, inequality will exacerbate distributive conflicts to the point of making democracy highly unlikely. Social and political elites will

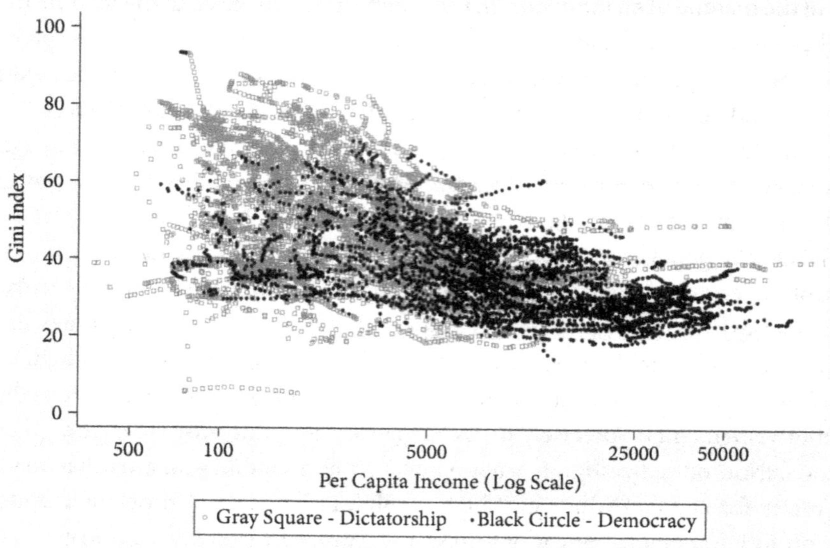

Figure 3.3 Democracy and its correlates—1900–2017

have a strong incentive to protect their economic assets and social status by blocking democracy. As growth takes place, however, the tolerance of all parties toward democracy will increase—by both attenuating the redistributive claims of the least advantaged and minimizing the utility losses of high earners.

Figure 3.3 plots data of per capita income and Gini coefficients across the world from 1900 to 2017. Each point represents the value for a country-year. In addition, Figure 3.3 marks with a gray square those countries that were authoritarian, and with a black circle those that were democratic in each year. The measure of development is a country's real gross domestic product per capita (in 2011 USD) based on the Maddison project database, revision 2020.[34] The Gini coefficients come from Beramendi and coauthors.[35] The political regime classification follows the Boix, Miller, and Rosato criteria, version 3.0 (updated to cover years until 2019).[36]

Figure 3.3 shows that development and inequality are negatively correlated. An increment of $1,000 is associated with a fall of 0.6 points in the Gini index. The correlation is statistically significant. In addition, cross-country variance in the distribution of income declines also with development. Whereas Gini values range from 25 to above 80 percent among poor countries, they fluctuate between 20 and 45 percent in high-income nations.

In line with the previous discussion, democratic regimes are more frequent both among more equal economies (even for relative low levels of per capita income) and developed countries (where authoritarian regimes are exceptional and mainly correspond to oil-exporting economies). Both economic development and economic equality are statistically significant and correlated with the presence of democracy in estimation models, including fixed country and year effects. Moreover, economic development attenuates the negative effect of economic inequality.

Is This Time Different?

Which could be the consequences of an acceleration and intensification of the current process of automation (brought about by artificial intelligence, which I will refer to as AI) for democratic capitalism? Will we go back to the stark incompatibility between democracy and capitalism that prevailed during the nineteenth century? Or, are there ways to reconcile both of them as in the past decades? To explore these questions, I first consider the probable effects of AI on labor and capital, and then reflect on the broader political implications of those changes.

AI and Labor Demand and Supply

The effect of AI on labor can take the form of two main scenarios. In the first one, AI simply intensifies the skilled-biased nature of current technological changes. In a second one, AI perfectly substitutes labor.

Consider the partial-substitution scenario first. In a widely cited paper, Frey and Osborne correlate vulnerability to computerization with the level of skills—extremely high "for low-skill and low-wage jobs in the near future," and much less so for "high-skill and high-wage occupations" (267).[37] With demand for unskilled and semi-skilled labor declining, their wages will fall too. The result should be, in principle, more inequality. Nevertheless, the final effects of AI on wages and income will depend on the behavior of labor supply. If the labor force can be upskilled, there will be a re-matching of jobs and workers (provided enough AI-complementary jobs are available) and relative equality. Otherwise, a fraction of the workforce will remain unemployed or employed but lowly paid. With labor supply not matching labor demand, inequality will persist over time.[38]

Consider now the second scenario. Although machines are far from reproducing the manual and cognitive tasks performed by humans in many tasks, in recent surveys AI experts give a 50 percent chance to the possibility that humans will be technologically redundant between 2040 and the early 2060s.[39] Here, the distributional split will not take place between capitalist and high-skilled individuals on one side and the rest of labor on the other, but rather between capital and labor.

Most discussions about the impact of AI on labor refer to advanced countries. Nonetheless, its consequences are likely to be stronger in emerging economies. Globalization 2.0, which coincided with and in fact was fostered by the informational and computational revolution that began in the 1980s, facilitated the industrialization of a subset of developing countries. Multinational corporations unbundled their production structure to exploit the specific comparative advantage of each country across the world—moving or subcontracting tasks performed by less skilled labor to the developing world. Indeed, the very economic transformations that increased the level of political tension within advanced economies (namely, a process of globalization that has eroded the position of their industrial working class) were arguably responsible for the reduction of political conflict (and perhaps the process of democratization) in newly industrialized countries.

By contrast, an acceleration in the process of technological change may reverse the economic and political gains enjoyed by developing nations so far. If machines replace all low-skilled labor, fully robotized plants will be relocated from "periphery" countries back to the consumer markets of advanced economies—to minimize distribution and transportation costs. Unless newly industrialized economies move up in the production ladder from low-value-added to high-value-added activities, they will be unable to catch up with advanced economies, and may even experience some economic backsliding in absolute terms. With full capital-labor substitution, firms will have an even stronger incentive to relocate their production close to their consumers—probably exacerbating the negative economic shock to emerging economies.

AI and Capital

In principle, automation should benefit capital owners—both for the partial-substitution scenario where particular forms of labor are more complementary to AI than others and for the full-substitution scenario where substituting machines for human work is economically efficient. A growing body of work points to a fall in the labor share of income since the 1980s, particularly in economic sectors with high R&D intensity.[40]

How this may translate into the internal concentration of assets ownership—and therefore on the internal composition of the returns to capital, will depend on two factors: barriers to innovation and information costs. If the barriers to AI innovation and implementation are high, capital should become concentrated in a limited number of owners. AI may lower, however, the costs of producing machines (i.e., of capital investment) directly—to the point of enabling everybody to set up some heavily automatized or robotized shop. Mobile phones have reduced the costs of production and distribution of African farmers. Independent truck drivers employ digital platforms to coordinate more efficiently the transportation and distribution of goods. Social media have facilitated the emergence of a decentralized rental market between tourists and private homeowners, competing directly with hotel chains.

As for the information effects, AI technologies may lead to larger firms by minimizing the costs of both collecting information about (present and future) preferences of buyers/consumers and integrating production chains. In 2023, for example, Google has over 90 percent of the search engine market, Facebook controls almost 70 percent of social networks, and three top firms concentrate almost one-third of all the US e-commerce. On the other hand, AI may push down the costs of monitoring production across tasks, weakening the incentives to integrate all jobs in a single plant or under a single firm, and fostering subcontracting.

AI and Democratic Capitalism

In light of our discussion of the economic consequences of AI, its effects on democracy are likely double sided. By widening the gap between capital owners and labor or, at least, between capital owners and high-skilled individuals on the one hand and the rest of labor on the other, it should affect negatively everyone's incentives to have democracy. However, its positive effect on income growth, via productivity gains and (in advanced economies) a potential reshoring of manufacturing, should reduce the political impact of more inequality.

Consider first AI's potentially negative consequences. Throughout the twentieth century, advanced democracies responded to the political and social tensions generated by industrial capitalism with policies that, while having a redistributive component, benefited businesses too. Public spending on health and education improved the living standards of citizens directly and, perhaps more important, indirectly: it allowed them to take advantage of social mobility opportunities offered by a booming economy. In addition, it generated the kind of well-trained labor force that second-industrial-revolution employers needed to be fully productive. In short, in the world of Detroit capitalism, welfare states were complementary to most or all firms. By contrast, if AI firms only hire a fraction of the labor force, they may resist supporting universal spending and investment programs that are of little use to them. The past complementarity of democratic-base welfare states and capitalism could then give way to more contentious forms of politics, where voters with no access to well-paid AI jobs may push for an intensification of redistributive policies (for example, in the form of a very extensive universal basic income) the winners of automation may resist.

AI may have a second negative effect on democratic governance. It may reinforce the position and resources of its beneficiaries to such an extent that, even if they are an electoral minority, they may have the power and influence to block both democracy and redistribution. The growing concentration of wealth that has taken place in the last few decades does not bode well for the future. During the last decades, campaign contributions in US federal elections have gradually become concentrated among the super-wealthy. The top 0.01 percent of households (in the income distribution) donated between 10 and 15 percent of all campaign contributions until the early 1990s. In 2012, the proportion was 40 percent.[41]

AI should have positive effects on democracy too. First, as discussed earlier in the paper, a richer economy implies having more resources available to minimize the disruptive effects of technological change. Second, given the declining marginal value of additional income among high-income voters, the extra wealth due to AI may make redistributive policies (to compensate any losers) less contentious than in the past.

Which of these effects may prevail is at this point unclear. Still, in developed countries, there are two reasons why the likelihood of a democratic breakdown seems low. On the one hand, a growing economy has historically played a stabilizing role on democratic institutions. On the other hand, well-performing democracies tend to engage in what we may want to call "re-equilibrating" policy dynamics in response to economic and political shocks. In representative regimes where policymakers are accountable to voters, politicians have an incentive to develop policy solutions in response to any new political and economic challenges harming the electorate (or, at least, the decisive voter). In the specific case of technological change, those policy responses can range from deploying new programs to help workers adapt to technological change (through, for example, new educational investments) to passing new regulations blocking technological innovation. If these policy interventions are successful, making the labor force complementary to ITs and AI and reducing any initial income disparities due to those technological changes, democracy should remain in place.

By contrast, the introduction of AI may prove more disruptive in emerging economies. First, if it results in some economic de-growth, the incentives to combine democracy and capitalism will decrease. Second, because authoritarian regimes are more common in the developing world, the process of policy re-equilibration through which democratic procedures foster, via elections, the adoption of measures to sustain a pro-democracy majority, will be less likely to take place.

Concluding Remarks: Mapping Policy Interventions

We know little about the future. On the one hand, an increasing number of experts forecast technological developments whose consequences prefigure a much more contentious relationship between democracy and capitalism than the one that existed during the golden age of democratic capitalism. On the other hand, even if what we experience today are the pains associated with the birth of a new political and economic world, we do not know much about the timing, pace, or final consequences of this technological transformation. The future may be waiting for us ten or perhaps one hundred years from now. The rate of transformation may be fast and unwieldy, or slow enough to allow us to adjust in a leisurely way. Robotization may be universal in its reach or limited to a few sectors. Still, it seems advisable to suggest three main types of interventions to respond to automation (to be modulated as a function of the extent of change).

First, reinforcing educational investments (including vocational training) should facilitate the transition of the workforce from routine jobs, which are at the highest risk of automation, to non-routine occupations or, at least, jobs that are complementary to AI tasks. If the process of capital-labor substitution speeds up to the point of generating some persistent unemployment, policymakers may consider introducing a "universal basic capital" (UBC), that is, granting each person some fixed capital at birth. To incentivize prudential behavior, its recipients would have free disposition only over its returns (and only after becoming legally adult). That solution would combine the supporting component of a universal basic income (UBI), with an individual incentive to manage it actively; that is, to apply some effort instead of consuming an income flow (like the one coming from an UBI) passively. A tax on robots could fund the UBC.

Second, policymakers should strengthen a regulatory and institutional system that pre-empts the formation of a closed elite. In the economic sphere, this calls for an active antitrust policy to maintain competitive markets. In the political sphere, it requires several reforms, such as limiting campaign donations by corporations, distributing electoral funds along the lines of the Ackerman-Ayres proposal,[42] disclosing the (ownership and marketing) relations between media and large firms, and so on.

Third, states should consider a generous system of migration between the North and the South. If AI harms less developed economies (through the process of automation and reshoring) more than advanced economies, and given how difficult it seems to reform political and legal institutions in the South, migration may become the main way for people in the South to escape poverty or, in other words, the only redistributive tool in our hands to equalize life chances across the world. Given the political backlash that such an open-border system may create, migration should be probably gradual. Still, because of the current demographic trends in advanced economies (pointing to negative natural population growth in the near future), immigration from the South seems advisable from an economic point of view—including the goal of sustaining welfare states.

Notes

1. Thomas Macaulay, "Speech before the House of Commons" (*Hansard Parliamentary Debates*, 3d series, 1842) vol. 63, cols. 45–49.
2. Quoted in Alan Kahan, *Liberalism in Nineteenth Century Europe: The Political Culture of Limited Suffrage* (New York: Palgrave Macmillan), 79.
3. Karl Marx, *The Class Struggles in France, 1848 to 1850* (New York: International Publishers, 1934), 69–70.
4. Daniel Bell, *The End of Ideology*, 2nd ed. (Cambridge, MA: Harvard University Press, 1988), 402–3.
5. John. Stuart Mill, "Recent Writers on Reform" (The Collected Works of John Stuart Mill, 33 vols, edited by John M. Robson (Toronto, 1963–1991), XIX, 364) Quoted in William Selinger and Greg Conti, "Reappraising Walter Bagehot's Liberalism: Discussion, Public Opinion, and the Meaning of Parliamentary Government," *History of European Ideas* 41, no. 2 (2015): 291. This assumption about the presence of a fundamental friction between capitalism and democracy is not accepted universally, either because democracy guarantees the property rights that sustain a market economy, or because the liberal values that animate democracy are essential to the operation of capitalism. See, for example, Milton Friedman, *Capitalism and Freedom* (Chicago: The University of Chicago Press, 1962) and Tabarrok, this volume. The problem with this position is that it cannot account for those historical periods in which capitalism and democracy have been at odds with each other.
6. For an extended discussion, both theoretical and historical, about the relationship between capitalism and democracy, see Carles Boix, *Democratic Capitalism at the Crossroads* (Princeton: Princeton University Press, 2019).
7. Karl Polanyi, *The Great Transformation: The Political and Economic Origins of Our Time* (New York: Farrar & Rinehart, 1944).
8. See Eric Hobsbawn, *Industry and Empire: An Economic History of Britain since 1750* (London: Weidenfeld and Nicolson, 1968); Kevin H. O'Rourke and Jeffrey G. Williamson, *Globalization and History: The Evolution of a Nineteenth-Century Atlantic Economy* (Cambridge, MA: MIT Press, 2001); and Richard Baldwin, *The Great Convergence: Information Technology and the New Globalization* (Cambridge, MA: Belknap Press, 2016).
9. The data on investment by state-owned businesses comes from Robert P Short, "The Role of Public Enterprises: An International Statistical Comparison," in *Public Enterprise in Mixed Economies: Some Macroeconomic Aspects*, ed. Robert H. Floyd, Clive S. Gray, and Robert P. Short (Washington, D.C.: International Monetary Fund, 1984), Table 1, pages 116–122.
10. The data covers around 115 for an extended series, before yearly measurement started in 1970. Starting in 1970, the data contains 86 in 1970 and then increases gradually to cover 168 in 2020. The data is available from the Fraser Institute in https://efotw.org/sites/all/modules/custom/ftw_maps_pages/files/efotw-2024-master-index-data-for-researchers-iso.xlsx
11. Joel Mokyr, ed., *The British Industrial Revolution: An Economic Perspective* (New York: Routledge, 2009).
12. Andrew Ure, *The Philosophy of Manufactures; or, an Exposition of the Scientific, Moral, and Commercial Economy of the Factory System of Great Britain, with Illustrations* (London: Charles Knight, 1835), 35 and 20.
13. Charles H. Feinstein, "Pessimism Perpetuated: Real Wages and the Standard of Living in Britain during and after the Industrial Revolution," *Journal of Economic History* 58, no. 3 (1998): 625–58.

14. Simon Szreter and Graham Mooney, "Urbanization, Mortality, and the Standard of Living Debate: New Estimates of the Expectation of Life at Birth in Nineteenth-Century British Cities," *Economic History Review* 51, no. 1 (1998): 84–112.
15. Roderick Floud, Kenneth Wachter, and Annabel Gregory, *Height, Health and History: Nutritional Status in the United Kingdom, 1750–1980* (New York: Cambridge University Press, 1990); and John Komlos, "Shrinking in a Growing Economy?: The Mystery of Physical Stature during the Industrial Revolution," *Journal of Economic History* 58, no. 3 (1998): 779–802.
16. Harry Jerome, *Mechanization in Industry* (New York: NBER, 1934), 63.
17. Goldin, Claudia, and Lawrence F. Katz. "The origins of technology-skill complementarity." *The Quarterly journal of economics* 113, no. 3 (1998): 693–732.
18. Lawrence F. Katz and Robert A. Margo, "Technical Change and the Relative Demand for Skilled Labor: The United States in Historical Perspective," in *Human Capital in History: The American Record*, ed. Leah Platt Boustan, Carola Frydman, and Robert A. Margo (Chicago: University of Chicago Press, 2014), 15–57.
19. David Nye, *America's Assembly Line* (Cambridge, MA: MIT Press, 2000), 53.
20. Robert J. Gordon. *The Rise and Fall of American Growth: The US Standard of Living since the Civil War* (Princeton, NJ: Princeton University Press, 2016).
21. As I show in Boix, *Democratic Capitalism at the Crossroads*, 69–81, that process of equalization cannot be explained by either war or unionization, generally hailed as the big equalizers of the twentieth century by the existing literature. See Kenneth F. Scheve and David Stasavage, "Institutions, Partisanship, and Inequality in the Long Run," *World Politics* 61, no 2 (2009): 215–53; and, Thomas Piketty, *Capital in the Twenty-First Century* (Cambridge, MA: Belknap, 2014).
22. Sources for Figure 3.2. For the US data: for the nineteenth century, Peter H. Lindert and Jeffrey G. Williamson, "Unequal Gains: American Growth and Inequality since 1700," *Juncture* 22, no. 4 (2016): 276–83; for 1913–63, Robert D. Plotnick, Eugene Smolensky, Eirik Evenhouse, and Siobhan Reilly, "The Twentieth Century Record of Inequality and Poverty in the United States," University of Wisconsin-Madison, Institute for Research on Poverty, Discussion paper no. 1166-98 (1998): Figure 3.2; after 1963, Branko Milanovic, *Global Inequality: A New Approach for the Age of Globalization* (Cambridge, MA: Harvard University Press, 2016). Sources for the United Kingdom: up to 1913, Lindert and Williamson, "Unequal Gains: American Growth and Inequality since 1700"; after 1960, Milanovic, *Global Inequality: A New Approach for the Age of Globalization.* Sources for Japan: before World War II, Ryoshin Minami, "Income Distribution of Japan: Historical Perspective and Its Implications," *Japan Labor Review* 5, no. 4 (2008): 5–20; after World War II, UNU-WIDER, 'World Income Inequality Database (WIID3c)', September 2015, /project/wiid-world-income-inequality-database'., 2015.
23. Bell, *The End of Ideology*, 31.
24. Guido M. Cortes, Nir Jaimovisch, and Henry E. Siu, "Disappearing Routine Jobs: Who, How, and Why?," *Journal of Monetary Economics* 91 (November 2017): 69–87.
25. Katz and Margo, "Technical Change and the Relative Demand for Skilled Labor."
26. In addition to technological change and globalization, economic deregulation may have also contributed to the transformation of labor markets and the rise of income inequality. Income distribution widened the most in highly deregulated market economies (cf. Figure 3.2). In those European countries where earnings inequality remained unchanged, the cost was, however, tepid private employment growth in net terms.
27. Boix, *Democratic Capitalism at the Crossroads*; and Carles Boix, "Electoral Realignments Across the Atlantic," in *Who Gets What? The New Politics of Insecurity*, eds. Frances Rosenbluth and Margaret Weir (New York: Cambridge University Press, 2020), ch. 9, 213–36.
28. Notice that part of the research community does not link the political malaise of the last decades to technological and economic change. For a line of research, the former comes from a spreading "cultural discomfort" generated by a set of factors that range from immigration to the dissolution of communitarian and moral ties produced by social media (and not directly related to any changes in the production process)—see Yotam Margalit, Shir Raviv, and Omer Solodoch, "The Cultural Origins of Populism," *The Journal of Politics* (2024)

https://doi.org/10.1086/732985. For a different line of argument, it derives from trade competition affecting uncompetitive economic factors or sectors in North America and Europe—see Ron Rogowski, *Commerce and Coalitions* (Princeton: Princeton University Press, 1989). Globalization can be traced back, however, to the fall in information and transportation costs due to the technological innovations of the last decades.

29. Nancy Bermeo, "On democratic backsliding," *Journal of Democracy* 27, no 1 (2016): 5–19. Steven Levitsky and Daniel Ziblatt, *How Democracies Die* (New York: Crown, 2019).
30. Larry M. Bartels, *Democracy Erodes from the Top: Leaders, Citizens, and the Challenge of Populism in Europe* (Princeton: Princeton University Press, 2023). Anne Meng and Andrew T. Little, "Measuring Democratic Backsliding," *PS: Political Science & Politics* 57, no. 2 (2023): 1–13. Daniel Treisman, "How Great Is the Current Danger to Democracy? Assessing the Risk with Historical Data," *Comparative Political Studies* 56, no. 12 (2023): 1924–52.
31. For a formal treatment of the conditions under which political self-restraint increases the chances of democratic capitalism, see Adam Przeworski and Michael Wallerstein, "Democratic Capitalism at the Crossroads," in *Capitalism and Social Democracy*, ed. Adam Przeworski (Cambridge: Cambridge University Press, 1986), 205–17; and Carles Boix, *Democracy and Redistribution* (New York: Cambridge University Press, 2003), 131–39.
32. R. Layard, G. Mayraz, and S. Nickell, "The marginal utility of income," *Journal of Public Economics* 92, no. 8–9 (2008): 1846–57.
33. See Pablo Beramendi, Carles Boix, and Daniel Stegmueller, "Resilient democracies," *Journal of Politics* (2025, forthcoming), for a formal discussion and empirical testing of this mechanism.
34. Jutta Bolt and Jan Luiten van Zanden, "The Maddison Project: Collaborative Research on Historical National Accounts," Maddison Project Database, version 2013, *Economic History Review* 67, no. 3 (2014): 627–51.
35. Beramendi et al., "Resilient Democracies." The data used in the construction of our total inequality measure are country time-series on (i) rural inequality as defined by Ben W. Ansell and D. J. Samuels, *Inequality and Democratization* (Cambridge: Cambridge University Press, 2014); (ii) disposable household income inequality from the SWIID database in Frederick Solt, "The Standardized World Income Inequality Database," *Social Science Quarterly* 97, no. 5 (2016): 1267–81; and (iii) the share of the labor force employed in agriculture from A. M. Wingender, "Structural Transformation in the 20th Century: A New Database on Agricultural Employment around the World," Discussion Paper No. 14-28 (Department of Economics, University of Copenhagen, 2014). Missing observations time-series observations are extrapolated backwardly using a flexible semiparametric model (with model terms tailored to each specific country).
36. Carles Boix, Michael Miller, and Sebastian Rosato, "A Complete Data Set of Political Regimes, 1800–2007," *Comparative Political Studies* 46, no 12 (2013): 1523–54.
37. Carl Benedikt Frey and Michael A. Osborne, "The Future of Employment: How Susceptible Are Jobs to Computerisation?," *Technological Forecasting and Social Change* 114 (January 2017): 254–80. According to the World Development Report of 2016, two-thirds of jobs in developing countries and between 50 and 60 percent in Europe and the United States could be automated over the coming decades (World Bank Group. *World development report 2016: Digital dividends.* World Bank Publications, 2016. Page 126). Employing different criteria may lead, however, to sharply different results—Melanie Arntz, Terry Gregory, and Ulrich Zierahn, "The Risk of Automation for Jobs in OECD Countries: A Comparative Analysis," *OECD Social, Employment and Migration* Working Papers, no. 189 (Paris: OECD, 2016), estimate that only 9 percent of jobs in OECD countries are highly automatable.
38. As discussed in Boix, *Democratic Capitalism at the Crossroads*, consider a world where the final skills of any person are a function of two factors: the individual's natural talents, and some know-how acquired through education. Natural talents include the genetic endowment at birth and the intelligence nurtured by a particular family environment. The educational know-how is, instead, the result of an investment made through formal institutions. Assume that the distribution of natural talents among the population is unequal, and that formal education reduces the deficiencies in the initial endowment of talents, and therefore the "natural" inequalities in the population imperfectly. Because the job qualifications needed during the first and second industrial capitalisms (prevalent in the nineteenth and twentieth centuries)

were not demanding (most jobs required low to medium skills), the remedial effect of education (even when the investment on human capital was low to moderate) was successful. If the skills needed for future jobs are very high, the initial distribution of natural talents may be more relevant in determining final wages and incomes.

39. Anton Korinek and Megan Juelfs, "Preparing for the (Non-existent?) Future of Work," *National Bureau of Economic Research* Working Paper 30172 (2022). For a much more skeptical position, see Stuart Armstrong and Kaj Sotala, *How We're Predicting AI—Or Failing To* (Oxford: Future of Humanity Institute, Oxford University, 2012), who identified up to 95 such forecasts published between 1950 and 2012 and show that the year they predict ranges from 1970 to 2107, with most of those studies dating the advent of AI between 15 and 20 years from the time they were published.
40. Loukas Karabarbounis and Brent Neiman, "The Global Decline of the Labor Share," *Quarterly Journal of Economics* 129, no 1 (2014): 61–103; Gene M. Grossman and Ezra Oberfield, "The Elusive Explanation for the Declining Labor Share," *Annual Review of Economics* 14 (2022): 93–124; Dominique Guellec and Carolina Paunov, "Digital Innovation and the Distribution of Income," Working Paper 23987 (National Bureau of Economic Research, 2017).
41. Adam Bonica, Nolan McCarty, Keith T. Poole, and Howard Rosenthal, "Why Hasn't Democracy Slowed Rising Inequality?," *Journal of Economic Perspectives* 27, no 3 (2013): 103–23.
42. See Bruce Ackerman and Ian Ayres, *Voting with Dollars: A New Paradigm for Campaign Finance* (New Haven, CT: Yale University Press, 2018). The Ackerman and Ayres' system consists in giving to each citizen a fixed number of dollars to be spent in the electoral campaign in the way (that is, on the candidate) everyone prefers. That proposal is complemented with the decision to establish a blind trust in which all private donations are put—to be transferred to the candidate or parties chosen by the donor. As with the secret ballot, the secrecy of donations should reduce the lobbying by well-identified donors.

SECTION II

ENVIRONMENTAL DEGRADATION

Democratic Capitalism, Industrial Policy, and the Challenge of Climate Change

MICHAEL JAMES LENOX

Winston Churchill famously quipped that "It has been said that democracy is the worst form of government except all the others that have been tried."[1] His point is obvious: despite all its flaws and limitations, democracy has proven itself best to advance the human condition when compared to the alternatives. One could easily extend Churchill's logic to capitalism. Over the course of the past century, despite numerous concerns about its pathologies and excesses, capitalism has generated vast improvements in human welfare and well-being. And it is only logical to extend this reasoning to the union of democracy and capitalism. Together, democratic capitalism has demonstrated repeatedly, in practice, its superiority to other political economic systems.

However, are all prepared to declare this a universal truth? The superiority of democratic capitalism has been contested from its genesis. At least since the time of Marx, scholars have suggested that its constituent parts, democracy and capitalism, are incompatible—often arguing that the latter will undermine the former.[2] More recently, writers have called into question whether democratic capitalism is up to the task of addressing our most pressing challenges, such as climate change.[3] Our self-interested capitalistic markets lack the incentives to provide solutions and our politically divided democratic institutions lack the will to require markets to do so. Perhaps, an enlightened authoritarianism is needed to bring about the necessary change, either through the reining-in and shaping of market forces or from outright ownership and direction of the means of production.

In this essay, I will explore the pressing threat of climate change, and advance the argument that democratic capitalist nations are best positioned to deliver the changes necessary to avert or, at the very least, moderate a crisis. This includes the capacity for such nations to lead in the creation and scaling of technological innovations necessary to address climate change, as well as the potential to motivate action and adoption among more authoritarian and socialist regimes. While by no means a panacea, democratic capitalism gives us the best path forward to tackling our climate crisis when compared to the alternatives.

The Breadth of Our Challenge

Climate change is a decidedly wicked problem.[4] Since the dawn of the industrial revolution, we have seen a massive increase in the concentration of greenhouse gases in the atmosphere largely due to the burning of fossil fuels such as oil, natural gas, and coal. The increase in greenhouse gases, largely carbon dioxide but also potent chemicals such as methane and nitrox oxide, have already increased global average temperatures by approximately 1 degree Celsius in the past century.[5] If current growth patterns in emissions continue, we will likely be looking at global warming greater than 4 degrees Celsius by the end of this century.[6]

While to some that may not seem like much, the implications are concerning if not outright frightening. Rising sea levels, as ice on glaciated land melts in Greenland and Antarctica, may swamp major global cities and population centers. Increases in droughts and heatwaves making some regions barely inhabitable during parts of the year. Extreme weather events such as major hurricanes, tornados, and floods becoming routine, wreaking havoc on communities in their paths. Climate refugees fleeing their homelands, crossing borders, and destabilizing governments.

While adaptation to a new climate-altered world will assuredly be necessary—such adaptation is already occurring—the need for mitigating greenhouse gas emissions remains paramount. The global community came together to establish the Paris Accords in 2015 to set a target of reducing greenhouse gas emissions such that global warming would not exceed 1.5 degrees Celsius.[7] Given cumulative emissions to date, we will need to reduce annual global greenhouse gas emissions to net-zero by 2050 if not sooner. With every year that emissions increase rather than decrease that date gets closer and closer. Some scientists believe we may have already passed the opportunity to arrest warming to less than 1.5 degrees Celsius, and the deadline for limiting warming to 2 degrees Celsius is fast approaching.[8]

Fortunately, there is an emerging vision for what needs to happen to be able to achieve net-zero emissions by 2050, if not sooner. At the heart of this vision is electrifying as many processes as possible that currently use fossil fuels and then "decarbonizing" the production of electricity using renewables.[9] Five sectors account for virtually all anthropocentric greenhouse gas emissions around the world: transportation, buildings, industrials, energy, and agricultural. Let's consider each in turn.

Transportation—planes, trains, ships, and automobiles—makes up approximately 15 percent of global emissions with automobiles representing by far the largest share of these emissions.[10] For automobiles, the emerging solution centers around electrification—most likely battery-powered electric vehicles (BPEVs) though there continues to be interest in alternatives, such as hydrogen fuel cells. For planes and ships, electrification may provide a partial solution though is limited in some applications like long-haul flights. Hydrogen and sustainable aviation fuel (SAF) are some of the options being explored.

Electrification is likely the best approach for buildings as well. The built environment such as commercial and residential real estate contributed roughly 6 percent of global emissions directly from the burning of fossil fuels for heating and cooking.[11] Fortunately, there are market-viable alternatives such as electric stoves and heat pumps that can decarbonize the sector. The challenge is two-fold: (1) improving the economics of these electrified alternatives so they are desirable in all regions such as the cold Northeast United States, and (2) motivating a massive retrofit of existing buildings with these technologies.

Industrials includes the vast array of manufacturing operations in the world and constitutes a fifth of global greenhouse gas emissions. In many instances, processes currently using fossil fuels can be electrified similar to transportation and buildings. However, three critical industries are particularly hard to decarbonize: steel, cement, and petrochemicals. All three are vital backbones of our industrialized world. They are not easily substituted, and they make up a significant amount of the emissions from industrials more broadly (greater than 60 percent).[12] Each will likely require innovative new approaches to decarbonize.

Of course, electrification is only greenhouse gas reducing if we decarbonize the production of electricity. Energy production represents about a quarter of all global emissions largely from the burning of coal and natural gas to produce electricity. The solution here centers largely around renewables, specifically solar and wind. Fortunately, the cost of solar and wind have come down dramatically in the past decade and, as a result, have become an important and growing part of our electricity generation capacity. However, many challenges remain—first and foremost, dealing with the intermittent nature of these technologies. A fully decarbonized electric grid will require massive storage capacity as well as new transmission lines, and what is referred to as smart grid technology to handle a highly decentralized network of generation sources.

Last, but certainly not least, is the agriculture and land-use sector. Surprisingly to many, this sector makes up nearly 25 percent of global greenhouse gas emissions largely from (1) the raising of live-stock, especially beef, which produces methane, and (2) the use of nitrogen-based fertilizers that release nitrox oxide.[13] There are many technological solutions being pursued from precision agricultural to vertical farming to lab-grown meat, but these are all a long way from providing truly scalable solutions. Fortunately, agricultural and land use also provides opportunities for creating carbon sinks—such as growing trees or restoring wetlands—that may help offset emissions.

Overall, what is clear is that we need massive technology and market transitions from fossil fuel-based approaches to so-called clean technologies that eliminate greenhouse gas emissions. We need to convert our automobile fleets from gasoline to EVs. We need to convert our electricity generation from coal and natural gas to renewables and battery storage. We need to convert our gas-powered water heaters and stoves to electric. We need to innovate new carbon-free technologies and approaches for producing steel and cement and growing the food needed to feed a growing world. And we need to see such transitions across the globe in virtually every nation and marketplace. Climate change is the ultimate commons problem. Efforts by one country to reduce emissions does nothing if other nations are increasing their emissions by similar amounts.

The Role of the Market

It is obvious that such a massive transition of the global economy will require the active involvement and participation by market players. Capitalist markets are particularly well suited for driving technology change. Joseph Schumpeter keenly observed that the success of market players in achieving and, often locking-in, favorable market positions creates the incentives for entrepreneurs, broadly defined, to seek new technologies that disrupt and replace the status quo—allowing them to forge new favorable market positions for themselves.[14] In the words of Schumpeter, capitalistic markets fuel the "gales of creative destruction."[15]

Studies of industry dynamics confirm Schumpeter's insight.[16] Early in the lifecycle of a new technology, intrepid entrepreneurs—new ventures and established firms alike—experiment with the technology, perhaps investing R&D dollars to advance its performance both technically and economically. While the returns on these investments may seem limited at first, for the technology to be disruptive, there will come a point where we see increasing returns to development and with it, exponential growth in adoption.

Underlying these dynamics are learning curves—paths of improvement that come from experimentation and experience.[17] We see learning curves everywhere. Over the past decade, we have seen a massive decrease in the cost of lithium-ion batteries, as the underlying chemistry of batteries improves and production becomes more efficient with experience (not to mention the gains from simple economies of scale). We have some similar trajectories for solar photovoltaic cells and wind turbines. Technologies that were once too inefficient and costly to see significant adoption, have moved down the learning curve, and are seeing exponential growth in adoption.

The prevalence of learning curves fuels underlying competitive dynamics that ultimately drive technology transitions. As the new technology improves, a competitive race ensues where economic actors enter the market in an attempt to capture valuable competitive positions in this new emerging market. This often leads to a crowded marketplace and a competitive shakeout where many entrants fail and exit the market, leaving a handful of market players left to compete.[18] Depending on the industry structure, these survivors may be able to secure competitive advantages that allow them to realize sustainable economic rents.

The possibility of securing these entrepreneurial, or Schumpeterian, rents are central to motivating economic actors to make the risky investments of capital necessary to innovate, experiment, and to move down the learning curve. The persistence of these rents may be the result of securing intellectual property rights such as patents, capturing economies of scale as a first-mover, or developing unique capabilities that are hard for competitors to imitate (among many other sources). Eventually these rents may dissipate in the face of competition. Just as likely, however, is that they disappear only when confronted with a new technology that once again fuels the gales of creative destruction.

This feature of innovation and competitive renewal is one of the reasons market economies typically outperform socialistic, planned economies. Planners have limited knowledge about which technology trajectories will ultimately prove successful. Investing in a limited number of pathways does not guarantee that any will prove successful. Capitalistic economies provide the incentives for massive experimentation. Within an industry, dozens, if not hundreds, of innovators may pursue new technologies to disrupt the status quo. Each one likely pursuing a slightly, or some cases radically, different approach to new technology. Each one exploring a different branch of the technology trajectory, if you will.

The vast majority of these experiments will fail. In the case of entrepreneurial ventures, roughly 90 percent go out of business.[19] However, the possibility exists that one will move down the learning curve and develop a new technology that disrupts the existing status quo. This possibility gives capitalistic economies a significant advantage over planned economies—the freedom of capital to pursue innovative and disruptive ends. Venture capitalists know this intuitively, typically expecting positive returns to be generated by a small number of investments in their portfolio. They seek "home runs" that provide 10x returns to help offset the losses generated from most of their investments.

While capitalistic markets create critical incentives to innovate, there is a less well developed understanding of the direction in which this innovative activity will proceed. History is littered with promising technologies that never achieved market viability, at least not yet. Nuclear fusion holds great promise as a cure-all for our energy needs, yet despite progress in the underlying technology it has not proven viable at a commercial scale. Hydrogen fuel cells have been experimented on for over half a century, and yet have found only limited and niche adoption. It can be a fool's errand to try to correctly predict the direction of innovation.

Markets evolve, but the direction of that evolution is not exogenously delivered from on high. What drives progress down a particular technology trajectory may be influenced by a host of idiosyncratic forces in the larger social, economic, and political environment. Take the earliest days of the automobile. There were several competing drivetrains being experimented with, from the Stanley Steamer (a steam-driven vehicle) to electric vehicles to internal combustion engines powered by kerosine and, of course, gasoline. Historians suggest that it is not clear that the gasoline-powered internal combustion engine (ICE) won out due to inherent technological superiority.[20] Rather a set of idiosyncratic events, including policy choices, drove experimentation such that the gas ICE moved faster down its learning curve than its rivals. Only a hundred years later did we begin to significantly experiment again with electric vehicles and discover that its learning curve may in fact be more attractive than that of the gas ICE.

This inherent uncertainty in learning curves places significant importance on the role of attention. In other words, which technological trajectories attract the attention of would-be innovators? In a world of arguably infinite innovative possibilities, why are certain technologies experimented on when others are not? For investors and innovators alike, they face a world of Knightian uncertainty where well-defined probability distributions on the future attractiveness of one technology versus another cannot be formed. They often don't know what they don't know.

One particularly interesting stream of research finds that market failures can serve as way to focus attention.[21] One could say that the history of innovation is marked by attempts to address the pathologies of the past. The automobile was hailed by some as an environmental good as it addressed a salient environment issue of the time—manure from horse-drawn carriages.[22] In major cities, like New York, the collection and disposal of manure created a major human health risk and a huge logistical challenge. The "horse-less carriage" was an environmental savior to the manure problem.

In this way, when a new technology creates harm that is not priced in the market, that is, a negative externality, this attracts the attention of would-be innovators who begin experimenting with new technologies that both address the externality and provide a path to becoming market viable. Market viability in these cases may be driven by a combination of competing with the dominant technology on the current dimensions of merit (e.g., better quality, lower cost) and by capturing a greater willingness to pay by some consumers for the public-good nature of the new technology (e.g., paying a price premium for a "green" product).

Such a logic seems to have played an important role in the growing market of green products and services that help reduce greenhouse gas emissions. From electrical vehicles to renewable energy, the desire to address climate change is frequently cited by innovators for turning their attention toward these technologies. Elon Musk has been very explicit about this in his leadership of Tesla, recently releasing a new master plan to achieve worldwide energy sustainability, stating, "There is a clear path to a fully sustainable Earth—with abundance."[23]

Interestingly, concerns about social and environmental harms caused by the production of otherwise green technologies are motivating further innovation. For example, the use of cobalt in the production of lithium-ion batteries has raised concerns due to the social and environmental costs of mining cobalt in Africa.[24] As a result, there are concerted efforts to "invent-out" cobalt from the battery architecture while preserving, if not improving, the performance and cost profile of lithium-ion batteries.

Of course, one should not assume that the mere presence of negative externalities is sufficient to motivate market-viable innovations that address those concerns. Markets for innovation can be plagued by several forms of market failure. Early investments in basic research and development are often characterized by significant knowledge spillovers that reduce private incentives to invest. These investments often resemble public goods that are non-rivalrous and non-excludable. Even when patents may be secured, the lack of enforceability and the time path to market diffusion, when longer than the patent life, may undermine investment.

Even in the presence of strong private incentives, the inherent uncertainty in investing in novel disruptive technologies may lead to lock-in to less promising paths. Consider the classic two-armed bandit problem, where a gambler must decide between two "bandit" slot-machines of unequal payouts.[25] With no prior information, the gambler will begin to experiment with the two machines. Initial random variance—a winning streak—may lead the gambler to falsely assume one machine has a higher payout than the other. This in turn leads to lock-in, playing the wrongly presumed better-paying machine and failing to experiment with the truly superior machine.

This inherent uncertainty means that there is no guarantee that the market, left free to its own devices, will generate innovative solutions to existing negative externalities. There is no way to know a prior if market-viable alternatives even exist—technologies that can outcompete the current dominant technology on the current dimensions of merit such as quality and cost while simultaneously addressing the externality. Additional incentives to experiment—such as a price-premium for green goods—may not be sufficient to overcome these risks of investment. Ultimately, the ability to capture entrepreneurial rents from a market-viable alternative, if it did exist, is not guaranteed as it may be subject to knowledge spillovers and other competitive pressures that undermine the private incentives to invest.

The Role of the Nation-State

All of this raises a fundamental question. If the market left to its own devices is unlikely to innovate the solutions necessary to address climate change, what role should the state play in driving the direction of innovative activity toward publicly desired ends?

Since the rise of neoliberalism in the latter half of the twentieth century, it has been generally agreed that the state choosing winners and losers in the marketplace for technology is a dangerous proposition. In the same way that the entrepreneur faces a myriad of uncertain—in the Knightian sense—paths before them, how can the state effectively choose? Even worse, how do you avoid the incentives for members of the political class to shape innovation policy to their own private gains, perhaps lavishing investment on their districts or favoring market actors who fund their elections?

As an alternative, perhaps the state can provide "guardrails" to innovation—to encourage investment down certain desired paths and discourage progress down non-desired paths. While not designating specific technologies, the state could guide innovation broadly, creating incentives for investing in innovation in a general direction, perhaps investing in public goods that lowers the barriers to adoption of new clean technologies. Could the state be a catalyst for innovations that address climate change?

Arguably, such a logic is at play when economists and policymakers advocate for putting a price on carbon. Either through a carbon tax or through a cap-and-trade scheme, those who emit greenhouse gases could be charged for the amount they emit. Pricing the externality directly will raise the cost of pollution and cause producers to seek alternatives. In this way, pricing carbon creates broad incentives to invent alternatives that avoid the costs of emitting greenhouse gases in the first place.

In a static market, this arguably introduces an inefficiency into the marketplace—a deadweight loss—that is accepted to address the negative externality and enhance overall welfare, but an inefficiency nonetheless. Given that climate change is a global commons problem, it is not clear why one state would accept the negative market impacts of a price intervention in the absence of action by all other states, since the welfare benefits are only realized with full global adoption. Hence, we often see arguments that addressing climate change is simply too costly. Carbon pricing will increase the costs of production, raising consumer prices, and creating unacceptable economic harm.

In a dynamic market, however, the outlook is brighter. Any inefficiency created in the current market by a carbon price may be overcome by pushing the technology-possibility frontier out through new innovations. Rather than raise the cost of production of say, coal-fired power plants, we encourage investment in innovations such as solar PVCs that simultaneously eliminate emissions while lowering the cost of production—potentially lower than coal in the absence of a carbon price. While some deride this as an impossible "free-lunch," history has proven repeatedly that such market-driven innovations are possible.

This possibility has transformed the prospective of the state from one where they are bearing a cost for the greater good of humanity to one where they are investing in the technologies and industries of the future. Investments in green technology are justified because they will drive economic growth and job creation and make domestic products and services more globally competitive. In the global marketplace, such nationalistic claims tend to resonate with elected officials across the political spectrum.

Yet not all state interventions are viewed equally. In the United States, there is political aversion to anything that can be labeled a "tax." Despite repeated attempts, the US Congress has failed to pass a national carbon tax. Alternatives such as a cap-and-trade scheme, despite being pitched as "market-based," have also failed to gain traction. The prospects remain dim in the current political environment. While the European Union has made progress on pricing carbon, they remain an outlier on the global stage where few countries have acted.

Perhaps as a result, national governments have been experimenting with other interventions, broadly characterized as industrial policy. In the United States, the Biden Administration successfully passed the Inflation Reduction Act (IRA) which, despite its name, is the most ambitious climate legislation passed in the United States to date. The IRA uses a mix of carrots and sticks to encourage investments in electrical vehicles, batteries, renewables, and other green technologies. Items include funding for basic research, subsidies for purchases of EVs and renewables, and investment in a national charging infrastructure and in building-out of smart-grid electrical infrastructure.

The IRA highlights several ways that the state can help solve various market failures for innovation. They can help address the public good nature of early-stage R&D by funding national labs and university research. They can solve the knowledge spillover problem by giving limited monopoly rights over intellectual property. They can address the disincentives to experiment on highly speculative technology by guaranteeing price premiums through purchase subsidies and tax breaks. They can address the need for innovation and investment in complementary goods such as charging infrastructure and smart electric grids.

The IRA also includes several provisions that are blatantly nationalist, or at least regionalist, and seek to ensure that large parts of the supply chain for green technologies are produced in the United States, or by our close allies. These are largely in reaction to China's efforts at dominating the green technology market through their own industrial policy interventions. China released their 14th five-year plan (FYP) on renewable energy development in 2021 providing a comprehensive blueprint with specific goals and investments.[26] China is quite explicit about its intentions to dominate the global market for clean technologies, including renewables and electric vehicles.

This raises the question of which approach is best. The United States benefits from largely liberalized markets which create powerful incentives for entrepreneurship and innovation. Left to its own, however, the market is unlikely to drive the innovations necessary to address climate change. The government, in our messy politically divided democracy, seems ill-equipped to respond to the scale of the challenge. The same push for liberalized markets also makes the United States resistant to attempts by the state to shape the direction of innovative activity. Despite the passing of the IRA, there is increasing political resistance to the type of technology policy it represents.

Some have looked to China as an alternative. Over the past few decades, China has pursued a mix of state-owned and sponsored businesses and simultaneously pushing some liberalization of its markets. The state has had a heavy hand in the direction of innovation. This approach has led to an incredible increase in economic growth lifting millions out of poverty. Simultaneously, it has allowed China to become a global leader in numerous industries including several emerging green technology sectors such as EVs, solar, and batteries. China's capacity for innovation is perhaps best exemplified by the rise of tech giants such as Alibaba and Tencent.

However, the nature of this success also highlights the limits to this approach. Questions abound about the fundamental nature of their innovation; whether the advances made have largely been through imitation of others. More significantly, the rise of a powerful entrepreneurial class has created a political backlash best exemplified by the harassment of Alibaba founder, Jack Ma. Whether an authoritarian regime with a socialist heritage can generate and sustain the necessary innovation to address climate change seems very much in doubt.

The competitive dynamics between the United States and China highlights the challenges with industrial policy. On one hand nationalism creates the political will to invest in innovation. On the other hand, that same nationalism can undermine global innovation. If the goal is to catalyze the innovations necessary to address our global climate crisis, protectionist efforts are counterproductive. Climate change knows no boundaries. We need green technologies to diffuse around the world. A large part of the economic growth in the latter half of the twentieth century was fueled by the increasing global exchange of products and services allowing for regional specialization and market efficiencies. The recent push to decouple global trade will likely hinder our ability to address climate change.

The Innovation Imperative

Global efforts to address climate change to date have largely centered around securing pledges by nations states to reduce national emissions negotiated in large United Nations sponsored Conferences of Parties (COP). Despite important progress, such as the establishment of a global target establish in the 2014 COP in Paris (the Paris Accords), the world has made limited progress toward net-zero emissions.

The effectiveness of the COP approach is increasingly being called in to question. Even the most lauded effort at international coordination, the Montreal Protocol to address the ozone hole, only gained traction when major market players such as Dupont felt confident that they had a desirable alternative to CFCs (specifically, HFCs). The political will to act was bolstered by a recognition that a market-viable alternative existed.

I would argue that the focus on national emissions targets largely distracts us from the task at hand: innovating alternative clean technologies that can compete with and ultimately replace existing fossil-fuel based technologies. Only when new clean technologies can compete on the current dimensions of merit—higher quality, lower cost—can we feel confident that global markets will adopt new climate friendly technologies over current technologies.

The beauty of this approach is that it does not necessarily rely on all nations passing legislation and pursing clean innovation. In fact, a small handful of countries could have a big impact. For example, innovations in low-cost battery technology in the United States could diffuse to countries in the global south. We are arguably seeing such a dynamic in the growing adoption of EVs across major global markets.

Of course, we should not underestimate the transitional challenges even under the most optimistic technology regimes. Adoption of low-cost solar and wind electrical generation will require massive capital expenditures and investment in complementary goods such as electrical lines and smart grid technology. This, however, only highlights the needs for innovation in both core green technologies as well as complementary infrastructure. Increasing market-viability will lower the barriers to adoption and help ease political resistant to investment.

So, which countries are best positioned to generate such innovations? Once again, capitalism provides a set of high-powered private incentives to disrupt existing markets and push technology transitions. The challenging is knowing what direction such efforts will push technology. Hence, the need of the state to place guard-rails on innovation and catalyzing it down a path towards decarbonization.

As we argued, state interventions on the direction of innovation can be fraught. Democracies must deal with a multitude of competing interests trying to push such interventions towards their private desires. Incumbent businesses may resist the push to disrupt their current market positions actively resisting government interventions and promoting disinformation to undermine the very belief in the severity of the challenge faced. This has especially been true in the case of climate change.

However, the alternative, authoritarian regimes, seem just as likely to be subject to such gaming and rent seeking. Industrial policy creates opportunity for profiteering by government officials include outright bribery and corruption. The existence of state-open enterprises only further acerbates these challenges. Lastly, the pressure on authoritarian regimes to quite dissent increases the likelihood of reigning in, if not outright demonizing, successful private market entrepreneurs who may otherwise leverage their success to exercise political power.

As messy as democracies can be, they are best positioned to adjudicate the numerous competing interests while unleashing the full innovative power of market economies. They have demonstrated the capacity to invest in basic R&D and other upstream innovations that the market would not pursue on their own. In some cases, they have created incentives, such as subsidies, to help de-risk early-stage development of novel technologies. In other cases, they have invested in complementary goods, such as infrastructure, to help reduce the barriers to adoption of new technology.

Climate change is a race against time. While adaptation to climate change is already needed, mitigation remains an imperative as a world of increasing GHG concentrations will be increasingly inhospitable. Solutions like geo-engineering and carbon capture and storage (CCS) may very well need to be part of the mix, however, the fact is that reductions in the burning of fossil fuels remains essential. As such, we need massive, disruptive innovations across a wide number of sectors.[27]

Democratic capitalism provides the best environment for catalyzing such innovation. The sooner, the better. Ironically, this system best positioned to help us address our climate challenge may be the one most at risk due to climate change. As sea levels rise and various regions become less hospitable, climate refugees will be more likely, crossing borders, and destabilizing countries. Will democratic capitalist nations revert to more authoritarian political and socialistic economic systems under such pressures, undermining the very innovation needed? The race is on.

Notes

1. Winston S. Churchill, 11 November 1947 in a speech to the House of Commons. https://winstonchurchill.org/resources/quotes/the-worst-form-of-government/ (accessed on August 14, 2024).
2. Karl Marx, *Capital: Volume 1* (Chicago: H. Regnery, 1959, originally 1867).
3. P. S. Adler, "Capitalism, Socialism, and the Climate Crisis," *Organization Theory*, 3, no. 1 (2022): 1-16
4. L. Rafael Reif—MIT President, "OpEd: The 'super wicked problem' of Climate Change Is our Earthshot," *Boston Globe*, April 19, 2021, https://www.bostonglobe.com/2021/04/19/opinion/super-wicked-problem-climate-change-is-our-earthshot/.
5. United Nations Environment Programme, *Emissions Gap Report 2023*, November 20, 2023, https://wedocs.unep.org/bitstream/handle/20.500.11822/43922/EGR2023.pdf (accessed on August 14, 2024).
6. United Nations Environment Programme, *Emissions Gap Report 2023.*
7. Paris Agreement to the United Nations Framework Convention on Climate Change, December 12, 2015, T.I.A.S. No. 16-1104.
8. Taejin Park, Hirofumi Hashimoto, Weile Wang, Bridget Thrasher, Andrew R. Michaelis, Tsengdar Lee, Ian G. Brosnan, "What Does Global Land Climate Look Like at 2°C Warming?," *Earth's Future* 11, no. 5 (May 2023): 1-16
9. Michael Lenox and Rebecca Duff, *The Decarbonization Imperative: Transforming the Global Economy by 2050* (Palo Alto: Stanford Press, 2021).
10. Lenox and Duff, *The Decarbonization Imperative.*
11. Lenox and Duff, *The Decarbonization Imperative.*
12. Lenox and Duff, *The Decarbonization Imperative.*
13. Lenox and Duff, *The Decarbonization Imperative.*
14. Joseph A. Schumpeter, *Capitalism, Socialism, and Democracy* (New York: Harper & Row, 1962).
15. Schumpeter, *Capitalism, Socialism, and Democracy.*
16. Michael Gort and Steven Klepper, "Time Paths in the Diffusion of Product Innovations," *The Economic Journal* 92, no. 367 (1982): 630–53.
17. Linda Argote and Dennis Epple, "Learning Curves in Manufacturing," *Science* 247, no. 4945 (1990): 920–24.
18. Michael J. Lenox, Scott F. Rockart, and Arie Y. Lewin. "Interdependency, Competition, and Industry Dynamics," *Management Science* 53, no. 4 (2007): 599–615.
19. Josh Howarth, "Startup Failure Rate Statistics," November 3, 2023, https://explodingtopics.com/blog/startup-failure-stats (accessed on August 14, 2024).
20. David A. Kirsch, "The Electric Car and the Burden of History: Studies in Automotive Systems Rivalry in America, 1890–1996," *Business and Economic History* (1997): 304–10.
21. Jeremy K. Hall, Gregory A. Daneke, and Michael J. Lenox, "Sustainable Development and Entrepreneurship: Past Contributions and Future Directions," *Journal of Business Venturing* 25, no. 5 (2010): 439–48.
22. Gijs Mom and David A. Kirsch. "Technologies in Tension: Horses, Electric Trucks, and the Motorization of American Cities, 1900–1925," *Technology and Culture* 42 no. 3 (2001): 489–518.
23. Elon Musk, Tesla Investor Presentation, March 2023, https://www.youtube.com/watch?v=Hl1zEzVUV7w.
24. Lena Mucha, Todd C. Frankel, and Karly Domb Sadof, "The Hidden Costs of Cobalt Mining," *Washington Post*, February 28, 2018, https://www.washingtonpost.com/news/in-sight/wp/2018/02/28/the-cost-of-cobalt/.
25. Dorian Feldman, "Contributions to the" two-armed bandit" Problem," *The Annals of Mathematical Statistics* 33, no. 3 (1962): 847–56.

26. World Economic Forum, "Fostering Effective Energy Transition 2023," June 28, 2023, https://www.weforum.org/publications/fostering-effective-energy-transition-2023/in-full/china/ (accessed on August 14, 2024).
27. Michael J. Lenox and Ronnie Chatterji, *Can Business Save the Earth? Innovating Our Way to Sustainability* (Palo Alto: Stanford, 2019).

4

Can Democratic Capitalism Protect the Climate?

BARRY G. RABE

Climate change poses a profound test for democratic capitalism. A uniquely wicked problem, climate change features enormous scientific, technological, and political complexity, requiring that industries and governments around the world whose behavior contributes to the problem make far-reaching adjustments to that behavior. Climate mitigation imposes costs that are substantial and concentrated in the near term, whereas resulting benefits are difficult to measure and likely evident only in future decades if at all. As a collective action challenge, unilateral efforts by specific continents, nations, and industries to reduce their climate impacts may have little if any discernible impacts at any point unless integrated into a functional global system. Shirking incentives and opportunities abound, proposed policy tool and technology panaceas frequently underperform expectations, and numerous early opportunities for constructive engagement have been largely squandered. Unlike the COVID pandemic, withdrawal and isolation from other humans is not a credible option as the effects of a changing climate will be global in scope.

Climate change reflects dramatic post-industrial era growth in the atmospheric concentration of greenhouse gases. This includes the long-lived climate pollutant carbon dioxide, which is responsible for more than half of the global warming that has occurred to date. Carbon dioxide is primarily generated through the combustion of fossil fuels (coal, oil, and natural gas) and remains in the atmosphere for between 300 to 1,000 years. There is no established method for removing carbon from the atmosphere or neutralizing its climate impacts once released. At the same time, there are additional greenhouse gases that also force climate impacts. These include methane, hydrofluorocarbons (HFCs), nitrous oxide, and black carbon, collectively responsible for nearly half of global

Barry G. Rabe, *Can Democratic Capitalism Protect the Climate?*. In: *Can Democracy and Capitalism Be Reconciled?*. Edited by: Sidney M. Milkis and Scott C. Miller, Oxford University Press. © Oxford University Press (2025). DOI: 10.1093/9780197774731.003.0005 warming to date.[1] These contaminants linger in the atmosphere for shorter periods than carbon dioxide but have a far more intensive near-term impact. Methane, for example, packs more than 85 times the climate-heating impact of carbon dioxide during its first two decades in the atmosphere. These shorter-lived climate pollutants can be generated through fossil fuel use but also have many other contributing sources. Methane is released through the energy sector as vented, flared, or leaked gas, but also emanates from the livestock, agricultural, and waste management sectors. HFCs represent a suite of chemicals used largely in refrigeration and air conditioning systems as well as various sprays. Nitrous oxide arises from varied industrial uses, including fertilizer application in agriculture. Black carbon emerges from incomplete combustion of fossil and bio-based fuels in engines, furnaces, forest fires, and cooking. Fossil fuels are thus a major factor in climate change but are not the exclusive contributor to warming.

Such pollutants converge to transform the climate through elevated temperatures and a cascade of related weather shifts. These disrupt established systems for food production and distribution, water supplies, transportation, flood protection, plant and animal species resilience, public safety, and much more. Impacts will vary by region, with a strong likelihood that they will be most disruptive in global regions with the least historic contribution of greenhouse gases and the least resource capacity to adapt to future challenges. This raises innumerable issues of fairness and justice in both climate mitigation and adaptation. Global temperatures have already risen 1.3 degrees Celsius (2.3 degrees Fahrenheit) from pre-industrial levels and may pass 1.5 degrees Celsius (2.7 degrees Fahrenheit) by 2030.

Under current policies, the United Nations reports that the world is heading toward a temperature increase of 2.8 degrees Celsius by century end.[2] Even if all nations fully honored their existing greenhouse gas emission reduction or stabilization pledges made under the Paris Agreement, global temperatures would still rise 2.4 to 2.6 degrees Celsius, well beyond the Paris target to contain temperature growth to 2.0 degrees Celsius, much less its "stretch goal" of limiting increases to 1.5 degrees Celsius.[3] Global emissions would need to be reduced by 25 percent from 2010 levels by 2030 to reach the 2.0 degree Celsius target and by 45 percent for the 1.5 degree Celsius target.[4] There is very little indication, however, that these existing pledges will be honored much less bolstered, suggesting additional warming. Each gradation of temperature increase elevates and compounds climate risks, with rises of 3.0 or more degrees Celsius remaining plausible.

Numerous technological and policy ideas to address climate change have surfaced in past decades, but no silver bullets have emerged. Global emissions have dropped markedly twice during this century, following the economic contraction of the late 2000s and the pandemic of the early 2020s. Both episodes triggered hopes that they might launch sustained reductions. In both instances, however, emissions rapidly rebounded once social and economic activity recovered. Attempts to devise a viable global governance system began more than three decades ago, resulting in the abject failure of the 1997 Kyoto Protocol and the uncertain path ahead for the 2015 Paris Agreement that endures as a model of soft international law reliant on voluntary national pledges rather than hard multinational commitments.

This chapter considers the capacity of democratic capitalism to play a constructive role in containing these risks through collective action to reduce greenhouse gas emissions in the coming decades. It explores exceptional cases where substantial progress has been made through the tools of democratic capitalism. On a global scale, coolant sector transformation has been driven by a mixture of policies, scientific advances, and technology diffusion guided by advanced democracies through an ongoing and adaptive international policy regime. On a continental scale, the European Union has increasingly led the world in establishing policies to achieve significant greenhouse gas emission reductions over multiple decades. These examples demonstrate that democratic capitalism has considerable potential for far-reaching climate protection.

These cases generally remain outliers, however, with limited indication of far-reaching diffusion to other economic sectors or nations. Instead, deep political and economic dependence upon fossil fuels endures globally, repeated attempts to deploy market-based policies to guide emissions reduction have encountered formidable political challenges, and nationalistic absorption with domestic political and economic interests have mightily compromised efforts to develop credible global regimes to address greenhouse gases. In turn, democratic capitalism in the climate case must confront the reality that a steadily-growing portion of annual emissions emanate from authoritarian regimes. Many such nations, including China and Russia, have poor climate protection records, reminding that any long-term international climate strategy must markedly accelerate mitigation efforts among both democratic and non-democratic political systems. This is no small task in an era where the divides between these systems deepen across multiple issue domains, and many democracies have become increasingly preoccupied with advancing national interests in energy production and use while eschewing broad trade agreements.

Reasons for Optimism: A Global Model and Continental Leader

In theory, democratic capitalism could be well suited to address climate change. Nations such as the United States possess formidable wealth, abundant natural resources, and robust technological research and development capacity in major universities and corporations that could be deployed in such an effort.

Few constitutions guiding democracies specifically address environmental or climate concerns, but none formally restrict use of a wide range of taxation, regulatory, or spending authorities that could be applied to climate change. Democracies have long-standing histories for cross-national alliance on military and trade issues, in some instances leading to the development of effective and durable policy regimes. There have been stunning technological advances in climate-relevant arenas in the last decade, such as major reductions in solar and wind energy costs and satellite monitoring to measure methane releases.

Democratic capitalism has already registered some significant environmental protection advances, reflected in a large array of national, continental, and global policies to address air and water quality, hazardous waste management, chemical production and use safety, species and habitat protection, among others. This includes some demonstrated capacity for alliances between democracies and non-democratic systems, including resource sharing and technology transition assistance. The United States has ratified more than 50 environmental treaties in the last half a century, many of which have proven durable and effective. It also played a pivotal role in promoting air quality through development of a suite of policies and technologies via the Clean Air Act that could be extended to address greenhouse gases.[5]

Effective Global Climate Governance: Cooling Sector Chemicals

The predominant model of the potential of democratic capitalism to foster global environmental protection remains the 1987 Montreal Protocol on Substances that Deplete the Ozone Layer. All nations have ratified Montreal, amid mounting evidence that a series of chemicals used commonly in air conditioning and refrigeration systems were depleting the ozone layer and posing a series of global environmental and public health threats. Protocol development and implementation was led by a cross-national coalition of government, industry, and scholarly leaders from major democracies who recognized the gravity of these environmental and public health risks, and accelerated development and distribution of a suite of alternative chemical coolants that were far more ozone friendly.[6] The Montreal process has maintained significant transitional funding through a Multilateral Fund established by large democracies to support emerging nations in securing access to these alternatives. In turn, Montreal was designed to be flexible in response to evolving scientific developments and was amended four times during the 1990s with broad political support. Nearly four decades since its inception, this process has delivered significant ozone restoration benefits.

Less recognized is that Montreal is the most effective climate protection policy ever established globally or nationally. Chemical substitution designed for ozone layer protection also served to protect vegetation from heightened ultraviolet radiation, which would compromise its capacity to store carbon through photosynthesis. This protection has already reduced additional global warming by an estimated 0.5 to 1.0 degrees Celsius over what is projected to have occurred without the global pact,[7] a climate benefit that increases over time as the ozone layer stabilizes. Nonetheless, the ozone and climate benefits via global HFC use ushered in by Montreal have been offset by some climate downsides. These coolants are exceptionally good at protecting the ozone layer, but remain short-lived climate pollutants like their predecessors, albeit modest overall when weighed against impacts posed by carbon dioxide and methane.

The broad political and industrial coalition supporting Montreal and subsequent amendments pivoted in the 2010s to further cooling sector transition to address this issue. The adaptive Montreal process added HFCs to its list of controlled substances, and launched a phase-down process for 150 participating nations through the 2016 Kigali Amendment. For developed nations, this represents a commitment to reduce HFC production and use by 85 percent by the mid-2030s, with more flexible transition terms for less developed nations. Full global participation in Kigali would reduce twenty-first-century global warming a projected 0.5 degrees Celsius below temperatures anticipated under continued HFC use.

Initial ratification lags by some major national economies, particularly the United States, China, and India, led to considerable uncertainties about Kigali's effectiveness, despite the impressive Montreal track record. Global HFC emissions had been growing at an 8 percent annual rate and were poised to soar in a world expected to expand from 3.6 billion cooling appliances in 2020 to 9.5 billion by 2050 without a major transition to next-generation coolants.[8] However, the United States has since embraced Kigali, pivoting from global laggard to leader. With broad bipartisan support, Congress adopted the American Innovation and Manufacturing (AIM) Act in 2020, signed into law by President Donald Trump. AIM outlined an American path toward full compliance, followed in 2022 by overwhelming Senate approval of the Kigali Amendment. China and India have also joined Kigali, creating a broad base of cross-national support that ranges alphabetically from Albania to Zambia. This case demonstrates that it is indeed possible to establish a global climate governance structure that can draw on the strengths of democratic capitalism, engage both democratic and authoritarian systems, and prove durable and effective.

Even in hyper-partisan America, a broad and diverse coalition of legislators backed AIM and Kigali. American firms and trade associations recognized major scientific advances in developing HFC alternatives, mindful that Kigali trade restrictions on non-participants would constrain their ability to engage global markets. Proliferation of individual state policies in the late 2010s indicated the likelihood of fragmented regional standards without unifying federal policy. Consequently, many industry leaders became active AIM and Kigali proponents. The United States has moved rapidly to implement all key provisions, including the creation of a multi-agency force to deter HFC smuggling that surfaced initially in Europe and Asia.

Democratic capitalism has worked spectacularly well throughout the Montreal and Kigali processes. However, this feat has yet to be emulated for other greenhouse gases where political hurdles to global collective action remain far greater. The Paris Agreement was formalized at the same time as Kigali, reliant upon "nationally defined contributions" (emission reduction pledges) without such punitive measures as financial penalties or restricted trade access for non-compliance. The Global Methane Pledge was launched in 2021 by the United States and the European Union, imploring nations to pledge to support global efforts to reduce methane releases from all sources by 30 percent from 2020 levels by 2030, while not requiring any formal actions or emission reductions within their own borders. Unlike the hard law of Kigali, both Paris and the Global Methane Pledge are soft international agreements that fall far short of binding treaties. These allow the United States to participate via executive action by supportive presidents rather than Senate treaty ratification, thereby risking exits by less-supportive chief executives. American climate policy engagement has become increasingly contingent on executive preferences in recent decades.[9] This has reflected the challenges of engaging a polarized Congress, leaving the most powerful democracy an unreliable player in the international arena. The first day of Donald Trump's second presidential term illustrated this phenomenon anew, as he withdrew the United States from Paris, as was the case in his initial term.

Climate Policy Leader: The European Union

There are numerous national and sub-national cases in which significant reductions of greenhouse gases other than HFCs have already occurred. These are concentrated exclusively among nations defined by the Democracy Index of the Economist Intelligence Unit as either "full" or "flawed" democracies rather than authoritarian nations or hybrids blending democratic and authoritarian system features. Twenty-four nations have reduced their emissions over recent decades, all located in Europe excepting Jamaica and the United States. In most of these cases, electricity and heat generation sectors have generally achieved far larger emission reductions than transportation and other large industrial sectors. This includes cases where emission reductions began in the 1970s and have continued over time (including Finland, Germany, Sweden, and the United Kingdom), declined markedly during post-Cold War transition and continued dropping (including Bulgaria, the Czech Republic, Hungary, and Ukraine), or began to fall after 2000 and have continued to do so (including Italy, Spain, and the United States). "While the total GHG reductions of these 24 countries are trivial compared to recent global emissions growth, some have achieved a decline of up to 50 percent in their annual emissions, showing what is possible even under very moderate climate action," noted a 2022 analysis of national trends. Most of these nations maintained economic growth during their periods of emissions decline and some "approached the fast annual rates of change that will be needed across the world in the coming decades to limit warming" to 2.0 degrees Celsius.[10]

Political scientist Daniel Fiorino confirms these general patterns in his insightful book, *Can Democracy Handle Climate Change?* He considers the uneven national emissions and policy record among nations around the globe, including democracies, and acknowledges numerous future challenges. But Fiorino also underscores lessons to be derived from "small, more consensus-based, high-functioning democracies like Sweden, Norway, and Denmark," as well as select sub-federal states and provinces that have pursued comparable policies and achieved sustained emission reductions.[11] The Environmental Performance Index (EPI) also supports this interpretation with its extensive set of environmental indicators that measure policy and environmental outcomes across all nations. Democracies consistently dominate the upper third of EPI national ranking categories, many addressing climate change.[12] In North America, Canada has been most effective in keeping pace with European nations in these assessments and a subset of provinces and American states have particularly strong records.

The European Union (EU) looms as particularly significant, given its unique ability to achieve significant emission cuts through sustained implementation of a durable suite of climate mitigation policies that include pricing, regulation, and subsidies. The EU has demonstrated the potential for a quasi-federal or multi-state democratic system to integrate national policies with continent-wide ones in achieving major greenhouse gas emission reductions. It has featured many differing national strategies on climate policy, most evident in the electricity sector where many nations have achieved significant transition to renewables while reducing fossil fuel use.[13] Some of these have been particularly innovative and effective; Finland, for example, has flourished economically while registering average annual emission reductions of 3 percent in recent decades. This reflects significant transition to cleaner electricity sources and major energy efficiency. Finland is also expanding the use of nuclear power, a non-carbon electricity source, through a pioneering process for siting the world's first permanent nuclear waste repository alongside new reactors.[14]

The European Union has complemented these national steps with continent-wide policies, most notably an Emissions Trading System (ETS) that has effectively combined durable political support for carbon pricing with adaptive management that has improved system performance over time. It built on earlier experimentation with carbon taxes in many European nations, most notably Nordic democracies. Initially dismissed as a failure following a series of early administrative stumbles and political accommodations, the ETS has steadily evolved into a global model for a market-based pricing system by auctioning allowances under a steadily declining emissions cap.[15] This includes a Market Stability Reserve to withdraw excessive allowances and stabilize the carbon market. ETS has played a central but not exclusive role in EU emission reductions in the electricity, heat generation, and energy-intensive industry sectors of 43 percent between 2005 and 2021. It is designed to be a driving force in the next planned stages of EU climate mitigation, a 61 percent reduction from 2005 to 2030 in sectors under the ETS umbrella. Proposed expansion includes the maritime, building, and road transport sectors. ETS allowance prices increased nearly three-fold during 2021 and have averaged between 60 and 100 Euros per ton since 2021. The United Kingdom has generally kept pace with the EU on climate despite Brexit upheavals with a parallel ETS and complementary policies.

The ETS also generates substantial revenue to fund subsidies to accelerate transition toward cleaner energy sources and greater energy efficiency. Auction proceeds have increased markedly alongside its growing carbon price, with revenues divided between individual member states and continent-wide projects. Nations use approximately 80 percent of their ETS-generated revenue for complementary climate purposes, while the EU uses its auction share to support continental energy technology development and energy transition assistance for lower-income nations. Growing ETS robustness has also positioned the EU to play a lead role in using trade policy to incentivize stronger climate performance by other nations, through carbon tariffs (or "border adjustments") on imported goods from nations lacking a comparable carbon price or carbon emissions intensity.

Reasons for Pessimism: Political Stumbling Blocks

The Kigali treaty and promising European cases provide evidence that democratic capitalism has some capacity to address climate change. These policies include a range of institutional, economic, and technological elements that can, at least in some instances, converge to significantly reduce greenhouse gas releases. Their promise, however, is offset by substantial evidence suggesting that democratic capitalism has more generally struggled to achieve deeper and broader emission reductions necessary to approach Paris climate protection goals. In turn, there is minimal evidence indicating that authoritarian regimes, prominent alternatives to democratic political systems, are more effective in addressing climate change.

Both Paris and the global methane regime have secured scores of national pledges from both democratic and non-democratic governments but these would result in warming above a 2.0 degree Celsius target even if fully honored. There is little indication that such national implementation success is in the offing, particularly in the all-important energy sector. Nearly all 55 global energy system sub-sectors are off-track to meet mid-century Paris targets, with the lone exceptions being electric vehicles and lighting.[16] In 2021, fossil fuel demand and use rebounded dramatically after the first year of the global pandemic. This included a 6.6 percent increase in coal use, with 36.6 percent reliance on coal for global electricity despite major reductions in the United States and some other nations. Despite some expanded demand for electric vehicles, over 91 percent of global transportation energy continued to come from oil. In turn, energy sector methane emissions rose 5 percent in 2021, the very year that the Global Methane Pledge was launched.

As a result, climate policy advances through Kigali and exceptional national cases are consequential but largely overshadowed by considerably less progress in numerous other sectors and nations that also contribute substantial greenhouse gas emissions. Much policy and technological experimentation continues, but follows decades of dawdling during which global emissions loading proliferated. These delays reflect several major political stumbling blocks that have constrained the ability of democratic capitalism to credibly address climate change on national, continental, and global scales. These challenges endure, showing no immediate signs of resolution.

Fossil Fuels and the Carbon Trap

The global abundance of fossil fuels has provided relatively abundant and inexpensive energy that has underpinned industrial and economic expansion for generations. Coal, oil, and natural gas each features its own political, economic, and technological story in terms of extraction, refinement, and distribution. These individual fuels converged in fostering major global economic expansion during the nineteenth and twentieth centuries. They continue to play dominant roles in twenty-first-century energy use, despite mounting concerns about climate change and other negative externalities that they generate. No nation has banned fossil fuel use and most nations and sub-national jurisdictions with extractable fuels continue to support their production for use and export. The relatively small set of nations that have formally prohibited coal mining or oil and gas drilling, including some European emission reduction leaders, have remained dependent on imported fossil fuels for much of their energy supply. This ongoing import dependence became particularly evident during the Ukraine War, as Europe aggressively sought alternatives to Russian supplies, and expanded capacity to import liquified natural gas from the United States and other producing nations.

Fossil fuels have provided enormous economic benefits to many nations, communities, and industries, leading to the maintenance of protective political regimes supporting continued production, distribution, and use. This engages massive private firms that operate globally to unlock localized fossil fuel deposits, as well as platoons of smaller entities providing specific technologies or services. Collectively, these firms employ millions of workers around the world, including corporate executives, petroleum engineers, drill rig workers, refinery operators, truck drivers, and many others across supply chains for individual fuels. Such organizations have an enduring political interest in retaining their social license, preserving supportive tax and regulatory policies, and thwarting policies to reduce fossil fuel production and use.[17]

Such private entities have secured formidable political allies, including industries and labor unions that also benefit economically from sustained fossil fuel use.[18] These groups often maintain broad and durable coalitions that oppose climate policy proposals, frequently cutting across political party divides. Heavy sunk costs in labor, training, facilities, and transportation linked to easy access to low-cost energy create a foundation for a vast array of businesses and industries that can prove easy to stir into active opposition to policy proposals that would threaten their routines and potentially challenge their capacity to continue operations. This can then trigger far-reaching political actions, ranging from high-scale investments in lobbying and campaign contributions to promotion of narratives challenging the integrity of climate science.

Political hostility toward any proposed transition from fossil fuels may well be shared and advanced by governments closely allied with industry preferences.[19] In jurisdictions such as Texas and Alberta, so-called "petrostates" have long operated within political systems providing intensive support to sustain subsidies for fossil fuel production while thwarting sub-national and national policies that might undermine their continued preeminence. Such petrostates can become dependent on revenue provided through taxes and royalties paid by fossil fuel-based firms and their employees, including levies on property, income, and extraction. At the same time, global fossil fuel production is frequently managed by public rather than private entities, in a few democracies such as Norway and

Mexico but more commonly in autocratic nations such as China, Iran, Russia, Qatar, Saudi Arabia, and Venezuela. Sixty percent of global oil production and half of natural gas production is attributable to such nationally operated firms, with investment and production decisions directly aligned with the political interests of a given nation or state. Jurisdictions with such energy production systems hold nearly two-thirds of global fossil fuel reserves; their preeminence may only grow if private firms based in democracies pivot away from fossil fuels for either economic or political reasons.

Regardless of the form of energy production control, governments frequently protect these interests and can deter the entrance of competitive energy sources, such as renewables. Collectively, these private and public forces converge in creating a "carbon trap" that secures political support for sustaining fossil fuel production and use for as long as possible.[20] As legal scholar Andrew Green has explained, "We are locked in politically, economically, technologically, and culturally to the use of fossil fuels from local to global. The dependence at each level reinforces the lock-in at others."[21] Under a carbon (or methane) trap, a large and unified coalition assiduously protects sustained fossil fuel production and use, mightily complicating any transition toward cleaner alternatives.

Policy Panaceas

Much earlier climate policy scholarship assumed that the world would inexorably establish robust national carbon pricing regimes that would be integrated into a sustained global assault on carbon emissions. This expectation animated the 1997 Kyoto Protocol, reflecting recent experience with market-based tools used for sulfur dioxide in the United States and carbon dioxide in five Nordic nations. Pricing was embraced by global trade and monetary authorities, as well as innumerable economists of varied ideological stripes. In theory, carbon price adoption could reduce fossil fuel consumption, heighten demand for non-carbon energy sources, and propel technological transition toward cleaner energy production. It featured a distinct choice between a direct tax across fuel types or a cap-and-trade system with bargaining over allowance purchases auctioned under a firm emissions cap. Both taxes and trading system auctions generated government revenue that could be used for numerous purposes, including transition to cleaner energy production or greater energy efficiency. The underlying argument behind carbon pricing as the primary policy tool to address climate change was economic efficiency, allowing markets to find the lowest-cost emission reductions to stimulate a complex transformation from fossil fuels, all seemingly within the democratic capitalism wheelhouse.

In practice, carbon pricing has faced major political adoption challenges around the world.[22] The wicked problem nature of climate change means that any short-term action to increase energy prices represents a form of direct pain imposition in the short term for few obvious near-term gains. Even though carbon pricing was billed as a market-based policy to contain overall costs, fossil fuel interests routinely opposed it and many pricing systems that were adopted were replete with exemptions. Durability was also a significant and unanticipated problem, as numerous early pricing experiments faced withering opposition and were delayed, downsized, or reversed. This included major energy-producing democracies, such as the United States, Australia, and Canada.

There has been no groundswell to adopt robust carbon pricing regimes in most developed or emerging nations, including the United States, much less weave them into an integrated global system. Studies of numerous pricing programs indicate modest annual emission reductions.[23] In 2023, 75 pricing systems operated around the world, covering 24 percent of global emissions, and producing $104 billion in annual revenue.[24] Most were modest in scope, imposing prices below $10 per ton and laden with exemptions. However, a small but growing set of initiatives have pushed well beyond this level in recent years, including Europe, Canada, and the United Kingdom. Some studies indicate more substantial reduction patterns, particularly in Nordic cases with relatively high rates sustained over time.[25]

Carbon pricing continues to face significant limits in its global impact, although there are some possibilities of expanding its future role in concert with trade reforms. At the same time, alternative policies such as regulations and subsidies have also frequently struggled politically and, where approved, their capacity to drive significant emission reductions is also quite uneven. Subsidies and their potential to underpin the broader idea of transformational energy industrial policy have received new visibility through American adoption of the 2022 Inflation Reduction Act. This includes a vast set of programs intended to offset some costs associated with clean energy production and use. Its future durability and performance will represent an important test of the climate impacts of a policy approach reliant primarily on heavy government spending rather than pricing or regulation, reflecting the considerable US political challenges facing the former and legal obstacles confronting the latter. Thus far, only the European Union among democracies has successfully operated all three policy types simultaneously over an extended time period.

Energy Nationalism versus Global Needs

The emergence of populism and nationalism in many democracies raises further questions about their capacity to launch and sustain effective climate policies and support global climate governance. Common backlashes against proposed and adopted climate policies in many democracies suggest deep partisan divides with one or more major political parties commonly decrying active climate engagement as a threat to national economic well-being. A report from a 2022 international climate policy conference concluded that "Climate policy could become a 'wedge issue' for populists as immigration had been previously; populists could say that climate policy served elite interests; that it was technical and abstract; and that policy makers disdained or ignored the interests of ordinary people."[26]

This pattern has been increasingly evident among democracies with less advanced economies where recent emissions growth is often quite high. Nations such as Brazil and Mexico are major national greenhouse gas emission sources, ranking far behind most democracies with advanced economies in performance measures of climate policy. In Brazil, former President Jair Bolsonaro frequently dismissed climate change as a central policy concern during his tenure, particularly as he resisted global pressures to protect the Amazon, a crucial ecological link in climate protection. Brazil also backtracked from other prior climate protection policies during his tenure.

In North America, Mexico made a massive pivot away from climate protection following the 2018 Presidential election of Andrés Manuel López Obrador. Mexico previously had adopted new policies accelerating transition toward renewable energy, including collaboration with external private firms. It also adopted methane mitigation legislation for its large oil and gas sector, earning global notoriety. Much of that was reversed under López Obrador, alongside costly restoration of long-standing national firms to dominate Mexican energy production and electricity generation. This promoted expanded oil and gas exploration and production, billed as fostering greater Mexican energy self-reliance. Electricity production pivoted back toward traditional fossil fuel use, including expanded use of coal and oil for power. Mexico has largely abandoned its methane regulatory strategy in an all-out effort to expand oil and gas production on land and offshore, resulting in substantial methane release increases.[27] Much like Bolsonaro on the populist right, López Obrador on the populist left downplayed climate change in favor of greater domestic fossil fuel output, demonstrating that energy nationalism from either side of the partisan divide can serve to undermine climate policy. There were some early indications that climate protection might re-emerge as a policy concern as Claudia Sheinbaum, an energy engineer, assumed the presidency in 2024.

Such patterns have also been evident in democracies with advanced economies, including both terms of Donald Trump's presidency in the United States. Trump demonstrated the ability of an elected executive devoted to energy nationalism to eschew the legislative branch and pursue an aggressive agenda to increase domestic fossil fuel output, encourage exports, and reverse nearly all major climate initiatives taken by prior administrations. This anti-climate strategy included the formal American withdrawal from Paris on two separate occasions, deep environmental agency staff and budget cuts, and the nomination of federal judges likely to constrain authority of future executives to pursue climate mitigation. Deep American partisan cleavages over climate change endure in survey findings and policy debates, with Republican Party opposition to many proposed climate policies often linked to economic concerns about reducing domestic oil and gas production or restricting energy exports. There have also been signs of climate policy backlash in other democratic nations such as Australia and Canada, and such EU member states as Hungary and Poland.

In turn, leading democracies have also struggled to support climate protection investments beyond their national boundaries despite the global nature of this issue. Long-promised commitments from democracies with advanced economies to provide at least $100 billion annually to support energy transition in emerging economies have never materialized. India's political leadership insists that it will require $1 trillion in external support by 2030 if it is to take significant first steps toward realizing 2050 net-zero emission goals. However, there is no credible global plan in place to begin to approach this level of support for India, much less other nations with emerging economies. This issue surfaced dramatically during global climate meetings in the 2020s, bringing new visibility to proposals for reparations or "loss-and-damage" provisions from nations that had caused the greatest climate damage historically to assist those least responsible for the crisis and least able to respond to it. European leaders expressed considerable support but the United States and other nations with advanced economies balked. The United States offered an alternative plan that proposed carbon offset and credit use to generate funds but these were largely dismissed as symbolic and lodged in past failures using comparable tools. It remained in arrears on Green Climate Fund pledges and failed to emerge as a credible player in reparation or loss-and-damage policy development during the Joe Biden presidency, with future American support likely to further erode during the second term of Donald Trump.

Instead, the United States has increasingly focused federal climate policy on subsidies to be invested almost exclusively within its boundaries, pitching new investment programs as beneficial for the domestic economy by reducing dependence on trade partners and fostering greater national energy self-reliance. Just as many major democracies concentrated COVID vaccine distribution at home rather than sharing with other nations, climate, energy, and trade nationalism increasingly converge in many democratic nations. This pattern was evident in American adoption of 2020 clean energy, 2021 infrastructure, and 2022 climate subsidy legislation, producing hundreds of billions of dollars for climate-friendly investments, nearly all intended exclusively for use within the United States. Purchasing incentives for electric vehicles, for example, are laden with preferences for products manufactured and assembled domestically while using minerals mined domestically. This triggered considerable concern from leading Asian and European nations that sell large numbers of vehicles in the United States, inviting potential retaliation that would discourage imports from the United States. This is consistent with a general pattern whereby climate-engaged democracies focus principally on their own emissions and related economic development advantages from unilateral action, without plans to share technologies or resources with other nations lacking such capacity. It appears increasingly likely that such aggressive promotion of national economic interests will continue to proliferate and complicate cross-national climate cooperation, potentially provoking formal challenges under international and multilateral trade agreements.

Energy nationalism also forestalls serious consideration of what "just transition" strategies might entail for communities likely to face profound economic and social challenges amid any major shift from fossil fuel to renewable energy sources. Parties supporting sustained fossil fuel production often view just transition discussions as a distraction and potential threat to pursuing all-out resource development for as long as possible. While many petrostates have benefited economically from intensive production, relatively few have set aside resources for long-term transition. Norway and several American states such as Texas and New Mexico are exceptions, having long diverted substantial royalty and severance tax revenue into sovereign wealth funds for long-term savings and investment that could support future diversification.[28] The petrostate norm is generally quite different, reflected historically in a series of boom-and-bust pivots, enduring dependence on energy sector tax revenue, and an abiding political emphasis on maintaining production for as long as possible. As Abdulaziz bin Salman, Saudi Arabia's energy minister, stated in 2022: "We are still going to be the last man standing, and every molecule of hydrocarbon will come out."[29] Brokering the global terms of energy transition remains in its earliest imaginable stages, further complicated by ascending patterns of energy nationalism and continued discoveries of major oil and gas deposits in developing nations.

Aggressive national protection of industry interests remains dominant and complicates climate policy in the agriculture and livestock sectors, representing about 10 percent of global carbon emissions and more than one-third of global methane and nitrous oxide emissions. In many democracies, this reflects energy-intensive crop production, substantial methane releases from animals providing beef and dairy products, heavy fertilizer use producing nitrous oxide releases, and the downplay of negative externalities linked to food production. These sectors are commonly buttressed economically by a dizzying series of durable government subsidies, backed by protectionist measures to discourage import competition. Agriculture may be the single sector under democratic capitalism where the least progress has been made in advancing credible climate policy alternatives; established interests remain systematically protected through policy rather than incentivized to address climate change. Denmark, the Netherlands, and New Zealand stand largely alone globally in developing far-reaching policy to reduce emissions from this sector, although these efforts have faced intense political opposition.

The Dismal Climate Record of Authoritarian Regimes

Just as much of the global population does not reside in a nation where democratic capitalism prevails, a growing amount of annual greenhouse gas emissions emanate from authoritarian nations that spurn both democracy and capitalism. China supplanted the United States as the world's largest annual source of greenhouse gases in 2006, and has generated more emissions annually than the entire developed world combined since 2019.[30] Russia and many Middle Eastern petrostates also combine high rankings in annual emissions alongside governance systems highly estranged from democratic capitalism. In 2020, Russia ranked fourth globally in national greenhouse gas emissions, followed by Iran in sixth place and Saudi Arabia in ninth place. Most of the world's leading national producers of oil and gas are authoritarian. No credible global plan to mitigate climate risks can operate without active engagement from authoritarian nations, and yet there are few signs of collaboration across these lines.

In theory, authoritarian systems may have natural advantages in addressing climate change.[31] They are thought to eschew short-term profit margins and election cycles in favor of long-term planning and stability. They can direct substantial revenues toward the development and use of new technologies and phase-out existing industries and practices deemed outdated without prolonged review. They can also be more aggressive in making land-use decisions establishing new energy or industrial facilities without prolonged public debate and court review. Authoritarian nations may also be more adroit at managing intergenerational transition than democratic nations, as the latter often give added political clout to older voters least supportive of societal change. In cases such as China, co-benefits from climate mitigation may abound given profound national air quality problems that far exceed those of most nations under democratic capitalism, making a rapid pivot from fossil fuels particularly attractive. China may also have considerable incentives to develop its own energy supplies from renewable sources and mined materials under its direct control. Such transition would give it considerably more latitude to pursue its broader international security and economic goals free of reliance on imported fuel.

There is evidence that China has made some significant progress in reducing its climate impact. This includes major advances in the production and distribution of lower-cost solar panels, building on initial technological and policy advances led by the United States and Germany, as well as relatively inexpensive electric vehicles.[32] In 2020, China pledged through Paris that its greenhouse gas emissions would peak in 2030 and that it would become carbon neutral by 2060, both accelerations from prior pledges. Surveys among international climate experts on the ambition and credibility of national emissions reduction pledges give China relatively high marks, second only to the European Union and ahead of the United States, India, and other democracies. As David Victor and colleagues noted, "in some models less-democratic countries offer more credible pledges after controlling for institutional quality and ambition. This finding may reflect the high degree of administrative and political control that exists within consolidated autocratic governments."[33]

At the same time, there is considerable reason to harbor doubts about China's commitment to addressing climate change. It has pursued major increases in coal production and use since making its Paris pledges, with more coal plants under development in 2024 than remain operational in the United States. It has increased its dependence on Russian oil and gas, indifferent to its exceptionally high rate of methane loss. Its environmental ministries remain under strong control by economic counterparts, and most of its industrial sectors remain far more carbon-intensive per unit of production than counterparts in the United States and advanced democracies.[34] Its capacity to flood the world with relatively inexpensive solar panels and electric vehicles has been challenged by American decisions to impose steep trade tariffs on these Chinese products. Even well-publicized policies such as China's emissions trading system remain experimental and quite modest in scope, trivial compared to Europe. China's increasing production of coal, oil, and gas has heightened its global leadership in annual methane emissions, generating more annually than all North America and European nations combined. It has refused to join more than 155 nations that have endorsed the new global methane regime, undermining the likely impact of that pact.

In Russia, evidence mounts of staggering emission rates in energy production and use, compounded by desperate efforts to maximize oil and gas output to sustain its economy.[35] Russia and many other nationalized energy production firms release prodigious amounts of methane through slipshod oversight, as indicated through international monitoring that discredits national reports.[36] Overall, authoritarian nations have struggled to develop and implement credible emission reduction policies to date across multiple sectors. Collectively, there is little indication that more authoritarian nations outside the orbit of democratic capitalism are credibly preparing to address climate change, amid continuing uncertainties as to how democratic capitalism might incentivize or prod them into action.

Possible Next Steps

There is little evidence that the Kigali model for global coolant sector transformation will be replicated any time soon for other greenhouse gas sectors. Kigali may well constitute a fluke case just as the European Union's record of significant decarbonization remains unique. Many democratic and authoritarian nations continue to struggle politically to mount credible climate policies and sustain them, while global loading of greenhouse gases continues and early opportunities to stave off the impacts of climate change have been largely squandered.

Alongside the continued domestic policy jockeying and development of the Paris Agreement and the Global Methane Pledge, several plausible and non-exclusive paths forward have emerged for future climate policy. Each presents unique challenges for democratic capitalism, but could play to some of its strengths.

Trade and Climate Leverage

The last decade suggests a growing shift away from pursuit of regional and international trade agreements, reflected in both the Trump and Biden presidencies, at the same time global carbon and methane regimes serve limited roles beyond gathering non-binding pledges. Major climate policy differences between trade partners have increasingly raised concerns over leakage problems, whereby investment and related emissions gravitate toward jurisdictions with easier policy compliance paths. This has spawned expanding discussion over whether nations with cleaner production and significant carbon prices might levy carbon border adjustments through tariffs on imported goods, both to protect their own industries facing higher standards and to financially incentivize exporting nations to improve their climate records. This is also emerging as a consideration in methane, where energy importing nations could add levies to imported oil and gas produced with high methane release rates.

The European Union has led the way in shifting border adjustments from economic theory to policy practice, a centerpiece of its strategy to secure deeper continental emission reductions while leveraging its ETS program to prompt comparable steps among trade partners. The EU launched its formal border program in 2024, gathering data to prepare for its 2027 launch. Canada, the United Kingdom, and several Asian democracies have expressed considerable interest in either joining the EU in a climate tariff partnership or developing their own programs, reflecting their own significant carbon prices. These developments were not well received by major trade partners, such as China, India, Russia, and the United States. American responses have divided along partisan lines, with a growing likelihood that the United States might continue to eschew any domestic carbon price while imposing its own tariffs on China and other trade partners with greater carbon emissions intensity in major industrial sectors.

Political, administrative, and economic uncertainties abound in contemplating potential linkages between trade and climate policy or establishing multinational "climate clubs" among allied nations imposing tariffs. But some form of border adjustment appears increasingly plausible in a world with deep carbon pricing and climate policy variation, and growing national preference for domestic economic protection through trade rather than multilateral trade agreements. Stiff global trade penalties remain a cornerstone of Kigali, but it remains uncertain whether a comparable process can be developed for carbon or other greenhouse gases in coming decades.

Climate Industrial Policy

The political challenges facing adoption of pricing and regulatory policies has fostered growing consideration of using government spending to subsidize climate transition as a primary alternative, particularly in the deep-pocketed United States. Unlike the sticks of pricing or regulation, an investment-based industrial policy strategy would use government revenue as carrots. This could involve any number of emphases, including direct support for industries producing cleaner energy or manufactured products, and assisting the public with the costs of purchasing them. In theory, revenues could be generated through general-purpose taxes where it is harder to attribute direct political blame to any program funded by them. At the same time, new funding could be used to confer benefits on specific groups, fostering a political constituency among recipients who want their benefits to continue or expand over time.

Subsidies have long been used in various forms of energy and climate policy, reflected in tax credits and incentives in sectors such as electricity, transportation, and agriculture. Oil and gas production has long been heavily subsidized around the world. But the idea of markedly expanding and increasing their scope for energy alternatives is newer in practice, reflecting major governmental shifts toward green investment in Europe and the United States. Passage of the massive US Inflation Reduction Act illustrates this model as an investment-centered climate strategy. However, it was adopted only with support from one political party and lacks complementary regulatory and pricing policies so central to European advances. This fledgling American approach also faced serious challenges as Donald Trump returned to the presidency in 2025. It has remained unclear how widely this approach might diffuse, given the need for substantial fiscal capacity to fund such programs that is highly uneven among democracies.

Other industrial policy approaches, involving major governmental investment in or direct ownership of specific industries, potentially operate alongside increased government disinvestment for other industries linked to fossil fuels. In some respects, China stands as a preeminent global model for this approach, reflecting significant political control over all greenhouse gas-intensive sectors and the possibility of substantial reallocation of government revenue to pursue climate initiatives. Much like carbon border adjustments, climate industrial policy is largely untested politically and economically on a large scale. In both cases, major uncertainties remain over potential impacts on emissions, cost effectiveness, political durability, and capacity to develop and deploy new technologies on a global scale.

High-Risk Technological Alternatives

Growing emphasis on industrial policy approaches in the United States and other nations has underscored the possibility that advanced economies might underwrite the development and deployment costs of a suite of far-reaching technological alternatives that have not yet experienced large-scale usage and evaluation in practice. These options have emerged primarily through applied research supported by public and private funds under democratic capitalism and remain both untested and controversial politically given potential risks linked to their use.

These alternatives include strategies to formally prevent carbon and methane from entering the atmosphere or withdraw it following release. Carbon sequestration and storage is intended to capture industrial emissions and deposit them below the surface of the earth in large, secure repositories. Direct air capture systems represent proposals to deploy powerful machines to withdraw emissions from the atmosphere and then contain them. In addition, solar geoengineering entails releasing particles into the atmosphere to attempt to block some of the most intensive heating effects of the sun and reduce global temperatures. Still other options include development of hydrogen-based energy and modular nuclear reactors.

Most of the research and early testing of such alternatives emanates from advanced economies and remains in early stages of development. All would be extremely expensive to deploy on any large scale, and each raises its own political and technical feasibility, cost effectiveness, and public health risk concerns. Sequestration and air capture could ultimately prove ineffective while undermining transition to clean energy by prolonging the case for fossil fuel use. Solar geoengineering raises countless questions of safety and public risk through a massive atmospheric experiment without precedent. Modular reactors suggest a possible path for nuclear energy expansion that would avoid carbon emissions but pose enduring uncertainties about nuclear waste management. Nonetheless, the growing inability to address climate change through effective mitigation policy has made each of these alternatives more visible and attractive, reflected in significant American subsidy support.

Pivoting to Adaptation

The enduring political challenge of climate mitigation has converged with the growing evidence that climate change is accelerating and having increasing consequences around the globe. This inevitably raises questions of whether mitigation policy may continue to lag and be supplanted by aggressive efforts to focus on adaptation, adjusting to emerging threats from a changing climate rather than attempting to reduce their frequency or intensity. Adaptation preparedness has been hard to spell out in policy terms and yet governments around the world are increasingly adjusting to reflect the new normal associated with a heating climate. It is theoretically possible to simultaneously pursue climate mitigation and adaptation, although continued struggle in the former may accelerate serious engagement in the latter.

In theory, democratic capitalism should prove particularly nimble in leading the way on adaptation, harnessing technology and both public and private resources to prepare for coming climate threats. This will include heightened weather risk detection capacity, new safety and reliability standards for buildings and transportation systems, expanded cooling capacity, and preparedness for migration of people and animals. In developed nations, adaptation also opens avenues for conflicts over resource use, including energy, land, and water. Such challenges only mount when contemplating adaptation in nations with emerging economies and limited resources, or governments with limited capacity to facilitate migration. Ironically, many of the very nations that have historically contributed the most to loading the atmosphere with greenhouse gases may prove most flexible and least directly harmed by this transition, raising an unprecedented series of questions about fairness in how the world responds and adapts.

Conclusion

Despite decades of mounting natural and physical science evidence, the continuing acceleration of climate change attributable to greenhouse gas accumulation has not been mitigated by democratic capitalism. Some policy and technological advances suggest considerable mitigation potential, providing models for potential emulation and diffusion. But these have largely been concentrated in relatively small sectors, such as refrigeration and air conditioning chemicals, or been unable thus far to achieve high levels of utilization across many jurisdictions, such as renewable energy.

Overall, the decades of the late twentieth and early twenty-first centuries generally reflect sustained failure by major emitting nations and economic sectors to achieve a path toward deep greenhouse gas emission reductions. Aside from the Kigali regime addressing cooling sector chemicals, no other credible global climate regime exists that formally drives rapid technological transformation across all nations. Only Kigali establishes a binding emission reduction framework, imposes major trade sanctions for non-compliance, and funds technological access by both advanced and emerging economies. For all other greenhouse gases, international policy remains a hodge-podge of loose mechanisms allowing nations to claim political credit for non-binding future emission reduction pledges that can prove easy to evade over time.

Nations in the forefront of democratic capitalism, including the United States, have continued to struggle with ongoing dependence upon fossil fuel production and use backed by formidable political support. Political polarization has confounded efforts to build broad and durable political coalitions to support effective mitigation policy; the European Union remains the primary exception to this pattern. Climate policy has also been dogged by political battles over competing policy approaches rather than efforts to sequence tools such as pricing, regulation, and subsidies in effective ways. Growing emphasis on nationalism in energy production and use may open some windows to expanded deployment of emerging technologies in individual domestic contexts, linking home-grown energy transition to local political economy benefits. However, this pattern increasingly undermines prospects for cross-jurisdictional coordination and credible global strategies, as nations with advanced economies show little appetite to shift resources and technologies to nations with emerging economies.

In turn, the reach of democratic capitalism to address climate change is further impaired by the ever-growing volume of annual greenhouse gas emissions that emanate from authoritarian nations. Many such nations have unusually dismal emission records, reflecting high rates of energy inefficiency, political preference to continue to pursue indigenous fossil fuel resources with little attention to methane loss, and indifferent commitments to global climate policy adoption and implementation. Alongside the challenge that democracies face in reducing their own greenhouse gas releases, any credible climate strategy must include active engagement by authoritarian nations.

These shortcomings of democratic capitalism and authoritarianism have triggered searches for alternative policy and technological options. These include heightened consideration of expanded use of trade policy to leverage climate-friendly reforms through import tariffs, new experiments in the use of climate subsidies and industrial policies that might ease domestic political opposition, and the emergence of largely untested, high-risk technologies to either capture and store carbon dioxide below ground or remove it from the atmosphere. None of these are proven alternatives but they underscore the growing consensus that existing political and economic systems have largely failed to date to deter profound risks posed by climate change. In turn, that realization has contributed to a growing focus on adaptation rather than mitigation, considering ways to attempt to manage the myriad and wrenching impacts of an ever-heating climate, given the enduring limitations to date of mitigation efforts.

Notes

1. Paul J. Young, Anna B. Harper, Chris Huntingford, et al., "The Montreal Protocol Protects the Terrestrial Carbon Sink," *Nature* 598, (August 19, 2021): 384–391; Gabrielle Dreyfus, Yangyang Xu, Drew Shindell, and Veerabhadran Ramanathan, "Mitigating Climate Disruption in Time," *PNAS* 119, (May 23, 2022): 1–12.
2. United Nations Environment Programme, *Emissions Gap Report*, 2022.
3. John Springford, Christian Odendahl, Elisabetta Cornago, and Zach Meyers, *Ditchley Conference Report: The Politics of Climate Change* (Center for European Reform, 2022).
4. Andrew Green, *Picking Up the Slack: Law, Institutions, and Canadian Climate Policy* (University of Toronto Press, 2022).
5. Ann Carlson and Dallas Burtraw, eds., *Lessons from the Clean Air Act* (Cambridge University Press, 2019).
6. Charles Sabel and David Victor, *Fixing the Climate: Strategies for an Uncertain World* (Princeton University Press, 2022), ch. 2.
7. Young, et al., "The Montreal Protocol Protects the Terrestrial Carbon Sink."
8. United Nations Environmental Program, *Cooling Emissions and Policy Synthesis Report* (2020); Saugat Bolakhe, "Rethinking Air Conditioning Amid Climate Change," *Knowable Magazine*, April 12, 2022.
9. Frank Thompson, Kenneth Wong, and Barry G. Rabe, *Trump, the Administrative Presidency, and Federalism* (Brookings Press, 2020).
10. William F. Lamb, Michael Grubb, Francesca Diluiso, and Jan C. Minx, et al., "Countries with Sustained Greenhouse Gas Emissions Reductions: An Analysis of Trends and Progress by Sector," *Climate Policy* 22:1 (2022): 1–17.
11. Daniel Fiorino, *Can Democracy Handle Climate Change?* (Polity, 2018).
12. Yale University Center for Environmental Law and Policy and Columbia University Center for International Earth Science Information Network, *Environmental Performance Index 2022: Ranking Country Performance on Sustainability Issues.*
13. Elin Lerum Boasson, Merethe Dotterud, and Jørgen Wettestad, eds., *Comparative Renewables Policy* (Palgrave, 2021).
14. Torben Mideska, "Pricing for a Cooler Planet," CESifo Working Papers 9172 (2021); Matti Kojo and Tapio Litmanen, eds., *The Renewal of Nuclear Power in Finland* (Palgrave, 2009).
15. Jørgen Wettestad and Torbjørg Jevnaker, *Rescuing EU Emissions Trading: The Climate Policy Flagship* (Palgrave, 2016); Andrew Jordan and Brendan Moore, *Durable by Design? Policy Feedback in a Changing Climate* (Cambridge University Press, 2020).
16. International Energy Agency, *Tracking Clean Energy Progress* (2022).
17. Fiorino, *Can Democracy Handle Climate Change?*; Roger Karapin, *Political Opportunities for Climate Policy* (Cambridge University Press, 2016).
18. Matto Mildenberger, *Carbon Captured* (MIT Press, 2020).

19. Paasha Mahdavi, *Power Grab: Political Survival through Extractive Resource Nationalization* (Cambridge University Press, 2020).
20. Steven Bernstein and Matthew Hoffman, "Climate Politics, Metaphors, and the Fractal Carbon Trap," *Nature Climate Change* 9 (2019): 919–25.
21. Green, *Picking Up the Slack*, p. 212.
22. Barry G. Rabe, *Carbon Pricing Enters Middle Age* (Wilson Center, 2023); Rabe, *Can We Price Carbon?* (MIT Press, 2018).
23. Jessica Green, "Does Carbon Pricing Reduce Emissions?," *Environmental Review Letters* 16 (2022): 1–17.
24. World Bank, *State and Trends of Carbon Pricing* (2024).
25. Julius Andersson, "Carbon Taxes and CO2 Emissions," *American Economic Journal: Economic Policy* 11 (2019): 1–30; Torben Mideska, "Pricing for a Cooler Planet," CESifo Working Paper 9172 (2021).
26. Springford, et al., *Ditchley Conference Report.*
27. Barry G. Rabe, *The Politics of Short-lived Climate Pollutants and North American Methane Policy* (International Policy Center, 2022).
28. Barry G. Rabe and Rachel Hampton, "The Re-emergence of State Trust Funds in the Shale Era," *Energy Research & Social Science* 20 (2016): 117–27; Gordon Clark, et al., *Sovereign Wealth Funds* (Princeton University Press, 2013).
29. "Nationally determined contributors," The *Economist*, July 30, 2022: 55-56
30. Kate Larsen, et al., *China's Greenhouse Gas Emissions Exceeded the Developed World for the First Time in 2019* (Rhodium Group, 2022).
31. Ross Mittiga, "Political Legitimacy, Authoritarianism, and Climate Change," *American Political Science Review* 116 (2022): 1–14.
32. Gregory F. Nemet, *How Solar Energy Became Cheap: A Model for Low-Carbon Innovation* (Routledge, 2019).
33. David G. Victor, Marcel Lumkowsky, and Astrid Dannenberg, "Determining the Credibility of Commitments in International Climate Policy," *Nature Climate Change* 12 (2022): 793–800.
34. Shuting Pomerleau, *Is the U.S. Really a Leader in Low-Carbon Intensity?* (Niskanen Center, 2023).
35. Adnan Vatansever, *Oil in Putin's Russia* (University of Toronto Press, 2021).
36. International Energy Agency, *Global Methane Tracker 2024.*

5

Recruiting Capitalism for Environmental Protection

SHI-LING HSU

This volume grapples with the question of whether capitalism and democracy are ultimately irreconcilable. There is a great deal of variation in these two broad terms, but the prevailing fear nowadays is notionally the same as that expressed by Smith, Marx, Polanyi, Schumpeter, and others: that the forces of capitalism attack and ultimately undermine social and political institutions. In our troubled modern times, the fear is that capitalist forces have already set about irreparably corroding the foundations of democracy. This chapter addresses the specific problem of environmental degradation, which appears to be just a variant of that age-old worry: capitalism seems to be undermining the governmental institutions responsible for environmental protection.

There is a bit of explanatory value in this line of thinking. Examples abound in which polluting industries translate economic might into political clout to weaken environmental law and the institutions protecting the environment. But the argument is problematic. For one thing, this narrative elides the different forms of capitalism in existence throughout the world. Some capitalist economies are better, sometimes far better, than others in minimizing the environmental footprint of market activity. For another thing, there is no counterfactual to this argument. As far as environmental protection is concerned, what is the alternative to capitalism? The most obvious candidate, socialism (also a vague concept) necessarily entails some slide toward authoritarianism as a means for centralized decision-making. Socialist-authoritarian countries have, in the several experiments thus far, performed much worse in terms of environmental outcomes.

There is a tempting (if troubling) logic in the appeal of socialism for environmental protection: democratic countries with capitalist economies inevitably

Shi-Ling Hsu, *Recruiting Capitalism for Environmental Protection.* In: *Can Democracy and Capitalism Be Reconciled?.* Edited by: Sidney M. Milkis and Scott C. Miller, Oxford University Press. © Oxford University Press (2025).
DOI: 10.1093/9780197774731.003.0006

suffer from rent-seeking and rent-preserving activities.[1] In fact, rent-seeking and rent-preserving activities seem to exploit the openness of democratic societies. Choking off such activities—many of which protect polluting industries—would necessarily involve restricting the openness of democratic societies, so the thinking goes.

Rent-seeking and rent-preserving activities represent a tension between democracy and capitalism, but this tension between governance and markets is not unique to democratic countries or capitalist economies. On the contrary, democratic societies with capitalist economies have generally been better at managing rent seeking and rent preserving than socialist-authoritarian countries. On balance, the openness of democratic societies has done more to reinforce a very broadly held norm for environmental protection than it has to encourage or enable rent-seeking or rent-preserving activities.

This chapter argues that it is possible, working fully within democratic institutions, to not only manage rent-seeking and rent-preserving activities, but to channel capitalist energies toward different, more environmentally oriented objectives. Capitalist economies are driven by prices, and the current pollution-heavy, fossil fuel-centered economy is a product of a sprawling network of prices that neglect to account for environmental harm. Redirecting capitalist energies to focus upon less environmentally harmful technologies and methods requires changing those prices. This chapter calls for changing prices by taxing pollution.

Pollution taxation (or "environmental taxation") is, of course, a familiar prescription and a perpetual political challenge. Prices could also be changed by subsidizing technologies and methods believed to reduce pollution. Subsidies are less economically efficient and less effective than pollution taxes, but are more politically expedient. Although capitalist economies are dynamic, they are still path-dependent with respect to industrial practices and methods. If subsidies can change the trajectory of capital investments, even subtly, they may change political economies enough to make pollution taxation more palatable. In other words, environmental subsidies, though inferior, may play a transitional role in easing political opposition to pollution taxation.

Socialism as an Alternative

There is a great deal of ambiguity in the terms "capitalism," and its opposing term "socialism." Both socialism and capitalism defy clean definitions, as the complexities of economic governance make categorization difficult. As a very general matter, in economies that are considered capitalist, prices tend to be considered as exogenous, and investment decisions are relatively unfettered by government influence.[2] A socialist economy, on the other hand, tends toward centralization of pricing and investment decisions. Countries tending toward socialist economies thus tend toward authoritarian government—the centralization of pricing and investment decisions makes this necessary.[3]

Some environmental progressives are troubled by what they see as unfettered market activity producing an inordinate amount of pollution. The centralization of decision-making in socialist-authoritarian countries seems to appeal to capitalism-skeptical environmental progressives that see market activity as causing environmental degradation. The environmental scholar Gus Speth, a top Carter Administration official, has written that capitalism is an "externalizing machine." While *rejecting* socialist solutions, Speth laments that the profit motive supplies a strong incentive to offload external costs, and that environmental costs are among the easiest to offload.[4]

But even where an explicit profit motive is absent, there remain many other motivations for externalizing environmental costs. In the few experiments with socialist-authoritarianism undertaken thus far, centralized, non-market government directives have created their own incentives for cost externalization that are at least as powerful as the profit motive. A centralized directive of the Soviet Union to make the country self-sufficient in cotton is responsible for the shrinking, by half, of the Aral Sea, the world's fourth-largest lake when the cotton growing began. The washing ashore of over 5,000 dead pigs just upriver from the most populous city in the world, Shanghai, can be traced not only to lax environmental enforcement but also to a stated Chinese "strategic imperative" to feed a national taste for pork. Venezuela's state-owned oil industry is the world's worst in terms of engaging in the wasteful practice of flaring excess gas during production, while its aging pipelines leak prodigiously. This argument is only anecdotal, but the list of anecdotes is very long, given the fairly small number of countries considered "socialist." To be sure, there are also instances in which capitalism appears to have led to environmental degradation, such as when countries transitioning from centrally planned economies to market-based ones experience a traumatic loss of a natural resource. But in general, the stark environmental contrast of socialist-authoritarian countries with the rest of the world suggests that a broad condemnation of capitalism misses the mark.

Why *might* socialist-authoritarian countries actually be worse polluters? Again, the experience with such countries is limited, but one common theme runs through all of them: they have been less prosperous and less productive than comparable democratic countries with capitalist economies. Centralized pricing and investment decisions simply do not move resources to their highest valued uses.[5] While some socialist-authoritarian countries have, at times, established environmental laws, economic crises have repeatedly pushed environmental concerns into the background.[6] And in hiding environmental harms, socialist-authoritarian governments are aided by opaque governance.

Political Choices

In a sense, blaming a system labeled as "capitalist" for environmental degradation is a prevarication, a rationalization for the political choices that have steered a capitalist economy in a particular direction. Different, less polluting and less fossil fuel-intensive directions are possible, but would require the making of different choices. Most political choices in the United States that have led to excess pollution have been driven by the Republican Party, but there is broad consensus across the political spectrum for many of these political choices. For example, ahead of the 2022 midterm elections, President Biden released 180 million barrels from the Strategic Petroleum Reserve to keep gasoline prices low. The energy crisis precipitated by the Russian invasion of Ukraine could have been, like the oil crisis of the 1970s, an opportunity to increase energy efficiency. But the Biden Administration calculated (probably correctly) that low gasoline prices would help the Democratic Party stem its losses in Congressional races. It has been an explicit bipartisan political choice that gasoline prices in the United States should remain much lower than that of similarly affluent countries such as Canada, Australia, New Zealand, Sweden, Finland, and even oil-rich Norway. All of those countries have lower population densities than the United States, so there is no structural reason that gasoline prices must be so low.

It has also been a political choice to tolerate the proliferation of chemical substances of unknown toxicity and carcinogenicity. It has been an explicit political choice to impose low regulatory costs of developing new chemicals, along with the attendant risks of knowing almost nothing about their properties. The primary means for regulating potentially toxic chemicals is the Toxic Substances Control Act, which was amended in 2016.[7] That amendment was bipartisan and the first significant instance of environmental lawmaking by Congress since 1990. It was a conscious legislative choice to avoid imposing mandatory testing requirements for new chemicals, and instead delegate to an understaffed and underfunded US Environmental Protection Agency the task of figuring out, among the hundreds of thousands of industrial chemicals in use, which warranted testing and which do not. It has also been a political choice to tolerate widespread water pollution and the loss of biological diversity in exchange for low food prices and the maintenance of a strange American agricultural sector, at one turn efficient and at another inefficient. It has been a choice for the United States to repeatedly eschew carbon taxation. Republicans have made opposition to carbon taxation a litmus test, but many environmental organizations have campaigned vigorously against environmental taxes on distributional grounds.

All of these choices were products of a democratic process, albeit a process very often tainted by rent seeking and rent preserving, and often driven by misinformation. Unlike decisions made in socialist-authoritarian countries, these choices have been formally susceptible to public input, and from time to time, influenced by a public interest acting in opposition to industries engaging in rent seeking and rent preserving. Environmental defeats have largely been political ones, not the inevitable product of capitalist economies.

It is true that some political choices are touted as improving capitalism, in which case it might be argued after all that an inherent tension exists between capitalism and environmental protection. The line between capitalism-enhancing and political choices can be blurry, as it is in antitrust law, which has always wrestled with the mixed political and economic question of industrial concentration. In the environmental realm, a widely circulated canard is that low energy prices, low food prices, and low chemical prices should be maintained so as to maximize economic activity and help capital migrate to their highest and best uses. The fact that these arguments are couched in economic terms does not mean that they are necessarily advancing the cause of capitalism, and it does not mean they are apolitical. Had the politics or the political economy of these choices been different, it is entirely possible that the choices would have been different. The variety of democratic countries that have made different choices suggests as much. Sweden taxes carbon dioxide emissions at about $135/ton,[8] the cost of water in Israel is roughly seven times that in California,[9] and the tiny country of New Zealand, which has 5.6 times as many sheep as people, has embarked upon a taxation scheme to tax livestock for their emissions of methane, a greenhouse gas that is generated by regurgitating animals.[10] US Senate ratification of the Kigali Amendment in 2022,[11] an international agreement to phase out hydrofluorocarbons, a powerful greenhouse gas, suggests that even in a polarized and dysfunctional United States, paths to pollution regulation still exist. It is also easy to forget and take for granted the flurry of federal environmental statutes passed in the United States in the 1970s, a series of political choices that have not been undone. While there is still too much pollution, those federal environmental statutes have certainly altered the path of the US economy, setting it on a different course than it might have taken otherwise.[12] Governance can be a mixed question of economics and politics, but allocations of the burdens and benefits of economic activity is a political choice.

Prices, Capitalism, and Path-dependence

The environmental outcomes of capitalist economies are thus determined by political choices. Regulations, taxes, subsidies, institutions, organizations, and government activity are all the products of political choices, and all affect economic activity. It is important to bear in mind that political choices do this by affecting prices, directly or indirectly. Taxes and subsidies, for example, directly affect the prices of the taxed or subsidized good or service, and indirectly of related products. Fossil fuel subsidies reduce the price of fossil fuel-generated electricity. Regulations—or the lack thereof—affect prices indirectly, such as when a pollution control requirement increases the production cost of a raw material, such as steel, and consequently products that contain steel.

The emphasis on prices is critical to understanding the outcomes of a capitalist economy. Although capitalism is only amorphously defined, there is wide agreement that it is a system of economic governance that embraces decentralized markets as a way of coordinating and allocating labor and resources.[13] Capitalism allows for investment, a means of connecting ideas with money, even money that happens to be far away. In extending markets to investment monies, capitalism allows vast sums of money to be directed quickly, sometimes too quickly. The prices of goods and services—sometimes implicit—play a central role in determining the flow of resources in a capitalist economy.

Inevitably, choices that influence prices are highly political. This volume asks the question of whether those political choices, heavily influenced by private industry and business, can undermine the democratic processes in which those choices are made. This chapter, pertaining specifically to environmental protection, does not follow this progression (or perhaps, digression) to an antidemocratic conclusion. Rather than treat capitalism as a force that corrupts democratic institutions, this chapter proposes instead a means of harnessing capitalist forces to transform a global, fossil fuel-centered economy. Such a capitalism-driven transformation would have to come about as a result of a change in prices resulting from taxation on pollution. I propose a system of environmental taxes: unitary levies on small, measurable amounts of pollution.

Environmental taxation, of course, is nothing new.[14] However, the case I make for environmental taxation differs from that of preceding scholars, which has mostly been to argue for striking a balance between marginal costs and marginal benefits, thereby achieving some optimal level of pollution. My argument for environmental taxation is capitalist economies can be said to have a *direction,* and environmental taxes are required to *steer* economies in a different direction: pushing economic activity toward environmentally sustainable technologies, methods, and industries. Prices play a central role in steering economies and environmental taxes in affecting prices, and do so in a way that most directly affects the pollution itself. A wide variety of other factors are important as well, such as political environments, but at bottom, consumption and capital flows are determined by prices, and a new network of prices *must* account for harm to the environment through environmental taxes.

As an example of how prices lend direction to a capitalist economy, consider the role of tax subsidies for fossil fuels in the United States. Congress enacted special tax treatment for the oil and gas industries in 1913. Unlike other heavy industries, the largest assets of energy industries were their energy deposits, so Congress allowed energy firms to claim some fraction of their energy reserves—once as high as 27.5 percent for oil—as capital expense, deductible against income.[15] Additionally, oil and gas firms were (and some still are) allowed to deduct *immediately*, not depreciate over a period of years, "intangible drilling costs," such as labor, fuel, power, materials, supplies, and drilling site preparation. This allowance, unavailable to other industries, essentially allows oil and gas firms to defer tax payments, tantamount to an interest-free loan.

These favorable tax rules and subsidies incentivized exploration and production, funneling far more capital investment than would otherwise have occurred.[16] One study estimated that from 1918 to 2009, oil and gas firms have received $447 billion in subsidies, measured in 2010 dollars, the equivalent of $4.85 billion per year.[17] As much money as that is, it does not represent the effect of subsidies on oil and gas activity, and how they steered the American economy down a particular path. A subsidy need only *affect* capital decisions, not finance the entire capital investment. Thus, a $4.85 billion injection (it was greater in earlier years) would have induced capital investment in excess of that amount. How much? In response to a 2013 Obama Administration proposal to phase out these subsidies, a study commissioned by the American Petroleum Institute estimated that just a *delay* of deductibility for $1 billion of intangible drilling costs would have reduced capital expenditures by $44 billion in 2019 (a 27% drop from the baseline case) and would have eliminated over 233,000 jobs. If that study is accurate within just an order of magnitude, then the amount of induced investment over a century in the oil and gas extraction industry is in the many trillions of dollars.

It seems banal to assert that prices play a central role in determining the direction taken by a capitalist economy, but the effects are surprisingly large and broad. Consider the effect of low oil and gas prices on adjacent industries. Petroleum-fed chemical industries have also benefited from low oil prices. Low fuel costs made highway construction seem more sensible. Land use development patterns throughout the United States were affected by the low cost of transportation, in turn resulting in much greater motor vehicle usage than all but a small number of countries in the world. Motor vehicles themselves have developed against the backdrop of low fuel prices.[18] Homes, businesses, and factories, and everything inside that consumes electricity have been designed with low electricity prices in mind. All of these effects and many others were the product of a political choice to grant favorable tax treatment to oil and gas industries (and later the coal industry), and the continuing choice not to repeal them. The enormous fossil fuel-centered footprint was a product of a political choice to keep energy prices low, despite ample evidence of the environmental harms of fossil fuel combustion.[19] Alternative technologies are more cost-effective because of lower environmental costs, but fossil fuels have persisted. The direction of the American economy has been difficult to change.

The persistence of fossil fuel-centered and fossil fuel-adjacent industries (such as chemical manufacturing or vehicle manufacturing) suggest a degree of path-dependence. One source of path-dependence stems from the cumulation of innovation. Acemoglu et al. found that in energy industries, research and development and resulting innovation was skewed toward incumbent industries with an already developed capital stock, in their case "dirty," fossil fuel-generated electricity. Since "dirty" incumbents enjoyed a head start over "clean" renewable energy technologies, and since innovation reduces production costs, it stood to reason that an effective barrier to entry was preventing renewable energy technologies from making more headway.[20] Similar results were obtained by Aghion, et al., which found, within the context of the automobile industry, that a larger stock of "dirty" innovation (internal combustion vehicles) was much larger than that of "clean" innovation (electric vehicles and hydrogen vehicles), and that only a very large carbon tax could cause clean technologies to catch up with dirty ones quickly.[21] The implication for both studies was clear: that the extant accumulation of capital investments in incumbent industries poses a barrier to innovation in newer, "cleaner" industries. For physical capital assets, innovation improves the efficiency of those assets over time, further lowering input prices. Capital investment in capitalist economies is thus a contest, not just among firms but among sectors. Innovation that is sector-wide or industry-wide will attract more capital to those sectors or industries. Moreover, and perhaps even more critically, investments in physical capital attract human capital, which also adds value to physical capital. Physical and human capital can develop a symbiotic relationship that enhances the value and productivity of both. Capital investments, and an accompanying knowledge stock, thus cumulate.

In addition to the path-dependence identified in Acemoglu et al. and Aghion et al., this chapter introduces an additional source of path-dependence: rent-seeking and rent-preserving activities that manipulate law and policy to preserve competitive advantage.[22] Long-lived and expensive capital assets may, at some point during their operating lives, confront new information or new technologies that render them suboptimal, or even obsolete. This dynamic creates incentives for the owners of expensive physical assets to protect their investments by engaging, sometimes aggressively, with the political process. Owners of capital may engage in political activities that amount to rent seeking or rent preserving. What is at stake for those owners of expensive capital assets are the streams of rents that they expected when making their investments, that may no longer be warranted. Perhaps of even greater political importance is the human capital that may be intertwined with threatened physical capital. Firms can diversify their physical capital stocks, but individuals have a limited number of opportunities during their lifetimes to obtain human capital. Threats to their human capital can seem existential to their holders, and may provide even greater impetus for rent-preserving activities.

Consider Figure 5.1, a very simple graphical illustration of this one dynamic of capital investment. The horizontal axis is time, and the vertical axis is cumulative profitability. At *t=0*, a capital investment is made for a physical asset, either a larger one with an instantaneous cost ***C1***, or a larger one with a smaller cost **C2**.

Conceptually, a capital investment at time *0* represents an immediate decrease in profits, but the capital investor expects that the asset will pay back over time, resulting in the increasing cumulative profitability lines, dotted for the small one and solid for the larger one. At the end of the useful life of both capital assets, at *t=h*, both assets would be retired, with the larger one having generated a larger profit.

However, at some time during the life of the asset, a new technology may emerge, new global trading patterns may emerge, or new information about negative externalities produced by the asset may be discovered. If this new development occurs at time *x*, at that point it could be beneficial for society but disadvantageous for the capital owner to abandon the asset. If that were to happen, the owners of large capital would be losing the larger amount ***L1*** and the small capital owners would be losing ***L2***.

In theory, capital owners should assume the risk that future profits fail to materialize. The reality is that capital owners engaging in rent-preserving activities

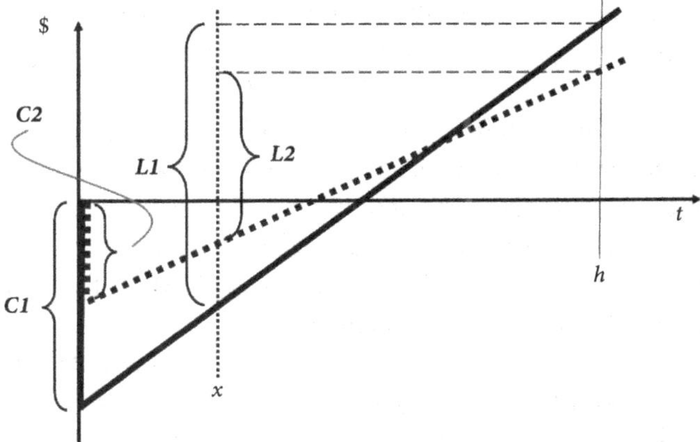

Figure 5.1 A dynamic of capital investment

often call upon, often successfully, government bodies to protect not just their capital outlays but also their expected stream of profits. Note that since ***L1*** and ***L2*** can be larger than original capital outlays ***C1*** and **C2**, it is entirely possible that capital owners may be willing to spend *more* than their original capital outlays to engage in rent-preserving activities to protect their capital investments. Political choices are made to protect capital investments from competition, trade, and environmental protection laws. I provide here three examples, but there are plenty more where these came from.

First, federal motor vehicle fuel efficiency standards have advanced only sporadically in the past few decades. In 2007, President George W. Bush created a special category for passenger trucks and sport-utility vehicles that were much more lenient than for cars,[23] leading to the evolution of enormous trucks and sport utility vehicles with dismal gas mileage and that threaten the safety of pedestrians, cyclists, and every other vehicle sharing the road with these behemoths.[24] The beneficiaries of this dichotomy were the Big Three US automakers, which make much larger profits on these gigantic, dangerous vehicles.[25] Second, under the Federal Insecticide, Fungicide, and Rodenticide Act, even after a pesticide is deemed to be dangerous enough to warrant prohibition, pesticide makers are allowed to sell existing stocks, and farmers are permitted to use them.[26] And third, in the US Supreme Court opinion in *West Virginia v. EPA* involving EPA regulations to reduce greenhouse gas emissions from power plants, Chief Justice Roberts lamented that the rule "would entail billions of dollars in compliance costs (to be paid in the form of higher energy prices), require the retirement of dozens of coal-fired plants, and eliminate tens of thousands of jobs across various sectors."[27] Almost all of that lament was inaccurate, but it indicated a deep-seated concern for incumbent industries and workers. The opinion has been heavily criticized[28] for its invocation of the little-used "major questions doctrine," but it is worth also remembering that the case stemmed from an Obama Administration regulation necessitated by Congressional refusal to legislate. Congressional intransigence on climate policy now spans multiple generations.

These are the kinds of political choices that are commonly made to avoid the disruptions characteristic of capitalism. This inertia is most pronounced in fossil fuel and fossil fuel-adjacent industries. Effectively, political choices are made to *insure* capital investors from unexpected setbacks from new information. Consider Table 5.1, which sets for a list of most of the NAICS 4-digit subsectors, ranked in descending order of capital intensity.[29]

Four caveats are in order. First, this table represents a snapshot in time: 2014, not a long-term representation. Second, this table only supports an inference, and is not offered as empirical proof. Third, in 2014, pipeline investment happened to be larger than it was in other periods of measurement; I chose 2014 because I draw the value-added data from Tschofen, Azevedo, and Muller. That said, pipeline investment generally tends to be very capital intensive. Fourth, some of these sectors are capital intensive because of their regulatory legal regime. For example, many utilities are capital intensive because they are governed by a regulated utility model, in which capital expenditures are allowed or disallowed by a public commission. This governance model is believed to

Table 5.1 **Ratio of 2014 Capital Expenditures/Value Added**

Pipeline transportation	1.185
Oil and gas extraction	0.824
Farms	0.515
Mining, except oil and gas	0.475
Rail transportation	0.458
Utilities	0.448
Water transportation	0.406
Other transportation equipment	0.303
Air transportation	0.194
Plastics and rubber products	0.182
Wood products	0.165
Other retail	0.152
Nonmetallic mineral products	0.151
Truck transportation	0.149
Forestry, fishing, and related activities	0.132
Hospitals	0.130
Waste management and remediation services	0.127
Chemical products	0.125
Food, beverage, and tobacco products	0.123
Educational services	0.121
Miscellaneous manufacturing	0.120
Paper products	0.118
Primary metals	0.115
Other transportation and support activities	0.104
Textile mills and textile product mills	0.102
Computer & electronic products	0.100
Machinery	0.097
Warehousing and storage	0.083
Petroleum & coal products	0.082
Fabricated metal products	0.082
Accommodation	0.081
Printing and related support activities	0.078
Electrical equipment, appliances, and components	0.064
Other services, except government	0.057
Motor vehicles, bodies, and trailers as well as parts	0.056
Food services and drinking places	0.055
Construction	0.052
Furniture and related products	0.046
Apparel and leather, also allied products	0.043
Wholesale trade	0.042
Transit and ground passenger transportation	0.041
Admin and support services	0.037
Support activities for mining	0.012

create an incentive to engage in excessive capital investment.[30] "Value added" is a purely economic term defined by the Bureau of Labor Statistics; as such it *does not* include costs external to industries.

While my point is only inferential—such a simple model can only be inferential—it is difficult to avoid noticing that the most capital-intensive industries tend to be the older ones, fossil fuel-related, and most tend to have large environmental externalities. Why do we tolerate both economic inefficiency and environmental externalities?

Path-dependence of economic activity in a capitalist economy poses a challenge to traditional notions of capital investment. The emphasis on innovation in Acemoglu et al. and Aghion et al. is path breaking not only because it enriches notions of capital investment but also because it lends credence to the notion that capitalist economies can have a *direction*. Given the relatively small fiscal cost of energy subsidies, it is astonishing that so much industrial and land use development has seemingly followed from low fossil fuel prices. Without a counterfactual, it is hard to know *exactly* how different the American fossil fuel-centered economy would have been, and how much of a role path-dependence has played. But the examples of countries such as Canada, Australia, New Zealand, Norway, Sweden, the United Kingdom, and many European countries serve as stark counterexamples. One study of gasoline prices over a 23-year period in OECD countries found that not only do low gasoline prices lead to high consumption but that high consumption begets low gasoline prices. In other words, the causality runs both ways! The authors conclude that high gasoline consumption leads to political pressure, perhaps implicit, to keep gasoline prices low.[31]

Environmental Taxation Revisited: Breadth of Innovation

This chapter proposes the imposition of a system of environmental taxes to account for pollution so as to overcome path-dependence, and to redirect economic activity and innovation to more environmentally benign methods and technologies. Environmental taxation is a means of changing the price of an input—in this cost of being able to pollute—to induce innovation. The notion that input prices can induce innovation dates back to *The Theory of Wages* by Sir John Hicks in 1932.[32] The suggestion that environmental taxation might stimulate innovation by changing input prices has been made by a number of researchers, including Popp,[33] Goulder and Schneider,[34] Acemoglu et al.,[35] and others.[36] If, as I assert, that a capitalist economy can be said to have a direction, then there are few indicators more fitting than where innovation is occurring. Environmental taxation is thus a way to induce innovation for reducing pollution and steering the American economy in a different direction.

Innovation is doubly important because it is now clear that several environmental crises cannot be adequately addressed without the development and implementation of new technologies. Chief among the environmental crises, climate change, will require a number of innovations on a number of fronts in order to steer economic development and growth onto a path that minimizes, as much as possible on this very late date, global exposure to climatic risks. In fact, global emissions trajectories may already be such that even unrealistically fast and drastic emissions reductions can no longer avert catastrophically climatic changes; to do that, carbon removal technologies must be developed and scaled up to remove extant greenhouse gases from the Earth's atmosphere. Those must be developed and implemented on a large scale, and innovation will be needed for that.

In addition to the familiar arguments that environmental taxation will stimulate innovation, I offer an additional one. An environmental tax has the advantage over previous regulatory efforts and over subsidies of formal agnosticism about the means of reducing pollution; this agnosticism preserves the maximum number of options for reducing pollution, and thus the maximum opportunity to innovate. Early environmental regulations defined compliance as the installation of some acceptably effective pollution control equipment, which would limit innovation to improvements in the specified technology. Modern regulation is more sophisticated and flexible, now usually specifying a level of pollution abatement consistent with the best-known technology, and thus permitting several options. But even that type of regulation assumes a class of approaches to reducing pollution. Subsidies must necessarily specify the technologies that can receive a benefit, thus narrowing innovation to the specified technology. By contrast, environmental taxation directly addresses the fundamental, underlying problem—too much pollution—without attempting to steer capital investment or innovation in any technological or methodological direction. This agnosticism is important, because as a general matter, innovation is maximized when the number and breadth of options for pollution reduction are maximized.[37] Any specificity in scope definition necessarily narrows the scope for inquiry and innovation.

For example, if a climate goal is stated as "the promotion of electric vehicles" (an explicit goal shared by several countries over decades),[38] and subsidies are directed toward the development of electric vehicles, then the universe of innovation resides entirely within the vehicle itself: the size and durability of the battery, the design of the engine, and perhaps other vehicle features that might increase the efficiency of energy conversion into movement. If, however, the goal is stated as "reducing emissions from motor vehicles," then the promotion of electric vehicles is less obviously the most environmentally beneficial or cost-effective way forward.[39] Even as countries and private firms worked on making electric vehicles practical for household use, Toyota's Prius hybrid electric vehicle became a best-seller and in its first two decades, and resulted in emissions reductions far, far greater than the slow-maturing electric vehicle industry. Going a bit further afield, if the climate goal is stated as "reducing emissions from transportation," then a much larger menu of options emerges, including the reduction of motor vehicle use itself. This might involve modal switching to bicycling and transit options, or it might involve land use changes to reduce the need for vehicular transportation. The now decades-old notion of "mixed use development" was motivated in part by a policy goal of reducing the need for vehicle trips altogether, and replacing them with pedestrian or bicycling transportation, with not only pollution reduction but also public health benefits. The COVID pandemic has clearly suggested ways to reduce the need for transportation that include the use of meeting technology.

In broadening the options, the potential scope for innovation increases, because *parts* of some emissions reduction strategies could be paired with parts of others. For example, electric vehicles can serve as household energy storage batteries; it could be that neither electric vehicle operation nor rooftop solar is economical for a particular household, but the combination might be. As another example, Northern California's Bay Area Rapid Transit system did not seek to replicate the New York City subway system; by developing BART train stops as parking lots, BART could greatly reduce vehicle emissions, even if it did not eliminate them entirely. By developing BART stops as business nodes, BART could also reduce the need for vehicular side trips, such as for groceries or dry-cleaning.

Environmental Subsidies Revisited: Changing the Political Economy of Environmental Taxation

Acemoglu et al. and Aghion et al. posit that capital investment and resulting knowledge stocks may cumulate, and thus create barriers to entry. In that sense, path-dependence is always a potential problem in capitalist economies. Moreover, democratic governments must always engage in open lawmaking, which creates problems with rent seeking and rent preserving. That would also tend to create barriers to entry and capital path-dependence. To address path-dependence, Acemoglu et al. suggest that as between "dirty" and "clean" industries, a small subsidy for clean industries might be warranted in order to compensate for the head start enjoyed by the dirty ones.

The efficiency arguments against subsidies, at least in comparison with environmental taxation, are well rehearsed.[40] But these arguments are usually made in the context of an idealized economic environment, a simplistic tax-versus-subsidy comparison that takes no account of political or social context, dynamic impacts, and without appreciation of path-dependence of capital investment. Those arguments still contain important lessons, but are incomplete. Drawing on work reviewed and presented above, several counter-arguments suggest that subsidization of environmentally beneficial technologies might be warranted under some circumstances after all.

First, environmental subsidies have always been politically easier to enact than environmental taxes. If environmental subsidies can be enacted more quickly, the severity and immediacy of the climate crisis suggest that the efficiency benefits of environmental taxation are far outweighed by the costs of waiting.[41] Second, there is ample reason to believe that research in technologies that confer positive externalities—such as technologies having the effect of reducing pollution—are systematically underfunded, and represent a market failure.[42] Subsidies may target suboptimal technologies and may be inefficient for other well-known reasons, but they can also divert capital flows away from polluting industries, partially offsetting the original market failure. Possibly, over time, subsidies may improve the political economy of environmental taxation. Third, given path-dependence in innovation and caused by rent seeking, simply correcting the original distortion by say, an environmental tax, will not be sufficient to correct a misallocation of capital investments produced by the original market failure.[43] Some *over-corrective* policy is required to correct the path of capital flows, and as between an environmental subsidy and a higher environmental tax, the former is more politically palatable. And fourth, path-dependence in capital investments also exists with respect to human capital, and given its symbiotic relationship with physical capital, may also require some over-correction to overcome market failure. Because human capital is difficult for workers to acquire, the injection of money represented by a subsidy may better facilitate the retraining required for workers to enter a new industry.

All of these counter-arguments address the political realities of environmental taxation. Since the primary obstacle to environmental taxation is political, changing the politics within the bounds of democratic processes and institutions would be vital to ensuring public acceptance of a policy that is generally unpopular.

The United States has taken some steps in this direction. The Inflation Reduction Act of 2022 contains over $300 billion of subsidies for a very wide variety of climate emissions reductions measures, as well as financing to help states and local governments adapt to the effects of climate change.[44] The Inflation Reduction Act was passed in a political environment extremely hostile to climate legislation, but it may not have passed at all without earlier passage of the Emergency Economic Stabilization Act of 2008,[45] which included an electric vehicle tax credit of $7,500, or of the American Recovery and Reinvestment Act of 2009,[46] which contained subsidies for alternative energy technologies, most prominently wind and solar energy. In the 13 years between the financial crisis-era legislation and the Inflation Reduction Act, technological advancements were surprisingly strong in wind and solar energy, electricity storage technology, and electric vehicle technology. It is challenging to imagine that the Inflation Reduction Act, facing a hostile Congress, would have passed without the technological advances of the preceding 13 years. It is also challenging to predict if or when truly meaningful climate policy, that would include carbon taxation as well as other measures, will pass in the United States. But if renewable energy technologies continue to develop and scale up with the benefit of subsidies, it will be an easier political lift than otherwise. The value of these subsidies was to change capital flows and alter the direction of the current fossil fuel-centered economy of the United States.

An Objection

An objection can be made that establishing a system of environmental taxation could be viewed cynically as a centralization of investment decisions after all. Certainly, if an agency charged with setting environmental tax rates viewed its mission as *engineering* a transformation of industry instead of *inducing* it, the danger is plausible. By setting high environmental taxation rates, or manipulating them, can't an agency in a democratic country practicing capitalism act, *de facto*, as a centralized decision-maker? Is it not true that a would-be authoritarian could, by levying unreasonably large environmental taxes achieve the same objective as by authoritarian impulse?

This objection underestimates the potential for good administrative lawmaking. It is possible, through careful lawmaking, to minimize the danger of skewing capital investment or more dramatically, authoritarian decision-making, through the guise of environmental taxation. In fact, given the complexities of environmental policy, there is no alternative to vesting an administrative agency with robust information-gathering and enforcement powers.

The proposal of this chapter is to legislatively authorize the US Environmental Protection Agency (EPA) to undertake a fact-finding, harm-measuring, and tax rate-setting process for demonstrably harmful pollutants. Administrative processes in the United States, and by the EPA in particular, are subject to *extreme* scrutiny, and are frequently the subject of litigation. The EPA has become accustomed, over the decades in which it has been sued thousands of times, to having their scientific and economic findings challenged. In this modern era of hyper-polarization, every single significant rule, and every single rule having anything to do with climate change, is litigated intensely—if not by private industry litigants, by state attorneys generally seeking to advance their ideological viewpoints.

Turning over a key process—that of identifying environmental externalities and assigning a cost to them—may be fraught and controversial, but not a recipe for authoritarianism. With courts overseeing virtually every single EPA decision of any significance, there is little chance that EPA, in the role of setting environmental tax rates, could conceal and carry out any ideological agenda or any mission of rent seeking. With a staff of tens of thousands, and an entire division of environmental economists, EPA was essentially created exactly for this kind of task: determining, quantifying, and monetizing the harmfulness of pollutants. If anything, the process will almost certainly be too slow, but there is no speedier alternative that is consistent with the principles of democratic government.

On a conceptual level, turning the regulatory orientation toward consideration of environmental externalities and their social costs would represent a paradigm shift in regulation. Any time that any legislative body or administrative agency has insinuated itself in a discussion of *how best* to achieve an environmental objective, it has gotten embroiled in political disputes. Considerations of efficacy or efficiency often cloak rent-preserving motivations. By straying too far from the environmental objective itself, legislators and regulators have lost sight of their core objectives and unwittingly attached themselves to some rent-seeking or rent-preserving objective. By refocusing the question upon the fundamental problem—the reduction of pollution—environmental taxation at least directs the discourse to a different domain, one that is at least focused on the environmental problem and not the technological solution. Even if the environmental tax-setting process would also be susceptible to rent seeking and rent preserving, it would represent, by virtue of the required information, a useful reorientation of the locus of dispute.

It is tempting, and difficult to avoid, equating authoritarian decision-making with the highly consequential environmental tax-setting decisions that must inevitably be made in a regime centered upon that very process. However, failure to make that distinction would rule out many meritorious laws and policies. The legal and policy basis for rulemaking is of supreme relevance for political legitimacy; to give up trying to distinguish would be a surrender to raw nihilism. It is one thing to revoke special land use and taxing prerogatives to Disney World because large private corporations should not enjoy special treatment; it is another thing to do so because "Florida is where Woke goes to die."[47]

Conclusion

Capitalist economies are supposed to be dynamic. In healthy capitalist economies there is—when technological, environmental, or social changes warrant—disruption and creative destruction.[48] However, those changes inevitably harm some people, sectors, or industries: that is the nature of economic change. Costly capital investments, both physical and human, that lose value with change create an incentive to resist change. In essence, capital investments create their own political economy, and generate rent-seeking or rent-preserving activities, creating some path-dependence. In a tangible sense, capitalist economies have a direction, or a trajectory.

Path-dependence in capital investment poses a challenge for those advocating for capitalism. The "steering" of a capitalist economy, as it turns out, can sometimes be a bit sticky. The implicit competition between sectors for capital may be biased, in the sense that some sectors and industries may have a large head start by virtue of innovation embedded in physical capital and human capital intertwined with it. Indisputably, fossil fuel industries have had an enormous head start over renewable energy technologies.

Environmental crises require modern capitalist economies to undergo a major course correction. The direction of the modern fossil fuel-centered and pollution-heavy economy was inadvertently set by an inefficient price environment, one that fails to reflect environmental harms. A course correction would involve changing errant prices, and the most efficient and the most effective way to accomplish that would be to impose a system of environmental taxes. Environmental taxes should be levied to closely track the estimated harm caused by the pollutant. Although a properly set tax level should produce an optimal amount of pollution, the greater significance is that capital investment patterns would change.

A strong argument can be made that because path-dependence in capital investment represents a barrier to entry, that some subsidization is needed to supplement the effects of a tax, to overcome the advantage enjoyed by incumbent industries. This argument is probably correct in the context of climate change. The costs of delay for climate change are likely greater than the deadweight losses of subsidizing suboptimal technologies to reduce climate change.

Environmental crises abound, with the climate crisis front and center in terms of the pressing need for economies worldwide to undergo change as soon as possible. But entrenched, heavily polluting industries such as the fossil fuel industry stand in the way. Dislodging them will require something powerful and disruptive. A dramatic and rapid course correction is required, in the form of wholesale replacement of large infrastructure and redeployment of large workforces. What else is out there, other than capitalism, that is up to the task?

Notes

1. Rent seeking is the seeking of favorable government policy securing above-normal wealth for members of a special interest group. Rent-preserving activities are the ex post analog of rent-seeking activities, and the exercise of protecting existing rents. Rent-preserving activities include lobbying or litigating, or prosecuting some public campaign to preserve its competitive position, which may be privately worthwhile but publicly costly. See, e.g., Mancur Olson, *The Rise and Decline of Nations* (Yale Univ. Press, 1982), 41–47. See also Gordon Tulloch & Charles Rowley, "The Rent-Seeking Society," in *The Selected Works of Gordon Tullock* (Liberty Fund, 2005).
2. See, e.g., Bruce R. Scott, *Capitalism: Its Origins and Evolution as a System of Governance* (Springer, 2011), 41–42.
3. Geoffrey Hodgson, *Is Socialism Feasible?* (Edward Elgar, 2019), 19.
4. James Gustave Speth, *America the Possible: Manifesto for a New Economy* (Yale University Press, 2012), 4.
5. Hodgson, *Is Socialism Feasible?*, 104, note 3.
6. See, e.g., Peter Pavlinek and John Pickles, "Environmental Pasts/Environmental Futures in Post-Socialist Europe," *Environmental. Politics* 13 (2007): 237, 242.
7. Frank R Lautenberg, Chemical Safety for the 21st Century Act, 130 Stat. 448, Pub. L. 114–82 (2016).
8. As of July 25, 2023, the Euro traded for $1.1054 USD. With a carbon tax of 122 Euros per metric ton of CO2, *see* Government Offices of Sweden, Sweden's Carbon Tax, https://perma.cc/26R2-DRW2 (last visited July 25, 2023), this translates to a carbon tax rate of $135 USD per metric ton.
9. Shi-Ling Hsu, *Capitalism and the Environment: A Proposal to Save the Planet* (Cambridge Univestity Press, 2021), 153.
10. Ministry for the Environment, Government of New Zealand, *Pricing Agricultural Emissions: Report under Section 215 of the Climate Change Response Act 2002* (2022), 11.
11. Amendment to the Montreal Protocol on Substances that Deplete the Ozone Layer, adopted at Kigali on October 15, 2016, by the Twenty-Eighth Meeting of the Parties to the Montreal Protocol, Ex. Rept. 117–2 (November 16, 2021).
12. For example, a cost-benefit analysis on the US Clean Air Act from 1990 to 2020 carried out by the EPA found that the benefits exceed the costs by 30 to 1. EPA Office of Air & Radiation, *The Benefits and Costs of the Clean Air Act from 1990 to 2020* (2011), 7–3, 7–8, https://www.epa.gov/clean-air-act-overview/benefits-and-costs-clean-air-act-1990-2020-second-prospective-study [https://perma.cc/VTC6-KEL8].
13. See, e.g., Geoffrey M. Hodgson, *Conceptualizing Capitalism: Institutions, Evolution, Future* (University of Chicago Press, 2015), 251–57.
14. See, e.g., Arthur Cecil Pigou, *The Economics of Welfare* (Macmillan, 1928), 131–35.
15. Owen L. Anderson, "Royalty Valuation: Should Royalty Obligations BE Determined Intrinsically, Theoretically, or Realistically?," *Natural Resources Journal* 37 (1997): 547, 554–56.
16. See, e.g., James C. Cox and Arthur W. Wright, "The Cost-effectiveness of Federal Tax Subsidies for Petroleum Reserves: Some Empirical Results and Their Implications," in *Studies in Energy Tax Policy*, ed. Gerard Brannon (Ballinger, 1975), 177, 188–89 (finding that special tax provisions induced the petroleum industry to maintain larger investments in proven reserves); Walter J. Mead, "The Performance of Government in Energy Regulations," *American Economic Revirew* 69 (1979): 352, 352.
17. Nancy Pfund and Ben Healey, *What Would Jefferson Do? The Historical Role of Federal Subsidies in Shaping America's Energy Future* (September 2011), 29, https://www.dbl.vc/wp-content/uploads/2012/09/What-Would-Jefferson-Do-2.4.pdf.
18. It should also be noted that federal fuel efficiency standards act as a counterweight to low fuel prices, but only a partial one. Vehicle fuel efficiency standards decrease the need for consumption, reducing the price of fuel, and in a "rebound," lead to small increases in consumption because of the resulting low prices. See e.g., Lorna A Greening, David L Greene, and Carmen Difiglio, "Energy Efficiency and Consumption—the Rebound Effect—a Survey," *Energy Policy* 28 (2000): 389, 399.

19. For example, fine particulate matter pollution emitted by coal-fired power plants has been estimated to cause at least 100,000 of premature deaths annually in the United States, Andrew L. Goodkind, Christopher W. Tessum, Jay Coggins, Jason D. Hill & Julian D. Marshall, "Fine-scale Damage Estimate of Particulate Matter Air Pollution Reveal Opportunities for Location-specific Mitigation of Emissions," *PNAS* 116 (2019): 8775 (citing Centers for Disease Control and Prevention, Underlying Cause of Death, 1999–2018 (2018), https://wonder.cdc.gov/ucd-icd10.html), and millions worldwide. *Burden of Disease from Ambient Air Pollution for 2016*, WHO (April 2016), https://www.who.int/airpollution/data/AAP_BoD_results_May2018_final.pdf?ua=1 [https://perma.cc/7N7D-3YY6].
20. Daron Acemoglu, Ufuk Akcigit, Douglas Hanley & William Kerr, "Transition to Clean Technology," *Journal of Political Economy* 124 (2016): 52.
21. Phillippe Aghion, Antoine Dechezlepretre, David Hemous, Ralf Martin & John Van Reenen, "Carbon Taxes, Path Dependency, and Directed Technical Change: Evidence from the Auto Industry," *Journal Of Political Economy* 124 (2016): 1.
22. See, e.g., Olson, *The Rise and Decline of Nations*, note 1.
23. See, *Passenger Automobile Average Fuel Economy Standards*, 49 CFR § 531; *Light Truck Fuel Economy Standards*, 49 CFR § 532; and *Medium- and Heavy-Duty Vehicle Fuel Efficiency Program*, 49 CFR § 535. It should be noted in fairness to the Bush Administration, prior to this rule, trucks were not covered at all by federal fuel efficiency standards.
24. See, e.g., Michael L. Anderson & Maximilian Aufhammer, "Pounds That Kill: The External Costs of Vehicle Weight," *Review of Economic Studies* 81 (2014): 535.
25. John Seabrook, "America's Favorite Pickup Truck Goes Electric," *New Yorker*, January 24, 2022. ("Analysis from the National Highway Traffic Safety Administration has shown that pedestrians who are hit by pickups or SUVs are two to three times more likely to die than those who are hit by cars.")
26. Sec 136d(a)(1).
27. *West Virginia v. EPA*, 597 U.S. 697 (2022).
28. *West Virginia v. EPA*, 597 U.S. at 758 (J. Kagan, dissenting); see also Michael Barsa and David Dana, "The Major Questions Doctrine's Upside for Combatting Climate Change," *N.Y.U. Environmental Law Journal* 32 (2024): 1.
29. Capital intensity is measured as capital expenditures from the year 2014, divided by value added from the same year. Capital expenditures are obtained from the 2015 Annual Capital Expenditures Survey (table 4b, revised for 2014), with the exception of farm capital expenditures, which are obtained from USDA Farm Production Expenditures. 2018 Summary, Farm Production Expenditures by Year, 2014–2018. Farm capital expenditures include (i) farm supplies and repairs, (ii) farm improvements and construction, (iii) tractors and self-propelled farm machinery, (iv) other farm machinery, (v) seeds and plants, (vi) trucks and autos, and (vii) miscellaneous capital expenses. Value added data was compiled by Peter Tschofen, Inês L. Azevedo, and Nicholas Z. Muller, "Fine Particulate Matter Damages and Value-added in the US Economy," *PNAS* 116 (2019): 19857, https://www.pnas.org/content/116/40/19857 [https://perma.cc/8UC2-GDQR].
30. Harvey Averch and Leland L. Johnson, "Behavior of the Firm under Regulatory Constraint," *American Economic Review* 52 (1962): 1052, 1053. Empirical evidence is generally supportive. See, e.g., H. Craig Peterson, "An Empirical Test of Regulatory Effects," *Bell Journal Of Economics & Management. Science* 6 (1975): 111; Donald F. Vitaliano and Gregory P. Stella, "A Frontier Approach to Testing the Averch-Johnson Hypothesis," *International. Journal of Economics & Business* 16 (2009): 347.
31. Henrik Hammar, Asa Lofgren, and Thomas Sterner, "Political Economy Obstacles to Fuel Taxation," *Energy Journal* 25 (2004): 1.
32. John R. Hicks, *The Theory of Wages* (Macmillan, 1932).
33. David Popp, "Induced Innovation and Energy Prices," *American Economic Review* 92 (2002): 160.
34. Lawrence H. Goulder and Stephen H. Schneider, "Induced Technological Change and the Attractiveness of CO2 Abatement Policies," *Resource & Energy Economics* 21 (1999): 211.
35. Acemoglu et al., "Transition to Clean Technology," 56, note 20.

36. See, e.g., Adam B. Jaffe, Richard Newell & Robert Stavins, "Technological Change and the Environment," *Handbook of Environmental Economics*, ch. 11, vol. 1 (2003), 462–504; Lawrence H. Goulder and Koshy Mathai, "Optimal CO2 Abatement in the Presence of Induced Technological Change," *Journal Of Environmental Economics & Management* 39 (2000): 1.
37. See, e.g., Shi-Ling Hsu, "On Electric Vehicles and Environmental Policies for Innovation (a Review of John Graham's The Global Rise of the Modern Plug-in Electric Vehicle)," *U.C. San Francisco Science & Technology Law. Journal* 14 (2023): 231.
38. John D. Graham, *The Global Rise of the Modern Plug-in Electric Vehicle: Public Policy, Innovation, and Strategy* (Edward Elgar, 2021).
39. See, e.g., Kenneth Gillingham & James H. Stock, "The Cost of Reducing Greenhouse Gas Emissions," *Journal of Economic Perspectives* 32 (2018): 53.
40. See, e.g., Gilbert Metcalf, "Tax Policies for Low-carbon Technologies," *National. Tax Journal* 62 (2009): 519; Per G. Fredriksson, "Environmental Policy Choice: Pollution Abatement Subsidies," *Resource & Energy Economics* 20 (1998): 51.
41. Acemoglu et al., "Transition to Clean Technology," 56, note 20.
42. See, e.g., David Popp, "Innovation and Climate Policy," *Annual Review of Resource Economics.* 2 (2010): 275, 277–78.
43. See, e.g., Daron Acemoglu, "Distorted Innovation: Does the Market Get the Direction of Technology Right?," NBER Working Paper 30922 (February 2023).
44. Pub. L. 117–169, 136 Stat. 1818 (2022).
45. Emergency Economic Stabilization Act of 2008, Pub. L. No. 110–343 (2008).
46. American Recovery and Reinvestment Act of 2009, Pub. L. No. 111–5, 123 Stat. 115 (2009).
47. Because the Disney Corporation publicly opposed Florida's laws restricting discussion of gender identity and sexual orientation in public schools, Florida governor Ron DeSantis revoked a special designation that Disney World in Orlando enjoyed that enabled it to levy local taxes and provide government functions, such as build and maintain roads, and provide transportation, fire and medical response services. See, e.g., Jesus Jiménez and Brooks Barnes, "What We Know About the DeSantis-Disney Dispute," *NewYork Times*, May 18, 2023, https://www.nytimes.com/article/disney-florida-desantis.html. DeSantis has frequently said "Florida is where woke goes to die." See, e.g., Philip Bump, "What Does 'Woke' Mean? Whatever Ron DeSantis Wants," *Washington Post.*, December 5, 2022, https://www.washingtonpost.com/politics/2022/12/05/desantis-florida-woke-critical-race-theory/.
48. Joseph A. Schumpeter, *Capitalism, Socialism, and Democracy* (Harper, 1950), 81–86.

SECTION III

GOVERNANCE AND CONSOLIDATION OF PRIVATE POWER

Can Democracy and Capitalism be Reconciled?

KENNETH G. ELZINGA

A Matter of Words

Whether Democracy and Capitalism can be reconciled is, at one level, a fair and fundamental question. Can they? And if so, under what conditions? However, behind that fair and fundamental question is the question of taxonomy. What do we mean by Democracy and what do we mean by Capitalism?

Democracy and Capitalism are both portmanteau expressions that require unpacking. For this reason, to address the prospect of reconciling Democracy and Capitalism involves how the two institutions are defined.

Many people would respond to the question, Can Democracy and Capitalism be reconciled with: "yes, they can," or "yes, I think so," if they get to define Democracy as a political system and Capitalism as a way of organizing economic activity. Otherwise, the two words—Democracy and Capitalism—have a Humpty Dumpty characteristic.

In *Through the Looking-Glass* (a sequel to *Alice in Wonderland*), Humpty Dumpty's most famous line is: "When *I* use a word, it means just what I choose it to mean—neither more nor less."[1] So long as Alice and Humpty Dumpty agree on how the word in question is defined, they can communicate with each other. Otherwise, not so much.

Further confounding the question whether Democracy and Capitalism can be reconciled is the endogeneity between the two: that is, how Democracy is structured and how it operates as a political system affects what a Capitalistic economy will be like. And vice versa. For example, if what goods and services are produced primarily is a decision reached collectively by voting in a Democracy, this limits the extent of the market: Capitalism will play less of a role in determining what goods and services will be produced because citizens will have less opportunity to "vote" with their dollars.

By way of further illustration, if Democracy as a political system is characterized by extensive rent seeking, this incentivizes business firms to curry political patronage and lessens their incentive to gain consumer patronage. Put differently, the degree of rent seeking in a Democracy will affect how Capitalism answers the fundamental economic questions of what goods and services will be produced, and by whom, and for whom. If a Democracy has an industrial policy offering grants and tax cuts favoring the market for computer chips rather than the market for potato chips, this will affect the choices made by investors differently than in a Democracy that has no policy of selecting "winners" in the economy.

If one considers rent seeking to be an inherent part of Capitalism, then any discussion of reconciling Capitalism with Democracy will have a different starting point—and probably a different ending point—than a discussion that considers rent seeking as part of Democracy's decision calculus and not part of Capitalism's market determination.

Voting with Dollars versus Voting with Ballots

A side-by-side comparison can be instructive in considering the extent one might wish to join Democracy and Capitalism at the hip—or expand the domain of one and restrict the scope of the other.[2] In tackling the question of rapprochement between Democracy and Capitalism, the reflections that follow compare the two institutions: how do consumers voting with dollars under Capitalism differ from citizens voting with ballots in a Democracy. I do so in the spirit of Isabel Sawhill's question at this conference of whether one-man, one-vote can be reconciled with one-dollar, one-vote.

One of the most fundamental differences between voting with dollars under Capitalism and voting with ballots under Democracy involves *competition*. In everyday parlance, the word competition refers to sports: competition on the field, or competition on the court. It is not so with economists.

Going back to the Adam Smith origins of "the dismal science," economists have spent their time and energy thinking about competition, but they do in a manner different than how most people think of the term. Competition, in economic analysis, is not about entertainment and sports. Competition and its absence—monopoly—are at the heart of microeconomics.

The degree of competition is an appropriate starting point in drawing the distinction between voting with dollars under Capitalism versus voting with ballots under Democracy. Capitalism involves much more competition than Democracy. Democracy involves much more monopoly than Capitalism. There are several reasons for this.

Under Capitalism, markets for goods and services are almost always contestable and do not have the high barriers to entry that characterize political markets in Democracy. Democracy (certainly in the United States) essentially is a duopoly with high barriers to entry for organizations other than the two incumbent political parties.

It takes some effort to come up with examples of markets for goods or services in the United States that have only two sellers, where both are protected by high barriers to entry. However, US political markets, at the state and federal level, are almost always duopolies.

The Phillips-Sawyer paper in this conference volume offers a summary of the efforts of government to restrain monopoly through the legal-economic institution of antitrust. Antitrust scholars consider US antitrust laws and their enforcement methods to be one of the prominent social exports the United States has sent to many other countries who have adopted their own version of trade regulation to promote competition and deter the exercise of market power. But the Sherman Act is hapless in its ability to reduce the barriers to entry erected by the two dominant political parties in the United States and to encourage new entrants.

Political theorists agree that a fundamental problem with Democracy is the tyranny of the majority. To the extent decision-making is done through markets under Capitalism, rather than by majoritarian Democracy, the tyranny of the majority is reduced. Unlike Democracies, the market system usually treats minorities on the same footing as it does the majority.

For example, the market for goods and services under Capitalism allows a range of ages to participate. Teenagers in the United States have enormous buying power in such markets as clothing and consumer durables, but Democracy generally is restricted to participants above 18 years of age. People with felony convictions have difficulty voting, but convicted felons who have done their time are welcome to vote with their dollars at literally millions of merchants.

Political competition—à la voting with ballots in a Democracy—generally is an all-or-nothing contest, a winner-take-all tournament. Whoever gets a majority of the vote for some office gets the entire "market." Market competition—à la voting with dollars under Capitalism—caters to (indeed welcomes) minority consumer preferences.

The relative treatment of majority preferences and minority preferences represents a major difference between Democracy and Capitalism. One corrective principle is to allow markets to help solve the tyranny of the majority. This works not only in principle but also in practice. Millions of times each day, Capitalism thwarts Democracy's authority over the minority by majority rule. Examples abound.

If a majority of fast-food customers prefer McDonalds, that does not mean Burger King, Five Guys, and Carl's Jr. must close up shop. If the highly popular BIC ballpoint pen does not confer the desired social status, Capitalism offers a Mont Blanc fountain pen alternative. Does a handbag by Coach seem too expensive? Purchase one from Brighton—or dozens of other vendors of women's fashion accessories. If Kentucky Fried Chicken once seemed like the only game in town, that did not last long. There is Chick-Fil-A, Bojangles, and others too numerous to list.

Under Capitalism, for a market to be a genuine monopoly—whether it be for land, labor, or capital—is rare. If a monopolistic market structure surfaces, it seldom has a long shelf life.[3] Consider companies that once were considered to have monopoly power in the United States: A&P for groceries (once called the Great Atlantic & Pacific Tea Company); United States Steel for steel products; Alcoa for aluminum; Xerox for copier machines; General Motors for automobiles; IBM for mainframe computers; Microsoft for personal computer operating systems.

At one point, there was an antitrust threat to break up General Motors because of the firm's share of the US automobile market. The Japanese and then the Koreans made such an antitrust action unnecessary. Xerox as a monopolist? One still hears the expression, "I'll make a xerox of that." But more than likely, the copy will be made on a non-Xerox machine. IBM as a monopolist? There is more computational power in cell phones and other mobile devices than IBM had in its System 360 mainframe computer. Microsoft as a monopolist? My students are puzzled when I tell them that when they were children, Microsoft was considered a monopolist.

Another consequential difference between Democracy and Capitalism: market competition under Capitalism is continuous; that is, rivalry among competing sellers goes on every day of the week. Political competition in a Democracy usually takes place only at discrete times.

If one considers intertemporal behavior: economic markets almost always work faster than political markets. "Kicking the can down the road" is not a descriptor of Capitalism but the expression often is used with regard to Democracies. In the United States, Congress regularly gets away with spending more than it takes in. Under Capitalism, business firms generally cannot get away with this—at least for long. The discipline of the market will intervene.

Capitalism almost always allows several firms in the same market to compete for consumer patronage—at the same time. Under Capitalism, my friends on the political right can subscribe to The New Criterion; my friends on the political left can subscribe to The New Yorker. My atheist friends can subscribe to The Skeptical Inquirer; my Christian friends can subscribe to First Things. As a Libertarian: I subscribe to all of them.

Under Capitalism, commitments are more transparent and accountable than they are under Democracy. For example, consumers can hold business firms liable to their promises. That is hard for a voter to do with an elected official. If an appliance company sells a washing machine that does not have a motor or a door, the buyer generally has legal recourse. In a Democracy, if a presidential candidate promises, "Watch my lips; no new taxes," and then raises taxes, disgruntled citizens who voted for this candidate do not have standing to sue.

Tocqueville, Downs, and Lewis

No paper on the subject of Democracy would be complete without reference to Alexis de Tocqueville—a French intellectual who admired America.[4] Tocqueville predicted that Democracy would degenerate into "soft despotism" and the "tyranny of the majority." He feared that:

> This immortal and more and more burning hatred, which animates democratic peoples against the least privileges, singularly

> favors the gradual concentration of all political rights in the hands of the sole representative of the State. The sovereign, necessarily and without dispute above all citizens, does not excite the envy of any one of them, and each one believes that all the prerogatives that he concedes to the sovereign are taken away from his equals.[5]

When Democracies govern by the will of the majority, this can spell trouble for minorities.

The economist's parallel to the tyranny of the majority is the *median voter theorem*. Anthony Downs introduced this theorem in his book, "An Economic Theory of Democracy" (1957).[6] After more than 65 years, the book continues to offer an important insight into Democracy—and how political competition differs from competition in markets for goods and services.

Downs explained that any elected official who catered too much to the preferences of voters on the political right or the political left—whenever the majority of voters made up the middle (or median)—would likely not be elected again. The economic logic behind this proposition is not rocket science. An attempt by a politician to favor voter preferences on the left or the right opens an opportunity for a rival candidate to make an appeal to the median voter whose numbers (at least in a majoritarian system) will enable an electoral victory. Voters who have strong preferences but do not represent huge numbers lose out in this form of Democracy.

As Tyler Cowan put it:

> Politicians will respond to this dynamic, whether they are power-seeking demagogues or more benevolent types who use elected office to help the world. When it comes to the big issues, voters at the midpoint usually get the policies, if not always the exact outcomes, they want.[7]

Joining Tocqueville and Downs in fretting over Democracy's systemic problems is an unlikely public intellectual: C. S. Lewis. His concern was different. Lewis worried more about the kind of person who holds political office, and is thereby positioned to govern the lives of others. If voters cede power to public officials, Edmund Burke feared that "Power corrupts, and absolute power corrupts absolutely." Lewis feared even the beneficent public official in a Democracy. Here are Lewis's words if Democracy results in—or is tethered to—the welfare state:

> Of all the tyrannies, a tyranny exercised for the good of its victims may be the most oppressive. It may be better to live under robber barons than under omnipotent moral busy bodies. The robber baron's cruelty may sometimes sleep, his cupidity may at some point be satiated; but those who torment us for our own good will torment us without end for they do so with the approval of their own conscience . . . To be "cured" against one's will and cured of states which we may not regard as disease is to be put on a level of those who have not yet reached the age of reason or those who never will; to be classed with infants, imbeciles, and domestic animals.[8]

A tongue-in-cheek way to compare Capitalism with Democracy is to perform what Germans call a *Gedanken* experiment. Imagine the difference between the greeting one hears upon entering Chick-fil-A versus entering an office of the IRS. Upon entering Chick-fil-A, one may be asked: How can I help you? Upon entering the IRS, one may be told: Take a seat.[9]

If one considers how decisions are made in markets versus how decisions are made by central planning, the market wins—if the objective of the economy is promoting consumer welfare and the objective of Democracy is protecting individual liberty. If these dual objectives of Democracy and Capitalism are to be met, this requires a Democracy with a smaller State and a Capitalism with a larger private sector: one more in accord with what Adam Smith called the "simple and obvious system of natural liberty."

Rent Seeking and Antitrust

When I encounter students who can restrain their enthusiasm for Capitalism, what I often find is that, to them, Capitalism is an economic system where the private sector is in bed with the public sector. By that taxonomy, Capitalism means an economic system involving a complex alliance between government and business and coalitions between government and organized labor—all designed to siphon economic welfare away from consumers. These students do not recognize that the gravamen of their complaint about Capitalism is rent seeking, which is not a necessary condition for Capitalism or Democracy.

Rent seeking, as the phenomenon was developed by my former colleague Gordon Tullock[10] and by Anne Krueger[11], generally entails the use of lobbying the state for economic gain, rather than "building a better mousetrap" as a means of capturing economic gain. The economic perversity of rent seeking is that it uses up society's scarce resources, but it does not add to society's enjoyment of more goods and services.

Frederick Engels claimed that markets under Capitalism and rent seeking by the State were joined at the hip. He wrote:

> The modern state, no matter what its form, is essentially a capitalistic machine . . . The more it proceeds to the taking over of productive forces, the more does it actually become the nationalist capitalist. . .[12]

But rent seeking actually is foreign and inessential to the functioning of markets under Capitalism. The social perversity of rent seeking is that its existence turns many people against Capitalism—because they consider rent seeking a part of Capitalism.

To the extent Democracies have significant resources under the domain of the State, it follows as a proposition of economic logic that the incentive to engage in rent seeking will increase. That is, the proportion of the economy controlled by the State will influence the amount of rent seeking. *Ceteris paribus*, a Democracy where the State controls and organizes 50% of the economy's GDP is twice an attractive plum for rent seeking as a State that controls 25% of the economy's GDP.

The Lamoreaux-Wallis paper in this conference volume offers a quantitative analysis of rent seeking at the individual state level. The thesis of the paper—that deterring rent seeking through government favoritism enhances economic growth—would not surprise most economists familiar with the rent-seeking literature. What is striking is that Lamoreaux and Wallis demonstrate how consequential state mandate laws can be as a form of rent seeking.[13]

In reading the Lamoreaux-Wallis paper, one is reminded that when economists model the self-interested, profit-maximizing motivation of business owners, whatever zeal for economic gain is lurking in that model can be matched by the rent-seeking avarice of some who hold political office.

One of the greatest challenges in reconciling Democracy with Capitalism is organizing governance that disincentivizes rent seeking by business firms, labor unions, and consumer groups. An ancillary challenge is explaining that rent seeking is neither a sufficient nor a necessary component of Capitalism. Quite the contrary, rent seeking is a perversion of how the free market allocates society's scarce resources among competing uses in a manner that enhances consumer welfare.

The Phillips-Sawyer paper packs a great deal of antitrust history into a few pages. Given the complex mix of law, economics, and politics that makes up antitrust, this is no easy task. If a student wanted an introduction to antitrust—by way of an efficient summary of case law, schools of thought, and the continuing issues—the Phillips-Sawyer paper does the job.

Antitrust, like any institution, can be tempted by mission creep. To reconcile Democracy and Capitalism, it is best that antitrust stick to its knitting: promoting competition in a manner that increases consumer welfare rather than the pursuit of other objectives that may incentivize business firms to pursue Government patronage rather than consumer patronage.

The remarkable characteristic of antitrust is that the language of the Sherman Act does not change. Section 1 and Section 2 are essentially the same today as they were when the Sherman Act was passed in 1890. Antitrust enforcement, however, has changed significantly. It continues to attack price-fixing and market-sharing cartels—a perverse form of Capitalism that provokes consumers to think the game is rigged against them. But as antitrust enforcement evolved in the courts and enforcement agencies and became influenced by the economic analysis of competition and monopoly, antitrust now takes more seriously the task of protecting competition, rather than protecting competitors. In the world of antitrust, as the Phillips-Sawyer paper makes clear, ideas have had consequences.

A Lewisian Conclusion

Can Democracy coexist with Capitalism? Yes, if Democracy's political power is diffused and does not have the wherewithal to dictate life's meaning to its citizens. Can Capitalism coexist with Democracies? Yes, if Capitalism's markets are not monopolized and economic agents on the demand and supply side of the market are thwarted from rent-seeking alliances with the State.

In concluding these reflections, let me return to C. S. Lewis who made a case for Democracy, one of constrained enthusiasm, and one that has nothing to do with the median voter theory or an analysis of rent seeking. Lewis's case for Democracy was based on the story of Adam and Eve. He wrote:

> I am a democrat because I believe in the Fall of Man. I think most people are democrats for the opposite reason. A great deal of democratic enthusiasm descends from the ideas of people like Rousseau, who believed in democracy because they thought mankind so wise and good that everyone deserved a share in the government. The danger of defending democracy on those grounds is that they're not true . . . I find that they're not true without looking further than myself. I don't deserve a share in governing a hen-roost, much less a nation. Nor do most people . . . The real reason for democracy is just the reverse. Mankind is so fallen that no man can be trusted with unchecked power over his fellows. Aristotle said that some people were only fit to be slaves. I do not contradict him. But I reject slavery because I see no men fit to be masters.[14]

To return to the question before the house: can Democracy and Capitalism be reconciled? The question is an important one, but not a consuming one. For the academic scribblers who write about Capitalism and Democracy and ponder how the one can support—or thwart—the other, it is both comforting and humbling to consider the words of the Irish poet Oliver Goldsmith: "*How small, of all that human hearts endure,/ That part which laws of kings can cause or cure.*"[15]

Notes

1. Lewis Carroll, "Humpty Dumpty," in *Through the Looking-Glass* (MacMillan and Co., 1872), 124, 113–136.
2. My paper has a debt to my former colleague, James M. Buchanan. See, in particular, James M. Buchanan, "Individual Choice in Voting and the Market," in *Fiscal Theory and Political Economy* (University of North Carolina Press, 1960), 90, 90–104. See also Kenneth Elzinga, "Capitalism and Democracy," *St. Croix Review* LVI (June 2023): 25–34, http://www.stcroixreview.org/index.php/current/itemlist/user/610-kennethgelzinga.
3. For purposes of argument, I set aside regulated industries, such as public utilities.

4. As an aside, one is left wondering: why is he the only one?
5. Alexis de Tocqueville, *Democracy in America: In Two Volumes*, ed. Eduardo Nolla (Liberty Fund, Inc., 2012), 1203–4. A highly regarded account of Tocqueville and Democracy is Olivier Zunz, *The Man Who Understood Democracy: The Life of Alexis de Tocqueville* (Princeton University Press, 2022).
6. Anthony Downs, *An Economic Theory of Democracy* (Harper and Brothers, 1957).
7. Tyler Cowen, "Why Politics Is Stuck in the Middle," *The New York Times*, February 6, 2010, https://www.nytimes.com/2010/02/07/business/economy/07view.html.
8. C. S. Lewis, *God in the Dock: Essays on Theology and Ethics*, ed. Walter Hooper (Eerdmans, 1970), 292.
9. One might argue the two illustrations constitute stacking the deck. Readers can substitute their own examples of a retail firm and a government agency.
10. Gordon Tullock, "The Welfare Costs of Tariffs, Monopolies and Theft," *Western Economic Journal* 5 (1967): 224–32.
11. Anne Krueger, "The Political Economy of the Rent-Seeking Society," *American Economic Review* 64, no. 3 (1974): 291–303.
12. Frederick Engels, *Socialism: Utopian and Scientific* (International Publishers, 1936), 67.
13. Three cheers go to Indiana for being the model in revising state mandate laws.
14. C. S. Lewis, "Equality," in *Present Concerns*, ed. Walter Hooper (Harper One, 1986), 7.
15. Oliver Goldsmith, *The Traveller; or, A Prospect of Society* (S. Harward, Colonade Library, 1764), 21.

6

The Problem of Market Power in Postwar America

Antitrust Law, Regulatory Discourse, and Changing Ideas of Market Power

LAURA PHILLIPS-SAWYER

Economic concentration is on the rise in the United States—in multiple industries fewer firms or enterprises account for a larger proportion of economic activity.[1] While this trend may be identifiable across the twentieth century, it accelerated in the early 1980s in both product markets and labor markets.[2] Consolidation can result from economies of scale, barriers to entry, or mergers and acquisitions. Sometimes, a smaller number of firms competing in a market may entail higher mark-ups, less innovation, and—in the case of monopsony, or buyer power—lower wages or benefits for workers.[3] Relatedly, economic power can facilitate undue political influence, usurping the majority's democratic will. In recent years, scholars and pundits have expressed concern that some digital platforms lend themselves to "winner-take-all" dynamics, further accelerating a trend toward concentration that appears evident in more traditional markets as well.[4] The depth of corporate coffers coupled with the extent of corporate lobbying, litigation, and campaign contributions has (again) revived calls for enhanced corporate accountability standards, generally, and stronger antitrust enforcement, more specifically.[5] These interrelated phenomena have brought economic regulation back to the forefront of democratic political discourse.

In the United States, the foundational statutory text for governing market exchanges is the Sherman Antitrust Act of 1890, which prohibits contracts, combinations, and conspiracies in restraint of trade (section 1) and monopolization and attempts to monopolize (section 2).[6] The act passed in response to heightened antimonopoly sentiment, which emanated from diverse regions and

Laura Phillips-Sawyer, *The Problem of Market Power in Postwar America*. In: *Can Democracy and Capitalism Be Reconciled?*. Edited by: Sidney M. Milkis and Scott C. Miller, Oxford University Press. © Oxford University Press (2025). DOI: 10.1093/9780197774731.003.0007 interests, including the Midwestern farmers, Southern agrarians, and urban good government reformers. Each group feared that rising economic concentration might stifle market competition, rendering citizens and consumers captive to the interests of consolidated corporate and financial behemoths—be it collusive cartels or monopolizing center firms. The purpose of the act was neither singular nor explicitly defined; however, historians have converged around the idea that Congress intended to protect competitive processes by prohibiting anticompetitive conduct and that Congress believed this would equalize the playing field and thereby, help protect small and independent businesses from unfair competition.[7]

Critically, however, the act did not prohibit monopoly itself; instead, it prohibited monopolization or attempts to monopolize. This created the requirement of some anticompetitive, monopolizing conduct by the defendant.[8] Thus, rather than attacking size itself, antitrust law has largely accommodated certain levels of concentration by focusing on the *exercise of market power*. In turn, the key question in an antitrust case is whether the defendant firm used its market power in order to anticompetitively exclude its competitors from the market, and thus enhance or prolong its own market power. Other areas of regulation, such as public utilities law, could address the problem of durable or natural monopoly by establishing long-term public oversight. Public utilities law resulted from statutory interventions; whereas, antitrust law has policed a wider variety of market exchanges and has focused on eliminating likely or actual anticompetitive conduct. Antitrust law could impose on a monopolist a "duty to deal," for example, by issuing an injunction mandating that the monopolist-owners of a railroad bridge offer nondiscriminatory access to competing railroads.[9] But, those cases have been relatively rare, especially today,[10] despite repeated calls for more proactive, prospective antitrust enforcement.

In 1890, Congress codified common law language against "restraints of trade," which brought some clarity, but the Sherman Act also went further. It empowered the Department of Justice to bring suit in equity; it also created a private right of action and a fee-shifting structure with treble damages, moving far beyond the common law's non-enforcement of anticompetitive restraints. How the law would be enforced was left to the Department of Justice's prosecutorial discretion, private litigants, and ultimately, generalist judges. And, by the early twentieth century, the Sherman Act appeared both uncertain and woefully insufficient to the task of preserving competitive processes. The great merger movement had occurred despite it and the Supreme Court's rule of reason decision in U.S. v. Standard Oil (1911) exacerbated lingering uncertainties regarding the extent of the law. In response, Congress passed new laws in 1914: the Federal Trade Commission (FTC) and the Clayton Acts. The former created an administrative body to oversee the application of the laws and empowered it to prohibit unfair methods of competition. The latter enumerated certain types of impermissible conduct if found "to lessen competition, or tend to create monopoly."[11] For better or worse, this admixture of decision-makers—agencies, private litigants, and judges—populated an institutional matrix that would come to dominate the regulatory discourse around US antitrust law and policy.

In the postwar period, Congress passed several notable antitrust laws and amendments—for example, revising agency merger review in 1950 and 1976—however, the dramatic reinterpretation of American antitrust law in the second half of the twentieth century largely occurred through judge-made law. While antitrust law is subject to *stare decisis*—or the control of precedent—it is less so than other areas of law. Since the early twentieth century, the Supreme Court has treated the Sherman Act as having "a generality and adaptability" that allows for rethinking the law given changes in economic thinking.[12]

This chapter analyzes antitrust law's reinterpretation across three eras of American antitrust enforcement—1940 through early 1970s; mid-1970s to 2010s; and, 2010s to the present. Each era is characterized by the ways in which a rough consensus seemingly emerged around a key variable in antitrust analysis—finding market power. Lacking market power, the Court has instructed, a firm is unlikely to have effectuated an anticompetitive restraint—i.e., some level of market power is required to force an anticompetitive agreement onto others. (The next step is then to evaluate the effect of the restraint.) And although we may prefer to have direct evidence of market power, such as a restraint that reduces output or increases prices without the monopolist losing market share, we often lack such incontrovertible evidence. Instead, each era has had to grapple with the perplexing and often divisive question of the prevalence of market power across various industries—is market power a problem, or not? The answer to that question reverberates through law and politics, but is acutely felt within antitrust law. On the one hand, what one believes about the prevalence and durability of market power informs presumptions that judges use to more easily administer the law. On the other hand, those beliefs are often a reflection not only of economic training but also of one's political preferences regarding the relationship between business and government. Thus, answering this fundamental question has helped craft a forward-looking consistency, even as the law has been rethought and reshaped, and has allowed antitrust law's rethinking to fit neatly within larger movements in law and politics. This essay explains two preceding moments of rough consensus being forged within antitrust law, and then it shows how and why we are witnessing a similar rethinking today.

***

The Democratic Check on Market Power: Structuralism and the Making of Modern Anti-Monopolization Law, 1945–1974

The 1945 case of *U.S. v. Aluminum Company of American* (Alcoa) is typically taught as a foundational, modern anti-monopolization case even though much of its logic and its holding have been lightning rods of controversy. It marked a significant shift in American antitrust law and set the stage for the post-World War II era. A three-judge panel for the Second Circuit Court acted as the court of last resort because the Supreme Court could not reach a quorum. Judge Learned Hand delivered the opinion, and the Supreme Court affirmed its holding in subsequent cases.[13] Hand's ruling upheld the US Department of Justice complaint (originally issued in 1937, but frozen on appeal through the duration of World War II) that Alcoa had illegally monopolized the domestic virgin ingot market, reversing the lower court.[14] This prosecution, in combination with the anti-cartel *Socony-Vacuum* case,[15] marked a deliberate shift away from what the historian Ellis Hawley famously referred to as the New Deal's "ambivalence" toward antitrust law.[16] Rather than the "end of reform," this was a new era of structural reform.[17]

Despite Hand's "reluctance" to use the courts to reorder the US economy, the *Alcoa* ruling expanded section 2 liability in three important ways.[18] First, Hand forcefully interpreted Congress to have "forbad all" trusts and to have had more than "economic motives alone" in mind.[19] Hand wrote that "among the purposes of Congress in 1890 was a desire to put an end to great aggregations of capital because of the helplessness of the individual before them."[20] He then went on to explain that the current Congress was "still of the same mind," citing the Surplus Property Act and the Small Business Mobilization Act as well as the recent Supreme Court case, *U.S. v. Hutcheson,* as evidence that Congress intended to "perpetuate and preserve, for its own sake and in spite of possible cost, an organization of industry in small units which can effectively compete with each other."[21]

That interpretation of the act also reflected the moment's political anxiety about the deleterious effects that industrial concentration could pose to a well-functioning liberal democracy. The idea that economic decentralization facilitated political decentralization and, concomitantly, the protection of equal rights could be traced all the way back to the American founding. That idea was given renewed urgency in the early 1940s as a profusion of academic and government publications linked industrial concentration to the rise of fascist political organization in Europe.[22] According to this framing, the primary objective of American antitrust law was to protect liberal democratic capitalism, which was identified with market competition, from concentrations of economic power that could both lead to market failures and erode decentralized political power. The political and economic objectives of antitrust enforcement were deeply intertwined, and many of the institutionalist economists of that era structured their research agendas around those twin concerns. Ultimately, it was the combination of the two—pressing political concerns and mainstream economic thinking—that pushed antitrust doctrine toward new means of realizing both.

Secondly, Judge Hand carefully explained the court's finding of market power, which set the stage for novel means to intervene against economic concentration.[23] Today, Antitrust casebooks focus on explaining *how* Hand narrowly defined the relevant market—by excluding the secondary, or scrap, market for aluminum—which allowed the court to find that Alcoa possessed the requisite level of market power to fulfill the first step in an antimonopolization case. Yet, equally important is asking *why* he felt compelled to overrule the lower court and intervene in such a high-stakes case. Hand's market definition sparked an ongoing debate regarding the facts specific to the aluminum industry and, more generally, the methods used to determine substitutability or cross-elasticity of demand. Those debates have been important to advancing our thinking on market characterization and delineation—or, asking: what kind of market is this, and where are the boundaries of product and geographic competition? However, those technical debates obscure the way in which Hand distinguished previous monopolization cases that had relied less on finding market power and more on anticompetitive conduct—Hand flipped the script.

Hand conceded that "mere size is not an offense . . . but," he continued, "size carries with it an opportunity for abuse."[24] Alcoa's durable monopoly position, Hand wrote, "could only have resulted, as it did result, from a persistent determination to maintain the control."[25] Ultimately, the ruling expanded the category of anticompetitive conduct to include producing ahead of demand, which Hand hypothesized could be used to forestall competition by setting prices *below* the entry-inducing level and thus preserving Alcoa's market dominance.[26] Relatedly, Hand also rejected Alcoa's contention that its "ordinary" profit margins meant that it did not possess market power.[27] Instead, Hand insisted that monopoly power "deadens initiative [and] discourages thrift," which could thereby erode monopoly rents on an accountant's balance sheet.[28] (The Harvard-trained economist, Joe S. Bain, would make a similar argument in his 1956 textbook *Barriers to New Competition*.[29]) In other words, if monopoly power could be found, intent seemed to be immaterial and anticompetitive conduct flowed from the firm's power to control the market.

This new antimonopoly jurisprudence and its focus on market power was grounded in postwar economic thinking, which would animate antitrust law into the 1970s. Postwar economic structuralism borrowed from interwar institutional economics, which had rejected neoclassical models of perfect competition and *homo economicus* and instead, had endorsed the idea of managed competition and an active regulatory state. These ideas were debated and refined through the cataclysms of depression and war; the structuralism that emerged in the 1940s looked something like an economic consensus, though detractors on the left and right would remain. Building on the work of institutionalists, such as John Maurice Clark, Joan Robinson, and Gardiner Means, Harvard economist Edward Chamberlin explained that American firms were able to charge higher prices due to their spending on product differentiation (through branding and advertising), which in turn lowered their profits.[30] The resulting "monopolistic competition," which had an echo of Stuart Chase and Louis Brandeis from earlier in the twentieth century, was characterized by excessive product differentiation, consumer confusion, and high prices.[31] These studies discredited the idea of a self-regulating, competitive market, and pointed to market power as particularly problematic for price adjustments, stable employment, and consumer protection. The accepted means by which policymakers might intervene, however, was no longer the vast experiments of the First New Deal; now, lawyers and economists suggested that policymakers should intervene through more stringent regulatory efforts to protect competitive processes.

This nascent structuralism revised the classification scheme for thinking about types of markets, ranging from perfect competition to monopoly but now with a vast middle ground of imperfect competition. At the center of this developing system of economic thought was identifying the extent to which firms might anticompetitively exercise market power in that middle ground. In 1940, J. M. Clark's idea of "workable competition" narrowed this burgeoning list of problematic market types and clarified in which markets antitrust interventions might be most productive.[32] Writing ten years later, Joe Bain summarized Clark's contribution: "Fairly satisfactory competitive results may emerge from imperfect collusion or because of the long-run threat of entry."[33] Yet, he also criticized Clark's theory as "highly provisional and even personal . . . likely to rest heavily on the ad hoc assessment of obvious alternatives in given situations." Bain went on to extoll the "general signs of nonworkable competition in oligopoly." Although focused on the exercise of market power in oligopolistic markets, rather than monopolization as such, Bain began by identifying types of conduct that would suggest non-workable competition: "firms seriously outside the optimal range," excess capacity, excessive selling or advertising costs, and lags in the adoption of cost-saving technologies.[34] His main point came second "that the potential association of price results to market structure deserves primary emphasis."[35] In other words, "behavior may be in turn either influenced or determined by certain characteristics of the underlying market structure."[36]

Even though the DOJ did not secure a structural remedy against Alcoa, it was clear that antimonopolization doctrine had significantly changed.[37] In turn, those changes affected business strategies even when firms were not embroiled in an antitrust suit. As Edward Mason explained in 1959, "countless mergers and amalgamations might well have taken place in the absence of antitrust [but] have been scotched in the office of corporate counsel. It is, in fact, to the advice that lawyers give their clients that the laws against monopoly must look for their chief impact."[38] Indeed, some business historians have unearthed corporate archival materials that suggest IBM, for example, unbundled its software and mainframe hardware sales contracts in December 1968 for fear of antitrust scrutiny.[39]

This trend was felt perhaps most acutely in merger activity. In 1950 Congress had passed the Celler-Kefauver Merger Act, which amended the Clayton Act. It brought stock acquisitions as well as non-horizontal mergers, including vertical and conglomerate mergers, under the purview of the law if its effect "may be substantially to lessen competition, or tend to create a monopoly." The Supreme Court interpreted this "incipiency standard"—a preference to block anticompetitive mergers before consummation—into a "structural presumption," which is still with us today. The presumption holds that if merging parties capture a certain percentage of the relevant product or geographic market then it would be presumed anticompetitive.[40] Through the 1960s, the Court routinely upheld the Government's efforts to block mergers in markets it believed exhibited a trend toward consolidation. Over time, the Court blocked deals despite an efficiency defense[41] and deals where the post-merger market share was substantially below a threshold to presume anticompetitive harm.[42] The idea was to stymie trends in concentration.

For critics like Justice Potter Stewart, the result was an overly interventionist antitrust enforcement regime divorced from economic realities of price and output effects. In 1966, he famously opined "the Government always wins."[43] As we shall see, criticism of the Court's antitrust jurisprudence gained traction in the mid-1960s galvanized by business associations, academic scholarship, and new appointees to the Court.

Through the 1960s American antitrust law exhibited a deep skepticism of market power. That skepticism informed legislative proposals for "no-fault" monopoly liability. In 1968, President Lyndon Johnson's task force on antitrust laws endorsed the idea and, in 1971, it appeared in Senator Philip A. Hart's (D-MI) "Concentrated Industries Act."[44] Johnson's task force produced a report despite his announcement that he would not seek reelection. That document—commonly known as the "Neal Report" for its chair, Phil C. Neal—recommended that the government pursue breaking up large-scale firms (known as divestiture) wherever market power proved particularly sticky. In oligopolistic markets, "where monopoly power is shared by a few very large firms,"[45] the report recommended government-imposed market share caps of 12 percent, targeting the auto-industry, aluminum producers, and computer-makers.[46]

Writing in 1973, former FTC chairperson Earl Kintner cautioned business-people against attracting antitrust attention. He summarized: "if the firm occupies a substantial position of power, and if there is also evidence of the general intent to increase and strengthen this position, monopolization has occurred even though the firm's business practices are not unfair, unlawful, or forbidden by section 1 [of the Sherman Act]."[47] In fact, neither Congress nor the Court had adopted "no-fault" monopolization; and yet, through the 1960s the prevailing political sentiment and economic knowledge of the time seemed to tilt in this direction into the early 1970s.

Rethinking Antitrust Law and Economics: The Decline of Structuralism and the Rise of the Consumer Welfare Standard, 1974–2010

By the mid-1960s criticism of antitrust over-enforcement spread across both the mainstream popular press and academic publications. Business leaders decried the Court's interpretation of the "antimerger" law, insisting that American firms were unable to achieve efficient scale and scope.[48] In turn, they argued, firms pursued diversification strategies in unrelated industries to avoid antitrust scrutiny, and these inefficiencies contributed to higher prices.[49] American firms, however, were under pressure regardless of antitrust law—a combination of domestic inflation and increased international trade flows squeezed US firms' profits. By the early 1970s, US competitiveness lagged relative to its trade partners, which helped stoke a crisis mentality.[50] In response, newly-elected President Richard Nixon created his own blue-ribbon commission to counter Johnson's Neal Report. In 1971, the Stigler Report, eponymously named for the Chicago economist George Stigler who led the study, recommended relaxing antitrust enforcement. If the preceding era had been motivated by fear of market power and its erosion of competitive markets and political democracy, the Stigler Report focused exclusively on generating economic efficiencies to achieve higher productivity. The larger political climate mattered, too; the anti-regulation backlash within antitrust law coincided with the social conservative critique of the liberal Warren Court, which had rewritten the political balance of power.[51] Thus, the older objectives of antitrust law, which had gained traction since the 1940s, were being challenged both from within the law and economics discipline and from external political and business sources with different though overlapping concerns about the regulatory state.[52] It was this confluence of factors that produced the next rough consensus in antitrust law, significantly revising how to think about the plausibility of market power and, in turn, the likelihood of anticompetitive exclusion.

To be clear, structural presumptions have remained an important component of antitrust law, especially in merger review.[53] However, beginning in the mid-1970s, presumptions about the prevalence and problem of market power would be relaxed or qualified throughout antitrust law. A new, rough consensus would emerge that would change the law; however, there would always be those who wanted more or less enforcement.[54] Over time, economic structuralism's criticism of consolidated market power and skepticism of perfect competition would be replaced by new presumptions about the economic efficiencies generated by dominant firms and vertical integration, and about the resiliency of markets to move toward a competitive equilibrium. Those ideas are associated with libertarian-oriented scholars connected to the University of Chicago, such as George Stigler, Frank Easterbrook, and Richard Posner, but they would not rewrite precedent alone.[55] Critically, at the same time, scholars from the "Harvard School," which had once been a center for economic structuralism in policymaking, placed a new emphasis on "administrability." Donald Turner, Philip Areeda, and Stephen Breyer, for example, placed a renewed emphasis on antitrust rules that could be reasonably overseen and carried out in such a way as to restore competition. Each of these three elements informed the regulatory discourse and steered new economic policy in antitrust law.

At a broad level, these new presumptions had the effect of reining-in antitrust enforcement in two ways. First, it contributed to the take-off of error cost analysis that reordered antitrust law and still guides it today. Error cost analysis informed the idea that Type I Errors (false positives) in antitrust adjudication are more problematic than Type II Errors (false negatives) because the latter may be solved by market competition, whereas the former persists in both case precedent and business arrangements that are less efficient than the alternatives.[56] Second, it contributed to the abandonment of noneconomic concerns in antitrust adjudication because such elements could not easily be weighed and balanced, or translated into an "administrable" ruling. As early as the 1960s, Donald Turner, who led the DOJ Antitrust Division between 1965 and 1968, encouraged greater reliance on economic arguments to make the law both administrable and predictable. Thus, in order to understand how and why American antitrust law significantly changed its approach to market power and single-firm conduct, it is necessary to interrogate how and why both the dominant schools of thought contributed to this rethinking.[57]

Criticism of existing antitrust law—namely, its presumptions about market power and the resilience of competitive markets—found an easy ally in the University of Chicago law school's Free Market Study Group and later its Antitrust Group.[58] Both groups convened lawyers and economists, including Milton Friedman, Henry Simons, Aaron Director, Edward Levi, and George Stigler. This group of scholars self-identified as classical liberal and pursued research agendas concerned with minimizing "collectivism" and maximizing individual liberty (in the negative sense of the term).[59] Interestingly, through the 1930s and 1940s Chicago scholarship had supported antitrust interventions against dominant firms so as to preserve and protect a competitive market economy.[60] However, by the early 1950s the group adopted a decidedly anti-statist turn in their embrace of market competition over regulation. That turn drew from the earlier work of the economist George Stigler and his insistence that perfect competition was a reality worthy of pursuit in both economic theory and public policy—as opposed to much of the work on imperfect competition then in vogue.[61] And yet, Stigler still maintained a deep suspicion of large-scale industrial firms, particularly merger to monopoly.[62] Nevertheless, in a series of publications over the next several years, Stigler argued that the problem of market power, whether located in monopoly or oligopoly markets, was not as prevalent as commonly believed and that maintaining market power was more difficult—even for large-scale industrial firms with highly differentiated products—than commonly appreciated.[63]

Armed with Stigler's insights, a group of Chicago economists and lawyers took aim at the core idea in section 2 cases: exclusionary conduct. Prevailing wisdom held that a firm with market power could use that power to enact anticompetitive practices that might drive its competitors out of business (e.g., lowering prices to a predatory level to kill competition); and sometimes prosecutors prevailed simply by showing the defendant's intent to foreclose competition. However, what later became known as the "new learning" held that conduct such as predatory price-cutting was not very likely and, thus, not really a cause for judicial concern. Wayne Leeman, for example, argued that "in fact, most often [a dominant firm] can hold its dominant position in a dynamic economy only by acting in a very competitive manner."[64] Moreover, predatory pricing, "in actuality, . . . is a very costly method of preserving a dominant position and . . . probably in most cases in the long run the costs are prohibitive."[65] Thus, "potential entry or expansion may be as effective as actual entry or expansion in insuring [sic] that a large and dominant firm behaves competitively."[66]

Historic cases were recast as false positives. For example, John McGee reframed *U.S. v. Standard Oil* (1911) as erroneously attacking competitive conduct.[67] It was argued that the rational, profit-maximizing monopolist would choose to maintain its monopoly in the easiest, most lucrative market rather than attempt a risky, less profitable venture of expansion by means of predatory price-cutting. Moreover, if there are no regulatory hurdles to entry, then the monopolist's price-making should be limited by the threat of potential competition.[68] The same argument was applied to tie-in contracts, wherein a seller required the buyer to buy two separate products or services only as a combination sale, arguing that these contracts should not be considered illegal price discrimination instead they simply responded to consumers' various demand elasticities.[69] And so, a cottage industry was born that defended industrial concentration as a product of efficient scale and dismissed evidence of intent to predate as insufficient without more. While Bain's structuralist paradigm held that a positive association existed between concentration and profits and that market power begat anticompetitive conduct; now, scholars challenged both as incorrect.

The Neal Report and Sen. Hart's deconcentration bill thrust this academic debate into the public policy limelight, and substantially raised the stakes. Part of Sen. Hart's argument in favor of his deconcentration bill had to do with economic concentration being linked to rising prices. What had once been considered the domain of macroeconomists, of Keynesianism versus monetarism, was now a question of competition policy. The twin crises of international competition and domestic inflation displaced longstanding concerns about protecting the autonomy of independent proprietors and the second-order effects of political decentralization.

In response to these fundamental disagreements of national importance, in early March 1974, Columbia University law school convened a two-day conference on industrial concentration.[70] The Airlie House conference yielded an edited collection, which displayed the division among economists regarding diagnosing economic concentration and prescribing antitrust policy. Each of these scholarly presentations were paired with a Harvard School interlocutor, who invariably examined the same question and similar evidence and came to precisely the opposite conclusions. Nevertheless, the conference has been interpreted as a catalyst for antitrust reform—it marked a turning point in academic debates by bringing Chicago scholars into the mainstream conversation and failing to vanquish them.[71]

A few years later, Richard Posner summarized the new literature's presumption on market power and its effect on enforcement trends:

> . . .firms cannot in general obtain or enhance monopoly power by unilateral action . . . Consequently, the focus of the antitrust laws should not be on unilateral action; it should instead be on: (1) cartels and (2) horizontal mergers large enough either to create monopoly directly . . . or to facilitate cartelization[72]

There would remain some "'diehard Chicagoans' (such as Bork and Bowman),"[73] who rarely saw any need for regulatory interventions, but on the whole, Posner explained, Chicago's neoclassical price theory had displaced Harvard's industrial organization.

Perhaps the clearest example of this displacement was the 1978 antitrust treatise by Harvard's Donald Turner and Philip Areeda.[74]The Areeda-Turner treatise had incorporated Chicago insights to evaluate whether market power could be maintained or enhanced through tie-in contracts, vertical integration, and predatory pricing. Critically, their recommended tests shifted judicial scrutiny of these types of restraints away from a categorical condemnation and toward the rule of reason, where the court would consider the defendant's rebuttal.[75] Areeda and Turner were the main scholars cited by the Supreme Court in this shifting doctrinal landscape.[76] For example, they approached existing predatory pricing doctrine with skepticism in two ways. First, they argued that only prices below marginal cost should be registered as predatory. This was the case because prices above that measure denoted more efficient production than rivals, or competition on the merits. Marginal costs, however, presented an evidentiary problem because firms did not readily have that information available. This threatened to render their insights unworkable by courts and so they adopted an alternative measure: average variable costs.[77] Second, they noted that what qualified conduct as predatory was the temporary economic sacrifice plus "the expectation of greater future gains." In 1980, Areeda formalized these insights by suggesting that the plaintiff must also show that the predator could likely recoup the lost profits from the predation period. Thus, predation alone was not sufficient to find a violation of the law—the predator had to succeed, or at least success had to be plausible. Such a test raised the evidentiary standard for plaintiffs, allowing judges to more frequently dismiss such claims as implausible.[78]

Judge Stephen Breyer, a former Harvard Law professor and a Democratic appointee to the First Circuit, helped write this new test into law.[79] When he approached a case of allegedly predatory price-cutting, he took the opportunity to explore the current state of antitrust economic knowledge. "In an economy with a significant number of concentrated industries," he explained, "price cutting limits the ability of large firms to exercise their 'market power.'"[80] In other words, price-cutting could be benign or even beneficial to the public—turning previous presumptions on their head. "Thus, a legal precedent or rule of law that prevents a firm from unilaterally cutting its prices risks interference with one of the Sherman Act's most basic objectives: the low price levels that one would find in well-functioning competitive markets."[81] We might pause and note that Breyer is not saying that low prices are the sole goal of antitrust law, but rather that the process by which we determine whether anticompetitive conduct has occurred in the particular case is by asking how prices might act in a competitive market where market power cannot be exercised. For Breyer, who had devoted his career to studying economic regulation, a competitive market ensured efficiencies that served citizens and consumers. And, critically, where a competitive market could not be attained, such as in the case of market failure, then regulation was warranted.[82]

Chicago scholars went further; McGee and Posner insisted that predation was rare, irrational, and maybe even beneficial to consumers.[83] Breyer rejected those arguments and instead noted that "there is general agreement that a profit-maximizing firm might sometimes find it rational to engage in predatory pricing," and thus the courts needed a test to determine if the alleged price-cutting violated the law.[84] However—and this was a critical point—in devising such a test the judiciary needed to be careful to avoid Type I Errors, or false positives.[85] "For, unlike economics, law is an administrative system the effects of which depend upon the content of rules and precedents only as they are applied by judges and juries in courts and by lawyers advising their clients."[86] Channeling Areeda and Turner, Breyer rejected the Chicago preference for per se legality while he embraced a strict test to prove that predation could have occurred and had an anticompetitive, monopolizing effect in the relevant market.

Ten years later, in 1993, the Supreme Court adopted a new test for predatory pricing, but now it was endorsed by a conservative majority.[87] "As a threshold matter," the second prong of the predatory pricing test—the "dangerous probability" of recoupment—must be shown as likely given the characteristics of the market. Yet even with economic evidence of sales below cost and a plausible case for recoupment the court fell back on neoclassical theory, demonstrating the majority's willingness to intervene and reinterpret the economic evidence.[88] But, now the Court held that "'predatory pricing schemes are rarely tried, and even more rarely successful,' . . . and the costs of an erroneous finding of liability are high."[89] In other words, in the vast majority of predation cases a judge's summary dismissal should prevail, rather than allowing the case to go to a jury, and they largely have.[90]

Nevertheless, even as Breyer and other Democrats helped narrow antitrust law's ambit, significant differences persisted in how the two schools of thought approached the problem of market power. Indeed, through the late 1970s, Areeda and Turner maintained that "no-fault" monopoly should remain an option for the Department of Justice (though not private litigants) to break up durable monopolies through equity proceedings. In other words, echoing Judge Hand's dicta in *Alcoa*, the government should be able to sue a durable monopoly for a court-ordered injunction to break up the firm even without evidence of anticompetitive conduct.[91] Not only does this suggest that they believed efficiencies could be reached by way of divestiture, such as higher output or lower costs and prices, it also suggests that they believed that the courts could and should adjudicate the matter.[92]

Nevertheless, even as price theory and transaction cost economics displaced the older economic structuralism, and narrowed the scope of antitrust injuries, the Court did intervene in a handful of antimonopolization cases, setting important precedents and often citing Areeda and Turner. Most notably, the Supreme Court upheld interventions against a monopolist's exclusionary conduct that "'not only tends to impair the opportunities of rivals, but also either does not further competition on the merits or does so in an unnecessarily restrictive way.'"[93] Although ordinarily there is no "duty to deal," the possession of market power changes the evaluative standards for determining illegal exclusion by asking what specific intent "other than superior efficiency" a monopolist had when enacting an exclusionary strategy.[94] "Post-Chicago" scholars, also trained in price theory and transaction cost analysis, pursued this line of study. This group of scholars has challenged the presumptions of implausibility in section 2 cases, arguing that dominant firms might successfully deploy tie-ins, vertical restraints, or predatory pricing to illegally maintain or enhance their market position.[95]

The rough consensus forged through the Chicago-Harvard antitrust discourse produced the consumer welfare standard. And, although it is a standard and not a rule, it is fair to characterize it as focused on measuring output effects—namely, the question is often, does this restraint raise consumer prices or lower output, quality-adjusted?[96] As such, antitrust analysis became increasingly reliant solely on economic expertise. Within the academic community, microeconomics experienced a shift in presumptions about market power and the plausibility of anticompetitive exclusion. Chicago scholars deemphasized market power—its prevalence, durability, and effects on general welfare—as a threat to market competition. Harvard and other pro-enforcement scholars agreed that antitrust enforcement of the 1960s had overreached, but they did not adopt the libertarian-leaning Chicago approach to market power, or its critique of state interventions as obliquely bad. Instead, Turner and Areeda deployed price tests to help determine where market power might be leveraged to exclude rivals and thereby create antitrust injuries to competitors and the public. They were focused on efficiencies in that they demoted noneconomic concerns and focused on output effects largely limited to consumer prices and quantity changes. They worried about limited institutional capacity of the state, which complemented the rise of Chicago law and economics in the 1970s and '80s; however, they also maintained that a far greater range of state regulation and enforcement was necessary, and productive, particularly when compared to their Chicago counterparts. Despite their differences, the resulting consumer welfare standard that came to encapsulate these debates in law and economics exerted a gravitational force across antitrust doctrines and tests. This non-interventionist approach hardened in 1990s as the US-led Washington Consensus embraced liberalizing "free" markets worldwide.

Reassessing the Problem of Market Power for the Twenty-First Century

By the turn of the century, the consumer welfare standard was firmly ensconced as antitrust law's guiding principle, and it would become the bête noire of twenty-first century progressive reformers who demanded a reconsideration of market power itself as well as its effects on markets and society. This section briefly sketches three key changes to antitrust law, each of which progressive critics have lambasted as both uneconomic and antidemocratic; it then surveys how the antitrust community has fractured—not only regarding the changes wrought by the consumer welfare standard but also with regard to how antitrust law should approach the digital economy moving forward.

First, as we've seen, where formal legal rules had once prohibited certain business conduct that had been deemed anticompetitive generally, such as non-price and price vertical restraints, under the consumer welfare standard more cases were tried under the rule of reason.[97] Within that burden-shifting framework, plaintiffs must show that the defendant possesses some level of market power necessary to show likely anticompetitive effects. Then, defendants may dispute those allegations or offer procompetitive justifications—such as lower consumer prices or increased output—to redeem an allegedly anticompetitive restraint. This has increased the reliance on dueling economic experts, costs, and lengths of trials.[98] Second, the Supreme Court restricted antitrust standing (or, who may sue) by narrowing the definition of an "antitrust injury" and by requiring plaintiffs seeking damages to be "direct purchasers."[99] Third, the consumer welfare standard has empowered judges to declare certain allegedly anticompetitive schemes—such as predatory pricing—"implausible," and then to grant summary judgment for the defense as a matter of law.[100] Antitrust law became more technocratic, more inward-looking at each turn.

The result of these broad changes has been that, between 1999 and 2009, "courts dispose[d] of 97% of [rule of reason] cases at the first stage, on the grounds that there is no anticompetitive effect."[101] This startling figure does not reflect a change in enforcement against illegal per se actions (e.g., price fixing), which did not wane. Instead, it shows how reconfiguring the presumptions about the prevalence and persistence of market power has made showing a likely anticompetitive effect increasingly difficult, if not impossible, for most antitrust plaintiffs.

Some corners of the antitrust community, however, have seemingly celebrated market power as proof of superior business methods and products.[102] And, the Supreme Court has tacked further toward non-intervention. For example, in *American Express v. Ohio*, The Supreme Court rewrote the boundaries of the market in order to dismiss direct evidence of anti-competitive effects. American Express required that its merchant-customers abide by a "no-steering" rule, which prohibited them from steering customers toward credit cards with lower fees. The attorneys general argued that this violated the law by prohibiting price competition; and they found that the restraint increased consumer prices, while American Express did not experience any decline in merchant-customers. Such direct evidence of market power should have shifted the burden to the defense, but the Supreme Court intervened and redrew the boundaries of the relevant market. Instead, Justice Clarence Thomas, writing for the Court, held that the relevant market must also include cardholder-customers as well, and the plaintiffs had not proven anticompetitive harm across *both* sides of the market—thus, they failed.[103] This ruling led antitrust scholar Herbert Hovenkamp, the keeper of the Areeda treatise, to lament that the Court's holding failed to implement the true consumer welfare standard.[104] Instead, *American Express* and other recent rulings suggested that antitrust analysis from the conservative wing of the Court had ossified into a noninterventionist stance, belying the intent and purpose of the law.[105]

And so, the antitrust community exhibited a familiar fracturing, harkening back to older divisions between Harvard's welfare economics and Chicago's libertarian orientation; simultaneously, however, a new group of scholars offered a critique of antitrust law that challenged the validity of the consumer welfare standard itself. The New Brandeis Movement (NBM), as it has become known, was incubated in Washington, D.C., think-tanks and academic centers; and it exploded on the scene with Lina Khan's law school paper, "Amazon's Antitrust Paradox."[106] That article argued that antitrust law's consumer welfare standard had failed to arrest anticompetitive conduct and consolidations, and that it desperately needed to be updated to deal with twenty-first century realities. For example, digital platforms (like Amazon) adopted business models that had deployed predatory tactics to undercut its rival-sellers on the platform and had delayed recoupment through its access to "patient capital" to achieve scale and dominance before paying shareholder dividends.[107] The result was a new behemoth, which those rival-sellers now depended upon to reach consumers.[108] For Khan and many others, the consumer welfare standard myopically focused on short-term prices rather than longer-term competitive processes, which had encouraged the rise of "winner-take-all" digital platforms, like Alphabet, Amazon, and Meta. Consolidation also reached more traditional markets, such as publishing, airlines, and health care (hospitals and insurance providers).[109] While consolidation could entail greater scale and efficiencies, it might also foreclose the possibility of new entrants who then would have to enter at scale to effectively compete. Lacking competitors or potential competitors might then drive down innovation while preserving the dominant firm's ability to raise prices or reduce output.

The NBM gained considerable political traction as it harnessed new social science data that suggested rising economic concentration helped explain the problem of increasing inequality.[110] Although some commentators initially dismissed this progressive movement as ephemeral, President Joe Biden brought many of its leaders into his administration (such as Khan, Jonathan Kanter, and Tim Wu), and embraced their critique of concentration, inequality, and cognitive capture.[111] For example, the movement urges that new economic data showing a decline in the labor share of income and real wage stagnation resulted, in part, from lax merger enforcement and permissive antimonopolization law. Breaking with its singular focus on product markets, antitrust scholars and regulators (not limited to the NBM) have turned their attention to the antitrust harms that can result from unchecked labor market power, or the power of employers in a given market over its employees.[112] Although antitrust law does not directly address the problem of inequality, it is a tool for deconcentration when specific anticompetitive conduct can be remedied and market competition restored—thus, diminishing concentration and empowering workers as a result.[113] With Khan chairing the FTC, the agency promulgated one of its first administrative rules in decades, prohibiting nearly all noncompete covenants in employment contracts in an effort to improve workers' wages, mobility, and bargaining power.[114]

To get at these problems in their incipiency, the agencies issued new merger guidelines, which significantly altered their stated approach to reviewing mergers and acquisitions.[115] The 2023 guidelines lowered the market power thresholds that trigger a presumption of illegality. More interestingly, the guidelines demoted econometric analysis for defining the relevant market and finding market power. Now the "hypothetical monopolist test," which defines a market according to the power to raise consumer prices or restrict output, is but one of many "practical indicia" for determining market power. Citing numerous cases from the structuralist era, such as *Brown Shoe*, the guidelines suggest that this noneconomic approach to evaluating power will more narrowly delineate markets to catch potentially anticompetitive exercises of power; these include harms to laborers and competitors, as well as to consumers.[116]

For NBM reformers, market power is ubiquitous and sticky, and its harms exceed the economic sphere. Effective antitrust enforcement requires more than ensuring low consumer prices or high output (quality-adjusted); it also must protect democracy's promise of self-governance, which cannot be attained in today's concentrated economic market. In turn, enhancing economic welfare alongside protecting democratic participation and economic liberty requires a more forceful deconcentration agenda, which might be achieved by jettisoning the consumer welfare standard in favor of bright-line rules and greater attention to competitor harms. Lacking a statutory intervention by Congress, however, reorienting antitrust law will undoubtedly require corroboration from a conservative Supreme Court schooled in Chicago-style thinking. That said, the movement has already exerted a significant pull on antitrust discourse, reopening questions and cases that had been long ignored. Indeed, a new rough consensus seems poised for ascendance, even as president Trump reenters the White House.

***

The historical development of antitrust law's approach to market power has profound implications for current policy debates and the future of American democracy. The resurgence of concern about economic concentration, exemplified by the New Brandeis Movement, presents a direct challenge to the consumer welfare standard that has dominated antitrust thinking for decades.

This shift is not merely academic—it has already begun to influence enforcement actions and policy proposals—the stakes of this debate are immense. If the critics are correct that the consumer welfare standard has allowed excessive concentration of economic power, the implications go far beyond consumer prices. Issues of labor market monopsony, regional economic inequality, and the political influence of large corporations are all implicated in these antitrust debates. Moreover, the rise of digital platform economies presents novel challenges that may require rethinking traditional antitrust frameworks. The network effects and data advantages of large tech companies raise pressing questions about whether current antitrust tools are sufficient to maintain dynamic competition in the digital age.

As policymakers grapple with these issues, they must weigh competing priorities. More aggressive enforcement may risk chilling innovation or efficiencies that benefit consumers. On the other hand, failure to address abuses of market power will have long-term consequences for economic dynamism, faith in market competition, and democratic governance. As such, current antitrust debates are not merely technical disagreements, but the latest chapter in a long American tradition of grappling with how to reconcile democratic values with a capitalist economic system.

Acknowledgments

The author would like to thank Sid Milkis, Scott Miller, and others at the U.Va. Democracy Project for organizing the conference in March 2023. Additionally, the author thanks Brian Balogh, Brian Callaci, Kenneth Elzinga, Ariel Ezrachi, Eleanor Fox, Derek Hoff, Herbert Hovenkamp, Naomi Lamoreaux, Scott R. Nelson, Logan E. Sawyer, Spencer Weber Waller, and other conference participants for their insightful comments and questions. Portions of this paper were presented in 2024 at New York University Law School's 2024 Next

Generation of Antitrust; University of Oxford's Centre for Competition Law and Policy; Stanford University Law School's Legal Histories of American Governance: Institutions and the State; and the Business History Conference.

Notes

1. Economic activity may be measured by sales receipts, assets, or employment. See OECD Glossary of Statistical Terms (2008).
2. David Autor, David Dorn, Lawrence F. Katz, Christina Patterson, and John Van Reenen, "The Fall of Labor Share and the Rise of Superstar Firms," *Quarterly Journal of Economics* 135, no. 2 (May 2020): 645–709; Spencer Y. Kwon, Yueran Ma, and Kaspar Zimmermann, "100 Years of Rising Corporate Concentration" (unpublished manuscript, February 2023), PDF file. Available at: https://businessconcentration.com/ See also Laura Phillips-Sawyer, "Restructuring American Antitrust Law: Institutionalist Economics and the Antitrust Labor Immunity, 1890–1940s," *University of Chicago Law Review* 90, no. 2 (2023): 659–702.
3. See Denise Hearn, *Harms from Concentrated Industries: A Primer* (February 2024). Available at https://ccsi.columbia.edu/news/harms-concentrated-industries-primer.
4. On "winner-takes-all," or most, markets see Vinod Jain, "Understanding The Dynamics Of Winner-Take-All Markets," *Forbes* (March 5, 2024). Available at https://www.forbes.com/councils/forbesbusinesscouncil/2024/03/05/understanding-the-dynamics-of-winner-take-all-markets/.
5. See David Weil, *Fissured Workplace: Why Work Became So Bad for So Many and What Can Be Done to Improve It* (Harvard University Press, 2018); Adam Winkler, *We the Corporations: How American Businesses Won Their Civil Rights* (Liverlight, 2018); Filippo Lancieri, Eric A. Posner, and Luigi Zingales, "The Political Economy of the Decline in Antitrust Enforcement in the United States" (working paper, July 29, 2022). Available at https://ssrn.com/abstract=4011335
6. Sherman Antitrust Act, ch. 647, §§1–2, 26 Stat. 209, 209 (1890).
7. See William Letwin, *Law and Economic Policy in America: The Evolution of the Sherman Antitrust Act*, rev. ed. (New York: Random House, 1965).
8. Most states had already moved away from exclusive charters, and embraced general incorporation laws. Thus, the Sherman Act concerned private market power. (See Naomi Lamoreaux and John Wallis, Chapter 7 of this volume) See also U.S. v. U.S. Steel, 251 U.S. 417 (1920).
9. U.S. v. Terminal Railroad Association, 224 U.S. 383 (1912).
10. Verizon Communications, Inc. v. Law Offices of Curtis V. Trinko, 540 U.S. 398 (2003).
11. Clayton Act, ch. 323, 38 Stat. 730, 731–32 (1914); Federal Trade Commission Act, ch. 311, 38 Stat. 717 (1914). But see FTC v. Gratz, 253 U.S. 421 (1920).
12. Appalachian Coals, Inc. v. United States, 288 U.S. 344 (1933), at 359–60, as quoted in D. Daniel Sokol, "Antitrust's 'Curse of Bigness' Problem," *Michigan Law Review* 118 (2020): 1259. For a more recent exposition, see Kimble v. Marvel Entertainment, Inc., 135 S. Ct. 2401 (2015), at 2412–13.
13. American Tobacco Co. v. United States, 328 U.S. 781 (1946). See also U.S. v. Griffith, 334 U.S. 100 (1948).
14. United States v. Aluminum Co. of America, 148 F.2d 416 (2d Cir. 1945). The charges also included participation in an international cartel to divide global markets and fix prices. See Laura Phillips-Sawyer, "Jurisdiction Beyond Our Borders: *United States v. Alcoa* and the Extraterritorial Reach of American Antitrust, 1909–1945," in *Antimonopoly and American Democracy*, eds. Daniel A. Crane and William Novak (Oxford: Oxford University Press, 2023), 267–318.
15. United States v. Socony-Vacuum Oil Co., Inc., 310 U.S. 150 (1940).
16. Ellis W. Hawley, *The New Deal and the Problem of Monopoly: A Study in Economic Ambivalence* (Princeton: Princeton University Press, 1966).
17. Alan Brinkley, *End of Reform*

18. Mark Winerman and William E. Kovacic, "Learned Hand, '*Alcoa*,' and the Reluctant Application of The Sherman Act," *Antitrust Law Journal* 79, no. 1 (2013): 295–347.
19. United States v. Aluminum Co. of America, 148 F.2d 416, 427 (2d Cir. 1945).
20. *Alcoa*, 148 F.2d at 428.
21. *Alcoa*, 148 F.2d at 429.
22. See Phillips-Sawyer, "Jurisdiction Beyond Our Borders."
23. As a point of contrast, prior to 1945 section 2 adjudication followed a "tort theory" to enforce the law. Rather than emphasizing the first element of the modern anti-monopolization test (power), earlier cases emphasized exclusionary conduct and spent comparatively little time interrogating the extent of market power within a clearly delineated relevant market. See Standard Oil Co. v. United States, 221 U.S. 1 (1911). See also Donald F. Turner, "Antitrust Policy and the *Cellophane* Case," *Harvard Law Review* 70, no. 2 (1956): 281, 286–97.
24. *Alcoa*, 148 F.2d at 430.
25. *Alcoa*, 148 F.2d at 430.
26. *Alcoa*, 148 F.2d at 431 (producing ahead of demand). The case also upheld the allegations of a price squeeze in fabricated aluminum.
27. *Alcoa*, 148 F.2d at 427.
28. *Alcoa*, 148 F.2d at 427.
29. Joe S. Bain, *Barriers to New Competition* (Cambridge, MA: Harvard University Press, 1956), 36–37.
30. John Maurice Clark, *Studies in the Economics of Overhead Costs* (Chicago: University of Chicago Press, 1923); Joan Robinson, *Economics of Imperfect Competition* (New York: St. Martin's Press, 1933); Gardiner Means, "Notes on Inflexible Prices," *American Economic Review* 26, no. 1 (March, 1936): 23; John Maurice Clark, "Toward a Concept of Workable Competition," *American Economic Review* 30, no. 2 (June 1940): 241–256.
31. Edward Chamberlain, *Theory of Monopolistic Competition* (Cambridge, MA: Harvard University Press, 1933). See also Herbert Hovenkamp, *The Opening of American Law: Neoclassical Legal Thought, 1870–1970* (New York: Oxford University Press, 2014), 209; Laura Phillips-Sawyer, *American Fair Trade* (Cambridge: Cambridge University Press, 2018).
32. Clark, "Workable Competition."
33. Joe S. Bain, "Workable Competition in Oligopoly: Theoretical Considerations and Some Empirical Evidence," *American Economic Review* 40, no. 2 (May 1950): 35–47, 36.
34. Bain, "Workable Competition in Oligopoly," 37.
35. Bain, "Workable Competition in Oligopoly," 38.
36. Bain, "Workable Competition in Oligopoly," 38.
37. The federal government reshaped the aluminum industry after World War II by selling off its wartime production facilities, which in turn diminished Alcoa's market share. See Andrew Perchard, "This Thing Called Goodwill: The Reynolds Metals Company and Political Networking in Wartime America," *Enterprise & Society* 20 (December 2019): 1044–83.
38. Edward Mason, preface to *Antitrust Policy*, by Carl Kaysen and Donald Turner (Cambridge, MA: Harvard University Press, 1959), xii.
39. James Cortada, "Change and Continuity at IBM: Key Themes in Histories of IBM," *Business History Review* 92 (Spring, 2018): 117–48.
40. United States v. Philadelphia Nat'l Bank, 374 U.S. 321 (1963).
41. Brown Shoe Co., Inc. v. United States, 370 U.S. 294 (1962).
42. For example, the Department of Justice blocked Pabst's Brewing Company acquisition of rival Blatz, even though their combined market share totaled less than 5 percent of national beer sales. U.S. v. Pabst, 384 U.S. 546 (1966).
43. U.S. v. Von's Grocery Co., 384 U.S. 270 (1966), Justice Stewart dissenting, as quoted in "Antitrust: Anchor in the Past," *Time* (June 24, 1966). "The sole consistency that I can find is that, in litigation under [Clayton Act] § 7, the Government always wins."
44. Johnson convened the committee secretly, appointed University of Chicago Law School Dean Phil C. Neal to chair it, and shortly thereafter decided not to run for reelection. The report was leaked to the public in early 1969. For a brief introduction, see Herbert Hovenkamp, "The Neal Report and the Crisis in Antitrust" University of Iowa Legal Studies Research Paper No. 09-09, February 24, 2009. Available at https://ssrn.com/abstract=1348707.

45. Phil C. Neal, William F. Baxter, Robert H. Bork, and Carl H. Fulda, "Report of the White House Task Force on Antitrust Policy," *Antitrust Law & Economics Review* 2, no. 2 (Winter 1968–1969): 11–52. See also Yale Brozen, "The Antitrust Task Force Deconcentration Recommendation," *Journal of Law and Economics* 13, no. 2 (October 1970): 279–92. See also Edward F. Cox, Robert C. Fellmeth, and John E. Schulz, "The Nader Report on the Federal Trade Commission" (1969); Miles W. Kirkpatrick, "Report of the ABA Commission to Study the Federal Trade Commission," reprinted in supplement, *Antitrust & Trade Regulation Report* 427 (September 16, 1969).
46. "Antitrust: Surprise Formula," *Time* 93, no. 22 (Friday, May 30, 1969): 80.
47. Earl Kintner, *An Antitrust Primer: A Guide to Antitrust and Trade Regulation Laws for Businessmen*, 2nd ed. (New York: Macmillan, 1973), 108.
48. "GE Balks at Antitrust Decree," *Wall Street Journal*, June 16, 1961, 5; J. H. Carmical, "Antitrust Policy Scored by Oilmen: Industry Says Government Moves are Inconsistent," *The New York Times*, October 14, 1962, 155 (https://www.nytimes.com/1962/10/14/archives/antitrust-policy-scored-by-oilmen-industry-says-government-moves.html?smid=url-share); "Antitrust Tangle: Businessmen Call Laws, Enforcement a Growing Burden," *Wall Street Journal*, December 3, 1963, 18.
49. "Antitrust Enforcement Discussed at Parlay," *Washington Post*, April 10, 1965, E6; "Antitrust Zealotry," *Wall Street Journal*, September 14, 1960, 16.
50. Joseph D. Mathewson, "Tighter U.S. Laws Put American Companies at a Disadvantage Overseas, Critics Say," *Wall Street Journal*, May 10, 1963, 10; "Antitrust Laws Criticized as Obstacles to Business," *The New York Times*, July 23, 1964, 34 (https://nyti.ms/4bWulck). John S. McGee, *In Defense of Industrial Concentration* (New York: Praeger, 1971). See also George Stigler, "Working Paper for the Task Force on Productivity and Competition: Reciprocity," *Trade Regulation Reporter* 5 (June 24, 1969): 55525, 50252.
51. Under Chief Justice Earl Warren (1954–1969), for example, the Court struck down school segregation, created the "one man, one vote" principle, expanded the rights of the criminally accused, and recognized reproductive rights in constitutional law.
52. See Kim Phillips-Fein, *Invisible Hands: Businessmen's Crusade Against the New Deal* (New York: W. W. Norton, 2009); Rob Van Horn, "Reinventing Monopoly and the Role of Corporations: The Roots of Chicago Law and Economics," in *The Road to Mount Pèlerin: The Making of the Neoliberal Thought Collective*, eds. Philip Mirowski and Dieter Plehwe (Cambridge, MA: Harvard University Press, 2009), 204, 217; Rob Van Horn and Philip Mirowski, "The Rise of the Chicago School of Economics and the Birth of Neoliberalism," in *The Road from Mont Pelerin*, at 139; Gary Gerstle, *The Rise and Fall of the Neoliberal Order. America and the World in the Free Market Era* (Oxford: Oxford University Press, 2022).
53. Hart-Scott-Rodino Antitrust Improvements Act of 1976, 15 U.S.C. § 18a, required premerger clearance from either the DOJ or FTC for potential mergers or acquisitions above certain thresholds.
54. Brian Cheffins, "History and Turning the Antitrust Page," *Business History Review* 95 (2021): 805.
55. For example, see Tony A. Freyer, *Antitrust and Global Capitalism, 1930–2004* (Cambridge: Cambridge University Press, 2006), 6; Elizabeth Popp Berman, *Thinking Like an Economist: How Efficiency Replaced Equality in U.S. Public Policy* (Princeton: Princeton University Press, 2022); Benyamin Appelbaum, *The Economists' Hour: False Prophets, Free Markets, and the Fracture of Society* (Boston: Little, Brown, 2019).
56. On error cost analysis, see Frank Easterbrook, "The Limits of Antitrust Law," *Texas Law Review* 63, no. 1 (August 1984), 1–40.
57. See William E. Kovacic, "The Intellectual DNA of Modern U.S. Competition Law for Dominant Firm Conduct: The Chicago/Harvard Double Helix," *Columbia Business Law Review* 2007 (2007), 1-82. See also Herbert Hovenkamp, *The Antitrust Enterprise: Principle and Execution* (Cambridge, MA: Harvard University Press, 2008); William H. Page, "Areeda, Chicago, and Antitrust Inquiry: Economic Efficiency and Legal Process," *Antitrust Bulletin* 41, no. 4 (1996): 909.
58. See generally, *Building Chicago Economics: New Perspectives on the History of America's Most Powerful Economics Program*, eds. Robert Van Horn, Philip Mirowski, and Thomas A. Stapleford (Cambridge: Cambridge University Press, 2011).

59. See Angus Burgin, *The Great Persuasion: Reinventing Free Markets since the Depression* (Harvard University Press, 2012).
60. See Henry C. Simons, *A Positive Program for Laissez-Faire: Some Proposals for A Liberal Economic Policy* (Chicago: Chicago University Press, 1934); Henry C. Simons, *Economics Policy for a Free Society* (Chicago: Chicago University Press, 1948); Edward Levi, Wendell Berge, and James Martin, *Are We Against Monopoly?* (Chicago: University of Chicago Roundtable, 1947); George Stigler and Allen Wallis, letter to the editor, *The New York Times*, December 7, 1934.
61. George Stigler, "A Generalization of the Theory of Imperfect Competition," *Journal of Farm Economics* 19, no. 3 (August 1937): 707–17, 707–8, as cited in J. Daniel Hammond, "Milton Friedman and George J. Stigler: Early Interactions and connections," in *Milton Friedman: Contributions to Economics and Public Policy*, eds. Robert A. Cord and J. Daniel Hammond (Oxford: Oxford University Press, 2016), 680–702. For Chamberlin's scathing review of Stigler's book, see Edward H. Chamberlin, Review of *The Theory of Price*, by George Stigler, *American Economic Review* 37, no. 3 (June 1947): 414–8. On this debate, see Jan Horst Keppler, "The Genesis of 'Positive Economics' and the Rejection of Monopolistic Competition Theory: A Methodological Debate," *Cambridge Journal of Economics* 22, no. 3 (May 1998): 261–76.
62. George Stigler, *The Theory of Price* (New York: MacMillan, 1946), 206, as quoted in Hammond, "Milton Friedman and George J. Stigler," 687.
63. George Stigler, *Five Lectures on Economic Problems* (New York: Longmans, Green & Co., 1949); George Stigler, "Monopoly and Oligopoly by Merger," *American Economic Review* 40, no. 2 (May 1950): 23–34.
64. Wayne A. Leeman, "The Limitations of Local Price-Cutting as a Barrier to Entry," *Journal of Political Economy* 64, no. 4 (1956): 329.
65. Leeman, The Limitations of Local Price-Cutting," 330.
66. Leeman, The Limitations of Local Price-Cutting," 321, using John Rockefeller's management of Standard Oil Company as illustrative.
67. John S. McGee, "Predatory Price Cutting: The Standard Oil (N.J.) Case," *Journal of Law & Economics* 1 (1958): 137. The article's argument is based on the "one monopoly profit" theory. (McGee, "Predatory Price Cutting," 142.) For a direct contravention of McGee's argument, see Elizabeth Granitz and Benjamin Klein, "Monopolization by 'Raising Rivals' Costs': The *Standard Oil* Case," *Journal of Law & Economics* 39, no. 1 (April, 1996): 1–47.
68. For example, see John S. McGee, *In Defense of Industrial Concentration* (New York: Praeger, 1971).
69. Ward Bowman, "Tying Arrangements and the Leverage Problem," *Yale Law Journal* 67, no. 1 (November 1957).
70. Harvey J. Goldschmid, H. Michael Mann, and J. Fred Weston, eds., *Industrial Concentration: The New Learning*, (Boston: Little, Brown, 1974).
71. Miles W. Kirkpatrick, review of *Industrial Concentration: The New Learning*, by Harvey J. Goldschmid, H. Michael Mann, and Fred Weston, eds., *Columbia Law Review* 76, no. 6 (October 1976): 1048–51. See also Peter C. Carstensen, "How to Assess the Impact of Antitrust on the American Economy: Examining History or Theorizing," *Iowa Law Review* 74, no. 5 (July 1989): 1775.
72. Richard A. Posner, "The Chicago School of Antitrust Analysis," *University of Pennsylvania Law Review* 127 (April 1979): 925, 928.
73. Posner, "Chicago School Analysis," 932.
74. Posner, "Chicago School Analysis," 934. See also Kovacic, "The Intellectual DNA of Modern U.S. Competition Law," 40, fn.119.
75. Posner, "Chicago School Analysis," 936 (tie-ins), 938 (vertical integration) 940–1 (predatory pricing). See Phillip Areeda and Donald F. Turner, *Antitrust Law: An Analysis of Antitrust Principles and Their Application*, 1st ed. (Boston: Little, Brown, 1978), section 726B (vertical integration) and section 711 (predatory pricing).
76. Philip Areeda and Donald Turner, "Predatory Pricing and Related Practices Under Section 2 of the Sherman Act," *Harvard Law Review* 88, no. 4 (February 1975): 697–733.

77. Areeda and Turner, "Predatory Pricing."
78. Matsushita Electrical Industrial Co., Ltd. v. Zenith Radio Corp., 475 U.S. 574 (1986), granting summary judgment for defendants because the alleged predatory pricing scheme was deemed economically "implausible," 475 U.S. 587.
79. Barry Wright Corp. v ITT Grinnell Corp., 724 F.2d 227 (1st Cir. 1983), citing Areeda and Turner's 1978 treatise.
80. *Barry Wright*, 724 F.2d at 231, citing J. Bain, *Industrial Organization*, ch. 5 (2nd ed. 1968), 112–163; F. Scherer, *Industrial Market Structure and Economic Performance*, 56–70, 222–25 (2nd ed. 1980), and Areeda and Turner, *Antitrust Law*, 2:404.
81. *Barry Wright*, 724 F.2d at 231.
82. See Stephen Breyer, *Regulation and Its Reform* (Cambridge, MA: Harvard University Press, 1982).
83. John McGee, "Predatory Pricing Revisited," *Journal of Law and Economics* 23 (October 1980): 289–330; Richard A. Posner, "Exclusionary Practices and the Antitrust Laws," *University of Chicago Law Review* 41 (Spring 1974): 506, 516–17, among others.
84. *Barry Wright*, 724 F.2d at 231, citing only Areeda and Turner, "Predatory Pricing."
85. *Barry Wright*, 724 F.2d at 232. The judiciary must "avoid discouraging desirable price-cutting activity."
86. Ibid., 234, citing cases for the illegal per se rule and Derek Bok, "Section 7 of the Clayton Act and the Merging of Law and Economics," *Harvard Law Review* 74 no. 2 (December 1960): 226–355.
87. Brooke Group Ltd., v. Brown & Williamson Tobacco Corp., 509 U.S. 209 (1993). Now citing Phillip Areeda and Herbert Hovenkamp, *Antitrust Law: An Analysis of Antitrust Principles and Their Applications* (Boston: Little, Brown, 1992 supp.) secs. 714.2, 714.3. (Technically, *Brooke Group* arose under the Robinson-Patman Act primary-line product prohibition on price discrimination; however, the Court held that it would require the same evidentiary threshold as the Sherman Act. Justice Stevens dissented on this issue, too.)
88. Rebecca Haw Allensworth, "Economic Sense and Sensibility: *Matsushita* and the Rise of the Battle of the Experts," *Antitrust Law Journal*, 82.1 (2018), 47–80.
89. *Brooke Group*, at 226, quoting Matsushita Electric Industry Co. Ltd. v. Zenith Radio Corp., 475 U.S. 574 (1986).
90. See Michael A. Carrier, "The Real Rule of Reason: Bridging the Disconnect," *Brigham Young University Law Review* 1999, no. 4 (1999): 1265–365. See also Philip Areeda, "Monopolization, Mergers, and Markets: A Century Past and Future," *California Law Review* 75, no. 3 (May 1987): 959–81, 971, lamenting the twin problems of "vaguely instructed juries" and uncertain outcomes.
91. Areeda and Turner, *Antitrust Law* (1978, 1st ed.), vol. 3, ch. 6B.
92. For a discussion, see Areeda and Hovenkamp, *Antitrust Law* (1998, 3rd ed.), vol. 3, ch. 6B.
93. Aspen Skiing Co. v. Aspen Highlands Skiing Corp., 472 U.S. 585 (1985), fn.32 quoting Areeda and Turner, *Antitrust Law* (1978, 1st ed.), vol. 3, 78. See also U.S. v. Microsoft Corp., 147 F.3d 935 (D.C. Cir. 1998); U.S. v. Dentsply Int'l, Inc. 399 F.3d 181 (3d Cir, 2005), *cert.* denied, 546 U.S. 1089 (2006). But see Verizon Communications, Inc. v. Law Offices of Curtis V. Trinko, 540 U.S. 398 (2003), refusing to intervene where public regulation and administrative agency review already exists. Justice Scalia wrote, "*Aspen Skiing* is at or near the outer boundary of § 2 liability," *Trinko*, 540 U.S. at 409.
94. *Aspen Skiing*, 472 U.S. 585, fn.39, citing Robert H. Bork, *The Antitrust Paradox* (New York: Basic Books 1978), 157.
95. Thomas G. Krattenmaker and Steven C. Salop, "Anticompetitive Exclusion: Raising Rivals' Costs to Achieve Power over Price," *Yale Law Journal* 96, no. 2 (December 1986): 209–93. See also Patrick Bolton, Joseph F. Brodley, and Michael H. Riordan, "Predatory Pricing: Strategic Theory and Legal Policy," *Georgetown Law Journal* 88, no. 8 (August 2000): 2239–330.
96. Steven C. Salop, "Question: What is the Real and Proper Antirust Welfare Standard? Answer: The True Consumer Welfare Standard," *Loyola Consumer Law Review* 22, no. 3 (2010): 336–53. Note that the consumer welfare standard relies more on Areeda's emphasis on price and output than it does on Robert Bork's notion of total or aggregate welfare measures.

97. *Continental TV v. GTE Sylvania* (1977); State Oil Co. v. Khan, 522 U.S. 3 (1997), Leegin Creative Leather Products, Inc. v. PSKS, Inc., 551 U.S. 877 (2007).
98. Michael Salinger, "The Legacy of *Matsushita*: The Role of Economics in Antitrust Litigation," *Loyola University of Chicago Law Review* 38 (2007): 475–90.
99. Brunswick Corp. v. Pueblo Bowl-O-Mat, Inc., 429 U.S. 477 (1977), clarifying antitrust injury; Illinois Brick Co. v. Illinois, 431 U.S. 720 (1977), creating the direct purchaser rule.
100. See Matsushita v. Zenith Radio (1986), granting summary judgment; Bell Atlantic Corp. v. Twombly, 550 U.S. 544 (2007), granting motion to dismiss.
101. Michael Carrier, "The Rule of Reason: An Empirical Update for the 21st Century," *George Mason Law Review* 16 no. 4 (Summer 2009): 827–37, 828.
102. See Verizon Communications, Inc. v. Law Offices of Curtis V. Trinko, 540 U.S. 398 (2003), refusing to apply antitrust law to a regulated industry that already had agency oversight; the celebration of monopoly was dicta.
103. Ohio v. Am. Express Co., 138 S. Ct., at 2286.
104. Herbert Hovenkamp, "Platforms and the Rule of Reason: The *American Express* Case," *Columbia Business Law Review* (2019): 35–76. See also Daniel Crane, "Market Power Without Market Definition," *Notre Dame Law Review* 90, no. 1 (November 2014): 31–79.
105. See Herbert Hovenkamp, "The Looming Crisis in Antitrust Economics," *Boston University Law Review* 101 (2021): 489.
106. Lina Khan, "Amazon's Antitrust Paradox," *Yale Law Journal* 126 (2017): 564.
107. The term "patient capital" comes from K. Sabeel Rahman and Kathleen Thelen, "The Rise of The Platform Business Model and The Transformation of 21st-Century Capitalism," *Politics & Society* 47 (2019): 177.
108. K. Sabeel Rahman, "The New Utilities: Private Power, Social Infrastructure, and the Revival of the Public Utility Concept," *Cardozo Law Review* 39 (May 2018): 1621–92.
109. See Peter Brennan and Chris Hudgins, "Market-Leading US Companies Consolidate Power in Era of 'Superstar' Firms," *S&P Global*, January 2023. (This study excludes tradeable manufactured goods.) Available at https://www.spglobal.com/market-intelligence/en/news-insights/articles/2023/1/market-leading-us-companies-consolidate-power-in-era-of-superstar-firms-73773141.
110. See David Autor, David Dorn, Lawrence F. Katz, Christina Patterson, John Van Reenen, The Fall of the Labor Share and the Rise of Superstar Firms, *The Quarterly Journal of Economics*, Volume 135, Issue 2, May 2020, Pages 645–709, https://doi.org/10.1093/qje/qjaa004. See also Tim Sablik and Nicholas Trachter, "Are Markets Becoming Less Competitive?," Federal Reserve Bank of Richmond. Accessed July 21, 2023. https://www.richmondfed.org/publications/research/economic_brief/2019/eb_19-06.
111. Joseph R. Biden. *Executive Order 14036: Promoting Competition in the American Economy.* Federal Register 86, no. 121 (July 9, 2021). Available at: https://www.federalregister.gov/documents/2021/07/09/2021-14825/promoting-competition-in-the-american-economy.
112. José Azar, Ioana Marinescu, Marshall Steinbaum, "Measuring Labor Market Power Two Ways," *American Economic Association Papers and Proceedings* 109 (May 2019): 317–21; Laura Alexander and Steven Salop, "Antitrust Worker Protections: The Rule of Reason Does Not Allow Counting of Out-of-Market Benefits," *University of Chicago Law Review* 91, no. 2 (March 2023): 273–338; Ioana Marinescu and Herbert Hovenkamp, "Anticompetitive Mergers and Labor Markets," *Indiana Law Journal* 94, no. 3 (Summer 2019): 1031–63. See also Dan Papscun, "Companies Must Weigh Worker Impact Under New Merger Guidelines," *Bloomberg Law*, July 21, 2023.
113. See United States v. Anthem, Inc., 236 F. Supp. 3d 171 (D.D.C. 2017), *cert. dismissed*, 137 S. Ct. 2250 (2017) (affirming a district-court injunction against a merger due to labor market power effects).
114. Federal Trade Commission, non-compete clause rule (2023).
115. Department of Justice, Federal Trade Commission, Merger Guidelines (2023); Alexandra Alter and Elizabeth A. Harris, "Judge Blocks a Merger of Penguin Random House and Simon & Schuster," *The New York Times*, October 31, 2022. Available at https://www.nytimes.com/2022/10/31/books/penguin-random-house-simon-schuster.html?searchResultPosition=1.
116. Laura Phillips-Sawyer, "A Brief History of Labor Within Antitrust Law," *Competition Policy International*, June 2024. Available at https://ssrn.com/abstract=5053593.

7

Democracy, Capitalism, and Equality

The Importance of Impersonal Rules

NAOMI R. LAMOREAUX AND JOHN JOSEPH WALLIS

Introduction

There are ways of thinking about democracy and capitalism that make them seem irreconcilable. If capitalism is an economic system that allows a considerable degree of economic freedom and enables a small number of hard working or lucky individuals to accumulate substantial wealth, then capitalism may have an inherent tendency to increase inequality. If democracies gain legitimacy by leveling the playing field for their citizens, both politically and economically, then the unequal accumulation of wealth generated by a capitalist economic system may eventually erode the foundations of democracy. Viewed from this perspective, capitalism and democracy seem incompatible.[1]

To most economic historians, however, the answer to the question "Can democracy and capitalism be reconciled?" is an obvious "Yes." A glance around the world suggests that all of today's "advanced" capitalist societies are both rich and advanced democracies, and all of today's "advanced" democracies are rich and advanced capitalist societies. Indeed, democracy and capitalism developed together so closely over the last two centuries that asking whether democratic development caused modern economic development or modern economic development caused democratic development has long been a foundational question in economics, economic history, and political science. Few economic historians doubt that democracy and capitalism emerged in tandem. The debates are all about how and why.

The modifier "advanced" in the preceding paragraph is crucial. As we show in this chapter, only societies with *advanced democratic polities* are associated with *advanced capitalist economies*. If we define a democracy simply as a society that

Naomi R. Lamoreaux and John Joseph Wallis, *Democracy, Capitalism, and Equality.* In: *Can Democracy and Capitalism Be Reconciled?.* Edited by: Sidney M. Milkis and Scott C. Miller, Oxford University Press.
DOI: 10.1093/9780197774731.003.0008

selects leaders through some form of election, or if we define a capitalist society simply as one where economic actors pursue profits, then the relationship between democracy and economic development disappears. In other words, there is a strong association between advanced democracy and advanced capitalism, but little or no relationship between democracy and capitalism broadly defined. Why this is so is the subject of this essay. In brief, we argue that today's advanced capitalist democracies began to undergo changes in the late-nineteenth and early-twentieth centuries that transformed both their economic and political systems in mutually reinforcing ways. The changes in the organization of political institutions that occurred during this period would not have been sustainable without the corresponding changes that occurred in the organization of economic institutions, and vice versa. At the root of this double transformation was the adoption of impersonal legal rules—that is, rules that treated everyone (or, more accurately, broad categories of everyone) the same. Impersonal rules facilitated the free flow of resources to their most profitable economic uses that is the hallmark of advanced capitalism. They also made possible the emergence of the stable long-lived political parties that are the essential features of advanced democracies. Although they did not eliminate inequality or, for that matter, discrimination, they created peaceful, prosperous societies whose citizens benefited from a broad set of civil liberties.

Aside from the small number of advanced capitalist democracies, most societies around the world today have (and always have had) unstable political systems. Political elites in these societies try to stave off conflict by agreeing to allocate to each other what economists call "rents." The rents are created by "identity" rules—that is, rules that treat different members of the elite differently and whose form and enforcement depend upon the social identity of the individuals to whom they apply. Because the rents will be lost if these agreements collapse, the identity rules that enable them also create incentives not to violate them. The incentives are imperfect, however. Members of the elite are always jockeying for better deals, and the value of the rents can never be fixed through time. Indeed, rents can dissipate for completely idiosyncratic reasons. As a result, this kind of political manipulation of economic interests can be at best a source of short-run stability. At some point, the agreements will collapse.[2]

Although most writers consider it progress when countries begin to choose leaders by election, the move toward democracy can exacerbate problems of instability in a society governed by identity rules. Elections introduce considerable randomness to the choice of leaders, making it more difficult for elites to come to agreements in the first place and making the agreements they manage to reach less secure. The resulting uncertainty in turn increases the incentive for elites to solidify their coalitions by manufacturing new privileges they can distribute to their allies. Thus, the spread of electoral democracy can have the perverse effect of worsening both political instability and the extent of economic distortions.

Although opposition parties often promise to put a stop to this kind of corruption when they come to power, they rarely follow through because they too need to reward supporters to win elections. During the second half of the nineteenth century, however, a small group of countries found ways to limit significantly this kind of manipulation by mandating that the rules that governed their societies be impersonal. These countries became the advanced capitalist democracies of today. Each of them made the transition in its own way. There was no common route to change—no recipe that other countries could follow and become advanced. But in each of the countries that figured out how to do it, the adoption of impersonal rules set in motion a similar set of processes that transformed the way the economic and political systems worked and interacted. Most obviously, the resulting limits on rent-creation encouraged capitalist economic development by reducing the barriers that had inhibited the free movement of economic resources. Less obviously, the same developments strengthened the organizations—political parties—that mediated between the government and the electorate, directing political competition into channels that were no longer destabilizing.

In the next section of the chapter, "Definitions and Measurement," we define what we mean by advanced capitalism and advanced democracy, and document the association between these two systems using estimates of real per capita income and a widely used measure of democracy, the Polity V Score. The section "Why Identity Rules Cannot Support Advanced Capitalist Democracies" then explains why the association between democracy and capitalism does not hold below the set of advanced capitalist democracies. It begins by describing how societies governed by identity rules work, why they are plagued by instability, and why they constrain capitalist economic development. Next it explains how introducing democracy into such societies makes them more unstable and, often, poorer. The section "Impersonal Rules and Advanced Democracy" shows how mandating impersonal rules transforms these societies—how it removes the barriers that prevented resources from flowing to their best uses, allowing capitalism to thrive, and how it transforms the way the democratic political process works by giving rise to stable party systems. Finally, in "The Transition to Impersonal Rules and the Emergence of Consolidated Parties," we review the little that is known about how today's advanced capitalist democracies adopted impersonal rules, highlighting the difficult, context-specific character of these transitions by focusing on the cases of the United States, the United Kingdom, and Germany. The final section concludes.

Definitions and Measurement

To show that there is an association between advanced capitalist societies and advanced democracies, but not between capitalism and democracy more generally, requires that we be as clear as possible about our terms. Even so, measuring the extent to which countries fit our definitions is difficult because the available metrics are imperfect proxies for the characteristics we seek to capture. We are primarily interested, however, in the difference between advanced democratic capitalisms and all other societies, rather than with finely graded distinctions across the full spectrum of countries, so the measures are good enough for our purposes.

For all the discussion of capitalism in the literature, scholars have devoted relatively little effort to defining and measuring it. Marx, of course, conceived of capitalism as an economic system in which labor was the sole source of value in the economy, but workers did not own the means of production and had to sell their labor to the capitalists who did to survive.[3] Once the labor theory of value gave way to the idea that profits depend on the efficient combination of multiple factors of production, however, it became common for scholars to define capitalism very simply as a system where economic actors were motivated primarily by the pursuit of profits.[4] There are two problems with this definition. First, it does not allow us to distinguish societies that most people consider capitalist from others that most do not (like feudalism), where elites may also be motivated by the desire for economic gain. Second, it does not allow us to distinguish societies in which profit-oriented elites are able to cut rent-creating deals that limit the free flow of resources into profitable economic activities.[5] To avoid these problems, we prefer to categorize societies as more or less capitalist depending on the prevalence of such rent-creating arrangements. Advanced capitalist economies are those in which these kinds of barriers to entry have been largely removed, and entrepreneurs are free to invest their capital, workers are free to invest their labor, and resource owners are free to invest their property in almost any kind of venture they choose. In advanced capitalist societies, any person can form an organization, access government-enforced rules to structure it, and engage in a wide variety of activities without the explicit approval of the government. The forms of supported organizations are rich and varied, the scale of organizations can range from very small to very large, and new organizations, purposes, and products appear and disappear frequently.

There is a good deal of overlap between our definition of capitalism as an economic system in which individuals can use their capital, labor, land, and resources however they think best and the measures of economic freedom in Vincent Geloso and Alex Tabarrok's paper in this volume. However, in our view, even though advanced capitalist societies are characterized by the free movement of economic resources, they are not necessarily laissez-faire. As the "varieties of capitalism" literature has shown, such societies can differ considerably in the extent to which they regulate economic activity in the interests of health, safety, environmental sustainability, and other social goods, and in the extent to which they provide a social safety net.[6] Within the general constraints imposed by these types of regulatory policies, what matters is that capital, labor, and resources flow freely wherever their owners direct them. The key to *advanced capitalism* is not the absence of limits on economic activity, it is that *everyone* faces the *same* limits and enjoys the *same* freedoms.[7]

Although one can articulate the difference between advanced capitalist societies and their more basic capitalist counterparts, there are no comprehensive indices that capture these distinctions over space and time. We have chosen for our analysis what we think is the most reasonable metric available: real per capita income. The idea here is that, all other things being equal, societies with fewer barriers to the free flow of economic resources will be richer than those where profitable opportunities are limited to government favorites. We use the data on per capita income that Angus Maddison has compiled for a wide selection of countries over the last two centuries. Some of Maddison's estimates are little better than guesses, and coverage is spottier at the beginning of the period than at the end, but the data convey a general picture of trends in real income over time and across countries, which is all we need for our purposes.[8]

Scholars have devoted a great deal more effort to defining and measuring democracy than they have to capitalism. At the simplest level, democracy is a political system that selects leaders through elections. Joseph A. Schumpeter defined democracy this way in *Capitalism, Socialism, and Democracy,* contrasting it with the classical notion of democracy as a pure "ideal" type of political system in which elections somehow express the will of the people.[9] But democracy involves much more than elections. David Collier and Stephen Levitsky have specified a "procedural minimum" for being a democracy that presumes "fully contested elections with full suffrage and the absence of massive fraud, combined with effective guarantees of civil liberties, including freedom of speech, assembly, and association." Many countries that hold elections to select leaders are unable to meet even this basic standard. An "*expanded* procedural minimum" for democracy requires in addition that elected governments have effective power to govern. The expanded definition excludes political systems where elections are free, fair, and open, but the elected government does not fully control the state, as, for example, in countries where the military exercises independent power. In democracies that meet this expanded definition, the parties or coalitions that win elections are the organizations that control the government, which means that the policies governments put into effect and the rules they promulgate depend on the outcome of elections.[10]

What we call advanced democracies exhibit all the characteristics of electoral democracies that meet the expanded minimum standard. In addition, they have the enhanced stability that comes from the development of a relatively small number of major consolidated parties with durable lives.[11] These major parties neither suppress their opponents when they win elections nor disappear from the political scene when they lose them. Although one of the parties might prevail for a considerable period, in general they all have reasonable chances of winning elections, or of participating in a governing coalition, and therefore of determining the policies pursued by the state. Although advanced democracies all have consolidated party systems, other details of their political structures—the number of parties, whether they are parliamentary or characterized by separation of powers, whether representation is majoritarian or proportional, and so on—can vary significantly from one country to the next. Indeed, there is a literature on varieties of democracy that parallels, and feeds into, that on capitalism.[12]

Political scientists have constructed various indices that measure democracy numerically. The one we use here is the Polity V Score, which ranks countries on a 21-point scale ranging from −10 to +10. Negative numbers indicate how autocratic a society's political system is, positive numbers how democratic. The Polity V Score is built up from component indices that measure different aspects of a country's governance. It gives considerable weight to how the executive is chosen and to constraints on the power of the executive, as well as to the extent of political competition, and therefore highlights the characteristic features of democracies that meet the expanded minimum standard. Because its components are less able to detect the presence of consolidated political parties, some of the countries that receive Polity V Scores of +10 may not be advanced democracies by our definition. Nonetheless, the index is well designed to capture gradations of autocracy and democracy and, usefully for our purposes of correlating capitalism and democracy, is not confounded by the inclusion of variables that measure economic policy.[13]

For the purposes of this paper, we divide the political world conceptually into autocracies, electoral democracies, and advanced democracies. Our concern is with the line between advanced democracies and all other systems. Although we recognize that there is significant variation among countries on both sides of this line, we seek to understand how advanced democracies differ from all other democracies and to explain why it is advanced democracy in particular that is consistent with advanced capitalism.

Table 7.1 reports correlations between per capita income and Polity V Scores for countries for which both measures are available in 2000, broken down into various sub-samples. Because the Middle Eastern oil producers are rich despite being autocratic, we drop them from the analysis, but we report correlations that include them in the notes. At the top of the world income

Table 7.1 **Cross-Country Correlations Between Per Capita Income and Polity V Scores, Excluding Middle East Oil Producers, for 2000**

Subsample	*Average Per Capita Income*	*Average Polity V Score*	*Correlation Coefficient*	*p-value*
Richest 25 countries	$33,094	9.80	0.22	0.10
Richest 66 countries	$19,074	6.92	0.47	0.00
All countries	$10,835	3.10	0.55	0.00
Poorest 66 countries	$2,501	0.70	0.08	0.25

Sources: Per capita income (in 1990 Geary-Khamis dollars) is from Maddison (2010), https://ghdx.healthdata.org/record/statistics-world-population-gdp-and-capita-gdp-1-2008-ad. The Polity V Scores are from the Center for Systemic Peace, https://www.systemicpeace.org/polityproject.html.

Notes: The table includes the 132 countries for which we have both per capita income and Polity V Scores for 2000, not including the Middle Eastern oil producers Bahrain, Kuwait, Saudi Arabia, Oman, United Arab Republic, and Qatar. The averages are unweighted. If the oil countries are included in the sample, the relevant correlations (p-values) become: Richest 25 countries, −0.14 (0.25); Richest 66 countries, 0.14 (0.12); All countries, 0.34 (0.00).

distribution—the 25 richest countries, not including these oil producers—the correlation between our measures of capitalism and democracy is weakly positive and marginally significant; most of the countries in this group have Polity V Scores of 10, so there is little variation on the democracy side. However, as we expand the sample from the top 25 non-oil countries to the top 66 non-oil countries, and then to all the non-oil countries, the correlation coefficient rises from 0.22 to 0.47 to 0.55, and the statistical significance of the correlation increases. So long as the richest countries are in the sample, adding more poor countries increases the measured correlation, but the pattern is driven entirely by the richest set of countries. If we look only at the poorest 66 countries in the dataset, the correlation virtually disappears and becomes insignificant. The correlation coefficient is 0.08 with a p value of 0.25.

This lack of an association between our measures of capitalism and democracy for countries in the bottom half of the distribution can be seen graphically in Figure 7.1, which plots the income of the richest country in a given sample on the horizontal axis and the correlation between per capita income and the Polity V Score for that same sample on the vertical axis (the income numbers on the horizontal axis are negative to make the graph read from left to right). The first observation is the full sample of countries (excluding the Middle Eastern oil producers), ranging from Norway with a per capita income of $54,040 in 2000 to Afghanistan with an income of just $502. The second observation

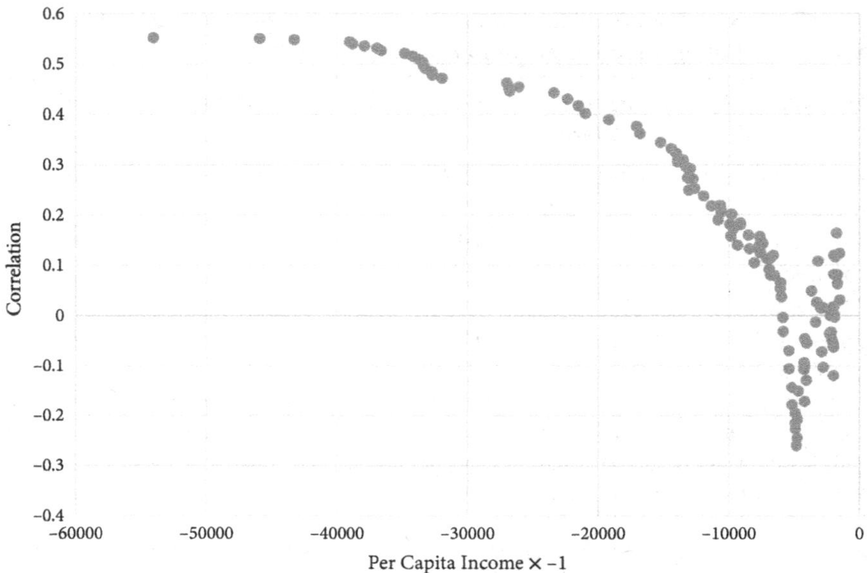

Figure 7.1 Correlation between the Polity V Score and per capita income in 2000, from $50,040 to $1,485.

Sources: See Table 7.1

Note: The figure reports the correlation coefficient between real per capita income and the Polity V Score for various samples of countries in 2000. The first point on the left is the coefficient for the entire sample of 132 countries, ranging from Norway, the richest country, to Afghanistan, the poorest, and excluding the specialized Middle Eastern oil producers. Each point to the right drops the richest country from the sample. The last point is the correlation coefficient for the poorest 27 countries from Bangladesh to Afghanistan. The horizontal axis demarcates the per capita income of the richest country in each sample, multiplied by −1. It uses negative numbers to make it easier to see how the correlation between democracy and per capita income declines as rich countries are dropped.

drops Norway and measures the correlation from the United States at $45,886 to Afghanistan. The last observation is the correlation for the poorest 27 countries (Bangladesh at $1,845 to Afghanistan). As the rich countries disappear from the sample, the correlation between per capita income and Polity V Scores declines, becoming statistically insignificant around a correlation of 0.2 and a top income in the range $10,000 to $12,000 (roughly the income of the Russian Federation). For the bottom three quarters of the countries there is little correlation between Polity V Scores and per capita income, and at the very lowest levels of the distribution the correlation actually becomes negative, suggesting that poor countries with autocratic governments may have higher incomes than those that are democracies. Those results are not statistically significant, however.

The association between advanced capitalism and advanced democracy that we have documented is just that—a correlation. We have not proven anything about the effect of democracy on capitalism or of capitalism on democracy. Nor have we ruled out the possibility that other phenomena are behind the correlation we observe. In the next two sections, we tackle the task of explanation.

Why Identity Rules Cannot Support Advanced Capitalist Democracies

As we suggested above, a distinguishing feature of advanced capitalist democracies is that they are governed by impersonal rules rather than identity rules. Indeed, we would go farther and assert that impersonal rules are a critical requirement for the positive association we observe between advanced democracy and advanced capitalism. In this section, we develop the logic of this claim. We first explain that autocracies and oligarchic republics always operate under identity rules because that is how ruling coalitions create the rents that give elites an interest in preserving social order. These coalitions are subject to collapse, however, because the deals that structure them are inherently unstable. They are also bad for capitalist development because rent-creation depends on the erection of barriers to the free flow of economic resources. We then show that the introduction of democracy typically makes both problems worse because the greater uncertainty of electoral outcomes increases political instability and hence the imperative to deploy rent-creating identity rules. In the next section, we round out the argument by showing how everything changes with the shift to impersonal rules.

The importance of identity rules is most obvious in autocracies and oligarchies. These societies are prone to coups, uprisings, and civil wars as different factions of the elite jockey for power. Agreements among powerful factions are vital to establishing and maintaining order, but they can only last if the elites involved in them have a stake in their continuance—if they earn valuable rents that will be lost if the arrangements fall apart. Thus, identity rules that create rents—that assign lucrative government offices or valuable monopoly privileges to strategically important political actors—are essential for preventing violent breakdowns.[14]

Coalitions organized by identity rules necessarily include groups with competing, even antagonistic interests. They are not just made up of allies. Maintaining social order depends on inducing the powerful factions that are most likely to fight each other to agree to cooperate. To give a recent example, former president Mwai Kibaki of Kenya was declared the winner of the 2007 elections despite the claims of his opponent, Raila Odinga, that the election had been manipulated. Violent protests broke out and Kenya seemed on the verge of civil war, but violence was forestalled by an agreement between the Kibaki and

Odinga organizations that allowed the former to assume the presidency. Entitled the National Accord and Reconciliation Act of 2008, the agreement rewrote the constitution and created the office of Prime Minister, which was given to Odinga. The Accord was an intra-elite agreement between enemies, not allies, and very consciously used identity rules to quell violence.[15]

Societies organized by identity rules are inherently "factional" in the sense that they are dominated by small groups of elites with distinct and different interests who join together to form coalitions to govern and to influence what the government does. These coalitions, and the factions that make them up, are fluid and constantly changing. As a result, intra-elite agreements can only maintain the peace for limited periods of time. Over the long run, changes in the relative power of the factions involved, or the emergence of a powerful faction from outside the agreement, can lead to outbreaks of violence. The rise of the Odinga organization in Kenya is a good example. Moreover, the rents that hold a coalition together can shift or even dissipate for exogenous reasons, forcing the agreement to be renegotiated and threatening violence. In eighteenth-century Britain, for example, a glut in the world market for tea led the crown to bolster the monopoly of the East India Company, whose investors formed a crucial part of the ruling coalition, at the cost of provoking a rebellion in British North America.[16]

Some ruling coalitions are autocracies, where one set of elites controls the government; some are oligarchies, where control is shared by a broader combination of elites. Although autocracies may appear to be more stable than oligarchies, they too are riven by factions. Autocrats always govern in the shadow of violence and must use rents to induce other powerful elites to refrain from using force against them. Nonetheless, in autocracies the person of the monarch or dictator provides a focal point that facilitates the coordination of agreements. In oligarchies, the coordination problem is more difficult. Agreements are both harder to reach and more prone to collapse.

Elites in oligarchies always fear that one faction among them will gain control of the government and will use that control to dominate or eliminate the other factions. In early modern Europe, this fear drove the development of the republican ideas and institutions that to this day claim the admiration of political theorists. To protect what they termed their "rights and liberties" from the tyranny that would result from such domination, republican thinkers advocated mixed and balanced government. They did not understand that what they called their rights and liberties were the product of identity rules; nor did they see factions as the characteristic outcome of societies structured by identity rules. To the contrary, they conceived of factions as natural phenomena—as products of human nature—and they could not imagine that societies could be organized without them. The mixed and balanced governments that republican thinkers promoted did nothing to eliminate factions; that, they thought, was impossible. Instead, the goal of these thinkers was to prevent tyranny by structuring the government so that factions counterbalanced one another and none was able to dominate.[17]

The republican thinkers who promoted mixed and balanced government did not advocate democracy, but their ideas nonetheless provided a critical foundation for the democratic reforms of the late eighteenth and early nineteenth centuries. Although these reforms are usually considered milestones of human progress, their introduction into societies structured by identity rules had the perverse effect of making problems of instability worse, as the violent conflicts of the age of revolutions suggest. Figure 7.2 shows that this effect is still evident in democratizing countries today. The figure graphs the relationship between Polity V Scores and political instability, measured in several ways. The vertical axis reports the likelihood that an unstable event will occur in a given year, and the horizontal axis the country's Polity V Score. As the figure shows, countries with very high Polity V Scores (advanced democracies) are the most stable in the world. Countries with very low Polity V Scores are also relatively stable. But as autocracies incorporate more democratic elements (mainly elections) into their political processes and move toward electoral democracies, they become less stable. Their chance of armed conflict and of backsliding into autocracy increases—that is, unless, against the odds, they manage to continue to democratize.[18]

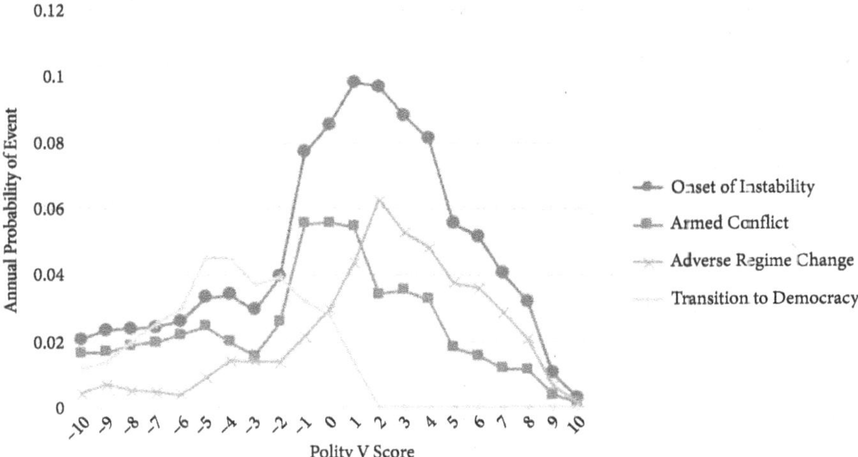

Figure 7.2 The Relationship between democratization and political instability.

Source: Center for Systemic Peace, https://www.systemicpeace.org/polityproject.html

Note: The vertical axis measures the likelihood that an unstable event will occur in a given year. The horizontal axis measures the country's Polity V Score.

Democratization makes achieving political stability more difficult for several reasons. In the first place, elections add an element of uncertainty to the selection of governments and, as a result, make agreements among elites more difficult to reach. More importantly, when the outcome of elections is determined by a majority vote (or another voting rule), groups have incentives to form coalitions of just enough factions to secure victory and to leave others (usually enemies) out of the rule-making process and the privileges that result from it. However, leaving antagonistic factions out of the agreement may doom it. The recent literature on civil wars shows that factionalized polities are more likely to be disrupted by violence when a group comes to feel that its interests cannot or will not be taken into account under the current governing arrangements.[19]

In addition, elections tend to worsen problems of factionalism and, as a corollary, encourage the proliferation of identity rules. The coalitions that elites form to compete in elections are typically called political parties, but they are really assemblages of factions, and they are riven by divisions and prone to collapse. To put together the majorities they need to win elections, party leaders must promise specific benefits to each faction in their coalition, which means that, if the party wins, it must manipulate the economy to ensure there are enough rents to fulfill the bargains. These coalitions, moreover, are difficult to hold together from election to election because groups dissatisfied with their share of the spoils can easily defect to another party that is eager to bid them away, or they can form a competing organization and try to build their own coalition. Hence in electoral democracies characterized by identity rules, parties form, dissolve, and reform, and elites dissipate state resources and impede economic development in the ongoing effort to hold their coalitions together.

Democratic elections can thus be doubly detrimental to economic growth. On the one hand, the combination of identity rules and elections inhibits capitalist enterprise by exacerbating rent seeking. On the other, the greater instability that results from the introduction of elections itself dampens growth. As Stephen Broadberry and John Wallis have shown, countries with more unstable polities also experience more frequent and more intense episodes of economic shrinking over time. Such shrinkages are a major cause of the low rates of economic growth that characterize so much of the Global South today. As a result, they help to explain the lack of a relationship between per capita income and a country's Polity V Score below the set of rich advanced democracies.[20]

Impersonal Rules and Advanced Democracy

As the so-called "pluralist" school of political science recognized as long ago as the 1950s and 1960s, politics in a given country tended to stabilize whenever the multiplicity of factions that characterized its early democracy gave way to a small number of consolidated, long-lived parties capable of accommodating diverse interests within their organizations.[21] The key to this development, we argue, was the shift from identity rules to impersonal rules. This shift changed the incentives that political actors faced in ways that facilitated the emergence of consolidated political parties. It also changed incentives in ways that helped to perpetuate the new political arrangements.

The immediate effect of the shift to impersonal rules was to reduce factionalism. The disappearance of identity rules and the rents that they created meant that it was no longer a simple matter for political leaders in one coalition to bid factions away from another. Nor was it easy for new parties to attract support by offering those who would join them a greater share of the spoils of victory. Although new parties might still form for programmatic reasons, the rewards to defecting from an existing party would shrink relative to the benefits of staying and working to reshape its agenda. Political stability would thus increase as the number of major parties declined and those that remained consolidated their organizations and achieved greater permanence.[22]

In regimes governed by impersonal rules, interests still had an important role to play in politics, but it was fundamentally different from their part in regimes governed by identity rules. Under identity rules, most laws were tailored to the needs of specifically named individuals, groups, organizations, or localities, and are the result of bargains among elites. Under impersonal rules, by contrast, laws apply uniformly to everyone, or at least to everyone in the relevant categories. Although one individual or group may benefit from a proposed law, others will as well, and still others may be harmed. As a result, those that expect to benefit and those that expect to be harmed have incentives to organize for and against the legislation and, in cases where the issues involved are likely to come up again and again, to form more permanent interest groups. These groups function very differently from the factions that disrupt early democracies. Their ability to secure their legislative goals depends not on achieving political power in their own names but in influencing the agendas of the major political parties. In societies governed by impersonal rules, parties respond to the emergence of these organizations by developing distinct programmatic identities that enable them to attract the support and resources of groups in sync with their agendas. These identities matter because the policies the government enacts depend on the party that is victorious. Parties that win elections seek to establish a record of achievement on behalf of the interest groups with which they are affiliated, and as they do, they pursue policies that build the capacity of the state.

The greater stability that comes from the establishment of long-lived political parties has positive effects on the economy by eliminating the episodes of shrinkage that result from political disruptions. At the same time, the shift to impersonal rules makes the economic system more dynamic, more competitive—more capitalist. Once lucrative opportunities (and the organizational tools needed to exploit them effectively) are no longer restricted to favored members of the elite, capital, labor, and resources can flow to their most profitable uses. The shift to impersonal rules does not preclude restrictions on what the owners of capital, labor, and resources can do. Policy does not necessarily become laissez-faire. Governments can still regulate economic activities to promote the health and welfare of their populations, a more equitable distribution of income and wealth, or whatever goals the parties that win elections set on behalf of their constituent groups. Under a regime of impersonal rules, however, these regulations apply to all economic actors in the affected categories. Powerful members of the elite must follow them, just like everyone else.

These positive effects on political stability and economic dynamism have a self-perpetuating character that helps to ensure that the regime of impersonal rules will persist. Of course, politicians always face the temptation to exchange favors for political support and to alter the rules in ways that disadvantage their opponents. But the changes set in motion by the new regime create countervailing forces that decrease the likelihood of significant backsliding. In the first place, the greater competitiveness of the economy means that there are now more firms with wealth and power in a position to challenge any effort to give advantages to their rivals. In other words, competition creates interests that are vested in defending the impersonal rules that sustain competition. Interest groups too can be counted on to mobilize against the award of special privileges that disadvantage their members; the more valuable the privileges, the more likely that multiple groups will mass together in protest and block the measure. In addition, consolidated political parties have long time horizons that give them a stake in maintaining the regime of impersonal rules. Their leaders understand that the uncertainties associated with electoral democracies mean that, at some point, they are likely to lose control of the government to the other party, and they want to be able to come back again and win. If they change the rules for short-term advantage, they will give their rivals the means to make their come-back more difficult.

It is an open question how strong these forces are in support of impersonal rules—whether they are enough to keep the temptation to backslide at bay. All we can say is that the first countries to adopt impersonal rules did so in the late nineteenth century. Over the ensuing century and a half, they have faced repeated challenges to their regimes of impersonal rules. So far, the forces that sustain these regimes have held.

The Transition to Impersonal Rules and the Emergence of Consolidated Parties

But how, in the first place, could a society change from identity rules to impersonal rules? What possibly could induce elites to relinquish the tools they had always considered essential for winning and holding on to power? In democracies characterized by identity rules, complaints about favoritism were ubiquitous. Although factions out of power campaigned on promises to reform the system, when they got control of the government they behaved in the same way. To do otherwise—to fail to reward the elites who played an essential role in their success—was political suicide. As a result, the system was very difficult to change. How could elites risk giving up the ability to create the rents they needed to hold their coalitions together?

Viewed in this way, the transition to impersonal rules seems like an impossible proposition. And yet, it happened—in at least a few places. In this section, we examine the very different ways in which two societies—the United States and the United Kingdom—transitioned to impersonal rules in the nineteenth century. We then contrast their experience with that of Germany, where partial reforms did not go far enough to bring about the necessary regime change. In all three cases, the beginnings of democratization made the problem of factionalism more severe, and exacerbated the use of identity rules for political ends. In all three cases, governments made initial, limited efforts to reduce the extent to which politicians could manipulate the economy, for example, by enacting general incorporation laws. That turned out not to be enough, however. In the United States and the United Kingdom, the shift to impersonal rules went far beyond general incorporation, transforming both the polity and the economy in the ways described in the last section. In Germany, however, the process stalled, with dire consequences for democracy and, it turned out, for the world.

The United States

The United States was born a republic. It was also born an electoral democracy. At the time of the American Revolution, both the number of offices chosen by election and the proportion of the population that could vote were already high by world standards, and they would grow higher still. By the middle of the nineteenth century, most legislative and executive offices and, in many states, judgeships were chosen in competitive elections in which all adult white males could vote.[23] At the same time, politics was becoming increasingly factionalized. Although textbook histories project our modern two-party system back on this early period, what the authors call parties were in fact little more than shifting coalitions of factions. And there were lots of them. At the height of the so-called second party system, in the state of New York alone the Democrats were divided into Barnburners, Hunkers, Hard-Shells, Soft-Shells, Free Soilers, Young Americans, Locfocos, and so on.[24]

As a quick glance at any legislative record from the founding era will reveal, identity rules played an important role in politics from the very beginning, and their importance only rose as the franchise expanded and the number of factions competing for power grew. Between 1830–31 and 1850–51, the number of pages of laws enacted by state legislatures nearly doubled, increasing from 12.6 thousand in 1830–31 to 21.3 thousand in 1850–51.[25] On the order of 80 to 90 percent of these bills were identity rules. That is, they benefited specifically named individuals, groups, organizations, or localities, granting them pensions, divorces, corporate charters, banking privileges, and the like. The favors that legislators awarded to political allies through these bills provoked outrage. Factions that were out of power promised to root out this kind of corruption if they were elected, but they never did and instead similarly dispensed legislative favors whenever they were in power.[26]

In the 1840s, however, the process of change was jumpstarted by a major crisis in public finance in which eight states and one territory defaulted on their bonded debt. The crisis was a direct result of the system of private bills. In Indiana, for example, advocates of a canal across the middle of the state had loaded up their public works bill with lots of little projects to secure the political support needed for passage. These sweeteners raised the aggregate cost of the project and the amount the state had to borrow to finance it. When the bank that Indiana used to market its bonds defaulted on its obligations, so did the state, and the resulting political earthquake propelled an effort to revise its constitution to prevent such catastrophes from recurring.[27] Among the top priorities of the delegates who assembled at the constitutional convention was to ban private and local legislation, and they delivered on that promise. The 1851 Indiana constitution prohibited the legislature from passing private or local bills in seventeen enumerated situations, banned special charters of incorporation, mandated that corporations could only be created by general laws, and, most significantly, required the legislature to enact general laws wherever possible. The change had a dramatic effect on what the legislature did. Instead of passing hundreds of laws in each session granting favors to specific individuals, groups, and localities, it concentrated on enacting a much smaller number of general laws that set the terms on which these privileges would be open to all. The number of laws enacted in each session fell from a range of 300 to 550 in the decade before the constitutional revision to around 150 in its aftermath. At the same time the percentage of the laws that were general rose from about 10 percent of the total in the 1840s to half to two-thirds in subsequent decades.[28]

Few of the other states that defaulted in the early 1840s initially went as far as Indiana in mandating that all laws be general, though most revised their constitutions to prohibit special charters of corporations.[29] That reform was important for the capitalist development of the economy but was not in itself enough to bring about the new institutional equilibrium. However, the mandate that laws be general spread rapidly in the last third of the century. Almost all the new states that joined the United States included general law mandates in their first constitutions. Moreover, there was another wave of constitutional revisions in the 1870s in which most of the remaining states in the union adopted Indiana's comprehensive general law provision or something very similar. There were a few exceptions (mainly in New England), but by 1900 impersonal rule provisions were pervasive in the United States.[30]

Why the 1870s? Factionalized political systems are always unstable but worries about instability seem to have reached a peak in the aftermath of the Civil War, when a resurgent South was endangering the achievements of what had been an extraordinarily bloody struggle and even threatening renewed conflict. In a broad swath of states stretching from the Middle Atlantic to the Middle West, the dominant Republican Party found itself facing rising competition from Democrats sympathetic to the South and, at the same time, internal divisions serious enough to hobble its ability to respond to this threat. We have studied the turmoil in Pennsylvania and found that, by the late 1860s, Republicans of all stripes had come to the realization that special legislation was fueling the factionalism that undermined their ability to hold power. Concluding that the only way to save their party was to follow Indiana's example (Indiana's Republicans were noticeably less divided), they spearheaded a move to call a constitutional convention for the sole purpose of adding a general law mandate to the state's fundamental law. Their effort to revise the constitution was successful, and they were able to use the reform to repress factionalism. Not only did the imposition of a general law mandate alter the way in which the legislature conducted business, but the Republican party was able to consolidate its organization and dominate the state's politics for decades to come.[31]

Something similar occurred in other states that revised their constitutions during this period, though sometimes it was the Democrats who benefited rather than the Republicans. In almost every case the reform led to a dramatic fall in the volume of laws, as legislatures devoted their time to enacting a much smaller number of general statutes.[32] Because general laws were broad in their effects, it was much more difficult to put together the majorities needed to pass them. Log rolling was still possible, but once all the bills in a legislative package had to be general, the added measures were as likely to exacerbate the problem as to build a majority for the bill. The key to cutting this gordian knot was the emergence of consolidated political parties that the ban on private bills made possible. Thanks to their longer time horizons, parties could work out legislative deals that played out over the long run.

There were several ways in which the ban on special bills facilitated the development of such modern parties, some of which were immediately apparent, others of which took longer to manifest themselves. In the short run, the ban stripped local politicians of an important source of goodies to dispense within their jurisdictions, making other sources of favors, such as patronage jobs, which were centrally controlled relatively more important. In Pennsylvania, this shift gave Simon Cameron, the state's lone Republican US senator, an initial advantage. So long as the Republicans controlled the White House, Cameron (and later his son, Donald, who succeeded him as senator) controlled the distribution of federal patronage in the state, including more than 200 positions at the Philadelphia customhouse and thousands more at the state's 3,000 plus post offices (the Philadelphia post office alone employed nearly 450 people).[33]

These short-run advantages could become sources of long-run dominance if the parties that benefited from them went on to develop programmatic identities that attracted the new interest groups that the shift to general laws also called into existence.[34] Large-scale businesses might have enough resources to lobby on their own, but small- and medium-sized enterprises had to join forces to advocate for the laws they wanted—laws that often conflicted with those that big businesses sought. In Pennsylvania, for instance, small-scale oil producers united to counter Standard Oil's dominance with a fair degree of success.[35] At the same time, voluntary associations for farmers and workers mushroomed into massive organizations that gave heft to what Elizabeth Clemens has dubbed a new and powerful "people's lobby."[36] In the 1890s, Pennsylvania Democrats sought to revive their fortunes by aligning with agricultural interests, but their opposition to tariffs hurt them with the state's labor movement at the same time as their embrace of inflationary policies did little to increase support. By embracing both gold and the tariff, Republicans were able to position themselves as the party of industrial prosperity and thereby secure support from both business and labor.[37]

Around the turn of the century, the two major parties were able further to entrench their dominance with the passage by most state legislatures of electoral reforms, such as the Australian ballot, stricter voter registration laws, and the requirement that party candidates be selected in primary elections. Although these general laws have conventionally been ascribed to progressives who targeted party practices they regarded as corrupt, the effect of the laws was to strengthen the major parties, not weaken them. As Shigeo Hirano and James M. Snyder have shown for the case of primaries, the process of enacting the new electoral procedures was partisan. The reforms enacted tended to favor Democrats when they were adopted by states with Democratic administrations and tended to favor Republicans when they were adopted by Republican states. Similar patterns have been documented for the Australian ballot and Anti-Fusion laws.[38] Although the new laws were initially enacted for partisan purposes, they were not reversed when control of the state switched to the other party, and instead became a permanent part of the electoral rules that both parties sustained. Once the political system stabilized around two major parties that would be around to compete against each other election after election, it was to the advantage of each to commit to a consistent set of election rules, and to the regime of general laws that underpinned them. Party officials knew they would lose some elections, but they also knew that when they did, they would return to power again in the future. Whatever temptation there was to undo the rules for short-term advantage was undercut by the realization such a move would empower the opposition to do likewise.

Some scholars have described the new electoral regime as antidemocratic, and certainly it altered the way voters related to the political system. Whereas politics in the late nineteenth century had been a participatory sport, in the twentieth century voters found themselves in the position of spectators, and many lost interest and stopped voting altogether.[39] However, although turnout dropped, so did electoral violence and corruption. The party system stabilized around two major parties, one dominating in some places and the other in other places, with control of the national government shifting from one to the other from time to time.[40]

As the political system stabilized, governments at all levels spent more money on public goods and took on a wider range of functions. In Pennsylvania, the state legislature poured resources into schools, hospitals, asylums, penitentiaries, and other public goods. It also developed the state's capacity to regulate corporations, banks, and railroads, and to assume new administrative functions through the creation of the agencies such as the Bureau of Labor Statistics, the Office of Insurance Commissioner, the Superintendent of Public Instruction, and more.[41] These investments were another way in which the political stability made possible by general laws had positive feedback effects on the economy.

United Kingdom

In the early nineteenth century, Parliament's main business, like that of the US state legislatures, was the enactment of private and local bills. Indeed, the states had inherited this practice, along with other British institutions, from their colonizer. Over the course of the century Parliament gradually curbed the passage of such special bills. The restrictions were not constitutionalized as in the case of the United States, or even explicitly formulated as a guiding legislative principle, but the change was nonetheless momentous and permanent. And it had similarly transformative effects on the economic and political systems, making the former more competitive and the latter more stable. By the late nineteenth century, the factionalized politics of the mid-nineteenth century had largely disappeared, and the political system was dominated by two major consolidated parties, the Conservatives and the Liberals.[42]

Although the transformation and its outcomes were similar in the two countries, the processes by which they occurred were very different, as was the timing of the change in relationship to democratization. The franchise expanded much more slowly in the United Kingdom than in the United States. Although a major reform bill enacted in 1832 fundamentally changed the electoral landscape by reallocating parliamentary representation to better fit the distribution of population, it only marginally increased the franchise. A second reform bill in 1867 made further improvements along the same lines, but as late as 1880, only about a third of the adult male population was eligible to vote. That proportion doubled after a reform bill enacted in 1884, but universal male (and then female) suffrage awaited the First World War.[43] Moreover, although it was generally the case that the party that won the most seats in Parliament controlled the government, that principle was sometimes contested. It became more firmly established over the course of the century, alongside the shift to impersonal rules.[44]

One effect of the 1832 reform bill was to increase the power of the business elite in Parliament at the expense of the gentry. Businesses had been chafing under the monopolistic privileges granted to a few "monied" corporations, such as the East India Company and the Bank of England, and they had long pushed Parliament to strip those enterprises of their monopolies.[45] They were eventually successful, but securing a corporate charter still required a special act of Parliament, which was very difficult to get. Although businesses often tried to operate as corporations without securing charters, this strategy potentially ensnared them in legal difficulties. Their growing clout in Parliament paid off, however, and they secured legislation that made the corporate form available by a simple registration process—without limited liability in 1844 and with limited liability in 1856. These measures freed large sectors of industry from government controls on entry, permitting capitalist enterprises to flourish there.[46]

Identity rules still prevailed in other areas of economic and political life, however. Indeed, the effect of the 1832 reform bill, much like the expansion of the franchise in the United States, was to increase the competitiveness of elections for Parliament and thus the incentives for Members of Parliament (MPs) to use their office to distribute favors to elite constituents. MPs flooded Parliament with private bills conferring on specifically named people charters for local railroads, utilities, and the like. Control of the government seesawed between the two most important parties, the Liberals and the Conservatives, but neither party was able to exert much discipline over its members. Indeed, the period is known as the golden age of the backbenchers, because individual MPs concentrated on bolstering their local bases of support, and voted for whatever they thought was in the interests of their district and their own reelection. After Sir Robert Peel pushed a bill repealing the corn laws through Parliament in 1846, the Conservative Party split so seriously that it faced the possibility of extinction, much like the Republicans in Pennsylvania in the years following the Civil War.[47]

By the mid-1840s, the flood of private bills was threatening MPs' ability to deliver favors to their constitutions in a timely way. In the case of railways alone, the number of bills presented for consideration jumped from about 150 per session in the late 1830s to more than 600 in 1846. Parliament convened a series of committees to consider the problem, and a consensus developed over the course of the 1830s that the solution was to enact a series of "clauses consolidation acts" to standardize the content of the private bills enacted for specified purposes. Over a short two-year period from 1845 to 1847, Parliament enacted many such acts: for railroads, waterworks, gasworks, companies, harbors, docks and piers, markets and fairs, cemeteries, police, and a variety of other areas in which private legislation was common. The clauses consolidation acts did not prevent MPs from doing favors for their constituents; to the contrary, they made the system of private bills more efficient. But the acts nonetheless moved the country toward impersonal rules by insuring, for example, that railroads would all operate under the same set of regulations. It was no longer easy, and perhaps not even possible, for businesses to secure especially favorable charter provisions with the help of their MPs. They could benefit from their aid in securing a charter, but the charter would be the same as everyone else's.[48]

The same press of business forced Parliament to grapple with the problem of dividing floor time between bills proposed by ministry, which was usually controlled by the party that won the most seats in Parliament, and bills introduced by rank-and-file members. Procedures worked out early in the nineteenth century allocated the two different kinds of business to different days of the week, which in practice came to mean that a couple of days each week were devoted to members' business, but otherwise the government controlled the agenda. Because members' bills were usually not of interest to anyone but the members involved, sessions on those days were increasingly poorly attended, and the ministry often encroached on them. The process was a gradual one, but by the end of the century MPs' access to the agenda became limited to twenty Fridays a year, and sometimes not even that.[49] Although the encroachments were not uncontested, the gradualness with which they occurred mitigated conflict and facilitated the reorganization of the political system. The factionalism of mid-century gave way to two major consolidated parties, the Conservatives and the Liberals, each with its own programmatic identity. With their ability to dispense favors to constituents curbed, MPs were increasingly beholden to the central party organization for the resources they needed to secure reelection. And the voters they courted cared less about them as individuals than they did the ideas and programs that their party stood for. MPs' fate was tied to that of their party.[50]

By 1900 private bills had almost completely disappeared from Parliament's record, and the United Kingdom had transformed itself into a society governed largely by impersonal rules without ever formally legislating the change. And yet the result was as durable as the constitutional shift to general laws mandated by most of the US states, and for much the same reason: because it transformed the economic and political institutions of society in ways that reinforced the new regime. In particular, the consolidation of the political system around two major political parties created organizations with an ongoing interest in preserving the regime of impersonal rules—of making sure that when they lost an election in the future, they would not also lose the chance to regain power.

Germany

The comparative cases of the United States and the United Kingdom highlight the divergent paths that even societies that shared a common legal tradition might follow as they negotiated the transition from identity to impersonal rules. In the mid-nineteenth century, both the United States and the United Kingdom enacted general laws that gave businesses ready access to the corporate form, and they both later expanded the scope of such impersonal rules to include most areas of law. This expansion occurred in very different ways in the two countries (and even in the various US states), but it was what made it possible for these nations to become advanced capitalist democracies. As a comparison with the case of Germany shows, merely opening access to the corporate form was not enough to bring about the political changes needed for this transformation. Germany adopted impersonal rules for forming business corporations circa 1870, but the rules did not spread into other areas of the law, and Germany's electoral democracy remained factionalized until it collapsed with the rise of Adolf Hitler and the formation of the Third Reich.

Until the late nineteenth century, businesses in the various German states needed the permission of their governments to form corporations. This system began to break down when some of the states competed to attract business investment by granting corporate charters more liberally than others, and it collapsed after 1861 when most of the states adopted a common code of business law that permitted them to enact general incorporation laws if they chose. Prussia's North German Confederation enacted a general incorporation statute in 1870, which became Reich law with the unification of Germany in 1871.[51] This liberalization did not, however, carry over to other kinds of organizations, or more generally into the legal system. Indeed, until the turn of the century German law severely restricted residents' right to associate without explicit permission. Just holding a meeting without authorization could result in criminal penalties.[52] The dangers were very real—so much so even purely economic organizations like credit cooperatives feared harassment and clamored for the extension of organizational rights to their associations.[53] The move toward impersonal rules that general incorporation represented, moreover, was undermined by other actions the government took to legalize cartels. Germany allowed businesses to form corporations at will, but it also allowed associations of corporations to reach intra-elite agreements that the state would enforce. The cartels were essentially bundles of identity rules that enabled businesses included in the arrangements to earn rents. They could effectively limit entry in their industries, and many did. By the time the Nazis came to power in the 1930s, large swaths of the German economy had been effectively monopolized with the approval and assistance of the state.[54]

In the period following unification, Germany took steps toward democratization, and the franchise expanded to include most adult males. Although the country's chancellor was not chosen democratically, and voting was weighted to give the wealthiest property owners significant advantages, turnout for elections to the Reichstag was high.[55] But the political system remained factionalized and became steadily more so over time as the number of parties proliferated. By the 1890s the conservative bloc that had supported Chancellor Otto von Bismarck—itself composed of three of the larger parties—no longer commanded even a third of the seats in the Reichstag.[56] As Daniel Ziblatt has shown, the government was forced to rely for its majorities on deals with local elites who dominated their areas through a combination of patron-client favoritism and outright repression and fraud. In exchange for their support, the central government showered local leaders in its coalition with infrastructure spending and other benefits.[57]

In Germany, as in other countries where elites continued to organize themselves using identity rules, consolidated political parties failed to emerge. Instead, as factions continued to proliferate and to combine and recombine in shifting coalitions, the political system showed increasing signs of instability. Rumors of coups and threats of uprising periodically swept the country from the late nineteenth century on. Sometimes they were more than threats, and in the 1930s, the Nazis took over.

Capitalism and Democracy

We have written more about democracy in this essay than about capitalism. In large measure this is because we have defined capitalism in a way that makes its development a direct consequence of the achievement of impersonal rules. But it is also because this achievement was part and parcel of the development of a new kind of political system that we call advanced democracy. Most political systems cannot deliver the impersonal rules that enable capitalism to thrive. Instead, elites depend on identity rules to achieve short-run political stability; that is how they create the rents that make maintaining the peace worthwhile, at least for a time. Introducing democratic elections in such societies does nothing to obviate such manipulations. To the contrary, as we have argued, the immediate effect is usually to worsen problems of factionalism, to increase the necessity of resorting to identity rules, and thus to exacerbate the economic distortions these rules entail. In such societies, therefore, the answer to the question of whether capitalism and democracy are reconcilable must sadly be no. Capitalism cannot thrive in polities where the pressure to hold factions together leads elites to manipulate the economy for political ends—where some elites gain access to profitable opportunities that are closed to everyone else. But neither are these polities likely to remain democracies. Prone to instability, their fate is often to slide back into autocracy.

Everything changes, however, in societies where the rules are impersonal. There the answer to the question of whether capitalism and democracy are reconcilable is a resounding yes. Capitalism thrives where opportunities that are open to some become open to all. Democracy thrives as well where factions give way to consolidated political parties whose longer time horizons give them a stake in the long-run stability of the political system. Getting from one equilibrium to the other is not easy, however. Only a relatively small number of countries have managed it—the rich advanced capitalist democracies of today. Because these countries made the transition in such different ways, their histories do not offer clear lessons that other countries can follow to become advanced. However, we can draw a couple of insights from the experience of two countries we have studied that successfully negotiated the transition—the United States and the United Kingdom. First, for idiosyncratic reasons, elites in these places responded to the increased instability associated with early democratization by making changes that they perceived to be in their interests but that had the effect of increasing the impersonality of the rules under which the society operated—first in the economic realm and then more broadly. Second, once these changes were in place, they had effects that were not idiosyncratic but common across all the countries that adopted impersonal rules. The emergence of durable consolidated political parties and party systems changed the operation of the political system in ways that made the new regime of impersonal rules sustainable over the long run.

Advanced democracies are societies in which open debate about the rules is an inherent part of the political process. One of the inevitable dimensions of debate is how "capitalistic" the rules should be—that is, how promotional versus how redistributive. What can easily be missed in all the heat generated by these discussions is that capitalism does not require low taxes, a small government, or rules that benefit the wealthy. What it requires are agreed upon rules that apply equally to everyone in the relevant categories. That is the kind of equality that matters to economic development, and it matters to political development as well. Democracy and capitalism are both threatened by identity rules. Their productive reconciliation depends on the achievement of impersonal rules, and we are more likely to maintain both peace and prosperity if we better understand this relationship.

Acknowledgments

We have benefited from the helpful comments of the volume editors as well as Abhay Aneja, Kenneth Ayotte, Hoyt Bleakley, Tracy Dennison, Kenneth Elzinga, Price Fishback, Martin Fiszbein, Philip Hoffman, Vikramaditya Khanna, Prasad Krishnamurthy, Robert Merges, Paul Rhode, Jean-Laurent Rosenthal, David Snyder, Christopher Tomlins, Francesca Trivellato, and Katrina Wang. Thanks too to participants in the conference "Can Democracy and Capitalism be Reconciled?" at the University of Virginia, the Caltech Finance and History Lunch, the Berkeley Law, Economics, and Business Workshop, the NBER 2023 Summer Institute (Development of the American Economy Group), the University of Michigan Business Law Lunch, the University of Wisconsin WHAT Workshop, the Yale Economic History Workshop, the University of Oslo seminar at the Institute for Archeology, Conservation, and History, and the 2024 Baltic Connections Conference held at the University of Jyväskylä. We are also grateful to Monty Marshall, Director of the Center for Systemic Peace, for sending us the data underlying Figure 7.2.

Notes

1. The idea that democracy and capitalism cannot coexist has a long history, as Göran Therborn has pointed out (Göran Therborn, "The Rule of Capital and the Rise of Democracy," *New Left Review* 103 (May/June 1977): 3).
2. The logic of this argument is laid out in Douglass C. North, John Joseph Wallis, and Barry R. Weingast, *Violence and Social Orders: A Conceptual Framework for Interpreting Recorded Human History* (New York: Cambridge University Press, 2009).

3. Karl Marx, *Capital: A Critique of Political Economy*, trans. from the 3rd German edition by Samuel Moore and Edward Aveling, ed. Frederick Engels, vol. 1 (London: Swan Sonnenschein, Lowrey, & Co., 1887).
4. See, for example, Joyce Appleby's definition (Joyce Appleby, *The Relentless Revolution: A History of Capitalism* (New York: W. W. Norton, 2010), 7). Although historians of capitalism have generally been reluctant to define their terms, when pushed they fall back on a similar definition. See Sven Beckert, Angus Burgin, Peter James Hudson, et al., "Interchange: The History of Capitalism," *Journal of American History* 101 (September 2014): 503–536. Jonathan Levy (*Ages of American Capitalism: A History of the United States* (New York: Random House, 2021), xiii–xx) defines capitalism essentially as the securitization of assets. His definition is creative but not very useful for our purposes.
5. On the importance of making this distinction, see William J. Baumol, "Entrepreneurship: Productive, Unproductive, and Destructive," *Journal of Political Economy* 98 (October 1990): 893–921.
6. The foundational work in this literature is Peter A. Hall and David Soskice, *Varieties of Capitalism: The Institutional Foundations of Comparative Advantage* (Oxford: Oxford University Press, 2001).
7. In many developing countries with weak state capacity there may be few formal regulations on economic activity. Nonetheless, the ability of individuals to use their resources may be severely limited by political arrangements.
8. We are using the 2010 version of Maddison's data, because there are benchmarking problems with the revised series.
9. Joseph A. Schumpeter, *Capitalism, Socialism, and Democracy* (New York: Harper & Brothers, 1942), chs. 21 and 22. For a brilliant discussion of how democracy as an ideal type differs from actual democracies, see Robert A. Dahl, *Polyarchy: Participation and Opposition* (New Haven: Yale University Press, 1971).
10. David Collier and Steven Levitsky, "Democracy with Adjectives: Conceptual Innovation in Comparative Research," *World Politics* 49 (April 1997): 430–51. For a similar typology, see Andreas Schedler, "What Is Democratic Consolidation?," *Journal of Democracy* 9 (April 1998): 91–107.
11. In a consolidated party system there are a small number of major parties with a reasonable chance of winning elections or participating in governing coalitions. The rules for forming parties, however, are open to anyone meeting minimal criteria. As a result, there may be many parties on the ballot, but few with any real chance of winning the election. See E. E. Schattschneider, *Party Government* (New Brunswick: Transaction Publishers, 1942).
12. For an example, see Arend Lijphart, *Patterns of Democracy: Government Forms and Performance in Thirty-Six Countries*, 2nd ed. (New Haven, CT: Yale University Press, 2012).
13. Another prominent measure of democracy, V-Dem, includes such confounding variables, as well as many that work against our ability to pick up the presence of consolidated political parties.
14. For the underlying logic, see North et al., *Violence and Social Orders*. For a similar understanding, see Stephen Haber, Noel Maurer, and Armando Razo, *The Politics of Property Rights: Political Instability, Credible Commitments, and Economic Growth in Mexico, 1876–1929* (New York: Cambridge University Press, 2003).
15. Jeffrey Gettleman, "Disputed Vote Plunges Kenya Into Bloodshed," *The New York Times*, December 31, 2007, https://www.nytimes.com/2007/12/31/world/africa/31kenya.html?searchResultPosition=2. See also Nic Cheeseman's introduction to the 2008 issue of the *Journal of Eastern African Studies*, which is devoted to the Kenyan election (Nic Cheeseman, "The Kenyan Elections of 2007: An Introduction," *Journal of Eastern African Studies* 2, no. 2 (2008): 166–84).
16. Arthur Meier Schlesinger, *The Colonial Merchants and the American Revolution, 1763–1776* (New York: Columbia University Press, 1918).
17. The literature on republican ideas is enormous. Two seminal books are J. G. A. Pocock, *The Machiavellian Moment: Florentine Political Thought and the Atlantic Republican Tradition* (Princeton, NJ: Princeton University Press, 1975) and Bernard Bailyn, *The Ideological Origins of the American Revolution* (Cambridge, MA: Harvard University Press, 1967).

18. Scholars have found that most civil wars occur in countries with Polity V Scores between –5 and +5, and call these places "anocracies" to emphasize the special dangers of this middle range. See, for example, Barbara F. Walter, *How Civil Wars Start: And How to Stop Them* (New York: Crown, 2022).
19. Walter, *How Civil Wars Start*, and Andreas Wimmer, *Waves of War: Nationalism, State Formation, and Ethnic Exclusion in the Modrn World* (New York: Cambridge University Press, 2013).
20. Stephen Broadberry and John Joseph Wallis, "Growing, Shrinking, and Long Run Economic Performance: Historical Perspectives on Economic Development," *Journal of Economic History*, forthcoming, June 2025.
21. The preface to Robert A. Dahl, ed., *Political Oppositions in Western Democracies* (New Haven, CT: Yale University Press, 1966) is an excellent introduction to this literature, as are the book's case studies. See also Seymour M. Lipset and Stein Rokkan, eds., *Party Systems and Voter Alignments: Cross National Perspectives* (New York: Free Press, 1967). Case studies in this tradition include Dankwart A. Rustow, *The Politics of Compromise: A Study of Parties and Cabinet Government in Sweden* (Princeton, NJ: Princeton University Press, 1955) and Arend Lijphart, *The Politics of Accommodation: Pluralism and Democracy in the Netherlands* (Berkeley: University of California Press, 1968). In recent years, political scientists have increasingly returned to this view, and it is common now to emphasize the importance for democratic development of consolidated political systems in which same parties compete against each other year after year, developing broad programmatic identities to cultivate voters' loyalty. See Didi Kuo, *Clientelism, Capitalism, and Democracy: The Rise of Programmatic Politics in the United States and Britain* (New York: Cambridge University Press, 2018), Frances McCall Rosenbluth and Ian Shapiro, *Responsible Parties: Saving Democracy from Itself* (New Haven, CT: Yale University Press, 2018), Daniel Ziblatt, *Conservative Parties and the Birth of Democracy* (New York: Cambridge University Press, 2017), Sheri E. Berman, *Democracy and Dictatorship in Europe: From the Ancien Régime to the Present Day* (New York: Oxford University Press, 2019), and Allen Hicken, *Building Party Systems in Developing Democracies* (New York: Cambridge University Press, 2009).
22. The United States and the UK became two-party systems, but other countries (the Nordics are good examples) underwent the same transformation with multiple parties. Impersonal rules for forming parties allowed anyone to do so, but the number of major parties with reasonable expectations of winning elections, or of being in a governing coalition in proportional representation systems, declined significantly.
23. Alexander Keyssar, *The Right to Vote: The Contested History of Democracy in the United States* (New York: Basic Books, 2000) and Stanley L. Engerman and Kenneth L. Sokoloff, "The Evolution of Suffrage Institutions in the New World," *Journal of Economic History* 65 (December 2005): 891–921.
24. Jack Furniss, "Devolved Democracy: Federalism and the Party Politics of the Late Antebellum North," *Journal of the Civil War Era* 9 (December 2019): 546–68. For a trenchant critique of the idea that there were modern political parties in this period, see Rachel A. Shelden and Erik B. Alexander, "Dismantling the Party System: Party Fluidity and the Mechanisms of Nineteenth-Century U.S. Politics," *Journal of American History* 110 (December 2023): 419–48.
25. To give a few examples, in New York they increased from 972 to 1,968, in Pennsylvania from 1,162 to 2,022, in Illinois from 218 to 534, in Kentucky from 468 to 2,086. The number of pages of bills enacted by state legislatures comes from the state session laws as listed on Heinonline, https://heinonline.org/HOL/Index?index=sslusstate&collection=ssl.
26. Robert M. Ireland, "The Problem of Local, Private, and Special Legislation in the Nineteenth-Century United States," *American Journal of Legal History* 46 (July 2004): 271–99 and Naomi R. Lamoreaux and John Joseph Wallis, "General Laws and the Emergence of Durable Political Parties: The Case of Pennsylvania," unpublished working paper, 2024.
27. Indiana had sold roughly $5 million in state bonds to the Morris Canal and Banking company on credit. The bank was to pay the state $500,000 every six months until all the bonds had been paid for, but the bank defaulted in the summer of 1839. For details, see John Joseph Wallis, "The Property Tax as a Coordinating Device: Financing Indiana's Mammoth

Internal Improvement System, 1835–1842," *Explorations in Economic History* 40 (July 2003): 223–50.

28. Naomi R. Lamoreaux and John Joseph Wallis, "Economic Crisis, General Laws, and the Mid-Nineteenth-Century Transformation of American Political Economy," *Journal of the Early Republic* 41 (Fall 2021): 403–33.
29. Many also prohibited their legislature from granting divorces and the privilege of running lotteries.
30. Lamoreaux and Wallis, "Economic Crisis, General Laws, and the Mid-Nineteenth-Century Transformation of American Political Economy." The general law mandates in these constitutions changed the norms for how legislatures should operate and affected practice in the few states that did not add general law provisions to their constitutions. There was no federal constitutional amendment mandating that laws be general and uniform, but Congress eventually codified the new norms in 1946 in the Administrative Procedures and Legislative Reorganization Acts. See Maggie McKinley, "Petitioning and the Making of the Administrative State," *Yale Law Journal* 127 (April 2018): 1538–637.
31. Lamoreaux and Wallis, "General Laws and the Emergence of Durable Political Parties."
32. Lamoreaux and Wallis, "General Laws and the Emergence of Durable Political Parties." On the emergence of dominant political parties in most states, see Shigeo Hirano and James M. Snyder Jr., *Primary Elections in the United States* (New York: Cambridge University Press, 2019), ch. 2.
33. Robert Harrison, "Blaine and the Camerons: A Study in the Limits of Machine Power," *Pennsylvania History* 49 (July 1982): 160–61.
34. Lamoreaux and Wallis, "General Laws and the Emergence of Durable Political Parties." For a related argument, see Kuo's 2018 discussion of the shift from clientelist to programmatic political parties.
35. The producers financed a *quo warranto* suit that Pennsylvania's attorney general brought against Standard Oil and used the state's partnership association law to keep Standard from picking them off with acquisitions. Chester McArthur Destler, *Roger Sherman and the Independent Oil Men* (Ithaca, NY: Cornell University Press, 1967), 83–193; and Naomi R. Lamoreaux, "Revisiting American Exceptionalism: Democracy and the Regulation of Corporate Governance: The Case of Nineteenth-Century Pennsylvania in Comparative Context," in *Enterprising America: Businesses, Banks, and Credit Markets in Historical Perspective*, ed. William J. Collins and Robert A. Margo, 25–71 (Chicago: University of Chicago Press, 2015), 53–54.
36. Elisabeth S. Clemens, *The People's Lobby: Organizational Innovation and the Rise of Interest Group Politics in the United States, 1890-1925* (Chicago: University of Chicago Press, 1997).
37. Lewis Wesley Rathgeber, "The Democratic Party in Pennsylvania, 1880–1896," unpublished PhD. dissertation, University of Pittsburgh (1956), William E. Lyons, "Populism in Pennsylvania, 1892–1901," *Pennsylvania History* 32 (January 1965): 49–65, and Peter McCaffery, *When Bosses Ruled Philadelphia: The Emergence of the Republican Machine, 1867–1933* (University Park: Pennsylvania State University Press, 1993), ch. 4.
38. Hirano and Snyder Jr., *Primary Elections in the United States*. See also Eric C. Alston, Lee J. Alston, Bernardo Mueller, and Thomas Nonnemacher, *Institutional and Organizational Analysis: Concepts and Applications* (New York: Cambridge University Press, 2018).
39. Mark Lawrence Kornbluh, *Why America Stopped Voting: The Decline of Participatory Democracy and the Emergence of Modern American Politics* (New York: New York University Press, 1999) and Michael E. McGerr, *The Decline of Popular Politics: The American North, 1865–1928* (New York: Oxford University Press, 1986).
40. Jon Grinspan, *The Age of Acrimony: How Americans Fought to Fix Their Democracy* (New York: Bloomsbury Publishing, 2021). Hirano and Snyder Jr., *Primary Elections in the United States*, 10–15, have shown that two-party competition was a national phenomenon rather than a state characteristic. They defined a state as uncompetitive if the eight-year moving average between the Democratic and Republican vote shares differed by at least 15 percentage points. Even by this rather extreme definition, 28 out of 45 states (62 percent) were uncompetitive in 1904.
41. Edward J. Davies II, "State Economic Policy and Region in Pennsylvania, 1853–1895," *Business and Economic History* 21 (1992): 280–89. On the growth of state capacity in the area of

antitrust, see Naomi R. Lamoreaux, "Antimonopoly and State Regulation of Corporations in the Gilded Age and Progressive Era" in *Antimonopoly and American Democracy*, ed. Daniel A. Crane and William J. Novak, 119–67 (New York: Oxford University Press, 2023).

42. Julian Hoppit, *Britain's Political Economies: Parliament and Economic Life, 1660–1800*, Cambridge: Cambridge University Press, 2017); Ramsay Muir, *How Britain Is Governed: A Critical Analysis of Modern Developments in the British System of Government*, 3rd rev. ed. (Boston: Houghton Mifflin, 1935), ch. 6. It is important to be aware that the word "public" was not synonymous with general in legislative records from the early nineteenth century. In the United States, state legislatures often published two volumes a year—one for private laws and one for public laws, but most of the laws in the public volume nonetheless applied only to specific individuals, groups, or localities. In Britain private laws were those that originated in a petition from an external party, who often paid fees to secure passage; public laws were introduced by MPs. Again, most of the public laws targeted specific individuals, groups, or localities.

43. Peter Flora and Jens Alber et al., *State, Economy, and Society in Western Europe, 1815–1975: A Data Handbook, Vol. 1, The Growth of Mass Democracies and Welfare States* (Chicago: St. James Press, 1983), 91–93, 148–151.

44. Kuo, *Clientelism, Capitalism, and Democracy*, 94–95; and Gary W. Cox, *The Efficient Secret: The Cabinet and the Development of Political Parties in Victorian England* (New York: Cambridge University Press, 1987), 10.

45. Dan Bogart, "The East Indian Monopoly and the Transition from Limited Access in England, 1600–1813," in *Organizations, Civil Society, and the Roots of Development*, ed. Naomi R. Lamoreaux and John Joseph Wallis (Chicago: University of Chicago Press, 2017), 23-49; J. Lawrence Broz and Richard S. Grossman, "Paying for Privilege: The Political Economy of Bank of England Charters, 1694–1844," *Explorations in Economic History* 41 (January 2004): 48–72; James R. Fichter, *So Great a Proffit: How the East Indies Trade Transformed Anglo-American Capitalism* (Cambridge, MA: Harvard University Press, 2010); and Naomi R. Lamoreaux, "Corporate Governance and the Expansion of the Democratic Franchise: Beyond Cross-Country Regressions," *Scandinavian Economic History Review* 64, no. 2 (2016): 103–21.

46. Mark Freeman, Robin Pearson, and James Taylor, *Shareholder Democracies? Corporate Governance in Britain and Ireland before 1850* (Chicago: University of Chicago Press, 2012), Ron Harris, *Industrializing English Law: Entrepreneurship and Business Organization, 1720–1844* (Cambridge: Cambridge University Press, 2000); Timothy W. Guinnane, Ron Harris, and Naomi R. Lamoreaux, "Contractual Freedom and Corporate Governance in Britain in the Late Nineteenth and Early Twentieth Centuries," *Business History Review* 91 (Summer 2017): 227–77.

47. Kuo, *Clientelism, Capitalism, and Democracy*; Cox, *The Efficient Secret*.

48. O. Cyprian Williams, *The Historical Development of Private Bill Procedure and Standing Orders in the House of Commons*, vol. 1 (London: His Majesty's Stationary Office, 1948); Sir Ivor Jennings, *Parliament*, 2nd ed. (Cambridge: Cambridge University Press, 1969), 463; James Foreman-Peck and Leslie Hannah, "UK Corporate Law and Corporate Governance before 1914: A Re-Interpretation," in *Complexity and Crisis in the Financial System: Critical Perspectives on the Evolution of American and British Banking*, ed. Matthew Hollow, Folarin Akinbami, and Ranald Michie (Cheltenham: Edward Elgar, 2016), 183-213.

49. Jennings, *Parliament*, esp. chs. XI and XIII; and Muir, *How Britain Is Governed*, ch. VI.

50. See especially Cox, *The Efficient Secret*, ch. 6.

51. Timothy W. Guinnane, Ron Harris, Naomi R. Lamoreaux, and Jean-Laurent Rosenthal, "Putting the Corporation in its Place," *Enterprise and Society* 8 (September 2007): 697.

52. Timothy W. Guinnane and Richard Brooks, "The Right to Associate and the Rights of Associations: Civil-Society Organizations in Prussia, 1794–1908," in Organizations, Civil Society and the Roots of Development, ed. Lamoreaux and Wallis, 291–329.

53. Timothy W. Guinnane, "New Law for New Enterprises: Cooperative Law in Germany, 1867–1889," *Jahrbuch für Wirtschaftsgeschichte* 61, no. 2 (2020): 377–401.

54. For histories of German cartels, see Steven B. Webb, "Tariffs, Cartels, Technology, and Growth in the German Steel Industry, 1879 to 1914," *Journal of Economic History* 40

(June 1980): 309–330; and Daniel A. Crane, "Fascism and Monopoly," *Michigan Law Review* 118 (May 2020): 1315–1370.

55. Flora et al., *State, Economy, and Society in Western Europe, 1815–1975*, 112–20; and Sheri E. Berman, "Modernization in Historical Perspective: The Case of Imperial Germany," *World Politics* 53 (April 2001): 431–62. See also Margaret Lavinia Anderson, *Practicing Democracy: Elections and Political Culture in Imperial Germany* (Princeton, NJ: Princeton University Press, 2000).
56. Berman, "Modernization in Historical Perspective," 446–49. Berman has argued that relaxation of restrictions on associational life in the twentieth century further contributed to this fragmentation. See Sheri E. Berman, "Civil Society and the Collapse of the Weimar Republic," *World Politics* 49 (April 1997): 401–29.
57. Daniel Ziblatt, *Conservative Parties and the Birth of Democracy* (New York: Cambridge University Press, 2017), esp. ch. 6, calls these local leaders caciques to connect the German pattern with similar factionalism in Spain, Portugal, Italy, and France in the same period and also in Latin America.

SECTION IV

INEQUALITY AND OPPORTUNITY

Can Capitalism Save Itself?

Capitalism's Looming Threats to Democracy and Practical Strategies to Step Back from the Brink

CHRISTINE MAHONEY

Democracy enables the existence of free-market capitalism. Under no other political system can private sector actors freely engage in open commerce. Capitalism, however, in its current form in the United States, presents a number of significant threats to democracy. In each case corporate actors are behaving in ways that maximize profits and concentrate wealth-accumulation, while also harming citizens, setting the stage for political instability. Corporations are engaging in lobbying against the interests of citizens in the legislative arena, take for instance the areas of tax law, privacy laws, agriculture policy, minimum wage, health insurance, and the regulation of disinformation. Corporate leaders, high-net-worth CEOs, corporate PACs and dark money are interfering in elections, swaying political outcomes against the interests of the public, and providing campaign finance as a quid pro quo for political access after the dust of an election has settled. Corporate actors, and the lobbying firms they hire, are working to undermine legislation passed by Congress during the implementation stage, taking the teeth out of regulations aimed at reining in greed or abuse. Corporations are engaging in unethical business practices, unchecked by insufficient, and sometimes complicit, federal oversight, as in the case of Purdue Pharma and the pumping of billions of pills of opioids into American communities; the financial sector knowingly lending to economically struggling Americans leading up to the 2008 housing crisis, foreclosing on and forcibly displacing millions of citizens;

and the private education industry predating on young hopeful Americans, taking billions in federal college loan dollars and providing sham higher-education programs and no prospects for citizens other than a lifetime of debt. Corporate c-suite pay continues to climb to unprecedented heights, while the average wage continues to be insufficient for survival, forcing millions of the working poor to depend on government programs for the basic necessities of life.

American Democracy was built on Jefferson's declaration: that "We hold these truths to be sacred & undeniable; that all men are created equal & independent, that from that equal creation they derive rights inherent & inalienable, among which are the preservation of life, & liberty, & the pursuit of happiness." Yet, in the practical application of today's capitalism, with corporate actors spending billions annually to undermine our elections, billions annually on lobbying to undermine our policy process, and making corporate decisions that undermine our citizen's livelihoods and well-being; tens of millions of American citizens are being denied the right to a life of liberty. Today's American Capitalism is a threat to America's Democracy.

Income inequality and wealth inequality continue to grow, and the middle class continues to shrink. The large political science literature on Democracy and Development has well documented the importance of a thriving middle class of engaged citizens for the maintenance of a healthy democracy. The United States is headed in the wrong direction. Large-scale inequality, mixed with identity politics, leads to grievance, uprising, and political violence. At this moment in history, it is critical that the United States strengthens its democratic institutions and reforms policies in ways that foster both economic equality and economic opportunity. It is the only way that free-market capitalism will survive.

Some of these reforms must come through the democratic process, especially those related to campaign finance and undue business lobbying influence. Libraries have been filled with academic discussion of the need for campaign finance reform and lobbying reform, but the practical reality is there is not the political will to do it, there has not been the political will to do it for decades, and with the winners of the status quo making the rules, there will not be political will to do it. If the health of our democracy rests on the political decision to rein in the democracy-destroying tendencies of capitalism, we are doomed.

The solution may be born out of the private sector itself. There are positive trends coming from a new generation of capitalists (ironically their ideas align with many of the concepts outlined by one of the original advocates of capitalism—Adam Smith, and his lesser-read *The Theory of Moral Sentiments* (1759).[1] The new generation of capitalists argues for a shift away from winner-take-all shareholder capitalism, toward stakeholder capitalism, where corporate behavior is guided by the needs of all stakeholders including employees/citizens, customer/citizens, supply chain partners/citizens, and the towns and communities hosting their activities. An entire industry has built up to support the growth, success, and expansion of these types of "conscious companies"—including the corporate social responsibility (CSR) profession, certification schemes, impact investing, and socially responsible investing. I discuss each of these in turn below. An evolution of capitalism, the movement argues, is needed that benefits all people, communities, and the planet, and they won't stop until all business is a force for good.

The 1960s was marked by activism by a range of social movements calling for environmental responsibility, civil rights, women's rights, antinuclear, an end to war and an end to poverty. These citizen movements called for a more equitable world, for racial justice, economic justice, and environmental justice. The government needed to respond to those pressures, but so too did the private sector. The roots of CSR began to take shape in the 1950s in the United States with the publication of Howard R. Bowen's *The Social Responsibilities of the Businessman,* but gained traction in the 1970s in response to the activism of the 1960s and the rise of new organizations like Public Citizen, started by Ralph Nader in 1971, advocating for consumer rights, pushing companies to protect citizen health and safety.[2] In the 1970s the Committee for Economic Development introduced the "social contract" between businesses and society, calling for companies to: "1. Provide jobs and economic growth through well run businesses. 2. Run the business fairly and honestly regarding employees and customers. And 3. Become more broadly involved in improving the conditions of the community and environment in which it operates."[3]

In 1984 Edward Freeman published his influential *Strategic Management: A Stakeholder Approach* arguing that companies should strive to create value for all stakeholders, not just shareholders.[4] Stakeholder Theory is a view of capitalism that stresses the connections between a firm and its customers, suppliers, employees, investors, communities, and others who have a stake in the organization and argues that for a company to be sustainable and successful its leadership must align the interests of all groups. Advocates of Stakeholder Capitalism argue the focus on shareholder wealth optimization leads to short-termism, unethical practices, and ultimately damages the health and sustainability of a firm.

By the 1990s CSR was a common topic of discussion in business schools and boardrooms, with enough companies engaging in CSR activities to review their impact. Donna J. Wood published "Corporate Social Performance Revisited" in the *Academy of Management Review*, which expanded on early CSR models and provided a framework for assessing the impact of CSR initiatives.[5] The same year Archie B. Carroll published his influential "The Pyramid of Corporate Social Responsibility: Toward the Moral Management of Organizational Stakeholders," which outlined a hierarchy of four areas of responsibility that a firm must consider.[6] First, Carroll argues, are economic responsibilities, which are the foundation on which all other responsibilities can be actualized; second, legal responsibilities, that is, complying with the laws of the countries where the firm is operating; third, ethical responsibilities, that is to do what is right, just and fair; and fourth, philanthropic responsibilities, to be a good corporate citizen.

CSR went mainstream in the first quarter of the twenty-first century. Fortune 500 companies now have CSR officers, professional associations for corporate citizenship experts have formed, and customers and citizens expect CSR to drive corporate behavior. But as one might expect, when something goes mainstream, it can also become watered down. Green washing and "impact washing" by less-than-ethical companies, has sprung up an entirely new set of actors in the ethical business space—certification and verification.

Over 400 certification schemes have been developed to signal to customers the ethical bona fides of firms like Fair Trade certification, LEED certified, USDA organic certification, Forest Stewardship Council, and more. Organizations like Slavery Footprint shine a light on companies that use modern-day slavery in their supply chains, Cruelty Free helps customers find companies that aren't engaging in animal abuse, and the Environmental Working Group certifies that personal care, cleaning products, and baby care products meet strict standards for transparency in ingredients and production practices.

The rise of CSR frameworks and hundreds of certification schemes, help move our capitalism toward a more "conscious capitalism," to use Raj Sisodia and John Mackey's term, but it also makes the work of the ethical consumer more difficult.[7] What does the young professional who is committed to fair trade, ethical production, and clean ingredients do?

Cross-referencing hundreds of certification schemes to find companies that aren't undermining the health of citizens and their biosphere can become a full-time job.

In 2006 the non-profit B Lab was founded to simplify and drive the movement toward a new, more ethical, capitalism forward. They launched the wholistic "B Corp" certification, a verified certification that a firm exhibits the highest levels of ethical responsibility across the categories of environment, employees, governance, supply chains, transparency, and which commit to ushering in a new economy—one in which "businesses should aspire to do no harm and benefit all" and understand that they are "responsible for each other and future generations."[8] They also launched the movement to introduce a new corporate form: Benefit Corporations, and have secured new laws in 36 US states that allow companies to register as a Benefit Corporation, and include their social and environmental commitments in their incorporation documents—locking their social mission in for future generations. There are now over 6000 B Corps operating around the world, creating sustainable products, improving access to education, health care, finance services, advancing sustainable agriculture, renewable energy, and more. Ultimately, they are part of a movement seeking to build a new form of capitalism that achieves a more equitable, healthy, and thriving citizenry. The building blocks for a healthy and thriving democracy.

These companies are not only sending signals to their customers, but also investors. Alongside the rise of this new breed of responsible business, we have seen the rise of a new kind of investing: Socially Responsible Investing (some people refer to it as SRI), or investing in companies that consider their Environmental, Social and Governance responsibilities (or ESG). Many people delineate between SRI and ESG in this way: SRI uses exclusionary filters to keep companies out of portfolios that do not meet certain criteria (i.e., you might opt to not invest in oil companies, extractive mining, weapons manufacturers, private prisons, or family detention centers), while ESG opts-in to companies that are making positive impacts in the three factor areas. Data on a company's environmental impact, social impact, and governance is used in tandem with traditional financial metrics to make investment decisions. In the Environmental category investors consider things like: carbon emissions, air and water pollution, deforestation, energy efficiency; in the Social category, investors consider a company's impact on people like gender and diversity, human rights abuses, labor standards, and customer data protection and privacy;

finally in the Governance category, investors consider metrics like: board composition, audit structure, bribery and corruption, executive compensation, whistleblower protection, and political contributions.

Many investors see ESG data as key information to assess a potential investment's risk/return profile. For example, lack of environmental responsibility by British Petroleum led to the Deepwater Horizon oil spill. That catastrophe led to loss of human life, the loss of hundreds of thousands of marine animals, long-term environmental devastation, loss of thousands of fishing industry jobs, and loss of revenues for hundreds of communities. In addition, it also had a "material" impact on investors—$4 billion in federal fines, and billions in losses for the company and thus their shareholders (share price fell by 55 percent). Volkswagen's rigging of millions of diesel vehicles to pass emissions tests similarly led to massive penalties and fines in the United States and Europe (over $30 billion), huge reputational costs and a hit to their shareholders (share prices lost nearly 40 percent of their value following the scandal). Finally, Facebook lost over $100 billion in value after it became public that they allowed the consulting firm Cambridge Analytica to lie to citizens/users and harvest psychological profile data from 87 million citizens/users without their consent, and then use that data for psychologically targeted political ads for the 2016 Trump campaign.[9] ESG risks are financial risks.

Just as hundreds of support organizations have sprung up to quantify, verify, and certify the social and environmental responsibility of companies for customers, a number of initiatives have developed to help investors on their path to invest in a more ethical and equitable form of capitalism (and avoid the type of spectacular losses just discussed). In early 2005, the then United Nations Secretary-General Kofi Annan invited a group of the world's largest institutional investors to join a process to develop the Principles for Responsible Investment (or PRI). These are a set of voluntary and aspirational investment principles and accompanying actions that support incorporating ESG issues into investment practice. There are now over 3000 investment managers, asset owners, and service providers that have become signatories to the PRI. Many credit Annan for launching the ESG movement.

In 2019, the Operating Principles for Impact Management were launched by the World Bank Group/IMF to provide a more complete framework for investors to ensure that impact considerations are purposefully integrated throughout the investment life cycle. They went a step further than the six UN Principles for Responsible Investing in that they are more concrete and call for independent verification.

The Global Impact Investing Network (GIIN) was founded in 2009 to support the development of the field of impact investing and they launched IRIS—their Impact Reporting and Investment Standards a decade ago. After ten years of research and improvement, they recently launched IRIS+, which is a generally accepted system for measuring, managing, and optimizing impact. Similarly, B Lab recently overhauled their GIIRS (Global Impact Investing Rating System). Also based on a decade of learning, the new system coincides with B Lab's process of certifying that companies are rigorously measuring and tracking their social and environmental impact (B Corp certification), and translating that framework for impact investors. The hope is that these resources support investors that manage their portfolio's impact with the same rigor as their financial performance.

The GIIN now estimates there is over $500 billion in assets globally being invested for social and environmental impact alongside financial return, and the US Forum for Sustainable and Responsible Investments estimates that $12 trillion in US assets are managed under some sustainable investing strategy, reflecting growing demand for investments that align with clients' social values. Investing in a new, more equitable and responsible capitalism is going mainstream. For example, the major asset manager Blackrock is stewarding its $8 trillion+ in assets under management, informed by financially material ESG data with the goal, not to be activist, but rather to enhance their risk-adjusted returns.[10] This massive financial institution is benefiting from the research of the Sustainability Accounting Standards Board (SASB) and the Task Force on Climate-Related Financial Disclosures—the impact measurement and management framework that looks most poised for widespread adoption by the industry.

At a time marked by partisanship and gridlock in Washington, D.C., prospects look weak for achieving more equitable, ethical, and environmentally sustainable outcomes through policy alone. Thankfully, the trends in the private market discussed here are promising. The movement for socially responsible business and finance has been growing for two decades, and it has gained significant ground and continues to push forward. A new frontier is a private sector approach to tackling the seemingly insurmountable problem of campaign finance reform and lobbying reform—the movement for Corporate *Political* Responsibility (CPR). As some of its key proponents note:

> it's disingenuous for companies to pretend they are passive observers of regulations, laws, or the political climate. Many have purposely contributed to the gridlock they bemoan, through conflicting messages, donations, and third-party affiliations. Political spending helps companies elect leaders who represent their interests and gain access when they need it. Social media, advertising, philanthropy, and public relations can shape civic discourse and cultural beliefs, influencing voting and behavior. And with direct lobbying, companies are not just playing by the rules of the game, they are *shaping* those rules and how they are enforced.[11]

This movement for more corporate political responsibility, driven forward by the CPR Taskforce at the University of Michigan "believes business has a shared interest in and a responsibility to support our nation's civic and political health." They are working to advance corporate political responsibility as a shared norm and ultimately strengthen trust in American civic institutions.

Equality, Opportunity, at the foundations of Democracy

At the formation of our American liberal democracy, capitalism was a key component of a system designed to advance individual freedom (for certain types of individuals). It was broadly understood that one of the roles of our democratic institutions was to balance the interests of those with and without property (or wealth)—for the government to help balance who got what, when, and how as Laswell put it. Madison argued in Federalist Papers No. 10 "the most common and durable source of factions has been the various and unequal distribution of property. Those who hold and those who are without property have ever formed distinct interests in society."[12] Advocates and activists fought for two centuries for more and more citizens to have basic rights, and for more equitable distribution of wealth. Yet despite nearly 250 years of advocacy for equity and opportunity, the twentieth-century version of capitalism, and its related corporate political interventions, have created a country and economy characterized by inequity. In this section, we hear from three scholars exploring the practical failure of our democratic institutions and our capitalistic economy to deliver the equity needed for a thriving democracy. In addition, they present us with philosophical and aspirational approaches we might use to realize a more perfect Union. Joel Mokyr, Robert H. Strotz Professor at the Departments of Economics and History at Northwestern University argues that a country will only be able to harness the power, creativity and promise of a diverse population, to achieve a thriving and equitable economy, if that system is endowed with good institutions. Deondra Rose, PhD., the Kevin D. Gorter Associate Professor of Public Policy, Political Science, and History at the Sanford School of Public Policy at Duke University documents the role of a failure of institutions—specifically private sector domination of our democratic system as an important piece of the puzzle. Policymakers' failure to advance equitable access to higher education in the 1800s, 1900s, and still today, has not only implications for income inequality, economic inequality, and wealth inequality but also unequal ability to effectively engage in democratic processes.

Danielle Allen, the James Bryant Conant University Professor and Director of the Edmond & Lily Safra Center for Ethics at Harvard University and author of *Justice By Means of Democracy* also discusses the importance of education in democratic participation, and further points out that our failure to foster broad-based democratic participation has major implications for our economy; resulting in monetary policy, fiscal policy, and economic policy that is not in the best interests of the people, ultimately threatening our democracy.

Allen proposes a set of design principles that can take us from the unequitable and undemocratic status quo, toward an equitable power-sharing liberal democracy along with an empowering economy. She paints a vision of an "egalitarian participatory constitutional democracy," and provides a blueprint for us to develop a key component of that vision—what she calls an "Empowering Economy" via: (1) free labor, democracy-supporting firms, and a good-jobs economy; (2) investment in bridging relationships; and (3) democratic steering of the economy. At a time when democracy seems in retreat around the world, and under attack here at home, the hopefullness of this vision is a welcomed breath of fresh air. Her first design principle—the need for free labor—implicitly highlights something important: "labor" is another word for citizens. If our corporations are engaging in wage theft from our citizens, that is a problem for our democracy. If our capitalistic system prohibits the movement of our citizens toward better opportunities, that is a problem for our democracy. "Democracy-supporting firms" are part of the solution—that is authentic purpose-driven firms that see their primary responsibility to the health of the social, institutional, and natural systems on which they rely. This definition is reminiscent of conscious companies, B Corporations and Benefit Corporations.

Allen sees a responsibility of firms to advance equity as well. Specifically, she highlights the importance of a company's pre-production, production, and post-production as three important and different areas for reform to achieve more equitable outcomes. I think she rightly highlights the outsized positive impacts that can be unlocked through changes in the traditional, as she refers to it, "authoritarian" black box of firms as they carry out their production. The movement toward purpose-driven companies, benefit corporations and certified B Corps is working to incorporate more ethical and equitable practices throughout their business models and supply chains, from pre- to post-production.

The rise of ESG Investing has driven unprecedented amounts of capital (now estimated at $30 trillion globally) toward companies committed to improving their environmental and social performance, including considering their impact on a broader set of stakeholders and their corporate political responsibility. The blueprint Allen lays out toward an Empowering Economy is in line with this movement and presciently calls for an evolution of firms in the direction of being "democracy supporting." Now ESG investing is under attack by some conservative politicians, attacking the very asset managers for which they are normally advocating. This development could damage the potential of the private sector to be allies in the fight for a more equitable economy as Professor Allen outlines.

Allen and Rose both highlight the importance of equitable access to education as an important pre-cursor to equitable access to democratic participation. Allen notes that "education is the causal force behind democracy." Rose demonstrates that achieving that goal has been hampered again and again by racism and biased support of the interests of private capital. Her chapter encourages us to consider what might be the most promising levers to change this status quo—at system change level, shifting the power of private sector interests through campaign finance reform and lobbying reform; or, at the issue-level of continuing the battle for equitable access to education, and protection against predatory lending and disingenuous marketing, or possibly action is needed at both levels simultaneously.

Since an educated citizenry is so essential to an engaged voting population, we need to question the unethical behavior of the for-profit education industry—not only in their unethical swindling of unsuspecting students, but also their extraction of taxpayer dollars and their manipulation of the policy process through campaign finance and lobbying spending. Rose's work encourages a new generation of scholars to dive deep into the counter factual analysis of what could have been the alternative history if the billions of dollars of federal aid had flowed instead to community colleges in small towns across the country. And we must all ask going forward, what role should the better-funded advocacy offices of our esteemed universities have in advocating for federal aid support to flow to our community colleges rather than to the shareholders of private education companies? What is the role of the academy in being part of this fight for equal access to education?

Rose notes in her piece that "it is a democratic imperative that the government intervene to ensure equal opportunity for and equal protection of its citizens." This argument could be extended to other issues areas that also have significant implications on the ability of citizens to effectively engage in democratic processes—such as access to affordable housing, childcare, health care, and justice through the policing and criminal justice systems. We might consider access to each of these also as key precursors to democratic participation. Ultimately, Rose suggests that, for democracy to thrive, the government has a critical role to play ensuring that our citizens have equal access to the tools they need to be thriving citizens.

Mokyr, like Rose and Allen, also advocates for better institutions, and like Allen, he sees power in "difference without domination." He proposes that the power of diversity (ethnic, racial, religious, ideological, linguistic...) can only be unlocked by "good institutions." Pluralist institutions he notes can be seen as "civilizing agents"—"they prevent intolerant people from acting on their aversions and instincts and overcome their 'natural' proclivity to be suspicious of others who look, behave, think, or talk differently." There is a good deal of evidence that cities that are necessarily more diverse are more economically productive, and many attribute the creative innovation of urban areas to the interaction of diverse viewpoints and ideas. In addition, we know refugees and immigrants are particularly entrepreneurial and job creating, regardless of the institutional setting they find themselves.[13] Mokyr notes that there is mixed quantitative evidence at both the micro- and macro-level on the relationship between diversity and economic performance and growth, but points to the historical record for evidence from a series of case studies where a minority incorporated into the economies of differing majorities, and created significant economic value such as Jewish communities across Europe, Roma, Armenian migrants in the Middle East, German settlers in southern and eastern Europe, and Chinese expatriates in the Far East.

Diversity, when coupled with pluralist and enlightened institutions, can drive economic growth and prosperity, which can be important preconditions for a thriving democracy. But Mokyr's work presents a warning as well—diversity, unsupported by good institutions—can lead to devastating outcomes like the bigoted Catholicism of Louis XIV and the genocidal policies of Hitler's Germany.

Conclusion

There is a vicious cycle at play, where wealth inequality drives political inequality, as wealthy and corporate interests finance the campaigns of business-friendly candidates and pour untold amounts of money into lobbying for policies that protect the status quo of inequity and further exacerbates it. Because of the incredibly high levels of money in politics, the American democratic system exacerbates the yawning gap between the rich and the poor rather than ameliorate it, as originally called for by Madison. This fundamental problem reverberates through every policy area and leads to policies that serve private capital and wealthy interests at the expense of regular citizens undermining equitable access to education, equitable access to health care, equitable access to housing, equitable access to childcare, equitable access to voting, and the list goes on.

Money in politics and the bias toward the will of wealthy interests undermine our citizens' ability to access the very foundations of a healthy and happy life. This tendency for winners to take all in our political system has been well documented by Hacker and Pierson's *Winner Take All Politics: How Washington made the Rich Richer and Turned Its Back on the Middle Class.*[14] It is not a foregone conclusion that wealthy interests will always dominate democracies unchecked. Comparative analysis of lobbying and political outcomes in advanced democratic economies demonstrates that there are processes and systems that result in more balanced policy outcomes, balancing citizen interests and those of private sector firms as my book *Brussels vs. the Beltway* shows.[15] The strategies laid out in Allen's work provide a roadmap for how we might begin righting the ship of American Democracy, and the players in the movement toward socially responsible capitalism provide ready and willing partners in that work.

Notes

1. Adam Smith, *The Theory of Moral Sentiments*, 1759.
2. Howard R. Bowen, *The Social Responsibilities of the Businessman* (Iowa City: University of Iowa Press, 1953).
3. "Corporate Social Responsibility: A Brief History," ACCP—Association of Corporate Citizenship Professionals, 2023, https://accp.org/resources/csr-resources/accp-insights-blog/corporate-social-responsibility-brief-history/.
4. Edward Freeman, *Strategic Management: A Stakeholder Approach* (Cambridge: Cambridge University Press, 1984).
5. Donna J. Wood, "Corporate Social Performance Revisited," *The Academy of Management Review* 16, no. 4 (October 1991), 691–718.
6. A. B. Carroll, "The Pyramid of Corporate Social Responsibility: Toward the Moral Management of Organizational Stakeholders," *Business Horizons* 34, no. 4 (July–August 1991), 39–48.
7. Raj Sisodia and John Mackey, *Conscious Capitalism: Liberating the Heroic Sprit of Business* (Boston: Harvard Business Review Press, 2013).
8. "Building the Movement," B Corporation, 2023, https://www.bcorporation.net/en-us/movement/.
9. Nicholas Confessore, "Cambridge Analytica and Facebook: The Scandal and the Fallout So Far—Revelations that digital consultants to the Trump campaign misused the data of millions of Facebook users set off a furor on both sides of the Atlantic," *New York Times*, April 4, 2018. https://www.nytimes.com/2018/04/04/us/politics/cambridge-analytica-scandal-fallout.html.
10. Blackrock, *2022 Sustainability Disclosure: Reporting under the Sustainability Accounting Standards Board ("SASB") Standards and Management Criteria* (New York: Blackrock, 2022). https://www.blackrock.com/corporate/literature/continuous-disclosure-and-important-information/blackrock-2022-sasb-disclosure.pdf.
11. Andrew Winston, Elizabeth Doty, and Thomas Lyon, "The Importance of Corporate Political Responsibility," *MIT Sloan Management Review*, October 24, 2022. https://sloanreview.mit.edu/article/the-importance-of-corporate-political-responsibility/.
12. Madison, James, "The Federalist Number 10," *Founders Online, National Archives*, 1787, https://founders.archives.gov/documents/Madison/01-10-02-0178
13. Christine Mahoney and John Kluge, "Building Inclusive Economies," *Rockefeller Foundation*, 2021. https://www.rockefellerfoundation.org/report/building-inclusive-economies-applications-of-refugee-lens-investing-refugee-investment-network/.
14. Jacob Hacker and Paul Pierson, *Winner Take All Politics: How Washington made the Rich Richer and Turned Its Back on the Middle Class* (New York: Simon & Schuster, 2011).
15. Christine Mahoney, *Brussels versus the Beltway: Advocacy in the United States and the European Union* (Washington, D.C.: Georgetown University Press, 2008).

8

Diversity, Pluralism and Tolerance

The Roots of Economic Prosperity?

JOEL MOKYR

Introduction

Are democracy and capitalism compatible? Any answer to this question depends almost entirely on one's definition of the two concepts. Democracy, of course, is more than just free and fair elections that determine who will run a country. It refers to a cluster of various freedoms and protections for citizens and various groups that cannot be easily removed by majority decisions, and most political scientists would insist that the cluster includes some measure of constraints on the executive, and checks and balances on all three branches and forms of power, as well as ways to map public opinions into policy (e.g., by referenda). Democracy and Capitalism have lived together in the recent past in the Anglo-Saxon world, parts of Continental Europe, and some Asian countries, but clearly one can exist without the other.

One aspect of the cluster of democratic institutions, which has become increasingly central to political thinking in the twenty-first century, is the question of the shares of various groups in the distribution of wealth, political power, desirable occupations, residential locations, and other valuable social assets. Equity implies that such distributions should reflect roughly their shares in the population, creating some measure of diversity. If in the past discrimination or other forms of mistreatment of certain groups has led to the systematic underrepresentation of some subsets of society, democratic principles could be seen as requiring policies intended to reverse such injustices. It is hard to see a well-functioning democratic state in which pluralist institutions (defined below) that support diversity do not play some kind of role. By that definition, nations that

Joel Mokyr, *Diversity, Pluralism and Tolerance*. In: *Can Democracy and Capitalism Be Reconciled?*.
Edited by: Sidney M. Milkis and Scott C. Miller, Oxford University Press. © Oxford University Press (2025).
DOI: 10.1093/9780197774731.003.0009

are subject to Jim Crow laws or Apartheid institutions are inconsistent with democracy.

Capitalism is even harder to define exactly, especially since one of its main characteristics is its adaptability and protean nature. It might be close to the consensus, however, to note that it is an economic system that involves in some form free markets in both commodities and factors of production, the acceptability of maximization of profits subject to the rule of law, and well-defined, enforced, and respected private property rights. In what follows I will be concerned with only one aspect of it, namely the emphasis of capitalism on efficiency and economic performance. Discrimination and the systematic oppression of minorities could be argued to be inconsistent with a reasonable definition of capitalism; after all, capitalism is about making money, and if discrimination, coerced labor, or the mistreatment of a minority are costly or inefficient, a pure form of capitalism ought to eschew it. Either way, both democracy and capitalism can be seen as sets of rules and norms by which modern societies operate, and which constrain the behavior of individuals and organizations, and therefore fall squarely into the Northian category of "institutions."

Diversity is widely seen today as a desirable objective. Universities have "diversity officers" whose job it is to increase diversity and encourage the inclusion of under-represented minorities. This policy has two sources of support, one is based on ethics, the other is on efficiency. The former justification is that low-diversity is the result of sins of the past such as colonialism and racism involving systemic discrimination against some groups that are now under-represented. Hence fairness and justice demand that these be addressed. A different idea is that low-diversity, whatever its causes, is inefficient. It is argued that higher diversity improves economic performance and stimulates creativity and growth by drawing on a larger pool of cultural material and a more diverse reservoir of experiences and attitudes, and thus increases the potential for innovation and effective management and cooperation.[1]

The enthusiasm of the supporters of diversity's positive efficiency effects notwithstanding, there are clearly *both* benefits and costs to greater diversity, and their net impact on economic performance and progress vary over time and across societies and industries. The literature on the topic is large, and in the chapter below I will only be able to deal with selected aspects of it, as exemplified by historical case studies. Before doing so, it is important to define carefully the differences between the three key concepts of diversity, tolerance, and pluralism, and take a closer look at what economic analysis has to add to our understanding of these three concepts. I will then argue how economic history sheds light on the complexities of the economic effects of diversity.

The basic answer to the question whether the economic effects of diversity are positive or negative can be summed up here. My answer is a variant on what is known in the history of technology as "Krantzberg's Law"—diversity is neither good nor bad, nor is it neutral.[2] What this statement means is that the effect of diversity can be substantial, but its net impact on economic efficiency and growth depends on the institutions of society. Much like the effects of innovation and natural resources, it can be either a curse or a blessing.

Some Definitions

Terms like "diversity," "tolerance," and "pluralism" are used frequently in this literature and need some careful definitions if we are to unpack the effects of diversity. By *diversity* I mean outcomes. A diverse society is composed of coherent groups that differ from one another in an important and observable characteristic shared by members of the group. Hence the aggregate has a higher variance in that dimension than a non-diverse society. Many traits are interchangeable with "identity," which is recognized by both those who have the traits and by "others," who do not. The pertinent question of diversity is how are different sub-populations sharing recognizable different traits represented across the economy and what are their relative socio-economic status, political power, and so on? Diversity is traditionally measured by a dispersion metric such as the Herfindahl index. What matters here is how these others regard and treat individuals that have a particular trait.[3]

Tolerance here will be defined as a pure matter of preferences, that is, culture. One natural way of defining it is by asking how much an individual objects to what others believe or what they look like. In the limit, perfect tolerance means we are utterly indifferent to what others believe as long as they do not act on it in a way that harms others. It measures a willingness to "let a hundred flowers bloom." It is also a measure of homophily, the degree to which we have a liking for others who resemble us in their religion, language, ethnic background, phenotype, and so on. Given that homophily (and hence an aversion of "others") appears to be hardwired into our preferences,[4] society has to set up institutions that constrain our behavior to act on those aversions. While these constraints may not necessarily make people more tolerant (that is, change their preferences), it will affect their behavior.[5]

The *institutions* that prevent people from realizing their homophilic preferences are what I what I mean by *pluralism*. Pluralist institutions can be seen as "civilizing agents"—they set the rules that prevent intolerant people from acting on their aversions and instincts, and overcome their "natural" proclivity to be suspicious of others who look, behave, think, or talk differently. Even countries with "good" institutions are subject to the consequences of homophily and intolerance. Pluralist institutions, by restraining individual behavior can attain the economic advantages of diversity while minimizing the costs.[6]

Pluralist institutions, unlike tolerance, are not individual choices and are taken parametrically, given by each individual. Examples include universal franchise, making minority languages official, complete freedom of worship and religion, and outlawing discriminatory practices such as redlining, higher education quotas, and similar rules that benefit specific groups at the expense of others.[7] The exact connection and interaction between tolerance (that is, culture) and pluralism (that is, institutions) is always complicated and the two co-evolve in subtle and complicated ways, as culture and institutions are apt to do.[8] Obviously, if an overwhelming majority of society is highly tolerant, this is likely to lead to pluralist institutions. But at times fanatically intolerant minorities that acquire power (for possibly unrelated reasons) may impose a highly antipluralist set of institutions, as happened in Germany in the 1930s. On the other hand, if individuals grow up in a society that has strongly pluralist institutions, they may internalize those in their preferences and become more tolerant. Optimally "good" pluralist institutions are the ones that permit people to hold and express idiosyncratic beliefs and expression, but prevent actions conditional on those beliefs if they have negative spillover effects.

Contemporary Evidence

Social scientists and economists have spent the past quarter century confronting the question of whether diversity is good for economic performance and growth, but a survey of the literature reveals that there are no simple one-line answers. For one thing, diversity is of course undefined unless we decide the diversity of *what*. It sounds reasonable, first, to distinguish between traits that are a matter of choice, such as religion, ideology, and cultural beliefs, as opposed to traits that are hardwired, that is, set at birth such as phenotype, ethnic origin, and genetics. Language falls in between. The two classes create different sources of resentment of "otherness." Traits that are a matter of choice may lead to resentment among the majority group precisely because a minority could have conformed to the traits of the majority but chose not to. Hardwired traits may breed resentment when they tap into much deeper sources of homophily and xenophobia, fear of the unfamiliar and so on. For the historian an obvious dimension of diversity is religion, to which I will return below.

The evidence of contemporary economies can be conveniently subdivided into macroeconomic and microeconomic evidence.[9] The macro evidence is largely based on cross-country or panel datasets and uses various measures of fractionalization as the proxy for diversity. Alberto Alesina and Eliana La Ferrara produce some useful estimates for religious, linguistic, and ethnic fractionalization and its input on GDP growth rates (or levels).[10] In Figure 8.1 I reproduce these figures, extended to 2019. They clearly show that the raw

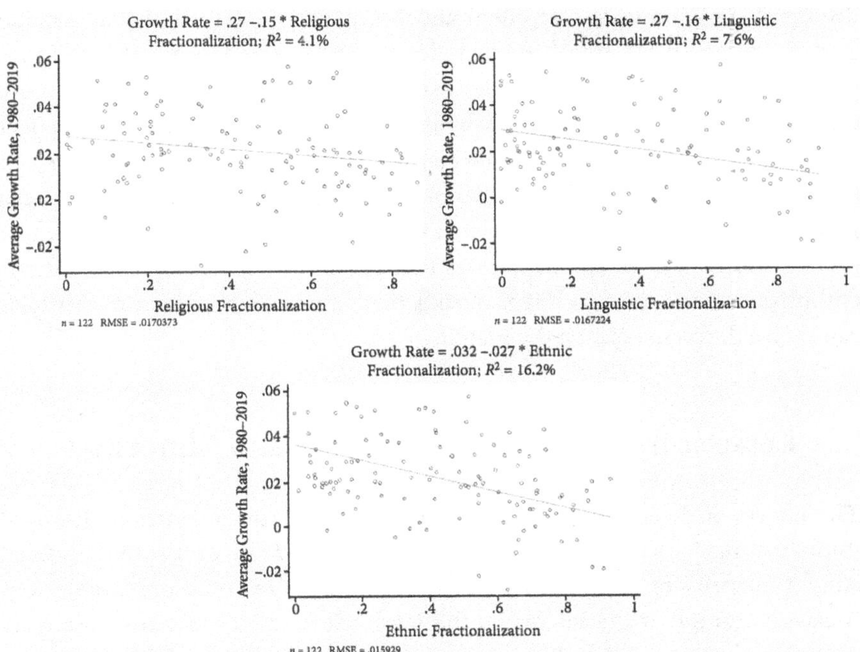

Figure 8.1 Ethnic fractionalization and GDP growth rates, extended to 2019

correlations are weak, and adding further controls (not reported) does nothing to improve them. All three slopes are negative, however, which probably indicates that on balance the negative factors of fractionalization slightly dominate the positive factors. Without specifying a much more detailed structural model, at this point the net effect of diversity on the macroeconomy is weak.[11] Detailed historical case studies of specific nations are few, but Balint Menyhert, in a detailed study of the highly diverse Hungarian part of the Habsburg Empire in 1910, finds that ethnolingual and religious diversity had a positive (if small) effect on economic development as approximated by the growth in the tax base.[12] Clearly, on the macro level, diversity has both salutary and deleterious effects, the latter focusing on its negative effect on social capital and trust.[13] It is not surprising, then, that well-designed studies still find contradictory results.

On the micro level, empirical research is extensive, but the evidence is equally mixed. One meta-analysis finds that cultural diversity at the firm level inherently involves trade-offs, meaning that the "optimal mix" may vary depending on the specific task at hand. Furthermore, culturally diverse teams had higher creativity (as postulated by Scott Page[14]), but also more conflict and less social integration. Cultural diversity does not have a direct impact on team performance, but the effect is indirect, mediated by "process variables" such as creativity, cohesion, and conflict; and is moderated by contextual factors such as team tenure, the complexity of the task, and whether the team is co-located or geographically dispersed. In another survey, Stahl and Maznevski (2021) find that a meta-analysis, based on 44 studies conducted between 1985 and early 2018, indicates that deep-level (cultural and knowledge-based) diversity is associated with more creativity due to its relationship with higher information diversity.[15] This effect tends to be stronger when the team is co-located or is engaging in a task with high interdependence. Surface-level (phenotypical) diversity, which can raise social identity threats, was negatively related to creativity and innovation for simple tasks.[16] In short, there are many cases that confirm Richard Florida and Page's enthusiasm about diversity but also many that do not. Perhaps historical studies can shed a different light on the matter.

Lessons from History I: Pluralism and Minorities

The effects of diversity on economic performance can be better understood from historical cases in which minorities of one kind or another dwelled amid a majority of people who differed from them in some observable way. A classic example is the history of the Jews, who until 1948 were a minority everywhere, and traditionally were subject to various forms of discrimination and persecution. Yet having Jews around was usually an economic benefit for the rest of the population. The reason was that in many cases Jews provided goods and services that the local population had difficulty providing. They were in the words of Yuri Slezkine, a "service minority"[17]—specialized in certain sectors (such as retail, estate management, finance, and medicine) that the majority would not or could not perform. Similar groups were the Roma, Armenian migrants in the Middle East, German settlers in southern and eastern Europe, and Chinese expatriates in the Far East.

In a remarkable paper, Saumitra Jha has written down the economics when a minority will be treated in a pluralist way, at least under normal circumstances. These can be summarized conveniently as Jha's five principles of pluralism, and list when and under what circumstances the minority will be well treated.[18]

1. *Complementarity*: If the two groups produce goods or services that are basically complementary, and if the majority recognizes these benefits, they are likely to allow the minority considerable freedoms and profit from their existence. The inhabitants of the Jewish *shtetls* in eastern Europe provided a host of valuable services in retail, transportation, finance, taverns, and more in a population that was heavily agricultural.[19] In eighteenth-century Germany, court-Jews provided administrative services and in Poland at that time they provided estate management.

2. *Locked-in specialization*: The majority (local) group should not be able to replicate or seize and then successfully deploy the resources that the other group uses more intensively. If the minority group, being politically weaker, derives its economic success from a resource that can be readily expropriated, the temptation for the majority to do so may be very strong. Service minorities had an incentive to specialize in activities that depended on human capital (such as medicine and management) or relied on networks of trusted in-group members.[20] When such lock-in conditions change, the pluralist equilibrium could be upset.[21]
3. *Size and inequality*: The "non-local" group should not be so small and/or so economically successful that it accumulates huge wealth, especially wealth that is transparent and easy to expropriate such as luxury homes and large estates. Such assets may give the larger and politically stronger group a temptation to seize them, and the vulnerable minority may be in a weak position to protect the assets.
4. *Redistribution*: Assuming the minority is economically successful, what is further conducive to a reasonably harmonious relation is a set of mechanisms that redistribute income between the two groups without violence while maintaining incentives. An example is a tax assessed on the successful minority (but not at confiscatory rates) and redistributed as rents to the people in power. This creates a powerful incentive for both sides to create a pluralist modus vivendi.[22]
5. *Intertemporal trade-off*: The discount rate of the ruling class is not too high for them to ignore the long-term effects of losing the benefits of the minority. In cases of national emergency the discount rate would peak, and the temptation to expropriate the vulnerable minorities would be too tempting.

To those five principles, all enunciated or implied by Jha, one could add one more of considerable historical importance.

6. *Political Entrepreneurs*: Pluralist institutional structures should be resistant to political entrepreneurs, usually populist demagogues or ideological fanatics, who exploit the culture of intolerance and xenophobia to draw political rents from inciting the majority population against some convenient target such as a vulnerable minority. These instances of the "economics of hatred"[23] are all too common and they can easily negate the substantial economic benefits of pluralism. The expulsion of non-Christian religious minorities from Spain, especially the Jews in 1492 and the Moriscos in 1609 are examples of such destructive political entrepreneurship.[24] Glaeser points out that pluralism may depend on the cost of disseminating false racist narratives as opposed to the costs of verifying them. This is correct, but we should keep in mind the great

danger of confirmation bias in these matters, which immunizes prejudiced people to evidence. Sadly, when it comes to racial hatred or religious bigotry, anything that could be regarded as evidence can be readily dismissed by those committed to an intolerant culture.

Lessons from History II: The Reformation

The Reformation in Europe provides an instructive example of the effects of diversity, in this case religious diversity. Unlike cases where "religious diversity" really was a proxy for ethnic or racial diversity, the Reformation in Europe created a severe shock to the low-diversity religious equilibrium that had reigned in Europe for at least eight centuries, in which, apart from a smattering of Jews and some outposts of non-conformist Christians, much of Europe was religiously homogeneous. All that changed dramatically in the first half of the sixteenth century.

What were the economic effects of this revolution? Clearly, for the first century after the Reformation, it is clear that religious diversity was mediated by antipluralist institutions. The principle of *cuius regio eius religio* formalized at the Peace of Augsburg in 1555 embodied the fundamental idea that "others" who did not share the religion of the ruler were not welcome anywhere. Germany (and Europe) was to be divided into Protestant and Catholic areas. That principle was never fully carried out on the ground, but it reflects the zeitgeist of religious intolerance in the middle of the sixteenth century. In 1562, the French Wars of Religion started with a massacre of Huguenots at Passy and were to last for 36 years. Elsewhere in Europe, too, massive violence between different brands of Christianity continued for many decades. These religious conflicts reached a crescendo of sorts with the Thirty Years War in Germany with devastating results for the economies of Central Europe. In short, the rise of religious diversity created a sharp rise in antipluralist institutions, with devastating human and economic consequences. Over time, European intellectuals and politicians, led by such clear-thinking writers as the French theologian Sebastian Castellio (1515–1563) began to recognize the cruelty and futility of intolerance.

Yet intolerance did not disappear magically with the 1648 Peace of Westphalia, not even in the most commercially advanced countries. Moreover, being "tolerated" was not the same as emancipation. Even the more pluralist institutions (formal and informal) of progressive Western societies were still quite remote from color/race/religion blind. In other words, the greater tolerance in much of enlightened eighteenth-century Europe did not preclude serious discrimination against minority groups at many levels. In the United Kingdom, dissenters such as Unitarians and Catholics could live and practice their religion after the Act of Toleration of 1689, but were excluded from many spheres until the Emancipation Act of 1829. Commerce and finance, where such discrimination was absent, prospered as a consequence.[25] All the same, even in the United Kingdom the move to a pluralist society was slow, uneven, and full of setbacks and retreats.[26] Profound prejudice remained deeply ensconced in British culture. In 1788, the enlightened English intellectual Edward Gibbon, observing the anti-Catholic Gordon Riots of 1780, wrote that they reflected "a dark and diabolical fanaticism, which I had supposed to be extinct, but which actually subsists in Great Britain." Two generations later, John Stuart Mill in his *On Liberty* felt the same way.[27]

Europe embarked on a growing commitment to pluralism in the nineteenth century, but only a growing ideology of tolerance constituted a solid cultural foundation of the legal and administrative reforms that established formal pluralism and gave minorities many rights beyond permission to simply reside in a given country. The eighteenth-century Enlightenment, by and large, supplied that foundation. While the *philosophes* whose work we identify as enlightened disagreed on many issues, there seems to be wide consensus among them as to the desirability of a "live and live" attitude that is, a culture of toleration. This is not to say that there were no important differences between Enlightenment intellectuals on this matter or that their support for pluralism was unqualified or entirely driven by ethics as opposed to pragmatism. Yet in the end there seems little to disagree with Ole Peter Grell and Roy Porter when they summarize the history of tolerance in Europe by declaring that "it was the thinkers of the Enlightenment who most clearly voiced those arguments for toleration, in all their strengths and weaknesses, which continue to envelop us in our present multicultural and multireligious societies. Here, as in so many other ways, we are the children of the Enlightenment."[28]

The importance of the Enlightenment for long-term economic development has long been underestimated, but today there are signs that its impact is being recognized.[29] The mechanisms through which an elite cultural movement could affect economic outcomes are varied. However, an emphasis on pluralism and on a tolerant attitude toward the publication of innovative material—no matter how disturbing to those committed to the conventional wisdom—can already be seen in the late seventeenth century with the "radical" writings of John Toland. Toland roundly condemned all forms of institutionalized Christianity in his 1696 book *Christianity not Mysterious*.[30] On the Continent, Pierre Bayle argued strenuously that a society of atheists could live a virtuous existence by honor and civility and did not need religion to keep people from misbehaving.[31]

What were the economic effects of pluralism? A comparison between the United Kingdom and France and their different levels of pluralism is instructive.

The role of dissenters and religious minorities in the British Industrial Revolution has been well documented.[32] Excluded from many career paths and the major universities, dissenters created their own educational institutions and many of them specialized in high-end artisanal occupations and commerce. In France, the bigoted Catholicism of Louis XIV in his later years led to the migration of some of the most skilled and productive members of the upper tail of the human capital distribution in France, among them Denis Papin, Abraham De Moivre, and John T. Desaguliers, who all found a home in the United Kingdom. Much of the clock- and watchmaking industry in France's neighbors originated with immigrants.[33] The favorable treatment of Huguenots in Prussia was demonstrated in a famous paper by Erik Hornung.[34] Similar phenomena can be observed in the Dutch United Provinces. Pluralism, no matter how incomplete, was a powerful tool in the competitive world of states in this era, and the migration of the footloose educated and skilled classes implied that any state whose anti-pluralist policies were dictated by intolerance would pay a high price.

Pluralism and the Industrial Revolution

Did British pluralism contribute to the Industrial Revolution? As noted, for many years after the Glorious Revolution religious minorities were still not considered part of the establishment that ran the country, but for that reason their human capital and energy were channeled into commercial and industrial activities. Scholars have long stressed the high proportion of dissenters among the most successful entrepreneurs and innovators in the Industrial Revolution. A particularly good example were Quakers. The most famous of them were the Darbys of Coalbrookdale in Shropshire, who famously pioneered the use of coke in iron smelting. In late eighteenth-century Birmingham, Quakers made up 1 percent of the town's population but one-third of its ironmasters and tanners.[35] Much like other minority groups in other pluralist societies, dissenters felt that they could trust their co-religionists more than others, which gave them an advantage in networked occupations in which trust was important. In this regard, homophily may have had its upside.

The other paradigmatic example of a tolerant culture leading to (relatively) pluralist institutions and from there to economic prosperity is the Netherlands in the Golden Age. Again, by modern standards, this was hardly an exemplary pluralist society. Many cities had strict prohibitions on the residence of people (many of them Protestants), who did not belong to the dominant Calvinist Church. The Dutch prominent liberal and pro-pluralist intellectual Dirck Coornhert (1522–1590) was born and remained a Catholic all his life, and had to move repeatedly to escape intolerant cities, until he settled in Gouda in 1588, at that time a relatively tolerant city. Pluralism in the Netherlands was a matter of geography.[36] In Utrecht, for example, Jews could not stay overnight until 1789 and had to live in Maarssen, a good two hours walking away. Again, however, formal regulations and the actual practice on the ground may have diverged. The pre-eminent historian of Dutch tolerance has argued that authorities often turned a blind eye to violations of residency limitations and other constraints on minorities, and concludes that "religious dissenters, however, enjoyed a de facto tolerance that made Dutch society religiously the most diverse and pluralistic in seventeenth-century Europe."[37] Non-Calvinists may have been barred from public office, but they could worship in so-called *schuilkerken* (illicit churches) and while they were at times subject to harassment, by and large people got along.

The Dutch Golden Age is a classic example of how capitalism and pluralism went hand-in-hand. It would be no exaggeration to say that in capitalist Netherlands in its Golden Age, religious diversity was a feature, not a bug of society. Pluralism, it turned out, was profitable. Local authorities were encouraged in their permissive attitudes toward other religions by substantial bribes for their connivance in semi-public rituals and quite overt houses of worship.[38] To be sure, exactly because of the uneven nature of pluralism in the Dutch Republic, some scholars have objected to the widespread description of contemporaries of the Netherlands as a model of tolerance. Yet it was precisely the decentralization of political power that made pluralism possible. Decentralized, polycentric government is typically more likely to be tolerant and diverse, simply because of coordination failures. More powerful autocrats like Ferdinand-Isabella, Louis XIV, or Czar Alexander III could carry out major acts of intolerance (at high cost). In the Netherlands this would have been far more difficult as local and provincial authorities would have had to coordinate their repressive policies. In that sense, the Dutch Republic was a miniature example of the political fragmentation argument, recently re-stated by Walter Scheidel in his *Escape from Rome*. In Europe, suppressing technological and intellectual innovation of any kind—including religion—was difficult simply because reactionary powers usually found it difficult to coordinate, and because there were always niches in which more tolerant rulers were willing to accept "apostates." Clever heterodox thinkers and religious skeptics inhabited the seams of Europe and skillfully played the states against one another.

The more difficult question is whether this pluralism actually represented a significant and positive factor in the "embarrassment of riches" of the Dutch Golden Age. Clearly, some contemporaries thought so, none more than the early political economist Pieter de la Court (1618–1685), who pointed out in his famous *Interests of Holland* that the Dutch economy depended on emigrants, and that religious pluralism "hath brought in many inhabitants and driven out but a few."[39] As an urban society, the Holland provinces required the constant infusion of immigrants on account of the high mortality rates in cities.[40] There is, however, little evidence that religious diversity *as such* contributed to its prosperity, and it was not able to prevent the economic decline of the Netherlands in the later eighteenth century. It seems more plausible that *both* pluralism and economic success were the result of a more rationalist and capitalist culture that emerged in the Netherlands in medieval times and that even the most benighted Calvinist fanatics could not suppress.[41] Dutch capitalism meant that profits trumped bigotry.[42] While the Dutch Republic in its heyday was hardly a democratic society by modern definitions, it was clearly an example of early capitalism, and its pluralism was a telltale sign of a nation that was ready for enlightenment ideology; democracy would follow eventually. While early capitalism provided the Dutch with a material motive for tolerance, the enlightenment added a moral base for it. In 1796, Dutch Jews were emancipated by the (French-dominated) Batavic Republic.

Competition and Pluralism

The Dutch example illustrates an important element in European History that no doubt played a role in the rise of religious pluralism, namely that internal competition in polycentric and decentralized political units is usually a salutary factor in the history of diversity. This is true even in the United States today, in which individuals who value a particular ideology have the option to settle anywhere they wish and thus vote with their feet. The Dutch Republic, despite its modest size, had a great deal of internal heterogeneity, which allowed minorities to pick and choose their location. What was true for the Netherlands was true for Europe as a whole. The competition did what it was supposed to do: antipluralist states such as France under Louis XIV eventually had no choice but to relent in their bigoted policies. In the eighteenth century after the death of Louis XIV, the persecution of Huguenots declined and some of them returned to France (one of them was the banker Jacques Necker, director-general of the finances of the Kingdom under Louis XVI). In 1787, just before the Revolution, Louis XVI signed the Edict of Versailles legitimized *de iure* certain civil rights for the Huguenots, even if it still denied them public worship and any political rights. A few years later the new revolutionary government officially invited them to return to France with full citizenship rights.

The other salutary effect of the Reformation and the competition among religions was that with the loss of the Latin Church's monopoly position in the European market for ideas, religions had to compete. In any market—including the market for ideas—competition is a salutary force if the competitors stick to agreed-upon rules that keep the competition civilized. Over time, the struggle between religions in Europe moved from violence to more productive channels. Much scholarly and educational work was undertaken for the purpose of demonstrating the superiority of and attaining a victory for a branch of the now divided Western Christianity.[43] The most important of those channels was education: Protestants such as Philipp Melanchton realized from the outset that education was a key to their success. One way the Catholic camp tried to fend off the threat of Protestants was to establish their own schooling system, primarily through Jesuit Schools. Whether this was a successful tactic to defend Catholicism remains to be seen, but clearly the Jesuits made a substantial contribution to the accumulation of human capital worldwide.[44] The Protestants responded by setting up their own schools, the most famous of which were the dissenting academies in England.[45] Many of the most prominent figures of the Industrial Revolution were educated at these academies, including the prominent ironmongers the Wilkinson brothers, and the chemists Joseph Priestley and John Dalton. Their graduates typically ended up in commerce, medicine, and industry. In a recent paper, Heyu Xiong and Yiling Zhao show that religious diversity and competition in the nineteenth century United States led to a proliferation of Colleges, and thus laid the foundation for the American system of higher education. A back-of-the-envelope calculation suggests that there would have been approximately 22 percent fewer colleges by 1890 if the United States had been dominated by a single denomination.[46] As long as pluralist institutions can mediate the competition and antipathy between rival religions and prevent them from reverting to violent conflicts, it can exploit the diversity and lead to significant economic improvements.

Once competition is regulated to exclude illegitimate means, and the playing ground made even, competition between minorities, whether religious, ethnic, or other, can indeed have salutary effects. In Imperial Germany, Jews were legally emancipated despite widespread antisemitism. While much of the culture was still intolerant, the pluralist institutions were able to restrain the behavior of anti-Jewish elements in the population. The net result was that Jews in Imperial Germany punched above their weight in their contribution to the industrial, commercial, and scientific development of the nation. While their share in the population was about 1 percent in 1871 and about 0.8 percent in 1933, they were over-represented in every sector associated with modernization, industrialization, and advanced science and technology. According to the 1933 German Census, Jews in Germany comprised 16.25 percent of lawyers, 15.05 percent of brokerage agents, and 10.88 percent of medical personnel.[47] This may not have amounted to the complete domination that Nazi propaganda screamed about, but it reflects the impact that pluralist policies had on Germany's development.[48] In the German banking sector,

Jews had a very powerful presence in both smaller private banks and the larger universal banks.

Examination of a small subsample of the Jews who materially contributed to Imperial Germany's economic and scientific successes confirms their central role in German economic development. Among the most notable were Albert Ballin, the son of a Danish Jewish immigrant who built a hugely successful shipping business and pioneered pleasure cruises catering to wealthy customers. He was personally close to the German Emperor and one of the Jews close to the imperial court known as *Kaiserjuden*. Equally prominent was Emil Rathenau, who purchased the European rights to Edison's inventions and founded Allgemeine-Elektrizitäts-Gesellschaft (later known as AEG) in 1887. He became known as the "Bismarck of the German electric industry," the person who introduced electric light and trams to most German cities. His son Walther ran the German command economy during World War I and served as foreign minister in the early days of the Weimar Republic.[49] In retailing, a chain of department stores was established by Hermann Tietz (1837–1907) and his nephews. The vast and luxurious stores were a huge success and had 10 branches in Germany, employing 13,000 employees. The bankers Abraham von Oppenheim and Gerson von Bleichröder were the first Jews to be ennobled in Germany on account of their financial support in the expensive military and political maneuvers that led to the unification of Germany. Bleichröder was particularly close to Bismarck, despite the chancellor's rather explicit antisemitism and he was known as Bismarck's *Privatjude*.[50]

In science and medicine, too, the contribution of Jews was way out of proportion, even if we leave out superstars such as Einstein and Freud. Perhaps the biggest contribution of all to the German nation was made by the chemist Fritz Haber, a fervent German nationalist, who famously perfected the nitrogen fixing process for which he won the Nobel prize in chemistry, and with which he did Germany the doubtful favor of securing a supply of nitrates that allowed it to stay in the war for four and a half years rather than a few months. Equally accomplished was the biologist Paul Ehrlich who won the Nobel Prize in 1908 for laying the foundations of what is now known as immunology, as well as developing the first effective treatment of syphilis.

And yet, German Jews violated the principles enunciated earlier that make pluralism work and diversity a blessing rather than a threat. Their skills were not strongly complementary to those of their gentile neighbors. They were good at activities that non-Jewish Germans were also good at. For every Emil Rathenau there was a Siemens and a Krupp and for every Tietz and Wertheim there were non-Jewish storeowners such as Rudolph Karstadt. In science, Einstein's success spurred the wrath and jealousy of non-Jewish competitors such as the physicist Philipp Lenard, who infamously dubbed Einstein's work as "Jewish physics." The culture of intolerance (that is antisemitism) was alive and well in Imperial and Weimar Germany, even as pluralism was still the law of the land. After the rise of the Nazis, Jewish assets were easily expropriated or bought at bargain basement prices by greedy Germans. The sharp turn of Germany from a nation of reluctant but effective pluralism to one of violent suppression of minorities demonstrates the fragility of pluralist institutions unless they rest on a firm cultural foundation of tolerance and willingness to co-exist with others.[51] It also shows how vulnerable pluralism is to demagogic political entrepreneurs who are willing to ride a wave of racism, exploiting the conscious and subconscious homophily that makes so many people uncomfortable with and suspicious of "others."

Much like the self-defeating bigotry of Louis XIV in the late seventeenth century, the Nazi racist policies were hugely harmful to Germany. Expelling the Jews, even if they were less than one percent of the population, drained a substantial proportion of Germany's upper-tail human capital, which was essential to its continued technological and scientific leadership.[52] In a series of brilliant papers, Fabian Waldinger has demonstrated that the loss of its intellectual elite in science and medicine left Germany permanently weakened. By his calculations, more than 1,000 academics were dismissed from German universities. This number included 15.0 percent of physicists, 14.1 percent of chemists, and 18.7 percent of mathematicians. It does not include the loss of other elite intellectuals from universities or top STEM workers employed by the government or the private sector. The loss of top Jewish scientists and physicians caused a large decline in research output and this loss was persistent, still noticeable as late as 1980. Fabian Waldinger estimates the total loss of top-rated scientific publications to be around 34 percent in the disciplines of physics, chemistry, and mathematics.[53]

Conclusions

Today's realities seem to be consistent with the notion that a high rate of diversity is economically beneficial when it is coupled to pluralist and enlightened institutions, but can be devastating when it is not. Some highly diverse nations have clearly paid a price for their ethnic or linguistic diversity with no obvious benefits. Ethiopia has 90 different ethnicities with anywhere between 77 and 92 languages spoken. Myanmar has 135 distinct ethnic groups grouped into eight "major national ethnic races." Has diversity been good for those "low institutional quality" countries? At the same time, it is equally clear that in some countries diversity is beneficial for the economy, provided they are firmly based on a pluralist culture of live and let live, even if perhaps not much love is lost between the different groups, as for example the Flemish- and French-speaking groups in Belgium or Francophone and Anglophone Canada. Perhaps the most underrated institution that makes diversity a success is the option of voluntary segregation, an application of Robert Frost's famous poem that in some cases tall fences make good neighbors.

All the same, the Page and Florida notion that mixing different ethnic and linguistic groups can stimulate creativity has merit when the institutional environment is favorable. In some countries, diversity seems demonstrably a net blessing even if there were substantial costs. Israel, for instance, is one of the world's most ethnically, linguistically, culturally, and religiously diverse countries. It is also one of the most creative countries, punching considerably above its weight in information technology, medicine, biotech, agricultural, and hydraulic technologies, to name but a few. It also has a rich and complex cuisine, a magnificent music scene (both popular and classical), and a highly original literary and theatre industry. Israeli culture is what syncretism is all about: creating "fusion" of diverse cultural traits, creating new entities by recombining and hybridizing ideas from different cultures. The modern Hebrew language, similarly, is a synthesis of many languages, giving it an uncommon power and flexibility. Dan Senor and Saul Singer single out Israel as "among the most heterogeneous in the world. Israel's tiny population is made up of some seventy different nationalities," which they credit with its hugely successful high-tech sector.[54] There is no doubt that the influx of Eastern European immigrants carrying a large amount of human capital in the late twentieth century sharply increased both diversity and creativity. In 2018, Israel was second only to Taiwan in patents per capita.[55] In 2022, its high-tech sector accounted for 54 percent of total exports and employed close to 10 percent of the labor force. Israel spent more on R&D than any other member of OECD, 5.4 percent of GDP.[56] All the same, the costs of Israeli diversity are just as salient, as the country's increasingly dysfunctional political system attests.

Another contemporary example of pluralism paying off to the economy is Singapore. Singapore is also quite diverse, with its population being a mixture of Chinese (74 percent), Malay (14 percent), and South Indian (9 percent) origin. It has no fewer than four official languages (English, Mandarin, Malay, and Tamil). It leaves nothing to chance: there is a government enforced ethnic integration policy known as EIP ("Ethnic Integration Policy"). The pluralist policies of Lee Kuan Yew were aimed at ethnic pacification, and were on balance a success even if they meant the curbing of some individual freedoms. The EIP was introduced in 1989 to counter the emergence of ethnic enclaves. The four categories of racial groups: Chinese, Malay, Indian, and "others" are allocated into apartment buildings according to quotas set by the EIP. Having most citizens in public housing allows the government to exercise a large degree of control over their social dynamics. The EIP is perhaps the most visible sign of this control.[57] But Singapore's government policy, best described as aggressive pluralism, is extended to education and employment as well.[58]

The Singaporean experience suggests above all that there is more than one path to pluralism. It is clear that forceful top-down policies can make a difference here. The Singapore government conceptualized the relationship between the different ethnic groups as four overlapping communities arranged as partially overlapping circles that maximized common ground but retains each race's separate identity.[59] When institutions are sufficiently strong to enforce an overall pluralist policy of peaceful and reasonably harmonious co-existence, the consequences are economic prosperity. Singapore's GDP per capita in 2021 was 106,000 Singapore dollar (S$) (right after Luxemburg, using PPP for comparison). It ranked seventh on the 2022 WIPO's Global Innovation Index (Israel ranked sixteenth).

None of this is to suggest that diversity is a necessary condition for economic success any more than any other part of the cluster of democratic institutions. Some of the most successful economies, such as the Scandinavian countries, South Korea, and Japan display little diversity. On the basis of either economic history or contemporary experience, it remains hard to argue that diversity in *any* dimension is a *major* (much less an *essential*) factor in any aspect of economic performance. The direction of its effect on the economy, moreover, depends on the quality of institutions. Perhaps this argues once again for a primary role for institutions in economic development, which seems to be a conclusion that much of the professions seem to gravitate towards.

Notes

1. The canonical sources for this argument in economics are Scott Page, 2007, *The Difference: How the Power of Diversity Creates Better Groups, Firms, Schools, and Societies* (Princeton: Princeton University Press, 2007) and Richard Florida, *The Rise of the Creative Class Revisited* (New York: Basic Books, 2012).
2. Melvin Kranzberg, "Technology and History: 'Kranzberg's Laws'," *Technology and Culture* 27, no. 3 (1986): 544–60.
3. Some "traits" actually define the identity of individuals through compound traits, for example, French Canadians or Orthodox Jews, thus created nested traits in which diversity can be defined over groups and subgroups.
4. Feng Fu, Martin A. Nowak, Nicholas A. Christakis, and James H. Fowler, "The Evolution of Homophily," Scientific Reports 2, article number: 845 (2012).
5. "Tolerance" will thus have to be distinguished from "toleration," which involves both the *belief* in religious freedom *and* its practice, and thus comprises both cultural and institutional elements. Cf. Perez Zagorin, *How the Idea of Religious Toleration Came to the West* (Princeton, NJ: Princeton University Press, 2003), 7.
6. While pluralist institutions are expected to be welfare enhancing in general, we cannot say for sure that they are inevitably strictly Pareto-improving, since those with strong homophilic preferences may be made unhappy by laws and arrangements that allow minorities to exercise their rights. This may seem a pedantic point if exercising such rights involves no externalities,

but when, for instance, the right of free speech permits offensive and hateful language, a welfare cost may be involved. Thus one can make the argument that holocaust-denial could be made illegal (as it is in Germany and Austria) on the basis of social welfare.

7. A possible exception is the use of quotas and other rules to compensate groups for past discrimination that have led to a long-run uneven playing field, such as affirmative action. Yet in a purely pluralist society, such compensating practices would be phased out eventually.
8. Alberto Alesina and Paola Giuliano, "Culture and Institutions," *Journal of Economic Literature* 53, no. 4 (2015): 898–944.
9. These are not new questions: Thomas Aquinas argued that diversity among creatures was necessary in order that "the divine goodness might the more perfectly be bestowed on things" and adds "there should be diversity among them, so that what could not be perfectly represented by one single thing, might be more perfectly represented in various ways by things of various kinds." Cited by João César das Neves and Domènec Melé, "Managing Ethically Cultural Diversity: Learning from Thomas Aquinas," *Journal of Business Ethics* 116, no. 4 (2013): 769–78.
10. Alberto Alesina and Eliana La Ferrara, "Ethnic Diversity and Economic Performance," *Journal of Economic Literature* 43 (2005): 762–800.
11. Fractionalization is related but distinct from the concept of "polarization," which is high when, for instance, society consists of two equally sized groups but low when society consists of many small groups. Polarization is strongly related to the onset of civil conflict (José G Montalvo and Marta Reynal-Querol, "Ethnic Polarization, Potential Conflict, and Civil Wars," *American Economic Review* 95, no. 3 (2005): 796–816).
12. Balint Menyhert, "Economic Growth Spurred by Diversity: Central Europe at the Turn of the 20th Century," Unpublished, presented to the 22nd Dubrovnik Economic Conference, 2016.
13. Alesina and La Ferrara, "Ethnic Diversity and Economic Performance."
14. Scott Page, *The Difference: How the Power of Diversity Creates Better Groups, Firms, Schools, and Societies* (Princeton: Princeton University Press, 2007).
15. Stahl, G., Maznevski, M., Voigt, A. *et al.* Unraveling the effects of cultural diversity in teams: A meta-analysis of research on multicultural work groups. *J Int Bus Stud* **41**, 690–709 (2010). https://doi.org/10.1057/jibs.2009.85
16. A good example of the ambiguity of diversity at the firm level is a survey by David Rock, Heidi Grant, and Jacqui Grey, "Diverse Teams Feel Less Comfortable," *Harvard Business Review* 95, no. 9 (September 22, 2016): 22–28. The paper argues strongly that more diversity leads to higher profitability, more innovation and more revenue, yet many companies that tried to recruit a more diverse workforce experienced that "success so far has been marginal." The reason, they argue, is that work in a diverse team is more strenuous and difficult, but that this higher effort—in some experiments—yielded better results. Bringing "different viewpoints" to the discussion was on the whole valuable, as opposed to different values, which they note, can produce corrosive conflict. The difference between "viewpoints" and "values" may be more elusive than they recognize.
17. Yuri Slezkine, *The Jewish Century* (Princeton: Princeton University Press, 2004).
18. Jha's test case is the position of Muslims in Hindu India, but his model works well for most minorities. Saumitra Jha, "Trade, Institutions and Religious Tolerance: Evidence from South Asia," *American Political Science Review* 107, no. 4 (November 2013): 806–32.
19. Yohanan Petrovsky-Shtern, *The Golden Age Shtetl: A New History of Jewish Life in East Europe* (Princeton: Princeton University Press, 2015).
20. The best-known example is the network of Maghribi traders, made famous by the classic work of Avner Greif, *Institutions and the Path to the Modern Economy: Lessons from Medieval Trade* (Cambridge: Cambridge University Press, 2005).
21. This is effectively the argument made by Sascha O. Becker and Luigi Pascali, "Religion, Division of Labor and Conflict: Anti-semitism in German Regions over 600 Years," *American Economic Review* 109, no. 5 (2019): 1764–804, who maintain that the Reformation weakened the prohibition on lending at interest in Protestant regions, and turned Jews and Christians from strong complements to weak substitutes, and hence reduced the economic gains from pluralism. The insight of Slezkine, *The Jewish Century* is similar: antisemitism in Eastern Europe flared up in the second half of the nineteenth century because the skills that Jews had

in service occupations could be more easily reproduced by non-Jews, who then used political power to displace Jews and keep them out.

22. An example of such an arrangement is provided by Maristella Botticini, "A Tale of 'Benevolent' Governments: Private Credit Markets, Public Finance, and the Role of Jewish Lenders in Medieval and Renaissance Italy," *Journal of Economic History* 60, no. 1 (2000): 166, who shows how the profits of Jewish moneylenders benefited the public finances of the communes in which they lived. Italian town governments, turned to Jewish lenders for funds, via taxation or loans.
23. Edward L. Glaeser, "The Political Economy of Hatred," *Quarterly Journal of Economics* 120, no. 1 (2005): 45–86.
24. Eric Chaney and Richard Hornbeck, "Economic Dynamics in the Malthusian Era: Evidence from the 1609 Spanish Expulsion of the Moriscos," *Economic Journal* 126, no. 594 (2016): 1404–40. Another instance would be political scapegoatism, in which a minority is blamed for some misfortune that occurs in society that otherwise seems to defy explanation. The persecution of Jews after the Black Death would be a well-documented example of such social scapegoatism.
25. In a famous passage in his sixth letter *Regarding the English Nation*, Voltaire exclaimed that at the London Royal Exchange "the Jew, the Mohammedan and the Christian negotiate with one another as if they were all of the same religion, and the only heretics are those who declare bankruptcy."
26. A 1753 bill that would give the United Kingdom's Jews after a residence qualification and the evidence of two supporting witnesses, the right to be naturalized "without receiving the Sacrament of the Lord's Supper" had to be withdrawn after furious opposition by bigoted Tories who felt it threatened the essence of a Christian Nation and indicates that pluralism had to tread cautiously because it remained contested deep in the age of Enlightenment (Justin Champion, "Toleration and Citizenship in Enlightenment England: John Toland and the Naturalization of the Jews, 1714–1753," in *Toleration in Enlightenment Europe*, ed. Ole Peter Grell and Roy Porter, 139 (Cambridge: Cambridge University Press, 2000)).
27. "Yet so natural to mankind is intolerance in whatever they really care about, that religious freedom has hardly anywhere been practically realized, except where religious indifference, which dislikes to have its peace disturbed by theological quarrels, has added its weight to the scale. In the minds of almost all religious persons, even in the most tolerant countries, the duty of toleration is admitted with tacit reserves . . . Wherever the sentiment of the majority is still genuine and intense, it is found to have abated little of its claim to be obeyed" (John Stuart Mill, *On Liberty*, The Project Gutenberg EBook of On Liberty [1859] 2011, https://www.gutenberg.org/files/34901/34901-h/34901-h.htm, 14).
28. Ole Peter Grell and Roy Porter, "Toleration in Enlightenment Europe," in Toleration in Enlightenment Europe, ed. Ole Peter Grell and Roy Porter, 19 (Cambridge: Cambridge University Press, 2000).
29. Joel Mokyr, "The Intellectual Origins of Modern Economic Growth" [Presidential address], *Journal of Economic History* 65, no. 2 (June 2005): 285–351; Mara P. Squicciarini and Nico Voigtländer, "Human Capital and Industrialization: Evidence from the Age of Enlightenment," *Quarterly Journal of Economics* 130, no. 4 (2015): 1825–83.
30. A century later, radical tolerance in the West had evolved; Thomas Paine famously wrote that "Toleration is not the *opposite* of Intolerance, but is the *counterfeit* of it. Both are despotisms. The one assumes to itself the right of withholding Liberty of Conscience and the other of granting it . . . The former is church and state, and the latter is church and traffic" (Thomas Paine, *The Rights of Man* (1791; repr., Minneapolis, First Avenue Editions, 2019), 272).
31. Grell and Porter, "Toleration in Enlightenment Europe," 8.
32. Joel Mokyr, *The Enlightened Economy* (London: Yale University Press, 2009), 361–63.
33. David S. Landes, *Revolution in Time: Clocks and the Making of the Modern World* (Cambridge, MA: Harvard University Press, 1983), 219.
34. E. Hornung, "Immigration and the Diffusion of Technology: The Huguenot Diaspora in Prussia," *American Economic Review* 104, no. 1 (2014): 84–122.
35. Peter M. Jones, *Industrial Enlightenment: Science, Technology, and Culture in Birmingham and the West Midlands, 1760–1820* (Manchester: Manchester University Press, 2008), 177;

Margaret Jacob, "Commerce, Industry, and the Laws of Newtonian Science: Weber Revisited and Revised," *Canadian Journal of History* 35, no. 2 (August. 2000): 275–92, has stressed the importance of unitarianism in the eighteenth-century British economy. Three of the most prominent figures of the Industrial Revolution, James Watt, Josiah Wedgwood and Joseph Priestley were unitarians, as were many others. Jacob summarizes the impact of this dissenting creed as offering "the conviction that a rational God—and not Calvin's inscrutable and judgmental one—would reward and replenish" (278).

36. Jonathan Israel, *The Dutch Republic: Its Rise, Greatness and Fall, 1477–1806* (Oxford: The Clarendon Press, 1995), 640–45.
37. Benjamin Kaplan, *Divided by Faith: Religious Conflict and the Practice of Toleration in Early Modern Europe* (Cambridge, MA: Harvard University Press, 2010), 174.
38. Willem Frijhoff, "Religious Toleration in the United Provinces: from 'case' to 'model'," in *Calvinism and Religious Toleration in the Dutch Golden Age*, ed. R. Po-Chia Hsia and Henk van Nierop (Cambridge: Cambridge University Press, 2002), 45.
39. Pieter De la Court, *The True Interests and Political Maxims of the Province of Holland* trans. John Campbell (1662; repr., London: printed for J. Nourse, 1746), 68; Jonathan Israel, *The Dutch Republic: Its Rise, Greatness and Fall, 1477–1806* (Oxford: The Clarendon Press, 1995), 786.
40. Frijhoff, "Religious Toleration in the United Provinces, 28, has noted that the organic connection between religious toleration and commercial prosperity was established as early as 1651 in Jean-Nicolas de Parival's *Les Délices de la Hollande*, a best-selling book translated into many languages. The commercial benefits of toleration became a cliché, "often repeated by later travellers, from Basnage to Montesquieu, from the Marquis d'Argenson to Voltaire and Diderot, even while Dutch prosperity was undergoing serious and lasting setbacks."
41. Maarten Prak and Jan Luiten van Zanden, *Pioneers of Capitalism: The Netherlands 1000–1800* (Princeton: Princeton University Press, 2023), 113–15.
42. Peter Stuyvesant, the intolerant Dutch governor of New Amsterdam asked in 1665 for permission from the West India Company to kick out the few Jews that had settled there. The governors wrote back coolly that such as request would be "unreasonable and unfair, especially because of the considerable loss sustained by this nation, with others" (Samuel Oppenheim, *The Early History of the Jews in New York* (New York: Printed for the Author and the American Jewish Historical Society, 1909), 8).
43. Anthony Grafton, "A Sketch Map of a Lost Continent: The Republic of Letters," *The Republic of Letters: A Journal for the Study of Knowledge, Politics, and the Arts* 1, no. 1 (2009): 1.
44. A striking example of the impact of Jesuit education on long-term economic welfare is provided by Felipe Valencia, "The Mission: Human Capital Transmission, Economic Persistence and Culture in South America," *The Quarterly Journal of Economics* 134, no. 1 (2019): 507–56, who shows that in the area of the Guaraní in South America, Jesuit education had a significant salutary effect.
45. Lawrence Stone, "Literacy and Education in England 1640–1900," *Past & Present* 42 (1969): 69–139.
46. Their conclusion is worth quoting: "The 'knowledge' industry remains, to this day, a key feature of 'American Exceptionalism'. US universities dominate global rankings: its top private research universities accumulate considerable wealth, attract talented students and faculty from abroad, and set the world's highest academic standards. This productive system is in part a consequence of unique circumstances in the 19th century: the absence of state-sponsored religion and the proliferation of Christian denominations" (Heyu Xiong and Yiling Zhao, "Sectarian Competition and the Market Provision of Human Capital," unpublished working paper, 2023).
47. G. Warburg, *Six Years of Hitler: The Jews under the Nazi Regime* (London: Allen and Unwin, 1939).
48. Amos Elon, *The Pity of it All: A Portrait of the German Jewish Epoch, 1743–1933* (New York: Picador, 2003, 6, notes: "In a relatively brief period [1870–1933], this small community [German Jews] produced a staggering array of entrepreneurs, artists, writers, wits, scholars, and radical political activists."
49. His contribution to the German war effort was remarkable: Elon, *The Pity of it All*, 314–15, notes: "In his eight months in this post, Rathenau established the first truly planned modern

economy in Europe. It is no exaggeration to say that, but for Rathenau and the gifted scientists, economists, and managers he engaged, Germany might have succumbed within months; its adversaries had greater stocks of food, minerals . . . bullets, and open supply lines if stocks ran out."

50. Elon, *The Pity of it All*, 193.
51. Both the Kaiser and Bismarck, despite their friendship with some Jews and their reliance on support from wealthy and influential Jewish citizens, were demonstrably antisemitic. Wilhelm fell under the influence of the rabid English racist Houston Stewart Chamberlain, and even proposed making his works required reading in German Schools (Elon, *The Pity of it All*, 267). Bismarck's ambivalent attitudes to Jews was equally obvious and open. At the Versailles peace conference he felt that his French counterparts must have been Jewish to judge from their physiognomy. "There was an insistent, harsh anti-Semitic tone at Versailles: at no other time in his life did Bismarck speak so often, so freely, so scathingly of the rootlessness of Jews, of their hustling, of their omnipresence" (Fritz Stern, *Gold and Iron: Bismarck, Bleichröder, and the Building of the German Empire* (New York: Vintage Books, 1979), 146).
52. For an exposition of the concept of upper-tail human capital, see Mokyr, *The Enlightened Economy*, 122, and Joel Mokyr, *A Culture of Growth: Origins of the Modern Economy* (Princeton: Princeton University Press, 2016), 121–26.
53. Strikingly, Waldinger shows that German science also suffered in the short term from the destruction of the physical plant and equipment due to allied bombing, but the loss of physical assets was less persistent and smaller than that of the upper-tail human capital. Fabian Waldinger, "Bombs, Brains, and Science: The Role of Human and Physical Capital for the creation of Scientific Knowledge," *Review of Economics and Statistics* 98, no. 5 (2013): 813.
54. Dan Senor and Saul Singer, *Start-up Nation: The Story of Israel's Economic Miracle* (New York: Twelve, 2009), 17. As the Irish economist and journalist Mark Levine explained in 2004, "Israel is quite the opposite of a uni-dimensional Jewish country . . . It is a monotheistic melting pot of a diaspora that brought back with it the culture, language and customs of the four corners of the earth . . . Worldwide, you can tell how diverse the population is by the food smells of the streets and the choice of menus. In Israel, you can eat almost any specialty, from Yemenite to Russian, from real Mediterranean to bagels. Immigrants cook and that is precisely what wave after wave of poor Jews did when they arrived having been kicked out of Baghdad, Berlin, and Bosnia" Mark Levine, "We're all Israelis Now," (2004) https://www.hnn.us/article/mark-levine-we-are-all-israelis-now
55. Alison DeNisco Rayome, "The 10 Most Innovative Countries in the World," *TechRepublic*, September 11, 2018, https://www.techrepublic.com/article/the-10-most-innovative-countries-in-the-world/.
56. John Jeffay, "Israeli High-tech Dominant Export Industry, but Investment Needed," *Israel21c*, May 12, 2022, https://www.israel21c.org/israeli-high-tech-becomes-dominant-export-industry-but-uncertainty-looms/.
57. Keshia Naurana Badalge, "The Country Where Diversity Is Enforced by Law," *We Are Not Divided*, October 22, 2020, https://wearenotdivided.reasonstobecheerful.world/the-country-where-diversity-is-enforced-by-law/.
58. Public schools in Singapore place great emphasis on developing a common national identity but remain "studiedly neutral" with regard to the promotion of group identities. The Singapore social studies curriculum emphasizes the promotion of a common citizen identity while assigning cultural and religious identities to the private sphere. In order to promote "social cohesion within a diverse society" and to ensure the survival of the nation-state, the Singapore government gives great emphasis to multicultural issues in the social studies curriculum and officially declares that a primary aim of the subject is to develop "citizens who have empathy towards others and will participate responsibly and sensibly in a multi-ethnic, multi-cultural and multi-religious society" (Theresa Alviar-Martin and Li-Ching Ho, "So, Where Do They Fit In?" Teachers' Perspectives of Multi-cultural Education and Diversity in Singapore," *Teaching and Teacher Education* 27 (2011): 127–35).
59. Alviar-Martin and Ho, "So, Where Do They Fit In?", 129.

9

For-profit Colleges and the Tension between Capitalism and American Democracy

DEONDRA ROSE

> Owners of for-profit entities get to keep any of the tuition money they don't spend—which means they have a strong drive to charge as much as the federal government will allow, to spend as little on education they can get away with, and to enroll as many students as possible regardless of their qualifications.
>
> —*Robert Shireman, Center for American Progress*[1]

During the 2021–22 academic year, 5 percent of American college students attended one of the nation's 2,270 private for-profit postsecondary institutions. Representing nearly 40 percent of degree-granting institutions in the United States that benefit from federal student aid, for-profit colleges—which include schools like Capella University, DeVry University, the University of Phoenix, and Walden University—have significantly altered the nation's higher educational landscape. Offering vocational and career courses in areas like culinary arts, medical assistance training, cosmetology, truck driving, teacher education, information technology, and more, for-profit colleges have been recognized for providing educational opportunity to low-income and first-generation college students as well as military veterans, groups that may go underserved by non-profit higher educational institutions. Given the substantial presence of low-income students in for-profit colleges, these schools receive a staggering proportion of the nation's student aid dollars. In 2015, for example, federal student loans provided approximately 86 percent of revenue at for-profit colleges throughout the United States.[2] By enrolling a substantial proportion of

Deondra Rose, *For-profit Colleges and the Tension between Capitalism and American Democracy*. In: *Can Democracy and Capitalism Be Reconciled?*. Edited by: Sidney M. Milkis and Scott C. Miller, Oxford University Press. © Oxford University Press (2025). DOI: 10.1093/9780197774731.003.0010 the nation's low-income and first-generation college students, for-profit colleges loom large in the nation's ongoing efforts to promote broad-reaching college access.

Since their emergence in the eighteenth century around the time that the nation's earliest private, non-profit higher educational institutions were founded, proprietary colleges have offered postsecondary training via a profit-seeking business model. Unlike their public and private non-profit counterparts that focus on the delivery of education that will lead to the acquisition of knowledge and skills that aid in the development of citizens and movement into gainful employment, privately owned colleges and universities are primarily concerned with earning profit and demonstrating business success to their shareholders. Unsurprisingly, for-profit colleges have higher-than-average net prices; their graduates tend to have significantly lower employment rates than their counterparts who graduate from other four-year colleges; and when they are employed, the graduates of for-profit colleges tend to earn less money than their counterparts who attended other four-year institutions.[3]

For-profit colleges have received substantial amounts of federal financial aid since becoming eligible to receive it in 1972; and recognizing the challenges that for-profit colleges bring to the educational landscape, policymakers have made some arguably modest efforts to regulate them. In 1992 as part of that year's Higher Education Act (HEA) reauthorization, lawmakers established the "90/10 rule," which capped the amount of revenue that for-profit colleges can accept from federal financial aid at 90 percent and required that at least 10 percent of revenue come from other sources. In 2014, lawmakers established the Gainful Employment (GE) regulation, which tied for-profit colleges' eligibility for federal student aid to their ability to meet debt-to-earnings thresholds for their graduates. The Obama-era GE regulation was scaled back in 2019 under Trump-appointed US Secretary of Education Betsy DeVos, demonstrating that the effectiveness of efforts to regulate for-profit colleges has been contingent on the ebbs and flows of changing political tides.

Why have lawmakers stopped short of using forceful government regulation to address the problematic, market-driven behavior of for-profit colleges and universities? This is particularly surprising considering the federal government's history of using regulatory policy to intervene when higher educational institutions have failed to subject students to fair treatment. Moreover, given the large amount of tax dollars that flow into for-profit colleges in the form of federal student financial aid, the government has an especial stake in ensuring that these funds are appropriated responsibly. Using historical analysis, this chapter investigates why federal policymakers have been reluctant to place strong regulations on for-profit colleges, despite the fact that the business model of for-profit higher education incentivizes prioritizing profit generation over ensuring student success. I argue that three forces have been particularly important to precluding firm regulation on for-profit colleges: the relative power differential between the major stakeholders—for-profit colleges and underserved college students; the sporadic nature of political leadership advocating on behalf of strong regulation; and a history of bipartisan resistance to cracking down on for-profit colleges. The federal government's reluctance to place adequate restrictions on for-profit colleges offers a powerful example of the connection between education policy and capitalism, a connection that has important implications for democracy.

The Growth of For-Profit Colleges

For-profit colleges have seen substantial growth since the early 1970s, as Americans have increasingly recognized higher education as a reliable pathway to economic stability and professional opportunity. Indeed, Americans who have higher levels of education tend to enjoy higher levels of income. In 2021, the median weekly income of an American whose highest level of educational attainment is a bachelor's degree was $1,334 compared to $809 for those with a high school diploma.[4] Americans who have more education also tend to enjoy greater job security. Only 3.5 percent of Americans with a bachelor's degree were unemployed in 2021, compared to 6.2 percent of those with a high school diploma.[5] Many students and families recognize the value of earning a college degree, but they often struggle to afford college due to the rising costs that have become a dominant feature of American higher education. The average student pursuing a bachelor's degree in the United States borrows $30,000, and nearly 43 million Americans have college debt.[6]

In addition to the socioeconomic benefits that tend to accompany higher education, scholars have shown that higher education provides knowledge, skills, and experiences that can promote democratic citizenship. Educational attainment is a powerful predictor of political and civic engagement, as people who have more education are significantly more likely to vote, to contact elected officials, to volunteer for political campaigns or other political causes, to contribute money to campaigns, and to participate in protests than their less educated counterparts.[7] Furthermore, political parties and candidates are significantly more likely to tap people who have more education to participate in political activities.[8]

Beyond the inherent risk that investing in higher education requires, students and families must navigate a higher educational landscape in which capitalist interests present an additional force making successful degree completion—and accessing the social, economic, and political benefits that tend to accompany college degrees—more difficult. The rise of for-profit colleges, which have been scrutinized due to inconsistencies in the quality of their programming and the frequency at which their graduates emerge unable to secure gainful employment has also challenged the US higher educational landscape.[9] For many supporters of for-profit colleges, a capitalist approach to higher education is a welcome innovation because market-based, profit-driven institutions are seen as more likely to optimize their services in hopes of succeeding in a competitive educational market. Given for-profit colleges' interest in maximizing profit, they have an incentive to admit large numbers of students, in some cases paying less attention to students' preparation for college or their performance on metrics typically used in non-profit higher educational admissions decisions, such as high school GPA and standardized test scores. For that reason, for-profit colleges offer higher educational access to some students who would be excluded from other colleges and universities. Thus, supporters often tout for-profit colleges as offering substantial higher educational opportunity to traditionally under-represented and otherwise marginalized groups.

But for traditionally underserved groups, such as first-generation college students, low-income students, and racial and ethnic minorities, for-profit colleges have brought especial risk. In their report on the returns to for-profit higher education, Justin Ortagus and Rodney Hughes describe nearly 80 percent of for-profit, four-year colleges as "high-price, low quality" institutions.[10] Since the Great Recession, underserved students have enrolled at for-profit colleges at particularly high rates; and this has been especially true in the last two decades as the market for online education has expanded.[11] As Hannah Appel and Astra Taylor note, "a whopping 96 percent of students who manage to graduate from for-profits leave owing money, and they typically carry twice the debt load of students from more traditional schools."[12] The debilitating student debt that many former for-profit college students hold is particularly problematic when we consider the challenge that many of them have when attempting to secure jobs that will enable them to pay it.

Many for-profit colleges have engaged in fraudulent and otherwise unscrupulous behavior that has called into question the quality of the education they provide, as well as their suitability to serve as stewards of federal education resources. In 2012, the Senate Health, Education, Labor, and Pensions (HELP) Committee released a report that investigated these unscrupulous practices. Their report echoed previous governmental and media investigations, revealing wide use of predatory recruitment techniques, demands for questionably steep tuition, high rates of student attrition, a record of saddling students with unwieldy debt, and sub-par student outcomes like difficulty attaining gainful employment upon graduation. Because for-profit colleges enroll a disproportionate number of low-income students, first-generation students, and racial and ethnic minorities, systematic failures and abuses would have important implications for equal opportunity and democratic citizenship.

If those who turn to for-profit institutions in hopes of achieving these benefits are systematically disadvantaged by their unscrupulous institutional practices, a failure of the federal government to crack down on for-profit colleges could constitute a gross failure to protect some of the nation's most vulnerable citizens. Moreover, the chronic shortcomings exhibited by many for-profit colleges are particularly troubling given the significance of educational attainment for people's ability and inclination to engage in political activities. Given the close relationship between education and democratic citizenship, the proliferation of for-profit higher educational institutions that have an incentive to maximize profits by offering the bare minimum in terms of educational services poses a challenge to democracy.

Understanding Federal Policy toward For-Profit Colleges

For understanding the government's failure to boldly address the problematic and market-driven behaviors of for-profit colleges, Anne Schneider and Helen Ingram's classic framework for understanding the politics of policymaking for targeted groups offers powerful insight.[13] According to Schneider and Ingram, one can often predict the type of policies that lawmakers will develop to engage with particular, targeted groups based on the nature of public impressions of the group and the group's power to advocate for itself in the political arena. Building on this insight, Schneider and Ingram crafted a powerful typology for classifying target groups based on their influence and how they are perceived; and these categories are useful for anticipating the types of policies that lawmakers will employ to engage with them.

For-profit college proprietors and leaders would fall into Schneider and Ingram's "Contenders" category—groups that are relatively powerful and able to advocate on behalf of their own interests but that are generally viewed negatively. According to Schneider and Ingram, policies addressing the behavior of Contenders like for-profit colleges "may depend on the extent of media and public attention, as well as variation in the cohesiveness and activity of the target groups."[14] Despite the public's wariness toward these groups, their level of political influence typically insulates them from burdensome policies.

Traditionally underserved college students and prospective college students, on the other hand, who have a particular interest in the development of meaningful regulations for for-profit colleges would fall into Schneider and Ingram's "Dependents" category. These groups are generally viewed favorably by the public, but they typically lack the power to effectively advocate on their own behalf in the political arena. While college students are typically viewed favorably by virtue of the fact that they are investing time and effort into education, they are not a powerful interest group that is well suited to advocating on behalf of their interests in the political arena. According to Schneider and Ingram, when public officials want to support their interests, Dependents' "lack of political power makes it difficult to direct resources toward them."[15] Instead, policies catering to this group tend to be symbolic or shaped in ways that place oversight away from the federal government.[16] For-profit college students who are often underserved students exemplify this characterization. The typical student enrolled in a for-profit postsecondary institution is African American, older than 24 years old, a holder of a GED, and female.[17]

Historical analysis illustrates how the differential relative influence of for-profit colleges and underserved students has tended to privilege capitalist interests by shielding for-profit colleges from substantial regulation. It also shows that an uncrowded field of advocates supporting greater government oversight and a tradition of bipartisan hesitation to regulate for-profit colleges are important forces behind this policy outcome. The federal government's failure to place adequate restrictions on for-profit colleges belies the commitment to equitable college access that federal policy precedents, like the Higher Education Act and Title IX have long demonstrated. While policymakers have taken small steps to crack down on the exploitative, profit-driven behaviors of for-profit colleges, political dynamics help to explain their unwillingness to move beyond superficial efforts to do so.

Public Policy and For-Profit Higher Education

Since the mid-twentieth century, as increasing numbers of Americans have pursued college degrees and as the federal government has taken a central role in helping students finance higher education, lawmakers have paid increasing attention to students' experiences at for-profit colleges. It is important to note that public policy has played an important role in the rise of for-profit higher education since the postwar era. The 1944 G.I. Bill contributed to an early spike in for-profit college enrollments when the federal government offered unprecedented student aid to returning veterans who were interested in enrolling in college and vocational training programs. At that point, proprietary colleges began the longstanding practice of aggressively targeting veterans who bring a reliable source of government aid.[18] With this influx of public investment during the postwar era came a marked increase in the number of proprietary programs and entrepreneurs entering the business of postsecondary training in order to offer veterans a place to spend their tuition dollars.

In addition to the G.I. Bill, a second public policy played a significant role in the dramatic increase of for-profit colleges during the twentieth century. In 1972, when reauthorizing the federal financial aid programs that had been created by the 1965 Higher Education Act, lawmakers made for-profit colleges eligible to receive Title IV federal student aid. This contributed to a dramatic increase in the number of proprietary institutions seeking to benefit from students' financial aid dollars.[19] This has had long-term consequences that continue to shape the higher educational landscape. For example, although for-profit colleges enroll approximately 13 percent of all college students in the United States, they account for a full 26 percent of all student loan borrowers and generate 35 percent of all student loan defaults.[20] As Constance Iloh notes, students attending for-profit colleges are "more likely to be older, women, students of color, and come from lower-income and less educated families."[21] By permitting students receiving need-based student aid to use their benefits at for-profit colleges, lawmakers unwittingly exposed them to aggressive recruiting tactics by institutions that have an incentive to place minimal resources into the education that they offer.

Scrutinizing For-Profit Colleges and Calls for Regulation in the 1970s

The 1970s marked an important period in the history of the government's relationship with for-profit colleges. In 1972, federal lawmakers reauthorized the 1965 Higher Education Act, thereby extending its Title IV financial aid programs. Part of the reauthorization was the decision to make proprietary colleges eligible to receive students' Pell Grant aid for the first time with the purpose of promoting greater diversity in US higher education by making student aid available to those who typically attend for-profit career programs.[22] Doing so opened a considerable new funding stream for profit-seeking schools.[23] National news outlets like *The New York Times*, the *Washington Post*, and the *Boston Globe* had begun to investigate unscrupulous behavior by proprietary schools, and high-profile news stories had attracted the attention of government officials.[24] They had revealed startling trends such as low graduation rates, high rates of student loan default, and students' difficulty achieving gainful employment upon graduation. During the summer of 1972, lawmakers made attempts to rein in unscrupulous behavior on the part of for-profit colleges using mechanisms like state licensing and accreditation requirements.[25] However, these attempts were not nearly enough to eliminate the chronic problems that students had with proprietary schools.

During the summer of 1974, the Special Studies Subcommittee of the US House Committee on Government Operations held hearings on the topic of proprietary schools. Bringing the opening session to order on July 16, 1974, subcommittee chairman Rep. Floyd Hicks (D-WA) offered an overview of the scope of the government's involvement with proprietary schools noting that the government engaged in a number of activities including "recogni[zing] accrediting agencies, providing funds for veterans education, insuring of student loans, and direct contracting with schools for training."[26] As his remarks indicated, the federal government interacted frequently with for-profit colleges. Rep. Hicks recognized the unique challenge that for-profit education posed to students, acknowledging "the danger that making money may become so important that it overshadows offering worthwhile training [and makes] consumer fraud . . . an ever-present possibility."[27]

The first witnesses to speak before the Special Studies subcommittee were Rep. Jerry Pettis (R-CA) and Rep. Alonzo Bell (R-CA) who had proposed legislation that would increase federal regulations on for-profit colleges the previous year. Rep. Pettis had been made aware of the problems that students attending for-profit colleges face by constituents who had attended Riverside University in his home state of California. When the school abruptly closed, many of the students were left without refunds and unable to receive transfer credit for the coursework that they had completed.[28] The legislation that Pettis and Bell proposed would relieve federal student loan recipients of their debt if it were determined that their school had engaged in unscrupulous behaviors that should have prevented their participation as stewards of federal financial aid funds.[29] Pettis and Bell's leadership on this issue illustrates the fact that Republicans in Congress were concerned about student exploitation by for-profit colleges and the affront that this posed to taxpayers who support federal student aid programs.

This is not to say that Republican Party colleagues always saw eye-to-eye on the issue. At one point during subcommittee hearings, Pettis and Bell seemed to disagree about the appropriate scope of government intervention to correct the behaviors of for-profit colleges. Bell expressed support for "a little bit of interest from the Federal Government," which, he argued "has acted like there was no problem [which] has led to the situation we have now."[30] Rep. Pettis responded that, while he was not "trying to get the Government to intervene in what are States' rights," he felt it worth pointing out that "historically we have solved some very serious problems by having the Government take cognizance of these problems when the State has not."[31] While there appeared to be some consensus among actively engaged lawmakers that something ought to be done to protect students and the financial aid programs from dishonest for-profit schools, lawmakers disagreed on the appropriate scope of government intervention.

At one point during deliberations, William Goddard, Executive Director of the National Association of Trade and Technical Schools, made a statement before the Special subcommittee in which he submitted a 1969 report on the emerging role of vocational schools in postsecondary education. The report—which was created with support from the Ford Foundation—emphasized the lack of full understanding regarding private vocational schools and their role in providing higher educational opportunity for groups that often go underrepresented in colleges and universities. The report offered an analysis of student characteristics, noting the significance of for-profit vocational schools for providing African American students with college access. At one point, the author speculated that most Black students enrolled in these institutions "probably" benefit from the financial aid provided by government agencies.[32] This is just one example of a technique that was often used by those lobbying on behalf of for-profit colleges: pointing to the significance of for-profit schools for extending higher educational opportunity to minorities and other historically marginalized groups.

On December 30, 1974, the Special Studies Subcommittee submitted a lengthy report titled "Reducing Abuses in Proprietary Vocational Education." In it, the special committee presented the findings of their investigation into "reported abuses on Government-supported students."[33] The report offered a detailed analysis of the problems exhibited by for-profit colleges, such as the use of deception when it comes to course quality, jobs, and earnings prospects for graduates; tuition and refund policies; accreditation; and attrition rates.

The deliberations during these hearings reveal that the attention placed on unscrupulous for-profit colleges was decidedly bipartisan. In their report, Rep. Chet Holifield (D-CA) and his colleagues on the Special Studies Subcommittee emphasized the lack of adequate regulation governing the behaviors of for-profit colleges saying:

> The present system of checks on proprietary school operations is inadequate. Even ethical schools of long standing, perhaps under competitive pressure, have sometimes used questionable advertising or recruitment tactics . . . . There has been too little cooperation among Federal agencies and between Federal and State organizations concerned with proprietary school operations.[34]

The committee strongly insisted that the government correct this problem by developing meaningful regulations that would enable agencies like the Office of

Education and the Veterans' Administration that invest heavily in higher education to more closely monitor how their financial aid dollars are spent. This list of suggested regulations included (1) empowering the US Department of Education to more forcefully regulate which schools have access to federal funds and to take action against those that do not offer quality education to their students. They also suggested that the government (2) place a limit on the proportion of a school's enrolled students who benefit from government support, and (3) that schools be required to implement more equitable refund policies. Finally, the committee suggested (4) that schools be required to disclose accurate graduation and placement data to prospective students. This call for the implementation of forceful regulations on for-profit colleges signaled lawmakers' awareness of the abuses perpetrated within the sector and their clear sense of policy actions that could help to address them.

By the end of the 1970s, lawmakers had managed to pass a policy that required the federal government to monitor educational institutions where more than 60 percent of students use federal student loans. The Federal Trade Commission also produced a rule aimed at preventing for-profit schools from making deceptive claims about their job placement record when recruiting students.[35] Although lawmakers succeeded in achieving some regulation, these policy changes pale in comparison to the full list of forceful regulations that advocates had suggested during committee and subcommittee deliberations.

Politics and the Reluctance to Make Forceful Policy Change in the 1980s

According to *The New York Times* writer, Jason DeParle, "Abuses at proprietary trade schools became a national scandal in the late 1980s with mounting evidence that many of the schools existed as diploma mills, set up simply to harvest Federal student aid."[36] At the beginning of the decade, the regulations created in the 1970s and the increasing awareness of unscrupulous behavior on the part of for-profit colleges had given way to renewed efforts by for-profit colleges to resist government regulation, and these efforts were enabled by bipartisan forces. Democrats, for example, had successfully worked to allow for-profit colleges to enroll students who had yet to complete a high school diploma. Similarly, Republicans had advocated for cuts to education that resulted in fewer resources that the government could devote to monitoring the behavior of for-profit colleges.[37]

During the early years of the Reagan Administration, officials became increasingly concerned about skyrocketing student loan default rates. President Reagan's Secretary of Education, William Bennett, prioritized addressing fraud and high default rates among for-profit schools.[38] In the winter of 1986, the Senate held hearings on higher education, and Secretary Bennett used the occasion to shed light on the need for more effective government regulations on for-profit colleges. These hearings revealed a clear lack of consensus regarding the need for more forceful regulation. Early in the hearings, Sen. Ted Kennedy (D-MA) emerged as a powerful voice in support of for-profit trade schools. He viewed them as significant for expanding higher educational opportunity to traditionally marginalized groups, particularly low-income and minority students asserting: "Many schools with high default rates also serve a very high percentage of minority and disadvantaged students. I am especially troubled by any proposal that would eliminate large numbers of these schools . . . ."[39] Kennedy's remarks echoed the arguments that for-profit colleges had long made, claiming that they provide educational opportunity to Americans who would otherwise be left behind.

In 1987, Secretary Bennett announced a plan to exclude schools with high student loan default rates from participating in financial aid programs.[40] By December of that year, the Senate held hearings on Problems of Default in the Guaranteed Student Loan Program. As the hearings got underway, senators on the Subcommittee on Education, Arts, and Humanities used their opening statements to express great esteem for the US system of higher education and appreciation of the government's commitment to ensuring that all Americans enjoy the opportunity to pursue postsecondary education if they wish to do so. During deliberations, lawmakers also discussed the chronic fraud and abuse that investigations of for-profit schools had uncovered. As was the case during previous hearings on this topic, much of the discussion centered on how best to hold for-profit schools accountable.

In his opening statement before the subcommittee, Sen. Strom Thurmond (D-SC) stated his willingness to take an open-minded approach to considering proposals for combating student loan defaults. But he also raised a point often made by advocates of for-profit schools: "As we examine these proposals," said Thurmond,

> we should keep in mind that there are a number of colleges which have traditionally served students from disadvantaged backgrounds. The Community and Historically Black Colleges have taken upon themselves a special responsibility to provide educational access to low-income students.
>
> Accordingly, any initiative in this area should recognize the unique role that these institutions play.[41]

In his own opening statement that day, Secretary Bennett addressed this notion that forceful regulations on for-profit colleges would lead to a decrease in higher educational access for minority and low-income students saying, "There are thousands of institutions throughout the country with low default rates, including proprietary institutions, historically Black colleges and universities, and other schools that enroll large numbers of low-income students."[42] In his comments, Bennett worked to correct the assumption that for-profit schools held an inevitable monopoly on minority students and those from other under-represented student groups. This discussion reveals the surprisingly narrow perceptions that many lawmakers held of higher educational opportunity for under-represented college students and the limited scope of approaches that they viewed as valid for expanding access. Rather than considering sweeping reforms like shifting government resources away from for-profit colleges and placing them in non-profit community colleges, state colleges, and HBCUs, lawmakers cautioned their colleagues about the consequences of cracking down on for-profit schools—namely, that doing so would restrict the number of options available to marginalized students.

In the course of deliberations, this issue of for-profit colleges and the access that they provide for disadvantaged students emerged as a key factor in lawmakers' hesitation to support various broad-reaching reforms. For example, Sen. Dan Quayle (R-IN) and Sen. Ted Kennedy (D-MA) had a telling exchange with Education Secretary Bennett and Deputy Undersecretary Bruce Carnes regarding the types of students who were targeted by for-profit schools with high default rates:

SENATOR QUAYLE: [C]an you give us a description of who these people are that are going to be affected [by efforts to decrease defaults]?

MR. CARNES: Yes, Senator. They tend to be low-income students. They tend to be students who are divorced or separated. There is a high representation of minorities here . . . . [T]hese particular individuals, it seems to me, are victimized and are taken advantage of. . .

SENATOR QUAYLE: Okay. Now, these are very important categories of people that you have just mentioned—low-income, children of divorced spouses, minorities.

SECRETARY BENNETT: Yes.

SENATOR QUAYLE: And we have got to make absolutely certain that as we institute some of these procedures—which I don't have any problem with—that these categories of people are the ones that really need our attention.

SECRETARY BENNETT: Right

SENATOR QUAYLE: I mean, you say that they have, in fact, been victimized; but if they don't have even a chance to do this, we have got to encourage some way to make sure that they get into the system.[43]

Secretary Bennett agreed with Sen. Quayle's point, but pointed out that "we are not doing anybody a favor, particularly not a poor kid or a low-income kid from a divorced or separated family, or whatever the category is, by allowing people to exploit him and the taxpayer at the same time."[44]

Sen. Kennedy eagerly followed up on this exchange, challenging Secretary Bennett's assertion that proprietary schools target low-income and minority young people:

> **SENATOR KENNEDY:** . . . Now we hear that we are going to save all these [minority, low-income, and divorced family] kids because we've got all these "hucksters" who are out there, pulling kids out of unemployment lines, throwing them into the proprietary schools and trying to make a buck on them. If you've got evidence of that, let's have it, Mr. Secretary, let's have it. Let's have it right now. Give me the documentation. Give me the studies that show in terms of proprietary schools, what percent of them are out there, huckstering young kids. I'd like to hear that right now.
>
> **SECRETARY BENNETT:** We'll have a study for you in four weeks—
>
> **SENATOR KENNEDY:** I don't want a study in some weeks. You have made the statement.
>
> **SECRETARY BENNETT:** Right.
>
> **SENATOR KENNEDY:** You have made the statement. You have made an indictment of all the proprietary schools of this country—
>
> **SECRETARY BENNETT:** Nonsense, nonsense. I certainly did not—
>
> **SENATOR KENNEDY:** Your staff has. I have the floor, Mr. Secretary, I have the floor. You'll have a chance.[45]

After this heated exchange, Senator Kennedy continued to pepper Secretary Bennett with questions about the prevalence of unscrupulous behaviors among proprietary schools that serve high proportions of disadvantaged and minority students and eventually focused on historically Black colleges:

> **SENATOR KENNEDY:** Could you tell us how many historically Black colleges have a high default rate?
>
> **SECRETARY BENNETT:** Using "high" as above 20 percent, I think it is something like two-thirds or three-quarters of the HBCUs are currently above 20 percent. But about half of those are within, I believe, the 20 to 30 percent range.
>
> **MR. CARNES:** That is correct.
>
> **SENATOR KENNEDY:** Are those Black colleges ripping the kids off?
>
> **SECRETARY BENNETT:** No, not for the most part, I don't think so. And I think we will see that default problem addressed by those institutions.[46]

Sen. Kennedy and other Democrats in the Senate, like Sen. Augustus Hawkins (D-LA), took issue with Bennett's endeavor to crack down on schools with high default rates because of the effect that it could have on the college completion rates of African Americans. They were concerned that a number of Historically Black Colleges and Universities (HBCUs), which provided substantial higher educational opportunity for African Americans, could be shut down under Bennett's proposal because they suffered from high student loan default rates.[47]

The following year, lawmakers continued to grapple with the task of addressing the problem of high student loan defaults and the prospect of placing more stringent regulations on for-profit colleges. As they considered how to move forward, the Reagan Administration's support for cutting federal financial aid loomed large in their minds. In June of 1988, the House Committee on Education and Labor's Subcommittee on Postsecondary Education again held hearings on the problem of student loan defaults. Shortly thereafter, Sen. Hawkins introduced a bill that would reverse the financial aid cuts that the Reagan Administration recommended. His bill also rejected the forceful regulations on colleges with high student loan default rates that Secretary Bennett had proposed.[48]

Efforts to crack down on for-profit colleges were weakened by the fact that William Bennett stepped down from his role as Secretary of Education in September of 1988, meaning that the effort lost a key policy entrepreneur. Moreover, when leaders of the Democrat-controlled House of Representatives produced an education proposal that would allocate more money to Pell grants and limit the Department of Education's authority to crack down on for-profit colleges, President Reagan and his new Education Secretary, Lauro Cavazos decided to strike a deal: they would essentially defer consideration of the education proposal to the next presidential administration if the Democrats dropped their bill.[49] Democrats accepted the deal. Thus, during the 1980s, the government's reluctance to effectively regulate for-profit colleges in the face of solid attempts made by Education Secretary William Bennett was a truly bipartisan phenomenon.

The Politics of a Tepid Crackdown in the Early 1990s

Taking office in January of 1989, President George H. W. Bush inherited the ongoing challenge of deciding how to address high student loan default rates and other problems wrought by unscrupulous for-profit colleges. Welfare reform during the late 1980s served to further entrench for-profit colleges into the social policy landscape, as the 1988 Family Support Act created new rules that required more welfare recipients to pursue work or job training programs.[50] In doing so, lawmakers provided additional impetus for hopeful students to turn to for-profit schools with their federal student loans and grants.

In June of 1989, the Bush Administration proposed regulations that would require for-profit colleges to produce "Teachout Arrangements" where they identify other institutions that offer similar programming in the case that the school closed or was otherwise unable to support students through the completion of their programs.[51] By the end of the decade as the range of abuses and fraud perpetrated by for-profit institutions were becoming increasingly well known, Democrats like Sen. Ted Kennedy and Rep. William Ford who had vocally advocated for for-profit schools had become more amenable to calls for meaningful regulation.[52]

Sen. Sam Nunn (D-GA) spearheaded the effort to place more exacting regulations on for-profit colleges as lawmakers worked to reauthorize the programs created under the Higher Education Act. From February through October of 1990, the Senate held hearings on the abuses of for-profit colleges. Sen. Nunn and the Senate Subcommittee on Investigations also produced a report that shed light on the continuing abuses perpetrated by proprietary colleges, noting that a disjointed and largely ineffectual system of oversight by federal, state, and non-governmental entities like accreditation agencies necessitated stronger federal intervention. The report provided a detailed overview of the unscrupulous and dishonest behavior in which for-profit schools engaged. For example, it quoted a former proprietary school recruiter who described the dominant approach to student recruitment:

> In the proprietary school business what you sell is 'dreams,' and so ninety-nine percent of the sales were made in poor, Black areas [at] welfare offices and unemployment lines, and in housing projects. My approach was that "if [a prospect] could breathe, scribble his name, had a driver's license, and was over 18 years of age," he was qualified for [the] program.[53]

As Suzanne Mettler notes, "this devastating report was signed by the subcommittee's bipartisan membership, a group that included a large number of both Republican and Democratic senators with strong records of working constructively with those in the other party."[54]

Witnesses representing for-profit trade and vocational schools engaged actively in these discussions, working to repair the reputation of the proprietary education sector. Among the participants providing information during hearings was Stephen Blair, president of the National Association of Trade and

Technical Schools. Blair argued that, although some for-profit trade schools engaged in questionable behaviors, this was not universally the case.[55] However, evidence from government agencies suggested that these behaviors were prevalent enough to warrant intervention. For example, a report from the US Department of Education claimed that for-profit colleges generated at least 75 percent of the fraud and abuse perpetrated against federal student loan programs.[56] Nevertheless, the House and Senate education committees failed to take serious action on the report that Sen. Nunn's subcommittee produced, but they did pass a budget bill that prevented schools with student loan default rates above 35 percent from participating in the program, with the understanding that the threshold would move to 30 percent in 1993.[57]

In addition to Sen. Nunn's efforts to reform government interaction with for-profit colleges, President George H. W. Bush's administration also worked toward this end. Bush's Secretary of Education, Lamar Alexander, agreed that reform was necessary to correct for for-profit schools' abuses of the federal student aid system.[58] In fact, in 1991, Alexander proposed that the government create a separate system of state assessment of for-profit schools that implemented federally established standards for things like degree completion, job placement, and other crucial student outcomes.[59]

In May of 1991, members of the House Committee on Education and Labor's Subcommittee on Postsecondary Education held hearings on program integrity and the reauthorizations of the 1965 Higher Education Act. Members of Congress brought forceful arguments about for-profit colleges and universities to the discussion. Representatives Maxine Waters (D-CA) and Bart Gordon (D-TN) were vocal advocates for reining in the unscrupulous behavior of for-profit schools. Rep. Waters offered a particularly powerful testimony in which she forcefully advocated for regulations against for-profit schools that were exploiting poor and overwhelmingly minority students in her East Los Angeles congressional district. She framed rigorous intervention as an imperative.

In her remarks before the subcommittee, Rep. Waters noted that she had worked to promote reform in for-profit recruitment and operation during her time as a state legislator in California saying, "most of my constituents are African American and Hispanic. Many of them are desperately looking for a better life. They're trying to achieve that dream by following the American way—educational advancement leading to job opportunities leading to economic betterment."[60] After describing some of the abuses that she had encountered and worked to combat in her California district, Waters made a point of addressing "two false issues frequently raised by vocational schools in attempting to hold on to the free flow of student loan dollars"[61]:

> These schools claim that they are the saviors of African American and Hispanic students who could not obtain any job training without their help. These schools attempt to intimidate political leaders from curbing their abuses by claiming that any reduction in money or increases in standards will create a system of educational apartheid, subjugating minority students to inferior or non-existent opportunities and foreclosing employment.
>
> This allegation is just nonsense; it's a lie. The current program only assures . . . vast profits to the unscrupulous and broken dreams to minority students.[62]

As they had during previous discussions of the issue, lobbyists representing trade schools objected to the charge that they were riddled with abuse. Stephen Blair of the National Association of Trade and Technical Schools agreed that reforms were necessary but emphasized the significance of these institutions for providing a pathway into skilled trades.[63] According to Blair, the Department of Education's emphasis on high default rates was problematic because such default rates could be a result of democratic admissions practices that offer opportunity to low-income, at-risk, urban students, as opposed to corruption.[64] In other words, Blair argued that the federal government could be trying to punish for-profit colleges for their efforts to diversify higher education.

Robert Beckwith, director of education policy for the Illinois State Chamber of Commerce similarly highlighted the importance of vocational education in his remarks, emphasizing the significance of for-profit schools for underrepresented minorities:

> From the 18th century to today private career schools have performed a vital service for an important part of our population. Private career schools educated a disproportionate percentage of women and minorities than other postsecondary education sectors. Nearly 40 percent of the students in private career schools are minorities and more than half are women. Nearly 45 percent of these students have an income of less than $11,000 and many have no other financial resources.[65]

Others echoed Beckwith's argument that for-profit colleges were a crucial avenue for upward mobility particularly for low-income, inner city students.[66] For example, Rep. William Ford (D-MI) who served as chairman of the House Education and Labor Committee took issue with the proposed regulations, arguing that for-profit trade schools represented the only higher educational opportunity available to many people.[67]

As lawmakers grappled with whether to incorporate increased regulation of non- profit colleges into their HEA reauthorization legislation, the media continued to shed light on the unscrupulous behaviors that had placed this issue on the political agenda in the first place. For example, one article in *The New York Times* noted that "Many of the trade schools aggressively recruit the poor, passing out leaflets in housing projects and welfare offices. School representatives help the students sign up for federally guaranteed loans for thousands of dollars, much of which is turned over to the schools."[68] Again, the issue of higher educational access for minorities and other under-represented students was used to sustain institutions that continued to subject these groups to deceptive recruitment tactics, subpar education, and lackluster job prospects.

Despite the rigorous discourse on for-profit colleges that occurred both within the halls of government and without, lawmakers declined to forcefully crack down on the sector. Instead, lawmakers passed light regulations aimed at addressing some of the fraud and corrupt behavior that had come to light in the previous decades. They made it illegal for proprietary colleges to tie their recruiters' pay to the number of students they enroll. They made it a policy to shut down colleges with student default rates that exceeded 25 percent for three consecutive years and created the aforementioned "90/10 rule," requiring schools receiving federal funds to generate at least 10 percent of its income from non-federal student aid sources.[69]

Nevertheless, the regulations stopped well short of the forceful reforms that were proposed during congressional hearings, including: (1) requiring colleges to demonstrate a proven record of success in student degree completion and job placement in order to receive funds, (2) requiring students to demonstrate their ability to benefit from the education that they plan to pursue, (3) ensuring that students are eligible for refunds if they withdraw from their courses of study, (4) discharging debt resulting from inadequate education and institutional misrepresentation, and (5) giving the US Department of Education the power to monitor the quality of schools and to ensure that they adhere to best practices.[70] When President Bush signed the HEA reauthorization bill into law on July 23, 1992, he highlighted the significance of the new provisions for addressing problems at for-profit schools, emphasizing that the legislation "contains a number of valuable program integrity and loan default prevention provisions. In particular, these provisions will crack down on sham schools that have defrauded students and the American taxpayer in the past."[71]

While the 1992 HRA reauthorization included some new provisions aimed at stemming abuse and fraud, these measures were modest and stopped short of the broad-reaching regulations that had been championed by former Education Secretary Bennett, Education Secretary Alexander, Rep. Maxine Waters, and others who fought for true reform.[72] As David Whitman notes, "increased oversight of for-profit schools was often avoided because, for distinct reasons, these institutions appeal to bipartisan sympathies."[73] The 1992 reauthorization of the Higher Education Act represents a powerful example of this phenomenon.

Conclusion

This historical case study suggests that politics has played a central role in federal lawmakers' failure to forcefully regulate for-profit colleges in the United States. Despite the sporadic efforts of executive branch agents and members of Congress since the 1970s, policymakers have only dabbled in light regulation, stopping short of the kind of reform necessary to counteract the profit-driven motives of for-profit educational institutions. Historical analysis of federal policy toward for-profit colleges suggests that the disparate political influence of for-profit colleges and underserved college students, the intermittent nature of strong advocacy for regulating for-profit colleges, and a history of Democratic and Republican reluctance to do so have shielded proprietary educational institutions from crucial oversight that would protect some of the nation's most vulnerable college students. Efforts to legitimize commodified higher education went so far as to appropriate the language of educational equity, casting their support for profit-driven education that often fell short of providing students with quality instruction as a mechanism for equal opportunity. In recent years, we have seen more concerted efforts by Democratic lawmakers to address the predatory actions of for-profit colleges, such as the Obama Administration's efforts to rein in those whose graduates are unqualified for gainful employment. Yet, shifts in political power have undone such efforts, and promoted a regression to the status quo of largely unregulated for-profit colleges.

Gaining insight into the tension between economic interests and efforts to promote equitable access to higher education that will promote economic empowerment for marginalized populations has important implications for democracy. Given that higher educational attainment is recognized as a central determinant of socioeconomic status and political engagement, correcting unscrupulous institutional behaviors that jeopardize Americans' ability to pursue quality education is a democratic imperative. Institutions that target vulnerable populations for their sub-optimal education actively oppose the legacy of government efforts to expand access to quality education and its democracy-supporting knowledge, skills, and experiences. As this analysis has shown, when in tension, capitalist interests have been prioritized over educational equity and, by extension, democratic interests. Yet and still, it is a democratic imperative that the government intervene to ensure equal opportunity for and equal protection of its citizens.

Notes

1. Robert Shireman, "The For-Profit College Story: Scandal, Regulate, Forget, Repeat," *The Century Foundation*, January 14, 2017: 4.
2. Hannah Appel and Astra Taylor, "Education with a Debt Sentence: For-Profit Colleges as American Dream Crushers and Factories of Debt," *New Labor Forum* 24, no. 1 (2015): 31–36, 32.
3. Suzanne Mettler, *Degrees of Inequality: How the Politics of Higher Education Sabotaged the American Dream* (New York: Basic Books, 2014); Justin Ortagus and Rodney Hughes, "Paying More for Less? A New Classification System to Prioritize Outcomes in Higher Education," *Third Way* [Report], March 3, 2021: 4–5, 8.
4. Bureau of Labor Statistics, "Education Pays" (2022), https://www.bls.gov/emp/chart-unemployment-earnings-education.htm.
5. Bureau of Labor Statistics, "Education Pays.
6. Jaleesa Bustamante, "Student Loan Debt Statistics," *EduationData.org, LLC*, 2020, https://educationdata.org/student-loan-debt-statistics
7. Sidney Verba, Kay Lehman Schlozman, and Henry E. Brady, *Voice and Equality: Civic Voluntarism in American Politics* (Cambridge, MA: Harvard University Press, 1995); Sidney Verba, Kay Lehman Schlozman, and Nancy Burns, *The Private Roots of Public Action: Gender, Equality, and Political Participation* (Cambridge, MA: Harvard University Press, 2001); Deondra Rose, *Citizens By Degree: Higher Education Policy and the Changing Gender Dynamics of American Citizenship* (New York: Oxford University Press, 2018).
8. Raymond E. Wolfinger and Steven J. Rosenstone, *Who Votes?* (New Haven, CT: Yale University Press, 1980), 33; Sidney Verba and Norman H. Nie, *Participation in America: Political Democracy and Social Equality* (Chicago, IL: University of Chicago Press, 1987); Stephen J. Rosenstone and John Marc Hansen, *Mobilization, Participation, and Democracy in America* (New York: Pearson, 2002).
9. Sarah Butrymowicz and Meredith Kolodner, "For-Profit Colleges, Long Troubled, See Surge Amid Pandemic," *The New York Times*, June 17, 2020. Available at: https://www.nytimes.com/2020/06/17/business/coronavirus-for-profit-colleges.html; Tressie McMillan Cottom, *Lower Ed: The Troubling Rise of For-Profit Colleges in the New Economy* (New York: The New Press, 2017); Mettler, *Degrees of Inequality*.
10. Ortagus and Hughes, "Paying More for Less?," 7.
11. Ortagus and Hughes, "Paying More for Less?," 5–7; see also Mettler, *Degrees of Inequality*.
12. Appel and Taylor, "Education with a Debt Sentence," 31–36, 32. Appel and Taylor illustrate the striking difference between the high cost of attendance at some for-profit colleges compared to their public community college counterparts: "The Medical Assistant program at for-profit Heald College in Fresno, California costs $22,275. A comparable program at Fresno City College costs $1,650. An associate degree in paralegal studies at Everest College in Ontario, California costs $41,149, compared with $2,392 for the same degree at Santa Ana College, a mere thirty-minute drive away" (31–32; see also David Deming et al., "For-Profit Colleges," *The Future of Children* 23, no. 1 2013: 137–63). Such comparisons highlight the fact that, although they target low-income students, for-profit colleges are not necessarily the most cost-effective alternatives.
13. Anne Schneider and Helen Ingram, "Social Construction of Target Populations: Implications for Politics and Policy," *American Political Science Review* 87, no. 2 (1993): 334–47.
14. Schneider and Ingram, "Social Construction of Target Populations," 334–347, 338.
15. Schneider and Ingram, "Social Construction of Target Populations," 334–347, 338.
16. Schneider and Ingram, "Social Construction of Target Populations," 334–347, 338.
17. Caren A. Arbeit and Laura Horn, "A Profile of the Enrollment Patterns and Demographic Characteristics of Undergraduates at For-Profit Institutions," *US Department of Education* [Report] (2017): 2. Available at: https://nces.ed.gov/pubs2017/2017416.pdf; see also Deming et al., "For-Profit Colleges," 137–63.
18. Christopher J. Salemme, 2018. "Unpatriotic Profit: How For-Profit Colleges Target Veterans and What the Government Must Do to Stop Them," *BYU Journal of Public Law* 32: 89–116.

19. Tiffany F. Boykin, "For Profit, For Success, For Black Men: A Review of Literature on Urban For-Profit Colleges and Universities," *Urban Education* 52, no. 9 (2017): 1140–62, 1144; Matthew Munro, "Where the Federal Government Fails State Legislatures Can Succeed: Eliminating Student Debt by Regulating For-Profit Colleges and Universities," *Journal of College and University Law* 41, no. 3 (2015): 627–55, 629.
20. Margaret Mattes, "8 Facts that Will Make You Think Twice Before Enrolling at a For-Profit College," *The Century Foundation*, May 30, 2017a. Available at: https://tcf.org/content/facts/8-facts-will-make-think-twice-enrolling-profit-college/?session=1
21. Constance Iloh, "Exploring the For-Profit Experience: An Ethnography of a For- Profit College," *American Educational Research Journal* 53, no. 3 (2016): 427–455, 428; see also Appel and Taylor, "Education with a Debt Sentence," 31–36, 32.
22. Lawrence E. Gladieux and Thomas R. Wolanin, *Congress and the Colleges: The National Politics of Higher Education* (Washington, D.C.: Lexington Books, 1976), 109.
23. Mettler, *Degrees of Inequality*, 92–93; Munro, "Where the Federal Government Fails State Legislatures Can Succeed," 629.
24. See, for example, David Whitman, "Vietnam Vets and a New Student Loan Program Bring New College Scams," *The Century Foundation*, February 13, 2017c. Available at: https://tcf.org/content/report/vietnam-vets-new-student-loan-program-bring-new-college-scams/
25. See, for example, "Proprietary Vocational Schools," Hearings Before a Subcommittee of the Committee on Government Operations, United States House of Representatives, 93d Congress, 2nd Session (Washington, D.C.: US Government Printing Office, July 16–25, 1974); "Reducing Abuses in Proprietary Vocational Education," 93d Congress, 2nd Session, House Report No. 93–1649 (Washington, D.C.: US Government Printing Office, 1974), 9.
26. "Proprietary Vocational Schools," 1.
27. "Proprietary Vocational Schools," 1.
28. "Proprietary Vocational Schools," 6.
29. Eric Wentworth, "Folding Schools Increase Loan Defaults," *The Washington Post*, June 24, 1974: A1.
30. "Proprietary Vocational Schools," 10.
31. "Proprietary Vocational Schools," 10.
32. "Proprietary Vocational Schools," 13.
33. "Reducing Abuses in Proprietary Vocational Education," 2.
34. "Reducing Abuses in Proprietary Vocational Education," 9.
35. David Whitman, "The Reagan Administration's Campaign to Rein in Predatory For-Profit Colleges," *The Century Foundation*, February 13, 2017a: 2. Available at: https://tcf.org/content/report/reagan-administrations-campaign-rein-predatory-profit-colleges/
36. Jason DeParle, "Trade Schools Near Success As They Lobby for Survival," *The New York Times*, March 25, 1992, A01.,
37. Whitman, "The Reagan Administration's Campaign to Rein in Predatory For-Profit Colleges," 2.
38. Mettler, *Degrees of Inequality*, 95.
39. Whitman, "The Reagan Administration's Campaign to Rein in Predatory For-Profit Colleges," 4.
40. Margaret Mattes, "The GOP Has a Long History of Cracking Down on "Sham Schools," *The Century Foundation*, January 12, 2017b: 4. Available at: https://tcf.org/content/commentary/gop-long-history-cracking-sham-schools/
41. "Problems of Default in the Guaranteed Student Loan Program," 100th Congress, 1st Session, Hearings Before the Subcommittee on Education, Arts and Humanities of the Committee on Labor and Human Resources, United States Senate (December 11 and 18, 1987), 25.
42. "Problems of Default in the Guaranteed Student Loan Program," 27.
43. "Problems of Default in the Guaranteed Student Loan Program," 80–81.
44. "Problems of Default in the Guaranteed Student Loan Program," 81.
45. "Problems of Default in the Guaranteed Student Loan Program," 82.
46. "Problems of Default in the Guaranteed Student Loan Program," 85.
47. Whitman, "The Reagan Administration's Campaign to Rein in Predatory For-Profit Colleges," 8.

48. Whitman, "The Reagan Administration's Campaign to Rein in Predatory For-Profit Colleges," 9.
49. Whitman, "The Reagan Administration's Campaign to Rein in Predatory For-Profit Colleges," 9.
50. Jason DeParle, "Trade Schools: Defaults and Broken Promises," *The New York Times*, August 9, 1990.
51. David Whitman, "When President George H. W. Bush 'Cracked Down' on Abuses at For-Profit Colleges," *The Century Foundation*, March 9, 2017b: 6. Available at: https://tcf.org/content/report/president-george-h-w-bush-cracked-abuses-profit-colleges/
52. Mettler, *Degrees of Inequality*, 95.
53. "Abuses in Federal Student Aid Programs. Report Made by the Permanent Subcommittee on Investigations of the Committee on Governmental Affairs United States Senate," Senate-R-102-58 (1991), 16–17. Available at: https://files.eric.ed.gov/fulltext/ED332631.pdf
54. Mettler, *Degrees of Inequality*, 97.
55. DeParle, "Trade Schools: Defaults and Broken Promises."
56. William Beaver, "For-Profit Higher Education: A Social and Historical Analysis," *Sociological Viewpoints* 25, no. 1 (2009): 53–73, 57.
57. Mettler, *Degrees of Inequality*, 17; Whitman, "When President George H. W. Bush 'Cracked Down' on Abuses at For-Profit Colleges," 7.
58. Jason DeParle, "Panel Finds Wide Abuse in Student Loan Program," *The New York Times*, May 21, 1991, A019.
59. Mattes, "The GOP Has a Long History of Cracking Down on "Sham Schools," 4.
60. "Hearings on the Reauthorization of the Higher Education Act of 1965: Program Integrity," Hearings Before the Subcommittee on Postsecondary Education of the Committee on Education and labor, US House of Representatives, 102d Congress, 1st Session. Serial No. 102-39 (Washington, D.C.: US Government Printing Office, May 21, 29, and 20, 1991), 49; see also Beaver, "For-Profit Higher Education: A Social and Historical Analysis," 53–73 and Mettler, *Degrees of Inequality*, 87–88.
61. "Hearings on the Reauthorization of the Higher Education Act of 1965: Program Integrity," 52.
62. "Hearings on the Reauthorization of the Higher Education Act of 1965: Program Integrity," 52.
63. DeParle, "Panel Finds Wide Abuse in Student Loan Program," A019.
64. Michael Winerip, "Billions for School are Lost in Fraud, Waste, and Abuse," *The New York Times*, February 2, 1994, A01.
65. "Hearings on the Reauthorization of the Higher Education Act of 1965: Program Integrity," 887.
66. Beaver, "For-Profit Higher Education: A Social and Historical Analysis," 53–73; Whitman, "When President George H. W. Bush 'Cracked Down' on Abuses at For-Profit Colleges," 10–13; "Hearings on the Reauthorization of the Higher Education Act of 1965: Program Integrity," 20–22.
67. "Hearings on the Reauthorization of the Higher Education Act of 1965: Program Integrity," 9–10.
68. DeParle, "Panel Finds Wide Abuse in Student Loan Program," A019.
69. Beaver, "For-Profit Higher Education: A Social and Historical Analysis," 53–73; James Dean Ward and William G. Tierney, "Regulatory Enforcement as Policy: Exploring Factors Related to State Lawsuits Against For-Profit Colleges," *American Behavioral Scientist* 61, no. 14 (2018): 1799–1823, 1800; Whitman, "When President George H. W. Bush 'Cracked Down' on Abuses at For-Profit Colleges," 15.
70. "Hearings on the Reauthorization of the Higher Education Act of 1965: Program Integrity," 56–57.
71. George H. W. Bush, "Statement on Signing the Higher Education Amendments of 1992," July 23, 1992. Online by Gerhard Peters and John T. Woolley, *The American Presidency Project* (1992). Available at: http://www.presidency.ucsb.edu/ws/index.php?pid=21259
72. The legislation made it a policy to shut down colleges with student default rates that exceeded 25 percent for three consecutive years. It created the "90/10 rule," which required schools

receiving federal funds to generate at least 10 percent of its income from non-federal student aid sources. It created State Postsecondary Review Entities (SPREs) that would supposedly tackle fraud, abuse, and high-default rates within for-profit colleges, and it required states to produce debt-to-earnings tests to help determine whether schools were providing a pathway to gainful employment. Beaver, "For-Profit Higher Education: A Social and Historical Analysis," 53–73; Whitman, "When President George H. W. Bush 'Cracked Down' on Abuses at For-Profit Colleges," 15.

73. Whitman, "When President George H. W. Bush 'Cracked Down' on Abuses at For-Profit Colleges," 14.

10

The Fourth Subsidiary Ideal

Empowering Economies

DANIELLE ALLEN

Introduction

This chapter seeks to address some difficult questions about how political equality should be weighed in a theory of justice. For instance, this question seems obvious: "Don't people need material supports for the political equality you have in mind?" And "How can you have social connectedness or *social* equality when great *material* inequality exists and power differences flow from that inequality?" In other words, my consistent focus on the theme of political equality may seem willfully avoidant, as if I were simply disregarding some of the hardest problems currently facing the citizens of developed democracies and their representatives—namely, problems of political economy. After all, our politics are beset by the consequences of significant increases in income and wealth inequality within the borders of any given developed democracy. Moreover, in the United States, other kinds of entrenched inequality—for instance, structural racism—seem to render the prospect of a truly connected society remote.

I argue that a discussion of political economy should be held in abeyance in order to discipline us to think about forms of equality other than the aterial, and to restore economic questions to a secondary place within the structure of human aspiration and theories of justice. This strategy borrows from the philosophical perspective of Hannah Arendt. I propose to view economic questions as critical to laying a foundation for political equality and human freedom, but not as ends in themselves. Whereas political equality and human freedom are intrinsically valuable, economic justice is an instrumental objective, in my account. We seek economic justice—or, I would say, economic egalitarianism—in

Danielle Allen, *The Fourth Subsidiary Ideal*. In: *Can Democracy and Capitalism Be Reconciled?*.
Edited by: Sidney M. Milkis and Scott C. Miller, Oxford University Press. © Oxford University Press (2025).
DOI: 10.1093/9780197774731.003.0011

order to secure political equality and human freedom. We can find our way to the necessary political economy only if we discipline ourselves to ask questions about the economy secondarily to clarifying for ourselves the content of political equality.

The goal of developing a political economy compatible with the principle of difference—"social and economic inequalities are to be arranged so that they are . . . to the greatest benefit of the least advantaged"[1]—without domination is to support political equality. This means the goal of political economy, on this account of justice, is to build empowering economies, economies that empower the citizenry broadly to succeed as civic participants. Let me further specify the ideal of an "empowering economy." An empowering economy provides the material bases of empowerment. To paraphrase George Marshall in his announcement of the post-World War II Marshall Plan, we need an economy that works—that delivers growth and productivity and stable transactions and prices (the opposite of Venezuela)—"so as to permit the emergence of political and social conditions in which *free institutions* can exist" (Marshall, 1947; emphasis added). On my definition, free institutions will incorporate the principle of full inclusion. Consequently, the goal is not only a dynamic but also an inclusive economy—where all are empowered. There is no room for domination in this economy. But how is this achieved?

Four design principles are key. First, an empowering economy organizes the productive structure of the economy in accordance with the principle of difference without domination; this means focusing on building an economy around free labor and democracy-supporting firms and aiming for a good-jobs economy. Second, an empowering economy supports investments in bridging relationships that cut across cleavages that otherwise emerge as a result of market competition or social competition; this commitment orients policy toward productive collaborations among the public sector, market organizations, and nonprofit concerns (including universities), avoiding domination by any one of those sectors.[2] Third, an empowering economy depends on democratic steering of the economy—through fiscal policy, public-goods investment, chartering authority over monetary policy, and rule-making—rather than on unchecked delegation to technocrats. Experts should be valued advisers but should not themselves rule. Fourth, an empowering economy rests on charters and rules that protect equal basic liberties, both positive and negative, both directly and indirectly.

An empowering economy protects equal basic liberties directly through securing the rights to property, private contract, and association as well as rights of political participation and political equality. It protects the basic liberties indirectly by choosing methods for securing those rights that steer the economy overall in directions that reinforce difference without domination in the political and social spheres. In other words, neither the productive structure nor the distributive framework of the economy should erode basic liberties or access to political equality. Taken as a whole, this goal of a dynamic and inclusive economy and these design principles constitute an ideal of a market-based economy whose rules and charters shape emergent social patterns in egalitarian directions and whose operations also benefit from those social patterns. *This is a power-sharing liberalism where a virtuous and mutual cycle of reinforcement has been set up among the political institutions of an egalitarian participatory constitutional democracy, the social institutions of a connected society, and market structures of the empowering* economy. The goal of this chapter is to specify further the design principles entailed by this ideal of an empowering economy, and also to specify the concrete policy choices that flow from them. The aspiration for this framework is to equip economists with the right questions to answer to support a flourishing democracy. I seek a paradigm change: a final section on the place of education in economic policy will help drive home the nature of that paradigm change.

As the eighteenth-century jurist and philosopher Cesare Beccaria put it: "In every human society, there is an effort continually tending to confer on one part the height of power and happiness, and to reduce the other to the extreme of weakness and misery. The intent of good laws is to oppose this effort and to diffuse their influence universally and equally" (Beccaria, 1872). I agree. Here let me offer a brief example of the role of law in constituting the framework for political economy. I draw on the figure of one of the founders of the American political order, Thomas Jefferson. He is famous not merely as the drafter of the Declaration of Independence, the first secretary of state, and the third president; he was also responsible for bringing an end in the infant United States to primogeniture laws of inheritance where property passes to the firstborn son. He understood this legal structure to secure Europe's system of large, aristocratic landed estates. He believed that preserving political equality required organizing land and capital in ways that worked against the concentrated accumulation of wealth by a small elite. He sought the fragmentation of large estates into a network of midsize properties. This was to secure the famous middling-class economy that Aristotle, like both Jefferson and Marshall, thought was necessary for a stable polity capable of securing conditions for human flourishing and the emergence of free institutions.

Land, labor, and capital should be organized by a legal framework that protects basic rights of contract, property, and association as well as positive rights of participation. As a matter of their ordinary, day-to-day workings, political institutions, even those of the most laissez-faire variety, establish the legal frameworks that organize land, labor, and capital. To identify arrangements for land, labor, and capital as part of the basic structure of society and to propose attending to these domains as a matter of basic right is not to propose new areas of intervention. It is, rather, to propose that we deploy already existing structures of intervention—in the form of the law—in directions that protect equal basic rights and political equality.

A Paradigm Change: Social Connectedness, the "Relational Turn," and Empowering Economies

Before turning to the specifics of an empowering economy and its related design principles, I want to pause to underscore that the over-arching principle of difference without domination changes the focus of economic analysis from transactions to social relations. This is a fundamental paradigm change. Here I am channeling the work of economist Glenn Loury, who begins a recent essay with an image of an economist who developed a tantra-like mantra to fend off the nightmare that the discipline of economics cannot explain or address racial inequality: "Relations before transactions; relations before transactions; relations before transactions. . . .(171)"[3] Loury's imagined economist chants this, trying to free himself from his discipline's insistent focus on transactions.

Loury uses this mantra to initiate a "relational turn" within the discipline of economics. When he scrutinizes the landscape of any society for inequalities, he begins by assuming that the explanation for the relevant inequality lies not in a series of exchanges or transactions but in an underlying structure of relationality that is itself generating the relevant, inegalitarian transactions. This is what it means to recognize the economy as embedded in society. Working with a colleague, Rajiv Sethi, on issues of crime and punishment, Loury makes the argument that stereotypes themselves can help generate harmful social equilibria capable of explaining disparities in criminality, sentencing, and incarceration. For Loury, when we see a nonrandom distribution of people in organizations and institutions, that observation is the starting point for an inquiry. We have a reason to ask, "What nonrandom process has led to this result?" The mere fact that a nonrandom process has led to a result—say, the percentage of national prizewinning poets from Poetry Lover Land is out of proportion to the percentage of the national population that lives in Poetry Lover Land—does not in itself delegitimize that result. One first has to know whether the nonrandom process that resulted in the failure of this distribution of national prizewinning poets to mirror the demographics of the national population is itself legitimate or illegitimate. To distinguish between legitimate and illegitimate social and institutional processes, we employ a principle of non-domination as an analytic tool. Legitimate social processes are those that, even if they lead to disparate outcomes, are free of domination. To address problems of material and social inequality, then, one must focus not merely on transactional approaches to distribution—the question of whether the transaction of the prize selection process functioned appropriately and without discrimination—but on achieving healthy processes and practices for the distribution of the opportunities that led to participation in the contest in the first place. Are these processes and practices characterized by non-domination? While the over-representation of people from Poetry Lover Land on the stage at poetry prize ceremonies may not be a cause for concern, the under-representation of women in the sciences will be. The former is unlikely to result from relational structures of domination; the latter, quite likely to do so.[4]

The principle of difference without domination, then, shifts our attention from transactions to relations. This shift of focus helps make visible a core problem with Rawls's difference principle. Rawls's difference principle lies at the heart of a great deal of contemporary policymaking in liberal democracies. Rawls wrote that social and economic inequalities must satisfy the condition that they be to the greatest benefit of the least-advantaged members of society.[5] This principle has been used almost exclusively to address questions of how the talented, who excel professionally, should be compensated, and how the rewards of a growth economy driven by those talented professionals should be distributed, and, even more importantly, redistributed. In other words, *the focus is wholly transactional* and oriented toward private compensation contracts and public social-welfare contracts. The point of Loury's mantra—"relations before transactions"—is that contemporary economics, like Rawlsian liberalism, overlooks the question of the structure of social relationships that lie beneath an economy and generate patterns of opportunity, modes of production, and emergent patterns of first-order distribution prior to any taxation-based redistribution.[6] The neoliberal economy—with increasing rates of return directed toward the holders of capital and the possessors of high levels of education—produces a skewed distribution, and the Rawlsian principle (or an extension of it, like guaranteed basic income) provides a way of remediating or mitigating that skew through redistribution. But the Rawlsian principle does not provide a means to address the underlying structures of relationality that generate the highly skewed distributions in the first place (and the same is true for a universal basic income).

In contrast, Loury asks us to shift our gaze to the underlying relational organization of the economy. If we see economic egalitarianism, the application of the principle of difference without domination in the social realm is the place to start. Particularly in conditions of pluralism, we can achieve an egalitarian economy that secures difference without domination only if the underlying pluralistic social structure is also egalitarian. The emergence of a connected society, in the social realm, can be expected to have egalitarian impacts on patterns in the distribution of economic resources, in the inverse of the situation of segregation.

Yet we can go beyond the ideal of a connected society. We might, Loury suggested, undertake a more comprehensive effort to identify and reform the laws structuring the forms of relationality undergirding any given economy. The next step is to convert the language of relationality and non-domination into the vocabulary of economic policy. The three policy domains of economics are preproduction, production, and postproduction. As economists Dani Rodrik and Stefanie Stantcheva put it : "Pre-production policies determine the endowments that people bring to the market, such as education and skills, financial capital, social networks and social capital. Production-stage policies are those that directly shape the employment, investment, and innovation decisions of firms." In contrast, postproduction policies "are ex post policies, that transfer income and wealth once they have been realized (e.g., redistributive transfers, progressive taxation, and social insurance). They reshape inequalities after the economic decisions regarding employment, investments, or innovations have been made."[7] The kinds of egalitarian policy available in each domain are listed in Table 10.1.

As in the social realm, in the economic realm, too, the standard of aspiring to achieve difference without domination does not necessarily generate a need for new domains of policy or services. Instead, it requires a review of current policies across preproductive, productive, and postproductive domains of the economy (investments in education, labor policy, trade policy, the organization of the firm, etc.) with a view to assessing how those current policies protect (or fail to protect) equal basic liberties. Where they fail to protect equal basic liberties or to pass a strict scrutiny test for the achievement of difference without domination, then we have found places where we need to adjust our policies.

The answer to how we can achieve an empowering economy, focusing on the relational above the transactional, emerges quickly: the most important relational aspects of the economy, in contrast to its transactional elements, reside in the domain of production. Indeed, when we apply the principle of strict scrutiny for difference *with* domination to the economic realm, we find that the most salient issues concern the domain of production: reduced labor mobility and job lock, problematic immigration policies, practices of domination that have developed inside firms, and the emergence of market concentrations, particularly in the technology sector. In addition, we will quickly see that democratic steering of the economy has been undermined across all three domains (preproduction, production, and postproduction) by the acquisition of political power by wealthy elites,[8] by technocratic independence, and by the technocratic orientation toward transactional rather than relational questions.

Table 10.1 **Types of egalitarian economic policy**

		At what stage of the economy does policy intervene?		
		Preproduction	**Production**	**Postproduction**
What kind of inequality do we care about?	*Bottom*	• Endowment polices (health, education) • Universal basic income	• Minimum wage • Job guarantee	• Transfers (e.g., EITC) • Full-employment macro policies
	Middle	• Public spending on higher education	• Good-jobs policies • Industrial relations and labor laws • Sectoral wage boards • Trade agreements • Innovation policies	• Safety nets • Social in-surance policies
	Top	• Inheritance/ estate taxes	• Regulation • Antitrust	

Source: Closing presentation by Dani Rodrik, Harvard University, at the conference "Combating Inequality: Rethinking Policies to Reduce Inequality in Advanced Economies," Peterson Institute for International Economics, October 17–18, 2019.

To clarify the nature of these challenges, and solutions to them, we will focus on three of the design principles for an empowering economy: (1) free labor, democracy-supporting firms, and a good-jobs economy; (2) investment in bridging relationships; and (3) democratic steering of the economy. With regard to the fourth design principle that I named at the start—direct rights protection—I am taking as given throughout this chapter that any policy that will align with justice by means of democracy will affirm direct protection of negative and positive liberties. Those protections are precompetitive matters, and so I assume them in what follows. The focus for the rest of this chapter will be on how the first three design principles for an empowering economy can help develop a political economy that not only directly but also indirectly supports positive and negative basic liberties—and on how, taken together, these add up to a paradigm change.

The First Design Principle: Free Labor, Democracy-Supporting Firms, and a Good-Jobs Economy

Free Labor

Building an empowering economy starts with a commitment to free labor, which we can update for the twenty-first century as a commitment to building a good-jobs economy. Focusing on overall GDP is not enough to measure whether we are building an inclusive and dynamic economy that connects all to opportunity and security, and thereby provides a foundation for political empowerment. In addition to measuring the overall output of the economy, we also need to track how well we are doing at creating good jobs and at ensuring that they are available across society. A good job enables a middle-class existence, by a region's standards, with enough income for housing, food, transportation, education, and other family expenses, as well as some saving. More broadly, good jobs provide workers with clear career paths, possibilities of self-development, flexibility, responsibility, fulfillment, and time and stability to support civic participation.[9]

But *the very first principle of a good-jobs economy is free labor*. This means ending enslavement—a problem that still exists worldwide, including in the United States[10]—and ending wage theft. After non-slavery, the next core requirement of free labor is labor mobility, the idea that workers need to be able to move to where opportunities are.[11] A striking feature of the contemporary American economy is the reversal of historical trends of high mobility. In the period from 1947 to 1970, roughly 20 percent of Americans a year changed residence. A steady decline began in 1971, and in 2018, for the first time since 1947, fewer than 10 percent of Americans moved.[12] Strikingly, the length and impact of the Great Recession of 2008 were not significantly resolved through mobility, as had been the case in previous economic downturns.[13] While the housing crisis of that period and underwater mortgages were among the drivers of this mobility decline, they were not the only causes. The decline has been steady since the early 1970s, with the exception of an increase for one year in the mid-1980s. Broader issues of housing costs in high-opportunity areas, transportation challenges, and job lock occasioned by our fragmented and nonportable health care system (the modern-day version of serfdom) have also contributed.[14]

Achieving free labor requires ensuring that workers are able to exit unsatisfactory work environments and move to alternatives.[15] If free labor is to be a reality, housing, transportation, and related policy areas must be organized to support the mobility of workers. There are answers to each of these problems—often cultivated at the level of city or state. Minneapolis is changing its zoning laws to permit greater density of housing and break the monopoly of the rich over residences near employment. Massachusetts is changing zoning to support density near transit. Mortgage insurance would be another mechanism to free people from currently existing housing traps. By maintaining the individual mandate for health insurance, Massachusetts continues to sustain a market that makes insurance both affordable and adequate with regard to the provision of care, including insurance independent of any employer. One can take a leap and quit a job in Massachusetts without having to forgo access to medical care. Policies that increase mobility end serfdom and affect the macroeconomy for the better. We need to develop a bundle of policies that invest in people, that break up the monopolies over opportunity held by a few, and that undo the housing and (in the United States) healthcare traps that keep people locked in place.[16]

Mobility on its own, however, is not enough. The principle of free labor requires supporting labor mobility with access to political voice. Workers who move without acquiring political voice find themselves easily dominated. The fact that the United States has approximately 11 million undocumented residents with no formal pathway to political voice has eroded the working-class component of the electorate and public discourse. Many have observed the erosion of labor's bargaining power over the past 50 years. The inability of a meaningful subset of the population to participate in the election of representatives who might take up labor issues has been a contributory factor, as political scientists Christopher Hare and Keith Poole argue.[17] Even more striking, they make the case that the absence of noncitizen workers from the pool of potential voters has contributed to polarization:

> The steady growth in income inequality and changes in immigration trends in the United States over the last half century also have implications for political polarization. Poorer citizens routinely exhibit lower levels of political participation, and the influx of immigrants who are low-income workers and/or non-citizens has further increased the proportion of non-voters at the bottom end of the income distribution. In effect, this has shifted the position of the median income voter upward along the income distribution and, thus, the active electorate is less supportive than the mass public of government spending on redistributive social welfare policies. This helps explain how the Republican Party has been able to move steadily rightward over the last 40 years without major electoral consequences, whereas Democrats have not been able to move further left than where the party was in the 1960s.[18]

Hare and Poole's argument suggests that we should think of the problem of polarization as, in part, reflecting a decline in political competitiveness as the range of opinion within the electorate shrinks through exclusion and the erosion of fully inclusive political equality. The health of democracy requires full inclusion. Now it turns out that the health of the economy does too. The protection of labor—and pursuit of the principle of free labor—depends on the access of workers to political voice. This ultimately requires a revised approach to immigration.

The policy proposal I prescribe calls for a sponsorship model of immigration, an expanded version of what Canada currently employs. The sponsorship model would secure political voice for migrants in the wealthy developed democracies that received them. But that picture of immigration policy requires one further detail. The effort to ensure that labor is free requires democracies that are receiving countries to invest in the conditions that enable free labor in the sending countries. Even foreign policy can be a matter of political economy. Securing free labor in wealthy countries may require supporting the development of the conditions for free labor in sending countries, lest we find ourselves building our own prosperity on extraction from others, for instance on the labor of workers who lack access to political voice in unstable societies. For instance, in the United States the question might be how to help stabilize functioning legal regimes in Central and South America. The goal is not to build democratic political institutions in other countries but merely, through investments in economies and a healthy civil society, to foster the conditions in which such institutions can exist—à la Marshall Plan.

In addition to securing both exit (via mobility) and voice for workers, and in order to realize in concrete form the design principle of a political economy built on free labor, a just political economy will give workers a meaningful opportunity for "loyalty" inside the firm. In Albert Hirschman's classic interpretation of social contract theory and its economic implications, the power that comes to members of an organization from "voice," specifically, can be exercised either on the outside (through protest or litigation, for instance) or on the inside. The latter occurs when the relevant organization functions to ensure that members are heard when they propose reforms or improvements and therefore that they have good reason to be "loyal." The idea that a healthy economy requires voice internally for members of organizations, such as firms, aligns with a theory of justice guided by an over-arching principle of difference without domination. A key element of realizing free labor will be ensuring democratization of the firm itself. This brings us to the need for democracy-supporting firms, a second key component of a good-jobs economy.

Democracy-Supporting Firms

I am not the first political philosopher to seek to address topics of political economy from within an account of justice that takes public autonomy, political equality, or democracy as its starting point. Both Elizabeth Anderson and

Carol Gould have already advanced this line of argument. They, too, argue for democratization of the firm.

Elizabeth Anderson famously opened up this line of work with her 1999 essay, "What Is the Point of Equality?" That essay, like this book, develops a critique of Rawls's *Theory of Justice* for its failure adequately to recognize and protect political equality. Over time, Anderson has expanded her analysis of equality into a theory of freedom, focusing on achieving a conjunction of negative freedom, positive freedom, and republican freedom—in her vocabulary, a combination of freedom from interference, freedom to participate, and freedom from domination. In her 2015 Tanner Lectures, "Liberty, Equality, and Private Government," Anderson argues for applying this theory of freedom to the organization of the capitalist firm and provides a framework for recon stituting labor rights. In the United States, she argues, "the boundary of the firm is defined as the point at which markets [and market freedoms] end and authoritarian centralized planning and direction begin."[19] She continues: "Why do we not recognize such a pervasive part of our social landscape for what it is? Should we not subject these forms of government to at least as much critical scrutiny as we pay to the democratic state?"[20] Anderson argues that justice requires us to ensure that the vertical or linking relationships within organizations, like firms or other units of economic activity, are not characterized by domination. Relevant issues can range from compensation, workplace governance, and firm ownership to matters like assignment of hours and access to time for bathroom breaks. The assignment of hours is particularly important from the point of view of whether workers can participate in civil society and political life versus having all their time consumed by the need to secure basic necessities or dominated by the arbitrariness of how hours are assigned, with the result that they cannot plan for other activities.[21] Anderson concludes by arguing for legal reform in support of worker freedom and worker participation in firm governance, holding up the German model of codetermination as one successful example.

Carol Gould also applies a theory of justice that starts from an argument for the good of democracy to political economy, arguing for, in her ideal framework, worker ownership and self-management of firms and, as second best, participatory and democratic management.[22] In other words, as developed by Anderson and Gould, an important step toward a political economy of empowering economies and achievement of free labor would be to reintroduce principles of human freedom to the legal structures used to frame employer-laborer relations and firm management. Changes such as these would help firms evolve in a democracy-supporting direction.

The arguments of both Anderson and Gould contain two particularly valuable ideas. First, they restore the possibility for the redevelopment of freedom and social equality inside the workplace, including even in workplaces with the necessary hierarchies of a division of labor. They advance the cause of difference without domination by identifying instruments that can be used to structure labor contracts so that the forms of differentiation that emerge in a capitalist economy do not articulate with domination. Second, and even more important, at the core of their economic argument is a shift of focus from transactions to relations. Their question is not, in the first instance, what wage structure or CEO compensation structure should obtain in a firm, but what structure of relations should obtain. The implicit presumption is that democracy-enhancing relationality inside the firm will drive transactions, too, in democracy-enhancing directions. Again, the German example provides some evidence in support of that hypothesis: worker ownership is linked to lower levels of CEO pay.

In *Capital in the Twenty-First Century*, French economist Thomas Piketty pursues a historical investigation of causes of income and wealth inequality. Part of his argument is much like that in the rest of the economics literature, namely, that skills-biased technological change has driven a wage premium on skill that has produced distributive inequality. Yet income growth at the highest end accruing to what he calls "supermanagers" reflects social acceptance of skyhigh executive pay. In his argument, such social norms constitute and reinforce a political ideology endorsing "hypermeritocracy." Reining in income inequality therefore requires social and political change—that is, a change in the values driving firm behavior.[23]

In the interest of spurring such a change in values, Harvard Business School professor Rebecca Henderson argues for the need to encourage the emergence of "purpose-driven" firms.[24] Her colleague Malcolm Salter argues that firms should, can, and sometimes do extend their sense of purpose beyond shareholder value maximization and profit maximization to what he calls "reciprocal justice." He makes these arguments as part of an effort to revive "stakeholder capitalism," in contrast to "share-holder" capitalism. Whereas shareholder capitalism orients all attention and transactional energy toward the owners of capital and profit, "stake-holder capitalism" takes its sense of purpose from the consequences of commercial operations not only for shareholders but also for labor, communities, and polities. Salter writes:

> In its most plain form, reciprocal justice is achieved when the standard of "fairness" or "fair return" governs relationships (or transactions) among various parties comprising the enterprise. By direct implication, legitimate corporate purpose according to the principle of reciprocal justice should reflect a fair balancing of interests of parties comprising the enterprise and affected by the enterprise, recognizing that each of these parties have different minimum thresholds of "fair returns" and fair treatment necessary to keep them as participants in, and supporters

> of, the enterprise. For employees that minimum is typically defined by the value of wages and benefits; for shareholders that minimum may be defined by their required rate of return on investment considering the riskiness of that investment; for the community affected by the enterprise the accounting may be less quantitative but no less critical.[25]

The new and increasingly frequent requirements that prompt business enterprises to produce environmental impact statements as part of justifying an investment provides an example of how innovative forms of accounting can help redirect capitalist behavior. Henderson has developed approaches to performance measurement to support evolution of firms in this direction. She argues that "reimagining capitalism requires embracing the idea that while firms must be profitable if they are to thrive, their purpose must be not only to make money but also to build prosperity and freedom in the context of a livable planet and a healthy society."[26] She makes the case that firms of "authentic purpose" can indeed outperform firms focused only on profit maximization. Moreover, they outperform for a very specific reason—one having to do with relationality. They are better positioned to implement what she calls "high road organizational structures." Henderson writes:

> Authentic purpose must by definition be expensive since authenticity requires putting the purpose of the firm ahead of profits some significant fraction of the time. This would seem to imply that genuinely purpose driven firms would be routinely less profitable than their more conventional competitors, and thus that they would be much less likely to survive—suggesting that those firms who claim to be purpose driven must be largely greenwashing. But if authentically purpose driven firms are much better positioned to implement high road organizational structures—and if these structures are actually more productive then there's good reason to believe that purpose driven firms cannot only survive but thrive whilst routinely sacrificing profits in the service of purpose In the US, for example, on average the most productive plants in any given industry make almost twice as much output with the same measured inputs as the least productive. . . . These differences are strongly correlated with differences in the adoption of high performance management practices—differences in the degree to which firms pay a great deal of attention to skills development, implement incentive systems that use much more than simple quantitative metrics to measure performance, use self-directed teams to manage work and create widespread opportunities for distributed communication and problem solving.[27]

An authentic purpose-driven firm, then, will see its primary responsibility as being, to paraphrase Henderson, to the health of the social, institutional, and natural systems on which it relies. In a society organized around the principles of "justice by means of democracy," this would entail evolving firms in a democracy-supporting way. This involves elements of non-domination internal to the firm—for instance, the use of "self-directed teams" and "distributed communication." Henderson's theory of the purpose-driven firm makes the case that such firms will also be more productive, thereby contributing to a productive economy able to deliver the material bases of support for a democracy.

Democracy-supporting firms of this kind are a highly attractive prospect. What, then, would it take to achieve the evolution of firms in this direction? As Salter sees it, in the United States some industries have indeed come to adopt a "more reciprocally just conception of institutional purpose" and capacities to negotiate across complex fields of interest that include the interests of the democratic community at large. The motivation has often been political. He writes:

> Some industries (automotive, civil aircraft, textile, semiconductor, telecommunications, healthcare, just to name a few) have been forced by economic and political circumstances to adopt at various stages in their history a more reciprocally just conception of institutional purpose and governance than that adopted by strict followers of shareholder capitalism. These circumstances include a range of factors that (a) require fair exchanges of value among multiple contracting parties comprising and affecting the firm for the firm to continue operating and (b) where the opportunities and benefits of intimidation and predation are low. . .[28]

The first factor on Salter's list, generating a more reciprocally just conception of institutional purpose, is the "political salience of the industry." He continues ():

> Of all these factors, political salience seems to play a key role triggering dynamic reciprocity. While the direct effects of the remaining factors deserve further inspection, what prior research in the industries referenced above indicates that in politically salient industries, firms tend to be (and are required to be) more politically attuned. Such firms therefore tend to view themselves as entities that have participants with both overlapping and competing claims on its resources. Thus, in addition to shareholders (and bondholders), customers, employees at all levels, and members of the community affected by the firm's business policies all represent legitimate interests that need to be negotiated and

> mediated in the context of the organization's purposes and industry dynamics.[29]

Achieving free labor, via democracy-supporting firms, will turn out to require the engagement of a democratic citizenry. This underscores the need for democratic steering of the economy. I'll return to that design principle of democratic steering in the next section, but there is still a bit more to say about what it takes to achieve a good-jobs economy.

Supplying Good Jobs

The ideal of an empowering economy is realized first through focus on free labor and democracy-supporting firms, both key elements of production and productivity. But the success of the free-labor principle also depends on an adequate supply of "good jobs" to provide the material bases of empowerment. Here I draw on a framework developed by Dani Rodrik and political scientist and legal scholar Charles Sabel. They write:

> The definition of "good job" is necessarily slippery. We have in mind in the first instance stable, formal-sector employment that comes with core labor protections such as safe working conditions, collective bargaining rights, and regulations against arbitrary dismissal. A good job enables at least a middle-class existence, by a region's standards, with enough income for housing, food, transportation, education, and other family expenses, as well as some saving. More broadly, good jobs provide workers with clear career paths, possibilities of self-development, flexibility, responsibility, and fulfillment. The depth and range of such characteristics may depend on context: the prevailing levels of productivity and economic development, costs of living, prevailing income gaps, and so on. We expect each community to set its own standards and aspirations, which will evolve over time.[30]

Importantly, economic policy as currently formulated—with a focus on monetary-policy-driven capital growth and redistribution—has left us with a real economy that innovates with and assimilates technology unevenly, "bottlenecking" opportunity in urban areas and leaving rural areas with lower productivity contexts. Rodrik and Sabel write: "We do not view this simply as a problem of inequality and exclusion, but also as a problem of gross economic inefficiency—a case of operating deep inside the production possibility frontier."[31] The question is what approach to economic policy can integrate a population fully into technology-driven opportunities. Rodrik and Sabel suggest that whereas GDP has been the metric of economic success for the past generation, a better metric would be the number of good jobs generated year over year. Success at generating jobs of the kind they have in mind would pull the real economy back in the direction of a middle-class economy, thereby securing the material base for justice by means of democracy.

But how can we achieve that supply of good jobs? Free labor cannot now rest on expropriation and exploitation, as it did in the nineteenth century with the Georgia Land Lottery and the Homestead Act.[32] Here is where Rodrik and Sabel make their most significant contribution: their answer is, in effect, that good jobs will come from democratization of decision-making around economic investment and experimentation. They argue for public-private partnerships, involving the full range of stakeholders, to make decisions in participatory regulatory processes about how firms might best invest in good jobs. They draw on preexisting governance models for decision-making in conditions of uncertainty, in particular the cases of fostering advanced technologies (as in DARPA, a federal government program that invests in defense technologies) and crafting environmental regulations (Rodrik and Sabel's example uses the case of Irish dairy farming). In these domains, private-public partnerships support active project management, collaborative review, adjustment of milestones, peer assessment of local problems, and "new forms of collaboration with networks of extension experts." Techniques of these kinds might be used, they argue, with place-based specificity, to help firms produce more good jobs and evolve their own firm practices in directions supportive of free labor. In short, the goal is participation-based regulatory processes in conditions of uncertainty. Firms' development of capacity to participate in these rule-making processes would be another dimension of their evolution toward increased democracy support. Rodrik and Sabel write:

> The concept of "good job," like clean water, is imprecise and needs to be operationalized in a way that is both evolving and context-dependent. Reasonable, attainable targets for good-job creation must remain provisional, to be revised under new information. . . . Achieving the targets depends on decisions on investment, technological choice, and business organization, the consequences of which are unknowable ex ante. Governance under uncertainty takes as its starting point the provisionality of ends and means and the need for disciplined review and revision. . . . Fostering good jobs depends at least as much on solving highly idiosyncratic, place-specific problems: failures of coordination between local firms and training institutions; between firms and their (potential) supply-chain partners; and the managerial breakdowns or

> skill gaps within individual firms and institutions to which the coordination problems point.[33]

Firms ready to participate in these sorts of collaborative, participatory rule-making processes are what we need in a world where we are pursuing justice by means of democracy.

For several decades now, economic policymakers have focused on jobs from the perspective of what skills firms need to support productivity and how to match workers to skill acquisition and firm need. This is a highly instrumentalizing approach—as if people were but tools to be fitted to the needs of capital. What about the question of whether the jobs on offer fit the needs of the people to be employed? No economy can be healthier than the people who power it. It's time for us to organize our economic policy from the ground up by asking what opportunities can help people live the lives they seek while also contributing to the greater good of a healthy economy—and how can we ensure these opportunities are equitable and inclusive. It's not just that workers should acquire the skills that firms need; it's that firms should offer the job experiences that people need. A good-jobs economy would include tailored supports and strategic investments that broadly spread opportunity to participate in an inclusive, dynamic economy. This includes attention to issues like housing and transportation. Wherever policymakers are focused on "job training" and "skills development," they should shift focus to achieving "opportunity with equity," and ensuring that all residents are connected to the good jobs of today and tomorrow in ways that deliver to workers an experience of opportunity and dignity, not instrumentalization.[34] The strategic work necessary to build these good jobs requires multistakeholder collaboration. In other words, an economy based on free labor requires power-sharing liberalism.

A good-jobs strategy focuses on the economy's productive structure, so that the economy itself can deliver the bases of well-being, in the form of a sufficient number of good, purpose-sustaining jobs. The goal is to put behind us approaches to political economy that leave significant portions of the citizenry highly exposed to the cold winds of political fights over redistribution. Let's instead choose a path that integrates all sectors of society into productivity. Importantly, the free-labor principle, when pursued in the United States in the nineteenth century, built a strong middle-class economy for white Americans only. In the wake of the end of Reconstruction in 1876, African Americans and other minorities were excluded. Realization of the principle depended on the expropriation of land from Native Americans. These same kinds of exclusion characterized the GI Bill after World War II that helped deliver a good-jobs economy to some in the middle of the twentieth century. Our twenty-first-century approach to the free-labor principle must finally be fully inclusive. Recognizing that, then, we can say that what land was to the nineteenth century, technology is to the twenty-first century: a new frontier, a source of innovation and fresh productive possibilities. In order to achieve the equivalent of allocating homestead plots to entrepreneurial workers ready to build on opportunity, we now have to build collaborative participatory processes, based on public-private partnerships, to generate, in the form of "good jobs," an equivalent to those nineteenth-century plots of land. Democracy-supporting firms are necessary actors in the pursuit of a free-labor economy. And so too is democracy itself. Just as the provision of homesteads in support of an empowering economy was steered in the nineteenth century by democratic processes, so too the achievement of a good-jobs economy will be the result of successful democratic steering of economic policy in the twenty-first. This has to include steering of the technology sector, which has yet to recognize its own responsibilities to inclusivity or to recognize that egalitarian participatory constitutional democracy, as the main vehicle of rights protection, is itself infrastructure for a healthy economy.

The Second Design Principle: Investment in Bridging

The need to be more explicit about inclusion in the project of building an empowering economy brings us to the second design principle. The collaborative, participatory rule-making processes necessary to navigate toward a good-jobs economy require investment in bridging relationships.

Scholars have recognized bridging ties as economically productive. For instance, in the case of Irish dairy farming explored by Rodrik and Sabel,[35] farmers, scientific experts, and government regulators had to be brought into productive synergies with each other, and relationships developed linking public and private sector, market firms and NGOs, for instance universities and think tanks. Bridge-building has been shown to support economic dynamism in the tech sector as well. As AnnaLee Saxenian puts it in *The New Argonauts,* Silicon Valley surpassed the Route 128 technology corridor in Massachusetts, and the entrepreneurial West surpassed the "hierarchy of established East Coast corporations," because they created "an industrial system distinguished by open labor markets, continuous entrepreneurship, and information exchange both within and between firms—all the direct opposite of the modern corporation with its hierarchical control of information, detailed division of labor and internal labor markets, and corporate secrecy and self-sufficiency."[36] In the Silicon Valley case, the striking detail is that information is exchanged not only within but also between firms. This upended a model of competition that shut down information flow and replaced it with a model of networking and cross-pollination that strengthened a whole ecosystem.

Bridges linking immigrants in the United States who then chose to return home also helped power the extension of Silicon Valley's entrepreneurial culture to new hubs of technological growth and development such as Taiwan and Israel. Saxenian tells the story of the repeated creation, in the wake of Silicon Valley's influence, of "cross-regional communities" driven by bridge builders able to bring together technical know-how with cultural competencies across a range of diverse communities—from the United States to Taiwan to Israel to India to China. Importantly, the strongest success cases for the mobilization of technology sector dynamism in support of economic development also bridged to the public sector to achieve support for a "well-functioning physical and communications infrastructure" and space for a private sector to "support venture capital funding and provide viable liquidity options." In these success cases, all parties across private-public lines were invested in collaborations and bridge-building relationships, not merely in narrowly defined competitive activities. Often the prime movers of these bridge-building relationships were immigrant professional associations. They linked Silicon Valley to new hubs of development in their members' countries of origin.

The bridging model to spur economic dynamism is powerful and can be extended to contexts beyond the technological. For such bridge-building work to generate not only a dynamic but also an inclusive economy within any society, investments in bridge-building as a matter of economic policy should also be directed within regions, not merely between regions. Subpopulations that are currently disconnected from economic participation—whether the urban poor or rural communities—need basic investment in bridging relationships. For entrepreneurs and policymakers to know what assets are available in different communities to drive innovation, dynamism, and good jobs, connection, not competition, may be the answer—not industrial espionage but creative and nontraditional trade associations that incorporate participation by historically marginalized entities and people. For members of marginalized communities to be able to leverage opportunities of which they are aware in their local context, they need "market knowledge and connections as well as technology and skill."[37] It's not enough just to give workers skills-training opportunities predefined by others. They should be integrated into innovation networks of existing entrepreneurs, investors, managers, and others with domain-specific expertise and offered the opportunity to lead in shaping a development agenda. Public sector investment in such bridge-building advances an empowering economy.

The Third Design Principle: Democratic Steering

It is time now to turn to the next design principle of an empowering economy: democratic steering. The pursuit of the design principles of free labor, democracy-supporting firms, and a good-jobs economy led to a focus on the domain of production within the economy. While the focus on the relational, rather than the transactional, components of the economy, led us in this direction, Rodrik and Sabel, starting from a different theoretical point, also eloquently articulate the relational stakes of the domain of production:

> In contrast to standard remedies that deal with the pre-production (e.g. schooling) or post-production (e.g. taxation) stages of the economy, our approach directly targets production. The motivation is that private producers, left to their own, do not take the social costs of the scarcity of good jobs into account. In the absence of government action, production is not efficient. An important implication is that the traditional distinction between distribution and production no longer makes sense. Efficient production and distributive inclusion are two sides of the same coin. One cannot achieve one without the other. Questions of production—how goods and services are provided, which types of investments are made, what is the direction of technological change—are placed right at the heart of political economy and justice analysis.[38]

The fundamental relational question about how the economy is structured is whether it generates empowering forms of relationality. To provide the material bases of empowerment, an economy must generate good jobs; to pursue this via participatory processes is also to maximize productive efficiency. We took that idea a step further by proposing investment in bridging as one of the key design principles of an empowering economy. And, importantly, bridging investments must be fully inclusive. The goal with the successful production of good jobs and inclusive bridge-building is to take the economy to its productive limits and thereby deliver the material basis of democratic empowerment. This does not mean that preproduction investment or postproduction redistribution are off the table, only that they are complements to the core goal of fostering empowering relations of production.

To reiterate, successful production of good jobs is a desideratum of democracy specifically. This is because democracies need good jobs to achieve an empowered citizenry. For this reason, it is above all a democracy's representatives who will recognize this goal, and who must be charged with pursuing and protecting it. Achieving a good-jobs economy will therefore require steering of the economy by those elected representatives. Only such democratic steering can be expected consistently to deliver good-jobs policy that puts questions of production and relationality front and center in policy-making. An economy steered primarily by firms or by the holders of capital may lose sight of the important foundation of justice in free labor. As a result, the ideal of an empowering economy consists not just of the empowerment of individual residents of the polity, as supported by free labor and democracy-supporting firms, but also of the empowerment of the national legislature, specifically, to steer the national economy.

This is a strong claim. For much of the past few decades, the goal has been to insulate economic policy-making from politics by entrusting it to independent bodies such as the Federal Reserve. The requirement for democratic steering is not that we should abandon such independent bodies but, rather, that the legislature should more actively take responsibility for establishing the objectives of those agencies. When the Federal Reserve was originally chartered in the early twentieth century, it was to be rechartered every twenty years. This has not occurred. Yet policy targets of independent central banks should not be assumed to be permanently stable, and any given set of policy targets involves trade-offs that have political implications.[39] Annual legislative review of credit guidance and an every-twenty-year rechartering of the central bank would permit appropriate democratic accountability over the direction of monetary policy, balanced with respect for the role of technocratic expertise in managing monetary policy.[40] In recent years it became common to observe that the fundamentals of the economy in the years 2000–2020 suggested that inflation cannot be understood merely as it was in the 1970s. This observation led to an exploration of the idea that central banks should perhaps not have inflation targeting as their primary duty. Central banks took up study of this question, investigating potential alternative areas of work pertaining to the stability of the financial system and climate change. They began exploring individual accounts and digital currencies. And now, of course, robust postpandemic inflation has returned their attention to that original inflation-fighting mission. But while central banks should tee up the analysis, they should not be the ones to make the final call on the trade-offs that face them as they set new directions for their policy work. Elected representatives should have a routinely established opportunity to review and approve the objectives selected by central banks.

Monetary policy—and the trade-offs it establishes between inflation and jobs—is not the only aspect where democratic steering is pertinent. The specific forms of private-public partnership that can accelerate and expand the development of good jobs will be place-specific. Success will require aligning natural and actual polities. The work of building and steering these partnerships should therefore proceed by means of devolution to states, cities, and towns.

Democratic steering of the economy should also occur across all three domains of the economy: preproductive and postproductive as well as the productive domain. In no domain should the democratic legislature abdicate to technocrats, even if it should routinely call on their expertise and advice. To propose democratic steering of the economy's productive structure is, as we have seen, to introduce a focus on public-private partnerships for rule-making in support of good jobs. It is to call attention back to the role of fiscal policy in steering a healthy economy, via investments in infrastructure that supports productivity. It is also to foreground the need for democratic steering of antimonopoly and competition policy. Finally, the ideal of an empowering economy ought to include a jobs guarantee, a form of stabilization of the economy in periods of economic contraction that avoids the erosion of skill and capacity, and therefore of empowerment, in the citizenry.

As Rodrik and Sabel point out, current policy regimes have the following problems:

> Ex post redistribution through taxes and transfers accepts the productive structure as given, and merely ameliorates the results through handouts. Investments in education, universal basic income (UBI), and social wealth funds seek to enhance the endowments of the work-force, without ensuring productive integration. Broadly speaking the same can be said about the Keynesian approach to job creation, through aggregate demand management.[41]

An empowering economy seeks productive integration, as Rodrik and Sabel put it. The combination of the design principles—for free labor, a good-jobs economy, investments in bridging relationships, and democratic steering—add up to a fundamentally different economic vision than has reigned in the United States for the past forty years—to a paradigm change, in effect. We can best see how the different elements of the paradigm change come together by looking closely at how the "empowering economies" framework yields an alternative view about the place of education within economic policy, a critical preproductive investment.

Economy and Education

The question of whether an economy integrates all members and sectors in productivity itself and thereby directly in the gains of productivity is answered by political decisions made by that nation's legislatures. Yet mainstream scholarship in political economy has not focused on restoring political capacity within the citizenry as a method of correcting problematic patterns of production and distribution. Instead, the main line of technocratic attack on inequality has served to erode the foundation for political equality.

In the late 1980s, economists began to notice a dramatic increase in wealth and income inequality, particularly in the United States and Canada. By the early 1990s, economists had identified technological change, which biased available jobs toward highskilled workers, as the primary culprit. From this diagnosis, they then took a short step to an argument that education—specifically, vocational education and education in science, technology, engineering, and math (STEM)—was the remedy. That is the lesson of Claudia Goldin and Larry Katz's important book *The Race between Education and Technology*. They argue that the best way of reducing the wage premium on education is to disseminate technological skills as broadly as possible throughout a population; this dissemination of skills would be expected to drive down the wage premium on expertise and compress the income distribution.

Indeed, in the United States, starting with the Cold War competition with the Soviet Union, educational policymakers have steered educational institutions toward increasing vocationalism and emphasis on science and technology. The argument from economists that the only way to reverse the dynamics of income inequality is to accelerate the dissemination of technological skills through the population further entrenched this policy direction. It has been widely adopted at the highest levels of government. President Obama, in his 2013 State of the Union address, announced a competition to "redesign America's high schools." Rewards would go, he said, to schools that develop more classes "that focus on science, technology, engineering, and math—the skills today's employers are looking for to fill jobs right now and in the future."[42] And in his 2016 State of the Union address, Obama announced a Computer Science for All initiative that would make students "jobready on day one."[43] A result of this focus, one shared by Obama's predecessors, has been a precipitous decline in the United States, over the past twenty years, of time spent in school on social studies, the arts and humanities, and programs like Model United Nations, youth simulation of politics and policymaking.[44] In parallel, colleges and universities have seen a precipitous decline of enrollments in these areas, as students flock to the "big four" fields of business, computer science, economics, and medicine.

Piketty, too, has pursued this line of technocratic response to inequality. Leaving aside his global wealth tax, his other proposals for addressing inequality fit squarely within this now conventional frame, focused on the dissemination of technological skills. He writes, "Historical experience suggests that the principal mechanism for convergence [of incomes and wealth] at the international as well as the domestic level is the diffusion of knowledge. In other words, the poor catch up with the rich to the extent that they achieve the same level of technological knowhow, skill, and education."[45] To the degree that Piketty's recommendations turn to educational policy, he focuses on access. When he considers curriculum, he is explicit only about vocational goals. He argues that educational institutions should be made broadly accessible; elite institutions, which serve mainly privileged youth from the highest income brackets, should draw students from other backgrounds; schools should be run efficiently; and states should increase investment in "high-quality professional training."

But there is a flaw in the argument that technology's inexorable forward march, and its creation of inequality, can be remediated only through the dissemination of technological skills and transactional practices of redistribution. As economists Daron Acemoglu and Jim Robinson argue,

> The quest for general laws of capitalism is misguided because it ignores the key forces shaping how an economy functions: the endogenous evolution of technology and of the institutions and the political equilibrium that influence not only technology but also how markets function and how the gains from various different economic arrangements are distributed.[46]

Similarly, as Rodrik puts it, "Today's world economy is the product of explicit decisions that governments had made in the past . . . . It was the choice of governments to loosen regulations on finance and aim for full cross-border capital mobility, just as it was a choice to maintain these policies largely intact, despite a massive global financial crisis."[47] Again, these economists are making the point that the economy is embedded in society.

The pursuit of free labor, democracy-supporting firms, a good-jobs economy, and bridging investments constitutes a powerful alternative framework for government decision-making in support of an economy that would be not only productive but also egalitarian. Yet achieving that policy framework depends on advocacy on its behalf by a democratic citizenry. Rather than supporting such advocacy, however, the standard policy response to income inequality—the dissemination of STEM skills—actually erodes political equality. The very modes of education advanced by the technocratic policy fail to prepare people for democratic participation. In the United States, at least, attainment in the humanities and social sciences correlates with increased engagement in politics, but attainment in STEM fields correlates with lower political engagement. Data from the Department of Education reveal that, among 2008 college graduates, 92.8 percent of humanities majors have voted at least once since finishing university. Among STEM majors, that number is 83.5 percent. And, within ten years of graduation from university, 44.1 percent of 1993 humanities graduates had written to public officials, compared to 30.1 percent of STEM majors.[48] These are statistically significant differences. These college graduates are generally of similar socioeconomic backgrounds, suggesting that factors other than relative wealth or income must account for the difference in political engagement. The emphasis on STEM appears to leave people underprepared for civic engagement and empowerment. The technocratic policy we have is working against the ends we need.

Of course, the self-selection of students into the humanities and STEM majors may mean that these data reflect only underlying features of the students rather than the effects of teaching they receive. Yet the same pattern appears in a study by political scientist Sunshine Hillygus (2005), which controls for students' preexisting levels of interest in politics. Hillygus also finds that the differences in political engagement among college graduates are mirrored in primary education.[49] High verbal scores on the SAT (an achievement test used for college entrance exams in the United States) correlate with increased likelihood of political participation, while high math scores on the SAT correlate with decreased likelihood of participation. Again, since socioeconomic effects on SAT scores move both verbal and math scores in the same direction, this difference between the effects of high verbal and high math scores on the likelihood of participation must be telling us something about the relationship between attainment in specific subject domains and participatory readiness. Moreover, the SAT effect endures even when college-level curricular choices are controlled for.

In a 2006 article, "Why Does Democracy Need Education?," economists Edward L. Glaeser, Giacomo Ponzetto, and Andrei Shleifer[50] argue that education is a causal force behind democracy. Specifically, they point to a causal relationship between education and participation, considering three hypotheses for why the former might be a source of the latter. They consider whether education drives up participation through indoctrination, through the cultivation of skills that facilitate participation (reading and writing and "soft skills" of collaboration and interaction), and through the increased material benefits of participation. (On the last, the idea is that education increases income, and participation correlates to socioeconomic status.) The authors reject the first and third hypotheses in favor of the second. Education, they argue, fosters participation because it prepares people for democratic engagement. Reading, writing, and collaboration are, after all, the basic instruments of political action. In short, Glaeser, Ponzetto, and Shleifer conclude that it is indeed attainment in the verbal domain that correlates with participatory readiness.[51]

To identify a correlation is not, of course, to identify, let alone prove, causation. But those with more sophisticated verbal skills and dexterity at sociopolitical analysis are clearly more ready to participate in civic life. Another source of motivation may have engaged them in politics, leading them, once engaged, to seek out the verbal and analytical skills needed to thrive as civic participants. Or verbal competence and social analytical skills may make engagement easier in the first place. We don't have a study that considers levels of engagement before and after significant increases in these kinds of competence. Nonetheless, data suggest that the work of the humanities and social sciences on verbal empowerment and social analysis is intrinsically related to the development of participatory readiness.

Of course, science, technology, engineering, math, and medicine have done much to create the contemporary condition in which we find ourselves residents of mass democracies. Thanks to the industrial, aeronautical, biomedical, and digital revolutions, the world's population has grown from one to seven billion in little more than 200 years, a profound historical transformation. We surely need the STEM fields to navigate this new landscape. But if the STEM fields gave us the mass in "mass democracy," the humanities and social sciences gave us the democracy.

The European and American colonists who designed systems of representative democracy capable of achieving a continental scale—also tragically employing genocidal techniques—were broadly and deeply educated in history, geography, philosophy, literature, and art. This is the sort of education necessary for citizenship. After all, citizens must judge whether their governments are fulfilling the responsibility to secure basic liberties and the conditions in which private and public autonomy can emerge. If a government fails in its core purposes, citizens have the job of figuring this out and deciding how to change direction. When those early founders failed at inclusion, it was figures steeped in the humanities and social sciences who pointed this out—from Abigail Adams to Frederick Douglass to Ida B. Wells to Martin Luther King Jr. Changing direction requires diagnosing social circumstances and making judgments about grounding principles for the political order and about possible alternatives to the formal organization of state power. Properly conducted, the citizen's intellectual labor should result in a probabilistic judgment answering this critical question: what combination of principles and organizational form is most likely to secure collective freedom, safety, and happiness? Such labor is best supported not by the STEM components of an education but by the humanistic, social scientific, and critical components.[52] Rather than blindly "following the science" in political decision-making, we need to cultivate capacities for judgments based on actionable intelligence. Such equality as the world has managed to achieve—whether political or economic—can often be traced to the operations of these latter human capacities. This is not an argument that we should have education in the humanities and social sciences *instead of* STEM education but, rather, an argument that *we need both.*

Democracies cannot afford to dispense with those kinds of education that nourish the capacities needed in a democracy. And to the degree that science education as currently practiced undermines democracy, we ought to revisit our STEM instructional strategies.

In contrast to the technocratic, transactional approach to the role of education in combating income and wealth inequality, this line of argument, which returns to the relational, introduces significantly different needs for an educational system. If political choices determine the rules that shape productive and distributive patterns, it makes sense to focus on ensuring the emergence of political equality and forms of democratic empowerment in which citizens are equipped to secure modes of economic arrangement that in turn reinforce their freedom. If we choose political equality as our orienting ideal—empowering all to participate capably in the life of a polity—a different view of education's purpose, content, and consequence comes into view. We clearly need not only technology-oriented but also civic education. This means investment in all those liberal arts subjects described above. But not only that; at this point, digital literacies, not merely STEM knowledge, are a form of linguistic competence that itself can work powerfully in support of democracy. Education in the technological infrastructure of democracy needs to be incorporated into the other core building blocks of civic education. STEM education itself can be reconfigured in support of empowering, rather than neoliberalizing, economies.

Implicit in my argument thus far is that a civic education will not only support political equality but also lead to increased economic fairness—by lodging decisions about the steering of the economy with a broadly engaged public of ordinary citizens. As Acemoglu and Robinson argue, the expansion of political participation drove egalitarian economic reforms in the United Kingdom in the nineteenth century and in the United States in the early twentieth. We are currently seeing a resurgence of participation on both the right and left. These movements, dubbed populist by many commentators, are putting issues of distributive justice on the agenda once again. Their populist dangers flow from their direct connection with charismatic party leaders, aspirations to unchecked majoritarianism, and alienation from respect for legislatures, processes of representation, full inclusion, minority-protecting mechanisms, and synthesis and compromise. In other words, populists reject egalitarian participatory constitutional democracy.

Nonetheless, in the cases of the United States, the United Kingdom, and France, the populists have restored valid questions, marginalized for too long, to the agenda of political economy. They have raised questions about the structure of the labor market and its relation to migration. They have raised questions about the fairness of the distribution of the gains from productivity. The question is whether populism can evolve from the expectation that a charismatic leader will change things by executive fiat into an embrace of egalitarian participatory constitutional democracy, where representatives seek compromises that permit them to steer the economy in ways that rest on the perspectives of the polity's diverse stakeholders. This resurgence of populism increases the stakes of educating people for civic participation. While the technological view of the link between education and equality reinforces a vocational approach to curriculum and pedagogy, a civic view demands a renewed focus on the humanities and social sciences and a civics-oriented approach to technology. Justice by means of democracy will depend on investments in public goods, among them education, and, even more specifically, civic education.

Conclusion

In order to develop a political economy for "empowering economies," I have turned away from the transactional and toward the relational, asking how the overarching principle of difference without domination might be extended to the economic realm. Following Rodrik and Sabel, I identified the productive sector of the economy—the job-creating sector—as that portion of the economy that can generate both productivity and reasonably egalitarian distribution of its fruits. I used the principles of free labor, democracy-supporting firms, and good jobs; of investment in bridge-building; and of democratic steering of the economy as guides to the specific policies we might pursue. Throughout I have assumed as a basic requirement of any policy that it must be structured to protect the positive and negative basic liberties both directly and indirectly.

A focus on achieving difference without domination in the economic realm widens the lens beyond Rawls's redistributive questions and, as in the social realm, requires recognizing a broader swath of the policy landscape than we typically acknowledge as relevant to the question of how to protect equal basic liberties. In this sense, the principle of difference without domination is more strenuously egalitarian than the difference principle. It establishes a higher standard for our decisions about how we protect our equal basic liberties and pulls a larger swath of the policy landscape under the umbrella of that to which the equal basic liberties pertain.

This approach to political economy protects freedom of contract and property, but seeks to ensure that the relational environment in which contracts are developed supports stakeholder, not shareholder, capitalism. This requires egalitarian political empowerment, social connectedness, and a standard of disconnecting difference and hierarchy from domination in all contexts—public and private. This political economy also identifies the policies that organize land, labor, and capital as elements of the structure necessary to secure the basic liberties, positive and negative, and therefore to secure private and public autonomy. The combination of egalitarian political empowerment, social connectedness, and a relationally oriented political economy should result in a productive structure that secures more egalitarian distributive outcomes than our current productive structure.

But even under this egalitarian political economy, the patterns of distribution that flow from underlying arrangements of production will not escape the problem of those who would fall outside the structure of employment and, therefore, absent a foundation for flourishing, would fall below the threshold of material security necessary for political empowerment. This political economy, too, will need to secure a transactional welfare state, but the design of services should be understood conceptually as a second step after the design of the relational infrastructure. Moreover, the design should focus on providing a foundation for participation in economy and society—not a safety net in which to become entangled but a stable floor, anchored by housing security, on which to stand and thrive. The goal is an economy organized such that the least well-off still have access to egalitarian political empowerment, and this means a foundation for flourishing through access to housing, transportation, education, and health. But it also means a system of employment and a market economy compatible with political agency and democratic social connectedness. Thus conceived, we might develop a political economy aimed at securing freedom in its fullest sense—including not only private but also public autonomy, with both strands aligned with freedom from domination. This is a political economy for power-sharing liberalism.

Finally, there is the question of how a vicious cycle of income and wealth inequality and political domination of democratic institutions by wealthy elites can be converted into the virtuous circle of egalitarian empowerment, social connectedness, relational economies, and stakeholder capitalism that I have sought to describe here. The answer is through the democratic exercise of power in political institutions. We need to pursue justice by means of democracy. For this, we need to focus on the practice of democratic citizenship.

References

Acemoglu, Daron and James A Robinson. "The Rise and Decline of General Laws of Capitalism." *Journal of Economic Perspectives* 29, no. 1 (Winter 2015): 3–28.

Allen, Danielle. *Education and Equality*. University of Chicago Press, 2016.

Allen, Danielle, Adam Gerard, Danielle Cerny, et al. "One Commonwealth Agendas: Good Jobs Agenda." 2021–2022. AllenforMA. https://allenforma.com/agendas.

Anderson, Elizabeth. *Private Government: How Employers Rule Our Lives (and Why We Don't Talk about It)*. Princeton, NJ: Princeton University Press, 2017.

Bartels, Larry. *Unequal Democracy: The Political Economy of the New Gilded Age*. Princeton, NJ: Princeton University Press, 2010.

Becaria, Ceasare. *An Essay on Crimes and Punishments. By the Marquis Beccaria of Milan. With a Commentary by M. de Voltaire. A New Edition Corrected.* Albany: W.C. Little & Co., 1872.

Bloom, Nicholas and John Van Reenen. "Why Do Management Practices Differ Across Firms and Countries?" *Journal of Economic Perspectives* 24, no. 1 (Winter 2010): 203–24.

Bowles, Samuel and Wendy Carlin. "Shrinking Capitalism: Components of a New Political Economy Paradigm." CEPR Discussion Paper no. DP16515, 2021. https://ssrn.com/abstract=3928826.

Caruana, R., A. Crane, S. Gold, and G. LeBaron. "Modern Slavery in Business: The Sad and Sorry State of a Non-field." *Business & Society* 60, no. 2 (2021): 251–87.

Downey, Leah. "Delegation in Democracy: A Temporal Analysis." *Journal of Political Philosophy* 29, no. 3 (2021): 305–29.

Downey, Leah. "Governing Money Democratically: Re-chartering the Federal Reserve." In *Political Economy of Justice*, edited by Danielle Allen, Yochai Benkler, Leah Downey, Rebecca Henderson, and Josh Simons. University of Chicago Press, 2022: 340–366.

Downey, Leah. *When Democracies Make Money*. Princeton, NJ: Princeton University Press, forthcoming.

Gilens, Martin. *Affluence and Influence: Economic Inequality and Political Power in America*. Princeton, NJ: Princeton University Press, 2012.

Goldin, Claudia and Lawrence Katz. *The Race between Education and Technology*. Cambridge, MA: Belknap, 2008.

Gould, Carol. *Globalizing Democracy and Human Rights*. Cambridge, UK: Cambridge University Press, 2004.

Gould, Carol. "Structuring Global Democracy: Political Communities, Universal Human Rights, and Transnational Representation." *Metaphilosophy* 40, no. 1 (2009): 24–41.

Gould, Carol. *Interactive Democracy: The Social Roots of Global Justice*. New York: Cambridge University Press, 2014.

Gould, Carol. "Democratic Management and International Labor Rights." In *Global Justice and International Labour Rights*, edited by Yossi Dahan, Hanna Lerner, and Faina Milman-Sivan. New York: Cambridge University Press, 2016: 266-284.

Gruber, Jonathan and Brigitte C. Madrian. "Health Insurance and Job Mobility: The Effects of Public Policy on Job-Lock." *Industrial and Labor Relations Review* 48, no. 1 (1994): 86–102.

Hacker, Jacob. "The Institutional Foundations of Middle-Class Democracy." *Policy Network* 6 (2011): 33–37.

Hare, Christopher and Keith T. Poole. "The Polarization of Contemporary American Politics." *Polity* 46, no. 3 (2014): 411–29.

Henderson, Rebecca. *Reimagining Capitalism in a World on Fire*. New York: Public Affairs, 2020.

Henderson, Rebecca. "Interrogating Corporate Purpose: Values-Based Firms and the Struggle to Build a Just and Sustainable World" (2022). Paper presented at the Edmond J. Safra Center Workshop on the Political Economy of Justice, February 2020. Manuscript on file with author.

Hillygus, Sunshine. "The Missing Link: Exploring the Relationship Between Higher Education and Political Engagement." *Political Behavior* 27, no. 1 (2005): 25–47.

Hirschman, Albert O *Exit, Voice, and Loyalty: Responses to Decline in Firms, Organizations, and States*. Cambridge, MA: Harvard University Press, 1970.

Ichniowski, Casey and Kathryn Shaw. "The Effects of Human Resource Management Systems on Economic Performance: An International Comparison of U.S. and Japanese Plants." Management Science, May 1999, https://pubsonline.informs.org/doi/epdf/10.1287/mnsc.45.5.704

Inchauste, G., J. Karver, Y. S. Kim, and M. A. Jelil. *Living and Leaving: Housing, Mobility and Welfare in the European Union*. Washington, D.C.: World Bank, 2018.

Jackson, Matthew O. "Social Structure, Segregation, and Economic Behavior." Presented as the Nancy Schwartz Memorial Lecture in April of 2007 (2009). http://papers.ssrn.com/abstract=1530885.

Katz, Lawrence. 2010. "Long-Term Unemployment in the Great Recession." Testimony for the Joint Economic Committee, US Congress Hearing on Long-Term Unemployment: Causes, Consequences, Solutions. https://scholar.harvard.edu/files/lkatz/files/long_term_unemployment_in_the_great_recession.pdf.

Katz, Michael S. *A History of Compulsory Education Laws*. Bloomington, IN: Phi Delta Kappa, 1976.

Loury, Glenn C. "Relations before Transactions: A Personal Plea." In *Difference without Domination: Pursuing Justice in Diverse Democracies*, edited by Danielle Allen and Rohini Somanathan. Chicago: University of Chicago Press, 2020: 171-187.

Marshall, George. 1947. "The Marshall Plan Speech": https://www.oecd.org/en/about/history/the-marshall-plan-speech-at-harvard-university-5-june-1947.html.

National Center for Education Statistics. *1993/03 Baccalaureate and Beyond Longitudinal Study* (2009). https://nces.ed.gov/pubs2006/2006166.pdf.

National Center for Education Statistics. *2008/09 Baccalaureate and Beyond Longitudinal Study* (2011). https://nces.ed.gov/pubs2011/2011236.pdf.

Okin, Susan.1991. *Justice, Gender, and the Family*. New York: Basic Books.

Piketty, Thomas. *Capital in the Twenty-First Century*. Cambridge, MA: Harvard University Press, 2014.

Polanyi, Karl. *The Great Transformation: The Political and Economic Origins of Our Time*. 2nd ed. 1944; repr. Boston: Beacon, 2001.

Posner, Eric A. and Glen Weyl. *Radical Markets: Uprooting Capitalism and Democracy for a Just Society*. Princeton, NJ: Princeton University Press, 2018. and K. Jacobs. "*All Economics is Local*." *The New York Times*, March 22, 2014. http://opinionator.blogs.nytimes.com/2014/03/22/all-economics-is-local/#more-152533.

Rawls, John 1971. *A Theory of Justice*. Cambridge, MA: Belknap.

Rawls, John (1993) 2011. *Political Liberalism*. Expanded ed. New York: Columbia University Press.

Rodrik, Dani. "The Politics of Anger." *Project Syndicate*, March 9, 2016. https://www.project-syndicate.org/commentary/the-politics-of-anger-by-dani-rodrik-2016-03.

Rodrik, Dani, and Charles Sabel. "Building a Good Jobs Economy." In *Political Economy of Justice*, edited by Danielle Allen, Yochai Benkler, Leah Downey, Rebecca Henderson, and Josh Simons. Chicago: University of Chicago Press, 2022: 61–95.

Rodrik, Dani and Stefanie Stantcheva. "A Policy Matrix for Inclusive Prosperity." NBER Working Paper no. 28736. Cambridge, MA: National Bureau of Economic Research, 2021.

Rose, Julie. *Free Time*. Princeton, NJ: Princeton University Press, 2016.

Salter, Malcolm S. "Implications of Reciprocal Justice Theory for Corporate Purpose." Unpublished manuscript. (2017).

Salter, Malcolm S. "Corporate Purpose in a Post-Covid World." In *Political Economy of Justice*, edited by Danielle Allen, Yochai Benkler, Leah Downey, Rebecca Henderson, and Josh Simons. Chicago: University of Chicago Press, 2022: 210–236.

Saxenian, AnnaLee. *The New Argonauts: Regional Advantage in a Global Economy*. Cambridge, MA: Harvard University Press, 2006.

Scanlon, T. M. "Why Does Inequality Matter?" In *Combating Inequality: Rethinking Government's Role*, edited by D. Rodrik and O. Blanchard. Cambridge, MA: MIT Press, 2021: 59–64.

Shambaugh, Jay and Ryan Nunn, eds. *Place-Based Policies for Shared Economic Growth*. Washington, DC: Brookings Institution, 2018.

United States Census. CPS Historical Migration/Geographic Mobility Tables. Table A-1, "Annual Geographic Mobility Rates, by Type of Movement: 1948–2019." 2019. https://www2.census.gov/programs-surveys/demo/tables/geographic-mobility/time-series/historic/tab-a-1.xls.

Weyl, Glen. "Why I Am a Pluralist." RadicalXChange (blog), February 10, 2022a. https://www.radicalxchange.org/media/blog/why-i-am-a-pluralist/.

Weyl, Glen. "The Political Philosophy of RadicalXChange." In *Political Economy of Justice*, edited by Danielle Allen, Yochai Benkler, Leah Downey, Rebecca Henderson, and Josh Simons. Chicago: University of Chicago Press, 2022b: 96–117.

Notes

1. John Rawls, 1971, 266.
2. The important triadic model of collaboration among these three sectors developed by Samuel Bowles and Wendy Carlin (2021) is at the base of the political economy I sketch here ("Shrinking Capitalism: Components of a New Political Economy Paradigm," CEPR Discussion Paper no. DP16515 (2021), https://ssrn.com/abstract=3928826). It has also been captured in the work of Glen Weyl (e.g., Glen Weyl, "Why I Am a Pluralist," RadicalX-Change (blog), February 10, 2022a, https://www.radicalxchange.org/media/blog/why-i-am-a-pluralist/; Glen Weyl, "The Political Philosophy of RadicalXChange," in *Political Economy of Justice*, ed. Danielle Allen, Yochai Benkler, Leah Downey, Rebecca Henderson, and Josh Simons (Chicago: University of Chicago Press, 2022b). Bowles and Carlin call their model "shrinking capitalism." I call it "embedded liberalism." Weyl calls it "pluralism." A name has yet to stabilize for this paradigm.
3. Glenn C. Loury, "Relations before Transactions: A Personal Plea," in *Difference without Domination: Pursuing Justice in Diverse Democracies*, ed. Danielle Allen and Rohini Somanathan (Chicago: University of Chicago Press, 2020).
4. If you protect the basic liberties, both negative and positive, social difference will emerge, and "difference" is another word for "inequality." To paraphrase Tim Scanlon, the important question is whether the emergent differences are justified or not. To make this determination, I rely on the principle of difference without domination. If the relevant inequality subjects individuals or groups to the arbitrary reserve control of others, or in other ways undermines political equality, then that inequality is problematic and needs to be redressed, undone, or mitigated, depending on circumstances. The goal is a world in which social difference does not articulate with domination of any one person, or any group, by any other person or group. Scanlon, in his essay, identifies six kinds of inequality to which we might object: inequality of status, unacceptable control of some by others; interference with equality of opportunity; interference with the fairness of political institutions; unequal provision of benefits owed to all; and institutions that generate unequal incomes without adequate justification. Notably, the first four objections capture problems of political or social inequality; the last two, problems of material inequality. This underscores how important political equality is within a picture of human flourishing. The goal of economic policy, or political economy, should be to treat political empowerment or equality as what we're aiming for, and then to ask the question of how we also work toward social and economic egalitarianism in support of political empowerment. To reiterate, the reason to prioritize institutional, social, and economic bases for political equality or empowerment is that this concept fully captures human purposiveness. Tim Scanlon, "Why Does Inequality Matter?," in *Combating Inequality: Rethinking Government's Role*, edited by D. Rodrik and O. Blanchard (Cambridge, MA: MIT Press, 2021).
5. I paraphrase from Rawls ([1993] 2011, 6): "Social and economic inequalities are to satisfy two conditions: first, they are to be attached to positions and offices open to all under conditions of fair equality of opportunity; and second, they are to be to the greatest benefit of the least advantaged members of society."
6. See also Okin 1991; Cohen 2009.
7. Dani Rodrik and Stefanie Stantcheva, "A Policy Matrix for Inclusive Prosperity," NBER Working Paper no. 28736 (Cambridge, MA: National Bureau of Economic Research, 2021), 1–2.
8. Martin Gilens, *Affluence and Influence: Economic Inequality and Political Power in America* (Princeton, NJ: Princeton University Press, 2012). See also Larry Bartels (*Unequal Democracy: The Political Economy of the New Gilded Age* (Princeton, NJ: Princeton University Press,

2010), who has shown how, in the case of the United States, policy outcomes closely track the policy preferences of the wealthy.

9. Dani Rodrik and Charles Sabel, "Building a Good Jobs Economy," in *Political Economy of Justice*, ed. Danielle Allen, Yochai Benkler, Leah Downey, Rebecca Henderson, and Josh Simons (Chicago: University of Chicago Press, 2022): 61-95; Danielle Allen, Adam Gerard, Danielle Cerny, et al., "One Commonwealth Agendas: Good Jobs Agenda," 2021–2022, AllenforMA, https://allenforma.com/agendas.
10. R. Caruana, A. Crane, S. Gold, and G. LeBaron, "Modern Slavery in Business: The Sad and Sorry State of a Non-field," *Business & Society* 60, no. 2 (2021): 251–87.
11. Eric A. Posner and Glen Weyl, *Radical Markets: Uprooting Capitalism and Democracy for a Just Society* (Princeton, NJ: Princeton University Press, 2018); Caruana et al. (2021).
12. United States Census, @CPS Historical Migration/Geographic Mobility Tables. Table A-1, 'Annual Geographic Mobility Rates, by Type of Movement: 1948–2019'" (2019), https://www2.census.gov/programs-surveys/demo/tables/geographic-mobility/time-series/historic/tab-a-1.xls.
13. Katz, Lawrence. 2010. "Long-Term Unemployment in the Great Recession." Testimony for the Joint Economic Committee, US Congress Hearing on Long-Term Unemployment: Causes, Consequences, Solutions. https://scholar.harvard.edu/files/lkatz/files/long_term_unemployment_in_the_great_recession.pdf.
14. On health-insurance-related job lock, see Jonathan Gruber and Brigitte C. Madrian, "Health Insurance and Job Mobility: The Effects of Public Policy on Job-Lock," *Industrial and Labor Relations Review* 48, no. 1 (1994): 86–102.
15. Albert O. Hirschman, *Exit, Voice, and Loyalty: Responses to Decline in Firms, Organizations, and States* (Cambridge, MA: Harvard University Press, 1970).
16. Economists in the Unted States have begun to focus on "place-based" models of economic policy. See, for instance, M. Reich and K. Jacobs, "All Economics is Local," *The New York Times*, March 22, 2014, http://opinionator.blogs.nytimes.com/2014/03/22/all-economics-is-local/#more-152533; Jay Shambaugh and Ryan Nunn, eds., *Place-Based Policies for Shared Economic Growth* (Washington, D.C.: Brookings Institution, 2018). On housing, mobility, and productivity, see G. Inchauste, J. Karver, Y. S. Kim, and M. A. Jelil, *Living and Leaving: Housing, Mobility and Welfare in the European Union* (Washington, D.C.: World Bank, 2018).
17. Christopher Hare and Keith T. Poole, "The Polarization of Contemporary American Politics," *Polity* 46, no. 3 (2014): 411–29.
18. Hare and Poole, "The Polarization of Contemporary American Politics," 417.
19. Elizabeth Anderson, *Private Government: How Employers Rule Our Lives (and Why We Don't Talk about It)* (Princeton, NJ: Princeton University Press, 2017), 39.
20. Anderson, *Private Government*, 40.
21. cf. Julie Rose, *Free Time* (Princeton, NJ: Princeton University Press, 2016).
22. Carol Gould, "Democratic Management and International Labor Rights," in *Global Justice and International Labour Rights*, ed. Yossi Dahan, Hanna Lerner, and Faina Milman-Sivan (New York: Cambridge University Press, 2016); see also *Globalizing Democracy and Human Rights* (Cambridge, UK: Cambridge University Press, 2004); "Structuring Global Democracy: Political Communities, Universal Human Rights, and Transnational Representation," *Metaphilosophy* 40, no. 1 (2009): 24–41; *Interactive Democracy: The Social Roots of Global Justice*, chapters 4, 11–15 (New York: Cambridge University Press, 2014); cf. Jacob Hacker, "The Institutional Foundations of Middle-Class Democracy," *Policy Network* 6 (2011): 33–37; Karl Polanyi, *The Great Transformation: The Political and Economic Origins of Our Time*, 2nd ed. (1944; repr., Boston: Beacon, 2001).
23. Thomas Piketty, *Capital in the Twenty-First Century* (Cambridge, MA: Harvard University Press, 2014).
24. R. Henderson, "Reimagining Capitalism," lecture for the Edmond J. Safra Center for Ethics, April 2017.
25. Malcolm S. Salter, "Implications of Reciprocal Justice Theory for Corporate Purpose," Unpublished manuscript, 2017, 2; cf. "Corporate Purpose in a Post-Covid World," in *Political Economy of Justice*, ed. Danielle Allen, Yochai Benkler, Leah Downey, Rebecca Henderson, and Josh Simons (Chicago: University of Chicago Press, 2022): 210-236.

26. Rebecca Henderson, *Reimagining Capitalism in a World on Fire* (New York: Public Affairs, 2020), 36.
27. Henderson, *Reimagining Capitalism in a World on Fire*, 9; see also Rebecca Henderson, "Interrogating Corporate Purpose: Values-Based Firms and the Struggle to Build a Just and Sustainable World," Paper presented at the Edmond J. Safra Center Workshop on the Political Economy of Justice, February 2020, 196–97). The quote cited Bloom and Van Reenan, 2007; "Why Do Management Practices Differ Across Firms and Countries?," *Journal of Economic Perspectives* 24, no. 1 (Winter 2010): 203–24; 2011, Bloom et al., 2019; Jon, Ichniowski and Shaw, 2002; Casey Ichnioswski and Kathryn Shaw, "The Effects of Human Resource Management Systems on Economic Performance: An International Comparison of U.S. and Japanese Plants," Management Science, May 1999, https://pubsonline.informs.org/doi/epdf/10.1287/mnsc.45.5.704.
28. Malcolm S. Salter, "Implications of Reciprocal Justice Theory for Corporate Purpose," unpublished manuscript, 2017, 4; cf. Malcolm S. Salter, "Corporate Purpose in a Post-Covid World," in *Political Economy of Justice*, ed. Danielle Allen, Yochai Benkler, Leah Downey, Rebecca Henderson, and Josh Simons (Chicago: University of Chicago Press).
29. Salter, "Implications of Reciprocal Justice Theory for Corporate Purpose," 4–5.
30. Rodrik and Sabel, "Building a Good Jobs Economy." 62.
31. Rodrik and Sabel, "Building a Good Jobs Economy." 65.
32. Caruana et al. "Modern Slavery in Business": 251–87.
33. Rodrik and Sabel, "Building a Good Jobs Economy." 80.
34. Allen et al. "One Commonwealth Agendas: Good Jobs Agenda."
35. Rodrik and Sabel, "Building a Good Jobs Economy."
36. AnnaLee Saxenian, *The New Argonauts: Regional Advantage in a Global Economy* (Cambridge, MA: Harvard University Press, 2006), 29.
37. Saxenian, *The New Argonauts*, 116.
38. Rodrik and Sabel, "Building a Good Jobs Economy," 88.
39. Leah Downey, "Delegation in Democracy: A Temporal Analysis," *Journal of Political Philosophy* 29, no. (3 (2021): 305–29; "Governing Money Democratically: Re-chartering the Federal Reserve," in *Political Economy of Justice*, edited by Danielle Allen, Yochai Benkler, Leah Downey, Rebecca Henderson, and Josh Simons (University of Chicago Press, 2022): 340-366; *When Democracies Make Money* (Princeton, NJ: Princeton University Press, forthcoming).
40. Downey, "Delegation in Democracy;" "Governing Money Democratically;" *When Democracies Make Money*.
41. Rodrik and Sabel, "Building a Good Jobs Economy," 62.
42. Barack Obama, 2013 State of the Union Message, February 13, https://millercenter.org/the-presidency/presidential-speeches/february-13-2013-2013-state-union-address
43. Barack Obamsa, 2016 State of the Union Address, January 20, https://millercenter.org/the-presidency/presidential-speeches/january-12-2016-2016-state-union-address.
44. Danielle Allen, *Education and Equality* (University of Chicago Press, 2016).
45. Thomas Piketty, *Capital in the Twenty-First Century* (Cambridge, MA: Harvard University Press, 2014).
46. Daron Acemoglu and James A Robinson, "The Rise and Decline of General Laws of Capitalism," *Journal of Economic Perspectives* 29, no. 1 (Winter 2015): 3.
47. Dani Rodrik, "The Politics of Anger," *Project Syndicate*, March 9, 2016, https://www.project-syndicate.org/commentary/the-politics-of-anger-by-dani-rodrik-2016-03.
48. College graduates' civic engagement. data from the American Academy of Arts and Sciences. Figures calculated according to the National Center for Education Statistics (National Center for Education Statistics, *1993/03 Baccalaureate and Beyond Longitudinal Study* (2009), https://nces.ed.gov/pubs2006/2006166.pdf; *2008/09 Baccalaureate and Beyond Longitudinal Study* (2011). https://nces.ed.gov/pubs2011/2011236.pdf).
49. Sunshine Hillygus, "The Missing Link: Exploring the Relationship Between Higher Education and Political Engagement," *Political Behavior* 27, no. 1 (2005): 25–47.

50. Glaeser, Edward L, Giacomo AM Ponzetto, and Andrei Shleifer. 2007. "Why Does Democracy Need Education?" *Journal of Economic Growth* 12 (2): 77–99.
51. Edward L. Glaeser, Giacomo Ponetto, and Andre Shleifer. 2006. "Why Does Democracy Need Education? NBER Working Paper no, 12128. Cambridge, MA: National Bureau of Economic Research.
52. Saxenian, *The New Argonauts*, 86–87.

SECTION V

POLARIZATION

In Polanyi's Shadow

Race, Capitalism, and Democracy in Our Time

Robert C. Lieberman

Writing at a moment of cataclysmic fear and uncertainty for the fate of both capitalism and democracy, the political economist and historian Karl Polanyi warned that fascism, which had already swept across Europe and was knocking at the rest of the world's door, arose not just because national politics failed but because "the fascist solution of the *impasse* reached by liberal capitalism," which "can be described as . . . a reform of the market economy at the price of the extirpation of all democratic institutions" was always a shadow possibility in liberal, democratic, and capitalist countries.[1] Polanyi was perhaps the essential theorist of the imbrication of capitalism and democracy. His magnum opus, *The Great Transformation,* conceived during the Great Depression and published during World War II, sought to find the root causes of the convulsive terror of the mid-twentieth century—the political and economic origins of our time, as his subtitle declares—by excavating an earlier moment of similarly broad and deep economic, social, and ultimately political change: the industrial revolution of late-eighteenth and early-nineteenth-century England. Polanyi's theme was the political construction of both markets and democracy in the process of industrialization through the famous "double movement" of marketization and commodification, on the one hand, and the drive for protection against these phenomena, on the other. In Polanyi's hands, the development of both markets and democracy were rendered as contingent and connected events, achieved only through intense and often conflictual struggle.

Polanyi famously recounts the turmoil unleashed by the decision of the local magistrates of the parish of Speenhamland, Berkshire, to tie poor relief rates to the rising price of bread beginning in 1795. The Speenhamland system, which in Polanyi's narration led to the depression of rural wages and the pauperization of the local countryside, encapsulated a gathering confrontation between old and new social, economic, and political orders that lasted for several turbulent decades, until the Reform Act of 1832 and the New Poor Law of 1834 consolidated an emerging liberal equilibrium around the twin poles of a national market for wage labor and representative democracy that embraced the rising bourgeoisie. But that development, in turn, generated its own version of the double movement, the emergence of a working-class movement that challenged the dominance of the democratic-capitalist order on new terms.[2] In Polanyi's own time, it was becoming clear that the double movement of the liberal era would not necessarily end on terms that preserved either democracy or capitalism. Countries across Europe and beyond met the crisis of the interwar years by turning toward varieties of totalitarianism, and the liberal democratic holdouts in the Anglo-American world (where Polanyi himself lived and worked after he left Vienna in 1933) were gripped with fear about the intertwined fates of both liberal democracy and capitalism.[3]

Once again, both American democracy and capitalism find themselves at a moment of uncertainty and inflection, and Polanyi's fundamental insight might again prove a useful guide to understanding how a contemporary variant of this double movement—particularly the neoliberal push toward the marketization of, well, pretty much everything and the continuing resistance that this drive has provoked—is playing out in the postindustrial transformation of American (and, indeed, global) capitalism and the threat that this transformation might pose to democracy, in the United States and around the world.[4] As in Speenhamland, we are living through a clash between old and new political and economic orders that has found visible expression in seemingly intractable conflicts over global issues such as climate change, migration, and global markets that pose existential challenges to the post-World War II global order, and has given rise to a rising and dangerous populist challenge to liberal democracy. It is far from clear whether either democracy or capitalism will survive. In the United States, this conflict is playing out, ominously, at a moment when political, economic, partisan, and especially racial conflicts largely coincide in unprecedented ways. As Suzanne Mettler and I have argued elsewhere, the contemporary combination of political polarization, racial conflict, economic inequality, and growing executive power (in the face of legislative dysfunction) poses an especially grave risk to American democracy, and it is against this backdrop that I assess the perpetually fraught relationship between democracy and capitalism in the United States.[5]

The last few decades have seen a decline in both democracy's capacity to provide accountable government and capitalism's capacity to generate broadly shared prosperity. This process of mutual degradation, I suggest, is not accidental, and there are numerous factors that connect these two things. A recent revival of political economy in American politics scholarship has pointed toward a new synthesis that seeks to probe the critical connections between America's distinctive political and economic systems, and a wide range of recent work—both inside and outside of the emerging "American political economy" tent—has elucidated much about the politics-economy nexus.[6] To some extent, the "rediscovery" of American political economy as a core topic in American politics is reminiscent of Monsieur Jourdain, the protagonist of Molière's *Le Bourgeois Gentilhomme*, who finds himself astonished to learn from his tutor that he has been speaking prose his entire life. Like M. Jourdain, it turns out that political science has been speaking political economy for a long time. The systematic relationship between democracy and capitalism has, at least intermittently, occupied the discipline for nearly a century, if not more.[7] But a political-economy perspective on American politics has long contended with approaches that regarded politics and the economy as separate spheres, and effectively wrote considerations of capitalism out of the study of American democracy (and vice versa), so the new concerted attention to this relationship is welcome.

In the American context, alongside the basic variables that often populate accounts of political economy—class formation, business power, labor organization, economic voting, and the like—we must consider one inescapable factor that has been integral to the development of both capitalism and democracy in the United States and that continues to shape the connection between them: race. It is simply impossible to arrive at a full understanding of the American democracy-capitalism nexus without incorporating the role that racial inequality has long played in each. The role that race has played in shaping American democracy has been well documented, from the earliest connections between enslavement and ideas of liberty and the compromises that embedded the protection of slavery and the power of enslavers in the Constitution to authoritarian enclaves in the twentieth-century South along with the persistence of what Vesla Weaver and Gwen Prowse have called "racial authoritarianism."[8]

On the capitalism side, the record is nearly as long. Some have argued that capitalism as it evolved, particularly in Europe, was inherently racialized, built upon and intimately connected to imperialism and enslavement.[9] But even if we relax the strongest claims of the "racial capitalism" school that capitalism is inherently racial, we can still acknowledge that the particular historical and political circumstances that gave rise to *American* capitalism, alongside *American* democracy, owe a great deal to the role that race has long played in structuring economic relations and patterns of work, income, wealth, and inequality in the United States in ways that we have yet to fully fathom.[10] All too often, racial inequality is treated as the product of unfortunate beliefs or attitudes on the part of Americans rather than as a constitutive, structural feature of American politics and society.[11] I want to propose that it is a mistake to treat racial conflict and inequality as somehow merely incidental to contemporary polarization and the distemper of American democratic capitalism.

W. E. B. DuBois made the case for the inextricable connections among American race, capitalism, and democracy in his masterwork *Black Reconstruction.*[12] Du Bois sought to challenge the racist Dunning school of Reconstruction historiography, which held that the federal government's attempt after the Civil War to enforce rights for formerly enslaved Black Americans in the South had been a shameful episode of federal overreach that promoted corruption, and empowered people who were incapable of responsible self-government.[13] In Du Bois's reinterpretation, Reconstruction was an opportunity to remake the South in both political and economic terms, and he emphasized the agency of Black southerners themselves in attempting to build a Black working class that could form a foundation for economic autonomy, political empowerment, and ultimately citizenship in a democratic society.[14] And he documents how in response, white Southerners sought to recreate the exploitative pre-Civil War labor system, or at least to reconstitute it on somewhat altered terms, replacing chattel slavery with practices such as debt peonage, convict leasing, and sharecropping, backed by widespread organized violence and authoritarian politics.[15] The white reaction to Reconstruction effectively undermined the possibility of cross-racial working-class solidarity to construct instead a cross-class coalition of whites against African Americans, subsidized by what Du Bois called the "psychological wage" that whites of all classes received from their status in a racial hierarchy.[16] The effect of the reaction was both to undermine democracy and reinstate authoritarian regimes in the South, as southern states systematically disenfranchised Black men in the 1890s and 1900s, and to suppress the south's economic development and foreclose the emergence of the class politics that is characteristic of capitalist political economies.[17]

As these developments unfolded in the South's political economy, industrial capitalism was flourishing in the North along with the rising inequality, urban problems, and labor strife that are characteristic of industrializing economies. These pressures provoked movements for social and economic reform in the late nineteenth and early twentieth centuries. While many other countries responded to similar pressures by beginning to build welfare states as a way of taming the most egregious social and economic impacts of industrialization and either protecting the legitimacy of democratizing regimes or forestalling democratizing pressure, in the United States these movements generally foundered at the national level until the emergency of the Great Depression.[18] To the extent that such early welfare state policies emerged in the United States, mostly in the states, they generally restricted access to benefits for racial minorities, establishing a template that would continue to shape American welfare state development.[19]

The New Deal proved to be a critical inflection point for both capitalism and liberal democracy in the United States. When Franklin Roosevelt became president in March 1933, the depression economy was at its lowest ebb, and it seemed plausible that liberal democracy was not equal to the challenge of restoring the economy to equilibrium and prosperity. Deeply fearful, many Americans looked approvingly across the Atlantic, where emerging authoritarian regimes seemed better able to meet the emergency with vigor and clarity, as opposed to the muddled American response that seemed to have produced only lassitude and confusion.[20] In the face of this crisis, the Roosevelt Administration responded by establishing many of the building blocks of a national welfare state, including retirement pensions, unemployment insurance, expanded labor protections, and income support for the poor. As Roosevelt articulated in his famous 1941 "four freedoms" speech, he saw these protections as essential not only for the prevention of privation and despair but also as "the foundations of a healthy and strong democracy. The basic things expected by our people of their political and economic systems," he continued, "are simple." Chief among the items he went on to enumerate were economic: jobs, opportunity, and security—encapsulated later in the speech as "freedom from want."[21]

But we know that saving American democracy and capitalism from the political and economic emergency of the 1930s came at a price: this was a welfare state designed for white working men.[22] The New Deal did little to dislodge the structural racial inequality that remained embedded in the political system, and its social and labor policies were generally carefully designed to avoid upsetting the racial balance of power in the country, and particularly in the authoritarian enclaves of the American South.[23] In particular, the mechanisms that effectively excluded Black Americans from the protection of the emerging welfare state were centered particularly on the rural South: the widespread exclusion of farm workers from coverage and the preservation of localized administration of public assistance programs, which allowed southern states to direct benefits away from African Americans and to preserve the equilibrium of the rural labor market.[24]

In their chapter, Suzanne Mettler and Trevor Brown are certainly right to identify New Deal agricultural policy as a critical origin point for the rural-urban divide that has come to infect American democracy over the past few decades. The New Deal's deep commitment to rural development arose out of Roosevelt's belief that the health of the rural economy was essential both to national recovery and his own political fortunes.[25] As Mettler and Brown carefully document, the apparent decay of that commitment over time along with the decimation of much of the rural economy in the contemporary era have certainly combined to create for many rural Americans the sense that both democracy and capitalism have failed them, creating the conditions that have given rise to the antidemocratic mistrust and resentment that widely characterize rural politics today.

Like the welfare state, New Deal rural and agricultural policy were, of course, devised and enacted by a racially structured state that empowered southern whites, and even though some rural Black southerners benefited from policies such as rural electrification and farm security programs, these policies, like other New Deal programs, did little to fundamentally restructure racial power relations in the South. Moreover, the unfolding of these policies coincided with the Great Migration of African Americans from rural South to urban North. In short, the commitment to rural redevelopment came just as rural America was becoming whiter. In 1900, only 22.7 percent of the country's Black population lived in urban areas. By 1930, after the first wave of South-North migration, that figure nearly doubled, to 43.7 percent, and by 1960 it was 73.2 percent. (The urban share of the white population also grew over that span, but considerably less dramatically: from 43 percent in 1900 to 65.5 percent in 1960).[26]

The economic shifts and resulting political resentments that have reshaped rural America can thus be reinterpreted as an attack on an economic class that benefited not just from a close attachment to the state but also from a certain kind of privileged, politically constructed whiteness. As an axis of polarization, this racial divide was long suppressed by the party system, especially the New Deal coalition that brought the rural South and urban North into an uneasy political alliance and was bound together by an organizationally strong, if programmatically amorphous, party.[27] But the racial conflict that was largely masked by the midcentury party system became inescapable later in the twentieth century as the political claims of African Americans moved to the center of the national agenda. This new axis of racial conflict was about both democracy and capitalism. The claims that animated the civil rights revolution were not just political claims about rights and power but also *economic* claims, about access to jobs, housing, and the kind of economic security that midcentury prosperity and policy had offered to the white working class, rural as well as urban, but that largely eluded Black Americans.[28] From the work of A. Philip Randolph and his Brotherhood of Sleeping Car Porters to the 1963 March on Washington, which was billed as a march for jobs and freedom, to Martin Luther King's Chicago Freedom movement, which focused particularly on the stifling of economic opportunity through job and housing discrimination, the civil rights movement targeted both democracy and capitalism.[29] The movement's early successes included advances in jobs and wages for African American workers, especially (and ironically) in industries that were nearing their death throes in the American economy, such as steel and manufacturing, and in public-sector jobs that have increasingly come under attack in the neoliberal order that was just beginning to gestate.[30]

The contemporary neoliberal era of political and economic stress is equally entangled with the legacies of racial inequality. As Hacker and Pierson describe in their chapter, the transformation from an industrial to a knowledge-based economy has wrought tremendous changes in American politics, as the sticky policies and institutions that were designed in the twentieth century to govern an industrial country have proven ill-equipped for the postindustrial, globally interconnected present, and that transformation has broadly given rise to a political economy that is heavily tilted in favor of wealthy, educated elites and has proven severely dislocating for many others who have channeled their political, economic, and cultural resentment into an oppositional politics that has taken dead aim at the political establishment of an earlier era.[31]

In many ways, the transition to a postindustrial economy is reminiscent of the earlier transition to industrial capitalism in the nineteenth century, which proved extremely economically and political unsettling, as Polanyi demonstrated. In both cases, economic transformation was closely linked to advances in science and technology, and relied on a newly educated work force. Both depended on innovation-friendly legal and regulatory systems and efficient financial markets that proved contentious and tended to widen the inequality gap between the beneficiaries and victims of the new economic order. Patterns of urban transformation, labor mobility, and relatively open immigration policies—which produced severe racialized backlash in both eras in the United States and elsewhere—also played important roles in both eras. As Hacker and Pierson have argued persuasively before, the very policies that once protected the American working class from the risks of industrial capitalism have withered through a combination of neglect, stasis, technological change, and willful confrontation, shifting risk onto the shoulders of those least able to bear it.[32]

But the notion that American political institutions and policies were better suited to govern an earlier era of industrial dislocation than the current era of postindustrial neoliberalism seems true only if one ignores the structural and systemic racial exclusion of the New Deal order and its aftermath. Compared with the contemporary era, mid-twentieth-century American democracy seemed more stable than today's version and the excesses of capitalism were largely tamed—for white Americans. The resolution of democratic instability in the United States by either initiating or reinforcing racial exclusion from the polity is a recurring pattern in American politics, and the mid-twentieth century was no exception.[33] Moreover, the transformation of American capitalism has been especially dislocating for African Americans and other minorities. As I suggested above, concerted national action to address racial inequalities in the economy largely came about just as the hollowing out of the industrial economy began to render these hard-won protections less secure and valuable. And racial minorities have been largely cut off from much of the new gains of the knowledge economy through the cumulative effects of historic discrimination in housing and education, as well as employment and through the growth of a carceral state that has drastically limited economic mobility for many. Again, both democracy and capitalism are compromised in the neoliberal era by the persistence and reconfiguration of racial inequality.

As Polanyi observed of industrialization, the transition to a new neoliberal political-economic order has provoked a double movement, the construction and consolidation of a new order and resistance to its effects, which has taken a variety of forms. Particularly prominent in this reaction is the "new right" that William Galston identifies, which seems to be coalescing around a culturally conservative skepticism about neoliberal capitalism and at best a cavalier attitude toward democracy. Galston offers an extremely convincing synthesis of this latest in a series of "new right" waves that have cropped up periodically, and his historical and intellectual exegesis shows quite clearly how this trend emerged as a challenge to both capitalism and democracy in their current forms.

But it is worth considering that these developments, and the form that this conservative resistance has taken, have themselves been shaped by the recurring conflict over the boundaries of membership in American society, particularly conflicts over race and immigration.[34] Much of the new conservative resistance seems to trace its origins to the election and presidency of Barack Obama. Obama was not only the first Black president (Toni Morrison's quip about Bill Clinton notwithstanding) but for many he also embodied the uncomfortable marriage of neoliberal political-economic consensus and racially progressive cosmopolitanism that drove a polarizing wedge deeper into the heart of American opinion and identity than had happened in a long time.[35] The Obama era unleashed not only the new right of economic dislocation and resentment in response to the long-run decline of manufacturing jobs and the hollowing out of many places that had been dependent on those jobs, but also a corrosive politics of racial resentment, white identity, and reaction.[36] In this regard, the rise of the contemporary new right echoes a previous incarnation of the new right that emerged out of the turmoil of the 1960s in its mingling of cultural, religious, and decidedly racial anxieties that were encapsulated in the presidential candidacy of George Wallace, Richard Nixon's "southern strategy" and his appeal to a "silent majority," and finally Ronald Reagan's rather miraculous alchemy that fused these elements of resentment into a deceptively sunny and amiable electoral formula.[37]

To return, finally, to Polanyi's penetrating analysis, the association between democracy and capitalism is fraught, changeable, and historically contingent. Whether they can coexist depends less on their inherent properties than on the specific contours of the struggles around equality, inclusion, and political and economic power that demarcate their relationship. In the United States, these recurring struggles have typically played out against the backdrop of the country's foundational and continuing history of racial inequality, and if they are to coexist and flourish in the future, they will have to confront that history.

Notes

1. Karl Polanyi, *The Great Transformation: The Political and Economic Origins of Our Time* (New York: Farrar & Rinehart, 1944), 237.
2. E. P. Thompson, *The Making of the English Working Class* (London: Victor Gollancz, 1963); Barrington Moore Jr., *Social Origins of Dictatorship and Democracy: Lord and Peasant in the Making of the Modern World* (Boston: Beacon Press, 1966); Daniel Ziblatt, *Conservative Parties and the Birth of Democracy* (Cambridge: Cambridge University Press, 2017).
3. See Ira Katznelson, *Fear Itself: The New Deal and the Origins of Our Time* (New York: Liveright, 2013). Note the echoes of Polanyi's subtitle in Katznelson's. On Polanyi's life and politics, see Gareth Dale, *Karl Polanyi: A Life on the Left* (New York: Columbia University Press, 2016), and Fred Block's Introduction to the 2001 edition of *The Great Transformation* (Boston: Beacon Press, 2001).
4. Gary Gerstle, *The Rise and Fall of the Neoliberal Order: America and the World in the Free Market Era* (Oxford: Oxford University Press, 2022); Frances McCall Rosenbluth and Margaret Weir, eds., *Who Gets What? The New Politics of Insecurity* (Cambridge: Cambridge University Press, 2021); Robert Kuttner, *Can Democracy Survive Global Capitalism?* (New York: W. W. Norton, 2018).
5. Suzanne Mettler and Robert C. Lieberman, *Four Threats: The Recurring Crises of American Democracy* (New York: St. Martin's, 2020).
6. Jacob S. Hacker, Alexander Hertel-Fernandez, Paul Pierson, and Kathleen Thelen, eds., *The American Political Economy: Politics, Markets, and Power* (Cambridge: Cambridge University Press, 2022); Alexander Hertel-Fernandez, *State Capture: How Conservative Activists, Big Businesses, and Wealthy Donors Reshaped the American States—and the Nation* (New York: Oxford University Press, 2018); Alexander Hertel-Fernandez, Suresh Naidu, and Adam Reich, "Schooled by Strikes? The Effects of Large-Scale Labor Unrest on Mass Attitudes toward the Labor Movement," *Perspectives on Politics* 19, no. 1 (March 2021): 73–91; Larry M. Bartels, *Unequal Democracy: The Political Economy of the New Gilded Age* (New York: Russell Sage Foundation; Princeton: Princeton University Press, 2008); Martin Gilens, *Affluence and Influence: Economic Inequality and Political Power in America* (New York: Russell Sage Foundation; Princeton: Princeton University Press, 2012); Benjamin I. Page, Jason Seawright, and Matthew J. Lacombe, *Billionaires and Stealth Politics* (Chicago: University of Chicago Press,

2019); Nicholas Carnes and Noam Lupu, "The White Working Class and the 2016 Election," *Perspectives on Politics* 19, no. 1 (March 2021): 55–72.

7. For just a few classic examples, see E. E. Schattschneider, *Politics, Pressures, and the Tariff* (New York: Prentice-Hall, 1935); Charles E. Lindblom, *Politics and Markets: The World's Political-Economic Systems* (New York: Basic Books, 1977); Albert O. Hirschman, *The Passions and the Interests: Political Arguments for Capitalism before Its Triumph* (Princeton: Princeton University Press, 1977); Peter A. Hall and David W. Soskice, eds., *Varieties of Capitalism: The Institutional Foundations of Comparative Advantage* (Oxford: Oxford University Press, 2001).
8. Edmund S. Morgan, *American Slavery, American Freedom: The Ordeal of Colonial Virginia* (New York: W. W. Norton, 1975); David Brian Robertson, *The Constitution and America's Destiny* (Cambridge: Cambridge University Press, 2005); Robert Mickey, *Paths Out of Dixie: The Democratization of Authoritarian Enclaves in America's Deep South, 1944–1972* (Princeton: Princeton University Press, 2015); Vesla M. Weaver and Gwen Prowse, "Racial Authoritarianism in U.S. Democracy," *Science* 369, no. 6508 (September 4, 2020): 1176–78. In general, see Desmond S. King and Rogers M. Smith, *Still a House Divided: Race and Politics in Obama's America* (Princeton: Princeton University Press, 2011).
9. See Eric Williams, *Capitalism and Slavery* (Chapel Hill: University of North Carolina Press, 1944); Oliver Cromwell Cox, *Caste, Class, and Race: A Study in Social Dynamics* (New York: Monthly Review, 1948); Cedric J. Robinson, *Black Marxism: The Making of the Black Radical Tradition* (London: Zed Press, 1983). For a nuanced approach to the concept of "racial capitalism" and its historical and intellectual genealogy, see Inés Valdez, "Socialism and Empire: Labor Mobility, Racial Capitalism, and the Political Theory of Migration," *Political Theory* 49, no. 6 (December 2021): 902–33.
10. See Chloe Thurston, "Racial Inequality, Market Inequality, and the American Political Economy," in *The American Political Economy*, ed. Hacker et al.; David Bateman, Jacob M. Grumbach, and Chloe Thurston, "Race and Historical Political Economy," in *The Oxford Handbook of Historical Political Economy*, ed. Jeffery A. Jenkins and Jared Rubin (Oxford: Oxford University Press, 2024); Michael C. Dawson and Megan Ming Francis, "Black Politics and the Neoliberal Racial Order," *Public Culture* 28, no. 1 (January 2016): 23–62.
11. See Fredrick C. Harris and Robert C. Lieberman, eds., *Beyond Discrimination: Racial Inequality in a Post-Racist Era* (New York: Russell Sage Foundation, 2013).
12. W. E. Burghardt Du Bois, *Black Reconstruction in America: An Essay toward a History of the Part Which Black Folk Played in the Attempt to Reconstruct Democracy in America, 1860–1880* (New York: Harcourt, Brace, 1935).
13. On the Dunning School and its harmful effects, both as an interpretation of Reconstruction and as part of the ideology that undergirded Jim Crow, see Eric Foner, *Reconstruction: America's Unfinished Revolution, 1863–1877* (New York: Harper & Row, 1988), esp. xix–xxi.
14. On voting and earning as the twin pillars of American citizenship, see Judith N. Shklar, *American Citizenship: The Quest for Inclusion* (Cambridge: Harvard University Press, 1991).
15. Douglas A. Blackmon, *Slavery by Another Name: The Re-Enslavement of Black Americans from the Civil War to World War II* (New York: Doubleday, 2008); Mickey, *Paths Out of Dixie*.
16. Du Bois, *Black Reconstruction*, 700–1. See also Joel Olson, "Whiteness and the Participation-Inclusion Dilemma," *Political Theory* 30, no. 3 (June 2002): 384–409.
17. See V. O. Key Jr., *Southern Politics in State and Nation* (New York: Alfred A. Knopf, 1949).
18. Theda Skocpol, *Protecting Soldiers and Mothers: The Political Origins of Social Policy in the United States* (Cambridge: Harvard University Press, 1992).
19. Linda Faye Williams, *The Constraint of Race: Legacies of White Skin Privilege in America* (University Park: Pennsylvania State University Press, 2003); Deborah E. Ward, *The White Welfare State: The Racialization of U.S. Welfare Policy* (Ann Arbor: University of Michigan Press, 2005); Cybelle Fox, *Three Worlds of Relief: Race, Immigration, and the American Welfare State from the Progressive Era to the New Deal* (Princeton: Princeton University Press, 2012).
20. Katznelson, *Fear Itself*; Mettler and Lieberman, *Four Threats*, ch. 5.
21. Franklin D. Roosevelt, "The Annual Message to the Congress, January 6, 1941," in *The Public Papers and Addresses of Franklin D. Roosevelt*, ed. Samuel I. Rosenman (New York: Macmillan, 1941), 9: 671–2.

22. See Suzanne Mettler, *Dividing Citizens: Gender and Federalism in New Deal Social Policy* (Ithaca: Cornell University Press, 1998).
23. Robert C. Lieberman, *Shifting the Color Line: Race and the American Welfare State* (Cambridge: Harvard University Press, 1998); Ira Katznelson, *When Affirmative Action Was White: An Untold Story of Racial Inequality in Twentieth-Century America* (New York: W. W. Norton, 2005).
24. Robert C. Lieberman and John S. Lapinski, "American Federalism, Race, and the Administration of Welfare," *British Journal of Political Science* 31, no. 2 (April 2001): 303–29.
25. Sarah Phillips, *This Land, This Nation: Conservation, Rural America, and the New Deal* (Cambridge: Cambridge University Press, 2007).
26. Daniel O. Price, "Urbanization of the Blacks," *Milbank Memorial Fund Quarterly* 48, no. 2 (April 1970): 48.
27. See Daniel Schlozman and Sam Rosenfeld, *The Hollow Parties: The Many Pasts and Disordered Present of American Party Politics* (Princeton: Princeton University Press, 2024).
28. See Taylor Branch, *At Canaan's Edge: America in the King Years, 1965–68* (New York: Simon and Schuster, 2006); Jonathan Eig, *King: A Life* (New York: Farrar, Straus and Giroux, 2023).
29. See Sidney Milkis and Katherine Rader, "The March on Washington Movement, the Fair Employment Practices Commission, and the Long Quest for Racial Justice," *Studies in American Political Development* 38, no. 1 (April 2024): 16–35.
30. See Judith Stein, *Running Steel, Running America: Race, Economic Policy, and the Decline of Liberalism* (Chapel Hill: University of North Carolina Press, 1998).
31. Robert C. Lieberman, Suzanne Mettler, Thomas B. Pepinsky, Kenneth M. Roberts, and Richard Valelly, "The Trump Presidency and American Democracy: A Historical and Comparative Analysis," *Perspectives on Politics* 17, no. 2 (June 2019): 470–79.
32. Jacob S. Hacker and Paul Pierson, *Winner-Take-All Politics: How Washington Made the Rich Richer—and Turned Its Back on the Middle Class* (New York: Simon and Schuster, 2010). See also Rosenbluth and Weir, eds., *Who Gets What?*; Torben Iversen and Philipp Rehm, *Big Data and the Welfare State: How the Information Revolution Threatens Social Solidarity* (Cambridge: Cambridge University Press, 2022).
33. Mettler and Lieberman, *Four Threats*; David A. Bateman, *Disenfranchising Democracy: Constructing the Electorate in the United States, the United Kingdom, and France* (Cambridge: Cambridge University Press, 2018).
34. Mettler and Lieberman, *Four Threats.*
35. Toni Morrison, "The Talk of the Town," *New Yorker*, October 5, 1998, 32; Fredrick C. Harris, *The Price of the Ticket: Barack Obama and the Rise and Decline of Black Politics* (Oxford: Oxford University Press, 2012).
36. Michael Tesler, *Post-Racial or Most-Racial: Race and Politics in the Obama Era* (Chicago: University of Chicago Press, 2016); Christopher S. Parker and Matthew Barreto, *Change They Can't Believe In: The Tea Party and Reactionary Politics in America* (Princeton: Princeton University Press, 2013); Arlie Russell Hochschild, *Strangers in Their Own Land: Anger and Mourning on the American Right* (New York: New Press, 2016); Lilliana Mason, *Uncivil Agreement: How Politics Became Our Identity* (Chicago: University of Chicago Press, 2018); Ashley Jardina, *White Identity Politics* (Cambridge: Cambridge University Press, 2019); Rogers M. Smith and Desmond King, *America's New Racial Battle Lines: Protect versus Repair* (Chicago: University of Chicago Press, 2024).
37. Kevin Phillips, *The Emerging Republican Majority* (New Rochelle, NY: Arlington House, 1969); Daniel Schlozman, *When Movements Anchor Parties: Electoral Alignments in American History* (Princeton: Princeton University Press, 2015), ch. 8; Rick Perlstein, *Nixonland: The Rise of a President and the Fracturing of America* (New York: Scribner, 2008); Rick Perlstein, *The Invisible Bridge: The Fall of Nixon and the Rise of Reagan* (New York: Simon and Schuster, 2014).

11

From Leader to Laggard? American Democratic Capitalism in the Knowledge Economy

JACOB S. HACKER AND PAUL PIERSON

Worries about the future of US "democratic capitalism" typically center on one side of the phrase: democracy or capitalism. Yet democratic capitalism—the mix of responsive governance and regulated markets that, for all its flaws, dramatically advanced prosperity and democracy in the twentieth century—should be seen as a set of evolving interrelationships. To assess its performance and prospects, we need to examine not just whether elections are free or markets competitive, but how well the interplay of capitalism and democracy is working. Is our democracy fostering a vibrant economy? Is our economy fostering a strong democracy? In short, is American democratic capitalism continuing to produce the virtuous circle of broadly increasing prosperity and strengthened democracy that generally marked its ascent?

In this chapter, we argue that American democratic capitalism is not performing so well—and, indeed, is caught in an increasingly worrisome cycle of dysfunctional politics and diminishing capacity to generate broad-based prosperity. The consequences have included declining social performance in key areas relative to other rich democracies (such as health, education, and inequality); stalemated or hamstrung national policymaking in the face of mounting economic challenges, including the existential challenge of climate change; and escalating crises of governance that increasingly threaten democratic capitalism itself.

At root, we argue, there is a widening chasm between the kind of governance our economy needs for Americans to thrive and the kind of governance our

Jacob S. Hacker and Paul Pierson, *From Leader to Laggard?*. In: *Can Democracy and Capitalism Be Reconciled?*.
Edited by: Sidney M. Milkis and Scott C. Miller, Oxford University Press. © Oxford University Press (2025).
DOI: 10.1093/9780197774731.003.0012

polity is producing. The postindustrial knowledge economy has thrown up a set of policy challenges that require active democratic governance. Such a response has been hobbled, however, by the ongoing transformation of American politics. The nationalization and polarization of the nation's two parties—the degree to which they have become national teams of elites, groups, and voters hostile to the other side—has placed huge strains on a constitutional order not well designed to deal with such deep polarization.[1]

When analysts speak of "polarization," they tend to highlight the gridlock and dysfunction caused by the movement of both parties from the center. Because our lawmaking institutions require broad agreement to function, a widening partisan gulf is a huge problem in an economic context where active governance is needed. The US constitutional order also assumes a constructive tension between the legislative, executive, and judicial branches. When political leaders act solely as members of partisan teams rather than as defenders of their branches' powers (in addition to partisan politicians), key safeguards against the dominance of powerful minority interests and executive and judicial aggrandizement are compromised. Finally, if national lawmaking is stymied by gridlock, other actors—from the president using unilateral powers to the federal courts to the states—take on greater importance. When these actors also act as partisan team players, there is the possibility that parties will face cumulative advantages (or disadvantages) based on whether they are systematically favored or disfavored in these other domains. As we shall see, the increased role of the courts, and in particular the Supreme Court, has greatly compounded the challenge of adapting to new economic realities.

The problem of polarization, however, is intensified by its asymmetric character. While both parties have retreated from moderation, it is Republicans who have moved further from the center, it is Republicans who have grown hostile to active democratic governance, and it is Republicans who have capitalized on and fanned the powerful right-wing populist backlash that has accompanied the transition to the knowledge economy and the nation's uneasy steps toward becoming a truly multi-racial democracy.[2] Fatefully, it is also Republicans who have been advantaged by a constitutional order that simultaneously makes active lawmaking difficult and weakens the representation of the diverse metropolitan centers now driving prosperity. As Trevor Brown and Suzanne Mettler argue in this volume, the parties are increasingly cleaved between the dense metro areas that fuel prosperity in the knowledge economy (increasingly aligned with the Democratic Party) and the less dense non-metro areas that struggle to adapt (increasingly aligned with the GOP). In various ways we shall discuss, American electoral and political institutions disadvantage the former and advantage the latter, imposing what amounts to a representational "density tax" on metro voters and the Democratic Party. (The particular challenge posed by the Supreme

Court reflects this density tax, which has allowed Republicans to forge a 6–3 conservative majority while regularly failing to win national popular majorities.) Republicans have found sustenance in these institutions, while Democrats have struggled to overcome their biases.

The Democrats' struggle is not just a result of institutional biases that favor the status quo and disadvantage a metro-based party. The party is marked by its own divides, which have hamstrung its response to the distinctive challenges of the knowledge economy—even in places and during moments when it has relatively unified control of governing power. Nowhere is this clearer than in the housing crisis (homelessness, unaffordability, inadequate supply for potential new arrivals) that afflicts fast-growing knowledge economy hubs like San Francisco, Seattle, and New York. Within the party, strong defenders of the status quo operate alongside newly empowered groups that seek greater incorporation within the American polity. All too often, these tensions within the coalition result in hobbled efforts to overcome entrenched incumbents, whether they be homeowners who resist denser and more affordable housing or concentrated industries that seek to preserve monopoly profits at the expense of workers and competitors (and, in the case of the fossil fuel industry, the future of a rapidly warming planet).

In the next section, we lay out our basic framework for understanding the American response to the evolving knowledge economy. That framework leans heavily on recent work in Comparative Political Economy and the emerging field of American Political Economy. We then outline why the United States—global leader in the initial transition to the knowledge economy—is facing increasing difficulties managing the challenges that are emerging from the interplay of capitalism and democracy. Fundamentally, we offer a *developmental* argument: epochal changes in the American economy, the demographic makeup of the nation, and the US party system have made longstanding political institutions less capable of promoting shared prosperity. The poor match between what the evolving economy needs and what our institutions can supply is growing worse, as forces alarmed by economic, cultural, and demographic (that is, racial and ethnic) trends have come together to create a "backlash coalition" centered within the contemporary Republican Party. This backlash coalition includes those concerned with a loss of social status as well as those fearful of losing privileged economic power; it includes voters dissatisfied with economic and demographic shifts as well as key segments of the American economic elite. And this backlash coalition has exploited core features of our political institutions in ways that accentuate, rather than reduce, the threat to shared prosperity and a vibrant democracy.

We focus on this backlash coalition because it is the largest and most immediate threat to democratic capitalism. We want to make clear, however, that the dynamics we identify in the Democratic Party—which has its own powerful defenders of the status quo—are also corrosive to the nation's continuing successful adaptation to changing realities. Thus we close the chapter by considering how it might be possible not just to diminish the threat of the backlash coalition, but also to combine a genuine politics of inclusion with a pragmatic but tough effort to overcome entrenched incumbents that stand in the way of a more vibrant democratic capitalism.

American Democratic Capitalism and the Knowledge Economy

To assess how well democratic capitalism is functioning, we draw on the emerging field of American Political Economy.[3] Like the more established field of Comparative Political Economy (CPE), American Political Economy (APE) focuses on the study of how economic and political systems are linked—that is, how political structures shape economic development and economic structures shape political development.

From these fields we take two insights. The first is that modern capitalist economies—the United States very much included—are *mixed* economies, in which democratic governments necessarily pursue an extensive range of public policies to manage the complex interdependence of contemporary life. To be successful, these policies must evolve over time to foster sustained growth and to deal with the shifting challenges that producing shared prosperity entails. This makes it crucial that political systems have the necessary incentives and capacities to be responsive to broad majorities and update policies in response to changing realities—incentives and capacities that have greatly weakened in the United States.

The second insight is that, while all capitalist democracies are mixed economies, the United States is unusual. Our political institutions, the structure of our economy, and the relationship between the two all look particularly exceptional today. So too do the consequences of this exceptionalism for the well-being of Americans. Put bluntly, our distinctive political institutions do not seem capable of managing our mounting challenges. This growing mismatch is generating many of the cross-nationally subpar economic and social outcomes discussed in other chapters of this volume—outcomes that are at once deeply troubling markers of political dysfunction, and key contributors to the vicious cycle we identify.

More specifically, we argue that the United States is failing to tackle effectively the challenges created by the ongoing transition from an industrial economy toward a so-called knowledge economy (KE). This transformation —comparable in scale and impact to the transition to the industrial economy itself—has involved a dramatic reshuffling of both relevant skills and economic space.[4] Among the winners have been highly educated workers, KE firms, and the favorably situated cities where they congregate (so-called urban agglomeration hubs). These inequality-promoting changes, operating in tandem with the financialization and globalization of business, have had a profound impact on the structure, behavior, and preferences of leading firms. In general, this transformation has increased the resources of business and the wealthy, and made them less interested in or capable of pursuing positive-sum solutions that put priority on the well-being of American workers.[5]

This transition has not only created big winners. It has also created big losers, particularly the large numbers of "left behind" workers and communities.[6] Concentrated in the declining manufacturing industries of the Northeast and Midwest, organized labor in the private sector has virtually collapsed. In turn, these changes in the balance of power have reconfigured political alliances and the dimensions and character of partisan contestation—all of which have fed back into policymaking in ways that threaten to undermine further successful adaptation to the shifting contours of the world economy.

The Knowledge Economy's Distinctive Opportunities and Risks

Comparative political economists have emphasized that quite different models of democratic capitalism can be broadly functional.[7] This argument rests on the expectation that, in the relatively small number of countries that have made the leap into the top ranks of economic performance, markets and democracy are largely complementary: the need for growth disciplines democracy (for example, by discouraging excessive rent-seeking); the need to satisfy voters constrains even powerful market actors, while encouraging policymakers to focus on generating broad prosperity and helping those negatively affected by the "creative destruction" of dynamic capitalism. Although the particular institutions that developed to manage these complementarities varied across rich democracies, they showed a common and unprecedented capacity to promote growing and reasonably widely shared affluence over decades.

Crucially, the transition to the knowledge economy creates a set of challenges that are often very different from those associated with an industrial economy. How and how well can we expect rich capitalist democracies to adapt to these new realities? Torben Iversen and David Soskice offer perhaps the most systematic (and optimistic) case: Over time, they argue, the interplay between markets and politics in advanced capitalist economies is likely to produce policies and institutions consistent with both high levels of economic performance and democratic stability.[8] Crucial to their argument is the claim that voters who benefit from the KE and those who seek to share in its rewards (what they call "aspirational voters") will be a decisive voting bloc that encourages parties across the spectrum to develop policies and institutions conducive to prosperity. It is essential to highlight these policies and institutions, without assuming they will be identical (or even present) in all rich democracies. They include:

- *Promotion of science and advanced education.* Social arrangements need to support an infrastructure for high-quality R&D and develop a highly skilled workforce.
- *Legal and regulatory systems that encourage and reward innovation,* including "strong" state institutions capable of "enforcing competition on advanced capitalist companies (who would prefer protection and stable profits)."[9]
- *Policies and arrangements supporting vibrant urban agglomerations,* the incubators of the KE. This includes the social infrastructure (transportation, education, housing) and amenities (cultural vitality, a clean environment, low crime) necessary to attract and retain highly skilled workers and innovative firms.
- *Sufficient levels of generational, class, and geographic mobility of labor to encourage upskilling and secure the support of aspirational voters,* voters who want to become a part of the KE or want their children to become part of it.
- *Effective management of growing social diversity.* The global KE recenters production in cities, and involves denser social connections across firms and individuals. As a result, knowledge production requires, or at least encourages, greater diversity and tolerance. In the context of increased immigration, these trends place acute strains on frameworks for encouraging social integration created in earlier eras.

How well has the United States done at constructing and sustaining these foundational elements of the emerging economic order? The United States was clearly at the forefront of the transition, and a strong argument can be made that its distinctive political institutions were a crucial reason why. It developed a highly flexible and decentralized system of R&D funding and higher education (with strong ties to federal defense and health research imperatives), a flexible high-end labor market, and an equally flexible and decentralized system of business and innovation financing. These systems were pivotal to US leadership in the radical innovation that marked the rise of the digital- and biomedical-centered KE.[10] No less important, despite the decentralization of many decisions about allocation and innovation, both federal and state governments invested enormous sums in higher education and R&D, overcoming the well-known free-rider problems inherent in activities with such enormous shared benefits.

While the United States clearly led the transition to the knowledge economy, developments of the past two decades provide a much more mixed picture. On the one hand, American firms continue to play an outsized role in key sectors: digital technology, bio-technology, professional services, and so on. Indeed, the grip of American companies on leading digital platforms—Facebook, Amazon, Google—has no real analogue in the recent past or in other rich democracies (though we will argue this poses barriers to innovation today). The scale and successful history of the infrastructure for start-ups and the scope and quality of American R&D and institutions of higher education—all remain impressive as well, in both absolute and relative terms, though not as impressive as in earlier years. And the United States has outpaced other rich nations in aggregate GDP growth and its economic recovery from the COVID-19 pandemic.

At the same time, there are good reasons to be concerned. Despite the first-mover status of the United States, distinctive features of the American polity have made it difficult to sustain and adapt the appropriate institutions and policies over time, especially as more and more countries position themselves to compete in the same economic space. With the rise of competition from poorer countries that are not capitalist democracies, especially China, all rich nations are facing new and intensified challenges. As we show in the next section, however, these challenges have proved especially disruptive in the United States, because they have generated a distinctive political response. When we broaden our perspective to take in the shifting interplay of politics and markets in the United States, there is reason to fear a virtuous cycle of success is giving way to a vicious cycle of pathology.

Signs of Strain

The knowledge economy creates distinctive challenges. *Political* economy, however, stresses that meeting those demands doesn't happen automatically; sustained prosperity requires supportive politics. Making sense of such politics requires attention to the way that evolving arrangements affect political coalitions and contestation, including the preferences of voters, the relative power of organized groups, and (especially) the changing contours of partisan contestation. As emphasized, it also requires attention to developmental issues. As the knowledge economy evolves, does it produce virtuous cycles or vicious ones?

The political-economic evolution of the United States over the past few decades gives reason for pessimism. First, institutions that were well adapted to the challenges of launching a knowledge economy may not work as well at adapting and supporting it over time, particularly as it creates new challenges. Second, to the extent that such challenges are not well addressed, those can help promote a sociopolitical response that further undermines the KE's successful evolution—what we call a backlash coalition. Finally, this backlash coalition can in turn exploit weaknesses in American institutions (weaknesses that were not as relevant in earlier periods) in ways that undermine the economy and threaten democracy. Each of these threats is growing.

In this section, we discuss three sources of increasing strain that are emerging as a result: (1) the growing concentration of prosperity in metro areas and the dislocations and resentments generated outside them; (2) the growing inability—due mostly to federal gridlock, but also to local political dynamics that directly implicate the Democratic Party—to sustain investments in R&D and higher education while updating policies to manage the growing interdependence of metro agglomeration hubs; and (3) the failure to moderate the growing concentration of key sectors of the American economy, which has produced a set of "modern robber barons" with both the resources and incentives to tilt policies and markets to quell competition.[11] After laying out these strains, we turn to the backlash coalition that they are fueling, and then to the ways in which US institutions have empowered it—intensifying, rather than moderating, the tensions between advanced capitalism and democracy.

Growing Geographic inequality

It is now well recognized that the United States, with its extreme inequality and more limited protections against job insecurity and skill displacement, has done a particularly poor job helping workers displaced by the rise of the global knowledge economy. Workers without college degrees in particular have been caught between dwindling opportunities for "good jobs" of yesteryear and the penuries and precarities of lower-wage service employment. Tellingly, the typically sunny Iversen and Soskice note that compared with other affluent democracies the United States is likely to be *relatively* vulnerable to a populist backlash. They stress that the highly stratified American systems of education and social provision do comparatively little for those most threatened by the decline of the industrial economy. These newly vulnerable citizens (which they term the "old middle classes") constitute the potential electoral base for a strong reaction to the evolving KE.[12]

As already noted, the dislocations facing this old middle class are extremely localized. Job and income growth, as well as opportunities for skill acquisition, have been concentrated in a smaller number of dense urban hubs. These areas have expanded in population and wealth—and would have expanded even more if they were better able to deal with their huge housing supply problems, which we shall take up shortly. The places left behind have hollowed out, with older and less mobile workers staying put. These "stayers," overwhelmingly white, are increasingly resentful of urban, multiracial America. Labor force participation of prime-age workers has also fallen, and union membership—critical to moderating racial resentment and focusing workers on national policy responses—has plummeted.[13] Little wonder that when these places suffer large job losses they typically shift dramatically toward the Republican Party.[14]

The growing concentration of affluence in urban centers is hardly unique to the United States. But it matters more in the United States than elsewhere. First, in contrast with countries that have proportional representation, the United States has a territorial electoral system that requires that parties construct geographically contiguous coalitions—partisan contestation focuses on winning *voters who live in particular places.* Second, compared with other rich democracies with single member district systems, such as Australia, Canada, and the U.K., there is a stronger relationship between the population density of districts and their partisanship.[15] Third, as discussed in the next section, America's long history of deep racial divisions—which have a pronounced spatial dimension, with most of rural America still overwhelmingly white—adds fuel to the ethnonationalist, anti-immigrant character of right-wing populism everywhere.

Finally, the American electoral system is unique among rich democracies in the degree to which representation is tilted toward less dense areas—what we call a density tax, because voters in denser areas (and the party that represents them) are penalized. The Senate is starkly biased toward less populous states, and the Electoral College carries over some of this bias. Even the House, with districts roughly equal in population, imposes a density tax because Democratic voters are so clustered in dense metro areas. Such clustering naturally results in more "wasted votes" for the Democratic Party in metro districts, and it makes it easier to "pack" such voters into a small number of districts, reducing their representation.[16]

The unusual degree of state control over election administration in the United States (in most countries, this is a national concern) facilitates such GOP-favorable gerrymandering, as does the fact that state legislatures display the same pro-rural bias and are also prone to acute gerrymandering themselves. In recent years, the House-level advantage of Republicans appears to be fading due to Democrats' growing strength in the suburbs of major metros and the growing edge of Republicans in rural areas (which leads Republicans to waste more votes than they once did). Still, the American system of representation continues to impose a sizable density tax.

Declining Investment

The successful American formula combined decentralization with massive government spending on R&D and higher education. Some aspects of decentralization now appear more pathological—it is a prime reason for the stratification and segregation of opportunity—but the biggest problem is sustained underinvestment. The American system has always made agreement difficult at the federal level, but the continuing rise of partisan polarization and the concomitant emergence of the Senate filibuster as a firm "rule of sixty" (meaning sixty votes for all but fast-tracked legislation) has made the gridlock problem much worse. Federal R&D spending as share of GDP has fallen from its peaks to a fraction of earlier levels. Meanwhile, higher education has increasingly relied on students themselves taking on debt, which both increases insecurity and reduces the chance a college degree will be a ticket to upward mobility. Once the world leader in college completion, the United States is now a middling performer.[17]

During the first two years of the Biden Administration (2021–22), there was a notable burst of long-term investment in infrastructure and clean energy, which we will discuss at the end of this chapter. For now, the important point is that these reforms were relatively modest given the backlog and required a now-rare window of opportunity for passing new laws. As much as they signaled awareness of the problem, they do not change the conclusion that ongoing investment on the scale needed is unlikely under current conditions.

This is especially true because it is not just areas left behind that need investment. Thriving metros are feeling the strains brought on by growing population and economic interdependence. Decentralization has allowed local incumbents, particularly wealthy homeowners, to resist reforms that would make possible the denser housing necessary to accommodate these places' growing populations, much less to bring in those who would like to move into these metro regions (two leading economists estimate that the resulting hit to the economy is on the order of a third of total US GDP).[18] For the most part, these difficulties cannot be blamed on polarization, because the most affected areas are governed almost exclusively by Democrats. Rather, they signal the Democrat's own failure to overcome powerful entrenched interests within their diverse cross-class coalition. This is precisely a situation in which higher-level governance—federal but also state—is needed to ensure positive-sum solutions are achieved, rather than held up by concentrated interests that enjoy a privileged role in local policymaking. In short, just as non-metro areas require assistance, metro areas need help exercising public authority on behalf of diffuse rather than concentrated interests. This political conflict—where wealthy incumbents block the policies that would foster shared prosperity—comes into even clearer view when we turn to the modern robber barons.

The Modern Robber Barons

The knowledge economy relies on innovation, and innovation relies on competition. But inherent features of the knowledge economy—particularly the fundamental importance of intellectual property and the prominence of network effects—also push toward consolidation. The information technology (IT) industry is dominated by a handful of firms and platforms, which seek to keep their domestic labor force relatively immobile (through, e.g., non-compete clauses) and buy up or discourage competitors. Stock values attributable to monopoly control have risen dramatically since 1985, and nine of the ten firms with the largest share of monopoly wealth are in IT-related industries.[19]

Yet the dominance of the "modern robber barons"—firms or sectors heavily dependent on rent-seeking (which includes the generation of profits through massive negative externalities)—is by no means limited to the tech industry.[20] The tendency is pervasive across all types of sectors from energy to IT-enabled finance to health care. These trends, according to recent research, lower wages and employment and increase inequality.[21] Less well recognized, they are heavily implicated in the growing divergence of *regional* economies. Corporate consolidation has "deprived many cities and towns of the corporate headquarters and local businesses that used to be a source of high paying jobs and demand for professional business services."[22] The problem is especially pronounced in rural areas. Indeed, just the consolidation of agriculture—which has more than halved the share of dollars spent on food that actually goes to farmers—can explain a "substantial" part of rural America's travails.[23]

The modern robber barons do not just change the market; they seek to use their political influence to change policies, too. In many cases, this means holding public authority at bay and allowing "drift"—change in economic and social realities alongside stasis in policy—to bolster their position.[24] Of course, large companies can bring about these changes through their own aggressive market actions. There is a reason the tech industry is known for extolling its first-mover advantages ("move fast and break things;" "ask forgiveness, not permission"). Whole spheres of technology that could threaten shared prosperity, such as AI, seem largely beyond democratic control. Meanwhile, fossil fuel companies have contributed greatly to America's halting response to the existential crisis of climate change. In health care, meanwhile, the United States spends vastly more as a share of its economy and per person despite dramatically falling behind other rich nations in life expectancy gains (a trend driven by higher death rates among younger Americans). Despite this, a bloated and self-dealing medical industry has managed to both obtain extensive public supports and keep at bay the kinds of cost control that every other rich democracy employs. Such policy-enabled profit-seeking based on rent extraction further undermines both capitalism and democracy.

The most important political-economic consequence of these trends is the concentration of wealth in the hands of a small number of powerful companies and corporate leaders eager to protect their monopoly rents. The results have been particularly apparent at the state level, where corporate-funded efforts to protect incumbent companies and hurt potential sources of countervailing power (including labor unions) have had notable impact.[25] While plenty of corporations align with the Democratic Party, the lion's share of corporate money has bankrolled Republicans and conservative causes. (We consider whether this is changing in the conclusion.) Moreover, the effect of corporate money is to reduce the incentive for *either* party to challenge consolidated incumbents—as the climate change and health care stories suggest. Democrats are cross-pressured, while Republicans are emboldened.[26] In both cases, distortions of the market that hurt the knowledge economy fester.

Corporate America, in other words, does not just fuel the backlash coalition through its market behavior. It fuels it directly through its political behavior. We now turn to that coalition.

The Ascending Backlash Coalition

Many of the developments just described have a pronounced impact on political cleavages in the United States. Taken together, these trends create a strong foundation for what the journalist Ronald Brownstein has called a "coalition of restoration," and what we have shorthanded as a backlash coalition.[27] Electorally, this coalition is concentrated in left-behind regions that find themselves excluded from the main centers of the KE. While forces of right-wing populism have emerged in many countries, the United States is one of the few where these forces have gained political power—and of course the only one that is also at the core of the modern global economy. Distinctively, too, these forces also find themselves allied with the most potent business coalitions and the lion's share of politically active wealth. Bolstered by electoral arrangements that amplify the political power of non-metro areas, this coalition constitutes a formidable challenge to the knowledge economy. In this section, we trace out three salient features of this challenge: its rejection of problem-solving governance, its embrace of ethnonationalism, and its alliance with the modern robber barons.

The Rise of an Anti-System Party

It is well known that Republicans have moved sharply right on policy areas fundamental to the KE, including taxation, regulation, and public investment.[28]

The GOP's retreat from the principles of the mixed economy has meant that major new initiatives to provide critical public goods and regulate major externalities, like carbon emissions require at a minimum full control of the federal government by Democrats. But even then, the explosion of the use of the filibuster in the Senate means that (vanishingly rare) Democratic super-majorities are typically required to pass major legislation, unless that legislation can be shoehorned into the budget process, which prevents filibusters but also places significant restrictions on what bills can contain.

But the reason to view Republicans as vanguards of a backlash coalition goes beyond their move toward the ideological extreme. No less important has been the growing willingness of the party to play what Mark Tushnet has called "constitutional hardball" and even to challenge democracy itself.[29] Repeated government shutdowns, debt-ceiling hostage taking, highly partisan investigations, aggressive off-cycle gerrymandering, restrictions on voting rights, failure to confirm executive and judicial nominees, and repeated reprisals against GOP officials who consider compromise or seek accountability for anti-democratic behavior—these are a few of the results of a turn away from governing and toward anti-system confrontation. This confrontational politics, inimical to the disagreement-laden but ultimately constructive pattern of bipartisan lawmaking that built the knowledge economy, is not just a threat to the US economy. As the events of January 6, 2021, starkly show, it is a threat to American democracy, denying as it does not just the result of an election, but the increasingly multiracial majority that decided it.

Rejecting Multiracial America

Racial divisions in the United States run deep. The relevant cross-national comparisons can be found in the racially cleaved countries of Latin America, not within Europe. Structures of public policy developed over generations have reinforced and intensified these divisions. Powerful incentives for spatial segregation stem from and in turn exacerbate differences in economic opportunity and public goods among communities. A bifurcated welfare state separates a largely white core of social insurance and tax-subsidized private provision from a disproportionately minority periphery of limited means-tested benefits. These factors, along with the decline of industrial cities, have also contributed to America's exceptional expansion of incarceration and the intense stigmatization of "race-class subjugated communities."[30]

These policy structures cast a long shadow over the American polity.[31] They have widened the opening for the race-based political appeals that have proven central to the emerging backlash coalition.[32] Voters' perceptions of public protections are highly racialized and have become more so.[33] The growth of immigration has also contributed to this backlash, especially in areas that are still overwhelming white. All of this has created tremendous opportunities for a political strategy that plays on racial and cultural resentments among many of those on the losing side of the KE transition.

One other factor virtually unique to the United States is highly profitable, extensive, and influential right-wing media. Political science and economics were slow to see the importance of this factor, in part because technology has rapidly amplified its influence. But their research now offers clear conclusions: right-wing media has an enormous effect on voters who watch it and on the politicians who seek their votes, creating a self-reinforcing loop of escalating extremism on the right.[34] Importantly, right-wing media exists in a distinctive media ecosystem, not shared by liberal media, that encourages the dissemination of extreme and false messages.[35] Such conspiratorial and oppositional messaging not only undercuts the accurate information on which electoral accountability relies; it also feeds the kind of anti-system mobilization and elite outbidding associated with the debt ceiling crisis, efforts at voter suppression (justified by false claims of voter fraud), and, on the far fringes, the January 6 attack on Capitol Hill. Moreover, right-wing outlets are strongly implicated in the strategic use of racial and ethnic animus associated with the backlash coalition.

The reality is that the American economy cannot continue to function without a baseline acceptance of multi-ethnicity. This fact is accepted across large swaths of corporate America. Unfortunately, it is not accepted by the party that corporate America often bankrolls.

The Role of Reactionary Elites

A final striking element of the emerging backlash coalition is the prominent role of *economic elites* within it.[36] The growth of organized, partisan action among the wealthy and major corporations on behalf of the Republican coalition has been a prominent feature of recent politics in the United States. As the GOP's right wing, with its emphasis on culture war issues, has taken over the party, some business actors have weakened their alignment with the GOP. KE industries have historically been closer to Democrats, and while the tech industry is split politically—with the world's richest man, Elon Musk, anchoring the right side of the sector's ideological spectrum—many tech leaders are best seen as socially progressive but skeptical of government regulation and labor unions. We take up the potentially shifting orientation of business and the superrich in the conclusion. For now we want to emphasize that, to an underappreciated extent, the conservative side of the business community—including its most powerful organizations—has backed the Republican Party even as it has become more oppositional and ethnonationalist. A study of CEOs as donors between 2007 and 2017, for example, found three times as many CEOs (57 percent) gave most of their money to Republicans as opposed to Democrats (21 percent).[37] Another looking at voter registration files found growing partisan polarization among top executives within S&P 1500 firms (that is, top executives at specific firms are increasingly aligned with each other). Still, nearly 70 percent of these executives backed the GOP.[38] In the 2022 midterm cycle, billionaires donated over $1 billion, with the top 15 billionaire donors accounting for nearly two-thirds of the total. (Out of those 15, 11 backed Republicans.) In the eight most competitive Senate races, billionaires favored Republicans over Democrats by an almost 5–1 margin.[39]

For those stressing the functional links between capitalism and democracy the central role of victorious capitalists and leading firms in backing a revanchist, rural-based party generates a puzzle. Shouldn't these actors have a big stake in supporting the policy infrastructure of the knowledge economy? In the American political economy, however, several factors militate against elite collective action of this sort. For one, the wealthy and leading firms who have been the economy's biggest winners have a strong desire to protect the spectacular concentration of resources that is supported by the policy status quo (including very favorable policies for executive compensation and for the sheltering of income and wealth from taxation). For another, the facilitation of wealth generation through rent extraction strengthens the incentive to oppose active governance (except when it increases rents). Donald Trump was criticized by leading figures within the conservative business community, such as Charles Koch—the driving force and funder behind a set of highly resourced organized conservative groups. Yet those within the Koch network profited spectacularly under President Trump due to the 2017 tax cuts and an aggressive deregulatory agenda, much of it spearheaded by Republican Congressional leaders and allied officials in the executive branch. At the end of Trump's first year, Mitch McConnell—no great friend of Trump's political brand and hardly a culture warrior—described 2017 as the best year for conservatives in thirty years. Charles Koch said his conservative movement made more progress than it had in fifty years.[40]

Finally, American electoral arrangements, especially when combined with growing polarization, place pressure on economic elites to pick a party. In multiparty systems right-wing populists and plutocrats have generally found different partisan homes; in the United States, they face incentives to coalesce in a single party coalition. Even compared with other majoritarian liberal market systems, the American system is an extreme example of a two-party system (the U.K. and Canada, for example, have long featured at least one sizable third party). The election of a single president through a single winner-take-all election creates unusually strong incentives to consolidate around two major political parties.

The degree to which polarization has become organized combat between cohesive partisan teams makes these developments acutely threatening to democratic capitalism. As we argue in the next section, American political institutions are not well designed to handle the stresses created by highly polarized and nationalized teams of voters, groups, and politicians that operate at all levels of government.[41] This is especially true because one team—the team associated with the backlash coalition—enjoys systemic advantages within those institutions that it is using to entrench its power.

How American Political Institutions (Often) Exacerbate the Threat

We return, then, to the most serious risk highlighted by our developmental perspective: the prospect that the backlash coalition could feed on itself and become more deeply resistant to normal mechanisms of accountability and moderation—and even perhaps immune to them. The United States has seen a marked intensification of polarization over time, in part because of such feedback processes. Political parties, interest groups, and media structures have been nationalized, giving politics an increasingly zero-sum character. Notably, these polarizing trends have reinforced existing cleavages, "stacking" cultural, racial, religious, and geographic divides one on top of the other.[42] In the process, they have transformed perceived disagreements on issues into something more like identity politics, again with a pronounced spatial dimension.

This acute polarization, with a powerful party increasingly hostile to core arrangements of the mixed economy, creates severe challenges for economic governance. In the past, cross-cutting cleavages (usually a reflection of local and regional party diversity embodying sectional divisions) provided the opening for cross-party deals of the sort the US constitutional system requires to function effectively. With polarization now "all the way down," such openings for moderate governance are far rarer.

Similarly, polarized partisan teams operating across the branches of the federal government creates a Janus-faced problem for active democratic governance. On the one hand, partisan teamsmanship increases the likelihood of gridlock, which stymies the responsive lawmaking essential to update democratic capitalism over time. On the other hand, it threatens the healthy tension between the branches that the Founders believed would protect against sustained partisan policymaking, as well as the even greater threats to democracy posed by party-driven executive or judicial aggrandizement. The Constitution was premised on weak or non-existent partisan bonds, but even in the age of strong parties, its successful operation has depended on limiting the degree to which partisan identities and goals overwhelm the systemic incentives to protect the distinctive powers of the branches. When a party will not police other branches and levels of government if they are controlled by the same party, the Constitution's protections against executive or judicial overreach are rendered toothless and even democracy itself is at risk.

Moreover, there are clear prospects that the institutionally advantaged but (increasingly) outnumbered GOP may seek to further consolidate its hold on power through tactics like gerrymandering and voting restrictions. The United States leaves far more power over elections in the hands of local authorities, and Republicans have used this power much more aggressively, particularly in crucial statehouse elections that in turn determine the scope for future electoral manipulation. While the direct effects of prevailing voter restrictions may be modest, not least because they generally spark countervailing efforts, these restrictions occur in a system with a very close overall partisan balance and, at a minimum, divert out-party resources that might be used to mobilize broader turnout. The effects of gerrymandering are not so modest: legislatures in states that constitute the battleground in national presidential elections, such as Wisconsin and Ohio, are effectively sewn up for the GOP even when Democrats win a clear majority of the vote. The wave of electoral changes in response to the party's 2020 presidential loss is likely to further entrench GOP advantages.

The federal courts, and especially the Supreme Court, provide the clearest example of how such cumulative advantages can upend the political balance necessary for the mixed economy to flourish. In this realm, we see all the forces of backlash come together in a potentially self-reinforcing spiral—one that, by the very nature of the American judicial system, is both distinctly capable of rewriting the rules of American democratic capitalism and distinctly resistant to the normal corrective pressures of democratic elections.

A Supreme Threat to Democratic Capitalism

The outsized power of courts in the United States is often missed by those who do not study policymaking in other nations. In no other rich democracy are courts (and lawyers) as influential—not just with regard to constitutional matters but also on statutory and regulatory issues. Moreover, this impressive influence powerfully shapes the American political economy. The courts' role in big social fights—abortion, affirmative action, gay marriage—gets most of the headlines, and it is a crucial part of the culture wars that have animated the backlash coalition. (Indeed, the ability of populist cultural forces and business-oriented conservatives to form a logroll focused on appointments to the Supreme Court is a key reason why this coalition has held together.) Yet while receiving less notice, US courts are also far more involved in shaping the *political economy* in the United States than in other rich nations. This difference has enormous implications for policy outcomes because the courts provide a low-profile arena in which concentrated interests, entrenched incumbents, and other well-resourced "repeat players" are often able to pursue their interests even in the wake of unwanted legislation or administrative interventions.[43]

The courts are not just powerful; they are also partisan. By this we mean mainly (but not merely) that judges and other key judicial actors—such as state attorney generals—are appointed by politicians or elected directly, and their great power makes them unavoidable sites of partisan contestation. Notably, lifetime appointments mean there is a considerable lag between shifting electoral outcomes and shifting judicial orientations. Moreover, this lag can be lengthened by aggressive behavior by the out-party to resist new appointments in the Senate (where presidential nominations are confirmed). The implications are particularly profound for the Supreme Court, because the biases across other institutions so influence the ability to nominate and confirm justices. Nothing illustrates this better than the fact that all six of the conservative members of the current court benefited from at least one of these biases, confirmed by Senators representing a minority of the population (Thomas), nominated by a president who did not win the popular vote (Roberts), or both (Alito, Gorsuch, Kavanaugh, and Barrett). Of course, Gorsuch's appointment was made possible by Senate Republicans' (who again represented a minority of the population) unprecedented refusal to consider a nomination during President Obama's final year in office.

We focus here on the Supreme Court because its role has become so crucial in our era of legislative gridlock and polarized partisan teams. We note in the conclusion, however, that the Supreme Court is part of a vast judicial system that both liberals and conservatives exploit—with a decided bias toward preventing, rather than facilitating, active governance. The Supreme Court is special, however, because it has so much scope to shape the balance of power between actors in the market (business, labor, consumers, particular firms), between the branches and levels of government (Congress, the president, executive agencies, states, and localities), and between the parties (party elites, allied groups, partisan voting blocs). In other words, the Court has exercised its power on both sides of the capitalism-democracy equation in ways that have increasingly undermined a healthy relationship between the two.

On the market side, the court has expanded the ability of business to insulate itself from class-action lawsuits, accountability to customers (through, for example, mandatory arbitration), and challenges from competitors. KE industries in particular have used the courts to shield themselves from competition, particularly through aggressive litigation over intellectual property. In other words, the courts have not just been mostly pro-business—according to historical data, the current Supreme Court has sided with corporations against alternative claimants at a record rate—but also pro-incumbent.[44] Both because they are the incumbents and because they have vast legal resources, the modern robber barons have been big beneficiaries.

Bridging the market and politics, the current Supreme Court has also strengthened the ability of corporations (and wealthy individuals and interests more broadly) to use money to affect American elections and policy. A growing body of research shows that the 2010 Citizens United decision encouraged Republicans to shift to the right and aided their electoral fortunes, as well as pushed policy to the right in states where the decision had the most impact on existing rules.[45] (The serious ethics questions currently swirling around Justice Clarence Thomas involve close ties between the justices and the very organizations and individuals taking advantage of the 2010 ruling—most notably, the conservative donor network founded by David and Charles Koch.) At the same time, the Supreme Court has hobbled labor unions in both the public and private sectors, further strengthening the hand of business and the wealthy.

The extreme weakness of unions in the private sector in the United States clearly hurts democratic capitalism. Unions play two roles that are particularly important given the growing difficulty that diffuse interests face in sparking national action. First, they are important organized actors working on behalf of a broad working-class constituency—the only ones, in fact, in the United States. Historically, unions were an important part of the political coalition that ensured that public investments were made and the rewards of growth broadly distributed. The most far-sighted were also central to the broadening of citizenship in the 1960s, and, as noted, union membership continues to foster racial tolerance among white voters. Moreover, the extent to which unions pursue such positive-sum solutions depends in part on their scope: narrower unions are likely more prone to parochialism than more encompassing unions would be—another reason to worry about their decline.

Second, and less recognized, unions are a powerful source of *constraint* in the market. Where capital must contend with an independent democratic state and reasonably strong labor movement, business managers develop different expectations about which political demands are possible and which are not. Over time in repeated interactions with policymakers and unions, firms facing greater countervailing pressures adapt their business models to adopt a longer-term and more stakeholder-oriented perspective on production that underwrites a more efficient and equitable economic regime.[46] The courts, by reducing America's already weak "beneficial restraints," has given business titans fewer incentives to consider the legitimate demands of policymakers or stakeholders, nor do firms have much reason to adopt longer-term perspectives in their economic models or policy demands.

Such beneficial restraints encompass government authority as well. A capable bureaucracy, guided by democratically enacted legislation, is essential to ensuring that the goals of popular and successful statutes continue to be updated to present circumstances—and more and more so to the extent Congress is stalemated. Yet the Supreme Court—seizing the myriad opportunities provided by Republican state attorneys generals suing the federal government and by conservative district courts inclined to back such challenges—has increasingly taken aim at the administrative state, raising the prospect that it will no longer show deference to the structure of congressional delegation on which most contemporary regulation is founded.[47]

In the highest-profile recent case, the 6–3 conservative majority declared in 2022 that the Environmental Protection Agency (EPA) did not have sufficient powers to regulate carbon emissions in the coal industry, notwithstanding the broad mandate of and extensive delegation to the EPA contained in the Clean Air Act. Invoking the so-called "major questions" doctrine, the court majority said that any regulatory actions "transformational to the economy" were presumptively invalid unless they were spelled out in the statute—a ruling in conflict with the Court's prior ruling in *Massachusetts v. EPA* as well as decades of regulatory law that recognize the need to delegate to expert agencies that can update the implementation of legislation to meet its goals. Rhetorically, the conservative majority claims that such authority would be returned to its rightful home, Congress. Given the realities of polarization and gridlock already described, it is well understood by all involved that the practical impact of such a return would be a sharp curtailment of federal regulation.

Finally, and perhaps most fatefully, the Supreme Court is now the deciding factor in the political-structural battles that may determine the fate of democratic capitalism itself. There are two salient threats to our democracy today: an overreaching president, enabled by an allied partisan team, and what we might call "minoritarianism"—the intensification of biases in the system that allow a powerful party with minority support to insulate itself from popular control. The evidence suggests that the current court is much more likely to police the overreaching of Democratic presidents than Republican ones.[48] More ominous still, it has either backstopped or failed to respond to the ongoing efforts to further tilt America's state-run electoral system in favor of the Republican Party. In recent decisions, the court has essentially washed its hands of any role in stopping states from adopting extreme partisan electoral maps, after enabling such maps in many Republican-controlled states with its hobbling of the Voting Rights Act in 2013. The court's familiar rationale, that popular majorities can rectify problems, ignores the fact that these maps prevent the majority from having a real voice, creating an increasingly permissive environment for minoritarian entrenchment.

In short, the rise of a nationalized cross-institutional party team carrying the banner of backlash poses a real risk that American political institutions will continue to be weaponized on behalf of minoritarian ends. The modern robber barons will become more and more unbridled. Governing partisans hostile to the mixed economy will become more and more entrenched. Can an economy that requires ongoing public investments in skills, infrastructure, and other vital policies be expected to flourish in such a political setting? Can democratic capitalism?

Can a Virtuous Cycle be Restored?

Our economy has weathered substantial shocks in recent years. But we should not minimize the challenges to a healthy knowledge economy that have emerged in recent decades: stark inequality across geographic and class lines, persistent underinvestment in the seeds of future growth and opportunity, and the concentration of wealth and power in the hands of consolidated industries and those whose fortunes flow from them. Most important, we should not minimize the *political* challenges that our perspective, focused on the American political economy, bring into clearer view. As polarization of the parties increases and concentrated economic power spills over into politics, economic governance sputters and democratic institutions suffer. It is hard to be bullish about the American political economy when accountability to the people is eroding. No democracy, no democratic capitalism.

What are the prospects for reversal? Developmental processes are not destiny, and vicious cycles can give way to virtuous ones. The three most promising potential sources of corrective pressures are business, voters, and reform-minded leaders, empowered through organized citizens. Though their combined effect is needed, we believe only the last, yoked to a sustained program of political-economic structural reform, is capable of turning the tide.

The Republican Party has transited from a conventional center-right party aligned with business to a right-wing populist force whose leading figures attack corporate "wokeness" and threaten to sink the economy in struggles over the budget and debt ceiling (another unique US institution that gives extreme politicians leverage). We have argued elsewhere that organized business could play an important moderating role in our politics, as it has in the past.[49] There were signs of such a shift in the refusal of the biggest corporate PACs to fund Republicans who refused to certify the 2020 election, even with the rubble of the January 6 attacks around them.

Unfortunately, we are doubtful that the business-GOP "rift" is deep or real enough to change Republican behavior or empower Democrats who could challenge them. First, there remains ample support for the GOP among the American economic elite. Second, leading business groups continue to emphasize priorities that reflect their expectation that Republicans will provide them with deregulatory and tax-cut largesse, and that expectation has so far been met. Despite railing against particular high-profile corporate targets (virtually always firms that lean toward Democrats), the most extreme Republicans in the House continue to call for deep cuts in taxes and welfare state spending. Revealingly, the business PAC "boycott" of election denialists, always porous and belied by the continued flow of less visible sources of funding, has largely fizzled. Indeed, the ranks of denialist Republicans in the House only expanded after the 2022 midterms.

Third, even if corporate elites were to feel greater alarm about GOP governance, there is also a basic collective action problem. In rich democracies with a history of coordinated industrial negotiation, peak business associations exercise enormous collective power. At the same time, their temptation to pursue self-interested parochial aims is tempered by their need to work with labor and the state. In the United States, even the strongest business groups, such as the Chamber of Commerce, are comparatively fragmented and weak—and hence more likely to find common ground on narrow short-term aims than collective long-term stances. As a result, not only is the collective capacity and collective clout of US business leaders compromised, but individual corporate heads also rightfully worry that standing up on their own will result in their exclusion from GOP policymaking. Even more unsettling, Republicans in power can exercise the formidable authority of the US state to intimidate corporations seen as wayward. Democratic capitalism rests on equal application of the law, but a unified party operating across branches and levels of government can use unequal application to push back against those who might challenge it. The prospect of such pushback—even when not ultimately deployed—is a major and growing barrier to corporate collective action.

Finally, the growth of extremism within the GOP is now on its own self-reinforcing path, fueled mainly by primary voters and right-wing media. Business efforts to push back against it are likely to be ineffective; in fact, they might even raise the profile and standing of the most visible darlings of the populist right.

The Republican Party's poor showing in the 2022 midterms points to a second possible source of accountability: voters. In a two-party system in which one party advances highly unpopular proposals, the other party should gain ground, forcing it back to the center. (The 2018 Trump tax cuts polled worse than only one other major initiative of the past 25 years; that initiative was the 2017 repeal of the Affordable Care Act.)[50] As Representative Elissa Slotkin, Democrat of Michigan, explained after the election, "I desperately want two healthy parties in this country that are empathetic but have a different view of government in people's lives. I cannot fix the Republican Party. Only they can fix themselves But I can beat them at the ballot box again and again and again until they take a little trip together to rethink and revamp their approach."[51] Republicans themselves have frequently worried that they are on the losing end of demographic change—or, as Republican Senator Lindsay Graham colorfully put it, "not generating enough angry white guys to stay in business for the long term."[52] Even with their recent gains among working-class voters of color, Republicans have had to continually ramp up their support in non-metro areas to remain competitive. Tellingly, they have not won the popular vote in seven of the last eight presidential elections—a string of losses without historical precedent.

We think Graham's forecast of the long term is accurate. Absent major shifts in the turnout or partisan allegiance of specific demographic groups, Republicans are currently set to lose around 2 to 3 points in the national popular vote every four years as younger and more diverse voters become a larger part of the electorate.[53] But the long term may be a long way off, and enormous, perhaps irreversible, damage might be done in the meantime. For more than two decades, Republicans have been busy constructing dikes that protect them against unfavorable electoral tides: the drift toward minoritarianism is a direct challenge to popular control. Meanwhile, the rise of nationalized partisan teams that include intense voters and well-resourced media and groups makes the threat of intra-party primary and leadership challenges more pressing for most Republicans than out-party rebukes of the sort Slotkin celebrates. And then there are the structural advantages. So long as the link between population density and partisanship is tight and growing, the Senate will tilt toward even an unpopular Republican Party. So long as the Supreme Court is firmly in Republican hands, minoritarian strategies and attacks on the mixed economy will have strong backing from what is currently the most powerful policymaking institution in the United States.

We also think that the Democratic Party remains an inadequate vehicle for large-scale reform. At the national level, the burst of investment spearheaded by President Biden and congressional Democrats—much of it focused on sparking growth in non-metro regions—shows that Democrats have not succumbed to identity politics, as often charged, but remain highly focused on big economic issues and, indeed, have become more ambitious with regard to spending, "industrial policy," and redistribution, at least since the 1990s.[54] The 2021 Bipartisan Infrastructure Law and 2022 Inflation Reduction Act, as well as the 2022 COMPETES (Creating Opportunities to Meaningfully Promote Excellence in Technology, Education, and Science) Act all signal a promising orientation toward long-term shared prosperity. Had their control of the Senate not been so precarious (and dependent on a Senator from a deep red state) they would have done more. Under Biden, federal regulators have also sought to curb the power of the modern robber barons through more aggressive enforcement of antitrust laws, as well as to strengthen workers' bargaining power in sectors where it is weak. While these policies ultimately proved to be politically inadequate in the face of the global inflation surge, which clobbered incumbent governments across the world, they nonetheless suggest that national Democrats are reorienting their aims to bring them into closer alignment with the needs of ongoing economic adaptation.

At the state and local level, however, the situation is much less promising. It costs far more to build infrastructure in the United States than in other rich democracies, and the central problem is how easy it is to block or slow development—a problem that heavily implicates Democratic-aligned groups, such as environmental organizations.[55] Progressives have relied heavily on the courts in these efforts, further empowering a set of institutions not well suited for active democratic policymaking. And, as discussed, America's housing crisis—so corrosive to the urban agglomeration hubs that drive the knowledge economy—is primarily a "blue state" crisis. Without effective pressure from the states and especially the federal government, localities are not going to fix the endemic problems of "opportunity hoarding" and systemic inequality that hold back opportunity and limit metro-driven growth.

All this is not a brief for despair. Rather, we think it calls on the broad cross-section of engaged thinkers, activists, and leaders who worry about these trends to invest in organization-building and political-economic structural reform. This will not be a short-term task: it will require shifting the center of gravity of politics slowly over time, just as it has shifted toward its dangerous location today. There will be no single great breakthrough, but a series of hopefully self-reinforcing steps, in which advocates of reform build power, win changes that strengthen their hand, and then gain greater ground.

In this struggle, there must be a dialectic between political and economic reform. With their bare majority in the Senate, Democrats and President Biden rightly sought major economic changes through the budget process. But without major political reforms—starting with the curtailment of the blocking power of the filibuster and continuing through efforts to make electoral outcomes more representative of citizen preferences—not only will such economic changes be hard to achieve, but there is also limited guarantee that they will move polarized voters. No sustained program of economic reform is possible without fundamental changes to our increasingly creaky system of government. Ultimately, it is organizations that outlast election-year efforts that are needed to place continuing pressure on political elites. In designing policies and building coalitions, far more attention must be paid on building up organized citizen pressure for the ongoing adaptation of our economic and political institutions.

The essential precondition, however, is an accurate diagnosis. With the rise of the backlash coalition, the Republican Party has retreated as an active partner in problem-solving governance, and this retreat is accelerating. This loss is simultaneously threatening democratic capitalism and placing too much responsibility for rescuing it on a Democratic Party that itself needs renovation. The gap between American institutions and policies and Americans' evolving economic interests can only be closed by forging a multi-racial democracy that delivers what we have lost: accountability to popular majorities and responsiveness to genuine social problems that can serve to discipline both parties and direct their energies constructively as they did more often in the past. Our economic problems may seem to drive our political dysfunction. The message of political economy is that the relationship runs at least as much the other way. Fixing American democracy will help fix American capitalism.

Acknowledgments

We thank the other authors in this volume for their inspiration and feedback and Sid Milkis and Scott Miller for their astute editorial advice. For collaborative work that informed our argument, we thank Kathleen Thelen, Alexander Hertel-Fernandez, Eric Schickler, Jacob Grumbach, Amelia Malpas, and Sam Zacher, as well as the participants in the workshops that led to our 2022 volume (edited with Kathy and Alex), *The American Political Economy: Politics, Markets, and Power* (Cambridge University Press). Finally, we are grateful for the organizational and editorial acumen of Chrissy Linsinbigler, the Project Manager for the Democracy and Capitalism project at the Miller Center of Public Affairs.

Notes

1. Paul Pierson and Eric Schickler, *Partisan Nation: The Dangerous New Logic of American Politics in a Nationalized Era* (Chicago: University of Chicago Press, 2024).
2. Jacob S. Hacker and Paul Pierson, *Winner-Take-All Politics: How Washington Made the Rich Richer—And Turned Its Back on the Middle Class* (New York: Simon & Schuster, 2010); and *American Amnesia: How the War on Government Led Us to Forget What Made America Prosper* (New York: Simon & Schuster, 2016).
3. Jacob S. Hacker, Alexander Hertel-Fernandez, Paul Pierson, and Kathleen Thelen, "The American Political Economy: A Framework and Agenda for Research," in *The American Political Economy: Politics, Markets, and Power*, ed. Jacob S. Hacker, Alexander Hertel-Fernandez,

Paul Pierson, and Kathleen Thelen (New York: Cambridge University Press, 2022). (Hereafter *The American Political Economy.*)

4. Torben Iversen and David Soskice, *Democracy and Prosperity: Reinventing Capitalism through a Turbulent Century* (Princeton: Princeton University Press, 2019).
5. Gerald Davis, *Managed by Markets: How Finance Re-Shaped America* (New York: Oxford University Press, 2009); Mark Mizruchi, *The Fracturing of the American Corporate Elite* (Cambridge: Harvard University Press, 2013); Hacker and Pierson, *American Amnesia.*
6. David Autor, David Dorn, Gordon Hanson, and Kaveh Majlesi, "Importing Political Polarization? The Electoral Consequences of Rising Trade Exposure," *American Economic Review* 110, no. 10 (2020): 3139–83.
7. Peter A. Hall and David Soskice, "An Introduction to Varieties of Capitalism," in *Varieties of Capitalism: The Institutional Foundations of Comparative Advantage,* edited by Hall and Soskice (New York: Oxford University Press, 2002).
8. Iversen and Soskice, *Democracy and Prosperity.*
9. Iversen and Soskice *Democracy and Prosperity,* 6.
10. David Soskice, "The United States as Radical Innovation Driver: The Politics of Declining Dominance?," in *The American Political Economy.*
11. Hacker and Pierson, *American Amnesia,* 270–303.
12. Iversen and Soskice, *Democracy and Prosperity,* 222.
13. Paul Frymer and Jacob M. Grumbach, "Labor Unions and White Racial Politics," *American Journal of Political Science* 65, no. 1 (2021): 225–40.
14. Autor et al, "Importing Political Polarization."
15. Zack Taylor, Jack Lucas, David A. Armstrong, and Ryan Bakker, "The Development of the Urban-Rural Cleavage in Anglo-American Democracies," *Comparative Political Studies* 57, no. 8 (2023).
16. Jonathan Rodden, *Why Cities Lose: The Deep Roots of the Urban-Rural Political Divide* (New York: Basic Books, 2019).
17. Hacker and Pierson, *American Amnesia,* 33.
18. Chang-Tai Hsieh and Enrico Moretti, "Housing Constraints and Spatial Misallocation," *American Economic Journal: Macroeconomics* 11, no. 2 (2019): 1–39 [as corrected at http://www.econlib.org/a-correction-on-housing-regulation].
19. Mordecai Kurz, "The New Monopolists," *Project Syndicate,* September 22, 2017, https://www.project-syndicate.org/commentary/monopoly-power-wealth-income-inequality-by-mordecai-kurz-1-2017-09.
20. Hacker and Pierson, *American Amnesia,* 270–303.
21. For a review of the evidence, see Suresh Naidu, Eric Posner, and Glen Weyl, "More and More Companies have Monopoly Power over Workers' Wages. That's Killing the Economy," *Vox,* April 6, 2018, https://www.vox.com/the-big-idea/2018/4/6/17204808/wages-employers-workers-monopsony-growth-stagnation-inequality.
22. Robert Manduca, "Antitrust Enforcement as Federal Policy to Reduce Regional Economic Disparities," *ANNALS of the American Academy of Political and Social Science* 685, no. 1 (2019):162.
23. Manduca, "Antitrust Enforcement," 162.
24. Jacob S. Hacker, Paul Pierson, and Kathleen Thelen, "Drift and Conversion: Hidden Faces of Institutional Change," in *Advances in Comparative-Historical Analysis,* ed. James Morone and Kathleen Thelen (New York: Cambridge University Press, 2015).
25. Alexander Hertel-Fernandez, *State Capture: How Conservative Activists, Big Businesses, and Wealthy Donors Reshaped the American States—and the Nation* (New York: Oxford University Press, 2019).
26. Hacker and Pierson, *Winner-Take-All Politics.*
27. Ronald Brownstein, "The Coalition of Transformation vs. the Coalition of Restoration," *The Atlantic,* November 21, 2012, https://www.theatlantic.com/politics/archive/2012/11/the-coalition-of-transformation-vs-the-coalition-of-restoration/265512/.
28. Hacker and Pierson, *American Amnesia,* 242–44.
29. Mark V. Tushnet. "Constitutional Hardball," *John Marshall Law Review* 37 (2004): 523–53.

30. Joe Soss and Vesla Weaver, "Police Are Our Government: Politics, Political Science, and the Policing of Race–Class Subjugated Communities," *Annual Review of Political Science* 20 (2017): 565–91.
31. See, among many works, Ira Katznelson, *When Affirmative Action Was White* (New York: W. W. Norton, 2005); and Robert Lieberman, *Shifting the Color Line: Race and the American Welfare State* (Cambridge: Harvard University Press, 1998).
32. Ashley Jardina, *White Identity Politics* (New York: Cambridge University Press, 2019); John Sides, Michael Tesler, and Lynn Vavreck, *Identity Crisis: The 2016 Presidential Campaign and the Battle for the Meaning of America* (Princeton: Princeton University Press, 2018).
33. Jardina, *White Identity Politics*; Michael Tesler, "The Spillover of Racialization into Health Care: How President Obama Polarized Public Opinion by Racial Attitudes and Race," *American Journal of Political Science* 56, no. 3 (2012): 690–704.
34. For a summary and synthesis of this research, see Hacker and Pierson, *Let Them Eat Tweets: How the Right Rules in an Age of Extreme Inequality* (New York: Liveright, 2020), 97–107.
35. Yochai Benkler, Robert Faris, and Hal Roberts, *Network Propaganda: Manipulation, Disinformation, and Radicalization in American Politics* (New York: Oxford University Press, 2018).
36. Hacker and Pierson, *Let Them Eat Tweets.*
37. The rest split their money more or less equally. Alma Cohen, Moshe Hazan, Roberto Tallarita, and David Weiss, "The Politics of CEOs," *Journal of Legal Analysis* 11 (2019): 1–45.
38. Vyacheslav Fos, Elisabeth Kempf, and Margarita Tsoutsoura, "The Political Polarization of Corporate America," NBER Working Paper 30182, May 2023.
39. William Rice and Zachary Tashman, "The Best Democracy Money Can Buy? Billionaires Pumped over $1 Billion into the 2022 Elections," Americans for Tax Fairness, May 2023, https://americansfortaxfairness.org/report-billionaire-spending-topped-1-billion-first-time-2022-elections-2/.
40. Hacker and Pierson, *Let Them Eat Tweets*, 141–70.
41. Pierson and Schickler, *Partisan Nation.*
42. Lilliana Mason, *Uncivil Agreement* (Chicago: University of Chicago Press, 2018).
43. K. Sabeel Rahman and Kathleen Thelen, "The Role of Law in the American Political Economy," in *The American Political Economy: Politics, Markets, and Power*, ed. Jacob S. Hacker, Alexander Hertel-Fernandez, Paul Pierson, and Kathleen Thelen (New York: Cambridge University Press, 2022).
44. Lee Epstein and Mitu Gulati, "A Century of Business in the Supreme Court, 1920–2020," Virginia Public Law and Legal Theory Research Paper No. 2022-55, August 3, 2022, http://dx.doi.org/10.2139/ssrn.4178504
45. Martin Gilens, Shawn Patterson, Jr., and Pavielle Haines, "Campaign Finance Regulations and Public Policy," *American Political Science Review* 115, no. 3 (2022): 1074–81.
46. Hacker and Pierson, *American Amnesia*, 144–46; Wolfgang Streeck, "Educating Capitalists," *Socio-Economic Review* 2, no. 3 (2004): 425–38.
47. Jonathan S. Gould and Gregory Elinson, "The Politics of Deference," *Vanderbilt Law Review* 75, no. 2 (2022): 475–552.
48. Lee Epstein and Rebecca L. Brown, "Is the U.S. Supreme Court a Reliable Backstop for an Overreaching U.S. President? Maybe, but is an Overreaching (Partisan) Court Worse?" Working Paper, October 11, 2022, https://www.documentcloud.org/documents/23463365-politicalcourt.
49. Hacker and Pierson, *American Amnesia.*
50. Hacker and Pierson, *Let Them Eat Tweets*, 145–152.
51. Quoted in Jonathan Weisman, "Republicans Reckon with Midterm Election Fallout," *The New York Times*, November 11, 2022, https://www.nytimes.com/2022/11/11/us/politics/republicans-midterm-elections.html.
52. Quoted in Hacker and Pierson, *Let Them Eat Tweets*, 133.
53. Ronald Brownstein, "The Demographic Makeup of the Country's Voters Continues to Shift. That Creates Headwinds for Republicans," *CNN*, May 16, 2023, https://www.cnn.com/2023/05/16/politics/demographic-changes-voters-fault-lines/index.html.

54. Jacob S. Hacker, Amelia Malpas, Paul Pierson, and Sam Zacher, "Bridging the Blue Divide: The Democrats' New Metro Coalition and the Unexpected Prominence of Redistribution," *Perspectives on Politics* (2023): 1–21.
55. Leah Brooks and Zachary Liscow, "Infrastructure Costs," *American Economic Journal: Applied Economics* 15, no. 2 (2023): 1–30.

12

How the Transformation of the American Political Economy Spurred a Rural-Urban Political Divide

TREVOR E. BROWN AND SUZANNE METTLER

Since the 1990s, a new geographic political cleavage has emerged in the United States as rural non-Hispanic white people, who previously varied in their partisan leanings and included many Democrats, shifted increasingly to become strong supporters of Republican candidates, nationwide.[1] Urban dwellers, who long favored the Democratic Party, have become even more supportive of it. The result is a powerful place-based divide that figures centrally in fueling contemporary polarization, fostering an "us" versus "them" politics, and contributing to democratic dysfunction.[2]

Why did this sweeping political change occur when it did, and reorganize politics by place? We argue that transformations in American capitalism, promoted by public policy, prompted political change in both rural and urban places. As the dust settled, the rural-urban political divide began to emerge, and as it has intensified, it has imperiled democracy.

Scholars have given growing attention to contemporary place-based polarization. For example, some have illuminated the sense of resentment experienced by white rural dwellers, others have focused on political change in the South, and some have highlighted the divide's relationship to American electoral institutions.[3] Yet to date, scholars have yet to fully examine how this profound cleavage emerged nationwide, explain how it relates to changes in capitalism, or consider its consequences for democracy.[4]

Elsewhere we have shown that the rural-urban political divide, far from being a fixed feature of American politics or explained by a single cause, has arisen

Trevor E. Brown and Suzanne Mettler, *How the Transformation of the American Political Economy Spurred a Rural-Urban Political Divide.* In: *Can Democracy and Capitalism Be Reconciled?.* Edited by: Sidney M. Milkis and Scott C. Miller, Oxford University Press. © Oxford University Press (2025). DOI: 10.1093/9780197774731.003.0013 over time through a developmental process, one we have called "sequential polarization."[5] The first phase of the process began in the 1990s amid changing political-economic circumstances that pushed rural and urban places, albeit long unequal, to grow further and further apart. Many urban areas enjoyed soaring growth while rural places experienced stagnation at best and deterioration and mounting hardship at worst. Here we trace several elements of that transition and some of its political consequences.

We argue that rural places had long enjoyed a prominent location in US public policies, and that from the 1980s onward, they lost that status. This occurred as policymakers—including some in the Democratic Party, which had long been associated with policies that upheld rural economies—restructured the American political economy, removing previous constraints on capitalism. As a result, rural areas became increasingly "left behind" and delinked from the prosperity enjoyed in urban places, sparking resentment. White rural dwellers, many of whom had previously felt that Democratic lawmakers represented their best interests, became disenchanted with the party and gradually abandoned their support for it.

Once those ties were weakened, by the early 2000s and beyond, other dynamics encouraged rural people nationwide to become increasingly strong supporters of the Republican Party. Economic developments attracted growing numbers of highly educated people to urban areas, and this group increasingly identified with the Democratic Party. Rural people, structurally advantaged by several political institutions in the United States, then defined themselves in reaction to what they perceived as overbearing elites who were attempting to impose policies on them without their input. The Republican Party, catering to these demands, enthusiastically welcomed rural dwellers. Before long, these forces would threaten democracy.

Growing Economic and Political Divergence between Rural and Urban Places

Urbanization in the United States has long been associated with the rise of place-based inequality. In the early republic, the vast majority of Americans lived in rural places, and fully 75 percent of those in the workforce were employed in agriculture.[6] Capitalist development in the form of industrialization in the nineteenth century hastened the growth of cities, spurring greater economic inequality between rural and urban places and threatening democracy through the concentration of wealth. By the late nineteenth century, the agrarian or "Populist" movement, centered in the economic "periphery," demanded better terms for farmers in their relationship with industrialists in core cities. The latter relied on them to produce the raw materials that were the basis of their growing wealth.[7] During the Great Depression, New Dealers attempted to reduce rural poverty, convinced that it was harmful to the economy as a whole.[8] New Deal policies, as we show below, helped prevent the emergence of a rural-urban cleavage by bolstering rural economies.[9]

Yet a set of transformations that began in the late twentieth century rendered rural areas increasingly marginal. First, economic forces, driven by public policy reforms as well as technological developments, led to the demise of decent jobs for those with less formal education in both rural and urban areas. Many urban areas adjusted to these changes by embracing the so-called "knowledge economy" and expanding high-end service sectors. Most rural areas, by contrast, continued to struggle. Growing place-based inequality from 1970 to 2021 is evident in Figures 12.1 and 12.2. Using county-level data retrieved from the US Bureau of Economic Analysis (BEA) and definitions of rural and urban derived from the US Office of Management and Budget, both chart the ascendance of urban economies and the relative stagnation of rural ones.[10] Figure 12.1 displays, in inflation-adjusted terms, personal income per capita (excluding government transfer payments), back to 1969. Certainly urban dwellers on average were better off than rural dwellers in 1970, when $8,000 separated their incomes. The disparity has grown sharply over time, however, reaching nearly a $17,000 divergence by 2019. Figure 12.2 shows raw private sector employment growth, pegged to 1970, by place. Since 1970, employment in urban places has grown at roughly twice the rate in rural areas.[11] Finally, in analysis not presented here, we find that, dating back to at least 2001, roughly 86

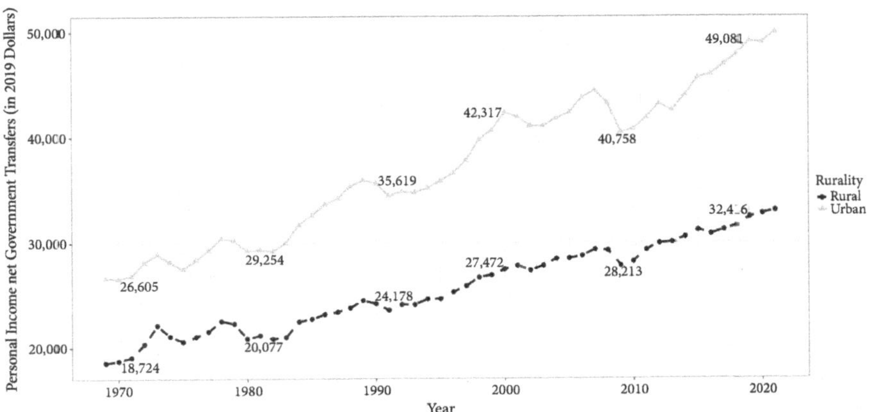

Figure 12.1 Private per capita income, over time and by place

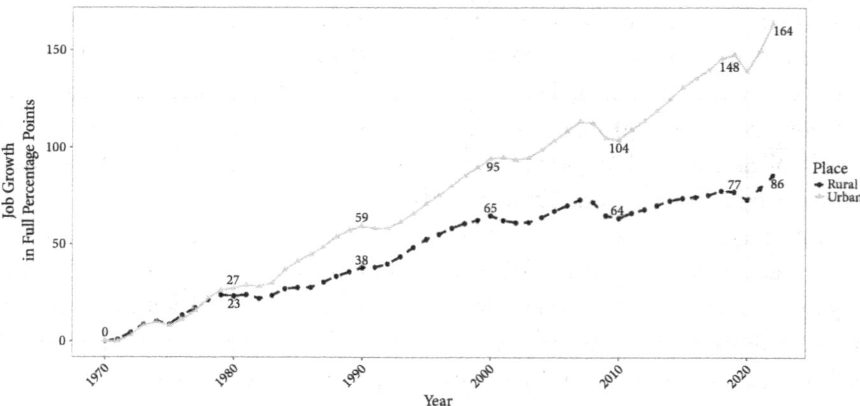

Figure 12.2 Private sector employment growth, over time and by place

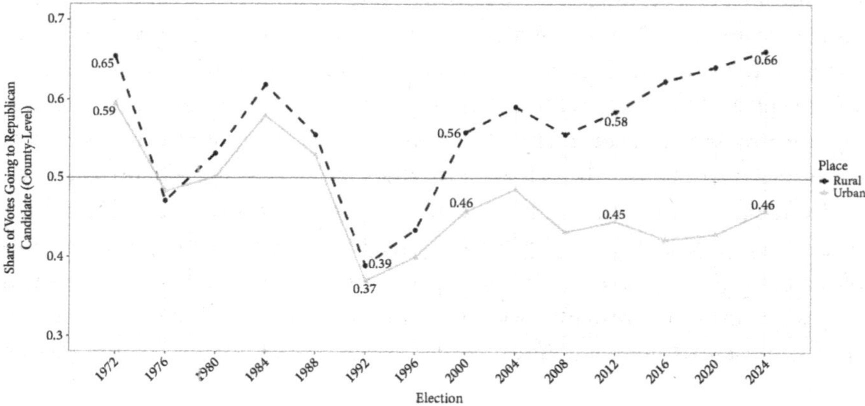

Figure 12.3 The rural-urban divide in presidential voting

percent of all the nation's gross domestic product (GDP) has been created in urban counties.[12] Rural well-being, in short, has become detached from urban fortunes.

Meanwhile, the politics of places has diverged as well. Figure 12.3 displays, in presidential elections, the share of votes going to Republican candidates from all rural and urban counties nationwide. From the 1970s into the 1990s, rural and urban dwellers tended to shift in tandem, supporting particular presidential candidates at very similar rates. Both areas offered strong support for Republican candidates Nixon and Reagan, and both threw their weight behind Democrat Bill Clinton. But from 2000 onward, a stark divide emerged as rural people increasingly supported the Republican candidate in each election. The gulf between them and urbanites grew from just 2 percent as recently as 1992 to 20 percentage points by 2024.[13]

Examining voting data at the regional level (not presented here), we find the rural-urban political divide has widened in all areas of the nation. Certainly, it is well known that dramatic political change has occurred in the South, where counties transitioned from overwhelming support for Democrats earlier in the twentieth century to growing support for Republicans. Less well known is that as the South changed, particularly since 1996, it acquired a striking divide between rural and urban counties that reached 20 percentage points in the 2024 presidential election. Each region of the country simultaneously experienced this divergence, which reached 21 points by 2024 in the Midwest, 18 points in the West, and a smaller but still formidable gap of 12 points in the Northeast.

These regional shifts in presidential voting are only one manifestation of this new geographic cleavage. The rural-urban divide in presidential voting has also widened in nearly all states over this same time period. More rural congressional seats that used to be represented or at least contested by Democrats have become safe havens for relatively extreme Republicans, who have fostered dysfunction and political polarization.[14]

In sum, rising place-based economic divergence has been followed by growing political polarization. Over the past half century, as many urban places have come to be the powerhouses of the nation's economy, they have solidified their loyalty to the Democratic Party. Rural places, by contrast, have found themselves further and further on the outer margins of the economy, and they have proceeded to move sharply in support of the Republican Party. Now the institutional advantages of sparsely populated places in the Electoral College, US Senate, and single-member geographically-defined districts are consolidated—as never before—in one party, giving it extra leverage throughout the political system.

Theorizing about the Relationship between Place, Capitalism, and Democracy

Over the past several decades, the United States was buffeted by a vast transformation in American capitalism, as well as by political and social changes. How did these changes affect rural and urban life politically? How might their timing and interplay have influenced the health of democracy?

We build on Seymour Martin Lipset and Stein Rokkan's classic insight[15] that two fundamental processes of change—a political-economic one and a territorial one—may drive partisan divisions.[16] We focus here on the political-economic dimension, featuring conflict over resources, products, or benefits in the economy. In Lipset and Rokkan's analysis, this involved an earlier transformation of capitalism: the late nineteenth and early twentieth century development of industrialization and the spread of global trade. As we show below, their analysis did not offer much explanatory power for the United States throughout most of the twentieth century because of the role public policies, among other things, played in bolstering rural economies. Yet this changed in the late twentieth century with the rise of post-industrial capitalism, including the shift from a goods producing- to service-based economy and the ascendance of the knowledge economy. We find that in the 1990s and early 2000s, such developments deepened an economic divide along rural and urban lines. Especially in counties that lost jobs and population, rural residents become more amenable to aligning with the Republican Party. Meanwhile, the growing ranks of highly educated Americans in urban areas reversed course began to support the Democratic Party.[17]

The territorial dimension, which can also create a new political cleavage, does so by spurring resistance by those in remote places to the encroachments of "dominant national elites and their bureaucracies . . . to the pressures of the centralizing, standardizing, and 'rationalizing' machinery of the nation-state."[18] Such dynamics have also contributed to the rise of the rural-urban divide, and involve promotion of national standards by the growing ranks of highly educated urban dwellers and rural resistance to it. This has occurred with respect to national laws and public policies that require states and localities to guarantee rights to all regardless of race, ethnicity, gender, or sexuality. Significant as well is the use of state power to address issues ranging from environmental concerns, such as protecting endangered species or regulating coal or solar production, for example, to gun control or liberalizing immigration. As the Democratic Party came to be perceived as the party promoting national adoption of such policies, resistance and alienation ensued among white rural Americans. On the face of it, they sought to limit government interference, but the impetus linking these issues involved rural dwellers' antipathy to what they perceived as the imposition of policies in which they had little input. Even worse, they came from the very people who benefited from the same transformed political economy that had marginalized them.

Crucially, this divide has been filtered through America's comparatively unique political institutions, giving rural areas extra power.[19] As the rural-urban divide has deepened and the Republican Party grown more extreme, the forces we outline here have converged to threaten democracy.[20]

The Long Tradition of Rural Prominence in US State Building

American state builders, from early on, gave rural areas—where the vast majority of citizens then lived—a prominent place in policy developments. Agriculture in particular received ample attention, and not surprisingly, given that it accounted for the livelihood of most Americans. The US Department of Agriculture came about in 1862, and in time it evolved into what Kenneth Finegold and Theda Skocpol called an "island of state strength in an ocean of weakness."[21] Also in 1862, President Abraham Lincoln signed into law the Morrill Act, granting federal land to states for the purpose of establishing agricultural universities, as well as the Homestead Act, offering public land to those willing to farm it. By 1887, the Hatch Act promoted cooperation between the federal and state governments in agricultural research by establishing experiment stations. The Smith-Lever Act of 1914 created a national agricultural extension service.[22] The Smith-Hughes Act of 1917 set up vocational education schools for farmers.

In addition, rural Americans generally—not only farmers—were served by the US Post Office. It reached far-flung communities as early as the Jacksonian Era, through a system of stage coaches that delivered mail to rural post offices. A more systematic and comprehensive approach began with the establishment of Rural Free Delivery in 1898.[23] Through such policies, lawmakers conveyed that the federal government was concerned with rural people and viewed the work they did as important to the life of the nation.

Rural Despair and Political Shifts in the 1920s

As industrialization intensified, however, rural dwellers grew more peripheral to the nation's economic life and struggled to find a political party to represent them. Between 1900 and 1930, the nation evolved from still being predominantly rural to predominantly urban as the rural population fell from 60 percent to 44 percent.[24] The proportion of the workforce employed in agriculture decreased from one in three to one in five.[25]

These downward trends were exacerbated by the 1920s farm crisis: while urban areas experienced the "Roaring Twenties," the price of agricultural products fell sharply, and rural Americans suffered. Paradoxically, the problem stemmed from overproduction, as farmers had increased production to meet needs during the Great War, but once it ended, demand for their crops fell and with it, so did the prices. Yet Republican President Calvin Coolidge expressed little interest in a government response, remarking, "Well, farmers have never made money. I don't believe we can do much about it."[26] He twice vetoed a popular bipartisan bill through which government would subsidize agriculture, raising the prices that farmers received and protecting them through tariffs.[27]

In the midst of this tumultuous period, when Al Smith ran as the Democratic nominee in the presidential election of 1928, some rural Americans who typically leaned Republican voted for him. They did so despite their antipathy to urban dwellers and immigrants, groups that supported Smith strongly.[28] And Smith, as Sundquist notes, "had scarcely even visited the West or South and admittedly knew nothing about agriculture," and "besides being a Catholic and a wet, he was a product of Tammany Hall and his manner of dress and speech could hardly have been more alien to rural and small-town America." In sum, "He was not the man to lead thousands of disgruntled Republican farmers into the Democratic party," or so it seemed. Yet, Smith made efforts to woo farmers, and he managed to carry 44 counties in Illinois, Iowa, Minnesota, and North Dakota, most of them rural, and only about half of which had large Catholic populations.[29] Democrats took note of how Smith had managed to subdue cultural antipathies with economic programs. Republican Herbert Hoover won the presidency, however, and as the Great Depression set in, he proved to be insensitive to the economic distress in rural areas and opposed to a stronger governmental response, such as through delivery of electric power.[30]

Farm incomes worsened as the Depression intensified, and once Roosevelt was inaugurated in 1933, farmers earned just half what they had in 1919. One third of farmers had lost their land. Amidst such discontent, the sub-regional shifts in voter support in 1928 would prove, in time, to be an entering wedge for the Democrats in rural areas of the Midwest.

Franklin D. Roosevelt Seeks to Build a Rural-Urban Alliance

In June 1931, when then-Governor of New York Franklin D. Roosevelt addressed a national gathering of governors about the economic crises facing the nation, he focused on what he called "the dislocation of a proper balance between urban and rural life." As historian Sarah Phillips explains, he described how many farmers "eked out an existence far below the 'American standard of living,'" often trying to work exhausted land.[31] One year later, as he campaigned for president, Roosevelt further developed his vision for a "rural renaissance built upon the proper use of land and the availability of hydroelectric power." He believed that the farm crisis of the 1920s had played a major role in causing the Great Depression and that rural poverty sustained it, saying: "Our economic life today is a seamless web. If we get back to the root of the difficulty, we will find that it is the present lack of equality for agriculture." Roosevelt saw rural economies as intertwined with those of urban areas—and he considered policy solutions accordingly. While he thought that the reduction of surplus production would provide short-term relief, he advocated permanent measures, such as national agricultural planning and rural electrification to lessen place-based inequality and to promote the nation's economic development.[32]

The Brain Trust that planned Roosevelt's campaign themes considered agriculture the top priority. Raymond Moley, who headed up the group, said that Roosevelt "advocated reforestation, land utilization, the relief of farmers from an inequitable tax burden, and the curative possibilities of diversifying our industrial life by sending a proportion of it into the rural districts."[33] Columbia University economist Rexford Tugwell, who served as architect of the farm strategy, emphasized the interdependence of rural and urban Americans, explaining that farmers were subject to what he called a "deranged" disparity between the price of farm and industrial goods such that they lacked the ability to be consumers themselves. This led, he argued, to unemployment among industrial workers in cities. At the urging of this group, Roosevelt declared in a speech in Topeka, Kansas, "This Nation cannot endure if it is half 'boom' and half 'broke.'" He called for agricultural benefits on par with the tariff protection bestowed on industry.[34]

When Election Day came, farmers in the Midwestern Plains states who typically voted Republican threw their support to Roosevelt, fueling his victory.[35] The president's coattails helped Democrats down the ticket prevail in many previously Republican-held districts. The election yielded the largest Democratic majorities ever to have served in Congress up to that point, with 60 in the Senate and 311 in the House.[36]

Now, it was time for action to address the needs of rural America, and none too soon, as increasingly angry farmers appeared on the verge of turning violent. In January 1933, Edward A. O'Neal, president of the Farm Bureau, predicted at a Senate committee hearing, "Unless something is done for the American farmer we will have revolution in the countryside within twelve months." [37] Farmers were banding together to prevent foreclosures as well as to impede the delivery of goods to market. The Farmers' Holiday Association, a militant group of Midwestern farmers, threatened a strike if Congress did not enact a relief measure promptly.[38] The Roosevelt Administration arrived in town ready to rise to the occasion, with strategies to save capitalism by mitigating its self-destructive tendencies. In doing so, such policy action would forestall a rural-urban cleavage from entering the party system, as Lipset and Rokkan's framework might otherwise predict.

A New Deal for Rural America

In the first Hundred Days, several new policies were adopted that aimed to raise rural incomes, based on the conviction that, as Phillips puts it, "the nation's prosperity rested on an agricultural base."[39] The Agricultural Adjustment

Act (AAA) sought to tackle the problem of overproduction in order to raise farm prices and incomes; it did so by permitting the federal government to set production quotas on major crops and by paying farmers to plant less. The Federal Emergency Relief Administration channeled a large portion of its efforts to rural areas, and by the end of 1933, officials announced that over five million people in farm families had benefited from the program's relief checks.[40] Aiming to stall the farm foreclosure crisis, Roosevelt used an executive order to consolidate all federal agencies dealing with agricultural credit into the Farm Credit Administration.[41] The Soil Erosion Service and National Industrial Recovery Act each also contained several provisions to address rural needs.

These programs quickly made a profound impression that government mattered in the lives of rural dwellers. As observed by Paul Landis, writing in the *American Sociological Review* in 1936, "National politics is no longer an abstract distant affair in Washington . . . The hand of the federal unit reaches every family. It meets them where they live . . . It has brought the activities of government into the concrete world of Mr. Everyman. The average farmer may not understand the intricate details of the 'New Deal', but when he gets his check for fifty dollars as a result of letting some of his acreage lie fallow, he feels that government is a real part of his life."[42] The Farm Credit Administration daily prevented 300 farms from foreclosure. One farmer wrote, "I would be without a roof over my head if it hadn't been for the government loan . . . God bless Mr. Roosevelt and the Democratic party who saved thousands of poor people all over this country from starvation."[43]

Other policies achieved Roosevelt's goal of bringing electricity to rural areas. Through the Tennessee Valley Authority (TVA), started in 1933, cheap electric power was quickly provided to homes, farms, and factories across seven states.[44] The Rural Electrification Administration (REA) transformed rural areas nationwide, as the rate of farms with electricity increased from one in ten when it began in 1935 to nine out of ten in 1950. As historian William E. Leuchtenburg noted of the REA, "Perhaps no single act of the Roosevelt years changed more directly the way people lived." At its inception, "The lack of electric power divided the United States into two nations: the city dwellers and the county folk." Farmers "toiled in a nineteenth century world," and their wives "performed their backbreaking chores like peasant women in a preindustrial age."[45] The REA "revolutionized rural life," and it did so in a strikingly visible manner, as Leuchtenburg notes:

> Finally, the great moment would come: farmers, their wives and children, would gather at night on a hillside in the Great Smokies, in a field in the Upper Michigan peninsula, on a slope of the Continental Divide,

> and, when the switch was pulled on a giant generator, see their homes, their barns, their schools, their churches, burst forth in dazzling light.

The REA likely made evident to many rural people the value of government generally and the impression that public officials in the Roosevelt Administration cared about people like them.

While the AAA benefited only property-owning farmers, especially those with more land, the Roosevelt Administration also aimed to help small farmers, tenant farmers, and sharecroppers. These efforts were less successful. The Resettlement Administration, created in 1935, attempted to give relief to poor farmers who worked unproductive land by purchasing the land, converting it to other purposes, and moving the inhabitants to better farms. In 1937, it was replaced by the Farm Security Administration, which shifted the emphasis to rehabilitating existing land. It issued a loan or grant to one in nine farmers in the nation, particularly higher-risk families in the South, and aimed to help tenants become owners.[46] Still, as Phillips observes, "When looking at the numbers, especially the racial differentials, it is hard to escape the conclusion that the rural New Deal," at least in "the South . . . served white rather than black, rich rather than poor."[47] Indeed, owing in part to such policy differences, Black Americans would continue to suffer from inequality for generations.

Despite its shortcomings, no presidential administration before or since focused so deliberately on the problems faced by rural dwellers. While a couple of the early laws were thrown out by the Supreme Court, one of those—the Agricultural Adjustment Act (AAA)—was replaced with a new version in 1938, and that endured, with price supports becoming a fixture of mid-century policies. Some others programs were combined or renamed, but their basic purposes were carried on. A half century later, the fundamentals of the rural New Deal remained intact.[48]

Preventing a Rural-Urban Political Divide

The New Deal responded sufficiently to rural areas to quell the resistance that had been fomenting since the 1920s. For many rural people who had sought a party that would do their bidding, the New Deal Democratic Party rose to the occasion, and in return, they lent it their support. This included lower-income producers, particularly those engaged in cotton, tobacco, rice, and peanut production in the South, as well as wheat growers in the Dakotas, Kansas, Nebraska, and the Pacific Northwest who had to deal with the risks of a semi-arid climate and highly variable yields. Others, particularly upper and middle-income farmers, remained in the Republican fold.[49] Through the next several decades, policymaking in Congress for rural areas typically involved bipartisan coalitions and log-rolling. At the local level, it consisted of a political patchwork, with Democratic strength not only in the South but also in numerous counties scattered throughout the Midwest. Republican candidates typically prevailed in many other rural areas, but even there, rural dwellers were willing to vote split ticket on occasion. These factors precluded a rural-urban political divide.

Such political patterns in rural areas did not emerge in the course of a single election, either in 1928 or in 1932: they took longer to coalesce. And in fact, many rural counties that had shifted away from their typical Republican leanings to support Roosevelt in 1932 subsequently returned to the GOP. A countermovement appeared, moreover, among some white Democratic rural voters in border states, who could not take "the spending, farm, and civil rights policies of the New Deal."[50] Gradually, conservative Democrats departed from the party.[51]

Certainly Republicans in Congress tried to scale back New Deal farm programs. Most had voted against them in the 1930s.[52] Subsequently, the Eisenhower Administration sought, unsuccessfully, to reduce agricultural subsidies. Then-Secretary of Agriculture Ezra Taft Benson later wrote, "We could not go on indefinitely under the old programs without piling up mountainous surpluses, losing markets, wasting resources, running up heavy dollar losses and, most important of all, endangering the economic independence of our farm people."[53] What the Republican Administration most worried about, according to Richard F. Bensel, was not just the size of federal spending on such programs or the limits they placed on the free market, but also the political ties they established between "the agrarian periphery and labor-oriented lower classes of the industrialized core." The GOP's aim was "to split asunder one of the political supports for the bipolar Democratic coalition."[54] Subsequently, by contrast, Democratic Presidents John F. Kennedy and Lyndon Johnson protected such programs.

Meanwhile, partisans in specific states continued to re-sort themselves politically, in what Sundquist calls the "aftershocks of the New Deal earthquake." Roosevelt aimed to build a coalition broader than Democratic Party stalwarts, and he reached out to Progressive Republicans and Farmer-Laborites in various states.[55] By the early 1950s, northern states that had supported Roosevelt but still elected Republicans further down the ballot shifted increasingly to favoring Democrats. In particular, voters in the upper Midwestern states of North Dakota, Wisconsin, and Minnesota, where Farmer-Labor parties had previously supported Republicans, shifted their allegiances to Democrats in a reaction against Eisenhower's farm policies.[56]

In the South, the political aftershocks occurred in urban areas, where the Republican Party made gains particularly among urban dwellers. This process intensified in 1948, when President Harry S. Truman came out in support of civil rights. In response, some white Southerners formed a "States' Rights Democratic Party," otherwise known as the Dixiecrats, and supported Strom Thurmond for president. As Hood and McKee note, the Dixiecrats' "fervent defense of white supremacy perhaps unwittingly eclipsed" the importance they also placed on "a conservative laissez-faire capitalist/free-market economic philosophy," with a platform that stressed the importance of "private employment without government interference."[57] In later years, when Dwight Eisenhower campaigned in the region, he specifically courted urban dwellers by stressing economic conservatism instead of segregation. Rural whites, however, continued to support Democrats.

In sum, at a time when rural Americans were under duress and shrinking as a portion of the electorate, Roosevelt and his administration prioritized them in their plans to stabilize and improve the American economy. Through a wide array of policies, the New Deal shored up rural communities. In the process, it conveyed to rural dwellers that public officials cared about people like them. Some never forgot how Roosevelt had rescued their family in a time of need or brought electricity to their farms, and they became devoted Democrats. Others, after voting for Roosevelt once or twice, returned to the Republican fold. The politics of the era, while saving capitalism from its own excesses, staved off the formation of a rural-urban divide and held it at bay for decades. Simultaneously, it helped democracy to survive, and by the 1960s and 1970s, to expand. But by the late twentieth century, politics changed, and with it, the relationship between rural and urban Americans.

The Demise of Rural Economies, the Rise of the Knowledge Economy, and the Making of a Place-Based Cleavage: 1980s to the Present

Beginning in the 1970s and accelerating throughout the last quarter of the twentieth century, multiple forces, including action taken by policymakers, undermined the well-being of rural economies, heightened the status of many urban ones, and ultimately increased inequality between them. Historically, rural areas have been dependent on natural resources and goods production, including not only agriculture, but other forms of resource extraction and, for a good part of the late twentieth century, manufacturing. Yet each of these industries have been hit hard in recent decades by global competition and consolidation, among other forces. Policy decisions including trade deregulation, relaxation of anti-trust enforcement, and the growth of environmental regulation have created or accelerated these trends. As lawmakers from across both sides of the aisle—including some Democrats—deprioritized the well-being of rural areas, they also began policy interventions that helped build up the knowledge economy in urban areas. These transformations effectively de-linked rural and urban economies and created a new type of economic sectionalism. They provoked resentment among rural people as they came to see Democratic lawmakers as no longer aligned with their material interests.

The Consolidation of Agriculture

Recent policy and technological changes have weakened the viability of agriculture as an industry that can produce widespread economic prosperity in most rural areas. Even though farming has been in secular decline since industrialization, as recently as the 1970s the agricultural industry served as an important source of economic security for rural areas. But it was a precarious arrangement that was held together largely by public policies. Tax policies and low interest rates during the Nixon Administration spurred investments in large-scale farming, including through the acquisition of land and machinery. The ethos of the decade was captured by Nixon's Secretary of Agriculture, Earl Butz, who famously told farmers to "Go big or get out."[58] Shortly thereafter, however, farmers were hit with a downturn the likes of which had not been experienced since the Great Depression. On the one hand, the Federal Reserve raised interest rates to curb inflation; this made the massive debt farmers had taken on to acquire more land and machinery even heavier and difficult to repay. On the other, Nixon strengthened the dollar internationally, rendering commodities far less competitive in the global marketplace.[59] During Ronald Reagan's presidency, between 1980 and 1988, some 200,000 to 300,000 farms—representing 8 to 12 percent of all farms at the time—either went bankrupt, were foreclosed on, or were financially restructured.[60] The prolonged destruction of such farms drew attention from national news outlets—including *The New York Times* and *Washington Post*—as well as federal lawmakers. These developments became widely known as the Farm Crisis.

Policy decisions combined with several other trends to heighten inequality within rural farming communities. In part because of technological changes and the growth of "lean" farming, agriculture consolidated significantly in the decades to come. Many mid-sized farms and supporting industries were squeezed out, large farms and companies continue to grow, and small ones stagnated and were largely relegated to become "hobby farms."[61] Virtually all of what is produced, from dairy to major crops, became the province of "big agriculture," as did most stages of production, including seed sourcing and retail.[62] Horizontal integration, meaning concentration of businesses *within* the same stage of the production process, has been joined by growing vertical integration, meaning concentration *across* areas of production.[63]

As with other industries, the consolidation of agriculture was intensified by deregulation and lax enforcement of antitrust.[64] By 2015, 51 percent of the value of US farm production came from farms with at least $1 million in sales, compared to just 31 percent in 1991, adjusted for price changes.[65] As agriculture became more concentrated, overall employment and income derived from farming continued to decline in rural areas.[66] By the end of the twentieth century, the sector employed fewer than 2 percent of the nation's workforce, and had in many ways become archetypical of what economists and political scientists have called the New Gilded Age, featuring high levels of economic concentration and power, and diminished opportunities for small producers and workers.[67] Furthermore, key provisions of New Deal farm policies were undercut throughout the 1980s and 1990s. The farm Bills of the 1980s and 1990s reduced federal commodity and income supports and helped move farm policy in a more market-oriented direction.[68] Though the impetus of these policies came from the Republican Party, a number of Democrats gave pivotal support—signaling to rural areas that the Democratic Party did not represent their interests.

Deindustrialization and of the Decline of Natural Resource Extraction Hit Rural America

Particularly after agriculture and related jobs dried up, manufacturing remained a crucial component of rural economies. It is well known that deindustrialization in major urban areas from the 1950s through the 1970s, and the resulting loss of jobs, was followed by greater poverty rates, unemployment, and even political demobilization. Black Americans especially were harmed.[69] Less well understood, however, is the impact of deindustrialization on rural areas, which were even more dependent on manufacturing into the early twenty-first century, in terms of both income and employment.[70] In fact, as manufacturers fled urban areas, they often landed in rural ones, particularly those transitioning to production that was done more efficiently in longer, single-story units. In addition to offering more space, rural areas were attractive because of their low-wage labor markets, cheap land, and an often hands-off regulatory environment. For a time, manufacturing employment thus grew at a higher rate in rural areas than urban ones.[71] Rural manufacturing was thus not necessarily ideal for workers: many plants relocated to rural areas to avoid union drives and regulations aimed at protecting workers. Nevertheless, the sector did offer many rural dwellers employment, typically in jobs with decent pay and benefits, especially relative to other industries that employ people with lower levels of formal education.

Starting in the 1990s, however, rural manufacturers became vulnerable to growing global competition and began to hemorrhage jobs. This occurred owing to trade liberalization and the rise of East Asian countries—first Japan and then China—as producers of electronics, furniture, and other consumer goods.[72] The North Atlantic Free Trade Agreement (NAFTA), ushered into law with bipartisan support in the mid-1990s, brought the United States into greater competition with Mexico, resulting in job losses and broader economic harm.[73] As David Autor and his colleagues have cataloged, the so-called "China Shock" had far-reaching implications in the communities it impacted, including employment displacement, stagnant wages, and the rise of premature deaths.[74] Indeed, these developments allowed foreign competitors to bypass the very conditions—low labor and regulatory costs—that made rural areas attractive to manufacturers to begin with.

To be sure, manufacturing continues to provide an important economic base for rural places. According to recent estimates from the USDA, as of 2015, 21 percent of non-farm earnings in rural areas came from manufacturing, compared to just 11 percent in urban counties.[75] And as of 2019, manufacturing offered a wage premium of 30 percent relative to other industries in rural areas, according to calculations from the Federal Reserve.[76] Yet rural communities' continued reliance on manufacturing and the waning importance of goods-production to the US economy point to the economic vulnerability of rural areas. This is apparent in the loss of industry they have suffered during the first decades of the twenty-first century, in no small part as a result of past trade policies. Rural workers in manufacturing were disproportionately impacted by the downturn in the early 2000s.[77] Further, on January 1, 2005, protections for domestic apparel and textile industries—which are disproportionately located in rural areas—expired as a result of trade negotiations reached in the 1990s, under then-President Bill Clinton. From 2000 to 2017, more than three-fourths of nonmetropolitan counties lost manufacturing jobs.[78]

Due to concerns related to privacy, county-level data on the sectoral base of local employment are hard to come by.[79] Yet one way to examine place-based industrial trends is by analyzing programs intended to help workers who have been displaced. The major program in the United States designed for such displacements is the Trade Adjustment Assistance Program (TAA), which offers training, employment, case management services, and various forms of income support to workers who are able to demonstrate they have been laid off or their employment terminated as a result of US trade policies. In Figure 12.4, using data from the filings with the Department of Labor, we weight the number of layoffs related to TAA claims at the county level, across rurality, over time. Of course, such data do not reflect the entire population of trade-related job displacements. Many workers do not file claims for various reasons, including

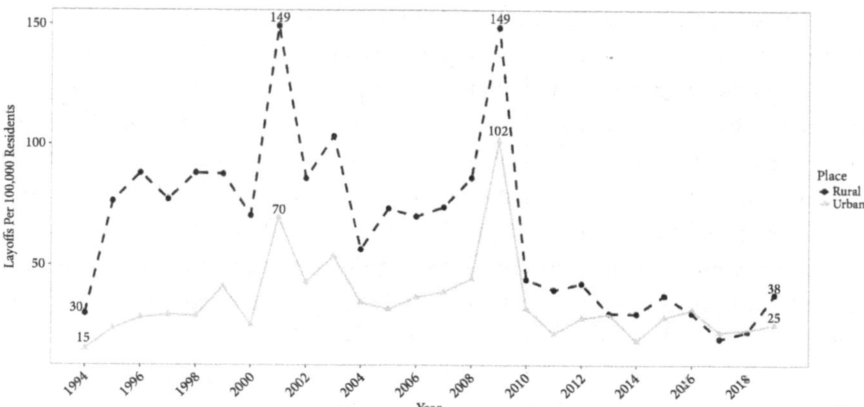

Figure 12.4 Population-weighted TAA-related job losses, over time and by place

administrative burden. Nevertheless, because we suspect that the drivers of administrative burden—such as lower levels of administrative capacity and fewer social networks—are likely more acute in rural areas, we consider this a relatively conservative measure. While the raw number of TAA-related jobs are more concentrated in urban areas, the population-weighted measure in Figure 12.4 shows that rural areas have been pummeled by recent trade policies. Increases in uptakes were especially high in the mid and late 1990s, following the implementation of NAFTA, and they often dwarfed rates in urban areas. In fact, adding all TAA-related claims up from 1994 to 2020, we find that rural areas lost nearly twice as many jobs per capita (85 percent more) than urban areas.

Along with manufacturing, rural areas particularly in the West and Appalachian regions have also been disproportionately reliant on the extraction of natural resources, including timber and natural energy. Certainly, such industries have offered rural people important sources of economic stability, but they also face both intrinsic and external constraints. Following trends in other sectors, many natural resource sectors have been subject to technological changes that reduced the number of jobs needed to support them, as global competition placed even more downward pressure on employment.[80] Even when such industries do flourish, they are highly subject to boom and bust cycles, and communities that exploit such industries can become overly reliant on them, a phenomenon known as the "resource curse."[81]

Efforts to Adapt to the Service and Knowledge Economy

Finally, if policy changes hastened the decline of rural areas, they also bolstered the growth of urban ones. The knowledge economy did not just develop naturally. Instead, it was constructed by policymakers at the national and state level.[82] Beginning in the 1980s and through the 1990s, when some Democrats were engaging in bi-partisan lawmaking that destabilized rural economies, they also commenced aggressive national and state-level policies to "incubate" urban knowledge economy hubs.[83] Such efforts were driven by factions within the Democratic Party that saw future national economic fortunes as being tied up with venture capital and university-industry consortiums in major cities; notably, they gave little attention to rural areas. While the knowledge economy does not account for all economic activity in urban areas, its policy-induced development certainly helped propel growth in many metro counties—and, in doing so, it spurred high levels of geographic inequality.

Several features of the contemporary knowledge economy exacerbate rural-urban inequality. First, the knowledge economy relies on a highly educated workforce, a workforce that rural areas have struggled to cultivate and retain. While residents of rural and urban counties had very similar levels of post-secondary education in 1970, since then the gap has grown tremendously. This has occurred as young people from rural areas who acquire more education—a potential resource for local economies—tend to migrate permanently to urban areas precisely for better job opportunities.[84] This so-called "brain drain" only hastens the decline of rural economies, contributes to population stagnation and loss, and promotes resentment among those residents who remain.

Furthermore, economic activity in the knowledge economy—even more than in industries of earlier eras—clusters in particular places. That is because such economies tend to benefit from or even thrive off of so-called "agglomeration" or spill-over effects that result from close proximity. In other words, firms and workers congregate so that they can partner with and learn from one another, engaging in idea formation, and draw on potential employee and employer pools. Cities, because of both their physical infrastructure and their amenities that draw in highly educated workers, are especially well suited for such industries. After an urban area has developed a solid base of the knowledge economy, it tends to build on its successes, and this can make place-based inequality soar.[85]

Rural areas, on the other hand, are far less well equipped to draw in such economic activity. Despite recent efforts to expand broadband to sparsely populated communities, rural places still tend to lag behind urban areas in terms of having the physical infrastructure necessary to support robust knowledge economies. As a result, many rural areas have been forced to rely disproportionately on the low-wage service sector jobs that are common in the contemporary labor market.[86]

Urban areas that are home to bustling knowledge economies are certainly not without their problems. These include high levels of economic and racial inequality, as well as other forms of dislocation, such as gentrification. And not all rural areas have been totally "left behind": some have successfully exploited their close proximity to natural amenities to foster economies based in tourism and recreation.[87] Counties with recreation-based economies have been less susceptible to appeals from conservative lawmakers and more likely to vote Democratic in recent elections, bucking the trends shown in Figure 12.3.[88] Yet such rural economies can create their own divides and frictions, pitting more affluent newcomers and vacationers against long-term residents, who may find themselves squeezed out of the housing market and other aspects of the economy. Moreover, economies rooted in natural amenities are simply not robust enough to foster sustainable, widespread growth.

The Political Effects of Rural Decline and Restructuring

How do these trends relate to political behavior broadly and, more specifically, the rightward shift of rural areas? We argue that they have converged not only to harm rural economies, but also in doing so, to spark political resentment among rural dwellers and open a window for them to become susceptible to appeals from the Republican Party. Especially given the geographic political advantage and the growing extremism of the Republican Party, this has endangered democracy.

The farm crisis of the 1980s and 1990s helped spur rural backlash and resentment. Farmers mobilized en masse, to resist foreclosures at the grassroots level and cuts to aid at the federal level. They banned together in state, local, and national level organizations, traveling to local sheriffs' departments, state legislatures, and even Washington, D.C. to call for relief.[89] As historian James Leiker sums up the farmer activism: "Each [movement] provided expressions of rage, manifestations of anger against government, consumers, and urban elites who understood little about farm life yet appeared to hold farmers' destiny in their hands."[90] While many of the cuts were eventually reversed, the farm bills of the 1980s and 1990s—all featuring some level of bipartisan support—included provisions that eviscerated support for farms and moved agriculture policy from the New Deal paradigm to a more market-oriented approach. Dairy farmers were especially vulnerable. The frustration, anger, and despair caused by the farm crisis and related economic policies of the 1990s endured for decades, particularly in the Midwest.[91] It led to heightened stress and depression among farmers, and appeared to be associated with a rash of farmer suicides.[92]

Similar trends were apparent in manufacturing and trade deregulation. Even though Republicans supported NAFTA in greater numbers, that many Democrats, including most prominently Bill Clinton—a Democrat from a relatively rural state, Arkansas—helped drive its passage likely pushed many white rural dwellers to see those in the party as no longer representing their interest.

A major grassroots effort emerged to oppose NAFTA. All major labor organizations opposed it vociferously, playing a "long overdue game of outside-the-Beltway hardball" that "successfully captured broad working-class anxiety and anger over the state of the economy."[93] A large coalition of organizations called the Citizens-Trade Campaign joined forces to defeat the agreement; it included a diverse array of labor environmental, consumer, human rights, and church groups from across the nation.[94] Labor unions invested millions in running television and radio ads against it and highlighted lists of jobs and companies that would be lost to Mexico.[95] The Clinton Administration promoted a debate on the subject between Vice President Al Gore and Ross Perot; televised on CNN in November 1993, it attracted the highest number of viewers CNN had ever had, and they heard Perot argue that the agreement would force blue collar jobs to depart the United States for Mexico.[96]

Ultimately, however, the opposition failed, and Congress successfully ratified NAFTA. Many Democratic members felt cross-pressured by strong support for Perot in their districts and opposition from organized labor, on the one hand, and Clinton's support for the trade agreement, on the other.[97] But the vote split Democrats in particular: in the Senate, it passed 61–38, but only 27 Democrats voted for it and 28 against it and one abstained, and in the House, it passed 234–200, with 102 Democrats in favor and 156 opposed. According to our analysis of roll call votes, several dozen rural Democrats voted in favor of it.[98] NAFTA had been a highly visible and deeply bruising battle, one that likely seared into the minds of many Americans that the Democratic Party was no longer the staunch defender of workers' interests that they had long assumed it to be. Rage ensued in some rural areas and small towns rocked by the decline of manufacturing and other goods-producing industries.[99] Communities felt betrayed not only by large corporations that outsourced jobs, but also by policymakers in Washington who facilitated changes that ruined much of what still protected their economic security.

As for natural resources, secular trends have certainly led to the decline of jobs in extractive industries for over a century. But in recent decades federal policies that aimed to regulate greenhouse emissions yielded highly visible examples of government intervention that, at least on their face, threaten local economic activity. While economic evidence is mixed on the true employment effects of such regulations, some—such as the Clean Air Act—do appear to have negative ones.[100] Moreover, Republican lawmakers have made rhetorical appeals against such laws on the basis that they "kill jobs." From the perspective of local residents, especially when they are not consulted, such regulations also seem invasive, sparking political resentment.[101]

Finally, the growing fortunes of many urban areas and their association with the Democratic Party likely further stoked resentment. As Katherine Cramer has shown, many rural dwellers feel like rural places do not get their fair share of economic growth. Other scholars have shown that rural resentment is a national phenomenon and underpinned by a sense of distributive injustice.[102] Given that key factions of the Democratic Party are now squarely aligned with highly educated knowledge economy workers and owners of such firms, it is perhaps no surprise that rural Americans have come to see Democrats as the party of urban elites.

Elsewhere we show how economic divergence in rural and urban areas has shaped the relationship between rurality and partisan political behavior over recent decades.[103] Using county-level data from the 1970s up until 2020, we explore the relationship between rurality (as defined by the OMB), support for Republican presidential candidates, and economic decline, the latter operationalized as population and job growth. We regress the share of votes going to the Republican presidential candidate on county-level job and population growth, respectively. Even after controlling for other potential confounders, such as election year, region, county-level educational attainment, age profile, and share of the population identifying as non-Hispanic white, we find that from the years 1992 to 2004, both job and population decline were associated with greater levels of Republican support in rural areas. The timing of such factors is particularly important, as they align with a number of the policy and economic developments described above, and helped pave the way for rural dwellers to be organized into the Republican Party in decades to come. In addition, during this period, highly educated urbanites aligned with the Democratic Party. Subsequently, after 2004, rural dwellers with less formal education responded in kind, reacting against what they viewed as the imposition of an urban elitist agenda. Importantly, the economic shifts of the earlier period fostered the resentment that intensified later on.

The Rural-Urban Divide: A Central Threat to American Democracy

The New Deal era was marked by a set of policies that aimed to mitigate the excesses of capitalism, not least by incorporating rural areas into the American political economy for decades to come. Yet beginning in the latter part of the twentieth century, technological and public policy changes—including the promotion of trade liberalization and the consolidation of agriculture—undermined the viability of many rural areas. Even more, the decline of raw goods production, the rise of imports, and the concentration of economic activity in urban knowledge hubs made rural and urban economies far less interdependent and reliant on one another. This, in turn, cultivated a new form of sectionalism, fostering divisions between rural and urban areas.

This transformed political economy was not inevitable. Just as lawmakers, including Democrats as well as Republicans, began embracing policies that harmed rural areas, they also helped build up urban ones. While many urban areas have been able to transition to the knowledge economy, rural areas have indeed been "left behind," leaving them susceptible to extremist and populist rhetoric from lawmakers.

What does the political rural-urban divide portend for the health of American democracy? In a sequential process, with political-economic developments leading the way and resentment of urban elites following, these forces have helped deepen polarization. We find that rural and urban white people diverge significantly in how they view particular social groups and actors, such as the National Rifle Association (NRA) and the police, and they both hold especially low opinions about members of the opposing party.[104] The rural-urban cleavage is now built into the US party system, fostering even greater levels of social polarization and "us" vs. "them" politics.[105]

Some scholars take a more sanguine view of recent capitalist development and argue that, despite the extremism it seems to help produce among those left out of economically prosperous cities, it does not necessarily pose a threat to democracy.[106] Our analysis suggests otherwise. The levels of out-group hostility and polarization certainly raise worries for those concerned with the health of civil society. Moreover, the current rural resentment is being amplified by US political institutions, which are unique in the extent to which they give additional power to sparsely populated areas.[107] The most well-known instances are the US Senate and the Electoral College, but it is also the case for federal and state House seats.[108] When one party dominates rural areas, as the Republican Party currently does, it gives that party extra power over key functions of American governance, including policymaking and judicial nominations, as we detail elsewhere.[109] If that party abandons small-d democratic principles, its additional leverage can be pivotal not only to winning elections outright, but also to "stacking the deck" in its favor, through gerrymandering, restrictive voting laws, and other means.[110] In brief, the growing place-based economic divisions and the resentment that follow have converged with America's political institutions to heighten the tensions between capitalism and democracy—posing a crucial threat to the latter.

Fortunately, the rural-urban political divide in the United States is not an ineluctable force of history. Just as politics and policymaking were once used to hold rural and urban areas together, they can be made to bridge the contemporary rural-urban divide. Such action will be key for safeguarding and ultimately strengthening American democracy.

Notes

1. Trevor E. Brown, Gisela Pedroza Jauregui, Suzanne Mettler, and Marissa Rivera, "A Rural-Urban Political Divide Among Whom? Race, Ethnicity, and Political Behavior Across Place," *Politics, Groups, and Identities* 13, no. 1 (2024): 229–242, https://doi.org/10.1080/21565503.2024.2328551
2. Trevor E. Brown, Suzanne Mettler, and Samantha Puzzi, "When Rural and Urban Become 'Us' versus 'Them': How a Growing Divide is Reshaping American Politics," *The Forum* 19, no. 3 (2021): 365–93, https://doi.org/10.1515/for-2021-2029.
3. Katherine J. Cramer, *The Politics of Resentment: Rural Consciousness in Wisconsin and the Rise of Scott Walker* (Chicago: University of Chicago Press, 2016); Robert Wuthnow, *The Left Behind: Decline and Rage in Rural America* (Princeton, NJ: Princeton University Press, 2018); M. V. Hood III and Seth C. McKee, *Rural Realignment in the Modern South: The Untold Story* (Columbia, SC: University of South Carolina Press, 2022); Jowei Chen and Jonathan Rodden, "Unintentional Gerrymandering: Political Geography and Electoral Bias in Legislatures," *Quarterly Journal of Political Science* 8, no. 3 (2013): 239–69.
4. For an importance exception, see Jonathan A. Rodden, *Why Cities Lose: The Deep Roots of the Urban-Rural Political Divide* (New York, NY: Basic Books, 2019).
5. Trevor E. Brown and Suzanne Mettler, "Sequential Polarization: The Development of the Rural-Urban Political Divide, 1976–2020," *Perspectives on Politics* 22, no. 3 (2023): 630–58, https://doi.org/10.1017/S1537592723002918
6. Steven Ruggles, "The Decline of Intergenerational Coresidence in the United States, 1850 to 2000," *American Sociological Review* 72, no. 6 (2007): 964–89, https://doi.org/10.1177/000312240707200606
7. Elizabeth Sanders, *Roots of Reform: Farmers, Workers, and the American State, 1877–1917* (Chicago, IL: University of Chicago Press, 1999).
8. Sarah T. Phillips, *This Land, This Nation: Conservation, Rural America, and the New Deal* (New York: Cambridge University Press, 2007).
9. Suzanne Mettler and Trevor E. Brown, *Rural Versus Urban: The Growing Divide that Threatens Democracy.* (Princeton, NJ: Princeton University Press, 2025).
10. "What is Rural?," US Department of Agriculture, Economic Research Service, last updated March 26, 2024, https://www.ers.usda.gov/topics/rural-economy-population/rural-classifications/what-is-rural/.
11. Estimates in Figure 12.1 and Figure 12.2 come from US Bureau of Economic Analysis, Economic Data by County (various years). Available at: https://www.bea.gov/data/by-place-county-metro-local
12. Unfortunately, data on GDP are not available prior to 2001, not allowing us to examine them at earlier points in time.
13. The county-level patterns in Figure 12.1 are generally reflected in individual-level survey data as well, particularly through the American National Election Studies (ANES) survey and Cooperative Election Survey (CES).
14. Mettler and Brown, *Rural Versus Urban.*
15. Seymour M. Lipset and Stein Rokkan, "Cleavage Structures, Party Systems, and Voter Alignments: An Introduction," in Seymour M. Lipset and Stein Rokkan, ed., *Party Systems and Voter Alignments: Cross-National Perspectives*, 1–65 (New York: The Free Press, 1967).
16. Lipset and Rokkan call the first a "functional" dimension, but we term it "political-economic," to highlight the interplay of policy change, political party development, and economic transformation. They call the second a "territorial" dimension.
17. Brown and Mettler, "Sequential Polarization."
18. Lipset and Rokkan, "Cleavage Structures, Party Systems, and Voter Alignments," 10.
19. For a detailed discussion of the United States's relatively maldistributed political institutions, see: Alfred Stepan and Juan J. Linz, "Comparative Perspectives on Inequality and the Quality of Democracy in the United States," *Perspectives on Politics* 9, no. 4 (2011): 841–56, https://doi.org/10.1017/S1537592711003756

20. Suzanne Mettler and Trevor Brown, "The Growing Rural-Urban Political Divide and Democratic Vulnerability," *The ANNALS of the American Academy of Political and Social Science* 699, no. 1 (2022): 130–42, https://doi.org/10.1177/00027162211070061.
21. Kenneth Finegold and Theda Skocpol, *State and Party in America's New Deal* (Madison, WI: University of Wisconsin Press, 1995), 58.
22. Daniel P. Carpenter, *The Forging of Bureaucratic Autonomy: Reputations, Networks, and Policy Innovation in Executive Agencies, 1862–1928* (Princeton, NJ: Princeton University Press, 2001), 226–54.
23. Carpenter, *The Forging of Bureaucratic Autonomy*, 68–76, 123–43.
24. Authors' analysis of US Census data, various years.
25. Ruggles, "The Decline of Intergenerational Coresidence in the United States, 1850 to 2000," 964–89.
26. James L. Sundquist, *Dynamics of the Party System: Alignment and Realignment of Political Parties in the United States*, rev. ed. (Washington, D.C.: Brookings Institution, 1983), 187.
27. Sundquist, *Dynamics of the Party System*, 187–88; Richard Franklin Bensel, *Sectionalism and American Political Development: 1880–1980* (Madison, WI: University of Wisconsin Press, 1984), 128–30, 137–46.
28. Charles W. Eagles, "Urban-Rural Conflict in the 1920s: A Historiographical Assessment," *The Historian*, 49, no. 1 (1986): 37.
29. Sundquist, *Dynamics of the Party System*, 189.
30. Phillips, *This Land, This Nation*, 23–24.
31. Phillips, *This Land, This Nation*, 21.
32. Phillips, *This Land, This Nation*, 63, 79.
33. Phillips, *This Land, This Nation*, 64.
34. Phillips, *This Land, This Nation*, 68–70.
35. David Darmofal, "The Political Geography of the New Deal Realignment," *American Politics Research* 36, no. 6 (2008): 943.
36. Phillips, *This Land, This Nation*, 76.
37. Quote in Kenneth S. Davis, *FDR: The New Deal Years, 1933–1937* (New York, NY: Random House, 1979), 71.
38. Davis, *FDR*, 71.
39. Phillips, *This Land, This Nation*, 79.
40. Phillips, *This Land, This Nation*, 78, 114, 116.
41. Wayne D Rasmussen, "The New Deal Farm Programs: What They Were and Why They Survived," *American Journal of Agricultural Economics* 65, no. 5 (1983): 1159.
42. Paul H. Landis, "The New Deal and Rural Life," *American Sociological Review* 1, no. 4 (1963): 592–603.
43. William E. Leuchtenburg, *Franklin D. Roosevelt and the New Deal, 1932–1940* (New York: Harper and Row, 1963), 193.
44. Phillips, *This Land, This Nation*, 100, 230.
45. Leuchtenburg, *Franklin D. Roosevelt and the New Deal, 1932–1940*, 157–58.
46. Richard S. Kirkendall, *Social Scientists and Farm Politics in the Age of Roosevelt* (Ames, Iowa: Iowa State University Press, 1966), 128–129.
47. Phillips, *This Land, This Nation*, 195.
48. Rasmussen, "The New Deal Farm Programs," 1158–62.
49. Bensel, *Sectionalism and American Political Development*, 214–15.
50. John H. Fenton, *Midwest Politics* (New York, NY: Holt, Rinehart, and Winston, 1957), 145.
51. Sundquist, *Dynamics of the Party System*, 225–27.
52. Sundquist, *Dynamics of the Party System*, 213.
53. Quote in Bensel, *Sectionalism and American Political Development: 1880–1980*, 194.
54. Bensel, *Sectionalism and American Political Development: 1880–1980*, 194.
55. Sidney Milkis, *The President and the Parties* (New York: Oxford University Press, 1993), 56–57, 76.
56. Bensel, *Sectionalism and American Political Development: 1880–1980*, 242–51.
57. Hood and McKee, *Rural Realignment in the Modern South*, 14.

58. Barry J. Barnett, "The U.S. Farm Financial Crisis of the 1980s," *Agricultural History* 74, no. 2 (2000): 366–80; quote on p. 373.
59. Barry J. Barnett, "The U.S. Farm Financial Crisis of the 1980s."
60. Estimates from the US Department of Agriculture (USDA). See Jerome M. Stam, Steven R. Koenig, Susan E. Bentley H., and Frederick Gale, Jr., "Farm Financial Stress, Farm Exits, and Public Sector Assistance to the Farm Sector in the 1980's," No. 645, US Department of Agriculture, Economic Research Service, 1991. Available at: https://naldc.nal.usda.gov/download/CAT91959390/PDF
61. James M. MacDonald, "Tracking the Consolidation of U.S. Agriculture," *Applied Economies Perspectives and Policy* 42, no. 3 (2020): 361–79.
62. James M. MacDonald, and Robert A. Hoppe, "Examining Consolidation in U.S. Agriculture," *Amber Waves*, US Department of Agriculture, Economic Research Service, 2018. Available at: https://www.ers.usda.gov/amber-waves/2018/march/examining-consolidation-in-us-agriculture/
63. David A. Domina and Robert C. Taylor, "The Debilitating Effects of Concentration in Markets Affecting Agriculture," *The Drake Journal of Agriculture Law* (2010): 81.
64. Cody McCracken, "Old MacDonald had a Trust: How Market Consolidation in the Agricultural Industry, Spurred on by a Lack of Antitrust Law Enforcement, is Destroying Small Agricultural Producers," *William & Mary Business Law Review* (2022); Domina and Taylor, "The Debilitating Effects of Concentration in Markets Affecting Agriculture."
65. MacDonald and Hoppe, "Examining Consolidation in U.S. Agriculture."
66. William A. Galston and Haren J. Baehler, *Rural Development in the United States: Connecting Theory, Practice, and Possibilities* (Washington, D.C.: Island Press, 1995), 93–94.
67. Carolyn Dimitri, Anne Effland, and Neilson Conklin, "The 20th Century Transformation of U.S. Agriculture and Farm Policy," US Department of Agriculture, Economic Research Service, 2005. Available at: https://www.ers.usda.gov/publications/pub-details/?pubid=44198
68. C. Edwin Young and Paul C. Wescott, "The 1996 U.S. Farm Act Increases Market Orientation," US Department of Agriculture, Economic Research Service, 1996, https://www.ers.usda.gov/webdocs/publications/42073/32953_aib726a_002.pdf?v=0.
69. Thomas J. Sugrue, *The Origins of the Urban Crisis: Race and Inequality in Postwar Detroit* (Princeton, NJ: Princeton University Press, 1998); William Julius Wilson, *When Work Disappears: The World of the New Urban Poor* (New York, NY: Knopf, 1996).
70. Sarah Low, "Manufacturing is Relatively More Important to the Rural Economy than the Urban Economy," US Department of Agriculture, Economic Research Service, 2021, https://www.usda.gov/media/blog/2017/09/12/manufacturing-relatively-more-important-rural-economy-urban-economy.
71. William A. Testa, "Trends and Prospects for Rural Manufacturing." Regional Economic Issues Working Paper Series, no. 92-12 (1992), https://www.chicagofed.org/publications/working-papers/1992/1992-12, p. 21, figure 4.
72. Nelson Lichtenstein and Judith Stein, *A Fabulous Failure: The Clinton Presidency and the Transformation of American Capitalism* (Princeton, NJ: Princeton University Press, 2023), 219.
73. Jiwon Choi, Ilyana Kuziemko, Ebonya Washington, and Gavin Wright, "Local Economic and Political Effects of Trade Deals: Evidence from NAFTA," *American Economic Review* 114, no. 6 (2024): 1540–75; Gavin Wright, "Voting Rights, Deindustrialization, and Republican Ascendancy in the South," Institute for New Economic Thinking, Working Paper no. 135, 2020, https://www.ineteconomics.org/uploads/papers/WP_135-Wright-VOTING-RIGHTS.pdf.
74. David H. Autor, David Dorn, and Gordon H. Hanson, "The China Shock: Learning from Labor-Market Adjustment to Large Changes in Trade," *Annual Review of Economics* 8, no. 1 (2016): 205–40, https://www.aeaweb.org/articles?id=10.1257/aeri.20180396; Justin R. Pierce and Peter K. Schott, "Trade Liberalization and Mortality: Evidence from US Counties," *American Economic Review: Insights* 2, no. 1 (2020): 47–64, https://www.aeaweb.org/articles?id=10.1257/aeri.20180396.
75. Low, "Manufacturing is Relatively More Important to the Rural Economy than the Urban Economy," 2021.

76. Adam Scavette, "The Role of Manufacturing in the Rural Fifth District," Federal Reserve Bank of Richmond, 2022, https://www.richmondfed.org/research/regional_economy/regional_matters/2022/rm_04_28_2022_manufacturing.
77. Amy Glasmeier and Priscilla Salant, "Low-Skill Workers in Rural America Face Permanent Job Loss," *Carsey Institute*, Policy Brief no. 2 (2006): 2, https://files.eric.ed.gov/fulltext/ED536116.pdf.
78. Gary P. Green, "Deindustrialization of Rural America: Economic Restructuring and the Rural Ghetto," *Local Development & Society* 1, no. 1 (2020): 19, https://doi.org/10.1080/26883597.2020.1801331.
79. Andrew M. Isserman and James Westervelt, "1.5 Million Missing Numbers: Overcoming Employment Suppression in County Business Patterns Data," *International Regional Science Review* 29, no. 3 (2006): 311–35, https://doi.org/10.1177/0160017606290359.
80. Richard S. Krannich, Brian Gentry, A.E. Luloff, and Peter G. Robertson, "Resource Dependency in Rural America: Continuities and Change," in *Rural America in a Globalizing World*, ed. Connor Bailey, Leif Jensen, and Elizabeth Ransom, 208–25 (Morgantown, WV: West Virginia University Press, 2014).
81. William R. Freudenburg, "Addictive Economies: Extractive Industries and Vulnerable Localities in a Changing World Economy," *Rural Sociology* 57, no. 3 (1992): 305–32, https://doi.org/10.1111/j.1549-0831.1992.tb00467.x.
82. Nicholas Short, "Antitrust Deregulation and the Politics of the American Knowledge Economy" unpublished manuscript (2022), https://nick-short.com/wp-content/uploads/2022/08/paper-4-antitrust-deregulation-and-the-politics-of-the-american-knowledge-economy.pdf; Nicholas Short, "The Politics of the American Knowledge Economy," *Studies in American Political Development* 36, no. 1 (2022): 41–60; Torben Iversen and David Soskice, *Democracy and Prosperity: Reinventing Capitalism through a Turbulent Century* (Princeton, NJ: Princeton University Press, 2019).
83. Short, "Antitrust Deregulation and the Politics of the American Knowledge Economy."
84. Wuthnow, *The Left Behind*. To be sure, this is also a problem in post-industrial urban areas without thriving economies (Moretti, *The New Geography of Jobs* (2012)). But note the pull is even stronger from rural areas, where fewer opportunities exist.
85. Enrico Moretti, *The New Geography of Jobs* (Boston: Houghton Mifflin Harcourt, 2012).
86. Arne L. Kalleberg, *Good Jobs, Bad Jobs: The Rise of Polarized and Precarious Employment Systems in the United States, 1970s–2000s* (New York, NY: Russell Sage Foundation, 2011); Amy K. Glasmeier, and Marie Howland, *From Combines to Computers: Rural Services and Development in the Age of Information Technology* (Albany NY: State University of New York Press, 1995); Alexander C. Vias and Peter B. Nelson. "Changing Livelihoods in Rural America," in *Population Change and Rural Society*, ed. William A. Kandel and David L. Brown, 75–102 (Dordrecht, The Netherlands: Routledge, 2006).
87. Galston and Baehler, *Rural Development in the United States*.
88. Dante J. Scala, Kenneth M. Johnson, and Luke T. Rogers, "Red Rural, Blue Rural? Presidential Voting Patterns in a Changing Rural America," *Political Geography* 48 (20150: 108–18.
89. Michael Stewart Foley, "'Everyone was Pounding on Us': Front Porch Politics and the American Farm Crisis of the 1970s and 1980s," *Sociology Lens* 28, no. 1 (2014): 104–24; James N. Leiker, "Rage of the Rural Minority: The High Plains Farm Crisis and Farmer Activism in Colorado and Kansas," *Great Plains Quarterly* 39, no. 3 (2019): 265–89.
90. Leiker, "Rage of the Rural Minority," 216–17; Jenny Barker Devine and David D. Vail, "Sustaining the Conversation: The Farm Crisis and the Midwest," *Middle West Review* 2, no. 1 (2015): 1–9.
91. For example, see: Paul Lasley, ed., *Beyond the Amber Waves of Grain: An Examination of Social And Economic Restructuring in the Heartland* (New York, NY: Routledge, 1995); Pamela Riney-Kehrberg, "Children of the Crisis: Farm Youth in Troubled Times," *Middle West Review* 2, no. 1 (2015): 11–25; Pamela Riney-Kehrberg, *When a Dream Dies: Agriculture, Iowa, and the Farm Crisis of the 1980s* (Lawrence, KS: University Press of Kansas, 2022).
92. Associated Press, "Farmer Suicide Rate Swells in 1980's, Study Says," October 14, 1991, https://www.nytimes.com/1991/10/14/us/farmer-suicide-rate-swells-in-1980-s-study-

says.html; Michael J. Belyea, and Linda M. Lobao, "Psychosocial Consequences of Agricultural Transformation: The Farm Crisis and Depression," *Rural Sociology* 55, no. 1 (1990): 58–75; Suzanne T. Ortega, David R. Johnson, Peter G. Beeson, and Betty J. Craft, "The Farm Crisis and Mental Health: A Longitudinal Study of the 1980s," *Rural Sociology* 59, no. 4 (1994): 598–619.

93. Rand Wilson, "Winning Lessons from the NAFTA Loss," *Labor Research Review* 1, no. 22 (1994): 29, 30–31.
94. Kay Tamara and Rhonda Evans, *Trade Battles: Activism and the Politicization of International Trade Policy* (New York, NY: Oxford University Press, 2018), 74, 102; Jennifer Merolla, Laura B. Stephenson, Carole J. Wilson, and Elizabeth J. Zechmeister, "Globalization, Globalizacion, Globalisation: Public Opinion and NAFTA," *Law and Business Review of the Americas* 11, no. 3&4 (2005): 568.
95. James McCann, "Afta' NAFTA: The Free Trade Debate and Party Politics in the United States," *Instituto Technologico de Estudios Superiores de Monterrey*, Mexico, 1999, 106.
96. Choi et al., "Local Economic and Political Effects of Trade Deals," 2024.
97. The fuller story of NAFTA's ratification appears in George W. Grayson, *The North American Free Trade Agreement: Regional Community and the New World Order* (New York: University Press of America, 1995), 195–221; Lichtenstein and Stein, *A Fabulous Failure*, 2023, 219–40.
98. Our analysis is based on voting data from VoteView and the share of the rural population from each representative's district, as defined by the US Census Bureau.
99. Wuthnow, *The Left Behind.*
100. Marc A. C. Hafstead and Roberton C. Williams III, "Jobs and Environmental Regulation," *Environmental and Energy Policy and the Economy* 1 (2020): 192–240, https://doi.org/10.1086/706799; W. Reed Walker, "Environmental Regulation and Labor Reallocation: Evidence from the Clean Air Act," *The American Economic Review* 101, no. 3 (2011): 442–47, http://www.jstor.org/stable/29783786; W. Reed Walker, "The Transitional Costs of Sectoral Reallocation: Evidence from the Clean Air Act and the Workforce," *The Quarterly Journal of Economics* 128, no. 4 (2013): https://doi.org/10.1093/qje/qjt022.
101. Arlie Russell Hochschild, *Strangers in Their Own Land: Anger and Mourning on the American Right* (New York, NY: The New Press, 2016).
102. B. Kal Munis, "Us Over Here Versus Them Over There . . . Literally: Measuring Place Resentment in American Politics," *Political Behavior* 44, no. 3 (2022): 1057–78.
103. Brown and Mettler, "Sequential Polarization."
104. Brown et al., "When Rural and Urban Become 'Us' versus 'Them'," 365–93.
105. Lilliana Mason, *Uncivil Agreement: How Politics Became Our Identity* (Chicago, IL: University of Chicago Press, 2018).
106. Torben Iversen and David Soskice, *Democracy and Prosperity: Reinventing Capitalism through a Turbulent Century* (Princeton, NJ: Princeton University Press, 2019), ch. 5.
107. Mettler and Brown, "The Growing Rural-Urban Political Divide and Democratic Vulnerability," 130–42.
108. Rodden, *Why Cities Lose.*
109. Mettler and Brown, *Rural Versus Urban.*
110. Jacob M. Grumbach, and Charlotte Hill, "Which States Adopt Election-Subversion Policies?," *The ANNALS of the American Academy of Political and Social Science* 708, no. 1 (2023): 243–56.

13

Capitalism, Democracy, and the Rise of the New Right

A Shifting Landscape

WILLIAM A. GALSTON

Introduction: Global Capitalism and the Rise of Polarization

Do liberal constitutional democracies tend to make rules and regulations that over time undermine the operation of capitalist markets? And conversely, do capitalist markets produce outcomes that over time make it impossible for societies to govern themselves democratically?

Throughout the twentieth century, major intellectuals and political movements in the West answered one (or both) of these questions in the affirmative. Some on the Right argued that the democratic commitment to equality would move economies beyond regulated markets to outright socialism, including public ownership of large productive sectors—and that socialism was incompatible with the individual liberty on which democracy depends. Some on the Left retorted that the capitalist effort to minimize restraints on markets would push economic inequality to outright oligarchy—and that oligarchy was incompatible with the civic equality that democracy requires.

For three decades after World War II, these tensions were muted. Western economies grew rapidly, and the fruits of growth were shared widely enough to reduce poverty and expand the middle class. European leaders drew a bright line between communism and social democracy, which was defended as a "Third Way" between communism and laissez-faire. The semi-socialist platform of the

William A. Galston, *Capitalism, Democracy, and the Rise of the New Right*. In: *Can Democracy and Capitalism Be Reconciled?*. Edited by: Sidney M. Milkis and Scott C. Miller, Oxford University Press. © Oxford University Press (2025). DOI: 10.1093/9780197774731.003.0014 post-war British Labour Party was as far left as most non-communist Europeans wanted to go.

Although the boundaries of political debate were different on the other side of the Atlantic, they took a similar form once the United States had overcome the Great Depression's threat to both capitalism and democracy. The failure of Henry Wallace and the Independent Progressive Party in 1948 showed that most Americans were in no mood to move left of the New Deal, and the victory of Dwight Eisenhower's "Modern Republicanism" over Robert Taft's Midwestern conservatism showed that most Americans had no desire to repudiate it either. Barry Goldwater's hostility to New Deal programs such as Social Security contributed to his landslide defeat in 1964, and Ronald Reagan, an ardent Goldwater supporter, made no serious effort to repeal New Deal programs after he became president in 1981. (He focused his attack on LBJ's Great Society instead.) Reagan's half-hearted attempt to cut Social Security benefits collapsed in 1981, as did George W. Bush's push to partially privatize the program in 2005.

The consensus extended to capitalism beyond national borders. Although there were always skirmishes about the effects of international competition on specific products such as steel and autos, the leading elements of both political parties endorsed free trade as the default setting for US policy, and the collapse of the Soviet Union extended this consensus to the free flow of capital and productive capacity.

To be sure, as Europe and Japan recovered from wartime devastation and began to compete effectively with the United States, opposition to this default setting emerged. On the Left, organized labor became increasingly skeptical about free trade and insisted, to considerable effect, that new agreements guarantee worker rights in all signatory countries and protect US workers against the negative effects of increased competition from abroad. On the Right, so-called "paleoconservatives" denounced the effects of globalization on the American communities in which sons expected to follow their fathers into secure manufacturing jobs and to preserve working-class cultural traditions. Patrick Buchanan, the leader of this revolt against conservative elites, declared that "the global capitalist and the true conservative are Cain and Abel."[1]

Still the consensus held long enough for elites across the ideological spectrum to back China's entrance into the World Trade Organization in 2001. The tide did not turn until the United States lost more than five million manufacturing jobs in the first decade of the new millennium. By 2016, Donald Trump, running on an America First agenda, routed his elite rivals for the Republican presidential nomination, and Hillary Clinton, who served as Barack Obama's

Secretary of State, thought it necessary to repudiate the Obama Administration's signature multilateral trade initiative, the Trans-Pacific Partnership, to secure the Democratic nomination.

As president, Donald Trump pursued the strategy he championed during the 2016 campaign. And to the surprise of many, Joe Biden mostly adhered to this strategy after he defeated Trump in 2020, so much so that his "Buy America" policy and subsidies for US industries have aroused consternation overseas, especially in Europe. During the first two decades of the twenty-first century, in short, anti-globalization insurgents triumphed over their adversaries in both political parties, and one consensus gave way to its opposite. A reasonable case can be made that the progressive critique of "neo-liberalism" is beating a dead horse.

This is not to suggest that there was a consensus across partisan and ideological lines about the domestic economic policies the United States should pursue. Although Bill Clinton embraced the traditional conservative goal of a balanced budget (and to everyone's surprise, achieved it for four consecutive years in his second term), he endured a government shutdown to hold the line against conservative efforts to slash taxes, regulations, and federal spending. This confrontation recurred in the third year of the Obama Administration after Republicans regained control of the House of Representative and again in the third year of the Biden administration.

This disagreement over the role of government in the economy has contributed to the partisan polarization that has diminished confidence in public institutions and eroded support for democracy itself. It would be a mistake, however, to suggest that this clash has been the sole or even principal source of rising polarization. Although the debate triggered by the New Deal has not yet ended, it has been overlaid by the new controversies about race, gender, culture, and patriotism that erupted in the 1960s and have raged ever since. Class consciousness has not disappeared, but it is manifested in cultural as well as economic terms. Much of the working class opposes upper-middle class professional elites as viscerally as it does the wealthy captains of industry and finance. Yes, they believe, the bosses don't offer the wages and working conditions we deserve, but the professionals want to take away our gas stoves and indoctrinate our kids.

In the United States. and throughout the West, the populist revolt draws strength from cultural resentment as well as economic disappointment. Some portions of the working class have moved left, but far more have moved right. In response, some conservatives are working to create an agenda that reflects the full spectrum of working-class concerns, economic as well as cultural. The rise of this New Right is among the most interesting—and potentially consequential—political developments of our time.

The Emergence of the New Right

During the Cold War, most American conservatives agreed that capitalism and liberal democracy were mutually supportive, a proposition that reached its apotheosis in Michael Novak's *The Spirit of Democratic Capitalism*.[2] Rejecting Daniel Bell's thesis that modern capitalism suffers from "cultural contradictions," Novak insisted that political democracy, a market economy, and a pluralistic culture work together in relations of mutual support. This is so, he said, because all reflect the same animating impulse—the quest for freedom. By building up the middle class, market economies bolster political liberties, which not only allow but also encourage the expression of cultural differences. Democratic stability requires economic growth, without which social mobility stalls and the promise of equal opportunity becomes hollow. Growth, he argued, moots claims based on "social justice," a concept more at home in steady-state economies where gains for some mean losses for others. Democratic capitalism does not guarantee equality of results, a goal shaped by envy and resentment.

Still, Novak admitted, unequal opportunity does yield a "legitimate grievance."[3] Novak acknowledged the cultural criticisms long leveled against capitalism—the corruptions of affluence and the denigration of excellence in favor of consumerism, among others—and the political criticisms, including the undue influence of corporations, but he downplayed their significance. He acknowledged, as well, that democratic capitalism favors dynamism over stability: "The spirit of democratic capitalism is the spirit of development, risk, experiment, adventure. It surrenders present security for future betterment."[4] But despite the pace of change, which many found dizzying, it was a trade-off worth making, Novak believed. For most democratic capitalist citizens, change would be their friend.

Democratic capitalism disrupts stable, traditional communities, Novak acknowledged. But it generates new forms of community—voluntary associations, which are consistent with geographic and economic mobility. These new communities do not require that their members know one another from birth, or that they share visions of God or the common good.[5] They are the form of associational life most compatible with the right of all individuals to pursue happiness as they themselves define it.[6] Novak admits that the transition from village life to new forms of association is "hard on all of us."[7] But it is worth it, because exercising individual freedom is the highest activity of the human spirit.

Democratic capitalism's commitment to individual freedom means rejecting unitary visions of the Good in favor of cultural, moral, and religious pluralism. In a pluralistic society, Novak argued, there is no one "sacred canopy." Instead, there are "radical experiences of human liberty."[8] If you believe in political liberty, he continued, there is no alternative to pluralism, because a unitary theory of the good (including the common good) requires a unitary political power capable of enforcing its theory on those who do not freely accept it.

Novak was a devout Catholic in constant dialogue with Church leaders. Nonetheless, he was alert to the potentially dangerous consequences of religion for free societies. Religious institutions, he believed, think they belong at the center of the polity with the power to bring their holistic vision into every aspect of human life.[9] But whatever the orthodoxy, free persons have the right to be different. "Those who wish the social order to be based upon commanded 'substantive' morality," he concluded, "cannot be in favor of pluralism. A democratic capitalist society is, in principle, uncommitted to any one vision of a social order."[10]

Traditionalists often saw Novak's pluralism as the road to anarchy, a fear he regarded as misguided. There can be a unity of practice without a unity of theory, he insisted. Citizens may disagree about the proper understanding of the "general welfare" while agreeing on constitutional institutions as the best way of managing this disagreement. And living within a democratic capitalist framework tends to encourage the virtues needed to sustain this form of public order. For example, Novak argued, "There is a strong consonance between the virtues required for successful commercial and industrial practice and the natural moral virtues."[11]

Novak believed that the moral consequences of capitalist life are preferable to those in ecclesiastical, aristocratic, and martial societies. Business activities, he claimed, are uniquely conducive to "rule by law, to liberty, to habits of regularity and moderation, to a healthy realism, and to demonstrated social progress."[12] But following Montesquieu and Adam Smith, he acknowledged that capitalism entails moral losses as well. For this reason, commercial systems need restraint and correction by a "moral-cultural system independent of commerce."[13]

This admission was the entering wedge for a traditionalist retort. If the commitment to individual liberty weakens the forces—religion and tradition—that act as a counterweight to the pursuit of profit and wealth, then Novak's confidence that capitalism and democracy are mutually supportive will turn out to be misplaced.

In 2017, R. R. Reno, a prominent religious conservative and editor of *First Things*, described the impact that Novak's book had had on him when he first encountered it 35 years earlier.[14] The book had helped him see that a market economy can make important moral and spiritual contributions to a healthy society. But now, Reno said, he had come to see Novak's emphasis on freedom as problematic. Toward the end of the book, Novak called for a brand of leadership that "inspires all to self-sacrifice for the common good." But the centrality of individual freedom, voluntary association, and social pluralism in Novak's conception of a healthy society provides no basis for a shared understanding of the common good, or for the exercise of authority needed to enforce this conception throughout society.

The limits on freedom are no longer the problem they were in American society after World War II, Reno argued. Today the problem is just the opposite—the excess of freedom, which erases moral boundaries. The part of our soul that craves liberation from all restraints has been unleashed, while the other part, which craves stability and relief from "the existential exhaustion of perpetual dynamism," is left to languish.

Emphasizing freedom made sense in the post-war period, which had a "closed, sealed quality" in economic and social life. But today we have the opposite problem: a fluidity that threatens to erase borders, sexual differences, and distinctions between good and bad. "We are drowning in freedom," Reno exclaimed. Traditional expectations about marriage and children have become optional, and we can even choose to become male or female. Novak's position, Reno concluded, was one-sided and unbalanced, stressing the virtues of dynamism but not the desire for permanence. If conservatism means nourishing the hunger for stability by preserving what is good about the past or at least slowing the pace of change, then a free society can be an antagonist of conservatism as well as its ally.

This ambivalent judgment applies as much to economic freedom as to social liberation. In retrospect, Reno said, conservatives underestimated the "flesh-eating character" of the market economy. The market is becoming the dominant mode of our social engagement, which "diminishes democratic culture."

Reno expressed the fear that the contemporary market was leading us away from democracy toward a new form of oligarchy. Globalization and the "rules-based international order" worked to the advantage of the advantaged but not for the interests of all citizens. This new order was undermining national sovereignty in favor of a transnational bureaucratic elite that operated without democratic accountability. And the ever-expanding corporations created by global markets were abusing their economic power to become engines of progressive social change, whatever local democratic majorities may want.

Reno's critique of Novak's Reagan-era paean to capitalism was an early voice in what became a swelling chorus. Conservative intellectuals charged that globalized capitalism had produced excessive concentrations of economic power at the expense of working and middle-class Americans—and that it created a post-industrial elite that perpetuated its own power while rejecting traditional values.

This anti-capitalist trend among conservatives occurred in response to the economic and social changes of the post-Cold War era. After the fall of the Berlin Wall and the collapse of the Soviet Union, the emergence of globalized capitalism with the freer movement of goods and capital facilitated the offshoring of production previously located in the United States and contributed to the loss of more than five million manufacturing jobs during the first decade of the twenty-first century. Working-class voters, long a key element of the Republican coalition, paid the biggest price.

Over the past decade, more and more conservatives insist, large corporations have embraced left-wing views on race, gender, diversity, and social responsibility and have opposed laws and practices that contradict these views. These conservatives have come to regard corporations as "oligarchic" forces at odds with popular democracy, and they advocate policies to rein in corporate behavior to promote domestic job-creation and reduce corporations' cultural influence.

In March of 2019, fifteen New Right intellectuals issued a manifesto, "Against the Dead Consensus," which argued that there could be no return to what they regarded as the obsolete Reagan-era brand of conservatism with its comfortable assumptions about the relation between capitalism and democracy. It was time to put workers first, they insisted:

> The Republican Party has for too long held investors and "job creators" above workers and citizens, dismissing vast swaths of Americans as takers unworthy of its time. Trump's victory, driven in part by his appeal to working-class voters, shows the potential of a political movement that heeds the cries of the working class as much as the demands of capital. Americans take more pride in their identity as workers than their identity as consumers. Economic and welfare policy should prioritize work over consumption.[15]

In short, the manifesto argues, the corporate push to reduce the cost of production works against average citizens and the national interest. Even if people who shop at Walmart must pay more for goods made in America, this is a price worth paying to bring manufacturing jobs back to this country and restore the dignity of work.

Since the publication of this manifesto, a steadily growing group of New Right intellectuals and activists have come together in a movement called "National Conservatism." In the summer of 2022, they issued a "Statement of Principles" that addresses (among many other questions) the relation between democracy and contemporary capitalism:

> [T]he free market cannot be absolute. Economic policy must serve the general welfare of the nation. Today, globalized markets allow foreign powers to despoil America and other countries of their manufacturing capacity, weakening them economically and dividing them internally. At the same time, trans-national corporations showing little loyalty to any nation damage public life by censoring political speech, flooding

> the country with dangerous and addictive substances and pornography, and promoting excessive, destructive personal habits.
>
> A prudent national economic policy should promote free enterprise, but it must also mitigate threats to the national interest, aggressively pursue economic independence from hostile powers, nurture industries crucial for national defense, and restore and upgrade manufacturing capabilities critical to the public welfare. Crony capitalism, the selective promotion of corporate profit-making by organs of state power, should be energetically exposed and opposed.[16]

In its opposition to corporate-dominated global capitalism, then, the New Right abandons the commitment to limited government that has long dominated American conservatism. In its place, this insurgent movement embraces a Hamiltonian stance toward the management of the economy and links this stance to the promotion of social conservatism.

The New Right rejects the core of Reagan-era conservatism—its belief that freedom is the highest good. The "autonomous self," they argue, knows no limits. It is inherently transgressive and undermines basic moral virtues such as self-restraint, solidarity with members of one's community, and the ability to commit to a cause higher than oneself. Just as government must restrain the excesses of capitalist freedom in the economy, it must also police the moral boundaries of the community.

These exercises of public authority are linked. If stable families and communities are the seedbeds of the moral virtues, as many conservatives inspired by Tocqueville believe, and if contemporary capitalism destabilizes families and communities, then restraints on capitalism serve moral as well as economic purposes. And if you believe that democratic societies need these virtues, then unrestrained capitalism must be reined in to preserve democracy.

The understanding of capitalism as inherently destabilizing has a distinguished pedigree. As we've seen, Michael Novak justifies the free market as a key site of human creativity. Inventors and entrepreneurs bring into being products, processes, and services that did not previously exist. In so doing, they improve our lives and expand opportunity for all.

A well-known twentieth century economic thinker, Joseph Schumpeter, offered a more complex view. Capitalism is not straightforwardly creative, he argued, because it destroys as it creates. As he famously wrote in *Capitalism, Socialism, and Democracy,*

> The opening up of new markets, foreign or domestic, and the organizational development from the craft shop and factory to such concerns as U.S. Steel illustrate the same process of industrial mutation—if I may use that biological term—that incessantly revolutionizes the economic

> structure from within, incessantly destroying the old one, incessantly creating a new one. This process of Creative Destruction is the essential fact about capitalism. It is what capitalism consists in and what every capitalist concern has got to live in. [17]

Post-industrial capitalist leaders are frank about this reality. Until 2014, Facebook's internal motto—created by Mark Zuckerberg—was "Move fast and break things." In the new ethos spawned by Silicon Valley, "disruption" is a term of praise. But this logic of capitalist economics is not always compatible with the needs of the individuals and communities who experience disruption as less than an unmixed blessing.

So long as conservatism was dominated by anti-communism, the tension between conservatism and capitalism was suppressed. But after the Soviet Union collapsed, this tension became harder to ignore. As originally understood, conservatism reflected the desire to preserve what exists, not for its own sake, but because what exists typically embodies practical wisdom about the institutions and norms that best serve the interests of society. Few conservatives believed that change could (or should) be resisted across the board, but they favored incremental changes at a pace to which most people could adjust. When change is too abrupt, it is disorienting and can evoke unproductive reactions.

The relation between conservatism and capitalism, then, is bound to be fraught. As thinkers from Marx to Schumpeter have observed, the quest for profit drives a process of innovation that relentlessly sweeps away established products and modes of production, often at a dizzying pace: "all that is solid melts into air." Although capitalism is creative, the new is not added to the old; it typically replaces the old—whence "creative destruction." And because social life organizes around economic life, the destruction of former modes of production often means the disruption of communities, as it did when mechanization drove farmers to seek jobs in the cities.

From the 1880s through the 1940s, defenders of agrarian communities were hostile to industrial capitalism. And after a period of continuity in the quarter century after World War II, the rise of trade competition and the information economy destabilized communities—large and small—that depended on factories for their livelihood. Understandably, the working class sought leaders who pledged to defend its embattled way of life rather than those who urged workers to adapt to change. And because preservation requires impeding the forces of change, the attempt to stabilize dynamic systems such as capitalism is an inherently conservative endeavor.

But stabilization is not an inherently democratic endeavor, because there is no guarantee that those who lose from change will outnumber those who gain. When the winners are in the majority, they often do not use even a portion of their gains to protect the losers, who are left with the choice between licking their wounds and engaging in undemocratic forms of resistance.

Constant destabilization is but one of several ways in which the outputs of a capitalist system may weaken democracy. Here's another: if democracy requires a large class of people who are neither rich nor poor, as theorists from Aristotle to Lipset have argued, and if the operation of capitalism in a specific time and place tends to weaken this class, a tension emerges between capitalism and democracy.

In the decades after World War II, the American middle class expanded dramatically. Not surprisingly, this was a period of high confidence that capitalism and democracy were mutually supportive. But since the 1970s, the middle class has been in relative decline. In 1971, 61 percent of US adults lived in middle-class households. By 2021, this figure had fallen to 50 percent. During this period, the share of household income commanded by the middle class fell even more, from 62 percent to 42 percent while the share going to upper-income households rose from 29 percent to 50 percent.[18]

These shifts have not meant the immiseration of the poor—far from it. After taxes and means-tested transfers, the lowest quintile of households have seen their income rise by 94 percent since 1979, and the post-tax and transfer poverty rate has fallen to the lowest level ever recorded. By contrast, middle-income household income grew more slowly, by a cumulative 59 percent, while income for households in the top quintile rose by 123 percent, even after transfer programs and the progressive income tax reduced their share of household income by 6 percentage points.[19]

The top 1 percent of households have done extremely well during this period, but the slogan of the Occupy Wall Street movement—"We are the 99 percent"—overlooked a key dynamic—the explosive growth of the new upper middle class of households with annual incomes between $200,000 and $570,000. These households, which constituted less than 1 percent of total households in 1971, now make up more than 10 percent—roughly speaking, the 89th to the 99th percentiles of all household), and their share of the national income has expanded even more.[20]

This changing class structure has had anti-democratic consequences, the New Right believes. Eight decades ago, James Burnham (then a Trotskyite, later a controversial leader in American conservatism) published *The Managerial Revolution*, which predicted the emergence of a new class of "managers" who were neither working-class nor the owners of capital. Instead, they would direct and coordinate the complex processes—technical, social, and political—on which a modern capitalist economy depends.

Although Burnham got the details wrong, the New Right argues, he nailed the big picture. Compared to half a century ago, the new upper-middle class has expanded its power and influence. This matters because the members of this new class share a characteristic outlook, a class consciousness—internationalist in economics, progressive in culture—rooted in the shift toward a post-industrial economy and a more highly regulated society.[21]

Because most do not work in sectors exposed to competition from abroad, they favor globalization and free trade. Because nearly all have bachelor's degrees, and many of them have advanced academic or professional degrees as well, they represent the values that most highly educated individuals espouse, in the United States and throughout the West. They are comfortable with geographic mobility, unlike their fellow citizens who are more rooted in local communities. They are comfortable with the racial, ethnic, and religious diversity they encounter during their education, workplaces, and travel. But because they live and work mainly with others of their class, they tend to be sealed off from the outlook (and problems) of less-educated people who work in agriculture, manufacturing, and routine services.

Non-conservative thinkers such as Richard Reeves, author of the *Dream Hoarders*, and Matthew Stewart, author of *The 9.9 Percent*, have explored this phenomenon in depth. "We are the people of good family, good health, good schools, and good jobs," Stewart writes, and the gap between this new class and the bottom 90 percent is widening. The members of this class believe that they owe their good lives to meritocratic competition, overlooking the many ways in which opportunity to succeed remains unequal. They use their advantages to ensure that their children prevail in the scramble for scarce slots in elite colleges and universities, a strategy that threatens to create a hereditary aristocracy. "Perhaps the best evidence for the power of an aristocracy," Stewart argues, is "the degree of resentment it provokes," adding that "[b]y that measure, the 9.9 percent are doing pretty well."[22]

New Right intellectuals argue that a subset of this new class—government bureaucrats, lawyers, corporate human relations managers, and school administrators—is mostly responsible for imposing the ideology of "wokeness" on key sectors of the US economy and society. Executives in national and international corporations are now pressured from without and within—by the new class and by their younger workers, whose educational institutions are dominated by progressive orthodoxy—to support woke causes they would rather avoid. The New Right views the new class as an anti-democratic minority bent on imposing its views on the majority, and the leaders of this new conservative movement are determined to use majoritarian political institutions to fight back. If this means picking fights with the corporate sector that traditional conservatives have long supported, so be it.

Conservatives have long been concerned with cultural issues, in part because of religious commitments, but also because they believe that individual morality is the basis of a healthy society. Throughout the Reagan era, they deplored what they saw as the declining influence of religious institutions, the weakening of family structures, and the evisceration of traditional moral norms in favor of an easy-going relativism.

In recent years, conservatives have focused less on moral drift per se and more on what they regard as the principal sources of moral decline—academia, the entertainment industry, and the media. In so doing, they echo the thought of Antonio Gramsci, an influential Italian neo-Marxist thinker best known today for his concept of "cultural hegemony." Modifying Marx, he regarded culture as more than a superstructural reflection of the economic base. It was, he argued, a partly autonomous source of power and legitimation within society.

In a penetrating analysis of Gramsci's significance for contemporary societies, Jackson Lears argues that the concept of cultural hegemony deepens the classic question, Who has power?

> The "who" includes parents, preachers, teachers, journalists, literati, "experts" of all kinds, as well as advertising executives, entertainment promoters, popular musicians, sports figures, and "celebrities"—all of whom are involved (albeit often unwittingly) in shaping the values and attitudes of a society. The "power" includes cultural as well as economic and political power—the power to help define the boundaries of common-sense "reality" either by ignoring views outside those boundaries or by labelling deviant opinions "tasteless" or "irresponsible".[23]

This analysis helps explain the New Right intellectuals' deepest fears. They believe that they have been all but excluded from the institutions that produce culture and, in so doing, define what is true and good. The conservatives of the Reagan era relied on limited government and the free market to safeguard a zone of liberty and on religion to shore up traditional values. Today's conservatives have lost confidence in this strategy, in part because market institutions advance cultural progressivism, but also because secular cultural influences are too strong for conservative religious forces to resist. The real choice is between retreating to enclave communities in which traditional values predominate—or going on offense to regain control of the culture by all necessary means, including deploying government power in the cultural sphere. The New Right has chosen the latter strategy, and its choice is gradually reshaping conservative politics.

The Politics of the New Right

On March 30, 2021, Representative Jim Banks, a rising conservative star, sent House Minority Leader Kevin McCarthy a confidential memo labelled "URGENT." Donald Trump, Banks said, had given Republicans a "political gift" by rallying working-class voters. The question now was whether Republicans would do what was necessary to "**permanently become the party of the working class**" (Banks's bold; copy on file with the author).

Banks's assessment was a bit misleading, because Republicans have enjoyed strong white working-class support for nearly six decades. Lyndon Johnson's landslide election in 1964 was the last time that Democrats commanded a significant majority of the white working class. The rightward shift of these voters began in 1968 in response to racial and cultural conflict and accelerated with George McGovern's nomination in 1972. (Richard Nixon received 70 percent of the white working class vote that year.) After a brief pause in 1976, the shift continued in the 1980s: Ronald Reagan averaged 61 percent among white working-class voters in his two presidential elections, and even the patrician George H. W. Bush received a solid majority in 1988. Bill Clinton averaged 41 percent of the white working-class vote in his two victories but eked out one-point pluralities over his Republican opponents in both 1992 and 1996. (Ross Perot got the rest.) But starting in the 2000 election, Democrats haven't come close to a plurality, let alone a majority, among these voters.[24]

To be sure, Democrats' performance among these voters took a further turn for the worse in 2016 and 2020. Hillary Clinton received a miserable 28 percent of their vote, and Joe Biden improved her showing only modestly, to 33 percent. Even in the 2018 midterm elections, a year of peak Democratic mobilization and large gains in the House, Democrats received only 36 percent of the white working-class vote.[25] Still, Donald Trump built on a longstanding trend that he did not initiate. The Republicans have been the party of choice for decades among white voters without college degrees.

But Trump did change the trajectory in two important respects: he substantially improved long-lagging turnout among white working-class voters, and he began to make inroads among working-class voters of color. One credible analysis showed that between 2012 and 2020, the Democrats' voter share among non-college men of color fell from 81 percent to 69 percent, and among non-college women of color, from 86 percent to 79 percent.[26]

Clearly, Jim Banks was on to something, and his argument reflected a historical shift that he did not mention. The main forces that began pushing the white working-class away from the Democratic Party were racial and cultural, not economic. This group was outraged by what it considered the unpatriotic stance of the anti-war movement and the immorality of the counterculture, and it was more affected by urban crime and violence than were upper-middle class whites who mostly lived in the suburbs. (The epithet "limousine liberal" was coined during this fraught period.) At the same time, income for working-class households of all races and ethnicity continued to rise, with recessionary interruptions, until the end of the century. This explains why the Republican appeal to white working-class voters was framed in overt cultural and covert racial terms throughout this period, while its economic agenda continued to reflect the outlook of business and small government advocates.

Then the economic pictured darkened. After peaking in 2000, working-class incomes stalled before declining sharply during the Great Recession. Adjusted for inflation, workers did not regain the incomes they had enjoyed at the end of the twentieth century until 2017. To be sure, they were not alone: median household income followed a similar path. But for families living from paycheck to check, the long income stall felt like the end of the American Dream, and the collapse of manufacturing employment in communities that had long depended on it underscored this sentiment.

It was against this backdrop that Donald Trump emerged as the Republican nominee in 2016. He appealed directly to working-class economic discontent as well as its cultural grievances, and he challenged the economic orthodoxy that had dominated conservatism since the emergence of the supply-side movement in the 1970s. He understood that workers had little interest in small government per se and that they opposed cuts in programs on which they depend, which Republicans had long advocated under the heading of "entitlement reform." Toward the end of the speech announcing his candidacy in 2015, Trump pledged to "save Medicare, Medicaid and Social Security—without cuts," adding for emphasis that we "have to do it."

Paul Ryan had been the Republicans' vice president nominee just three years earlier, and Trump's rejection of Ryan's brand of conservatism could not have been clearer. Nor could his break with the corporate agenda of globalization, free trade, and expansive immigration. Appealing to workers' beliefs that these policies had undermined their economic security and progress, he pledged to reverse them, promising that his personal wealth would immunize him from corporate lobbying.

When Jim Banks urged Kevin McCarthy to accelerate Republicans' transformation into the party of the working class, he had Trump's economic agenda in mind. "Republicans are pro-business and pro-worker, not pro-corporation," he insisted. By "business," Banks meant small business, as represented by the National Federation of Independent Businesses, not big business, represented by the Chamber of Commerce and the Business Roundtable. Small businesses are disproportionately hurt by regulations and shutdowns, and the government response to COVID-19 hurt non-college educated workers much worse than those with a BA or more. Unlike big businesses, small businesses must be sensitive to the culture of their local communities, not national and global elites.[27]

Embracing a working-class economic agenda meant hostility to the immigration and trade policies that elites had embraced. "For far too long," Banks told McCarthy, "both parties supported outsourcing working-class jobs overseas in the name of economic growth. [The result]: working Americans lost their jobs, while an already wealthy few profited off their decline."

A working-class agenda also meant taking seriously the link between concentrated economic power and anti-democratic social change. Corporations were promoting "wokeness," which reflected the outlook of educated elites rather than average Americans. Rep. Banks quoted Florida Senator Marco Rubio, who declared in a speech that "When the conflict is between working Americans and a company whose leadership has decided to wage culture war against working-class values, the choice is easy—I support the workers." Similar considerations supported Banks' recommendation to intensify the war against Big Tech, which he claimed engaged in "egregious suppression" of conservative speech.

For many conservative intellectuals, taking the working-class economic agenda seriously meant reconsidering long-held views. According to F. H. Buckley, a conservative professor at George Mason University's Antonin Scalia Law School, Reagan-era conservatives had assumed that the white working class had lost its jobs "because it smoked Oxy, because of moral poverty." But there's another explanation, he suggested, "Maybe they smoked Oxy because they had lost their jobs. Maybe it was really about jobs after all and not a sudden loss of virtue." Buckley drew an analogy between this job-centered explanation and the argument that the well-known sociologist William Julius Wilson had offered for the higher Black unwed birth rate: when jobs disappear, families and communities weaken, as do incentives to honor ordinary moral norms. In the end, Buckley concluded, "the best inducement to moral living is a good job." No progressive could have said it better.[28]

Buckley is not a household word, but Tucker Carlson is. In 2019, the conservative talk show host delivered a nationally televised critique of contemporary capitalism. "Any economic system that weakens and destroys families is not worth having," he declared. "A system like that is the enemy of a healthy society." He called for "a fair country. A decent country. A cohesive country. A country whose leaders don't accelerate the forces of change purely for their own profit and amusement." And he warned that a country where a shrinking percentage of the population is taking home an ever-expanding portion of the money is not a recipe for a stable society."

In a subsequent interview, Carlson acknowledged that his views had undergone a shift that paralleled Buckley's. It had gradually dawned on him that the poverty and decay that he encountered in white rural Maine resembled he had experienced growing up in Washington, D.C. "[W]hat I missed, what I think a lot of people missed, was that the economic system you're living under affects your culture," he said. "I was thinking, 'Wait a second; maybe when the jobs go away the culture changes. And the reason I didn't think of it before was because I was so blinded by the libertarian economic propaganda that I couldn't get past my own assumptions." He subsequently described the typical Republican politician as a "libertarian zealot controlled by the banks, yammering on about entrepreneurship."[29]

While Banks, Buckley, and Carlson are arresting examples, they are not outliers. In the fall of 2019, I attended the inaugural convention of the National Conservatism movement and was astounded to discover that the meeting's principal whipping-boys were libertarianism and neoliberalism. Leading National Conservative intellectuals saw no principled distinction between freedom-centered economic theories and the autonomous, unbounded self at the heart of progressive social theories. Freedom dissolves limits, they argued, and for this reason, it cannot be conservatives' highest principle. Only an ethos based on natural limits, responsibility to others, and the common good can provide the basis for decent lives and healthy societies. At times, political authority must be used to enforce this ethos, another reason freedom cannot take primacy over all other considerations.

As we've seen, this kind of conservatism is willing to challenge the free-market capitalism of the Reagan-Thatcher era and to advocate a much stronger role for government to regulate the excesses of capitalism and to secure decent conditions for families and communities. As the critique of global capital flows, free trade, generous immigration policies, and "woke" social policies intensifies, the coalition between conservative politicians and large corporations is weakening.

Although we do not know whether these cracks will widen into an irreparable breach, we do have evidence that the tectonics of American politics are shifting. As Jim Banks pointed out in his memo to Kevin McCarthy, in 2012, Wall Street donated three times as much to Mitt Romney as to Barack Obama. Eight years later, Wall Street contributed four times as much to Joe Biden as to Donald Trump. If the balance of power among conservatives is shifting away from the internationalist corporate sector toward a nationalist working-class economic and cultural agenda, can the conservative coalition hold together?

Other strong currents within contemporary conservatism further complicate this question. A portion of the revolt in the House of Representatives that almost derailed McCarthy's quest to become Speaker reflected personal animus and a struggle for power between the party's congressional leaders and its rank-and-file members. But there was a substantive issue as well: many members believed that current congressional procedures encourage excessive federal spending, and they were determined to change the rules to rein it in.

There is a potential clash between this latest iteration of small-government conservatism and the more expansive role for government that a working-class agenda would require. Measures to bolster working-class incomes and provide support for households with dependent children might well require expansive discretionary spending and expensive changes to the tax code. Small-government conservatives have given proposals for enhanced child tax credits a chilly reception, even the versions advanced by fellow conservatives on behalf of the working class.

Nor is it clear that conservatives can come together around efforts to reduce corporate power in the economy. These efforts must include a renewed attention to antitrust policy and enforcement, a tough sell for many on the Right. But if corporate oligarchy threatens working-class democracy, as some conservatives contend, then breaking up excessive concentrations of economic power is essential.

One may wonder whether conservative advocates of working-class economics are firmly enough committed to liberal constitutional democracy. In the name of restoring moral authority, National Conservatives support religious establishments wherever a polity contains a religious majority, as Christianity does in the United States, Judaism in Israel, Hinduism in India, and Islam in many countries throughout the Middle East, North Africa, and beyond. Parties and movements oriented toward working-class concerns are often impatient with the constraints on majorities created by individual rights and independent judiciaries.

Because corporations tend to be less comfortable with unconstrained majoritarian democracy (in part for reasons of self-interest), they are more comfortable with counter-majoritarian institutions. And because corporate leaders must function in (and often hail from) settings shaped by national and international cultural norms, they are more supportive of individual rights, even when the exercise of these rights leads to breaches of conventional morality. Corporate leaders gain status by contributing to the arts, which often value transgressive behavior that outrages the defenders of working-class morality.

The New Right has adopted what it believes is a working-class agenda on economics, culture, and even foreign policy. But its embrace of the working class in opposition to New Class elites is not necessarily evidence of a commitment to liberal democracy. Throughout the West, the rightward shift of the working class has strengthened political parties that attack liberal institutions such as constitutional courts and the free press. Here in the United States, figures aligned with the New Right have sought to deploy government power in ways that rub both libertarian and liberal sensibilities the wrong way, as when Florida Governor Ron DeSantis and the Republican legislature used Florida's power of the purse to punish the Walt Disney Corporation for its position on LGBT rights.

"I will not allow a woke corporation based in California to run our state," the governor said.[30]

Channeling the passions of aggrieved groups sometimes yields long-overdue reforms, but it can also weaken liberal democracy. Only unusually obdurate Marxists can view the working class as a reliably progressive force in contemporary politics, and there is little evidence that the aspiring new leaders of the working class are harnessing its grievances to liberal democratic ends. We will know that the threat to liberal democracy has subsided when conservative leaders work to remedy the legitimate economic and cultural grievances of the working class without using their resentment as a weapon against the institutions that safeguard the rule of law and protect liberty from majorities as well as special interests.

The Contradictions of Contemporary Conservatism: Small Government versus the Working Class

Meanwhile, it is not at all evident that the New Right's populist rhetoric, such as its attacks on "woke" corporations and global elites, is paired with an economic agenda that will actually improve the fortunes of working-class Americans. The Reagan-Thatcher catechism, with its synthesis of freedom, prosperity, dynamism, and optimism, undoubtedly had its flaws, and the New Right has drawn blood by pointing them out. What it has not yet done is embrace a constructive, coherent governing agenda that (for example) prevents plant shutdowns, revitalizes fading places and sectors, creates jobs on Main Street, and helps working families make ends meet.

The restraints on trade, immigration, and outsourcing that the New Right advocates are at most the beginning of such an agenda. But conservatives have yet to rethink their reflexive opposition to government programs that serve the material interests of their working-class supporters, although New Right policy intellectuals have produced a rich menu of proposals to do this. American Compass, a new economic think tank, has devised a child allowance for working families that would provide $400 per month for each child under the age of 6 and $250 per month thereafter until age 18.[31] This proposal would promote core conservative values such as family, work, and community. Nevertheless, it has gained little traction among right-wing elected officials, who are torn between their longtime commitment to limited government and the policies that would meet the needs of their working-class constituents.

Rep. Jim Banks, who urged Kevin McCarthy to lead the transformation of Republicans into a working-class party, symbolizes this tension. In 2023, the Republican Study Committee, which he headed, developed a plan to reach a balanced federal budget within seven years by slashing domestic programs. This plan proposed cutting Social Security and Medicare outlays by $3.5 trillion, in part by raising the normal Social Security retirement age in steps from 67 to 70, aligning the age of Medicare eligibility with the normal retirement age for Social Security, and then indexing both programs to life expectancy, which would probably mean further increases in the age of eligibility.[32] Because working-class adults are more likely to do jobs that wear down their bodies, and because they tend not to live as long as upscale professionals, they would be disproportionately harmed by these increases in the age threshold.

During the 15-ballot standoff in January, 2023 that preceded Rep. McCarthy's election as House Speaker, Rep. Banks and his RSC colleagues demanded and received a guarantee that their budget would be brought to a vote on the House floor. In response, former president Trump issued a preemptive rebuke to Republican lawmakers. "Under no circumstances should Republicans vote to cut a single penny from Medicare or Social Security," he warned. "Cut waste, fraud, and abuse everywhere we can find it . . . But do not cut the benefits our seniors worked for and paid for their entire lives."[33] Banks, now a U.S. senator, and his followers cannot have it both ways. They must choose between the fiscal policy of Paul Ryan and the economic strategy of Donald Trump.

This tension has continued unabated into President Trump's second term. While the budget resolution passed by the House and Senate Republicans in March, 2025 does not explicitly call for massive cuts in Medicaid, everyone knows that its target cannot be reached without such cuts, which Trump has rejected since he first announced his presidential candidacy a decade ago. Elon Musk's so-called "Department of Government Efficiency" has slashed employment at the Social Security Administration, which everyone knows will interfere with the prompt and accurate functioning of the program, even as the president and Republican leaders continue to insist that nothing will change. The tension between Musk's Silicon Valley "tech-bro" group and Trump advisor Steve Bannon's economic and cultural populist faction of the Trump coalition is intense.

Working-class Conservatism and Partisan Polarization

This clash within contemporary conservatism has consequences for polarization between the parties. On Social Security and Medicare, there is no disagreement between Joe Biden and Donald Trump. Conservatives and liberals might well be able to negotiate other elements of a working-class economic agenda. In the 117th Congress, they found common ground on a sectoral industrial policy that will invest $50 billion to boost domestic semiconductor manufacturing. And as we have seen, the parties are already converging on a deglobalization strategy that would regulate trade and encourage manufacturers to bring offshore production to the United States, even though business leaders are skeptical about the steep tariffs that President Trump is using to promote domestic reindustrialization. The threat from the Soviet Union moved the parties closer together on economic policy during much of the Cold War, and the threat from China seems to be having a similar effect today. If New Right populist conservatives can prevail over small government conservatives on fiscal policy, we might see a different relationship between the two parties, at least on economic issues. The 2024 presidential election witnessed a significant shift of non-white working class voters toward the Republican Party, leaving Democrats with a shrinking coalition of educated professionals and Civil Rights-era African Americans.

This partial convergence between the parties on economics does not mean that polarization would disappear, of course. But the principal axis of contestation would move from economics to culture, a shift that is already underway. This struggle would be bitter because fundamental issues of morality and identity are at stake. But it is possible that if the economic discontent of the working class could be addressed, the intensity of the cultural clash might diminish over time.

We do not know enough about the interplay between economics and culture to predict this outcome with confidence. Still, there are reasons to hope that if a group that has long felt marginalized is brought to the center of policy concerns, the resentment that fuels the culture war could gradually give way to more constructive sentiments. And this would augur well for the stability of liberal constitutional democracy in the United States.

Conclusion

The New Right's repudiation of laissez-faire in both economics and culture has triggered the latest change in the ever-shifting relationship between democracy and capitalism. But the mechanism of this change remains the same: when significant numbers of people become discontented with the outcome of the economic system, they turn to politics for redress of their grievances. Sometimes one of the major parties will choose to become the champion of the aggrieved. At other times, both parties will respond in distinct but overlapping ways.

Our current circumstances exemplify the latter. The political parties have come to agree that in recent decades the US working class has gotten the short end of the stick. Democrats blame corporate greed and the "billionaire class"; Republicans say that illegal immigrants are stealing working-class jobs and depressing wages. Both see globalization and unfettered trade as parts of the problem; both believe that China's admission into the global trading system has come at the expense of American workers. And both believe that a more interventionist government is needed to correct these ills.

While capitalism and democracy will always coexist in a state of dynamic tension, nothing in recent developments suggests that capitalism and democracy are incompatible, and nothing in the past two centuries suggests that they ever were. Economic inequality always yields charges of oligarchy, and no doubt wealthy individuals and large corporations can exercise disproportionate sway over key institutions and even electoral systems. But when they go too far, citizens of modest means find ways of mobilizing against them, using government to restrict wealth, regulate the sources of wealth, and create new policies and institutions that strengthen the power of ordinary people to stand against the power of wealth.

Citizens can also act on their own behalf, using instruments that previous waves of change created. For example, pandemic-related changes in the labor force have helped arrest the long decline of labor unions. New organizing efforts have gained momentum in previously non-unionized sectors of the economy, and long-established unions such as the United Auto Workers have displaced a level of militancy not seen for decades.

If "capitalism" means laissez-faire, then democracy is incompatible with capitalism. If "democracy" means that every citizen has an equal impact on political outcomes, then capitalism is incompatible with democracy (as is every known economic system). But it is a mistake to resolve profound political issues through stipulative definitions depicting worlds that no one has ever seen or ever will. Capitalism is a large category that undergoes historical change and embraces diverse policies and institutional forms; so is democracy.

Although these categories are capacious, they are not unbounded. Total public control of the economy is not capitalism; total domination of politics by an individual or small group is not democracy. But economic inequality is not the same as oligarchy, and government regulation of the economy does not set us on the road to serfdom. Claims to the contrary can be used to great political effect, but they do not describe the real world and real choices with which citizens and public officials throughout the world's imperfect democracies must endlessly grapple.

Notes

1. Peter Kolozi, *Conservatives Against Capitalism* (New York: Columbia, 2017), 167.
2. Michael Novak, *The Spirit of Democratic Capitalism* (New York: AEI/Simon & Schuster, 1982).
3. Novak, *The Spirit of Democratic Capitalism*, 124.

4. Novak, *The Spirit of Democratic Capitalism*, 47.
5. Novak, *The Spirit of Democratic Capitalism*, 140.
6. Novak, *The Spirit of Democratic Capitalism*, 142.
7. Novak, *The Spirit of Democratic Capitalism*, 137ff.
8. Novak, *The Spirit of Democratic Capitalism*, 53.
9. Novak, *The Spirit of Democratic Capitalism*, 69.
10. Novak, *The Spirit of Democratic Capitalism*, 67.
11. Novak, *The Spirit of Democratic Capitalism*, 181.
12. Novak, *The Spirit of Democratic Capitalism*, 91.
13. Novak, *The Spirit of Democratic Capitalism*, 120–21.
14. R. R. Reno, "The Spirit of Democratic Capitalism," *First Things*, October 2017, https://firstthings.com/the-spirit-of-democratic-capitalism/.
15. "Against the Dead Consensus," *First Things*, March 21, 2019.
16. National Conservatism: A Statement of Principles - National Conservatism
17. Joseph A. Schumpeter, *Capitalism, Socialism, and Democracy* (New York and London: Harper & Bros, 1942), 83.
18. How the American middle class has changed in the past five decades | Pew Research Center. Household income share of quintiles U.S. 2021 | Statista
19. The Distribution of Household Income, 2019 | Congressional Budget Office (cbo.gov)
20. (Income in the United States: 2021 (census.gov); and Household Income Percentile Calculator, US - DQYDJ
21. For an account and defense of Burnham's analysis, see Michael Lind, *The New Class War: Saving Democracy from the Managerial Elite* (New York: Penguin Random House, 2020).
22. Matthew Stuart, "The 9.9 Percent is the New American Aristocracy," *The Atlantic*, June 2018.
23. lears.pdf (virginia.edu), 572.
24. (The White Working Class and the Democratic Party (brookings.edu); PPS_2000126 55.72 (noamlupu.com)
25. Behind Biden's 2020 Victory | Pew Research Center
26. The College Degree Conundrum: Catalist Edition – Third Way
27. A remarkable Pew Research Center survey released on January 19, 2023, found that only 38 percent of Republicans have a positive view of banks and other financial institutions. The corresponding figure for large corporations is even lower—25 percent. How Republicans view their party, key issues as 118th Congress begins | Pew Research Center
28. Conservatism: Trump and Beyond - Intercollegiate Studies Institute (isi.org). F. H. Buckley, *Th Republican Workers Party: How the Trump Victory Drove Everybody Crazy, and Why It Was Just What We Needed* (New York: Encounter Books, 2018), p. 137.
29. Tucker Carlson has sparked the most interesting debate in conservative politics - Vox
30. Disney to lose special tax status for opposing Florida's 'don't say gay' bill | Florida | The Guardian
31. The Fisc: A Conservative Family Benefit Proposal | American Compass.
32. rsc_blueprint_to_save_america.pdf
33. Trump to GOP: Don't touch Medicare or Social Security in debt ceiling fight - POLITICO

SECTION VI

FRICTIONS AT THE INTERSECTION OF DEMOCRACY AND CAPITALISM

Popular Will and "Sound Policy"

Institutions as Interstices

Frictions at the Intersection of Democracy and Capitalism

JENNIFER BAIR

From May 1937 until June 1938, the US economy experienced a contraction that would come to be known as the Roosevelt Recession. In the context of a contentious debate about the causes of the downturn, and amid fears that it would derail the United States's recovery from the Great Depression, the President asked Congress to commission a study of the economy that would examine, among other topics, "the concentration of economic power in American industry." The body that would be created in response to Roosevelt's request, the Temporary National Economic Commission (TNEC), conducted research, held Congressional hearings, and produced dozens of technical reports over a span of more than two and a half years. By the time the TNEC completed its work in Spring 1941, increased defense spending was priming a recovering economy for what was soon to become full wartime mobilization, and the anxieties motivating the Commission's creation had largely faded from view. Nevertheless, its authors delivered their verdict about the anti-competitive effects of excessive economic concentration in strikingly straightforward and matter of fact prose:

> We know that most of the wealth and income of the country is owned by a few large corporations, that these corporations are owned in turn by an infinitesimally small number of people and that the profits from the operations of these corporations go to a very small group with the results that the opportunities for new enterprises, whether corporate or individual, are constantly being restricted.[1]

In a November 1941 essay for *The Atlantic* magazine, French journalist (and trenchant observer of American society) Raoul de Roussy de Sales quoted these lines from the Temporary National Economic Commission's report. His interest in the TNEC's conclusions made Roussy de Sales something of an outlier among journalists; overall, the report's release had barely registered in a news environment dominated by the escalating war in Europe. Roussy de Sales, however, thought the report worth mentioning precisely because he saw an important connection between the headline-grabbing international conflict and the TNEC's largely ignored report. In his view, the fact that a joint committee of Congress could reach such a dire conclusion about the consequences of concentrated economic power "at a moment when the United States is becoming daily involved in a war that is at the same time a world revolution" was evidence that "the long-drawn-out conflict between capitalism and democracy cannot be evaded or camouflaged much longer."[2]

Roussy de Sales understood the war in Europe as the latest and perhaps most consequential episode yet in a protracted conflict between democracy and capitalism. Hitler's rise had heightened the stakes in ways that revealed new fissures in the strained relationship between these two systems. Roussy de Sales observed that while national socialism was incompatible with democracy, it might well co-exist with capitalism, at least for a while, so long as there were enough capitalists who feared threats from the left more than they feared accommodation with fascism. Writing one month before the bombing of Pearl Harbor, when speculation about the United States's possible entrance into the war was intensifying daily, Roussy de Sales worried that some "important leaders of American industry and business" opposed Roosevelt's foreign policy because they recognized that participation in the conflict might entrench, or even accelerate, domestic changes unfavorable to their interests—changes that would, for example, strengthen the rights of workers to organize, or expand the social safety net by increasing government transfer programs. This suspicion on the part of Roosevelt's critics was correct, he argued, because the kind of total mobilization needed to defeat Hitler could only be achieved if "the masses are persuaded that the efforts and sacrifices required from them will benefit them" in the form of, say, higher wages or a more generous welfare state.[3]

For Roussy de Sales, managing the conflict between capitalism and democracy required the subordination of the economic system of capitalism to the political regime of democracy. Seeing World War II as a conflict that threatened the future of democracy in Europe (and elsewhere, if fascism prevailed), he drew a connection between the fight against anti-democratic forces abroad and the domestic struggles he saw in the United States over competing visions of the American political economy. Since "long historical experience has demonstrated that minorities, financially and economically powerful, tend to exert an influence over the affairs of the state completely disproportionate to their numerical strength," what is needed, Roussy de Sales argued, are institutions that "curb their power and reduce the abuses that stem from it."[4]

Institutions, and their role in mediating the frictions between capitalism and democracy, feature centrally in this section of the volume. Over the last few decades, it has become something of a truism that institutions are critical to the effective functioning of capitalism, and especially, to maintaining a healthy balance between capitalism and democracy. But if there is broad agreement *that* institutions matter, there is far less consensus about *which ones* are vital to the long-term success of capitalist democracies. Institutions that mitigate inequality and prevent the excessive accumulation of political power by economic elites are the ones Roussy de Sales believed were necessary for sustaining a positive tension between capitalism and democracy. Examples include collective bargaining, which attenuates the power imbalance between buyers and sellers of labor, or antitrust law, which preserves market competition by limiting economic concentration.

If the perspective championed by Roussy de Sales underscores the potential of institutions to mitigate inequality in market democracies, a different analytical tradition centers the role of (other) institutions in enabling economic development. Scholars aligned with what can be broadly termed the new institutional economics argue that the institutions most critical for facilitating development are those that reduce the risks and costs of transacting, potentially setting in motion a virtuous cycle of investment, accumulation, and, ultimately, growth. According to this view, the early emergence of institutions that secured property rights from the prerogatives of monarchs or other political elites is what enabled England, and eventually other Western European countries, to develop more rapidly than other parts of the world.[5] The new institutional economics privileges institutions associated with the other side of the equity-efficiency trade-off assumed in welfare economics—that is, those that incentivize economic growth rather than those that redress the inequalities that result in the course of that growth.

To be sure, both kinds of institutions are encompassed by the expansive definition offered by economic historian Douglass North, for whom institutions are "formal rules designed by states and cultural norms and informal codes of conduct that shape human interaction."[6] Yet many of the scholars working in the interdisciplinary field of new institutional economics that North's work helped inspire tend to focus on legal and judicial institutions (e.g., lex mercatoria) that support business interests by securing property rights and fostering credible commitments, as compared with institutions like collective bargaining or antitrust law that principally promote the interests of workers and consumers. These economic historians ask why property rights and other market institutions emerged in a particular time and place, how and why they enable economic growth, and via what mechanisms and with what effects they might diffuse to other parts of the world. In contrast, much of the conversation about how to mitigate the frictions between capitalism and democracy today is less about which institutions create the incentives necessary for capitalism to flourish, and more about how to address the negative effects of rising inequality and corporate concentration, not just on individual welfare but on our collective well-being and the state of our democracy. In short, the consensus that institutions matter may be impressively broad, but it is not particularly deep. What, then, does a focus on institutions offer for grappling with what Roussy de Sales described eighty years ago as "the long-drawn-out conflict between capitalism and democracy"?

Each of the three chapters in this section of the volume engages the theme of institutions, albeit in different ways. Two of them do so by examining the frictions between capitalism and democracy in particular times and places, and through the lens of a particular institution. For Dan Bogart and Kara Dimitruk, the time and place are late-seventeenth-century England, and the institution is Parliament. Their chapter examines the transition from mercantilism to capitalism in England, and the degree to which this transition was facilitated by changes in the political system associated with the Glorious Revolution of 1688. Under the then-prevailing model of mercantilism, economic success was understood to be a zero-sum competition among countries in which a nation's wealth was secured by maximizing exports and minimizing imports. Because, historically, military might was deployed as a tool to achieve international economic supremacy, a mercantilist system of the sort that existed in England in the late 1600s tends to center the state (rather than the market), and thus political (rather than economic) power.

Mercantilism created winners and losers within the English economy, and since the Glorious Revolution increased the power of (proto) democratic institutions through which losers might oppose mercantilist policies, Bogart and Dimitruk ask how the strengthening of Parliament after 1688 shaped England's transition from mercantilism to capitalism. The authors find that the elevation of Parliament vis-à-vis the Crown and the expanded role played by political parties (chiefly, Whigs and Tories) after the Revolution did not eliminate mercantilism, but it did create more space for competing interests to influence policies. In other words, institutional reforms introduced more dynamism into the political process, as reflected in changing constellations of coalitions between the monarch and parties, with alliances shifting according to the issue at hand. As Parliament met more regularly and thus the incentives to lobby members of Parliament increased, mercantilist legislation also became more explicitly and specifically protective of nascent manufacturing industries, as opposed to those industries generally promotive of shipping interests, which had previously been favored to promote England's overall commercial dominance vis-à-vis European rivals. While the authors do not identify a clear or clean transition from mercantilism to capitalism in the decade after the Glorious Revolution, they note several acts passed by Parliament over the period of their analysis (1660–1699) that limited or repealed mercantilist policies, perhaps because, in the case of these particular measures, there were no organized domestic constituencies clearly benefiting from them, and thus no one invested in mobilizing to defend the status quo.

In the period studied by Bogart and Dimitruk, both democracy and capitalism were systems in formation rather than robust regimes. However, the Glorious Revolution moved the country toward representative government, and the question their chapter addresses is how changes in England's political institutions affected the viability of mercantilism as an economic system. Overall, institutional reforms did not prove inimical to mercantilism, which persisted in a weakened form for another century and a half. But political reforms changed the nature of mercantilism as an economic regime, just as mercantilism shaped the incentives of actors to engage with the political process. Over the longue durée, this co-evolutionary dynamic facilitated the development of capitalism out of mercantilism, but the succession of mercantilism by capitalism was a "negotiated" process that was "not guaranteed". Bogart and Dimitruk's chapter is exemplary of institutional analyses in which actors have interests—such as securing patronage from the Crown, or shielding one's business from competition—and institutions, as "formal rules designed by states," structure the engagement between actors pursuing their interests in ways that drive long-term transformation in political economies.

Bob Bruner's chapter takes us from mercantilist era England to early-twentieth-century New York. Bruner's discussion of the 1907 financial crisis focuses on collective action, a problem that, whatever the advantages of capitalist and democratic regimes, is more likely to beset these systems than their dirigiste counterparts. Coordination is almost always difficult in complex environments, but this is particularly true in crises—moments when the stakes for successful collective action are particularly high, but circumstances make such action especially challenging. One factor contributing to this problem is what Bruner describes as a kind of institutional inertia: "institutions (organizations and orthodoxies) with some legacy from the past tend to be the default upon which initial efforts to mobilize collective action commence". In other words, the ability to respond promptly and effectively to a crisis like the financial panic Bruner studies may be hampered by an undue or inappropriate allegiance to outmoded or ineffective institutions.

At the same time, crises also create windows of opportunity for institutional innovation, as was the case with the panic of 1907, when a series of bank runs among large New York trusts threatened the viability of the financial sector. As Bruner explains, the response to the panic did more than simply forestall an even worse downturn in the economy; rather, the collective action mounted to contain the crisis put the American political economy on a new trajectory, changing "public attitudes towards government intervention". In this sense, the panic of 1907 and its aftermath created a precedent for the Roosevelt Administration's larger and more sustained response to the Great Depression, some two decades later. More immediately, it was also the key stimulant to the establishment of a federal central bank.

One reading, then, of the panic of 1907 is that it laid the groundwork for the New Deal and the establishment of the US Federal Reserve, key institutional innovations that were premised on an expanded role for the government in managing the frictions between capitalism and democracy. Yet Bruner's account reveals that most of the actions taken to quell the crisis in the days and weeks after the initial run on the trusts came not from government, but rather from the private sector. J. P. Morgan played a particularly outsized role, orchestrating to a greater or lesser degree all four of the collective responses outlined in Bruner's chapter. Morgan's titanic status in New York's financial sector enabled him to convene industry leaders to devise several ad hoc efforts. He coordinated an initial pooling of resources to create a rescue fund for two embattled trust companies, and shortly thereafter played a key role in negotiating a mutual aid pack among a larger set of trusts. Morgan was also at the nexus of collective action involving public sector officials. A promise on the part of the US Treasury Secretary, George Cortelyou, to inject liquidity into the system was made personally to Morgan as the banking industry's most powerful figure and its principal representative, and the mayor of New York City successfully made a similarly specific appeal to Morgan for help in covering the city's short-term debt.

A final example of public-private partnership that Bruner cites is the purchase by Morgan's US Steel of shareholdings in another steel concern, Tennessee Coal and Iron, that was threatened by the tumult in financial markets. President Theodore Roosevelt's promise not to enjoin the merger on antitrust grounds was a prerequisite for the acquisition, which, as Bruner notes, did much to allay anxieties on Wall Street and set the ground for a turn toward stability, if not rapid recovery. Yet while the merger helped calm panic in the markets, in other quarters it contributed to growing unease about the rise of industrial conglomerates and their relationship to the banking sector. Calls for increased scrutiny of trusts in the aftermath of the crisis led to the convening of a Congressional investigation that became known as the Pujo Committee. As Bruner notes, the Pujo Committee reflected (and contributed to) rising discontent with powerful elites who were perceived as exploiting an underregulated financial sector and manipulating it, to the detriment of the public, for their own benefit. Public criticism of economic elites gained traction, with the term "money trust" coming to function as a kind of shorthand for the excessive power wielded by corporate conglomerates. American newspapers used the "money trust" locution frequently in the years following the panic. The term's popularity peaked in 1913—the year that Congress passed legislation to create the US Federal Reserve—and then ebbed until the 1930s, when it reemerged among Americans grappling with the dislocations of a new and even more devastating financial crisis.

Bruner's analysis of the panic of 1907 powerfully illustrates how the "tortuous process of financial crisis and civic reaction" propelled institutional change, leading to a political realignment that consolidated Democratic Party control and institutionalized Progressive era reforms.[7] To be sure, the financial crisis had serious and protracted implications, but the tone of Bruner's discussion is largely optimistic because his account underscores the resilience of the US economy in the face of such challenges. Bruner's chapter emphasizes the way in which collaborative efforts, both among private actors and between private and public ones, overcame the obstacles to collective action. Yet another key theme emerging from his case study is the way in which episodes of particularly acute friction between democracy and capitalism can lead to the erosion of long-standing and widely shared beliefs about how the two systems work. Progressives had been challenging the reigning conservative orthodoxy for at least a decade before the panic of 1907, but the crisis crystallized many of these criticisms and increased their resonance, setting the stage for a shift in theory and practice.

Importantly, it was not just the uncertainty and hardships of the panic itself but also the very interventions highlighted in Bruner's chapter that contributed to the decline of the pre-crisis orthodoxy; paradoxically, the ability of J. P. Morgan to mobilize resources and instigate an effective response to the crisis ratcheted up concerns about the concentration of wealth and power that was occurring in the US economy. Just as journalists were writing about "the dark side of monopolistic industrial trusts", both the crisis and its resolution appeared to confirm such dangers. Together, the panic of 1907 and its aftermath eroded the hegemony of non-intervention as the government's default position toward the economy. Even some bankers and financial sector actors were converted to a different view of the government's role in markets, at least in times of crisis. This shift in ideology was, in tun, realized via the creation of new institutions, including the US Federal Reserve, perhaps the most concrete and consequential legacy of the panic of 1907, and a reflection of the symbiosis that Bruner's account reveals between ideological shifts and institutional reform as lubricants to the frictions between democracy and capitalism.

In contrast to Bruner's focused case study of the 1907 panic, Hannah Knox Tucker and R. Daniel Wadhwani's chapter ranges over some 250 years of American history. These authors share with Bruner an interest in the coevolution of ideas and institutions in mediating frictions, but they approach the theme from a different angle of vision. For them, "the deep political and economic tensions" in American life arise not from "fundamental, even irreconcilable, differences between democracy and capitalism," but rather from "inherent frictions within the practice of liberty that is common to both these societal forms." (p. X) Drawing inspiration from Charles Taylor's work on "modern social imaginaries," Tucker and Wadhwani propose the concept of entrepreneurial imaginaries as "the moral reasoning through which people understand their ventures as part of a mutually beneficial project of freedom from a constraining status quo." Entrepreneurial imaginaries implicate both democracy and capitalism because Americans understand liberty as intrinsically bound up with positive and negative freedoms that are experienced and expressed through both commercial activity and political engagement.

The authors identify three successive entrepreneurial imaginaries that structure American business history. They give the most fulsome treatment to the first, Entrepreneurial Society 1.0. Dating from the country's founding through to the 1870s, Entrepreneurial Society 1.0 lauded the virtues of ownership and celebrated the pursuit of freedom via property. Because this imaginary permitted a capacious understanding of ownership, it could accommodate two groups whose interests and ideologies might otherwise differ: farmers, whose property consisted of land, and artisans, whose property resided in their own labor and skills. For a nation experiencing growth and diversification, Entrepreneurial Society 1.0 provided a moral framework that created the sense of a shared American project: "While farmers and artisans engaged in very different material worlds, the language of liberty and the principle of property worked to blur the sharp edges of distinction into a mutually intelligible national community founded on common values". Over time, however, this imaginary was eroded by a fundamental contradiction between the conceptualization of property as an expression of positive liberty, and the negation of liberty inherent in the denial to enslaved peoples of property in their own person.

Entrepreneurial Society 1.0 was replaced by a new imaginary, Entrepreneurial Society 2.0, in which liberty was understood as the freedom to associate with others in pursuit of projects that would not be achievable by even the most industrious individual working alone. Association could take multiple forms within this schema, including cooperatives, trade unions, and what the authors refer to as "hierarchical organization" (i.e., the firm or modern business enterprise). Compared with its predecessor imaginary, the tensions implicit in Entrepreneurial Society 2.0 manifested more quickly in the form of conflict between different kinds of associations—for example, between trade unions and businesses, and between producers' cooperatives and hierarchical firms. Here, Tucker and Wadhwani's narrative intersects with Bruner's discussion of the panic of 1907—an event that did much to raise concerns about the dark side of association when represented by institutions like the money trust. Populist and progressive ideas gained traction in the opening decades of the twentieth century because a growing number of Americans worried that excessively powerful associations infringed upon, rather than extended, liberty.

Despite the early manifestations of freedom's frictions implicit in Entrepreneurial Society 2.0, this interpretive schema persisted as a unifying (if embattled) framework for several more decades, limping along until the middle of the century. It was ultimately undone some time between the 1950s and the 1980s, when Americans lost "faith in the ability of rationalized organizations to enrich the exercise of liberty". In Tucker and Wadhwani's telling, the denouement of Entrepreneurial Society 2.0 overlaps almost precisely with the "Trente Glorieuses," a term coined by French demographer Jean Fourastié to describe the three decades between 1945 and 1975 during which France enjoyed a fortuitous combination of rising average wages, high productivity, and expanded social benefits. Though the expression originated as a description of France's experience, the "Trente Glorieuses" is sometimes employed more expansively to describe the post-war trajectory of North Atlantic economies. This period marked the heyday of Fordism, a period in which the frictions between capitalism and democracy were mediated in a way that promoted stability and relatively broad-based prosperity in the United States and Western Europe. These decades also saw the "triumph of historical managerial capitalism" (p. X), represented by the hierarchy of the multinational corporation, as well as the expansion of government bureaucracy as embodied in the modern welfare state, both of which undermined Entrepreneurial

Society 2.0's vision of association as an expression of positive liberty.

Wadhwani and Tucker's argument about the decline of this second entrepreneurial imaginary echoes Schumpeter's well-known views on the enervating effects of excessive rationalization on capitalist societies. One year after Roussy de Sales voiced concerns about the fate of American democracy in the pages of *The Atlantic,* Schumpeter asked in *Capitalism, Socialism, and Democracy* if capitalism can survive. His succinct and understated answer—"No, I do not think it can"—reflected Schumpeter's belief that capitalism was evolving in ways that threatened the entrepreneurial spirit on which a vibrant capitalist system depends.[8] Reversing Marx's formulation, Schumpeter saw threats to capitalism emerging not from its economic foundation but from what he called its psychosocial superstructure; capitalism ushers in "psychological, moral and political changes which affect habits and attitudes" in ways that undermine capitalism's long-term prospects.[9] While Schumpeter believed that there was no economic basis for the concerns about growing concentration being expressed by critics like Roussy de Sales, he nevertheless saw changes in the institutional landscape that he believed were leading to the "obsolescence of the entrepreneurial function" so critical to capitalism's success[10]:

> Economically neither the case for competition nor the case against concentration of economic control is anything like as strong as this [anti-monopolization] argument implies. And, whether weak or strong, it misses the salient point. Even if the giant concerns were all managed so perfectly as to call forth applause from the angels in heaven, the political consequences of concentration would still be what they are. The political structure of a nation is profoundly affected by the elimination of a host of small and medium sized firms the owner-managers of which, together with their dependents, henchmen and connections, count quantitatively at the polls and have a hold on what we may term the foreman class that no management of a large unit can ever have; the very foundation of private property and free contracting wears away in a nation in which its most vital, most concrete, most meaningful types disappear from the moral horizon of the people.[11]

What Schumpeter is foretelling in the pages of *Capitalism, Socialism, and Democracy* is the declining allure of Entrepreneurial Society 2.0. For Tucker and Wadhwani, this imaginary, like the others, weakened over time due to emergent frictions between positive and negative freedoms. Specifically, the forms of association that Entrepreneurial Society 2.0 envisioned as routes to freedom created instead Weber's iron cage, giving rise to organizational forms that threatened liberty as they became "conventional, institutionalized, and dominant". As the apotheosis of the associative project, the modern shareholding corporation both expanded ownership and denuded it of meaning:

> The capitalist process, by substituting a mere parcel of shares for the walls of and the machines in a factory, takes the life out of the idea of property. It loosens the grip that once was so strong—the grip in the sense of the legal right and the actual ability to do as one pleases with one's own; the grip also in the sense that the holder of the title loses the will to fight, economically, physically, politically, for "his" factory and his control over it, to die if necessary on its steps.[12]

Schumpeter's predictions regarding capitalism's fate reveal an understanding of the affective, ideological and cultural, as well as the institutional dimension of capitalism as an economic and social system. His pessimism about the system's future is premised on what he described as the ongoing "Destruction of the Institutional Framework of Capitalist Society"—a process exemplified by changes not just in the business sector, but in other, interrelated domains, such as the family and the academy.[13]

As a forecast for capitalism's (and socialism's) future, Schumpeter's text fares poorly, in part because its author did not anticipate the success of challenges to the Keynesian consensus that would soon emerge. Tucker and Wadhwani note correctly that these criticisms of the post-war orthodoxy, which laid the foundation for a new imaginary, came from the left as well as the right. Yet their account of the transition to Entrepreneurial Society 3.0 seems to weigh more heavily the critical strand emerging from "liberationist countercultural movements" as compared with that deriving from the organized efforts of "conservative intellectuals like Frederich Hayek [who] worried that the growing American faith in planning by experts was not an aid to liberty but fundamentally undermining it".

Specifically, they emphasize the role of "activist entrepreneurs," who, as descendants of the "liberationist countercultural" critics of the post-war status quo, channeled widespread discontent with "corporate organizational values and practices" into a new business model. As founders of independent presses and organic grocery stores, they helped restore the figure of the entrepreneur to the heroic status that Schumpeter worried had been irretrievably lost.

Perhaps because Entrepreneurial Society 3.0 is the most familiar of the imaginaries presented by Tucker and Wadhwani, it is the least convincing as an interpretive schema that allows "people engaged in contradictory projects to imagine themselves as part of a joint American pursuit". The authors emphasize the deep contradictions that plague this imaginary, which celebrates the creative destruction unleashed by innovative entrepreneurs but effaces the massive reliance among Silicon Valley's pioneers on public funding for infrastructure development. Yet the ironies and tensions that permeate Entrepreneurial Society 3.0 reflect more than the obvious hypocrisy of its "techno-libertarian ethos." Arguably the persuasiveness of this imaginary is beset by what is, at root, an overwrought effort to position activist entrepreneurs as avatars of social change, battling the conformity and alienation of mainstream corporate capitalism by pursuing the "triple bottom line" rather than a narrower goal of profit maximization. Critics of conscientious consumption or mission-driven capitalism may be right that participation in the market should not be confused with engagement in the civic sphere, but the bigger problem with Tucker and Wadhwani's formulation of Entrepreneurial Society 3.0 is the weight it gives to liberationist countercultural critics-cum-activist entrepreneurs as a prime influence. The core ideas animating this imaginary descend more clearly from the ideas of Hayek than those of Herbert Marcuse.

Of course, this is in some sense to the point about entrepreneurial imaginaries; their power derives precisely from their multivalence, their ability to evoke a connection, however tenuous, between our diverse commercial pursuits—as owners, consumers, producers, workers—and a widely enough shared sense of a common civic project. The overarching ideas that animate the three schemata analyzed here—property, association, and innovation for the first, second, and third entrepreneurial imaginaries, respectively—are roomy enough to accommodate the myriad tensions that exist in how these concepts are interpreted and enacted in the world. For Tucker and Wadhwani, then, what erodes these constructs are not tensions inherent in their core ideas and the way they are put into practice, but rather the fact that "over time, as any particular model or belief becomes institutionalized, it increasingly comes to be understood as imposing a constraint on freedom rather than serving as a source of liberation". Frictions between positive and negative liberty are what propel Tucker and Wadhwani's narrative of American business history as a succession of entrepreneurial imaginaries. While this account emphasizes continuity, it may also underplay the degree of collective dissonance between these interpretive schemas and people's experience of a society in which income inequality and political polarization threaten the premise of any social imaginary: the sense of a shared social existence and a collective fate.

Like Bruner, Tucker and Wadhwani conclude their essay on an optimistic note. Recognizing that much recent scholarship has shown "how capital has moved historically, putting its powerful thumb on the scale of markets and elections," they propose instead "an agenda that renews interest in the emancipatory claims of the capitalist actors who moved that capital." Recognizing the exhaustion of Entrepreneurial Society 3.0, they nevertheless anticipate the "articulation of a new entrepreneurial imaginary embodying a reformulation of emancipatory promise to fulfill emergent moral values through the exercise of freedom". Their analysis intriguingly suggests that freedom's frictions are a kind of dialectic that propels new imaginaries into being, but while this account offers a fascinating description of the dynamics that undermine a prevailing formation, it is less clear where the content of the new imaginary comes from. This is particularly important for understanding what makes some emancipatory promises more compelling interpretive schemas than others. After all, entrepreneurial imaginaries exist in a field of competing moral visions and normative claims, including ones that privilege, say, solidarity or equality of opportunity as equally necessary to the realization of freedom as individual liberty.

As institutions, entrepreneurial imaginaries are aptly captured by one part of North's definition: "cultural norms and informal codes of conduct that shape human interaction". Yet to effectively guide and give meaning to human interaction, entrepreneurial imaginaries must exist in a positive tension with the other dimension of North's definition of institutions: the "formal rules designed by states." Such an observation returns us to the curiously underspecified consensus referred to at the beginning of this chapter wherein there is abundant agreement that institutions are important, but equally rife disagreement about which ones to privilege in analyzing the relationship between capitalism and democracy. This indeterminacy, however, is better understood as a feature than a bug—one that reflects an ongoing, fraught, and productively contentious debate about the frictions between capitalism and democracy. Institutions, then, are necessary interstices in two senses: they are spaces that intervene between capitalism and democracy, mediating their expression and often moderating their effects, but they are also expanses into which we can project our understanding of capitalism and democracy, and the frictions between them.

Notes

1. Raoul de Roussy de Sales, "The Conflict between Capitalism and Democracy," *The Atlantic Monthly*, November 1942, 538.
2. Roussy de Sales, "The Conflict between Capitalism and Democracy," 538.
3. Roussy de Sales, "The Conflict between Capitalism and Democracy," 535.
4. Roussy de Sales, "The Conflict between Capitalism and Democracy," 534.
5. Douglass C. North and Barry R. Weingast, "Constitutions and Commitment: The Evolution of Institutions Governing Public Choice in Seventeenth-Century England," *The Journal of Economic History* 49, no. 4 (December 1989): 803–832.
6. Douglass C. North. *Institutions, Institutional Change and Economic Performance* (New York: Cambridge University Press, 1990), 3.
7. Robert F. Bruner and Sean D. Carr, *The Panic of 1907: Heralding a New Era of Finance, Capitalism and Democracy* (Hoboken, NJ: Wiley, 2023), 257.
8. Joseph A. Schumpeter, *Capitalism, Socialism, and Democracy* (New York: Harper & Row, 1942), 61.
9. Cited in Richard Swedberg, "Can Capitalism Survive: Schumpeter's Answer and its Relevance for New Institutional Economics," *European Journal of Sociology*, 33, no. 2 (November 1992): 350.
10. Schumpeter, *Capitalism, Socialism, and Democracy*, 131.
11. Schumpeter, *Capitalism, Socialism, and Democracy*, 141.
12. Schumpeter, *Capitalism, Socialism, and Democracy*, 142.
13. Schumpeter, *Capitalism, Socialism, and Democracy*, 139.

14

Representative Government and Mercantilism in England

DAN BOGART AND KARA DIMITRUK

Introduction

England transitioned from having mercantilist to more capitalist institutions from 1600 to 1800. Mercantilism uses governmental regulation of the economy for the purpose of augmenting state power at the expense of rival national powers.[1] One principal aim is to promote exports and limit imports using tariffs and other trade restrictions. Mercantilism also calls for barriers to entry, by for example granting monopoly rights, if existing firms serving the market have a strategic purpose for the state. Mercantilism was the dominant economic system in many European and Western economies until the mid-nineteenth century. The mercantilist system in England, and eventually the United Kingdom, contributed to its rising international prominence over the course of two centuries with "important implications for the future of the international economy."[2] In some countries, mercantilism was slowly replaced by capitalism, defined to be a system where a country's trade and industry are controlled by private owners for profit and characterized by competition. We study part of this process in England.

We specifically examine the durability of mercantilism through England's early transition to representative government during the Restoration of the monarchy in 1660 and after the Glorious Revolution of 1688. The Restoration re-established parts of the traditional political order following the Civil Wars and Interregnum, during which the monarch lost influence and power. The Restoration was successful in maintaining order for several decades, yet rising political tensions in Europe and crisis concerning the succession of a Catholic monarch,

Dan Bogart and Kara Dimitruk, *Representative Government and Mercantilism in England.* In: *Can Democracy and Capitalism Be Reconciled?.* Edited by: Sidney M. Milkis and Scott C. Miller, Oxford University Press. © Oxford University Press (2025). DOI: 10.1093/9780197774731.003.0015

James II, led to its end with the Glorious Revolution of 1688. A new political order was established in which Parliament shared more power with the monarch. While the Glorious Revolution did not bring in democracy with full universal suffrage, it strengthened representative political institutions substantially. The best indicator is that the Parliament met regularly after 1688. Political parties and elections also played a greater role in policymaking with parliamentary supremacy. We use this history to offer insights into how economic and political systems evolved together, including mercantilism, capitalism, and aspects of democratic decision-making.

Mercantilist policies, like a tax on an imported good, could create an artificial wedge between the price paid by consumers and that received by producers. While such wedges benefited some producers and the government, there were clearly some losers, perhaps many. Herein lies a puzzle: how could mercantilist policies get selected in a political system where some of the losers have a political voice? For England, how could Parliament adopt mercantilist policies if there were losers who had Members of Parliament (MPs) representing or supporting their interests? One potential explanation is that the governments, led by the monarch, created dominant coalitions in Parliament which supported and expanded mercantilism.[3] Likewise, governments sought to weaken the opposition, which could represent the losers of mercantilism. If these government strategies were successful, then mercantilism could be durable, even with a functioning representative parliament. If the government was not successful, then it is possible to have mercantilist policies undone or weakened. The shape of institutions might also change with new dominant coalitions depending on the government's interests.

We examine the degree to which mercantilist policies persisted across the political transitions from the Restoration to the Glorious Revolution. We also examine how political support for mercantilist policies in Parliament evolved. We study acts of parliament, which strengthened or weakened mercantilism, and quantify the share of MPs on committees which were from the dominant political coalition for these acts. In this setting, the dominant coalition was organized by political parties, so our coalition measures are party strength on committees.[4]

Our analysis provides two lessons. First, consistent with previous research, we show mercantilism survived the political regime changes associated with the Restoration and Revolution.[5] It was common to use legislation to implement taxes, prohibitions, and grant monopoly rights to support domestic industry and weaken international rivals both before and after 1688. Yet, some aspects of mercantilist policies were weakened after 1688. For example, there were some policies that promoted more free trade. Broadly, we find that mercantilism was durable over the transition to more representative institutions. Our analysis shows that the replacement of mercantilism with capitalism was not guaranteed or the result of some law of motion. Rather, it was a negotiated process between domestic political economic actors and depended on international relations.

Second, we find that representative government, particularly with the supremacy of Parliament after 1688, shaped mercantilism in new ways. The structural shift altered the rival powers that were targeted by mercantilism, generally the Dutch Republic before 1688 and France after.[6] It also led to some shifts in the domestic industries that were protected, with shipping and the East India Company more favored before 1688 and domestic industry more after.

The political-economic 'equilibrium' of mercantilism also shifted. Before 1688, the monarchs successfully packed Parliament with supporters who helped implement its favored mercantilist policies. After 1688, the new monarchs negotiated with the two political parties (the Whigs and the Tories) to implement policies.[7] Even as one party allied with the monarch in the dominant coalition, the other served as an effective opposition, which sometimes weakened a mercantilist agenda or reshaped it to address losses created by policies.

Background on Mercantilism, Political Institutions, and Actors

As noted earlier, mercantilism used economic regulation for the purpose of improving state power at the expense of rival nation powers.[8] Contemporary scholarship tended to study errors in the logic of mercantilist ideas, particularly around the flow of specie, regulation of trade, population growth, and wages.[9] More recent scholars have studied the ways in which the machinery of the state was employed to grant monopoly rights that were central to the regulation of the domestic economy and the ways in which international conflict could secure resources for European powers.[10] This chapter falls into this latter political economic tradition.

Legislation

In England, the monarch and Parliament were central to the supply of rights that regulated the economy and trade in a variety of ways. We discuss examples in case studies below. These policies and regulations were embodied in legislation called acts of parliament.[11] Bills originated from interest groups, like trading companies or domestic manufacturers, who petitioned the government. Bills could also originate from government ministers, who acted on behalf of the monarch and varied other interests. Bills could start in either the Commons or the Lords. Each was reviewed by a committee. The committee could be an ad hoc committee with named members or a committee of the whole house, where it was reviewed by all present members in the respective houses. If a bill passed both houses and was approved by the monarch, it became a law (an act of parliament). Bills must have supporters in the government to become laws. Supporters have been identified by studying the legislative process, for example, which members were appointed to a committee, who introduced a bill, and if a group petitioned a bill.[12]

International Competition and Internal Political Changes

The English government used regulation (acts of parliament) to compete with other European powers, primarily the Dutch Republic, Spain, and France. The English governments were not only concerned with using regulation to compete with international rivals on the continent. Rivalries also extended to their colonial holdings. England and the other European powers increasingly imported from and exported to colonies.[13] Because England also ruled over three separate kingdoms (England and Wales, Scotland, and Ireland), regulation also sought to address strategic and competitive concerns with interests in these kingdoms.

The nature of alliances and competition with international rivals depended on the identity of the monarchs and their governments.[14] The relationship between monarch and Parliament evolved significantly. The period from 1660 to 1702 saw four regime changes: Charles II (1660–1684), James II (1685–1688), William and Mary (1689–1694), and William III (1695–1702).[15] Charles II and James II generally supported France and fought against the Dutch Republic, the predecessor state of the Netherlands.[16] The first war with the Dutch in 1652 was linked with the Navigation Act, the first significant piece of legislation aimed at promoting English shipping at the expense of rivals like the Dutch. Charles II led two more wars against the Dutch (Second Anglo Dutch War 1665–1667 and the Third Anglo Dutch War 1672–1674). These two wars were also linked with Navigation Acts. England allied with France during the third War. Charles II and James II's reigns were characterized by few general elections and increasing conflict over religion and the monarchy's constitutional place in government. Charles II ruled from 1681 to 1684 without Parliament and James II ruled for most of his reign from 1685 until the Revolution of 1688 without calling Parliament.

After the Glorious Revolution of 1688, William and Mary ruled England and Wales. It is generally agreed that the Revolution created more representative institutions in England because it led to the supremacy of Parliament, which had more frequent elections after 1688 and saw the emergence of two political parties (discussed next). The Revolution also shifted England's international alliances and rivals.[17] William was the leader of the Dutch Republic. England thus became allied with the Dutch and the Spanish. William led the Nine Years War against France (1688–1697). William's successor, Queen Anne, continued in fighting the French during the War of Spanish Succession (1702–1714).

Monarchs traditionally had influence over policymaking in the Parliament at Westminster (English and Welsh parliament), and thus sought to pack it with supporters (often called Courtiers or Court supporters). Political parties with whom the monarch had to negotiate became key actors after 1679. The Whigs emerged in the 1680s to constrain Charles II. They coalesced on concerns over religion, his alliance with France, and government excess, which included surveying government accounts over war spending and restricting patronage. The Court and Tories supported Charles II. After the Revolution, the Whigs argued more strongly for a constitutional monarchy, enshrined in the Bill of Rights. In foreign policy, there was continuity after the Revolution in that Whigs supported wars against France. The Tories were more ambivalent but did become the party that sought to avoid war expenses, which were thought to increase taxes on the landed gentry, its main constituents.

Domestic Economic Interests and Mercantilist Policies

Mercantilist regulation was shaped by England's economic interests. The economy was primarily agricultural: producing cereals and livestock. Its main domestic manufacturing industry was woolen textiles. The main service sector was shipping, which was led by international trading companies, like the East India Company and Royal African company. Colonial goods, like sugar, did not directly compete with domestic agriculture. Others, like textile silks from India and France, did compete with some parts of domestic textile production.

Government policies generally sought to use import and export regulations (bans and taxes) to maintain prices of commodities and encourage production. Here we discuss a few examples that related to agriculture and textiles. The Restoration period "saw the first time in English history that English agriculture was protected by high import corn duties."[18] One act of parliament in 1663 allowed exporting cereals only when domestic prices were below a certain low level, while charging a high duty on imports at the same time. The late nineteenth century is famous for the repeal of such protective mercantilist measures known as the Corn Laws. To protect textile manufactures from competition on the Continent, there was a ban on the export of raw wool from 1614 to 1824.

This ban was debated after the Restoration and the Revolution. It was re-enacted in 1660 and 1662, debated in 1668, 1670–78, 1685 and strengthened with new acts of parliament in 1688, 1695–96, and 1698.[19]

Analysis of Mercantilist Legislation

We examine the interests on major pieces of mercantilist bills and acts in four sessions of parliament (1660, 1670, 1690, 1699). We collect information from the *Journals* of the Parliament. Table 14.1 summarizes the sessions. It provides information on the monarch, dates of sitting, date of most recent election, session length, and the majority and minority parties.

We measure party interests on mercantilist policies to better understand the interests represented in the policymaking process. It is not straightforward to classify party strength during this period, in part because parties were forming for the first time. Nevertheless, scholars have estimated the strength of a specific party at various dates by studying the affiliations of Members of Parliament (MPs in the House of Commons). Prior to 1660, MPs were either affiliated with groups that supported the monarch or with the opposition. The estimates indicate that the monarch had strong support in Parliament for much of the period. In the 1660 parliament, the largest party was known as the Royalists, a group of MPs who had broadly supported the monarch Charles I during the Civil Wars. Approximately 48 percent of MPs were Royalists. In the 1661 parliament, which sat until 1679 without a general election, 57.3 percent of MPs were aligned with the Court that supported the monarch. The opposition was relatively small at that time, having only 18 percent of MPs.[20] It is generally agreed that the Opposition grew and became increasingly well organized by 1678.

After 1688, MP support for the Whigs and Tories was generally evenly divided, with neither party consistently in the majority. In the 1690 parliament, Holmes states that a Tory majority was narrowly returned but its size cannot be stated. The divided Commons is consistent with the mixed Whig and Tory ministries early in William and Mary's reign. In the 1698 parliament, which included the 1699 session that we study, it is estimated that 47 percent of MPs were affiliated with the Court Whigs, which were organized to support William's push to not disband the army at the end of the Nine Years' War (1688–1697). Court Whigs had a slight edge over the Tories, who wanted to disband the army. Holmes has estimated that 44.2 percent of MPs were affiliated with the Tories. The Whigs also held a majority of the ministry positions, and collectively they were known as the 'Junta,' then a Hispano-Portuguese term for an administrative council.

Table 14.1 **Sessions selected for analysis**

session (from 1660)	*monarch*	*session dates*	*parliament*	*most recent general election*	*session length (# of days)*	*majority party*	*minority party*
1	Charles II	25 Apr 1660–29 Dec 1660	Convention, 1660	1660	294	Royalists, Court	Presbyterian Opposition
10	Charles II	14 Feb 1670–22 Apr 1671	Cavalier, 1661	1661	234	Court	Opposition
26	William and Mary	20 Mar 1690–23 May 1690	1690 Parliament	1690	65	Tory	Whig
35	William III	6 Dec 1698–4 May 1699	1698 Parliament	1698	141	Whig	Tory

Notes: See text.

Recent research has further classified *individual* MPs as being aligned with the majority or largest party in each parliament from 1660 to 1741.[21] We use this data on majority party affiliations below to study committee composition on mercantilist policies. We document party representation on committees and whether representation evolved after the Revolution.

As a first step, we identify major mercantilist legislation based on the short titles of the acts. We study those related to international trade (e.g., exports or imports, taxation) and some domestic economic issues closely affected by trade (e.g., employment). Broadly we identified acts that addressed (i) trade restrictions, like imposing duties, and (ii) barriers to entry in markets involving international trade. Two examples include in 1660 "An Act for the encouraging and increasing of Shipping and Navigation" (12 Charles II, c. 15) and in 1698 "An Act to prevent the Exportation of Wool out of the Kingdoms of Ireland and England into foreign Parts; and for the Encouragement of the Woollen Manufactures in the Kingdom of England" (10&11 William III, c. 37).

For each session, we then study acts (bills passed by Parliament). We identify whether the act was committed to a committee of the whole house or to a select committee in the House of Commons. If committed to the whole house, we interpret that the act was supported by the monarch who wished to control the bill, either by aligning with the majority party or relying on the disorganization of the whole house and particularly the opposition. If the bill was committed to a select committee, then it is less clear if the monarch supported it, so we describe the share of MPs affiliated with the majority party on select committees. We use data on majority party affiliations to identify majority party MPs on select committee lists.

Table 14.2 summarizes the number of mercantilist bills we identify in each session, whether they were committed to a committee of the whole house or to a select committee, and the average share of MPs affiliated with the majority party on the select committee. The data indicate that the move to representative government after 1688 did not "do away" with mercantilist legislation immediately.

Table 14.2 **Mercantilist acts and committees**

Session	*# mercantilist acts*	*# bill committee of whole house*	*# select committee (S.C.)*	*av. share of MPs with majority on S.C.*
1660	5	1	4	0.5
1670	8	1	7	0.9
1690	7	1	6	0.41
1699	15	8	7	0.48

Notes: See text.

Recall the examples of mercantilist acts in 1690 and 1699 prohibiting trade with France and the exports of wool. One caveat is that some of these regulations weakened mercantilist institutions, which we discuss in the case studies below. The table also illustrates that the processes by which mercantilist policies were adopted changed. During the Restoration era, Charles II was able to pack mercantilist legislation with his supporters (the Court party). On average 90 percent of select committee (S.C.) members were affiliated with the Court majority in the 1670 session. The 90 percent figure on mercantilist select committees greatly exceeds the 57 percent Court majority in the whole House of Commons.

After 1688, when both Whigs and Tories competed for majorities in parliament, William III relied on the committee of the whole house to review legislation in the 1699 session. We find that a little over half of mercantilist acts were reviewed by the committee of the whole house in 1699. Recall that the Whigs had a narrow majority among all MPs and faced a well-organized Tory opposition. We conjecture that King William's government, led by the Whig Junto, used the disorganized nature of the Committee of the Whole to push through various mercantilist bills. We also see that after 1688, in contrast to under Charles II in 1670, half of select committee members processing mercantilist acts were affiliated with the Tory majority in 1690 and the Whig majority in 1699, which suggests that William and Mary and William III had to negotiate with both parties to carry out their mercantilist goals.

Case Studies

We now turn to case studies of the four sessions. The added context helps interpret the interests that supported the mercantilist policies, and the interests that the policies affected. Our analysis shows that the Revolution, which was a distinct move toward more representative government with the supremacy of parliament and governing under two parties, did not undo mercantilism. Rather, the move toward representative government shaped mercantilist institutions by changing the interests in power. Capitalist and democratic institutions co-evolved in England in the long run. The findings illustrate that this was a negotiated process and not guaranteed.

1660: Restoration

The five mercantilist acts we identify in 1660 were passed after the Restoration of the monarchy, which had been abolished along with the House of Lords during the Commonwealth period after the Civil Wars (1640s–1650s). Charles II regained power and returned to England from France after the Commonwealth devolved into near military rule under Richard Cromwell. England and the Dutch Republic had been fighting over control of trade and shipping.

The most important of the mercantilist acts in the 1660 session implemented one of the commonly known Navigation Laws, "An Act for the encouraging and increasing of Shipping and Navigation" (12 Charles II, c. 15). Broadly, it required that goods be transported on ships made in England, Wales, Ireland, or in the colonies and required that at least three-fourths of the mariners be English. Thus, the colonial staples were to be traded only with England initially, which could then re-export to other countries. Colonies could import from other European powers, but these goods would be subject to other discriminatory duties.[22] It was meant to bolster English shipping and was effectively targeting England's two largest commercial rivals, the Dutch and Spanish.[23] It did target French shipping, but to a lesser degree. While imperfectly enforced, the Navigation Laws were costly to those not affiliated with English shipping. The Act forced goods to be shipped extra distances (say from France to England and then the British West Indies).[24] The Act also reduced the share of the market served by the most cost-efficient shippers, generally the Dutch at this time.

For our purposes it is interesting to examine how the Navigation Act of 1660 came into being. Our analysis shows that the Navigation bill was sent to a select committee, which had 54 percent of its members affiliated with the Royalist coalition. That was larger than the whole House, which had 44 percent Royalists. We conjecture that committees were designed to have a majority of government/Royalist supporters to ensure that mercantilist bills were enacted.

Another example of a mercantilist policy during this session is "An Act for the better ordering the selling of Wines by Retail." It forbade the selling of wine without a license, which could only be obtained from the monarch in exchange for a fee. Thus, it effectively restricted entry into the retailing of wine. The law seems to have recognized that prices would be affected, and thus it set a maximum price for wine. Whether the price ceiling was binding is not clear, however, it is unlikely to have assuaged wine consumers. Our analysis shows that 48 percent of the MPs on the select committee for this bill were Royalist/Court compared to the 44 percent in the entire Commons. The narrow majority might have been necessary for its passage.

1670: Charles II

The 1670 session took place in the middle of Charles II's reign. The Court party, a coalition of MPs that relied on patronage to support the monarch's initiatives, was becoming better organized. The Dutch were still seen as the greatest rival to England. The Second Anglo Dutch War was fought from 1665 to 1667 and the Third Anglo Dutch War would begin in 1672.

There were eight mercantilist acts during the session, seven of which were sent to a select committee. These committees were very biased toward the majority Court coalition. On average, 90 percent of committee members were affiliated with the majority Court party. In the House as a whole approximately 60 percent of MPs were Court aligned.

The mercantilist acts during this period served various functions. One prevented the planting of tobacco in England (22&23 Charles II, c. 37), which illustrates the need to consider colonial production and interests in the mercantilist system. Another imposed duties on brandy imports (22 Charles II, c. 7). Another allowed beer to be exported (22 Charles II, c. 30). Brewing had become an urban occupation and larger brewers were emerging in London. The legislation was designed to start exports from the larger brewers.[25] Two other acts reinstated the licensing system for wine imports (22&23 Charles II, c. 28) and added to the Navigation Laws as they related to fighting piracy. One interesting feature is that mercantilist acts in 1670 did not especially target French imports over other countries. This would change with the Glorious Revolution and the new monarchs William and Mary.

1690: The Glorious Revolution

The Revolution of 1688 resulted in the overthrow of James II who was replaced by William and Mary. They jointly ruled until Mary's death in 1694. William was the stadholder of the Dutch Republic. Mary, who married William in 1677, was the daughter of James II and had a claim to the English throne. The Revolution created more democratic institutions in England in the sense that it confirmed the supremacy of parliament, a representative institution, led to more frequent elections and the emergence of two political parties.

Mercantilist legislation survived after the Revolution as we will further document below, but with the accession of William and Mary the shape and degree of England's mercantilist institutions changed. As Parliament sat more regularly, there were more petitions about economic issues.[26] These lobbying efforts came from local manufacturers or artificers who sought to influence or limit mercantilist legislation. The organized interests found MPs who would advocate for them in designing policies in Parliament. Under William III's reign, which lasted to 1702, there was "a considerable modification of the mercantilist system and the emergence of freer-trade policies."[27] The post-Revolution parliament was more open to the losers from mercantilist policies. Perhaps the monarch and its dominant coalition could not ignore their interests at a moment of political change.

Due to the nature of parliamentary politics, which now relied on bargaining with the Whigs and Tories, the types of mercantilist policies also changed. William III was engaged in a broader war with France.[28] Following this objective, the monarch argued for restrictions on French imports very early in the Nine Years' War: "England as for years received great damage by consuming

French commodities and exporting English bullion and coin."[29] Such sentiment was incorporated into a 1689 act prohibiting all Trade and Commerce with France:

> It hath been found by long experience, that the importing of French wines, vinegar, brandy, linen, silks, salt, paper, and other commodities . . . hath much exhausted the treasure of this nation, lessened the value of native commodities . . . and greatly impoverished the English artificers and handicrafts and caused great detriment to the kingdom in general.[30]

The Whigs supported William's goal of closing trade with France. Broadly they were concerned with limiting France's potential to undermine the Protestant religion in England. The last Stuart monarch and Catholic James II had been exiled to France and still posed a threat. The Whigs were an ideal partner for William to shift mercantilism in an anti-French direction. The Tories, who held a narrow majority in the 1690 parliament, were less ideal as they were more ambivalent about the French-Stuart threat. Significantly, our calculations show that only 25 percent of the MPs on the select committee working on the act prohibiting trade with France were Tories.

The mercantilist acts we identify were not uniformly supported by the majority Tory party based on our measure. Rather, some pieces of legislation had Tories in the majority on the select committee, while others had the Whig party as the majority. This can be seen in the committee composition of two mercantilist acts that regard silk production and trade. Broadly, the evidence suggests that both parties shaped mercantilist institutions and may have either sought to further their agenda and support the monarch or protect potential losers.

The first was mercantilist legislation that targeted thrown silk and silk products. Silk throwing was the process of reeling raw silk into skeins and bobbins so that it could be used in the production of silk cloths. Such measures that restricted imports, it was argued, protected the domestic wool industry, improved trade with Turkey, and encouraged domestic silk throwing in England. The preamble to "An Act for the discouraging the Importation of Thrown Silk" (2 W&M c. 24), states that there was concern that "great quantities of thrown silk have been imported from several parts and places in Europe, which are not the places of its growth or production." It only allowed importation of thrown silks from the Italian peninsula, like Sicily and Naples.[31] It effectively prevented imports of thrown silk from Turkey, China, and the East Indies. It was intended to protect the domestic silk throwing industry, largely in London. Our calculations show that the select committee had 50 percent Whig MPs (who were narrowly in the minority) and 33 percent Tory MPs. As with the prohibition on French trade, the Whigs were the stronger proponent of this mercantilist policy.

The Tories played a stronger role in "An Act for granting to Their Majesties certain Impositions upon all East India Goods and Manufactures, and upon all wrought Silks, and several other Goods and Merchandize" (2&3 W&M, c. 10). The Act granted duties for war both with Ireland and France. It also provided protection for domestic textile industries.[32] It laid out different duties for Indian and Chinese linens, calicoes, and raw silks and those imported from the Spanish Netherlands and United Provinces.[33] The East India Company's textile imports were especially targeted with higher duties. The Tory MPs likely played a greater role shaping this Act because the select committee had 52 percent Tory and 30 percent Whigs. The greater role for Tories requires more research. This Act was made when the East India Company's monopoly was being questioned. The Tories generally supported the Company and their presence on the committee may have helped to protect the Company from further legislation restricting its trade.

Broadly, the Whigs and Tories both played a role in shaping the different mercantilist policies introduced during the 1690 Parliament. There was a shift to policies that sought to weaken France, where previously the Dutch were the target. Also, there were more mercantilist policies which protected domestic industries explicitly. Several of these patterns would continue in the 1699 Parliament to which we now turn.

1699: After the Nine Years' War, Whig Junta

The 1699 session saw the most acts (15) dealing with mercantilism among the four sessions that we study. While it is not straightforward to classify their function, our estimation is that seven acts expanded mercantilism, say by adding trade restrictions, while six reversed or curtailed mercantilist policies, like eliminating duties. Two acts were a mixture of expansion and reversal.

An example of an act that expanded mercantilism was "An Act to prevent the Exportation of Wool out of the Kingdoms of Ireland and England into foreign Parts; and for the Encouragement of the Woollen Manufactures in the Kingdom of England" (10 WIII, c. 16). The Act introduced trade restrictions to effectively cheapen raw materials for the domestic woolen manufacturing industry, a very important sector at that time. Another example was "An Act for the more effectual employment of the Poor, by encouraging the Manufactures of this Kingdom" (11 WIII, c. 10). It effectively banned or restricted imports of textiles from China and India brought to England on East India Company ships. It is considered one of the important "Calico Acts," which helped protect the domestic textile industry, both woolen and cotton. An example reversing mercantilism policies was "An Act for taking off the remaining Duties upon Glass Wares" (10 WIII, c. 24). Such duties were introduced to finance the Nine Years War. Once the War ended in 1697 there were pressures to eliminate such duties which benefited the government but restrained trade. In this case, there was not an important or organized domestic industry which benefited from the protection offered by such duties, so they were easier to eliminate politically.

Our calculations show that the Whigs and Tories were both involved in the making of acts affecting mercantilism in 1699. The "Act to prevent the export of wool" noted above had an equal share of Whig and Tory MPs on the select committee. The Act to employ the poor by banning East India Company textile imports had more Whigs at 56 percent. The Act to eliminate duties on Glass had an equal share of Whigs and Tories.

The Whigs influenced policymaking in 1699 with the solidification of the Whig Junta in the ministry and the disorganization/lack of unity among Tory party leaders.[34] The leaders of the Whig Junta were concerned about the ability to pass William III's agenda, particularly around military goals related to disbanding the army.[35] William III sought to prevent disbanding the army in the event that there was renewed conflict with France.[36] Wary of executive power, England historically did not have a standing army. Many argued for the army to be disbanded with the conclusion of the Nine Years' War. William III found it challenging to find a Tory alternative to the Whig Junta that embraced his policy goals. Though Parliament did pass mercantilist legislation in 1699, the provisions in them and the failure of others were not aligned with William III's policy aims.[37] Some examples include acts which reversed mercantilist policies by eliminating duties introduced during the Nine Years War.

There was an interesting shift in the way some mercantilist acts were made in the 1699 Parliament. About half were committed to the committee of the whole house, not select committees which was common in earlier sessions that we study. Most of the acts committed to the whole house were for acts that expanded mercantilism. One example is "An Act for laying further Duties upon wrought Silks, Muslins and some other Commodities of the East Indies" (11 W. c. 3). More research is needed to explain this political strategy of using the committee of the whole House. We hypothesize that it was difficult for the monarch's government to rely on political parties to implement mercantilist policies. William III and the Whig Junta could better secure passage of key pieces of mercantilist legislation, by discussion in the whole House, if the opposition to such policies was disorganized.

Conclusion

Mercantilism was the dominant economic system operating before capitalism. It lasted for several centuries in most of Europe and slowly eroded in England during the 1700s and 1800s. Mercantilism was persistent because it promised the government higher tax revenues and weaker international rivals. It also persisted because monarchs were generally successful in constructing coalitions to support their agenda. Organized opposition to mercantilism was generally weak. As democratic institutions grew in England, mercantilism potentially lost some of its durability. The losers from mercantilism might find support from opposition parties who could challenge the dominant coalition and its policies that restricted trade and erected barriers to entry.

We examine the durability of mercantilism and its political support in England between the Restoration of the monarchy in 1660 and the decade following the Glorious Revolution of 1688. It was a moment when representative institutions, like Parliament, grew in importance. Political parties also emerged, which could represent the interests of different groups in society. Previously coalitions existed largely to support the monarch and in return MPs shared in the spoils of rule. We give several examples showing that mercantilism survived in this period of political transition.

That said, mercantilist policies were shaped by the post-Revolution environment. The foreign targets shifted from the Dutch to the French. Domestic manufacturing industries were more likely to be protected, where previously shipping was more favored. There were also broader coalitions of political actors who participated in making mercantilist policy. Before 1688 most MPs making acts were part of the monarch's ruling coalition. Afterwards, it included MPs from both the Whig and Tory parties, even when they were not part of the majority. The broader participation sometimes reversed or weakened aspects of mercantilism. We hesitate to predict whether capitalism will prove to be as durable as mercantilism. An optimistic reading of the history presented here suggests that those aspects of capitalism that benefit the narrowest interests will be hard to sustain in systems with organized political parties and effective representative institutions.

Acknowledgments

We thank participants at the Democracy and Capitalism workshop at the University of Virginia for helpful comments. We are also grateful to Scott Miller, Jenn Bair, Joel Mokyr, Naomi Lamoreaux, and John Wallis for comments.

Primary Records

Journal of the House of Commons Various volumes, 1660–1699 (London, 1802), British History Online, https://www.british-history.ac.uk/commons-jrnl/vol7?page=11

Pickering, Danby. *The Statutes at Large, from the First Year of K. William and Q. Mary, to the Eighth Year of K. William III*. Vol. 9. Cambridge: Printed by Joseph Bentham, printer to the University, 1764). https://books.google.co.uk/books?id=0ecuAAAAIAAJ

Notes

1. *Encyclopedia Britannica*, s.v. "Mercantilism," accessed December 3, 2023, https://www.britannica.com/money/mercantilism.
2. John J. McCusker and Kenneth Morgan, "Introduction," in *The Early Modern Atlantic Economy*, ed. John J. McCusker and Kenneth Morgan (Cambridge: Cambridge University Press, 2001), 1–12; Ronald Findlay and K. H. O'Rourke, *Power and Plenty: Trade, War, and the World Economy in the Second Millennium* (Princeton: Princeton University Press, 2007), 229.
3. Douglass C. North, John Joseph Wallis, and Barry R. Weingast, *Violence and Social Orders: A Conceptual Framework for Interpreting Recorded Human History* (Cambridge: Cambridge University Press, 2009).
4. Tim Harris, *Politics Under the Later Stuarts: Party Conflict in a Divided Society* (London: Routledge, 1993); David Stasavage, "Partisan Politics and Public Debt: The Importance of the 'Whig Supremacy' for Britain's Financial Revolution," *European Review of Economic History* 11, no. 1 (April 2007): 123–53; Steve Pincus, *1688: The First Modern Revolution* (New Haven: Yale University Press, 2009).
5. Raymond Sickinger, "Regulation or Ruination: Parliament's Consistent Pattern of Mercantilist Regulation of the English Textile Trade, 1669–1800," *Parliamentary History* 19, no. 2 (2000): 211–32.
6. Makio Yamada, "Foreigner Kings as Local Kingmakers: How the 'Unusual' Marginalization of Conservative Political Groups Occurred in pre-Industrial Revolution Britain," *Journal of Institutional Economics* 19, no. 4 (2023): 511–25.
7. Harris, *Politics Under the Later Stuarts*; Gary Cox, *Marketing Sovereign Promises: Monopoly Brokerage and the Growth of the English State*, Political Economy of Institutions and Decisions (New York: Cambridge University Press, 2016).
8. McCusker and Morgan, *The Early Modern Atlantic Economy*.
9. Robert B. Ekelund and Robert D. Tollison, *Mercantilism as a Rent-Seeking Society: Economic Regulation in Historical Perspective* (College Station: Texas A&M University Press, 1981).
10. Ekelund and Tollison, *Mercantilism*; Findlay and O'Rourke, *Power and Plenty*.
11. Julian Hoppit, *Britain's Political Economies: Parliament and Economic Life, 1660–1800* (Cambridge: Cambridge University Press, 2017); Sickinger, "Regulation or Ruination."
12. Dan Bogart, "Party Connections, Interest Groups and The Slow Diffusion Of Infrastructure: Evidence From Britain's First Transport Revolution," *The Economic Journal* 128 (March 2018): 541–75; Kara Dimitruk, "The Glorious Revolution and Access to Parliament," *The Journal of Economic History* 83, no. 3 (2023): 676–708.
13. Findlay and O'Rourke, *Power and Plenty*, ch. 5.
14. Yamada, "Foreigner Kings."
15. William and Mary co-ruled from 1689 until Mary's death in 1694. William (William III) ruled from 1694 until his death in 1701).
16. Findlay and O'Rourke, *Power and Plenty*, 240.
17. Yamada, "Foreigner Kings."
18. Gras quoted in Joan Thirsk, "Agricultural Policy: Public Debate and Legislation," in *The Agrarian History of England and Wales Volume VII*, ed. Joan Thirsk (Cambridge: Cambridge University Press, 1985), 328–29.
19. Thirsk, "Agricultural Policy," 364–66.
20. Geoffrey Holmes, *The Making of a Great Power: Late Stuart and Early Georgian Britain, 1660–1722* (London: Longman, 1993).
21. Dan Bogart, "Political Party Representation and Electoral Politics in England and Wales, 1690–1747," *Social Science History* 40, no. 2 (2016): 271–303; Kara Dimitruk, "Political

Coalitions in the House of Commons, 1660–1690: New Data and Applications," *Historical Methods: A Journal of Quantitative and Interdisciplinary History* 54, no. 3 (2021): 172–87.

22. Edward Channing, "The Navigation Laws," *Proceedings of the American Antiquarian Society* 6, no. 2 (1890): 160–79.
23. Findlay and O'Rourke, *Power and Plenty*, 242–43.
24. It should be noted that enforcement of the mercantilist policies we study was challenging throughout this period as argued in Hoppit, *Britain's Political Economies*.
25. Thirsk, "Agricultural Policy."
26. Steven C. A. Pincus and James A. Robinson, "What Really Happened During the Glorious Revolution?," in *Institutions, Property Rights, and Economic Growth: The Legacy of Douglass North*, ed. Sebastián Galiani and Itai Sened (New York: Cambridge University Press, 2014), 192–222.
27. George L. Cherry, "The Development of the English Free-Trade Movement in Parliament, 1660–1702," *The Journal of Modern History* 25, no. 2 (1953): 119.
28. Findlay and O'Rourke, *Power and Plenty*, 246.
29. As explained in Cherry, "Free-Trade Movement," 109.
30. Quoted in Cherry, "Free-Trade Movement," 109.
31. Danby Pickering, *The Statutes at Large, from the First Year of K. William and Q. Mary, to the Eighth Year of K. William III*, vol. 9 (Cambridge: Printed by Joseph Bentham, printer to the University, 1764), 85.
32. Findlay and O'Rourke, *Power and Plenty*, 249.
33. Pickering, *Statutes at Large*, 87.
34. Henry Horwitz, *Parliament, Policy, and the Politics in the Reign of William III* (Manchester: Manchester University Press, 1977), 257.
35. Horwitz, *Parliament, Policy, and Politics*, 148.
36. Findlay and O'Rourke, *Power and Plenty*, 247.
37. Horwitz, *Parliament, Policy, and Politics*, 255–56.

15

Freedom's Frictions

Entrepreneurial Imaginaries in the Making of American Capitalism and Democracy

HANNAH KNOX TUCKER AND R. DANIEL WADHWANI

In early 2023, Harvard Business School finance professor Mihir Desai penned an editorial in *The New York Times* to celebrate the "Crypto Crash." Desai welcomed the plummeting prices of crypto, grumbling that they reflected the "magical thinking that had come to infect part of the generation who grew up in the aftermath of the Great Recession—and American capitalism, more broadly." Magical thinking of this sort assumed "that favored conditions will continue on forever without regard for history," he explained, and was based in an impractical "conflation of virtue with commerce."[1]

Desai's characterization will be familiar to anyone who has encountered the social worlds of contemporary technology entrepreneurship. The "idea of revolutionary social change is common topos within the discussion around decentralised technologies," explains STS scholar Moritz Becker.[2] Essential to this revolutionary entrepreneurial rhetoric is a moral vision, one that Desai describes as conflating "virtue with commerce." It does so, explains one legal scholar, by making the "claim to free the individual subject from all institutional and other . . . constraints."[3] Crypto is not the only such entrepreneurial innovation that has arisen to animate the entrepreneurial imagination in recent years. The promises of the metaverse and the circular economy, to name just two others, are examples of a host of imaginary constructs promising futures free from the constraints of the present.[4] How do we make sense of the rise of such entrepreneurial imaginaries?

In contrast to Desai, however, we will argue that magical thinking that integrates virtue with commerce has been central to the evolution of American

Hannah Knox Tucker and R Daniel Wadhwani, *Freedom's Frictions*. In: *Can Democracy and Capitalism Be Reconciled?*. Edited by: Sidney M. Milkis and Scott C. Miller, Oxford University Press. © Oxford University Press (2025).
DOI: 10.1093/9780197774731.003.0016

democracy and American capitalism. The entrepreneurial visions of crypto and similar constructs have in common a social and political vision of a future free from the constraints of the present. "Entrepreneurial imaginaries," the name we will use for the construct, conjures visions of enterprise and inspires business models that promise freedom from the constraints of a collectively imagined status quo. As constructs, entrepreneurial imaginaries are protean enough to mask tangible differences, tensions, and contradictions in the people, resources, circumstances, and ventures they describe. But their broadly liberatory promises allow individuals to vest their ventures with shared moral and political meaning and justify business models that—at least for a while—are seen as resolving tensions inherent to the practice of freedom in democratic and capitalistic social relationships. Over time, however, these business models themselves come to be seen as constraining, creating the conditions for the emergence of new imaginaries.

Our chapter begins by developing more fully what we mean by entrepreneurial imaginaries. We then use the construct to venture a synthesis of American business history unfolding over three periods. We conclude by drawing out some of the implications of our construct for understanding the relationship between democracy and capitalism, particularly as they relate to the development of the nation.

Entrepreneurial Imaginaries

Democracy and capitalism, as social systems that emerged in the modern era, have in common the principle of freedom. The emergence of republican and subsequently democratic political principles rested on the promise of an independent citizenry's right and ability to self-govern, not only politically but also economically and culturally.[5] Capitalism, as an economic system defined by relatively free markets, rested on the promise that an economy in which private entrepreneurs are at liberty to judge and pursue ventures they deem worthwhile is more likely to produce a thriving nation than one in which such ventures are owned or closely controlled by the state.[6] Modern conversations around capitalism justly emphasize its tendency to encourage capital accumulation and subsequent inequality. Of less interest in these accounts, however, is an examination of the "freedom to" that precedes "deploy capital" in definitions of capitalism. By exploring how people understood this freedom as a moral discourse embodied in entrepreneurial practice, we aim to channel the conversation on capitalism in an entrepreneurial direction.

Freedom, however, was more problematic in practice than in principle. Most notably, freedom in practice struggled with the contradictory distinction between America's free citizens and unfree dependents, an enduring tension that continues to challenge American capitalism and American democracy. Even for those who claimed the rights of free citizens inherent tensions pervaded the practice of freedom as the exercise of liberty by some often threatened the liberty of others. Elaborated most famously in Isaiah Berlin's *Two Concepts of Freedom*, the tensions between positive freedom ("freedom to") and negative freedom ("freedom from") lay at the heart of the frictions involved in translating liberty as a principle into the practices of a free society.[7]

For much of American history, these tensions between positive and negative liberty have manifested themselves in the frictions between competing forms and practices of private enterprise. Entrepreneurship in practice unleashed the exercise of "freedom to," that is, *to* develop new products that drive out a competitor, *to* acquire land to build a railroad, or *to* consolidate an industry. The positive "freedom to" pursue such ventures empowered entrepreneurs to change the status quo and to, in Joseph Schumpeter's evocative description, not only create new worlds but also destroy old ones.[8] Yet, these same acts of entrepreneurial liberty could and were plausibly interpreted as threats to negative freedom for others. Models of enterprise—e.g., small proprietors in the mid-nineteenth century, management-led corporations in the mid-twentieth century, and tech entrepreneurship today—that were once considered commercially virtuous for the freedom they brought from old ways of organizing a venture came to be seen as violations of negative freedom as they became conventional, institutionalized, and dominant. Responses to these violations arose from within the competitive dynamics of capitalism, as new entrepreneurs experimented with new organizational models and business practices. But responses also took the form of democratic engagement, as critiques of older forms of capitalist enterprise became the basis of social movements and seeped into the language and tactics of electoral politics.

How, then, might we understand the deep political and economic tensions that have erupted in the American past? Whereas a long tradition in historical scholarship locates these tensions in American life in fundamental, even irreconcilable, differences between democracy and capitalism, we argue that they emerged from inherent frictions within the practice of liberty that is common to both these societal forms. Models of enterprise once understood as intrinsically virtuous expressions of positive freedom could come to be seen as constraining as they became dominant and impinged on Americans' negative freedoms. These frictions could be powerfully expressed and mobilized both in the marketplace and at the ballot box by what we call *entrepreneurial imaginaries*. The construct draws on philosopher Charles Taylor's concept of "modern social imaginaries." A student of Berlin's, Taylor defined a "social imaginary" as a widely held conception of "moral order" that defines the way people "imagine their social existence, how they fit together with others, how things go on between them and their fellows, the expectations that are normally met, and the deeper normative notions and images that underlie all these expectations."[9] According to Taylor, modern Western social imaginaries in which self-determined humans acting as individuals pursue their own ends in ways that result in mutual benefit replaced classical and pre-modern imaginaries in which one's place was divinely determined and hierarchically organized.

Extending Taylor's construct, *we define modern entrepreneurial imaginaries as the moral reasoning through which people understand their ventures as part of a mutually beneficial project of freedom from a constraining status quo*. Entrepreneurial imaginaries, we emphasize, are not specific ideas or enterprises, which are tremendously varied and heterogeneous across US history. Rather entrepreneurial imaginaries embody the moral principles and reasoning behind why some forms and practices come to be seen as threats to liberty, and others are imagined to be virtuous because they are understood as freeing individuals and society from those constraints. Entrepreneurial imaginaries are made manifest in prevailing models of enterprise and political movements that are imagined as promoting mutually beneficial liberty in particular historical situations. As such, they underlie public discourse on the virtues of some forms and enterprise and the threats of others. In the lived experience of the imaginary, individual political and economic practices created frictions between the ideal of positive liberty to pursue given ends and the reality of threats to negative liberties that these pursuits created.

The dynamic and evolving nature of the forms that entrepreneurial imaginaries take, we contend, arises from the fact that over time, as any particular model or belief becomes institutionalized, it increasingly comes to be understood as imposing a constraint on freedom rather than serving as a source of liberation. Drawing on Berlin, we contend that forms once deemed virtuous for promising to free stakeholders from a status quo can come to be understood as undermining freedom as they become institutionalized. Models once understood as virtuous commercial expressions of "freedom to" come to be understood as commercial vice as they come to be seen as constraining. Tensions inherent within the practice of freedom hence unleash a dynamic friction within free society that drives change.

Democracy and capitalism, in this account, are alternative social forms through which these moral tensions are worked out, propelling the organization of the economy and polity over time. Within markets, new organizational models and practices arise that compete with older models not only on the narrow basis of economic utility but also for the claims they represent about moral virtue. Within democratic practice, political movements coalesce around the moral framing enabled by modern entrepreneurial imaginaries, and electoral politics distill these situated moral concerns and claims into platforms and policies. Rather than irreconcilable worldviews, these moral tensions within and between capitalism and democracy constitute the intrinsic dynamics of freedom's frictions.

In the sections that follow, we sketch out a synthesis of American business history that uses our construct as the primary interpretive device. A summary of our sketch can be found in Table 15.1.

Entrepreneurial Society 1.0

The positive language of liberty took center stage in the preambles to the America's Revolutionary era foundational documents. The Declaration of Independence announced, "Life, Liberty, and the pursuit of Happiness" as inalienable rights, and the Constitution-writers justified the document's necessity by claiming it would "secure the Blessings of Liberty to ourselves and our Posterity." These expressions stressed the future-oriented promise of prosperity that free people might create through the exercise of positive freedom. But beyond the flourish of their opening lines, these texts more often glanced backward in enumerating violations of their negative freedoms experienced through colonial-era tyrannies and forward in implicit allusions to the dangers of future tyrannies possible without a sufficiently powerful but circumscribed government. In their Janus-faced expressions of freedom, the documents embodied the moral language at the heart of the Revolutionary movement and the emergent entrepreneurial imaginary.

During the late eighteenth century, the language of moral virtue infused commercial and political behavior in ways that moved Americans to exercise their independence, crystalizing a new entrepreneurial imaginary. This cauldron of liberatory politics sharpened latent moral principles that had emerged gradually over the colonial period in the daily practices of economic activity. In the 169 years between colonization at Jamestown and the Declaration of Independence, American colonizers developed two legitimized models of entrepreneurship each formed in its own distinct way on principles of political and economic liberty.

In one legitimized model, landed entrepreneurs conceived of their independence as based in their ownership of tangible property. Their capital consisted of land and human beings, property deemed alienable and collateralizable by

Table 15.1 **The United States' entrepreneurial imaginaries**

	Entrepreneurial society 1.0	*Entrepreneurial society 2.0*	*Entrepreneurial society 3.0*
Period	1770s–1870s	1880s–1960s	1970s–present
Freedom from . . .	Arbitrary governance	Isolated individualism	Stifling organization
Freedom to . . .	Individual independence	Associative independence	Creative independence
Belief in . . .	Property	Association	Innovation
Business model 1	Planter	Cooperative	Activist entrepreneur
Business model 2	Independent artisan	Hierarchy of expertise	Small business
Internal tensions	Landed vs. embodied property	Mutual vs. hierarchical organization	Innovation vs. disruption
Decline	End of Western dispossession, deskilling Labor	Stagnation, alienation	Chaos?Inequality/immobility?

colonial America's distinctly credit-oriented legal environment.[10] These men created value by laboring in fields with their families or enslaving people who did and managing their way to market success. They conceived of their plantations and farms as enterprises. While they often pursued safety-first agriculture, they sought meaningful growth through experimentation and marketing, eagerly testing and adopting new crops, techniques, and management practices, and expanding through the acquisition of more land.[11] Thomas Jefferson became the prophet and embodiment of this kind of landed independence. He conceived of America as a nation built on the efforts of independent planter patriarchs and smallholders, working for themselves and serving no master.

Artisans and merchants forged the second entrepreneurial model by producing and trading their way to market success. Their capital consisted primarily of stock, ships, and tools of the trade, but more importantly, they also conceived of an inalienable property in the self. It was their embodied skill and creativity that gave their stocks and ships value. These entrepreneurs valorized human proficiency and discipline as the foundation for independence. Benjamin Franklin, master printer and philosopher of American entrepreneurialism, was the prophet of personal diligence, discipline, and expertise and popularized these commercial virtues in his prolific and popular writing. Franklin's *Poor Richard's Almanac,* full of reprintable aphorisms espousing the benefits of hard work, and *The Way to Wealth,* his guide for young people, instructed his audience to cultivate industry, frugality, and prudence.[12] For Franklin, these qualities of self-mastery formed the foundations for a citizenry sufficiently commercially independent to be capable of self-governance. *The Way to Wealth* gained global renown as a practical polemic and influenced practical economic thought long after his death. By 1850, printers disseminated 1,100 separate editions into the public domain and translated the guide into 26 languages.[13]

Though these types of enterprise had been important cornerstones of the colonial American economy, in the years after the Seven Years War, these models were infused with sharper moral meaning as imperial policies increasingly encroached on colonizers' negative freedoms. Landed entrepreneurs responded with outrage at the imposition of the Proclamation Line in 1763, which prevented colonizers from dispossessing Indigenous people of their land and cultivating it as productive farms and plantations. Imperial officials designed the Proclamation line as a boundary along colonial America's Western edge to placate their Indigenous allies and stem the rolling tide of unruly settlement beyond imperial control.[14] Artisans and merchants objected to the increasing enforcement of rules that had long been on the books as well as the imposition of new ones. Stamps, molasses, sugar, and tea became the daily material manifestations of parliamentary overreach that contributed to colonists' discontent. In the new post-1763 environment, colonizers began to interpret these developments not just as economic infringements but as moral violations of their negative freedoms as citizens. The intolerability of the Crown's actions found expression in the natural rights of citizens to improve the property they held in land and in themselves: farmers could no longer occupy new lands, printers could not print, sailors could not sail, merchants could not trade, and assemblies could not govern as they had.[15]

In response to these perceived overreaches, American colonizers amplified strands of politically motivated moral reasoning to imbue the two existing models of enterprise with profound moral meaning. Drawing on 1720s era political rhetoric articulated by Trenchard and Gordon in *Cato's Letters* and other "country" critics, American writers articulated that centralizing power dangerously corrupted, which made independent property owners, especially farmers, the ideal republican citizens. While a fringe perspective in Britain, this morally charged political rhetoric became increasingly mainstream in America, where Revolutionary newspapers and pamphlets often cited *Cato's Letters* to articulate their own virtue and Britons' vices.[16] Although slower to develop, Revolutionary-era writers also articulated notions of a broadening base of political virtue that extended to artisans. Though he himself did not easily abandon hierarchical notions of social order, Franklin's colonial-era writings began to redefine independent artisans and others among the middling sort as potential vessels of virtue. These people, he reasoned, might claim a legitimate place in an emerging America through habitually practiced industry and frugality.[17] Americans articulated that their representative assemblies had long functioned to protect these virtuous peoples' positive freedoms to colonize, form enterprises, and reap the rewards of their efforts. In this view, freed from the restraints arbitrarily and, in their view, unconstitutionally imposed by Parliamentary interference, a larger group of white, male Americans could pursue entrepreneurial opportunities.[18]

Colonists built their political logic of independence on a common belief in property in land and the self as the twin pillars of value-creation. While farmers and artisans engaged in very different material worlds, the language of liberty and the principle of property worked to blur the sharp edges of distinction into a mutually intelligible national community founded on common values. Creating value transcended purely intrinsic property by requiring the will of human beings to envision and value opportunities, allocate and reconfigure resources, and legitimize novelty.[19] For this reason, advocates of the competing models of enterprise legitimized the alternative model as central to the practice of the entrepreneurial imaginary. Jefferson highlighted the virtue of merchants and artisans when he spoke of a nation, "spread over a wide and fruitful land, traversing all the seas with the rich productions of their industry" in his first inaugural address.[20] Similarly, Franklin's demographic study of colonial population growth argued that land supported the explosive growth of America's population and industry.[21] While these men built their own economic and political power on distinct foundations, they constructed an America with a shared view of the importance of property in land and the self. Though these different bases of virtue created frictions, the imaginary created credible appeals to unity that took shape in Washington's Farewell Address and the optimism and political calm that characterized Monroe's presidency.

Initially, the American Revolution did not radically change colonial-era organizational forms. Instead, it created the circumstances in which American entrepreneurs increasingly used governance as a tool to achieve their economic goals. As entrepreneurial farmers and land speculators began pursuing opportunities beyond the land resources they immediately controlled, they turned to their state to help facilitate their efforts.[22] In the years after the Revolution, American speculators pressured state and federal governments to legitimize their competing land claims and formulate regulations around land prices, sales terms, and taxation favorable to the consolidation of property in land.[23] In one example from the early 1800s, expansion-oriented entrepreneurs acquired Mississippi stock issued in the Yazoo claims settlement and redeemed it at land offices in Alabama and Mississippi for property newly dispossessed from the Creek, Cherokee, Choctaw, and Chickasaw.[24] In cases like these, the newly established republican governments aided entrepreneurship that facilitated dispossession.

Concurrently, merchant-underwriters took on new risks to support the high-risk ventures of the fledgling American state.[25] In turn, the nascent federal government stepped in to guarantee the validity of existing merchant practice and guarantee contracts in a way that legitimized property in land and the self that could form the basis of credit to a debtor nation.[26] Thus, a cycle emerged in which participation in democratic governance enhanced entrepreneurial activity. In turn, entrepreneurial activity guaranteed independence rooted in property in land and the self. This property allowed entrepreneurs to realign resources in ways that reimagined the world around them and created value for their societies, a common good. This public-mindedness, in turn, validated the emergent entrepreneurial imaginary that linked property to American citizenship and democratic participation.

Americans launched a new entrepreneurial society built on the broad principle of liberty founded on property, but the contradictions inherent in this entrepreneurial imaginary of propertied independence increasingly tested the fledgling society. The notion of property in the self created particular tension. Franklin described property in the self in terms of the wealth accruing to a person due to his or—occasionally for *feme sole* traders—her diligence and skill. These inalienable features appealed to people enslaved in the newly emancipated America. The notion of an inalienable self resonated with enslaved people's conceptions of their "soul value," a term coined by Daina Ramey Berry to encapsulate the deeply held stores of self-worth that sustained enslaved people amid the indignities of slavery.[27] Enslaved people drew on their own conceptions of property in the self to self-emancipate and produce for themselves, their communities, and the market.[28] For some, this entrepreneurial activity provided a path to legally sanctioned freedom.[29] For most, the terms of trade benefited enslavers such that enslaved people's entrepreneurial activity ultimately supported unfreedom.[30] Despite the efforts of enslavers to deny the legitimacy of enslaved people's property in the self, abolitionists rejected this as an unfounded distinction.

Thus, a fundamental disagreement about the nature of property in the self as a basis of independence festered at the heart of entrepreneurial society 1.0. Initially obscured by the broad entrepreneurial imaginary of the freedom to pursue propertied independence, this contestation continued to plague Americans as the nation expanded. In reality, few inhabitants of the United States could legitimately hope to achieve the dream of property in the self or land. Chattel slavery undermined enslaved people's rights to property in the self. *Feme covert* rendered a woman's property in land and the self the legal property of her husband. Wage workers of all sorts including white men, women, enslaved people, people with disabilities, and immigrants struggled to create the value needed to claim the independence that undergirded political participation.[31] Yet, the entrepreneurial imaginary of propertied independence contained sufficient flexibility and truth that many Americans held hope that they too could enjoy the economic prosperity it envisioned.

The friction between the two business models fanned the flames of political tension as some Americans increasingly understood their differing business models as manifestations of irreconcilable and regional conflicts. From its origins in the late-1830s antislavery Liberty Party, the Free Soil Movement built its political logic on the virtues of property in the self, but applied this principle to both the planter and artisan model. The movement valorized workers' liberty to freely contract their labor in ways that facilitated capital accumulation and upward mobility. Initially, the insurgent political movement formed a third party that attracted adherents from both the Whig and Democratic parties by drawing on the Democrats' egalitarian strain and the Whigs' Conscience strand.[32] In the 1848 election, the Free Soil Party won 12 congressional seats and a Senate seat, upsetting the balance and ushering in a period of political upheaval in the 1850s. The Free Soil Movement caused panic among Southern planters by undermining the logic of the planter business model that equated landed property with the freedom to enslave. These fears triggered disunion rhetoric as Southern Democrats accused the movement of advocating disunion, but also began to describe disunion as the only way to preserve their constitutionally inscribed freedom to deprive enslaved people of their liberty.[33] By the 1860 election, the Republican party embraced the logic of free soil and the Democrats embraced the logic of enslaver-liberty setting the stage for armed conflict.

The Civil War manifested as the ultimate contestation of property in the self, but its resolution paved the way for Americans to question the emancipatory claims at the heart of entrepreneurial imaginary 1.0. Toward the end of the war, Lincoln summarized the connection between regional business models and their plausible foundations in liberty but ultimately contradictory nature observing:

> The world has never had a good definition of the word liberty, and the American people, just now, are much in want of one. We all declare for liberty; but in using the same *word* we do not all mean the same *thing*. With some the word liberty may mean for each man to do as he pleases with himself, and the product of his labor; while with others the same word may mean for some men to do as they please with other men, and the product of other men's labor. Here are two, not only different, but incompatible things, called by the same name—liberty. And it follows that each of the things is, by the respective parties, called by two different and incompatible names—liberty and tyranny.[34]

Union loyalists fought a war based on the belief that the preservation of the Union best guaranteed their hope that free laborers might seek the rewards of property in the self.[35] In contrast, Confederates asserted a competing notion, property *of* the self. They believed in chattel and a slave-owning republic built on the belief that American liberty meant some people must be free to violate others' negative freedom from the tyranny of slavery.[36] These tensions at the heart of entrepreneurial society 1.0 resolved in the reassertion of property *in* the self and the rejection of property *of* the self. Yet, as property in the self triumphed, seemingly validating the emancipatory claims of positive freedom at the heart of the entrepreneurial imaginary, the value created by property in the self seemed increasingly elusive to the Union loyalists who had fought a war to legitimize it. To the south, Union victory affirmed that planters' freedom to enact their business model could not violate enslaved people's freedom from enslavement. Confederates decried this constraint as an unconstitutional violation of their liberties that, in their eyes, shattered the foundations of Planters' embodiment of the entrepreneurial imaginary, leaving them to seek a new path forward.[37]

Entrepreneurial Society 2.0

"No one, surely, proposes to revive the little business monarch who brooded watchfully over every operation in factory and office, calling his workingmen by their pet names," wrote journalist Walter Lippmann in his 1914 book *Drift and Mastery: An Attempt to Diagnose the Current Unrest.*[38] The book's title projected its thesis that old forms of democracy and capitalist practice—the unplanned drift of a society built on narrow self-interest and competition—could not achieve the promise of democracy in a complex, cosmopolitan world. Freedom came with a positive vision of mastery—a society that capitalized on association, cooperation, and organization in ways that empowered individuals to achieve things they could not accomplish on their own. Any lingering "current unrest" (as referred to in the subtitle) arose from the brooding "little business monarch" who was stubbornly bound to old ideas and old customs of atomized individual freedom. Lippmann's arguments reflected a new faith in the entrepreneurial freedom to associate and organize.

The new vision of associative America emerged during a period when the Revolutionary-Era entrepreneurial imaginary based on the liberating virtues of property became increasingly difficult to maintain. As Americans filled Western land rendered cheap through entrepreneurial dispossession, land became scarce, realizing founding-era fears that landless dependence undermined political and economic stability. The increasing scarcity of real property in the late nineteenth century made it more expensive, making mortgage loans more common—and more onerous for farmers as commodity prices fell.[39] The moral virtues attained by building property in oneself also became increasingly unattainable, as internal frontiers closed along with Western ones. Institutional and technological changes made it difficult for ordinary citizens to become independent tradesmen or proprietors.[40] Decline in the institutions of forced household labor on which some small proprietors had previously depended, and the skyrocketing costs of property and capital required for competing in markets, drove growing numbers into wage labor. By the 1890s, the expansion of capital-intensive industries combined with the Panic of 1893 and consequent price wars triggered a merger movement that left a greater share of business (and laborers) in a smaller number of hands.[41] Older forms of entrepreneurship persisted in some form, especially in parts of the country sheltered from these forces or where small proprietors managed to coordinate their strategic response.[42] But the broad trends in land and labor heightened moral worries that the Revolutionary-era pursuit of individual independence was no longer attainable.

As shifting material realities made autarkic understandings of freedom seem unrealistic, Americans critiqued the moral reasoning on which it was based. By the 1870s, Americans began to interpret older understandings of independence as a weight that mired them in toil without sufficient reward. Writing in 1888, Edward Bellamy's *Looking Backward* explained "Nearly every member was in a position of galling personal dependence upon others as to the very means of life, the poor upon the rich, employed upon employer, women upon men, children upon parents." In pursuit of individual independence, the new age of entrepreneurs had built a society of dependence characterized by "ruinous competition," and deskilled, degraded labor.[43] The Gilded Age revealed a distorted form of independence rendered grotesque by the excesses of hyper-rich robber barons. In this context, the once-buoyant dream of individual independence received increasing moral and political scrutiny.

Critics not only disparaged the hyper-individualistic moral vision as antiquated but also began to articulate a new entrepreneurial imaginary that interpreted organization as a positive exercise of Americans' freedom to associate in ways they believed best served their interests. Faith in property and individual independence as cornerstones of democratic freedom and capitalist enterprise did not fade entirely. Rather, these were recast as attainable not through autarkic isolation but through meaningful and mutually beneficial association of various kinds.[44] By the late nineteenth century, Americans increasingly experimented with the promise of association by embracing a variety of new forms of organization. Among other sources of inspiration, they drew on early and mid-nineteenth century utopian visions of individual sacrifice directed by disciplined management to promote human flourishing embodied in communities like New Harmony, Oneida, and Shaker societies.[45] In labor, industry, and democratic politics, Americans saw their positive freedom to associate as the key to building a free and favorable future. From these varied experiments, two models of entrepreneurial organization emerged: cooperatives and hierarchical corporations. Building on early utopian models of collective endeavor, these emergent business practices deemphasized the political virtues of autarkic individualism and instead embraced the political virtue of association.

Entrepreneurs formed the cooperative model based on the notion of diffuse power for mutual aid. As farmers and laborers faced a market with limited opportunities to avoid economic dependence, entrepreneurial proponents of cooperatives reasoned that pooling their resources could enable them to flourish together in ways that eluded them when they acted individually. While cooperatives did not reject management or expertise, they did make managers accountable to members and rejected the notion that workers lacked the ability to make savvy business decisions. The Knights of Labor, the leading labor union in the 1880s, made, "abolish[ing] as rapidly as possible, the wage system, substituting co-operation therefore," a leading part of their platform.[46]

Entrepreneurial cooperatives emerged broadly across the American economy advocating a radical transformation in the organization of enterprise. Leaders of the Knights of Labor including Leonora Barry and John Samuel argued for cooperatives and helped form them in diverse settings including cigar factories, print shops, and domestic work.[47] Agricultural and consumer cooperatives also emerged based on agitation from the Granger and Farmers' Alliance movements. Cooperative ventures like the Texas Farmers' Alliance, the Illinois Farmer's Mutual Benefit Association, and the California Fruit Growers' Exchange worked to establish centralized marketing and storage facilities, educate their members on new techniques, purchase machinery, set prices, and leverage the power of scale economies. Successful cooperatives like the Illinois State Dairymen's Association pooled $300 million in capital. In general, these cooperatives promoted equality among members that gave large and small landholders access to similar services designed to help them exploit new opportunities.[48] Americans also increasingly organized into fraternal organizations to deliver goods and services of mutual benefit. By 1910, one-third of adult men belonged to fraternal organizations that delivered a wide range of services, particularly in the areas of health care and social services.[49]

Enterprises built on the cooperative model of entrepreneurship could be innovative. For example, members owned and controlled building associations that provided increasingly innovative forms of mortgage lending to their middle- and working-class members. They forged financial practices that eventually became the long-term mortgage that made home ownership accessible for many. At a time when commercial banks rarely lent to working-class borrowers and offered only 50 percent loan-to-value ratios and three- to five-year maturities on mortgages, building and loans allowed members to finance home ownership over extended time frames at higher loan-to-value ratios.[50] Cooperative enterprise provided an attractive path forward to farmers and laborers who felt shunted into a state of dependence amid the crush of deflation, low-skilled positions, and low wages in the late nineteenth century.

Entrepreneurial organizers with faith in the hierarchical model of organization emerged in the same era as an alternative to the cooperative model of organization. Propelled by a belief in the promise of social, scientific, and technological innovation, hierarchical organizers worked to align all aspects of an enterprise to serve the top-down goals of the venture. The hierarchical model put expertise at its core and relied on the energy and effort of workers to serve that goal.[51] In business, Frederick Winslow Taylor's scientific management and proponents of a softer human relations movement devoted significant attention to improving managerial organization to promote efficiency. Their efforts concentrated planning, attempted to standardize labor, transformed laborers' relationship to time, and spawned the rapid expansion of the professional and managerial class.[52] A hierarchical model also emerged in labor. The American Federation of Labor (AFL), the leading labor union at the end of the nineteenth century, advocated a disciplined top-down approach in which planned strikes served unifying goals including higher wages and an eight-hour workday. The AFL zealously advocated for members' cultivation of the self by including only skilled workers among its rank and file, effectively excluding many women, Black, and immigrant laborers to advance a vision of cultivated self-worth through labor.[53]

Not everyone bought into the promise of association as the organizing principle for cultivating freedom. Prior to World War I, conflicts between labor and capital did turn violent in ways that suggested that new imaginaries could not work to ameliorate tensions between the dynamics of capitalism and the tenets of democracy. Wealthy industrialists like Rockefeller and Carnegie and financiers like J. P. Morgan wielded political and even police powers in ways that outstripped the principles of free societies. Meanwhile, the Industrial Workers of the World undertook a sustained strategic sabotage campaign designed to attack private property in an outright rejection of the capitalist foundations at the heart of the emergent imaginary. Indeed, clashes between American business and American labor were among the most violent in the industrialized world. Events like the 1886 Haymarket bombing, the battle of Homestead, the Pullman strike, and the 1914 Ludlow massacre, along with less well-known events like the 1887 massacre of striking Black sugar workers in Louisiana highlight that moral imaginaries were never completely divorced from pragmatic tests of material reality.[54]

Conflicts manifested not only from people and organizations that rejected the imaginary altogether but also from tensions within the imaginary. Unlike in the previous era, which obscured contradiction leaving these tensions to simmer slowly, the two business models that predominated in Entrepreneurial Society 2.0 created frictions from the start. The hierarchical model emphasized associative action as a response to relative human incapacity, while the cooperative model suggested a confidence in humans' ability to rise to new challenges. While most Americans shared the view that their best opportunity for prosperity lay in the exercise of their "freedom to associate," their rationales for and ideal forms of association seemed contradictory. Cooperatives and hierarchical organizations invoked the same associative moral reasoning, but the models came into conflict with one another as they became embodied in business practices. While Americans believed in the promises of association, they feared the dangers of its excesses and integrated this into their moral reasoning. Anti-monopoly sentiment pitted the cooperatives against the hierarchical model as each accused the other of monopolistic practices that violated the operation of free markets. Critics from cooperatives accused consolidated hierarchical firms of embodying monopoly by inflating prices and threatening rivals while hierarchical corporations accused the cooperatives of hypocrisy. Defending the cooperatives against their critics, Ben Terrell of the Farmer's Alliance announced, "If it is a monopoly we shall create a grand one. It will be a philanthropic monopoly. It will distribute wealth among the people." Both business models argued for their own virtue and their competitor's vice by drawing on a shared moral rhetoric that valorized the freedom to associate to realize the promises of a new age of innovation.

The tensions between the two models of freedom based on organized association and their implications for democracy were perhaps best reflected in the debate between Walter Lippmann and John Dewey. In *Public Opinion*, Lippmann argued that the early republican ideals of the well-informed citizen could not hold in a complex modern society where information overwhelmed the citizenry and, even more importantly, filtered through a distorting media.[55] The promise of organization was that it relied on specialization and expertise to make sense of complex information. This organizational form required citizens to relinquish decision-making over much of public life and leave it to experts. Hierarchical organization was therefore perfectly in line with a vision of democratic freedom. Dewey took a more optimistic view of human capacity and coordination. In *The Public and Its Problems*, Dewey argued that the public had the capacity to make rational judgments about the world, but this required the kind of engagement and association through debate and involvement that allowed citizens to develop as free individuals.[56] Far from removing decision-making from ordinary citizens, forms of association and organization that involved them in debate and governance formed precisely the kind of association that cultivated freedom.

To realize the promise of association swaths of Americans rallied around tangible political movements that transcended straightforward party politics. Shared belief in sacrificial association coalesced in the entrepreneurial imaginary, which defined the field within which Americans could engage in legitimate contestation both politically and economically. Just as Americans embodied the entrepreneurial imaginary in particular forms of economic organization, Americans responded to the imaginary in their political lives by envisioning new ways of influencing their political system. The Populists formed a broad-based political movement supporting farmers, wage laborers, and middle-class activists. Their movement built on the cooperative vision in economic organization by advocating for broader technical education, and government regulation of industry to realize the potential of new technology and infrastructure.[57] The Progressive movement also found a wide base of support, especially from middle-class reformers, across the political spectrum for broad and ambitious ideas like trust-busting, expanding suffrage, alleviating poverty, and environmentalism.[58]

While these movements transcended party politics, large swaths of Americans rallied behind the Populist and Progressive movements and their ideas made their way into electoral politics. Political actors transformed these broad movements into tangible political goals like soft money, nationalized trust-busting, suffrage, and government regulation. They contested these goals in key elections in 1896 and 1912. The election of 1896 brought Populist ideas into electoral politics by pitting hard-money, high-tariff, Republican William McKinley against bimetallic, pro-government-intervention, Democratic-Populist candidate William Jennings Bryan. The election of 1912 made the Progressive movement mainstream by pitting trust-busing Progressive candidate Theodore Roosevelt against Democrat Woodrow Wilson's New Freedom and Republican William Howard Taft. Americans broadly debated these and other issues over which they remained bitterly divided, but they invoked a shared moral understanding, asserting their freedom to associate to protect themselves from violations of their liberties.[59]

Amid the rising tide of organization, a positive role for government in entrepreneurship emerged from the tensions between Americans' entrepreneurial organizations.[60] In the late nineteenth century, America's democratic government had primarily taken an anti-trust stance informed by assumptions emergent in 1.0 of independent proprietors engaged in competition. Late-nineteenth century antimonopoly legislation created opportunities for litigation that broke up some large corporate trusts and monopolies, while also challenging small business cooperatives' efforts, and undermining efforts to unionize.[61] Louis Brandeis' vision, summarized in *Other People's Money* and popularized as Wilson's New Freedom articulated a different vision for the relationship between democratic governance and entrepreneurial organizations. Brandeis' New Freedom manifested a new accommodationist stance for democratic government that brought cooperatives, associations, corporate hierarchies, and labor hierarchies, into an uncomfortable détente.[62]

The events of the 1920s and 1930s created a more institutionalized relationship between capital, labor, and democratic government. The rise of welfare capitalist practices in the 1920s created a model that promised industrial workers many of the benefits that mutualism and fraternalism had once promised including insurance and credit, while denying them the control rights that the cooperative form allowed its members.[63] The New Deal, in many ways, addressed the economic crisis of the 1930s and war in the 1940s, by codifying organization and expertise at a new scale in ways that promoted the role of the state in the economy. In the triumph of hierarchical managerial capitalism, an accommodation emerged in which labor hierarchies allowed government intervention and increasingly ceded control and accepted management's right to manage in exchange for corporate benefits.[64] While labor unions continued to agitate and strike in the post-war years, they primarily limited their demands to issues of pay and the right to organize, issues well within the circumscribed limits of entrepreneurial society 2.0's imaginary.[65]

Entrepreneurial Society 3.0

Between the 1950s and the 1980s, faith in the ability of rationalized organizations to enrich the exercise of liberty eroded, making way for a new entrepreneurial imaginary based in the capacity of individuals to innovate. While belief in the kind of tech startup culture that infuses business and social rhetoric today came about as part of this shift, Entrepreneurship 3.0 had its roots in earlier critiques of the stifling character of large-scale organizations and the liberationist social movements of the 1960s. Entrepreneurial freedom of the innovation sort came to be clothed in the Schumpeterian rhetoric of "creative destruction," of "disruption," and of a style that looked upon notions of "social order" and "organization" with skepticism if not outright disdain.

In retrospect, the erosion of faith in effective rational organization as the principle for maintaining freedom can be traced to a critique of the New Deal order. Conservative intellectuals like Friedrich Hayek worried that the growing American faith in planning by experts was not an aid to liberty but was fundamentally undermining it.[66] Beginning as early as the interwar period but accelerating in the post-World War II years, they embraced and promoted an idea of entrepreneurship rooted in a "free market system" separated or even in opposition to a meaningful role for the state.[67] Intellectual and cultural critiques of organization quickly emerged from the Left as well. In the 1950s, critiques of the mediocrity and uniformity of the "organization man" became increasingly common. William Whyte coined this term, simultaneously popularizing the phrase and deriding corporate culture for eroding individuality and creativity in the pursuit of a homogenized workforce.[68] Other authors, such as Sloan Wilson in his novel *The Man in the Grey Flannel Suit,* echoed this critique, portraying the soul-crushing nature of white-collar work and the stifling effects of conformity on the individual.[69]

These arguments were part of a broader intellectual critique that challenged the status quo in postwar America. Sociologist C. Wright Mills, for example, argued in his book *White Collar* that the rise of the corporate bureaucracy had created a new class of managers and professionals who were disconnected from the working class and the political process.[70] He saw this new class as a threat to democracy and individual freedom, and called for a more participatory and democratic society. The German-American philosopher and political theorist Herbert Marcuse crafted similar critiques, arguing that a pervasive and oppressive system of social control characterized modern society, which he called "repressive tolerance."[71] Marcuse believed that this system was maintained through the manipulation of consciousness and the suppression of dissent, and he called for a radical restructuring of society that would break free from the constraints of the existing social order. Still, elite intellectual grumbling did not constitute an alternative imaginary nor did it provide a business model for how it could be manifest. As late as 1967, John Kenneth Galbraith could still credibly argue that "the entrepreneur no longer exists as an individual person in the mature industrial enterprise." Echoing broad mid-twentieth century faith in organization, Galbraith suggested that entrepreneurship was now part of a "technostructure" embodied in "all who bring specialized knowledge, talent, or experience to group decision making."[72]

It was not until "activist entrepreneurs" in the 1960s and 1970s translated liberationist countercultural movements that an emergent entrepreneurial imaginary based in the virtues of innovation came to be manifested in a business model. As historian Joshua Davis has shown, the social movements of the period spawned a host of new ventures that embraced entrepreneurship as a way to build commercial enterprises based on the values of the causes on which they drew.[73] These included African-American owned enterprises and real estate developers, feminist bookstores, and health food groceries that positioned themselves explicitly in opposition to corporate organizational values and practices.[74] For example, Baltimore-based Diana Press was founded in 1972 with the goal of "freeing women entirely from male printing establishments." In 1978, John Mackey and Renee Lawson founded the food store that would later be renamed Whole Foods to "make our country and world a better place to live." Mackey would later explain, "While the Vietnam War was foremost in many of our minds, human rights, food safety, and environmental deterioration were major concerns as well." The activist entrepreneurship model hence viewed entrepreneurial innovation as a means of social change. Early activist entrepreneurs saw their enterprises as growing directly out of the movements that inspired them, and their practices—the language used, their dress, and their ideas about mission-driven enterprises—were designed to distinguish them from the perceived soullessness of large corporations.[75]

In pursuing these ends, many activist entrepreneurs aimed to draw on the stream of the liberal tradition that saw a positive role for government in unleashing entrepreneurial energies.[76] For instance, in the late 1960s and 1970s, civil rights leaders appealed to local as well as federal government to provide financial and advisory resources for seeding minority-owned businesses and spurring urban entrepreneurship.[77] They also sought regulatory redress for institutions that had inhibited entrepreneurial venturing in underserved communities. For instance, the Community Reinvestment Act of 1977 aimed to reverse the long history of FHA-supported redlining that led to systematic disinvestment in minority communities.[78]

By then, a competing model had emerged that also promised innovative entrepreneurship as a way to disrupt the status quo and drive change. In the 1970s and 1980s, small business attracted increasing attention as policymakers, academics, and the public at large began to embrace it as a response to the decline of traditional manufacturing industries and the stagnating competitiveness of big business.[79] As these industries contracted, many workers turned to entrepreneurship as a means of creating their own jobs and economic opportunities.[80]

Though the "small business" movement gained momentum in the 1970s and 1980s, its political roots stretched back to the New Deal. During the Great Depression and World War II, associations representing small businesses complained that government policies and contracting unfairly favored large firms. As a concession to these concerns, the Truman Administration created the Small Defense Plants Administration during the Korean War to support small manufacturers' bids for defense contracts. The Eisenhower administration had sought to close down the SDPA along with the Reconstruction Finance Corporation, the New Deal era agency established to make loans to failing banks and large firms, but Republicans realized that they did not have sufficient political support across the business community for such a retrenchment. Established in 1953, the Small Business Administration was created as a political concession to garner support for politically important subsets of the business community.

In the 1950s and 1960s, small business was thus primarily understood as a political lobby. But as large industrial firms faltered during the economic stagnation of the 1970s, small business came to take on a mystique as more human-centered drivers of creativity and innovation. By the 1980s, individual entrepreneurs became celebrated increasingly as heroes and role models, and their stories of success became a fixture of popular culture.[81] The creative authenticity of entrepreneurship was formulated precisely to embrace everything that the "organization man" was not. "The entrepreneur is a misfit—he's out of step," explained the *Wall Street Journal*, that voice of counterculture. "Corporate executives get to the top by offending the least number of people, while entrepreneurs get to the top by stepping over those in the way." The Journal did its part to produce the archetype, explaining to the public in an extended 1986 report that entrepreneurs are "the mavericks, dreamers, and loners whose rough edges and uncompromising need to do it their own way set them in sharp contrast to senior executives in major American corporations."[82]

Small business entrepreneurs were lionized in the neoliberal political rhetoric of the Reagan years to put a human face on increasingly dogmatic ideas about free markets and in contrast to the goliaths of big business and big government. Reagan made these optimistic declarations of entrepreneurial capacity the centerpieces of his presidential campaigns in 1980 and 1984. "Freedom and incentives unleash the drive and entrepreneurial genius that are the core of human progress," Reagan declared during his second inaugural. "We have begun to increase the rewards for work, savings, and investment; reduce the increase in the cost and size of government and its interference in people's lives."[83] As the quote indicates, the small business model was based in a version of the entrepreneurial imaginary that emphasized negative liberties, not one that supported positive freedom. Indeed, the Reagan and Bush administration's primary entrepreneurial policies involved cutting taxes and reducing regulations rather than actively supporting small business. Ironically, funding to the SBA actually declined in the 1980s and the agency was almost closed.[84]

The small business model was based on shifts in government policy and corporate practices that ultimately left a growing number of Americans much more exposed to entrepreneurial risk. Critiques of the size and costs of large industrial firms led to a spate of calls for such firms to be led more entrepreneurially. CEOs were celebrated for "restructuring" their corporations by narrowing them down to focus on "core competencies" and hyper-lean cost structures. In effect, this meant that employment at large public corporations became increasingly precarious as corporations increasingly recategorized workers as independent "entrepreneurs." The growth of "independent contract" workers in effect also meant corporations increasingly shifted risks onto small businesses. The number of publicly traded corporations declined steeply, as "entrepreneurial leaders" sought the freedom to operate as private entities beyond the watchfulness of the public eye.

At the heart of Entrepreneurship 3.0's belief in innovation and disruption as expressions of freedom is a rejection of the status quo and a willingness to challenge established norms and conventions. This is seen as a necessary prerequisite for achieving autonomy and self-determination, and for creating a society that is more dynamic, innovative, and inclusive. It is also seen as a way to challenge the concentration of wealth and power in the hands of a few, and to promote greater economic and social equality.[85]

These goals sharpen the contradictions and ironies of Entrepreneurship 3.0. The mythology of entrepreneurial autonomy as envisioned in 3.0 embraced a suspicion of all forms of large organization, including government. Yet, it depended heavily on the state for policies and subsidies for its emergence. As Margaret O'Mara shows, Silicon Valley entrepreneurs espoused a techno-libertarian ethos despite depending on funding and programs from Washington, D.C., to produce the technology infrastructure and basic research that built the Valley.[86] Likewise, in the 1980s and 1990s, the US government played a significant role in supporting the development of startup culture and small business culture. This was in part a response to the economic challenges of the era, including high levels of unemployment and a decline in traditional manufacturing industries.

One way that the government supported small businesses and startups was through tax incentives and other financial incentives. This included the creation of Small Business Investment Companies (SBICs), which provided financing and support to small businesses and startups. The government also introduced tax breaks for small businesses, including the creation of the Small Business Administration (SBA), which provided loans and technical assistance to small businesses. The federal government also introduced programs to support small businesses and startups through regulatory and policy changes that made it easier for entrepreneurs to start and grow their businesses. This included the passage of the Bayh-Dole Act, which allowed universities and other research institutions to license their intellectual property to private companies, and the creation of the National Venture Capital Association (NVCA), which advocated for policies that supported entrepreneurship and venture capital investment, including unjustifiably favorable tax treatment of "carried interest."[87]

Even more ironic is the way in which its proponents used the rhetoric of entrepreneurial freedom and equality to justify increasing levels of economic inequality and declining prospects for social mobility. By 2020, "entrepreneur" was used to describe both Elon Musk, the richest man in the world, and precarious subcontractors like Uber drivers and temporary workers. Silicon Valley could still maintain its shiny glow as the Emerald City of entrepreneurial opportunity while its anchor tenants come under increasing scrutiny by the Justice Department for monopolistic practices. What has arguably become one of the most routinized business processes in the economy—that of starting up a firm—continues to embody the promise of innovation in an increasingly hierarchical society.[88]

Entrepreneurship 4.0?

The pursuit of particular kinds of freedom rests at the heart of each version of the entrepreneurial imaginary. As we have demonstrated, entrepreneurial imaginaries have funneled Americans' industry into exercises of positive freedom to pursue particular kinds of entrepreneurial ventures. These imaginaries have allowed people engaged in contradictory projects to imagine themselves as part of a joint American pursuit. In each version, contradictions challenged the loose entrepreneurial imaginary, while skeptics rejected it outright, but the imaginary exercised consensus influence. In each of our periods, crises slowly emerged as some Americans' exercise of positive freedom within the imaginary violated others' negative freedoms, leading to the formation of a new imaginary.

Perhaps the entrepreneurial imaginary that motivated 3.0 has run its course. As with previous imaginaries, Americans are expressing criticism, arguing that the pursuit of creative independence is actually undermining meaningful freedom, the kind required for a thriving, self-governing society that can effectively respond to emerging threats. Critics and skeptics see the imaginary as providing a language to justify and defend inequality as simply the worthy exercise of freedom. Broader discourse has begun to describe the once-lauded language of virtuous disruption as farcical. Amid this crisis, the 3.0 consensus may once again break down, paving the way for the articulation of a new entrepreneurial imaginary to meet the challenges posed by an emerging future.

Much of the criticism embedded in the charged rhetoric around the shortcomings of 3.0's entrepreneurial vision manifests as a critique of capitalism and its foundations in the seeming inevitability of capital accumulation. Critics can justly question the emancipatory promise of a social form in which the freedom to deploy capital toward independently chosen ends ultimately undermines freedom for many, but these criticisms are more about the nature of freedom than the nature of capital. Similar criticism might be levied for any social form resting on the exercise of freedom, like democracy. While recent work uncovers how capital has moved historically, putting its powerful thumb on the scale of markets and elections, we propose an agenda that renews interest in the emancipatory claims of the capitalist actors who moved that capital. Critical voices in our modern moment may tear down the social form of capitalism, but the articulation of a new entrepreneurial imaginary embodying a reformulation of emancipatory promise to fulfill emergent moral values through the exercise of freedom seems more likely. Historicizing the tensions between capitalism and democracy reveals that many of the tensions at the heart of both are really freedom's frictions.

Notes

1. Mihir A. Desai, "The Crypto Collapse and the End of the Magical Thinking That Infected Capitalism," *The New York Times*, January 16, 2023, sec. Opinion, https://www.nytimes.com/2023/01/16/opinion/the-crypto-collapse-magical-thinking-capitalism.html.
2. Moritz Becker, "Blockchain and the Promise(s) of Decentralisation: A Sociological Investigation of the Sociotechnical Imaginaries of Blockchain," in *Proceedings of the STS Conference* (Graz, 2019).
3. Katrin Becker, "Blockchain Matters—Lex Cryptographia and the Displacement of Legal Symbolics and Imaginaries," *Law and Critique* 33, no. 2 (July 1, 2022): 125, https://link.springer.com/article/10.1007/s10978-021-09317-8.
4. Tim Gorichanaz, "Being at Home in the Metaverse? Prospectus for a Social Imaginary," *AI and Ethics*, August 9, 2022, https://doi.org/10.1007/s43681-022-00198-w; Chiara Farné Fratini, Susse Georg, and Michael Søgaard Jørgensen, "Exploring Circular Economy Imaginaries in European Cities: A Research Agenda for the Governance of Urban Sustainability Transitions," *Journal of Cleaner Production* 228 (August 10, 2019): 974–89, https://doi.org/10.1016/j.jclepro.2019.04.193.
5. Drew R. McCoy, *The Elusive Republic: Political Economy in Jeffersonian America* (Chapel Hill, NC: University of North Carolina Press, 1980); Daniel T. Rodgers, "Republicanism: The Career of a Concept," in *Cicero and Modern Law*, ed. Richard O. Brooks (Routledge, 2009), 485–512; Gordon S. Wood, *The Radicalism of the American Revolution* (New York: Vintage Books, 1993).

6. Following in the tradition of Schumpeter (1942), our definition of modern capitalism emphasizes entrepreneurship, in contrast to definitions that build on Marx (1867) that focus on capital.
7. Isaiah Berlin, "Two Concepts of Liberty," in *Liberty Reader*, ed. David Miller (New York: Taylor & Francis, 2006).
8. Joseph A. Schumpeter, *Capitalism, Socialismand Democracy* (London: Routledge, 1976).
9. Charles Taylor, *Modern Social Imaginaries* (Durham, NC: Duke University Press, 2004), 23.
10. Claire Priest, *Credit Nation: Property Laws and Institutions in Early America* (Princeton, NJ: Princeton University Press, 2021).
11. Winifred Barr Rothenberg, *From Market-Places to a Market Economy: The Transformation of Rural Massachusetts, 1750–1850* (Chicago, IL: University of Chicago Press, 1992); S. Max Edelson, *Plantation Enterprise in Colonial South Carolina* (Cambridge, MA: Harvard University Press, 2006); Lorena S. Walsh, *Motives of Honor Pleasure & Profit: Plantation Management in the Colonial Chesapeake, 1607–1763* (The University of North Carolina Press, 2010).
12. Benjamin Franklin, *The Way to Wealth: As Clearly Shewn in the Preface of an Old Pennsylvanian Almanack, Intituled, Poor Richard Improved* (Edinburgh: Mundell and Wilson, 1782).
13. Sophus A. Reinert, "The Way to Wealth around the World: Benjamin Franklin and the Globalization of American Capitalism," *American Historical Review* 120, no. 1 (February 2015): 61–97, https://doi.org/10.1093/ahr/120.1.61.
14. Alan Taylor, *American Revolutions: A Continental History, 1750–1804* (New York: W. W. Norton, 2016).
15. "Letters from a Farmer in Pennsylvania to the Inhabitants of the British Colonies," in *Tracts of the American Revolution, 1763–1776*, ed. Merrill Jensen, 2nd ed. (Indianapolis, IN: Hackett Publishing Company, 2003).
16. Bernard Bailyn, *The Ideological Origins of the American Revolution* (Cambridge, MA: Harvard University Press, 1967), 35–37, 44, 51–53.
17. Benjamin Franklin, *The Autobiography of Benjamin Franklin* (P. F. Collier, 1909), 89–92; Norman S. Fiering, "Benjamin Franklin and the Way to Virtue," *American Quarterly* 30, no. 2 (1978): 199–223; Gordon S. Wood, *The Americanization of Benjamin Franklin* (Penguin, 2005); Wood, *The Radicalism of the American Revolution*. This "broadening" remained quite narrow, including only white, male, property owners.
18. Jack P. Greene, *The Constitutional Origins of the American Revolution* (Cambridge, UK: Cambridge University Press, 2011).
19. R. Daniel Wadhwani and Christina Lubinski, "Reinventing Entrepreneurial History," *Business History Review* 91, no. 4 (2017): 767–99, https://doi.org/10.1017/S0007680517001374.
20. Thomas Jefferson, "Speech of Mr. Jefferson at his inaugural," March 4, 1801, Library of Congress, https://www.loc.gov/item/rbpe.1900040a/
21. Benjamin Franklin, *The Papers of Benjamin Franklin, July 1, 1750 through June 30, 1753*, ed. Leonard W. Labaree, vol. 4 (New Haven, CT: Yale University Press, 1961), 225–34.
22. This suggestion draws on Howard Stevenson's formulation of entrepreneurship as "a process by which individuals—either on their own or inside organizations—pursue opportunities without regard to the resources they currently control." Howard H. Stevenson and J. Carlos Jarillo, "A Paradigm of Entrepreneurship: Entrepreneurial Management," *Strategic Management Journal* 11 (1990): 17–27.
23. Michael A Blaakman, "The Marketplace of American Federalism: Land Speculation across State Lines in the Early Republic," *Journal of American History* 107, no. 3 (December 1, 2020): 583–608, https://doi.org/10.1093/jahist/jaaa340; forthcoming in Michael A. Blaakman, *Speculation Nation: Land Mania in the Revolutionary American Republic*, Early American Studies (Philadelphia, PA: University of Pennsylvania Press, 2023).
24. Franklin Sammons, "'The Fruit of the Yazoo Compromise': Mississippi Stock and the Panic of 1819," *Journal of the Early Republic* 40, no. 4 (Winter 2020), https://doi.org/10.1353/jer.2020.0094.
25. Hannah Farber, *Underwriters of the United States: How Insurance Shaped the American Founding* (Chapel Hill, NC: The University of North Carolina Press, 2021).
26. Woody Holton, "The Capitalist Constitution," in *American Capitalism: New Histories*, ed. Sven Beckert and Christine Desan (New York: Columbia University Press, 2018), 35–62;

Scott Reynolds Nelson, *A Nation of Deadbeats: An Uncommon History of America's Financial Disasters* (New York: Vintage Books, 2012).

27. Daina Ramey Berry, "Soul Values and American Slavery," *Slavery & Abolition* 42, no. 2 (April 3, 2021): 201–18, https://doi.org/10.1080/0144039X.2021.1896188.
28. On self-emancipation as an act of personal liberation see David Williams, *I Freed Myself: African American Self-Emancipation in the Civil War Era* (New York: Cambridge University Press, 2014).
29. Richard Newman, *Freedom's Prophet: Bishop Richard Allen, the AME Church, and the Black Founding Fathers* (New York: New York University Press, 2008).
30. Justene Hill Edwards, *Unfree Markets: The Slaves' Economy and the Rise of Capitalism in South Carolina* (New York: Columbia University Press, 2021).
31. Seth Rockman, *Scraping By: Wage Labor, Slavery, and Survival in Early Baltimore* (Baltimore, MD: Johns Hopkins University Press, 2009).
32. Eric Foner, *Free Soil, Free Labor, Free Men: The Ideology of the Republican Party Before the Civil War*, 2nd ed. (Oxford, UK: Oxford University Press, 1995); Jonathan H. Earle, *Jacksonian Antislavery and the Politics of Free Soil, 1824–1854* (Chapel Hill, NC: University of North Carolina Press, 2005); Reinhard O. Johnson, *The Liberty Party, 1840–1848: Antislavery Third-Party Politics in the United States* (Baton Rouge: Louisiana State University Press, 2009).
33. Elizabeth R. Varon, *Disunion!: The Coming of the American Civil War, 1789–1859* (Chapel Hill, NC: University of North Carolina Press, 2008).
34. Abraham Lincoln, "Address at Sanitary Fair, Baltimore, Maryland," 18 April, 1864, *The Portable Abraham Lincoln*, ed. Andrew Delbanco (New York: Viking, 1992), 305–6.
35. Foner, *Free Soil, Free Labor, Free Men*; Gary W. Gallagher, *The Union War* (Cambridge, MA: Harvard University Press, 2012).
36. Caitlin Rosenthal, "Capitalism When Labor Was Capital: Slavery, Power, and Price in Antebellum America," *Capitalism: A Journal of History and Economics* 1, no. 2 (2020): 296–337, https://doi.org/10.1353/cap.2020.0002.
37. Caroline E. Janney, *Remembering the Civil War: Reunion and the Limits of Reconciliation* (Chapel Hill, NC: The University of North Carolina Press, 2013), 86–87, 113.
38. Walter Lippmann, *Drift and Mastery: An Attempt to Diagnose the Current Unrest* (New York: Mitchell Kennerley, 1914), 44.
39. Jonathan Levy, "The Mortgage Worked the Hardest: The Fate of Landed Independence in Nineteenth-Century America," in *Capitalism Takes Command: The Social Transformation of Nineteenth-Century America*, ed. Michael Zakim and Gary J. Kornblith (Chicago, IL: The University of Chicago Press, 2012), 39–67.
40. Michael B. Katz, Mark J. Stern, and Michael B. Doucet, *The Social Organization of Early Industrial Capitalism* (Cambridge, MA: Harvard University Press, 1982); Alexander Keyssar, *Out of Work: The First Century of Unemployment in Massachusetts* (New York: Cambridge University Press, 1986); Walter Licht, *Getting Work: Philadelphia, 1840–1950* (Cambridge: Harvard University Press, 1992); Martin Ruef, "The Household as a Source of Labor for Entrepreneurs: Evidence from New York City during Industrialization," *Strategic Entrepreneurship Journal* 14 (2020): 20–42; Walter Licht, *Industrializing America: The Nineteenth Century* (Baltimore: Johns Hopkins University, 1995).
41. Naomi R. Lamoreaux, *The Great Merger Movement in American Business, 1895–1904* (Cambridge: Cambridge University Press, 1985), https://doi.org/10.1017/CBO9780511665042.
42. Phil Scranton, *Figured Tapestry: Production, Markets and Power in Philadelphia Textiles, 1885–1941* (Cambridge: Cambridge University Press, 1989).
43. David Montgomery, *The Fall of the House of Labor: The Workplace, the State, and American Labor Activism, 1865–1925* (Cambridge, UK: Cambridge University Press, 1987), https://doi.org/10.1017/CBO9780511528774.
44. Berlin makes the case that simple want cannot undermine negative freedom, only coercion can do so.

45. Kenneth Lipartito, "The Utopian Corporation," in *Constructing Corporate America: History, Politics, Culture*, ed. David B. Sicilia and Kenneth Lipartito (Oxford University Press, 2004), 94–119.
46. Alex Gourevitch, *From Slavery to the Cooperative Commonwealth: Labor and Republican Liberty in the Nineteenth Century* (Cambridge, UK: Cambridge University Press, 2014), 119, https://doi.org/10.1017/CBO9781139519434.
47. Anne Meis Knupfer, *Food Co-Ops in America: Communities, Consumption, and Economic Democracy* (Ithaca, NY: Cornell University Press, 2013).
48. Jonathan Levy, *Ages of American Capitalism: A History of the United States* (New York: Random House, 2021), 303–8; Charles Postel, *The Populist Vision* (New York: Oxford University Press, 2007), 108–21.
49. David T. Beito, *From Mutual Aid to the Welfare State: Fraternal Societies and Social Services, 1890–1967* (Chapel Hill, NC: University of North Carolina Press, 2000).
50. David L. Mason, *From Buildings and Loans to Bail-Outs: A History of the American Savings and Loan Industry, 1831–1995* (Cambridge, UK: Cambridge University Press, 2004).
51. Alfred D. Chandler Jr., *The Visible Hand: The Managerial Revolution in American Business* (Cambridge, MA: Harvard University Press, 1977); Richard R. John, "Elaborations, Revisions, Dissents: Alfred D. Chandler, Jr.'s, 'The Visible Hand' after Twenty Years," *The Business History Review* 71, no. 2 (1997): 151–200, https://doi.org/10.2307/3116156. While organization certainly embodied an emergent trend in business, other forms endured and evolved alongside it, see Philip Scranton, "Small Business, Family Firms, and Batch Production: Three Axes for Development in American Business History," *Business and Economic History* 20 (1991): 99–106.
52. Daniel A. Wren, "The Centennial of Frederick W. Taylor's The Principles of Scientific Management: A Retrospective Commentary," *Journal of Business and Management* 17, no. 1 (2011): 11–22; Montgomery, *The Fall of the House of Labor*, 217–20.
53. David Montgomery, *The Fall of the House of Labor.*
54. Frederick Cooper, Thomas Cleveland Holt, and Rebecca J. Scott, *Beyond Slavery: Explorations of Race, Labor, and Citizenship in Postemancipation Societies* (Chapel Hill, NC: The University of North Carolina Press, 2000); Sean Wilentz, "Against Exceptionalism: Class Consciousness and the American Labor Movement, 1790–1920," *International Labor and Working-Class History*, no. 26 (1984): 1–24; Thomas G. Andrews, *Killing for Coal: America's Deadliest Labor War* (Cambridge, MA: Harvard University Press, 2010).
55. Walter Lippmann, *Public Opinion* (San Diego, CA: Harcourt, Brace & Co., 1922).
56. John Dewey, *The Public and Its Problems* (New York: Holt Publishers, 1927).
57. Postel, *The Populist Vision.*
58. Michael McGerr, *A Fierce Discontent: The Rise and Fall of the Progressive Movement in A* (Simon and Schuster, 2010).
59. Postel, *The Populist Vision.*
60. William J. Novak, "The Myth of the 'Weak' American State," *The American Historical Review* 113, no. 3 (2008): 752–72.
61. Laura Phillips Sawyer, *American Fair Trade: Proprietary Capitalism, Corporatism, and the "New Competition," 1890–1940* (Cambridge, UK: Cambridge University Press, 2018), https://doi.org/10.1017/9781139924658.
62. Sawyer, *American Fair Trade*, 107–9.
63. Margaret H. Schoenfeld and Anne Bezanson, "Trend of Wage Earners' Savings in Philadelphia," *The Annals of the American Academy of Political and Social Science* 121 (1925): i–65; Sanford M. Jacoby, *Modern Manors: Welfare Capitalism since the New Deal* (Princeton, NJ: Princeton University Press, 1997).
64. Lizabeth Cohen, *Making a New Deal: Industrial Workers in Chicago, 1919–1939*, 2nd ed. (Cambridge, UK: Cambridge University Press, 2008); Howell John Harris, *The Right to Manage: Industrial Relations Policies of American Business in the 1940s* (Madison, WI: University of Wisconsin Press, 1982).

65. Robert F. Freeland, *The Struggle for Control of the Modern Corporation: Organizational Change at General Motors, 1924–1970* (Cambridge, UK: Cambridge University Press, 2001); Robert H. Zieger, *The CIO, 1935–1955* (Chapel Hill, NC: University of North Carolina Press, 1995).
66. Angus Burgin, *The Great Persuasion: Reinventing Free Markets since the Depression* (Cambridge: Harvard University Press, 2012).
67. Lawrence Glickman, *Free Enterprise: An American History* (New Haven: Yale University Press, 2019).
68. William H. Whyte, *The Organization Man* (New York: Simon & Schuster, 1956).
69. Sloan Wilson, *The Man in the Gray Flannel Suit* (New York: Simon & Schuster, 1955).
70. C. Wright Mills, *White Collar: The American Middle Classes* (Oxford, UK: Oxford University Press, 1951).
71. Herbert Marcuse, *One-Dimensional Man: Studies in the Ideology of Advanced Industrial Society* (Beacon Press, 1964).
72. John Kenneth Galbraith, *The New Industrial State* (Houghton Mifflin Harcourt, 1967), 30.
73. Joshua Clark Davis, *From Head Shops to Whole Foods: The Rise and Fall of Activist Entrepreneurs*, Columbia Studies in the History of U.S. Capitalism (New York: Columbia University Press, 2017).
74. Thomas Frank, *The Conquest of Cool: Business Culture, Counterculture, and Rise of Hip Consumerism* (Chicago: University of Chicago Press, 1997); R. Daniel Wadhwani, "Kodak, FIGHT, and Civil Rights in Rochester, New York," *The Historian* 60, no. 1 (FALL 1997): 59–75.
75. Matthew G. Grimes, Jeffery S. McMullen, Timothy J. Vogus, and Toyah L. Miller, "Studying the Origins of Social Entrepreneurship: Compassion and the Role of Embedded Agency," *Academy of Management Review* 38, no. 3 (July 2013): 460–63, https://doi.org/10.5465/amr.2012.0429.
76. J. Willard Hurst, *Law and the Conditions of Freedom in the Nineteenth-Century United States* (Madison: University of Wisconsin Press, 1956).
77. Wadhwani, "Kodak."
78. Michael Barr, "Credit Where it Counts: The Community Reinvestment Act and Its Critics," *New York University Law Review* 80 (2005).
79. Hans Landstrom and Franz Lohrke, *Historical Foundations of Entrepreneurship Research* (Cheltenham: Edward Elgar, 2010).
80. David B. Audretsch, *The Entrepreneurial Society* (Oxford, UK: Oxford University Press USA, 2007).
81. Eric Godelier, "'Do You Have a Garage?' Discussion of Some Myths about Entrepreneurship," in *Business History Conference. Business and Economic History On-Line: Papers Presented at the BHC Annual Meeting*, vol. 5 (Wilmington, DE: Business History Conference, 2007), 1–20.
82. Ellen Graham, "Small Business (A Special Report): WSJ/Gallup Survey — The Entrepreneurial Mystique: A Gallup Survey Portrays The New Business Heroes As Mavericks and Loners With the Drive to Succeed," *Wall Street Journal*, May 20, 1985, Eastern edition.
83. Ronald Reagan, "Second Inaugural Address" (January 21,1985), The Avalon Project, https://avalon.law.yale.edu/20th_century/reagan2.asp
84. Steven K. Vogel, "Neoliberal Ideology and the Myth of the Self-Made Entrepreneur," *Research in the Sociology of Organizations* (August 13, 2020). Available at SSRN: https://ssrn.com/abstract=3698179 or http://dx.doi.org/10.2139/ssrn.3698179
85. MaryAnne M. Gobble, "The Case Against Disruptive Innovation," *Research-Technology Management* 58, no. 1 (January 1, 2015): 59–63, https://doi.org/10.5437/08956308X5801005; Lee Vinsel and Andrew L. Russell, *The Innovation Delusion: How Our Obsession with the New Has Disrupted the Work That Matters Most* (New York: Currency, 2020).
86. Margaret O'Mara, *The Code: Silicon Valley and the Remaking of America* (Penguin Publishing Group, 2019).
87. Jonathan J. Bean, *Beyond the Broker State: Federal Policies Toward Small Business, 1936–1961* (Chapel Hill, NC: University of North Carolina Press, 1996); Jonathan Bean, *Big Government and Affirmative Action: The Scandalous History of the Small Business Administration* (Lexington, KY: University Press of Kentucky, 2001).

88. Robert N. Eberhart, Stephen Barley, and Andrew Nelson, "Freedom Is Just Another Word for Nothing Left to Lose: Entrepreneurialism and the Changing Nature of Employment Relations," in *Entrepreneurialism and Society: New Theoretical Perspectives*, ed. Robert N. Eberhart, Michael Lounsbury, and Howard E. Aldrich, vol. 81, Research in the Sociology of Organizations (Emerald Publishing Limited, 2022), 13–41, https://doi.org/10.1108/S0733-558X20220000081002.

Financial Crises and the Coexistence of Democracy and Capitalism

The Case of the Panic of 1907

ROBERT F. BRUNER*

Introduction

Financial crises challenge the coexistence of democracy and capitalism by undermining their efficacy for delivering desirable social outcomes and hence, their legitimacy. For instance, asymmetric outcomes for rich and poor may erode norms of equality and fairness upon which democracy rests or faith in future prosperity upon which the acceptance of capitalism depends. At the heart of such challenges are doubts about the self-correcting nature of the two systems. This resilience, or the ability to self-correct, is one of the chief virtues of democratic capitalism over authoritarian governance and *dirigiste* economic oversight.[1] If democratic capitalism is so much nimbler than its alternatives, why does it struggle to quell financial crises? And what do the answers imply for the coexistence of democracy and capitalism?

I argue that answers to such questions are latent in systemic attributes that impede collective action. A study of the Panic of 1907, one of the pivotal financial crises in US history, highlights obstacles that both democracy and capitalism confront in mobilizing collective action in response to social problems. Such obstacles include disruptive innovation, information asymmetries, old institutions, incentives, interests, and competing ideologies. The chapter concludes that the two systems *can* coexist if they can manage and contain such sources of friction.

Robert F. Bruner, *Financial Crises and the Coexistence of Democracy and Capitalism*. In: *Can Democracy and Capitalism Be Reconciled?*. Edited by: Sidney M. Milkis and Scott C. Miller, Oxford University Press.
DOI: 10.1093/9780197774731.003.0017

The discussion here proceeds as follows. Part I frames the effort to quell a financial crisis as a problem in mobilizing collective action. Yet theory and empirical research on collective action point to attributes of democracy and capitalism as obstacles to effective crisis response. Of particular interest is the difficulty with which collaboration between public and private organizations can achieve socially desirable outcomes.

Part II discusses obstacles to collective action that challenge the ability to quell financial crises. Two centuries of financial crisis response in the United States display an *evolution* in public and private policies aimed at mitigating these obstacles. Part III summarizes the Panic of 1907 and highlights the obstacles to collective action that arose, as well as the subsequent reaction of democracy and capitalism to the crisis over the years 1908–1913. Part IV concludes with five implications for the coexistence of democracy and capitalism.

I. Collective Action Helps to Quell Financial Crises

A financial crisis is the destabilization of a financial system[2] after the rapid (and usually, panicked) withdrawal of funds from markets and institutions by bank depositors, investors, and lenders. Financial instruments plummet in value, and interest rates rise. Credit, the lifeblood of commerce, grows scarce. A financial crisis can spiral into an economic crisis because of spillovers from the financial sector into the real economy: a recession ensues; business revenues fall; price deflation makes it harder for debtors to honor their obligations; unemployment rises; consumer spending slows; and bankruptcies increase. At the core of such crises is declining confidence about the future: as President Franklin D. Roosevelt said at the nadir of the Great Depression, "the only thing we have to fear is fear itself—nameless, unreasoning, unjustified terror which paralyzes needed efforts to convert retreat into advance."[3]

The chief remedy to financial and economic crises is *rising confidence* about future conditions. And producing a turnaround in confidence depends on the mobilization of collective action to quell adverse trends. Successful collective action is concerted effort by enough participants to achieve a mutual goal. Examples include rescuing failing financial institutions and persuading market participants with enough resources to return. Collective action can be exercised through formal institutions, such as government agencies, and private sector organizations, such as clearing houses, and through informal institutions, such as community gatherings to rescue endangered banks or to provide social relief to needy individuals. To stop the vicious spiral of a financial crisis usually involves the support of influential individuals and institutions who will commit to quell the crisis. Such action must go beyond calming expressions of confidence (since talk is cheap) and instead should make tangible commitments of financial resources and reputation, which are large relative to the size of the crisis.[4]

The history of financial crises shows that public and private entities exercise collective action through policy choices of at least four kinds:

- Rescue. Any financial system depends on financial institutions of various sizes and types to function effectively. Stemming instability in the entire system may require preventing the collapse of constituent institutions, which, because of their large size or connectedness to other firms, could be conduits for contagion. Preventing the collapse of financially significant financial institutions through the injection of deposits or long-term capital can forestall the kinds of surprises that worsen a crisis.
- Recovery. Stimulating the return of buoyant economic and financial conditions is crucial to the recovery of confidence. Fiscal and monetary stimuli by the Federal Government are the most prominent examples of recovery-oriented policies. Also, private sector spending has a stimulative impact on the economy, as can the introduction of private currency substitutes.[5]
- Relief. Public agencies can provide social safety nets of various kinds to those individuals severely affected by a crisis: welfare payments, work relief programs, food stamps, housing vouchers. For-profit and not-for-profit institutions in the private sector have supported soup kitchens, food banks, and homeless shelters.
- Reform. Typically, a polity will demand remedies for the causes and accelerants of a financial crisis. These remedies and reforms might include changes in laws, regulations, norms, and best practices as well as the establishment of new government agencies or the reorganization of existing agencies. In the private sector, industry organizations may assert new norms and best practices.

Unfortunately, as Mancur Olson argued in his book, *The Logic of Collective Action*, the larger the community, the more difficult it will be to mobilize collective action.[6] Any of these four instruments typically entails recruiting support, aligning supporters around a vision, gaining commitment of financial, human, and political capital, and executing plans effectively.

II. Obstacles to Collective Action

Olson hinted at, but did not explore in detail, the specific obstacles (beyond size) that impede the mobilization of collective action. In this essay, I elaborate Olson's thesis by offering six obstacles to collective action that emerge in financial crises. These obstacles are informed by my case studies[7] of prominent European and American financial crises and include the following:

- Disruptive innovation. In conventional narratives, new markets, new instruments, new institutions, and other novelties figure prominently among the *causes* of financial crises.[8] I argue that innovations can also obstruct the ability to *quell* a crisis. First, innovations breed surprise: novelty tends to arise not in the center of the financial system but in the periphery (among the "shadow banks") where crises typically break out. Second, innovations tend to outpace the mandate of government regulators: in the depths of a crisis, it can become apparent that the old rules don't cover new conditions. And third, innovations breed increased complexity in the financial system, making it difficult for decision-makers to know what is going on.
- Asymmetric information. Charles Calomiris and Gary Gorton advanced the idea that information problems can trigger and worsen a financial crisis. Under rapidly changing crisis conditions, some members of a community are likely to be better informed about conditions than others. In his memoir, former Treasury Secretary Timothy Geithner referred to the "fog of war" that characterized the information that the most senior members of government had during the crisis of 2008.[9] This may lead the better-informed members to take actions at the expense of the less informed, a condition of market failure associated with the classic economic problems of adverse selection[10] and moral hazard.[11] Information problems contribute to the overoptimism associated with buoyant business expansion and the tendency of debtors to over-lever and of lenders to neglect time-honored credit standards. The architecture of a financial system links institutions to one another in a way that enables contagion of the crisis to spread. Trouble can travel. Safety buffers (such as cash reserves and capital) may prove inadequate to meet the coming crisis. Then, one or more shocks hit the economy and financial system, causing a sudden reversal in the outlook of investors and depositors. Confusion reigns. Public sentiment changes from optimism to pessimism that creates a self-reinforcing downward spiral in asset prices. In the vicious cycle, more bad news prompts more behavior that generates bad news. Collective action proves extraordinarily difficult to muster until the severity of the crisis and the insight and information held by a few actors prompts mutual response.

- Clinging to past institutions. Like generals, always trained to win the *last* war, crisis responders can tend to turn first to what worked in the last crisis. Institutions (organizations and orthodoxies) with some legacy from the past tend to be the default upon which initial efforts to mobilize collective action commence. Cost and urgency can drive responders first to the palliatives of past crises before embarking on finding new solutions to collective action. Thus, timely and effective collective action could be delayed by the need to prove why extant institutions will not suffice. And some policy advocates will cling to orthodoxies of the past in the belief that modern theories and approaches are just too complicated. For instance, theorists in the Classic and Austrian Schools of economics adhered to financial crisis remedies based on the price mechanism, and thus counseled governments to allow markets to fall until they discover a new equilibrium.[12] In response to such sentiments, John Maynard Keynes wrote in 1936, "Practical men, who believe themselves to be quite exempt from any intellectual influences, are usually the slaves of some defunct economists . . . in the field of economic and political philosophy there are not many who are influenced by new theories after they are twenty-five or thirty years of age."[13]
- Incentives. Financial crises disrupt expectations of future returns to participants in the markets. How participants perceive these payoffs might lead to worst-case outcomes for all. Game theoretic simulations show that modest changes in the payoffs in a competitive setting can tilt the likely outcome of a crisis toward or farther away from mutual assistance.[14] This is known as an "assurance" game: each player prefers to assist others if it can have the *assurance* that the others will also assist. But if it fears that the others will decline to help, it will also decline. Cooperation is needed to enable the participants to achieve the best outcome. Doubts about a player's willingness or ability to cooperate may prompt a decision to defect from mutual assistance. In the absence of cooperation, the game may end in the worst case. This is a classic failure of collective action, and amounts to a market failure: without coordination, the players arrive at an outcome that is suboptimal for all.
- Interests may cover a range of social and political values. By upsetting the status quo, financial crises can inflame interest groups. The ability to gain re-election, to protect a clan or ethnic minority, or to enlarge the influence of a political machine would be the kind of interests that a financial crisis can upset. Diversity of interests is the fuel for conspiracy theorists who assert that proposed remedies are the tools of domination by some groups over others—this was the thesis of the Tea Party and Occupy Wall Street movements shortly after the crisis of 2008.
- Ideologies. Crisis responses bear the hallmarks of reigning orthodoxies, systems of ideas or values that frame political and economic policies. For in-

stance, the gold standard (1870–1914) orthodoxy, placed high priority upon sustaining the convertibility of a nation's paper currency to gold at a stable rate of exchange. Stability promoted international trade, the aggregation of gold reserves within a country, the mercantilist interests of a country, and national creditworthiness in international markets. Sustaining the gold standard was typically coordinated with balanced government budgets, fidelity to meeting government debt obligations, and free trade. Under the Mundell-Fleming theory of the "impossible trinity,"[15] the ideology of the gold standard stabilized exchange rates, enabled the free flow of capital across borders, but forced nations to accept restrictions on their sovereign monetary policy.

In summary, the six "I's" (disruptive innovation, information asymmetry, past institutions, incentives, interests, and ideology) stood to thwart the ability and willingness of participants to unify around a mutual assistance pact.

III. The Panic of 1907: A Case Study of Obstacles to Regaining Systemic Stability

Crises before 1900 entailed little or no public sector response. The repair-and-correction activities following the Panic of 1907 marked a watershed in response to US financial crises. These activities were a blend of public and private collective action. Until the twentieth century, orthodox policy of the US Government regarding financial crises was simple: nonintervention. The regime shift that began in 1907 would be extended sharply during the economic strains of World War I and again with the activism of President Franklin D. Roosevelt during the Great Depression. The Panic of 1907 merits scrutiny not only because it is less well understood than subsequent crises, but also because it highlights insights into collective action in both the public and private sectors. Indeed, several of the initiatives of collective action were hybrids connecting both the public and private sectors, what in modern parlance is called a public-private partnership (PPP).[16]

The Panic of 1907 changed public attitudes toward government intervention. And it gave political opponents of the post-Civil War Republican hegemony an opportunity for large-scale attack. Furthermore, long-simmering discontent among farmers, laborers, and miners had already sprouted insurgent political movements and parties, all of whom coalesced around the appearance of collusion among powerful financial institutions and individuals. The disparate movements were the tinder; the Panic was the spark.

III.a. The Panic of 1907 and Emergent Public-Private Partnership

The Panic of 1907 occurred at the end of a long boom in the US economy. Economic output and industrial production surged from 1897 to 1906. Credit provided by banks and trust companies increased sharply, culminating in later years with rising prices in the stock markets and growing speculation. Forecasts of capital requirements for the growing US economy—particularly for the growth industry of the day, railroads—were so large as to prompt disbelief. Thus, in 1906, the financial system became strained: overextended credit was backed by inadequate cash reserves and capital. Most of the 21,000 banks in the United States were small and held undiversified loan portfolios in each local economy, such as agriculture or mining. In short, the American economy and financial system were vulnerable to economic shocks.

A massive shock hit on April 18, 1906. The San Francisco earthquake interrupted commerce and foreign trade, sent the US stock market into a slump, and triggered massive insurance claims and demand for bank credit. These demands rippled back to the central banks of France, Germany, and the United Kingdom, who raised interest rates and discouraged loans to the United States. What had been tight credit market conditions before the earthquake only worsened. By May 1907, the US economy had fallen into recession. Stock markets slumped and major borrowers found it difficult to roll over their debts or to raise fresh capital for new projects.

The grave conditions turned to panic on October 15, 1907, when an attempted speculation on the New York "Curb" exchange failed. The speculation was led by associates of Augustus Heinze and Charles Morse, who were insurgents (new competitors) in the New York financial community. Their associates had gambled substantially but neglected to gauge the true risk of their speculation. The failure of the speculation triggered the demise of two brokerage firms and then runs on banking interests of Heinze and Morse. Rumors fueled fears of other failures.

Into the crisis entered J. P. Morgan, on October 20, the same day that the New York Clearing House (NYCH)[17] agreed to assist the banks in the Heinze-Morse orbit, on condition that Heinze and Morse be ousted from all banking interests in the city. The acknowledged leader of the New York financial community, the 70-year-old Morgan, had been out of town and returned at the behest of partners in his firm. The next day runs began at the Knickerbocker, one of the largest trust companies in the city, following the announcement by the National Bank of Commerce that it would cease clearing payments at the NYCH for that trust company. Runs spread to two other large trust companies, Lincoln, and Trust Company of America (TCA).

On October 22, Morgan convened a crisis committee of financial leaders to audit the books of Knickerbocker and TCA. Based on a quick review of their assets, Morgan and the committee declined to aid Knickerbocker—news that inflamed fears of the public. Subsequently, Morgan commissioned reviews of TCA and Lincoln Trust Company and announced the formation of rescue pools of money for those trust companies.

As depositors ran on their banks and trust companies, those institutions had to call in loans. On October 24, the illiquidity of credit for traders on the New York Stock Exchange (NYSE) sent call money interest rates to 100 percent and threatened to crash the market. Morgan assembled a rescue pool for the NYSE and enlarged the pool the next day, along with increasing rescue funds for TCA and Lincoln.

US Treasury Secretary George Cortelyou, came to New York to review the situation and pledged to deposit $25 million in cash into national banks, to provide liquidity to the cash-starved system. (Subsequent deposits by Cortelyou ultimately raised the cash injection by the Treasury to $64 million.) This collaboration between Cortelyou and Morgan was the public-private partnership of consequence during the Panic of 1907 and arguably the spur to several other collective actions.

On October 28, the Mayor of New York appealed to Morgan for help. The city was unable to refund its short-term debts and would default unless rescue funds could be raised. Morgan raised them the next day.

From October 20 to November 1, Morgan struggled to organize a mutual assistance pact among the New York trust companies, another notable example of a private-sector response to financial crises. Such a pact was vitally important because the trust companies were not members of the NYCH, and therefore, could not look there for assistance—this was the result of a dispute a few years earlier between the banks and trust companies. On two occasions, Morgan gained an agreement for mutual assistance among trust companies, on which the trust companies reneged shortly after. Finally, in the early hours of November 3, Morgan succeeded in gaining a firm agreement among the trust companies for mutual assistance.

That same weekend, a new threat emerged: the brokerage firm of Moore and Schley was threatened with collapse, which would only set off a new round of panic. Morgan proposed that US Steel (of which Morgan was a director and primary organizer) should buy from Moore and Schley its shareholdings in a smaller steel company, Tennessee Coal and Iron (TCI). Following some arm-twisting by Morgan, the directors of US Steel agreed to buy the company, but on condition that President Theodore Roosevelt would not enjoin the acquisition on antitrust grounds. The next morning, Roosevelt consented, and anxieties in the New York financial community quickly receded. Roosevelt's consent was an additional dimension of public-private partnership in an effort to quell the crisis.

The announcement of the rescue of Moore and Schley began the turn toward recovery. Shipments of gold from Europe soon arrived in New York, affording the needed liquidity to assuage restive market participants. However, indicators of financial constraint continued in New York until January, and through the spring elsewhere in the country. The recession did not end until June 1908. Nor did the stock market return to pre-crisis levels until late 1909.

The *Commercial and Financial Chronicle* wrote, "It is probably no exaggeration to say that the industrial paralysis and the prostration was the very worst ever experienced in the country's history."[18] Milton Friedman and Anna Schwartz concluded that the recession was "among the five or six most severe."[19] Bruner and Carr show that the growth of gross domestic product per capita performed below trend for at least two decades later.[20] Economists call this "hysteresis," which means the persistence of slower growth, well after the shock that precipitated the slowdown.

III.b. Collectives and Public-Private Partnerships in 1907

Four collectives (of which two were public-private partnerships) figured prominently in the resolution of the Panic:

- J. P. Morgan and the New York banking community, especially the NYCH. Morgan's firm, a private bank, was not a member of the NYCH. But he held influence over the banking community by virtue of the resources he could command and his official role as a director or officer in banks and trust companies. He criticized banks that hastily withdrew support for other institutions and cautioned patience among the banks toward the evolving conditions.
- J. P. Morgan and George Cortelyou. The informal alliance between the US Treasury Secretary and the *de facto* leader of the New York Financial community was vitally important. The Treasury deposited gold reserves into nationally chartered banks (mainly in New York City) on the assumption that those banks would deploy the cash to points of greatest need. Given Morgan's influence with the leaders in the banking community, this strategy of deployment was essentially a partnership between Morgan and Cortelyou. This partnership spanned public and private interests and was the most prominent such partnership in the crisis.
- J. P. Morgan and the Trust Companies. The archives show that wrangling the diverse trust companies into a mutual assistance pact was the most challenging collective on which Morgan worked. A clue about the difficulty

of Morgan's negotiations was that he finally gained written agreement during an all-night meeting in which he *locked the door* to the meeting room, refusing to let anyone leave before signing.

- J. P. Morgan and Theodore Roosevelt. Created at the close of the frantic crisis stage in November 1907, Morgan gained the implicit endorsement of the US President for an acquisition of Tennessee Coal and Iron by US Steel that rescued a tottering brokerage firm and gained US Steel a larger share of the market. Though Roosevelt disavowed any deeper understanding between the two figures, progressives, and populists later pilloried Roosevelt for granting an antitrust exemption for the acquisition.[21]

III.c. Democracy Strives to Reform Capitalism

The Panic cast a bright light on defects of the US financial system. These included the "inelasticity" of the money supply; the pyramiding[22] of bank reserves; the immobility of rescue capital; the opacity of financial condition of institutions in the system; the tendency to focus on big banks to the neglect of small ones; the inadequacy of US Treasury gold reserves; the slow ability of clearinghouse loan certificates and other substitutes for cash to quell the panic; hoarding; and the absence of a clear successor to J. P. Morgan.

The civic reaction to the crisis slowly gathered steam. In December 1907, the US Senate demanded a report from the Secretary of the Treasury about government deposits in national banks during the panic. Two months later, the Senate authorized an investigation. In March 1908, progressive Senator Robert La Follette charged that the panic was deliberately planned by insurance companies with the Morgan and Standard Oil groups of banks—this marked a deepening divide between "Wall Street" and "Main Street" advocates in Congress.

To respond to the crisis before the Federal elections in November 1908, the Republican Party-led Congress passed the Aldrich-Vreeland Act, which empowered an expansion of the money supply in the event of a financial crisis. The Act also created the National Monetary Commission to study the problem of crises, which produced a multi-volume report in 1911 and the first government proposal to establish a central bank. In 1909, Congress passed the Postal Savings Bank Act, a weak nod to proposals by progressives and socialists for a government-owned financial institution.

Financial crises tend to be hard on elected officials. But 1908 broke precedents by seeming to reaffirm the hegemony of the Republican Party in Washington, D.C. This perhaps reflected the coattails of Roosevelt's popularity, and the absence up to that date of serious attacks by Democrats upon Roosevelt's

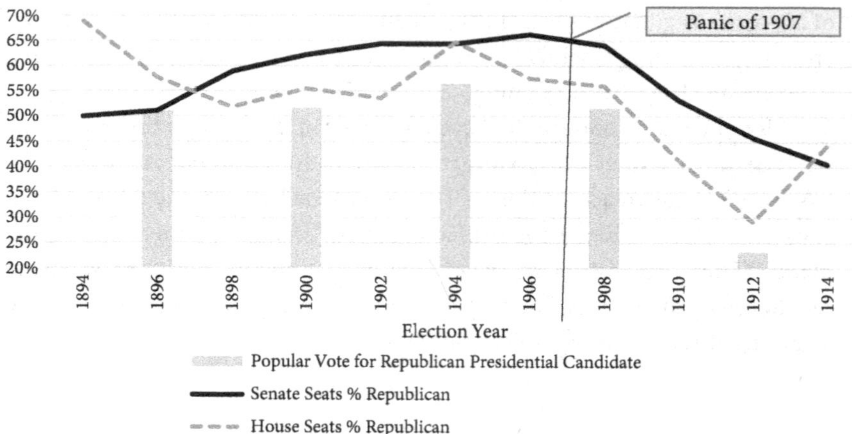

Source: Bruner and Carr (2023) page 228, used with permission of the authors.[i]

Figure 16.1 Republican Party election results, 1894–1914. *Source*: Bruner and Carr (2023) page 228, used with permission of the authors. Authors' figure based on data from the following sources: American Presidency Project (Santa Barbara: University of California Santa Barbara), downloaded May 12, 2022, from https://www.presidency.ucsb.edu/statistics/elections. Also, "Party Divisions of the House of Representatives, 1789 to Present," History, Art & Archives, United States House of Representatives, downloaded May 12, 2022, from https://history.house.gov/Institution/Party-Divisions/Party-Divisions/. And finally, "Party Division of the United States Senate" (Washington, D.C.: United States Senate), downloaded May 12, 2022, from https://www.senate.gov/history/partydiv.htm.

crisis policy. Roosevelt (who had declared that he would not run in 1908) engineered the Republican Party nomination of William Howard Taft for president. Taft was elected by a 52 percent popular majority. And the Party continued to hold majorities in the two houses of Congress. However, the election results began a weakening trend as depicted in Figure 16.1. At the next federal mid-term election in 1910, the Republican Party lost control of the House of Representatives. And in the pivotal election of 1912, the Republicans also lost the Senate and the White House. Thus, in the five years following the Panic of 1907, a massive political realignment took place.

Beginning in 1913, progressives stood at the levers of power. Why did it take six years for the change to occur? First, it may take a matter of years for a populace to realize the onset of hysteresis. Second, progressives and populists were slow to criticize the actions of Morgan and Roosevelt. Third, voters were slow to realize that Howard Taft was not the full-throated progressive that Roosevelt had been. And finally, the influential hearings held by the Democratic-controlled House of Representatives finally got moving only four and five years after the Panic (1911 and 1912).

In 1911, the Democratic Party-led House of Representatives embarked on two sets of hearings. The first (the "Stanley Hearings") was an investigation into US Steel's acquisition of TCI in 1911—this prodded the Taft Administration to sue US Steel for monopolizing the industry, and in effect chastised Theodore Roosevelt for blessing US Steel's acquisition of TCI.

The second was an investigation under the direction of Representative Arsene Pujo that focused on the existence of a "money trust," an alleged combination in restraint of trade particularly within the New York financial community.[23] The Pujo Committee never formally identified the members of the money trust, except to show that Morgan and other senior bankers worked together and held many corporate directorships. Populists, progressives, and socialists feared the power of big financial institutions and their leaders, particularly Morgan. Though Morgan had won plaudits for his leadership to quell the Panic of 1907, progressives and populists attacked him for earning profits on his rescue loans and even charged that he had engineered the crisis to discipline business adversaries.[24] When so much of the nation was affected by the Panic of 1907, public support for private-sector leadership of crisis fighting shifted support for public-sector leadership. The money trust hearing concluded that ". . . there exist[ed] an established and well-defined identity and community of interest between a few leaders of finance."[25] In 1914, Louis Brandeis concluded, "We must break the Money Trust or the Money Trust will break us."[26]

The "Money Trust" hearings proved to be enormously influential. They dominated newspaper headlines for months, as Wall Street leaders were called to testify before the committee. Of particular interest was the power of the New York Clearing House during the Panic of 1907 "to pronounce sentence of death upon every financial institution in [New York City]."[27] The findings of this hearing inflamed the public and seeped into the presidential election campaign of 1912. The Democratic Party candidate, Woodrow Wilson, said, "The great monopoly of this country is the monopoly of big credits."[28]

The hearings generated huge media coverage. A computer search of newspaper articles containing the phrase, "money trust," yielded 9,001 hits for 1911, 8,871 for 1912, and 7,989 for 1913.[29] As Figure 16.2 shows, the number of books mentioning the phrase spiked shortly after the panic, peaking in 1913, again in the 1930s, and remained in the public's mind for decades.

With the election in 1912 of Woodrow Wilson as President and with Democratic majorities in both houses of Congress, the drive toward central banking accelerated. Wilson ultimately entertained five proposals, reflecting different visions about governance of the central bank on two dimensions: (1) the extent of public versus private governance of the central bank, and (2) whether paper currency would be an obligation of the central bank. Wilson's compromise divided

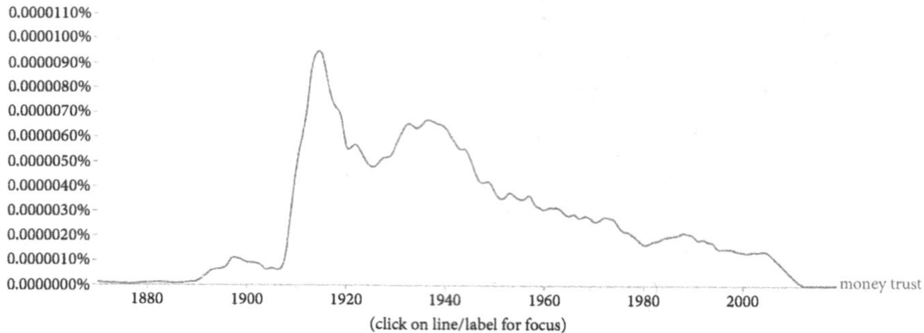

Figure 16.2 Frequency of occurrence of the phrase, "money trust" 1800–2020 *Note*: This graph displays the frequency of occurrence of the phrase "money trust" found in a corpus of English language printed sources

Source: Bruner and Carr (2023), 255, used with permission of the authors. Google Books Ngram viewer, downloaded June 21, 2022, from https://books.google.com/ngrams/graph?content=Money+trust&year_start=1800&year_end=2019&corpus=26&smoothing=3&direct_url=t1%3B%2CMoney%20trust%3B%2Cc0#t1%3B%2CMoney%20trust%3B%2Cc0.

the territory among the proposals, ensuring a majority for passage of the Federal Reserve act on December 23, 1913.

In all, the civic reaction to the crisis spanned six years, 1908–1913 inclusive, as the following figure shows. Notably, the more intensive activity of 1911 to 1913 coincided with the ascendancy of the political insurgent party, the Democrats, after the 1910 mid-term elections. Figure 16.3 shows that civic reactions to the Panic continued for years afterward. And it shows that the ultimate consequence, the Federal Reserve Act, did not spring immediately from the Panic of 1907. Rather, the design of a central bank advanced by stages in stop-gap laws (Aldrich-Vreeland, Postal Savings Bank), research (National Monetary Commission), hearings (Stanley and Pujo), lawsuit (*Department of Justice v. US Steel*), and trial balloon proposals (Glass, McAdoo, Owen).

Figure 16.3 depicts the legislative responses to the Panic of 1907 as a *cascade* of events, instead of a momentary pivot, as suggested in some popular accounts. The episode displays virtually all the obstacles to collective action that the crisis posed, and that those collectives eventually surmounted:

- Disruptive innovation: New institutions (such as chain banks[30] or trust companies that focused on consumer business), and new instruments (interest-bearing checking accounts) heralded a continuing gale of change. Entry by trust companies into the New York consumer banking market had begun to change the competitive equilibrium. The trusts gave insurgent players such as Augustus Heinze and Charles Morse footholds that challenged the incumbent firms. By their nature, the insurgents were wary of collective action and

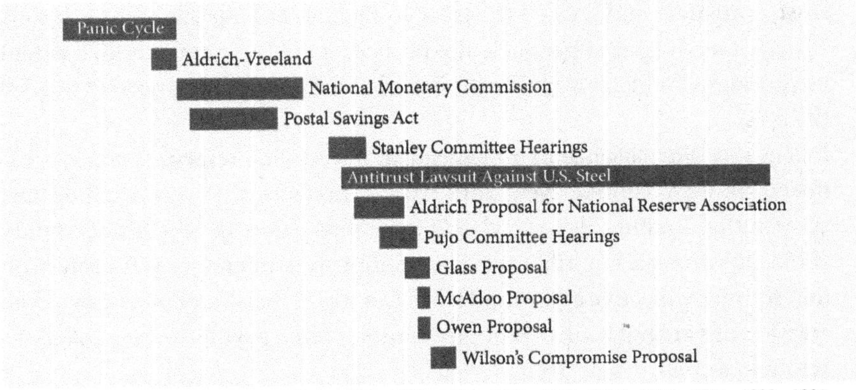

Figure 16.3 The cascade of congressional activity after the Panic of 1907 *Source*: Bruner and Carr (2023), 310, used with permission of the authors.

instead opportunistically sought advantage from independent action. This worked until it didn't. Morgan's leadership persuaded the trusts of the virtue of mutual assistance.

- Information asymmetry: Information was scarce; it was hard to tell what was going on within and among financial institutions. In 1907, financial statements of trust companies did not benefit from Generally Accepted Accounting Principles (GAAP), professional independent auditors, or government regulations of financial reporting. More generally, uncertainty owing to a lack of information or rumors and disinformation was a reliable obstacle to collective action. However, Morgan used the prospect of rescue funding to motivate banks and trust companies to divulge private information about their financial condition, thus surmounting the information asymmetry.
- Past institutions: Senator Nelson Aldrich, the powerful chair of the Senate committee overseeing banking and finance, was staunchly conservative and had been opposed to the concept of a central bank. The reigning orthodoxy of the day ("let the fires burn themselves out") was no longer useful, as the calamitous echoes of the Knickerbocker Trust's failure had shown. Yet, after the crisis, his National Monetary commission undertook research that illuminated the usefulness of central banks and gradually brought him around to supporting the idea. In October 1907, the trust companies could look to two other forms of collective action that already existed: the New York Clearing House, and J. P. Morgan's informal rescue committee. The NYCH was unwilling to resolve the standoff between the banks and trust companies or would otherwise raise funds to rescue distressed trust companies. And

Morgan's committee was already stretching its resources in support of the trust companies and wanted the trust companies to help themselves. It took 11 days for Morgan to persuade the recalcitrant trust companies that extant institutions would not mobilize the extent of collective action needed to quell the crisis.

- Incentives: The absence of a mechanism for pooling reserves created a cooperation game among New York trust companies that was tilted against cooperation—rather like the classic assurance game, in which uncertainty about the strategies of other players, prompts one to choose self-protection that stymies collective action and leads to a worst-case outcome. Instead, the creation of a central bank that pooled reserves tilted payoffs toward collective action in a crisis.
- Interests: The history of the Panic of 1907 highlights several differing interests among financial institutions, and indeed, the public: Wall Street banks (big, metropolitan, cosmopolitan, East Coast, and associated with Morgan) versus "Main Street" banks (smaller, domestic, more local in focus, and in the South, Midwest, and West); banks versus trust companies; and insurgents versus incumbents. Researchers have documented the diverse backgrounds of trust companies.[31] The wholesale-oriented trust companies were older, generally larger, and presumably content with the way business had always been conducted—they were *incumbents* in terms of intra-industry rivalry. The retail-oriented trust companies were younger, more aggressive, and reliant on a retail-oriented model that might displace the incumbents—these firms were *insurgents* in terms of rivalry. Divergent interests in terms of business model likely discouraged collective action by the trust companies. The rapid growth of the number of trust companies after 1895 and the entry of insurgents such as the Heinze–Morse group presaged division rather than alignment among them.
- Ideologies: Conservative orthodoxy in public policy, which had sustained the Republican hegemony since the Civil War had relied on austerity and deflation to return the US dollar to the gold standard in 1900, along with protective tariffs, trade surpluses, budget surpluses, resistance to unionization, lax antitrust enforcement, and a two-ocean navy. The realigning election of 1896 that sent McKinley to the White House seemed to affirm the public consensus around such values. Yet by 1907 the social dislocations of immigration, urbanization, technological change, industrialization, and rapid economic growth had eroded that consensus. Muckraking journalists exposed the dark side of monopolistic industrial trusts. The inklings of social science research emerging from universities suggested public policy interventions that would quell social ills. And Theodore Roosevelt caught the wave of a new ideology, progressivism, that suited his activist personality.

IV. Conclusion

Can democracy and capitalism coexist? This essay addresses the question by focusing on one of the most prominent frictions between the two systems: financial crises. Proponents of the systems claim a chief virtue to be their resilience, or capacities for self-repair and reform. But if democratic capitalism is so much nimbler than its autocratic and *dirigiste* alternatives, why does it struggle to quell crises? And what do the answers imply for the coexistence of democracy and capitalism?

First, democracy and capitalism *did* demonstrate resilience in their response to the Panic of 1907. Their capacities for self-repair and reform, as well as their abilities ultimately to mobilize collective action to fight the crises are consistent with the insight of researchers such as Markus Brunnermeier, Daron Acemoglu, and James Robinson about the resilience of democracy and capitalism.

Second, apparent delays in quelling a crisis can be explained at least in part by the obstacles to mobilizing collective action. This essay identified six obstacles: disruptive innovation, information asymmetries, past institutions, incentives, interests, and ideologies. Given the prevalence of such obstacles in democratic capitalism, it seems that delays in mobilizing collective action will be inevitable. The question is not whether delays will occur, but how long they will be. The answer is contingent on the effectiveness of leadership and the sufficiency of resources.

Third, it remains unclear whether democratic capitalism can mobilize collective action to *prevent* financial crises. Crises are sufficiently idiosyncratic that they cannot be forecasted practically. The important implication is that systems of democracy and capitalism should develop capabilities of *resilient response* to crises, rather than rely on a predetermined playbook. Research on business disasters characterizes such resilience as based on a preoccupation with failure, a reluctance to simplify, a continuous sensitivity to conditions, flexibility in addressing the conditions, and a deference to expertise.[32]

Fourth, struggles to respond to financial crises are not unique to democratic capitalism. Economists Carmen Reinhart and Kenneth Rogoff argued that financial crises are an "equal opportunity menace" afflicting rich and poor countries, and implicitly, political economic systems of all kinds.[33] None of the six obstacles to collective action is specific only to democratic capitalism.

Fifth, financial crises *have* changed both capitalism and democracy. The years following the Panic of 1907 featured a dramatic shift toward government oversight of the financial system and heightened antitrust enforcement. From the first US financial crisis in 1791 to the most recent, capitalism and democratic governance have morphed in response. Indeed, the long sequence of crises represents an extensive evolutionary process in which new ideas for regulation and crisis response were mooted, tested, and adapted. Democratic capitalism is a complex adaptive system. Hence, our understanding of its response to crises can benefit from historical analysis of its evolution. In 1907, such changes took at least three general forms:

- New orthodoxy. For the first time in US history, leaders in the public and private sector agreed that *rescues* of banks, trust companies, and the New York Stock Exchange were better than letting these organizations fail. Before then, the dominant orthodoxy of crisis response had been to let the fire burn itself out. Intervention by government into the marketplace in 1907 presaged the rise of the new progressive orthodoxy.
- New collaboration between public and private sectors. The crisis narrative of 1907 highlighted two important public-private collaborations: (a) the coordination between Cortelyou and Morgan in the allocation of public funds during the crisis, and (b) Roosevelt's acquiescence to Morgan's proposal for a takeover of Tennessee Coal and Iron by US Steel. Today, public-private partnerships are more common and may offer opportunities for crisis response.
- New forms of response included rescues, creation of a mutual assistance fund for trust companies, and strategic deployment of reserves by the US Treasury. In 1908, Congress enacted the Aldrich-Vreeland Act, which enabled the issuance of additional currency in the event of a bank panic. The next year, Congress passed the Postal Savings Bank Act, which created a new class of depository institution with limited government guarantees for deposits. And then in 1913, Congress passed the Federal Reserve Act, which created a government organization for systemic supervision and management of the money supply.

Within a fairly short time during the nadir of the Panic, Cortelyou, Morgan, and his circle of financial leaders managed to stanch the deepening spiral. They surmounted the obstacles to action across four collectives, the most groundbreaking of which was the informal public-private partnership between Morgan and Cortelyou.

Do financial crises of capitalism change democracy? And do the crisis-induced changes in democracy change capitalism? The case history answers "yes" to both questions. Antagonisms between the two systems emerged in the following six years: rising political polarization, conspiracy theories, lawsuits, slanders, and regime shift culminated in institutional change that wrested the resolution of financial crises from the private sector to the public sector. Arguably, both capitalism and democracy emerged from the long tail of the Panic of 1907 profoundly changed. Historian Robert Wiebe wrote: "The panic of 1907 acted as a catalyst in the [political] ferment. Most obviously, it convinced almost everyone, including the bankers, that financial reform was imperative . . . the panic released countless little pockets of pressure, turning concerned but comfortable citizens into active reformers, and opening many more to the calls for change."[34] With the end of the panic, the political landscape had changed: new political coalitions gained traction and a change of leadership was in the public mind.

Notes

* University Professor Emeritus, Distinguished Professor Emeritus, and Dean Emeritus, University of Virginia. This essay was prepared while the author was Compton Visiting Professor of World Politics and Faculty Chair of the Project on Democracy and Capitalism at UVA's Miller Center of Public Affairs. The author thanks participants at the Miller Center conference, "Can Democracy and Capitalism Coexist?" (March 7–9, 2023), and especially Jennifer Bair and Scott Miller for comments, as well as Sean D. Carr, my co-author of *The Panic of 1907: Heralding a New Era of Finance, Capitalism, and Democracy* (2023) from which some figures are drawn. This essay would not have been possible without support from the Miller Center of Public Affairs and the UVA Darden School Foundation.

1. The resilience of capitalist economies is a central theme of numerous writers ranging from Adam Smith and Joseph Schumpeter to Edmund Phelps (Adam Smith, An Inquiry into the Nature and Causes of the Wealth of Nations (1776; repr. New York, NY: Modern Library, 1937); Joseph A. Schumpeter, *Capitalism, Socialism, and Democracy* (New York: Harper & Row, 1942); Edmund Phelps, *Mass Flourishing: How Grassroots Innovation Created Jobs, Challenge, and Change* (Princeton, NJ: Princeton University Press, 2013)). Schumpeter cites the "gale of creative destruction" as the dominant force of self-correction in capitalism. The mutable—and indeed, revolutionary—nature of democracies figures prominently in writings ranging from Thomas Jefferson and Alexander Hamilton to Friedrich Hayek, Daron Acemoglu and James Robinson, and Anne Applebaum (Thomas Jefferson, "Letter from Thomas Jefferson to James Madison," (January 30, 1787) downloaded July 18, 2024 from (anonymous) Thomas Jefferson Encyclopedia, Charlottesville, VA: Monticello Research & Education, https://www.monticello.org/research-education/thomas-jefferson-encyclopedia/a-little-rebellionquotation/; Alexander Hamilton, "The Necessity of a Government as Energetic as the One Proposed to the Preservation of the Union," in Alexander Hamilton, John Jay, and James Madison, The Federalist Papers, Number 23 (U.S. Government National Archives, https://founders.archives.gov/documents/Hamilton/01-04-02-0180#ARHN-01-04-02-0180-fn-0001, accessed March 10, 2025); Friedrich Hayek, *The Road to Serfdom* (1944; repr., Chicago IL: University of Chicago Press, 1994); Daron Acemoglu and James A. Robinson, *Why Nations Fail: The Origins of Power, Prosperity, and Poverty* (New York: Currency, 2012); Anne Applebaum, *Twilight of Democracy: The Seductive Lure of Authoritarianism* (New York, NY: Doubleday, 2020)).
2. A financial system is populated with various kind of organizations, such as banks, trust companies, insurance firms, brokerages, investment firms, and markets in diverse assets. As the word "system" attests, these organizations are linked to one another by virtue of contractual commitments. The dark side of linkage is contagion. In a system, trouble can spread through linkages.
3. "March 4, 1933: First Inaugural Address, Franklin D. Roosevelt Presidency," University of Virginia Miller Center, https://millercenter.org/the-presidency/presidential-speeches/march-4-1933-first-inaugural-address.
4. During the Mexican Peso Crisis of 1994, Under Secretary of the Treasury, Larry Summers, advocated a massive US commitment in support of the peso, amounting to "shock and awe"

to quell the crisis. In 2008, Treasury Secretary Henry Paulson advocated a massive Congressional authorization of funds to convince markets that he had a "big bazooka" with which to support the financial system.

5. A currency substitute is defined by its acceptance by the public as a transaction medium and possibly a store of value. Examples from the Panic of 1907 were Clearing House Loan Certificates, trolley company fare tokens, and corporate "scrip" (IOUs issued by companies that promised to redeem in Legal Tender after the crisis ended).
6. Mancur Olson, *The Logic of Collective Action: Public Goods and the Theory of Groups* (Cambridge, MA: Harvard University Press, 1965), 35.
7. For a summary of these case studies, see Robert F. Bruner, "Case Studies about Financial Crises and Civic Reactions," December 18, 2020, https://ssrn.com/abstract=3752061.
8. For example, the Financial Crisis Inquiry Commission cited financial innovations as causes of the crisis of 2008. See US Government, Financial Crisis Inquiry Commission, *The Financial Crisis Inquiry Report* (New York: PublicAffairs, 2011), xix–xx, xxiv–xxv.
9. Timothy F. Geithner, *Stress Test: Reflections on Financial Crises* (New York: Crown Publishers, 2014), location 2714.
10. Adverse selection arises if a better-informed party in a transaction can exploit information to the disadvantage of the less well-informed party. Think of buying a used car (the seller knows more about the condition of the car, possibly a "lemon") or selling health insurance (the buyer knows more about his or her health outlook). Concern about adverse selection may drive parties out of the market, thus diminishing liquidity and the ability of the market to clear. Also, adverse selection might drive quality goods out of the market because sellers of high-quality goods cannot obtain the prices they deserve. In finance, "Gresham's Law" (i.e., bad money drives out good money) is an example of adverse selection. Charles W. Calomiris and Gary Gorton, "The Origins of Banking Panics: Models, Facts, and Bank Regulation," in *Financial Markets and Financial Crises*, ed. R. Glenn Hubbard (Chicago: University of Chicago Press, 1991, 109-174).
11. In the case of moral hazard, a party to an agreement fails to act in good faith and shifts risk onto counterparties. For instance, debtors who believe that the government will always bail them out in a crisis may simply borrow more, ultimately shifting risk onto taxpayers.
12. Herbert Hoover recounted that in 1930, his Treasury Secretary, Andrew Mellon, advocated such a policy: "Liquidate labor, liquidate stocks, liquidate the farmers, liquidate real estate . . . It will purge the rottenness out of the system. High costs of living and high living will come down. People will work harder, live a more moral life. Values will be adjusted, and enterprising people will pick up the wrecks from less competent people" Herbert Hoover, *The Memoirs of Herbert Hoover: The Great Depression 1929–1941* (New York: Macmillan, 1952). In 2008, Marc Faber, a prominent investment manager, touted "The best is to let the crisis burn itself out and clean the system, even if it means some pain for some people" Marc Faber, "Marc Faber: Let the Crisis Burn Itself Out," *CNBC* [Video interview], September 23, 2008, https://www.youtube.com/watch?v=kDxMtBlwNdE.
13. John Maynard Keynes, *The General Theory of Employment, Interest, and Money* (1936; repr., New York: Harcourt, 1964), 383–4.
14. Robert F. Bruner and Sean D. Carr, *The Panic of 1907: Heralding a New Era in Finance, Capitalism, and Democracy*, 2nd ed. (Hoboken, NJ: John Wiley & Sons, 2023), 307–9.
15. The "impossible trinity" is a hypothesis of international economics that it is not possible for a nation to have simultaneously the three following conditions: (1) a fixed foreign exchange rate; (2) an independent monetary policy; and (3) the absence of controls on the movement of capital across borders. Robert Mundell and John Fleming developed this theory independently in the early 1960s.
16. Of relevance to the coexistence of democracy and capitalism are examples of collaboration between the two systems in crisis-fighting. Theory and research suggest that public-private partnerships (PPPs) can help to resolve problems of urgent response, resource availability, agency costs, sunk costs, and/or expertise. Yet in a meta-analysis of extant research, Fabre and Straub conclude that the performance of PPPs present "a very mixed picture. The jury is still

very much out regarding the efficiency gains provided by PPPs. [which are] closely linked to the institutional context in which they are implemented, to the historical and political landscape in which they take place, and to the specific contracts and regulatory designs." Anais Fabre and Stephane Straub, "The Impact of Public-Private Partnerships (PPPs) in Infrastructure, Health, and Education," *Journal of Economic Literature*, 61, no. 2 (2023): 655–715. The ability of PPPs to achieve goals may be constrained by lack of skills, incomplete contracting, operating inefficiencies, rent extraction, and corruption.

17. The New York Clearing House was an institution that facilitated inter-bank payments and check settlement. To join the NYCH, a bank had to meet certain operating and financial standards and to open its books for monitoring periodically. In financial crises, the NYCH had agreed to assist member banks in distress, and thus performed the function of a risk-pooling organization. Also, during severe crises, the NYCH had issued Clearing House Certificates, a kind of fiat currency that served as a transaction medium when gold coin or Legal Tender were in short supply. The NYCH is significant in financial history as an example of a private-sector mechanism to forestall or mitigate financial crises. However, as the complexity of the US financial system increased and the US Federal Reserve was established, the significance of metropolitan clearing houses as crisis responders waned.
18. Quoted in Cahill, Kevin J. 1998. "The U.S. Bank Panic of 1907 and the Mexican Depression of 1908–1909." The Historian 60: 796.
19. Milton Friedman and Anna Schwartz, *A Monetary History of the United States, 1867–1960* (Princeton: Princeton University Press, 1963), 156.
20. Robert F. Bruner and Sean D. Carr, *The Panic of 1907: Heralding a New Era in Finance, Capitalism, and Democracy*, 2nd ed. (Hoboken, NJ: John Wiley & Sons, 2023), 221–23.
21. Theodore Roosevelt, *An Autobiography* (New York: Da Capo Press, 2017), 453–57.
22. "Pyramiding" of bank reserves stemmed from laws that enabled banks to keep excess reserves on deposit in major money center banks, where the reserves would earn higher interest. The problem with pyramiding was that it caused cash reserves of banks to reside in distant cities, rather than in local vaults when runs began.
23. Since the 1880s, industrial monopolies had been formed by bringing competitors under one organization called a "trust." Historian Naomi Lamoreaux found that from 1894 to 1904, more than 1,800 firms disappeared into the formation of 93 consolidated firms with an important, if not dominant, share of the market in their respective industries. The iconic trust of the Gilded Age was Standard Oil Company, whose practices and owners had been exposed by Ida Tarbell and other muckraking journalists. J. P. Morgan, the promoter of industrial combinations in fields as diverse as railroads, shipping, steel, and farm equipment, was a lightning rod for opponents of the trusts. Naomi R. Lamoreaux, *The Great Merger Movement in American Business, 1895–1904* (Cambridge, UK: Cambridge University Press, 1985).
24. Progressives such as Upton Sinclair, Charles Lindbergh Sr., and Robert La Follette alleged that Morgan and the NYCH engineered the Panic of 1907 to humble the insurgent trust companies. Robert M. La Follette, *Centralization and Community of Control in Industry, Franchise, Transportation and Finance: The Panic of October 1907 and Its Lessons* (Washington, D.C.: US Government Printing Office, 1908).
25. U.S. House of Representatives, *Subcommittee of the Committee on Banking and Currency, Money Trust Investigation: Investigation of Financial and Monetary Conditions in the United States under House Resolutions No. 429 and 504* (Washington, D.C.: U.S. Government Printing Office, 1913), 129.
26. Louis Brandeis, *Other People's Money and How the Bankers Use It* (New York: Frederick A. Stokes, 1914).
27. Quotation of chief investigator Louis Untermeyer in McCulley, Richard T. 1992 *Banks and Politics During the Progressive Era: The Origins of the Federal Reserve System, 1897-1913. New York, NY: Garland Publishing Inc.*, [repr. 2012, London, UK: Routledge] 266.
28. This quotation of Woodrow Wilson corresponds to statements made in his campaign speeches and is reproduced in his book, *The New Freedom: A Call for the Emancipation of the Generous Energies of a People* (New York and Garden City, NJ: Doubleday Page and Company, 1918), 185, https://books.google.com/books/about/The_New_Freedom.

html?id=MW8SAAAAIAAJ (accessed November 13, 2018). See also Woodrow Wilson, "Call for Freedom" [Speech], January 22, 1917, before joint session of Congress.

29. These numbers likely underestimate the volume of media attention to the phrase, "money trust," having been tallied from only 10 publications: *The New York Times, Wall Street Journal, Chicago Defender, Chicago Tribune, Norfolk Journal and Guide, Pittsburgh Courier, NY Amsterdam News, Baltimore Afro-American, Washington Post,* and *The Guardian & Observer.*
30. Chain banking aggregated several banks into one or more holding companies financed by loans secured by the stock of the various banks.
31. Bradley A. Hansen, "A Failure of Regulation? Reinterpreting the Panic of 1907," *Business History Review* (2014) 88(3): 545–569.; C. Frydman, E. Hilt, and L. Y. Zhou, "Economic Effects of Runs on Early 'Shadow Banks': Trust Companies and the Impact of the Panic of 1907," *Journal of Political Economy* (2015) 123(4): 902–40; C. Fohlin, T. Gehrig, and M. Haas, "Rumors and Runs in Opaque Markets: Evidence from the Panic of 1907," Center for Economic Policy and Research Discussion Paper 10497 (London, 2015); and Robert F. Bruner and Sean D. Carr, *The Panic of 1907: Heralding a New Era in Finance, Capitalism, and Democracy,*" 2nd ed. (Hoboken, NJ: John Wiley & Sons).
32. Robert F. Bruner, *Deals from Hell: M&A Lessons that Rise Above the Ashes* (Hoboken, NJ: John Wiley & Sons, 2005), 89.
33. Carmen M. Reinhart and Kenneth S. Rogoff, "Banking Crises: An Equal Opportunity Menace," Working Paper 14587 (Cambridge, MA: National Bureau of Economic Research, 2008).
34. Robert H. Wiebe, *The Search for Order 1877–1920* (New York: Hill & Wang, 1967), 201.

Conclusion

Can Democracy and Capitalism be Reconciled? Ten Conclusions in the Search for a Just Society

James A. Morone

Can democracy and capitalism be reconciled? Can they work together to help people flourish? The chapters in this volume answer those questions loud and clear: Yes and no.

No: Both democracy and capitalism are in deep peril—at least as they are practiced today in the United States. Each has drifted into a vicious cycle. Capitalism generates deep and selfish inequality. Democracy teethers toward minority rule and, perhaps, autocracy. Each reinforces pathologies in the other. Young people have seen only dysfunction in each system and value neither.

Yes. Of course, capitalism and democracy can be reconciled. They are deeply intertwined. A society cannot flourish if it does not link a just economy to robust democracy. We can't reform our politics without repairing our economy—and vice versa. What we need, more than anything, is the courage to imagine a more virtuous way forward.

What's next for democracy and capitalism? Here are ten principles that I draw from the preceding chapters. Together, they add up to a sobering view of our parlous political economy and an urgent call for change. The interconnection between capitalism and democracy once sustained a flourishing society. Yes, it people was deeply biased and woefully incomplete. But it boosted most people toward prosperity. All that is now endangered. The top soars, the rest are left behind. In the end the chapters of this volume ought to be read, not just as a diagnosis but as urgent calls to action.

James A. Morone, *Conclusion: Can Democracy and Capitalism be Reconciled?.* In: *Can Democracy and Capitalism Be Reconciled?.* Edited by: Sidney M. Milkis and Scott C. Miller, Oxford University Press.
DOI: 10.1093/9780197774731.003.0018

Here, then, are ten conclusions about politics, economics, the fix we're in and the potential path ahead.

Politics Make Markets

Democracy and capitalism are, of course, deeply interconnected. After all, a network of political decisions (and non-decisions) constructs the economic rules of play. Politics make markets.[1]

For example, when Elon Musk tried to impose his way on Swedish mechanics, they went on strike. One union after another stood up in solidarity. Dockworkers would not unload Tesla's automobiles, painters refused to touch up damaged cars, delivery services refused to handle the company's packages, and the list goes on. In contrast, American law rules out anything of the sort. The Taft Hartley Act (1947), passed by a conservative Congress over President Harry Truman's veto, flatly outlaws secondary strikes.[2] Different politics, different rules, different outcomes: Unions represent 90 percent of Swedish workers and 11.3 percent of American workers.[3]

Laws shape how firms compete, who gets rich, how workers organize, where money flows, and a thousand other details. American tax laws can be summed up by billionaire investor Warren Buffett's famous comment: Because of the favorable treatment for capital gains, his secretary—along with everyone else in his office—pays a higher tax rate than he does.[4]

Now, here's the ironic twist: A powerful political movement is rooted in the idea that politics and markets are opposites. President Ronald Reagan brilliantly committed this error when he swept into office with that famous declaration: "government is not the solution to our problem; government is the problem." If Reagan had cared about accuracy, he might have said "it's time to recalibrate the role played by government programs and market choices."[5]

The error informs policymakers at every level of politics. When the USSR collapsed, American economists raced in to help construct a market economy—without a thought to building the effective governance that would make capitalist markets possible. Without oversight, Russian economics quickly collapsed into a ruthless economic oligarchy.

Or, for another example, turn to the history of American health care policy. Over and over, conservative entrepreneurs imagined a great war between governments and markets. The efforts to empower the latter without the former led to a long series of flops and embarrassments as they failed to learn the old lesson: Health care markets require nimble and effective oversight if they are to work effectively. Without careful regulation, for example, entrepreneurs sign up elderly people for health plans with no facilities within 50 miles, or duck people who are likely to be sick (and expensive), or simply renege on their policies and refuse to pay for people with very high medical bills (a practice known as "recissions").[6]

Finally, as multiple papers in this volume note, right-wing members have left Congress in shambles by insisting that government is a monster to be drowned in the bathtub. Their antics diminish our democratic prospects in multiple ways. But they also hobble our economics. And all these troubles are rooted in the same foundational point: Politics and markets—democracy and capitalism—are not opposites but, rather, inextricably bound together.

Change! Change! Change!

The chapters in this volume pay sustained attention to history and its many unexpected twists. Taking the long view illustrates how swiftly the political economy evolves. Democracy and capitalism are always in motion.

Imagine, for example, if this volume had been written thirty years ago. The dark tone of this current moment would evaporate into a more optimistic story featuring the fall of the Berlin Wall, the crack up of the USSR, and the triumph of Democratic capitalism—with plenty of references to the end of history.

Or leap back thirty years before that and this volume might have reverberated with the idealism of John F Kennedy's new frontier and Lyndon Johnson's Great Society. Listen to the subtext of LBJ's most powerful speech, delivered after the bloody march in Selma: "Should we defeat every enemy, should we double our wealth, and conquer the stars, and still be unequal to [civil rights], then we will have failed as a people and a nation." Of course, the focus is on the treacherous issue of racial justice. But notice the implicit background to the president's challenge: we are a prosperous people self-confidently reaching for the stars.[7]

This book captures a fleeting present and places it in the long arc of the past. But every generalization made here—about democracy, about capitalism, about the United States—will soon be history. Things will change. The tone of these essays, for the most part, brace us for the tumble from bad to worse. We fear the loss of popular rule, galloping inequality, global warming, and the consequences of AI.

But readers who come to the volume with a glass-half-full frame of mind will draw some hope from the promise of change. This perilous moment is not the end of history either. There is a future to be made. The great question, of course, is—how? What might a reformist path look like?

Before we start imagining the future, we'd better be clear on where we are and how we got here.

Dilemmas of Capitalism in America

The preceding chapters add up to a clear economic story. Twentieth century capitalism recruited skilled and semi-skilled workers into a broad, comparatively egalitarian work force. Wage growth accelerated in the bottom and the middle of the income ladder. Each generation did better, made more, and lived longer than their parents. And then capitalism turned again.

A knowledge-based economy began to reward the well educated and left those with only a high school education in the dust. Globalization increased the disparities. One sector after another turned winner-take-all. The rewards rushed to the top—those on the economic bottom fell into precarity, the middle languished. The watchword of the new era became *inequality*—especially in the United States.

While the new knowledge-based capitalism squeezes every rich nation, most took action to limit inequality. In the 1970s, income distribution in the United States looked roughly similar to that in France, or Germany, or Canada. Today those nations have left us far behind in the quest for equality (or, for that matter, the chances of economic mobility). The United States has now drifted into the Latin American league, measuring a bit more equal than Mexico and a bit less than Argentina.

But the larger difference lies within the country. Densely populated cities are economic dynamos—generating innovation and gathering wealth. The vast rural heartlands fall behind—getting poorer, loosing population, and feeling mutinous.

Sociologists have launched a fleet of studies demonstrating how inequality changes everything from our universities (chasing wealthy donors) to our hospitals (owned by hedge funds). It alters how we eat, how we entertain, how we run elections, and the way we construct our skyscrapers.[8]

But the most formidable—and depressing—consequence falls on individuals. Average life expectancy in the United States has been tumbling since 2014. A toxic mix of COVID-19, opioids, alcohol, guns, suicide, vaccine denial, stress, and racism—the deaths of despair—takes a terrible toll. A child born in the United States can expect to live, on average, eight years less than a child born in Japan, seven years less than one born in Italy, six years less than one born in France, and five years less than one born in Chile. In Mississippi, life expectancy is six months lower than it is in Bangladesh.[9]

The dreary data is usually tagged "unprecedented." But as Carles Boix suggests in Chapter 3, something similar marked the rise of industrial capitalism in England during the nineteenth century. Back then, a turn in the means of production left people behind—with the same kinds of painful demographic consequences. But this time, you can't pin all the blame on evolving capitalism since the United States is a such a terrible outlier.

The roster of capitalism's troubles goes beyond individuals to the planet itself. Carbon emissions are rapidly warming the earth. Climate systems are unstable, the insect population is collapsing, larges mammals heading for extinction, oceans warming, agriculture failing in many places, and whole regions growing uninhabitable. The engines that power contemporary capitalism threaten our way of life—and even life itself.

Capitalism gets a lot of the blame for this rollcall of troubles. Even Business School students planning a life in finance are suddenly attacking capitalism for its injustice. "If *these* students are harboring doubts about the free market," writes conservative economist (and B-School Dean) Glenn Hubbard, "business leaders had better take notice." But perhaps we are blaming the wrong system. It's our political system that designs the economic rules. Which brings us to the anxieties of democracy.[10]

Dilemmas of Democracy in America

When Barack Obama won the presidency, his staff called veterans from previous administrations for advice. Both Democrats and Republicans agreed on one thing: "You guys are out of your fucking minds if you do health care." The health care system was in dreadful shape—with 50 million people uninsured and costs going through the roof. But the beltway wisdom waived all that aside with the confident assurance that Congress was not up to the job of designing reforms. Few themes blaze through the previous chapter as clearly as the breakdown of American politics and the peril to democracy. "Put bluntly," summarize Hacker and Pierson, "our distinctive political institutions do not seem capable of managing our mounting challenges."[11]

The problem lies in a fierce partisanship, the multiplicity of checks and balances, and the institutional tilt to minority rule. In the Senate, almost anything meaningful faces a filibuster and requires a supermajority of 60 votes. That's a high bar if the parties won't work together. The Democrats have had 60 members for only 7 months in the last 30 years; the Republicans have never reached that number in the party's entire history. Moreover, Republicans have held the

Senate exactly half the time since 2000 without winning a majority of the votes cast in any six-year election cycle.[12] Over in the House, the Republicans have evolved into the anti-government party. They have shut down the government three times in the last decade (for a total of 50 days) and constantly threaten to do it again.

The White House has been in Republican hands more than half the time between 2000 and 2028, though the party managed to win the popular vote (barely) just twice since 1988. And the Supreme Court wields its extensive powers (unmatched in any other nation) with a conservative supermajority appointed mostly by men who lost the popular vote and confirmed by a party in the Senate that represented a minority of the votes cast for that chamber.

The minority bias tilts toward the rural population. And with that we arrive at the anomaly detailed, especially in Chapter 12 by Brown and Mettler: A population left behind by the economy—rural, poor, and rebellious—dominates American politics.

Their sustained attack on American government, and government competence, has slowly gained purchase. The Supreme Court has launched a broad effort to hobble administrative agencies ruling, for example, that the EPA does not have the authority to regulate carbon emissions in the coal industry despite a broad delegation of power to the agency in the Clean Air Act. The court has developed a formidable new approach: If an agency decides to do something new and important, it must go back to (the gridlocked) Congress for the unlikely authority to do so.[13]

The Trump administration hit upon an even bolder attack on public administration. They planned to create an entirely new classification of federal employees who would have no civil service protection—they would serve at the discretion of the president. Known as *Schedule F*, it would permit an administration to turn any policymaking role into a political appointment. While the plan has not yet gone into effect, it has fired the populist imagination and offers a way to drain the swamp—or, put more accurately, to powerfully diminish government capacity and the role of expertise.

In 2020, the attack on government turned into an all-out assault on democracy itself. President Donald Trump famously conjured up a monster rally—which turned riotous—as part of the effort to overturn the election he lost. Two out of three Republican House members backed up his dishonesty and refused to certify Joe Biden's victory. Four years later, 70 percent of the Republican faithful told pollsters the election had been stolen—almost precisely the same number who claimed to believe (falsely, of course) that Barack Obama was a foreigner and therefore illegitimate.

And don't let Democrats off the hook. They suffer from their own civic shortcomings. Hacker and Pierson remind us that the vibrant cities, controlled entirely by Democrats, have priced the working class right out of town. Efforts to build affordable housing can't overcome the NIMBY resistance. The cities struggle to organize humane policing, address homelessness, or welcome the immigrants that their economies need.

Will American institutions continue to hold—as they did when both state officials and courts refused President Trump's effort to overthrow the election? Or will the angry tide swamp popular rule in the United States? It remains a close call. And, in any case, the angry, populist tide—against government, against Democrats, against majority rule—makes governing the economy almost impossible. It's hard to see how our government can be mobilized for the pressing tasks before us: reversing global warming or deep inequality or monopoly power or simply the crisis in affordable housing that casts families into the streets. At least, it is difficult to see—for now.

The Race Line: The Original Sin for Capitalism and Democracy in America

Almost every chapter acknowledges the importance of race in America. But none deal directly with the honking reality of our origins: in this country, both democracy and capitalism were founded on slavery. Two hundred years of slavery followed by another century of racial repression don't just fade away—they leave deep scars.

Start with the consequences for democracy. James Madison fretted about how to stop the (poorer) majority from the "temptation . . . to trample over the rules of justice" and tax the (richer) minority. Like a good political scientist, he figured carefully designed institutions might do the trick.[14] Subsequent observers, from W. E. B. DuBois to Edmund Morgan thought slavery acted as a deeper, more credal counterrevolutionary force. Slavery divided poor Americans. There was no working class primed to demand rights (as in England, France, or Germany). Rather, there were black slaves and white free people. And the latter squeezed privilege—a kind of wage, said DuBois—out of their very whiteness. They enjoyed a special social status—above the black workers at the social bottom. White workers were not about to upset the socio-economic order for that might result in racial equality—and the loss of their racial status. The blunt fact of slavery served as a bulwark of the socio-economic order. And was powerful enough to outlast slavery itself.[15]

A generation after slavery fell, southern populists lamented the racial straitjacket that still bound the poor south. Black and white tenant farmers "are made to hate one another," summed up Tom Watson of Georgia, "because upon that hatred rests the . . . financial despotism which enslaves [them] both."

Elites and their newspapers easily wrecked the populist coalition. All they had to do, lamented Watson, was to chant "Negro domination, negro domination, negro domination" and the hardscrabble white farmers lunged for their racial supremacy even if it divided the poor and consigned them all to wretched poverty. Watson soon followed the path of least resistance and turned into an ardent racist himself.[16]

Racial hierarchy defined the southern workforce and limited the democracy. In areas with large black populations, southern whites gave up popular rule altogether—trading off democracy for white supremacy. When the southern party (Democrats till 1941, Republicans after 1968) dominated national politics, they injected their racial phantoms into the mainstream.

Perhaps the deep Southern aversion to unions also reflects the long legacy of violently enslaved work force. And perhaps the legacy of enslaved workers helps explain why in both north and south, American capital resisted labor organizing with a violence unparalleled in any other industrial nation.[17]

In the North, a somewhat different kind of racial tension divided the working class. Immigrants—seen as racial groups—identified and with their own national compatriots (and lashed out, often violently, against people from other countries). When the great migration brought African Americans up from the south, another violent racial trench marked the northern cities. North and South, working-class solidarity cracked along racial and ethnic lines.[18]

Race Feeds Partisanship

Race and ethnicity turn contemporary party politics especially ferocious. Traditionally, the political parties split in their approach to the two most disruptive issues, race and immigration. Democrats embraced white supremacy but fought for immigrants; they eagerly distributed ballots to the newcomers almost before they had recovered from the sea voyage to the new world. Republicans, in contrast, were the party of civil rights but, at the same time, embraced American nativists. Of course, both race and immigration set off violent culture wars. But the political pattern—most black Americans in one party, most immigrants in the other—meant that the parties diffused the full force of the great battle over national identity.[19]

Then, through the twentieth century, a great political migration began to take place. Republicans gave up on Civil Rights—it was too hard, too bitter. And they had a safe national majority without the South (where most black Americans lived till the great migration of Black Americans to the North beginning in 1910 and changed everything). President William Howard Taft used his inaugural address in 1909 to announce that fighting for the right to vote or giving black people government jobs "does [them] more harm than good."[20] Eventually, blacks responded. Beginning in 1928, and gathering velocity in 1932 and 1936, African Americans in the North moved to the Democratic Party.

Newspaper editorials scoffed at their naivete—didn't these people realize they were moving into the party of white supremacy? The tone then precisely reflects the incredulity that greets African Americans turning to Republicans today. Back in the 1930s and 40s, black Democrats soon gathered enough influence to win an Executive Order opening the armaments industry to black workers (in 1941) and a dramatic civil rights plank at the Democratic Party convention (in 1948). By that point the black vote had turned decisively to the Democrats—and began to transform the party of white privilege into the party of civil rights. By the time of the classic Civil Rights Movement, in the mid 1960s, Democratic Party identification among black Americans had reached 90 percent.[21]

The Democrats had always been the party of immigrants. The Latino vote reflected this pattern. The Asian vote, in contrast, was safely Republican as late as 1996—it even went for the hapless Republican presidential candidate, Robert Dole. But in 2000, Asian Americans began to flip to the Democratic Party and became, like the Latino vote, over 60 percent Democratic. By the early 2000s, the Democratic Party had gathered all the so-called minorities. And just in time for the Census Bureau's controversial 2004 bombshell: The United States would be a majority minority nation in two generations.

On the other side of the party divide, liberal Republicans battled for the black votes in the northern cities. But slowly, northern conservative Republicans and southern conservative Democrats found themselves in the same political trench—resisting the "socialistic tendencies," as they saw it, of Democrats like Harry Truman and their labor union allies. In 1964, when Republicans nominated Barry Goldwater, one of only six Senate Republicans to vote against the Civil Rights Act, the Republican half of the new alignment was set: Most white voters turned Republican. Richard Nixon consciously took up the Goldwater move and turned it into his Southern strategy: the Democratic embrace of Civil Rights would deliver the South, and with it, a majority of the nation's white vote, from the Democrats to the New Republicans. Democrats running for the Presidency would average just 39 percent of the white vote between 1968 and 2020.

A vivid new pattern emerged. The Republican Party was, very roughly, 90 percent white. They confronted a Democratic Party that included almost all black voters, most recent immigrants, and white liberals. The parties—which had once separated the different features of identity politics now had electoral incentives to stress them. And stress them they did. The era of hyper partisanship was on us. The most violent conflicts in American history—race, immigration, national identity—were, for the first time, baked into the national political parties.

Party members ferociously express that identity. Most Democrats believe racial discrimination against black and Hispanics remains a major problem in American life. Republicans scoff. Most of them (73 percent) tell pollsters that discrimination against whites is as big a problem as discrimination against blacks.[22]

As the parties divided by race, their views of government changed sharply. The Republicans had saved the Civil Rights Act in 1964. But, after that, social welfare programs began to look like assistance to the great American other. Republicans turned fiercely against the government. The party had always been wary of too much government. But it may be racial hostility that pushed it toward the burn it all down nihilism we sometimes see today. Perhaps this is the foundation beneath William Galston's Chapter 13 charting contemporary politics as culture war.

Of course—recall point 2—the parties will continue to evolve and change. There is much speculation that Hispanic, Asian, and black voters are drifting from the Democratic Party. Perhaps, if they do so, they will calm our partisanship and lower the temperature of American politics. Muddling the racial configuration might finally turn the parties away from the ferocious fights over identity and back to negotiations over policy preferences. It might very well transform the Republican Party. After all, when new groups enter a coalition, they bring new perspectives and interests with them. Black voters barged into the party of Jefferson and in less than a generation shut down a 150-year legacy of championing white supremacy.

Of course, at this moment, the motion of black, Latino, and Asian voters toward the Republican Party is still only an intimation stirring across the voting data. But, at least for many minority voters, it would slip right into the global currents. Everywhere, working-class voters are abandoning the left. Why? Neoliberalism.

The Left's Road to Ruin: The Resistible Rise of Neo-liberalism

Shortly after President Bill Clinton took office in 1993, his economic team trooped into the Oval with long faces and difficult news. If he didn't quickly address the budget deficit, interest rates would rise, cripple the economy, and defeat him and everything he hoped to do. Clinton fancied himself a fresh kind of progressive and shocked his team with a red-faced, screaming rant: "I didn't get elected president to worry about the fucking deficit," he shouted. But, once he got that out of his system, he dutifully fell into line. Clinton whipped the Congressional Democrats into walking the plank on a tough budget (raising taxes and restraining the growth in spending); the unpopular bill squeaked through by two votes and famously destroyed Democratic political careers. Next, the administration thrust NAFTA, a trade agreement negotiated by Republican predecessors, through Congress largely on Republican votes—outraging unions, liberals, and Democrats who voted 156–102 *against* the pact. Few administrations have been more effective at smashing their own coalitions.[23]

The German Social Democrats lived through a parallel experience. They too came back into office in the 1990s after a long stretch of conservative rule. Prime Minister Gerhard Schroeder, who styled himself a new, third way, Democratic—like Bill Clinton and Tony Blair—fought bitterly with his traditional, big government, finance minister, Oskar Lafontaine. After four stormy months, Lafontaine resigned. Nothing quite reflected the new dispensation than the headlines that greeted his fall: *Lafontaine Resigns, Traders Cheer: German [Stock] Market Up 5.1%.*[24]

A change in the institutional rules—loosening the regulations on global (and currency) markets—changed politics. The newly treacherous economic tides threatened to swamp politicians who strayed from neoliberal strictures: deregulation, free trade, marketization, austerity, and reductions in government spending. Market thinking—a faith that market choices were superior to government fiats—came to dominate politics.

In the process, as Didi Kuo argues in Chapter 2, many left-center parties lost their connection to the working class. The big government, programs financed by taxes that they had once championed (Social Security, Medicare, Medicaid) were now out of bounds. When Democrats served up new programs, they were market-friendly concoctions scored (by the Congressional Budget Office) on the extent to which they could pay for themselves. They were easy to mock, hard to defend, and impossible for most people to understand. The most ambitious Democratic efforts of the era, the Clinton health care plan and Obamacare both illustrate the theme.[25]

Conservatives celebrated markets and bashed governments. They constantly discovered—but never managed to learn—that the former are only as effective as the latter.

On the other side, some democratic politicians clung to the old dream. Former President Barack Obama told me, unasked, that *Medicare for All* would have been the ideal health care option—but it wasn't remotely feasible. In fact, liberals tried to pursue markets with a fat asterisk. President Clinton, for example, declared "the era of big government is over . . . ." But—here was the asterisk—he insisted (three times in that famous speech) that markets, left to themselves, were cruel: "We cannot go back to the time that our citizens were left to fend for themselves." Still, despite the ambivalence, the left largely acquiesced (and often promulgated) the network of market rules that lifted poor nations abroad, stranded entire communities at home, and fostered screaming inequality (almost) everywhere.

Neoliberalism made for thin political gruel. As the preceding chapters show, neither party offered a program aimed at the working classes or the left behinds. Over time, politicians on the right seized on the culture wars to mobilize their side. And, not infrequently, the left answered in kind. Today, defending abortion from the right's culture war has become the American left's most reliable issue.

Still, there are little hints that the neoliberal era is closing. After all, it's harder to celebrate markets after the 2008 crash, the long slow economic recovery, the COVID-19 era and the excesses of the markets themselves. And as we shall see below, both the Trump and Biden administrations have shown signs of groping toward a new approach.

Capitalism Run Amuck Is a Failure of Democratic Governance—and Threatens Both

The question posed by this volume—is capitalism compatible with democracy—got its urgency by the rank excesses of contemporary capitalism. The problem is partially rooted in a reckless attitude, blessed by Milton Friedman and his allies: The firm's only duty is to make money for shareholders, and individuals are only responsible for themselves. But it is feckless government that licenses the reign of corporate plunder.

Examples are everywhere—and, taken together, they generate contempt for contemporary capitalism. Start with the for-profit universities vividly described above. They essentially harvest government support for college students, signing up first-generation college students, loading them with debt, offering minimal education, and graduating less than a fifth of enrolled students (only five percent in particularly egregious cases).[26] In Washington, D.C., Democratic administrations have generally tried to crack down on the sharp practices. But bringing real discipline to the sector is not high on the party's agenda and the efforts evaporate as soon as Republicans come back into power. The Trump Administration's Department of Education was especially solicitous of the sector.

The American health care sector offers an even more alarming case. Private equity firms have quietly gobbled up hospitals and physician practices—drawn, once again, by flow of federal funds into the sector. The firms bought 1,400 health units in 2021 alone. They raise prices, shut down less profitable services, and load the providers with debt. One creative practice is to spin off a hospital's land into a real estate investment trust and then require the hospital to pay rent. Another results in large and unexpected medical bills when the managers slip "out of network" personnel into emergency rooms; patients, who dutifully went to the hospital specified by their insurance network suddenly face surprise bills. The private equity firms are perfectly blunt about why health care is so appealing: plenty of federal funds with minimal oversight or regulation. Occasional outbursts (like one over surprise medical billing) move governments to act, but the reactions are haphazard and narrowly focused. Private equity's conquest of American medicine continues with little oversight—despite growing evidence that it lowers quality and increases costs.[27]

In a yet more dramatic example, people all over London suddenly got no water when they turned on their taps while raw sewage poured into the Thames River. This story began when the Thatcher government privatized the nation's water supply in 1989. In 2006, an Australian private equity firm, Macquarie, acquired the company responsible for London, Thames Water. Private observers and government officials immediately sounded the alarm over the company's practices. The regulators (OFWAT) ignored the alarms and approved the sale (accepting the Australian bid over one from Qatar—notice the globalization subtext). Over the next decade, Macquarie saddled Thames Water with over £10 billion of debt, dished out billions in dividends to its own investors, paid no corporate taxes, let the infrastructure erode, and sold out just before environmental agencies levied fines for environmental damage. Brazen private equity and feckless government oversight left English households with plenty of pollution but not enough clean water to drink.[28]

Of course, the most harrowing case of capitalist excess and feckless government lies in global climate change, described in the chapters above. One scientific report after another documents the alarming news: heat rises (breaking the record, year after year), the seas warm, storms grow more intense, entire insect populations collapse, large mammals face extinction, agriculture dries up in vast regions, and people flee injecting terrific political pressure on the United States and Europe. Gridlock generally blunts the (often half-hearted) Democratic efforts to address the emergency; negative partisanship prompts almost gleeful Republican efforts to reject and deny.

If this is capitalism then the answer to this volume's question is simple: No, it is not compatible with democracy. This capitalism corrupts our governments and devours the public sphere—from education to health care to drinking water to the planet itself. Small wonder that even business students excoriate the capitalism they see all around them. And the right undermines its own values when it dumbs down capitalism by crying "socialism" at every effort to ameliorate and reform.

The devastation we see all around is not the only capitalism—at home or abroad. If capitalism and democracy are going to survive, we will need to radically rethink each. And don't forget the first principle: we can't reform one without the other.

Restoring Democratic Capitalism Means Looking Around—and Remembering

In the 1990s, American health policy analysts swarmed into Germany touting—incredibly enough—the American way. Competition, they averred, would dissolve the problems of German health care. I was part of a team that followed in their wake, warning the Germans that this advice would lead to ruin. American rules, we told them, give insurance companies a very clear incentive: shun the sick. That's how we have 38 million (at the time) people with no health insurance at all. German audiences were stunned at all this. We have, they responded a solidarity culture: it's not acceptable, they insisted, to leave people behind in such a crass way. And then they'd shake their heads and ask how it could be that such a rich nation as the USA "permits"—as they kept putting it—so many people to languish without insurance protection.

The German incredulity reflects a theme that is often mentioned but rarely explored through this volume: The varieties of capitalism. Different societies run their capitalist economies with very different rules. Each economy is nestled in a different society with very different norms and expectations. While the global markets squeeze every rich nation, inequality is far lower in, say Belgium (with a Gini Index of .27) or Denmark (.27) or Germany (.31) or Japan (.33) than in the United States (.40 and rising). Health and education, taxes and pensions, are all distributed differently in different countries. But here's the bottom line: Few other rich nations follow the Americans (and the British) to such rampant precarity.

International comparisons stretch our imagination. But different countries are different along so many dimensions that what is normal over there may not always be possible here. Perhaps it's more useful to exercise our reformist imaginations by looking at America's own rich varieties of capitalism.

One touchstone lies in Franklin D. Roosevelt's New Deal vision. From the presidential campaign of 1932 to his four freedoms speech (in 1941) to the penultimate State of the Union Message (1944) he pressed for a bold new vision of rights. The original Bill of Rights laid out a series of important negative liberties: The government shall not interfere with your right to speak or pray or assemble. Now, insisted FDR, a modern era required the state to guarantee a bill of positive liberties. After all, no person is truly free if they are hungry or sick or impoverished. FDR put it clearly in his 1944 State of the Union Message when he described the economic bill of rights that we owe every citizen.

> Of these rights, the most fundamental . . . is the right to a useful and remunerative job in the industries or shops or farms or mines of the Nation. In turn, other . . . economic rights of American citizenship, such as the right to a decent home, to a good education, to good medical care, to social security, to reasonable farm income.[29]

Here's an image worth remembering. The people's government takes the negative freedoms of the Federal Constitution and grafts on a positive pledge of personal security: No hungry children, no uneducated youths, no needy families, no old people without a place to live, no suffering Americans turned away from health care because they cannot pay.

Today, such an expansive vision of rights would not fit under our dumbed-down rubric of capitalism. But not only did it once fit, it saved capitalism at a time when—much like today—it was under attack as mean and repressive and out of date. If Roosevelt and the New Deal seem long ago, consider what happened just yesterday.

The United States confronted the COVID-19 epidemic under both Republican and Democratic administrations. In the first year of the pandemic, Congress produced three tranches of relief. Americans making less than $60,000 a year (almost double the poverty line) saw an average of $3,450 in stimulus funds. Food assistance grew, child tax credits rose, evictions slowed, and unemployment relief increased by $600 per worker. The result: 4.5 million Americans rose out of poverty during the pandemic.[30] All that relief flipped the long-standing canons of American welfare spending: this time, payments went to those with the lowest incomes.

The same went for government sponsored health insurance. At the height of the pandemic, Medicaid covered over 92.3 million Americans (up from 47 million before the Affordable Care Act expanded the program).[31] Another 65 million were enrolled in Medicare. And increased premium support led a record 16 million people into the ACA insurance exchanges (for all the political tempests, notice how tiny the exchanges are compared to the more easily expandable big-government Medicaid programs). In most of the country, the pandemic produced a patchwork, shaky, temporary American version of that old liberal dream: a right to health care.

As we face the problems of capitalism run amuck and a democracy that is stuck, we ought to pay attention to how the COVID-19 crisis helped both parties to—briefly—leap over their enmity and think about what people needed to get through the hard time. The relief assisted both individuals and the economy negotiate the worst of the epidemic and the choppy recovery that followed it.

Still, as the crisis passed, these intimations of the good community quickly evaporated. Democrats could not muster a majority to keep them going—indeed, they seemed barely cognizant that they had briefly erected a real social safety net. Across the aisle, Republicans appeared to be chagrinned at their role at all that promiscuous spending. None of it was enough to protect the population from the deadly epidemic. But the Americans took a real step toward the good society and then, quickly, conspired to forget the intimations of social justice they had stumbled into during a moment of panic.

As we try to imagine a democratic capitalism that works, we ought to remember what we aimed for long ago and what we briefly managed very recently.

Ideas Change the World: Think Big, Think Small, Think Hard

To get the ACA through Congress, Democrats in the House were going to have to vote for the flawed, unpopular, conservative, deeply compromised Senate version of the bill. Many knew that a yay would cost them their seats. Just before the vote, President Obama went up to Capitol Hill for a pep talk. He reminded the fretting Democrats that even this version of the bill was a hell of a lot better than doing nothing—and stranding almost 50 million people without health insurance. "Every once in a while, he said softly, every once in a while, a moment comes where you have a chance to vindicate all those hopes that you had about yourself and about this country, where you have a chance to make good on those promises in all those town meetings . . . all those people you looked in the eye and said, you know what . . . I'm going to make it better. Well, this is one of those moments."[32] One member told me at the time that those words made the difference for him. He voted for the bill knowing it would mean the end of his Congressional career.

Take a step back and use the health reform as a template for change They would never have been there in the first place if liberals hadn't dreamed up a way to reconfigure a conservative health care plan that had been knocking around Washington for fifteen years. Or if Democrats and Republicans hadn't worked together to cook up a version in Massachusetts. By the time the Obama administration came to Washington, the idea had been fully baked. "I don't dream up new ideas," Congressman Barney Frank once told me. "I find a wave that's breaking and ride it into shore."

Well, that's the job for volumes like this one and the intellectuals who contribute to them. Dream up ideas that might gather velocity and, over time, create waves. Dreams of change show up in three different ways in the preceding chapters.

First, almost every chapter documents just how badly—and how widely—reforms are needed. A dysfunctional government has let a vicious version of capitalism run out of control—generating inequality and wrecking the public sphere. American Democracy itself also looks to be in danger. Our institutions—elections, courts, Congress, the parties, the bureaucracy—all need repairing. And while no one comes out and says so directly, almost every chapter depicts a rickety Constitution straitjacketing the polity.

At the same time, this volume quietly unfurls a more subtle story about reaching for reform. By digging into our history, the authors show that democracy did not spring fully formed out of James Madison's Constitution. It was over a century before anything approximating democratic representation emerged from American legislatures (as Lamoreaux and Wallis so vividly show, in Chapter 7). Over and again, we learn about the hard work of creating democracy, building equality, seeking racial justice. Sometimes the efforts succeeded, often they failed. But, either way, they remind us that the perplexities of democracy are as old as the republic.

Finally, most chapters suggest reforms, large and small. Taken together, they toss us back to the same truth: We can't fix capitalism without reforming the government. And reforming government will require new thinking about the economy and who it serves. Danielle Allen, in Chapter 10, goes furthest in thinking about an economy that supports a genuine democracy and rebuilds a robust communal sphere. The entire volume echoes the task she lays before us. That kind of fundamental change will need to draw on the talents of every sector and corner of our polity.

Including the people who most profit from the current version of capitalism. Our forty-year experiment with this variety—everyone for themselves (or greed is good)—has got us into our terrible fix. Yes, we need to build a government that rewrites those rules. But we're not going to manage that without some help from business itself. In the best case, firms will begin to think about empowering employees, about their effects on the public sphere, about what they are doing to the planet. But, as Rebecca Henderson has written, it must go further. Business influences governments. It is a powerful force for political change—good or ill. The old reflex to attack regulation, fight taxation, and bash government will, in the not so long run, sink democracy, wreck capitalism, and ruin us all.[33]

Yes, the dream of business pushing for government reform seems like a stretch. But capitalism itself is rapidly evolving. Today, a handful of asset managers control extraordinary piles of capital. They can and do create new requirements for all large businesses—insisting, for example, that firms include the effects on climate change when they report their results.

Of course, political change is going to need a lot more than business. It will have to reach far and wide. Where to even begin? Perhaps with the political parties themselves.

For Democrats, the task starts with building a fifty-state party. It's not just that Democratic ideas don't resonate in the heartlands. It's that the party, as an institution, has atrophied to nothing in deep red states. The Democrats no longer have any institutional existence at all in the mountain West—or swaths of the Deep South.[34] Time to rebuild. And then the really big job: the party must find a way to fight inequality and reconnect with the working class.

But a regime structured for two parties will never thrive if only one is serious about governing. The job facing contemporary Republicans is to cull conservatism from the white privilege and nativism that turns so many party officials into masters of outraged gesturing. Traditional Republicans will bristle at such talk. They fix their gaze on more honorable matters than race hatred: Lower taxes, fewer regulations, protections for the traditional family, religion, patriotism, and the military. What do any of those have to do with past segregation or anybody's racial dog whistles? The answer lies in the coalition. All those honorable positions get their political juice—generation after generation, north and south—from the energy of white anxiety. Racial demons have always crawled into the anti-government coalition.

Young conservatives may be especially eager to start the operation. It's one way they can rescue the party from the grandparents and connect it to the young. Rearrange the tribal loyalties—reconnect Republicans and people of color—and just watch our partisan rage ebb back into traditional, party competition. Impossible? Not for those who take the long, historical view. Ethnic and racial politics are always changing, populations shift, attitudes turn. Recall what lured the black vote into a party run by segregationists back in the 1930s. Local party leaders recruited them, labor allies organized with them, New Deal policy appealed to them, and their own party took them for granted.

Of course, fixing the parties is just the first step in a long process that will need to reach every broken institution in American political life. Each effort will have to be guided by a simple metric: Majorities ought to rule. And that means, they ought to be able to introduce change—without the thousand checks that sink almost every large effort today. Permitting majorities to pursue the policies they promise might very well nudge both parties back to responsible governing.

Is capitalism compatible with democracy? Some forms of capitalism are. Some are not. But, in the end, there is a better way to put the same question: How do we build an economy that nourishes a genuine democracy—that creates prosperity and spreads its benefits to everyone in the country? Or to put the same question in different words, how do we create a genuine democracy—one that extends liberty (positive and negative) and some prosperity to everyone in the nation?

Of course, it's a daunting climb. But what other choice do we have?

Notes

1. The classic statement of this point is Charles Lindblom, *Politics and Markets* (New York: Basic Books, 1977).
2. Harold Myerson, "At Tesla, Swedish Workers Can Do What American Workers Can't," *The American Prospect*, November 14, 2023, https://prospect.org/blogs-and-newsletters/tap/2023-11-14-tesla-swedish-workers-unions/
3. US Bureau of Labor Statistics, "Union Members—2022" USDL 23-0071," January 19, 2023, https://www.bls.gov/news.release/pdf/union2.pdf
4. Chris Isidore, "Buffett Says He's Still Paying Lower Tax Rate than his Secretary," *CNN Business*, March 4, 2013, https://money.cnn.com/2013/03/04/news/economy/buffett-secretary-taxes/index.html.
5. Ronald Reagan, "Inaugural Address," January 20, 1981.
6. James A. Morone, "Hidden Complications: Why Health Care Competition Needs Regulation," *The American Prospect*, 10, Summer 1992.
7. Lyndon Johnson, "Special Message to Congress: The American Promise," March 15, 1965, *Public Papers of the Presidents of the United States: Lyndon Johnson* (Washington, D.C.: Government Printing Office, 1965): 1:281–87. For discussion, James A Morone, "*Republic of Wrath: How American Politics Turned Tribal from George Washington to Donald Trump* (New York: Basic Books, 2020), ch. 7.
8. Charles Eaton, *Bankers in the Ivory Tower* (Chicago: University of Chicago Press, 2022); Matthew Soules, *Icebergs, Zombies and Ultrathins: Architecture and Capitalism in the Twenty-First Century* (Princeton Architectural Press, 2021); S. Margot Finn, *Discriminating Taste: How Class Anxiety Created the American Food Revolution* (New Brunswick, NJ: Rutgers University Press, 2017); Ashley Mears, *Very Important People: Status and Beauty in the Global Party Circuit* (Princeton, NJ: Princeton University Press, 2020).
9. Angus Deaton and Anne Case, *Deaths of Despair and the Future of Capitalism* (Princeton, NJ: Princeton University Press, 2020). Data from James A. Morone, "An Introduction to Health Politics," in *Health Politics and Policy*, 6th edition, ed. James Morone and Daniel Ehlke (Stamford, CT: Cengage, 2024). 12
10. Glenn Hubbard, "Even My Business School Students Have Doubts About Capitalism," *The Atlantic*, January 2, 2022. https://www.aei.org/articles/even-my-business-school-students-have-doubts-about-capitalism/
11. Quoted in David Blumenthal and James Morone, *Whiplash: From the Battle for Obamacare to the War on Science* (New Haven: Yale University Press, 2026).
12. Stephen Levitsky and Daniel Zieblatt, *Tyranny of the Minority: How to Reverse an Authoritarian Turn and Forge a Democracy for All* (New York: Viking, 2023).
13. *West Virginia v. EPA* (June, 2022).
14. James Madison, "Federalist Papers No. 10" (1787).
15. W. E. B. Du Bois, *Black Reconstruction in the America*, 1935; repr. New York: Athenaeum, 1992); Edmund Morgan, *American Slavery, American Freedom* (New York: W. W. Norton, 1975).

16. Tom Watson, "The Negro Question in the South," *Arena* 6 (1892): 540–50, quoted at 545. For discussion, see Morone, *Republic of Wrath*, ch. 5.
17. J. David Greenstone, *Labor in American Politics* (New York: Random House, 1970).
18. Ira Katznelson, *City Trenches: Urban Politics and the Patterning of Class in the US* (Chicago: The University of Chicago Press, 1981).
19. The next five paragraphs summarize the argument I made in *Republic of Wrath*.
20. William Howard Taft, Inaugural Address. Thursday, March 4, 1919.
21. Morone, *Republic of Wrath*, ch. 6.
22. Alex Samuels and Neil Lewis Jr., "How White Victim Hood Fuels Republican Politics," *The New York Times*, 538, May 21, 2022, https://fivethirtyeight.com/features/how-white-victimhood-fuels-republican-politics/.
23. Eric Planin and David S Hilzenrath, "House Passes Clinton Budget Plan by Two Votes," *The Washington Post*, August 6, 1993; James Gerstenzang and Michael Ross, "House Passes NAFTA, 234-200: Sometimes bitter debate over trade pact reflects hard fought battle among divided Democrats," *Los Angeles Times*, November 18, 1993. https://www.latimes.com/archives/la-xpm-1993-11-18-mn-58150-story.html
24. See, for one of many examples, Vanessa Fuhrman aand Michael Sesit, "Markets Cheer Lafontaine's Resignation, but European Economic Woes Remain," *Wall Street Journal*, March 15, 1999, https://www.wsj.com/articles/SB921471246905l3902.
25. Obama interview in David Blumenthal and James Morone, *From the Battle for Obamacare to the War on Science* (New Haven: Yale University Press, 2026). On Clinton, David Blumenthal, and James Morone, *The Heart of Power: President and Health Care from Franklin Roosevelt to George W Bush* (Berkeley: University of California Press, 2009).
26. Tamar Lewin, "Report Finds Low Graduation Rates at For-Profit Colleges," *The New York Times*, November 23, 2010, https://www.nytimes.com/2010/11/24/education/24colleges.html
27. Laura Katz Olson, *Ethically Challenged: Private Equity Storms US Health Care* (Baltimore: Johns Hopkins Press, 2022); Fred Schulte, "Sick Profit: Investigating Private Equity's Stealthy Takeover of Health Care Across Cities and Specialties," *KFF Health News*, November 14, 2022, https://kffhealthnews.org/news/article/private-equity-takeover-health-care-cities-specialties/.
28. Jony Bloom, "The Thames Water Scandal Is Another Disaster Inflicted by Our Don't Care Government," *The New European*, June 29, 2023. Columnists on the left-leaning *Guardian* were especially vociferous about Macquarie's practices—before, during, and after it took over Thames Water. https://www.theneweuropean.co.uk/the-thames-water-scandal-is-another-disaster-inflicted-by-our-dont-care-government/
29. Franklin D. Roosevelt, "State of the Union Address," January 11, 1944, Washington, D.C.
30. Joseph Dalaker, *Poverty in the United States in 2021*, Washington, D.C.: Congressional Research Service, December 27, 2022, https://crsreports.congress.gov/product/pdf/R/R47354. The fall in poverty rates appeared in the *Supplemental Policy Measure*, which is designed to factor in relief payments.
31. Bradley Corallo and Sophia Moreno, "Analysis of Recent National Trends In Mewdicaid and CHIP Enrollment," *Kaiser Family Foundation*, April 4, 2023. Table 1. https://www.kff.org/coronavirus-covid-19/issue-brief/analysis-of-recent-national-trends-in-medicaid-and-chip-enrollment/
32. Barack Obama, *The Promised Land* (New York: Penguin, 2020), 425.
33. Rebecca Henderson, *Reimaging Capitalism in a World on Fire* (New York: Public Affairs Press, 2020).
34. Robert Saldin and B. Kal Munis, "Go Local, Young Democrat: How Nationalization of Everything Is Widening the Urban-Rural Divide and What Democrats Can Do about It," *Democracy*, No. 64, Spring 2023, https://democracyjournal.org/magazine/64/go-local-young-democrat/

INDEX

Tables and figures are indicated by an italic *t* and *f* following the paragraph number.

For the benefit of digital users, indexed terms that span two pages (e.g., 52–53) may, on occasion, appear on only one of those pages.